ALL IN A WOMAN'S DAY

Volume 2

Including pages 411 through 792 and the index

Plants, trees prove natural for holidays

Christmas, the commemoration of the Holy Birth, long has been considered a lively holiday and a celebration of the joy of life. You can add to the liveliness and the loveliness of Christmas by bringing a little life into your home and the homes of friends. It's a natural thing to do at this season of the year with lovely, living plants and trees.

You can prolong the holiday cheer by getting a living Christmas tree you can replant in the New Year. Select a tree with sturdy root and keep it moist and cool in a shallow container away from heat outlets and fireplaces. After the holidays, plant it as soon as the ground can be dug. Then next Christmastime you can enjoy decorating two Christmas trees, one inside, one out.

To liven your Christmas giving, there are plants that fit almost everyone on your list. For homeowners, try giving ornamental shade trees or charming shrubs or bushes. Match plants with personalities; some of them are flowering house plants; delicate, exotic ferns, businesslike broadleaved plants; and hardy cacti.

For a child, a plant can be a learning experience. This will be the opportunity of learning more about nature; how to grow plants, what makes them green, what they can do for us, and at the same time, he or she can learn about the responsibility of caring for a living thing. Plants, however, for children are not for all childre. Be sure you know the child to whom you might be planning to give a plant.

Choose well-shaped Christmas trees for your own for for giving. They look better and are easier to decorate. You might even have to do a little trimming yourself. You might want to highlight a color or color combination or use a theme. Trim should always be simple; however, it should be distinctive. In decorating a tree place the lights on first, then the garlands, tree ornaments, glass ornaments and last the tree top and the skirt.

If you like to have snow on your tree, you can make your own. Just mix a cup of detergent or soap powder with half a cup of water. Beat with mixer or egg beater until stiff. Then daub it on the tree branches with a clean brush. It clings and dries. looking just like pretty frosty white snow. If you have an artifical vinyl tree, it washes off, too.

Remember the safety side and spray your Christmas tree with a reliable fire retardant.

Always leave the tree outside the house as long as possible, preferrably in a bucket of water with a commercial solution to keep it green. Use a sturdy stand and fill it daily with water.

Never place the tree near a fireplace, radiator or other sources of heat that will cause dryness. When purchasing a tree, always strike the bottom against a hard surface several times. If needles fall off, it is to dry. Choose another tree. When getting ready to place a tree in a stand, cut one-inch off of the trunk on a diagonal line to allow for better absorption of the water. Find a nice tree and treat it well this year.

Christmastime gives stars special meaning 

The stars in the sky seem to have a special meaning at Advent and Christmastime. In fact, they take on a new meaning. Everywhere in the world the people look up to the stars and the thoughts of the first Christmas comes into their minds. The warm glow of the stars seem to charm all hearts.

The beginnings of our own nation are rooted in the promise, the faith and the assurance given to people by the ever-lasting spirit that is the light of the Christmas Star.

It is a beautiful faith; the trusting faith of a child, the never failing trust of humanity in the miraculous. Yet, it is even more. It is the force against with the most powerful evil cannot prevail for long, nor which the most wicked can overpower in the end. Whether it is in the time of war or in the time of peace; whether in time of happiness or time of strife ... Christmas comes as the years come and go. The world, with all its cruelties, greed, hate, and yes, its blessings through the many years since man began to travel, has found that the star has lighted the way, has never altered the spirit of Christmas, nor dimmed the light of His star. the light in the heart is the light that lasts forever. The light of the world may go out, but the light in the heart warmly gleams. This Christmastime the star must surely shine brighter than ever in the darkness of a discouraged world. The world; however, is not lost for it was saved those many years ago in Bethlehem. this is what the Christmas Star is saying to us, and nothing, no nothing, will alter this fact.

It does, however, seem strange that with such a star in the sky at the birth of Christ, that thousands of people would surely have seen it, for it must have been very bright and in motion. But only those men from far off seem to have seen it as it came down so close to the chosen spot.

And the shepherds ... it took a voice from heaven and a light that brightened the sky as daylight to get them to hear the historic announcement.

The stars, yes, and His star are still in the sky, shining as brightly as ever, only some see and some don't. For individuals in general, the Christmas Star may be the dream, hope and fancy of loved ones. For the Christian, that special star is the call from on high for human beings to rise to the life that was destined for them when the first star shone out for the men from the East.

The stars remind us of the brotherhood of man under the fatherhood of God; that there is no East or West, North or South. Jesus came in the flesh to bring love and peace to mankind, and then taken in death to forgive and take away our sins. There can be no greater love for all mankind. This is the message of His Christmas Star. Shine on, O Star in all your glory!

* * *

May the Christmas Star shine on you at this season and throughout the coming year!

All in a Woman's Day--December 31, 1985

Epiphany brings a trifold message

The twelfth day after Christmas, Jan. 6, is called Epiphany. The time between Christmas Day and Epiphany is called Christmastide, and Epiphany is the last day of Christmastide.

It has been said that Epiphany marks three event sin the life of Jesus: His baptism, the visit of the Wise Men to Bethlehem and the miracle at Cana, when Jesus changed water to wine at the wedding feast.

Some people also believed that the Epiphany date was the birthday of Jesus. This, however, was before his birthday was set on Dec. 25.

Epiphany means "shining upon." The star of Bethlehem shone upon the Wise Men and guided them to the baby in Bethlehem. In the Bible Jesus is called "the light of the world." Therefore, Epiphany is a day to remind us that through Jesus, the light of God's love shines on all people. Jesus did not choose all people to love, he loved all people everywhere.

Perhaps the Wise Men may have each come from a different country and different race. One may have had black skin, one white skin and one brown. Since we cannot see the light of the star as the shepherds and Wise Men did, we make light in different ways to celebrate this special day. In many instances, however, it is celebrated on Epiphany Sunday.

Many people burn candles in thier homes and in churches to remind them of the light of Epiphany. This is a traditional time in some towns and cities for people to get together and burn all their Christmas greenery and Christmas trees in a big bonfire. They sing carols around the blazing branches and remember that Jesus brought the light of God's love into the world.

It is known that Epiphany has been observed as early as 194 A. D. Then by the fourth century the feast of Epiphany was widely accepted. King Alfred in England in the ninth century, made Epiphany a Saxon fixture, by decreeing that the Christmas season should include Christmas Day and the 12 days following.

When Charles II ascended to the throne, the Twelfth Night Cake was a standard tradition, along with the burning of Christmas greenery.

In the year 567 the Council of Tours officially declared the Twelve Days of Christmas as a holy festival and people celebrated all the days each year until the early 19th century.

The Twelfth Night refreshments always featured a beautifully decorated cake with a bean somewhere in it. Each recipient of a piece of cake would cautiously bite into his piece and then after a crunch someone would shout "I have the bean." A gold paper crown was placed on the head of the lucky fellow and the party was underway. The "bean king" would select his queen and the other revelers imitated their every action.

A favorite game at Twelfth Night parties made use of the still popular Christmas song, "A Partridge in a Pear Tree." A leader would speak the verse and the guests would repeat until all had tried. Anyone who got his tongue twisted on "seven swans a-swimming" or left out the "pipers piping" had to pay a forfeit. Originally, the song mentioned the partridge in both English and French. The French would pronounce (pear tree) "peardree." Gradually it became pear tree.

The importance of this special day Epiphany, is the emphasis on the Christian mission. Those Magi were the first Gentiles to whom Jesus manifested himself. Their coming to Bethlehem is the Bible's assurance that the Christ is God's revelation to all races and nations. The star is the scriptural sign that the "Love" born in Bethlehem can lead all men to the light of God's truth.

Epiphany seems the best time to declare the faith that Jesus is indeed "the light of the world."

Thoughts simplify 1986; advice must be followed

Most holiday decorations have been put back into storage for another year, and we are ready to move along to something else. It is time for doing a little relaxing and catching up with things that need to be done.

* * *

As we go into this new year, here are some thoughts that might make 1986 a little easier with which to cope, if we would but follow the advice given:

Take time to think … it is the price of success.

Take time to read … it is the fountain of wisdom.

Take time to be friendly … it is the road to happiness.

Take time to play … it is the secret of perpetual youth.

Take time to dream … it is hitching your wagon to a star.

Take time to be loved … it is the privilege of the gods.

Take time to savor beauty … it is your joie de vivre.

Take time to laugh … it is the music of the soul.

And

Take time to talk with God … it will draw you closer into the shelter of His arms.

—Author unknown

* * *

Cooking tasks never seem to let up regardless of the season, so I'll share a few hints that might help in that everyday job of homemaking.

Run orange peel through your garbage disposal to keep it smelling fresh.

This might be a good time to have some pancakes. By adding a teaspoon of sugar to the batter it will brown better.

If you are afraid that maybe your baking powder has lost some of its zip, just place one teaspoon into a cup of hot water. If it fizzes actively, it is not "dead." Just continue to use the contents of the can. Store the can upside down. When you turn it right side up this helps to stir up the ingredients.

A quick easy way to drain oil off canned tuna is with a potato masher (if you have the right kind). Just insert the masher into the open can of tuna, and press against the tuna while pouring off the oil.

When making a chocolate cake should you want to have a nice red color or just add one tablespoon vinegar to the milk and this will make the cake have a really red color.

Do you like chicken fried steak? Shape ground beef into flat patties and chill; then dip in milk and flour. Fry in hot grease, and salt and pepper to taste. Cook on each side until the coating is crisp and continue to flatten as they cook. This also is a good way to prepare minute steaks.

If your brown sugar has hardened, here is a different way of softening it. Simply place a lettuce leaf with the sugar in a tightly closed container and the sugar will soften up as it was when purchased.

If bananas are mashed before adding them to gelatin, they will not discolor.

Stuffed peppers will hold their shape well for baking if they are placed in muffin tins.

When filling cup cake liners, hold them over the bowl of batter. This saves a mess on the pans.

If parsley is washed in hot water instead of cold, it retains its flavor and is more easly chopped.

Before rolling anything, place the rolling pin in the refrigerator. This will prevent dough from sticking.

Raisins won't get hard when used in a cookie recipe if they are parboiled in one-fourth to one-half cup of water, and stirred often. The water will be absorbed and will not add to the liquid content of the recipe. Cookies will be moist and chewy with no hard, charred raisins.

Lard or shortening, the size of a pea, added to salted boiling water before adding rice, macaroni or lima beans, will keep them from foaming and boiling over.

If you don't know the formula for making the color orange, use one drop red coloring and four drops of yellow.

Whenever you have fresh oranges or lemons, peel them and put just the peeling into the blender, chopping very fine. Pour this into a small jar, and freeze. You will then have grated orange or lemon peel when needed.

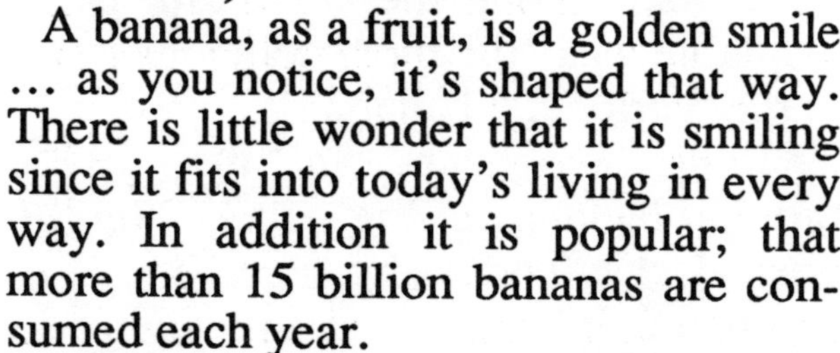

All in a Woman's Day--January 14, 1986

Golden smile fruit, banana, is delicious

A banana, as a fruit, is a golden smile … as you notice, it's shaped that way. There is little wonder that it is smiling since it fits into today's living in every way. In addition it is popular; that more than 15 billion bananas are consumed each year.

Bananas seem to go with things that help make our lives fun. They are great to eat when biking, hiking, picnicking, at the beach, barbecuing, entertaining, baseball and football stadium snacks, preparing eat-as-you go meals and used as a fondue dipper … bananas make a good appearance wherever they go.

This seedless fruit, that resembles a palm, is harvested when green, with food value and flavor the result of conditions and temperatures that are carefully controlled. As they ripen, their starch is converted into sugar.

The skin of a partly ripened banana is generally yellow; however, there also are red skinned varieties. In fact, there are some 30 species of this fruit and all look and taste different from the other.

There are bananas that are red, and also greenish, those with a flavor suggestive of the apples or peaches, and some with a more delicate or richer flavor. Some are not suited to be eaten raw, but must be cooked—fried, boiled or baked—to be palable. These are often used as a vegetable.

Originally the banana "tree" was native to tropical Asia, possibly India, and ancient Greece. Arabian writers have called bananas "the remarkable Indian fruit tree." Because of its botanical name, Musa sapientum, which means fruit of the Wise Men, it has been held in high esteem. However, it seems that people, wise or foolish, aren't the only creatures that finds bananas enjoyable. The tropical American oriole is fond of the fruit, and it is called the banana bird.

Although called a tree, and no doubt it looks to be such; however, the banana plant is a giant herb, and its leaves furl one upon another, to form the "trunk," as it would be called if it were a tree. A banana plant bears only one stem of fruit, and then it is cut down. Each root or rhizome produces many shoots or suckers which take over when the plant has borne its fruit, insuring a continuous crop. The new shoot, called the "daughter," arises from the base of the original stem. The daughter is cut down after its crop has been harvested, and gives rise to a "granddaughter" plant. The long pointed leaves generally hang in shreds, thus giving a rather disheveled look.

The banana plant helped the sages of India practice wisdom; they would sit under its shade, meditating. Seeing a Holy man sitting under a banana "tree" is the same as if he held up a "Do not disturb" sign. The sages were always too preoccupied to have meals. But there the beauty of the banana plant is revealed ... he would just reach up and pick a fruit without so much as a ripple in his meditating.

Bananas were first sold in New Orleans markets in the 1830s by traders from Honduras or Costa Rica. In May, 1943, a New York merchant, John Pearshall, imported 300 bunches of Cuban red bananas and sold them at 25 cents each, who!esale. And don't forget, then 25 cents had the value of more than $2 at today's prices. They remained an expensive luxury throughout the 19th century.

Many Americans were introduced to the banana at the Philadelphia 1876 Centennial Exposition, where individually tinfoil-wrapped bananas sold at 10 cents each.

The banana plant dates back to the Pliocene era, some one million years ago, which makes the banana the oldest of fruits. The Roman encyclopedist, Pliny (23-79 A.D.), first wrote about bananas, and stated they were of Indian origin. The Korans say the banana, not the apple, was the forbidden fruit in the Garden of Eden.

During the second century, Yan Fu, a Chinese scholar, wrote about the then exotic banana in "Record of Strange Things," describing it as "very sweet, like honey or sugar ... after eating, the flavor lingers on among the teeth."

The botanical name is said to be derived from the writings of Alexander the Great, who found wise men eating bananas when he crossed the Indus River in 327 B.C.

It is believed that Arab traders introduced the banana plant to the Middle East and Africa during the seventh century. The first record of a banana recipe comes from the writings of an Arab historian, Masudi, who in the 10th century wrote of an Egyptian treat consisting of almonds, honey and bananas.

Portuguese explorers in Africa during the 15th century, gave the banana its current name deriving from a variety of West African languages that called the fruit bana gbanan, abana, funana, and banane.

It was Portuguese traders, looking for a route to China some 500 years ago, who carried the plant from the Guinea Coast to the Canary Islands, where it still thrives today. Minister Benjamin Disraeli, who wrote from Cairo in 1831, that among the wonderful fruits available was "the most delicious thing in the world ... a banana."

Sailing schooners in the 1870s brought bananas in big bunches on the open decks. Today, however, they are pampered in ships that are equipped with special temperature controls. The schooners first came intermittently as they might catch the wind and land in Boston or New Orleans with a big cargo; however, oftentimes the ships encountered storms or becalms and would have to dump their fruit overboard because it didn't last until port was reached.

* * *

Banana Salad

20 marshmallows cut in fourths
1 cup halved seeded grapes
1/2 cup whipped cream or whipped topping (more if necessary)
2 cups shredded cabbage
1/2 cup chopped nuts
1/2 cup mayonnaise
2 bananas, diced

Mix thoroughly and lightly. Chill before serving it. Serves 6 to 8 persons.

All in a Woman's Day--January 21, 1986

Bananas; special handling is necessary

Bananas are such a delightful, honey-like fruit that has appeal to all generations. Also, they are available the year around; however, peak season is in March-June.

Have you ever seen a banana blossom? It is rather fantastic in shape and color, and is, well, almost exotic. A single fuschia colored bud pushes its way through the center of the leaf cluster. It has brilliant purple bracts in a rather strange abstract pattern, and as the bud grows longer it tends to bend over and then point upward. A few days later it begins to shed the purple bracts, and under each bract is a double row of small flowers. Each of these develops into a cluster of a banana called a "hand." All this exotic flora is framed in bluish green leaves, eight to 10 inches long. Finally there are 10 or 11 "hands" growing on the stem, and each "hand" has from 10 to 20 individual bananas or "fingers." At first they point downward, and as they grow they turn outward. Within a year the stems are ready to be harvested. There are about 150 fingers to each stem and it weighs about 85 pounds.

When the big stem of the banana is formed on the plant, it is covered completely with a transparent plastic bag to protect it from insects, birds, and against being scarred by tropical winds.

They are harvested in the plastic bags and sent to the boxing station, often on an overhead cable. There they are cut into clusters, placed in huge water tanks and washed several times to clean them before shipping. Women do this work because they have a more delicate touch with the fruit.

When purchasing bananas, look for firm, unblemished plump fruit, regardless of size. Choose the bananas according to the way you plan to serve them. They are sold in small bunches, mostly by weight. Purchase them by bunches instead of singly as a single banana will deteriorate more rapidly.

The green tipped banana, or one that is slightly underripe, is fine for broiling and sauteeing or, as some prefer, for eating out of hand. The full yellow banana is the degree of ripeness most commonly chosen for eating raw. Bananas, with brown-flecked skins, are usually the sweetest. They are fully ripe and should be used immediately.

Bananas also are sold packaged or dehydrated in powder, flakes or slices.

One medium banana, sliced, makes two-thirds cup; two medium bananas, sliced, make one cup and three medium bananas, mashed, make one cup.

Keep bananas at room temperature. They also may be refrigerated to keep them longer at the preferred stage of ripeness. The skins will darken in the refrigerator; however, the flesh will retain both color and flavor.

Bananas must ripen off the plant. If allowed to ripen on the plant, they will

417

split open and become tasteless. Even in the tropics, where they are grown, the bananas are cut green and stored to ripen slowly under the house where it is moist and shady.

To ripen green or slightly green bananas, they should be at room temperature and should ripen slowly to the desired degree. When bananas are green, they generally take about five days to ripen at room temperature.

A medium banana has 85 calories and provides vitamins A, C, B-6, plus thiamine, niacin, riboflavin and iron, in addition to potassium. It is very low in sodium, is cholesterol free, with a minimum amount of fat. It also is easily digested when fully ripe.

Firm, golden bananas have a sweet creamy taste. Try them with ice cream or yogurt in fruit salads or puddings. The underripe, or green-tipped banana, is not quite as sweet and is quite firm. The fully ripe bananas are the sweetest, and are perfect for baking, adding extra flavor and sweetness.

Most of the bananas received in this country come from Costa Rica, Honduras, Ecuador, Panama, Guatemala and other Central and South American countries.

Bananas are one of the diet mainstays in the West Indies and Central and tropical South America, the Pacific Islands and throughout Central America. Generally, there is only a small space for growing; however, this fruit will support more people than wheat. Most any house or hut in the banana growing countries will have its own little grove of trees nearby, where the fruit grows as weeds. Bananas for commercial use are grown on large plantations.

* * *

Banana Cake

1/2 cup butter or margarine
1/2 cup sugar
2 eggs
3/4 cup commercial sour cream
2 ripe bananas
1 teaspoon vanilla
2 scant cups sifted flour
1/4 teaspoon salt
1 teaspoon soda

Cream butter or margarine with sugar until smooth and creamy. Mix in eggs, sour cream, bananas and vanilla. (It might be well to measure the 2 cups of flour, then remove 2 tablespoons to make them "scant"). Sift dry ingredients together and add to batter. Mix just until well blended; do not overbeat. Pour into greased pans, a 9x12 and an 8x8. Bake at 375 degrees for 30 minutes or until it tests done with a cake tester.

Frost with a butter cream powdered sugar frosting that bas been flavored with banana extract.

All in a Woman's Day--January 28, 1986

Various ways used in caring for bananas

Sunny, smiling bananas are still on the agenda; however, this will conclude the series.

This week's column features hints on using and serving bananas.

To serve plain, just peel, slice and sprinkle immediately with lemon, orange, pineapple or other fruit juice or with an ascorbic acid mixture to prevent them from turning dark. Chill them two to three hours in the refrigerator before serving.

Green bananas will ripen a bit faster if placed next to some that are ripe. They just seem to take the hint.

The inside of a fresh banana peel is a

good polisher for leather shoes if wiped off with a woolen cloth.

Bananas can be frozen, and are good to have on hand for cakes, cookies and breads. Use ripe bananas, peel and mash. Place approximately two bananas in a sandwich-size freezer bag. These bags will lie flat and don't take up much space in the freezer. You also will have the proportional size to use in baking. Be sure to use an ascorbic acid mixture or lemon juice to keep them from turning brown.

Using a plastic knife to cut bananas will help them stay fresh longer than cut with a metal knife.

Save banana peelings and bury them around rose bushes as they will enrich the soil.

Wrap firm bananas separately in foil and place in a sack and set in a cool place (not refrigerator), and they will stay firm and not get over ripe. They will; however, get brown flecks on the skins.

A tasty combination is sliced ripe bananas served in glass bowls with lots of orange juice poured over them. Offer this as a first course at brunch or as a dessert.

Bananas are the perfect dress ups for the easiest, most ordinary desserts. Packaged puddings and fruit gelatines perk up with a crown of golden sliced bananas.

Next time you are dreaming up ideas for a kid's party ... think bananas. They make the neatest, edible place markers. Take a felt tip pen and print each child's name on the skin. Place these sunny markers at each setting and tell the kids they can eat their name cards.

Peel ripe bananas, brush with melted butter, and bake them at 375 degrees for 15 minutes for a different side dish that everyone will enjoy.

Banana pancakes make any breakfast special. Too, they are fast to fix. Just dice a banana into a favorite pancake batter. A few fresh bananas sliced atop the cooked hot cakes adds a bonus of healthful goodness.

Add sliced bananas to glazed carrots just before serving

Also add sliced bananas and chopped peanuts to coleslaw.

Here is a perfect chance to use those very ripe bananas, just waiting on your kitchen counter. Mash the fruit and add it to your packaged muffin mix in place of the liquid specified. While the muffins make wholesome breakfast fare, they are especially tasty at dinner as an accompaniment to roast pork or poultry, or as a surprise in a youngster's lunch box.

Try a peanut butter and sliced banana sandwich.

Top warm gingerbread with sliced bananas and lemon sauce.

Add sliced bananas to hot oatmeal.

Serve curried chicken or cream chipped beef over broiled bananas.

Add sliced bananas and crumbled cooked bacon to a cheese sandwich before grilling.

Ham and eggs and baked bananas are an unusual and delicious combination.

Slice one ripe banana onto a piece of buttered toast, then sprinkle with cinnamon and place it under a preheated broiler two minutes.

* * *

Banana Sticky Buns

10 teaspoons butter or margarine
2 bananas
10 teaspoons orange marmalade
1 package (10-count) refrigerated buttermilk biscuits

1/3 cup flaked coconut

Place one teaspoon of butter in each 10 muffin pan cups; place in a 400 degree oven until butter melts. Add 1 teaspoon marmalade and about 1 1/2 teaspoons of coconut to each muffin cup. Peel bananas and cut into slices, placing about three slices in each cup. Then press a biscuit into each cup. Bake in a 400 degree oven 20 minutes or until biscuits are golden brown and a cake tester inserted in center comes out clean. Cool 10 minutes, turn out of pan, and serve warm.

All in a Woman's Day--February 4, 1986

Remember nose tissues; and the old roller towel?

It always was difficult to carry a handkerchief without losing it. Often it was pinned to the dress; however, boys just about rebelled over a handkerchief. Sissy-like they would say!

Now, while those young men were no doubt wiping their nose on their shirt sleeves, or whatever they were wearing, just remember that the Japanese were sneezing and blowing into a paper tissue.

An Englishman, Peter Mundy, in writing about the Japanese in 1637, has noted that "They blow their Noses with a certaine soft and tough kind of paper which they carry about them in small pieces, which having used, they Fling away as a Filthy thing."

It was in the early 1600s that Hasekura Rokuemon, a Japanese envoy, visited France, and he amazed the French people by using a nose paper (hanagami). It was reported that in some places the citizens would rush to try and pick up his used nose papers, in some instances even fighting over them.

In one account, a French newspaper said this about the envoy's visit: "He was so amused at the people quarreling over his tossed away nose papers that he really used more than necessary for the souvenir hunters to have."

The first paper tissues in the United States appeared in 1924 and were called "Kleenex."

* * *

Have you ever wondered just what became of the roller towel?

Often it hung on the kitchen door, or it could be found at the side of the wash basin; sometimes it hung between a couple of brackets on the wall.

The towel was one continuous piece of cloth, perhaps 14 inches or so wide, and possibly four feet long. To put it in place you would pick up the roller, slide the towel on it, and then place it back in the brackets.

After washing your hands and face, you would hunt for a dry place on the towel; rolling it around until you found a dry spot. Sometimes the wet spots were used several times, depending, of course, on how dry a spot you wanted.

Eventually the towel was pulled around until all the dry spots were used, and a clean towel was hung in its place.

Remember, when company was coming, and then other times, too, the roller towel had to be clean.

At harvest time, the lady of the house was so busy getting food ready and on the table for the hungry workers that the roller towel was forgotten until someone would ask if they could have a dry towel. Do you know what she would remark? "What's the matter with you? Already 50 people have used that towel before you did, and you are the first to complain!"

* * *

Fruit Pizza

1 package sugar cookie mix
1 tub (8-ounces) Philadelphia cream cheese
1/2 cup sugar
1/2 teaspoon vanilla
2 tablespoons "minute" tapioca
1/2 cup orange juice
1 can mandarin oranges, drained
2 bananas, sliced and soaked in lemon juice to keep them from discoloring
1 bag frozen whole strawberries, sliced in half and drained when thawed, or fresh strawberries sliced in half
1 small can crushed pineapple, drained and save juice
White seedless grapes
Maraschino cherries, cut in half and drained

Prepare cookie dough as directed on package, spread on ungreased pizza pan. Bake 10 minutes at 350 degrees, or until lightly browned. Mix cream cheese, sugar and vanilla until creamy. Spread on COOLED crust. Start at the outside edge of the pan and arrange fruit in rows around the pan as listed, with pineapple in the center. Dot pizza with maraschino cherries.

Place reserved pineapple juice and 1/2 cup orange juice in small pan. Add tapioca and let it stand for five minutes. Cook and bring to a boil. Remove from heat and cool. Spread over entire pizza. This is somewhat difficult to do, just be patient. Spread to edge of crust using the back of a wet spoon. Refrigerate and let set for at least one hour before serving. Slice just like a regular pizza.

Month of Love; Caring, sharing time

I have always thought of February as the Month of Love. Perhaps it really is, with Valentine's Day coming this week, and, of course, that is a time for thinking of love and showing our affection.

Genuine love is the greatest thing that anyone can ever give to someone. Neither the most precious of jewels nor the highest of favors can compare with this greatest of Christian virtues. Too, genuine loving concern given to someone also is one of the greatest demonstrations of love.

Oftentimes we strive to give something different, and we may hope to receive something different; however, nothing will ever come near nor approach the giving and receiving of love.

We find that where love is, fear and loneliness cannot abide. Many of the ills of the world, I am sure, could be cured by love. You might convey your love to someone with a letter or a phone call, and it might be done at the proper time when someone was needing special concern.

Love brings happiness, and true love often manifests itself in many ways. As we know, love is patient, love is trusting and love is understanding. Husbands and wives can especially show their love for each other by remembering doing these three things—being patient, trusting and understanding.

It seems that by nature, love is the utmost in human desires.

Love makes it possible for people of different backgrounds and races, to get along. Because of love of country, persons respect the laws. And because of love, we pay the proper homage to God.

Love seems to understand all things; yes, and it even makes allowances, big or little. It takes faithfulness for granted; it is never unduly jealous; love can be reasoned with; it is never uncompromising.

God so loved the world that he gave His only begotten Son. There is no greater love than this.

* * *

There is a story that has been told concerning love in Muslim country. When individuals approach, each touches his own arms, lips, and then the area near the heart. The hands of the two firmly clasp with words of greeting, "Peace to you my friend." These actions have been explained thusly:

To touch the lips means "Of you I will speak no evil."

To touch the heart means "I wish you only love and goodwill."

To touch the hand means "I will do all I can to help you."

How wonderful it would be for each of us if we could meet our neighbors and friends in just such a way!

* * *

May you have a "Happy Valentine's Day!"

* * *

Here is a recipe your family might enjoy on this special day of the heart.

Peppermint Stick Dessert

1 cup vanilla wafer crumbs
1 (8-ounce carton) whipped topping or
1 pint heavy cream, whipped
1 cup miniature marshmallows
1/2 cup finely crushed old-fashioned sugar peppermint stick candy

Place 1/4 cup of crumbs in a buttered 9x13-inch pan. Combine remaining in-gredients and spread over the crumbs. Sprinkle the remaining 1/4 cup of crumbs over the top. Garnish with additional crushed peppermint candy. Chill 24-hours before serving.

All in a Woman's Day--February 18, 1986

Pancakes, whenever served, hit the spot

It makes no difference what season, pancakes, griddle cakes or waffles are always in season.

Somehow, they just seem to hit the spot, whether for breakfast, lunch or supper. Wherever you go, this country kitchen fare has universal appeal, and pancakes are found around the world in one form or another.

The French call them "crepes," a very thin pancake rolled up or folded with a filling; in Sweden it is "plattar"; and, in Holland, they are "flenjses." In Russia they are "blini" or "sirniki," a yeast raised and rolled around caviar. In Hungary, the "palacsinta," is spread with dairy sour cream and chopped ham, stacked 6 or 7 high, and served in wedges. In China a version of the egg roll is thin like a tortilla; while in Germany, they are called "pfannkucken," and in Austria, a souffle light "nocke-rin."

In Jewish cookery, it is the "blintz" that is similar to a crepe, and filled with cottage cheese, cream cheese or fruit. In Italy the "cannelloni" is seasoned with well-cooked meat or fish, and moistened with a little gravy or egg yolks.

Wherever pancakes come from, or whatever variety they come in, they can be made delectable, served for a main dinner course or family favorites for breakfast or dessert.

No doubt you have heard of and probably have made flannel cakes.

They are like the New England griddle cakes, except the baking powder is increased to six teaspoons and the egg yolks and whites are beaten separately, with the batter folded in at the last.

Oh, yes, and "Johnny Cakes." According to legend, these were called "journey cakes" as they were carried for sustenance on various tedious journeys. They are made by pouring two cups boiling water over two cups white corn meal, adding one teaspoon of salt, a half cup of milk and one-fourth cup of melted butter or margarine. More water may be added as the batter should be soft, but not thin. Bake the cakes on a griddle and serve with maple syrup and butter. You might try them sometime without syrup and served with broiled ham, fried chicken or creamed turkey.

Pancakes are such a popular food that they even have a special day set aside for them. Shrove Tuesday or the day before Lent, is traditionally set aside for pancakes. It also is called "Pancake Tuesday."

Eating pancakes on Shrove Tuesday is an old English custom that goes back centuries, when people practiced strict religious laws. That day was the time to confess sins for the Lenten season. It also was the day to use up all the milk, eggs and fat that were not allowed to be eaten during those days of Lent. Still a custom in Oleny, England, and dating back to 1445, a church bell is rung to call the parishoners to the church to confession. This bell is known as the "pancake bell."

A woman was making pancakes when the bell rang, and, grabbing her frying pan, she ran out into the street toward the church, letting the pancakes cook as she went. From this, developed among the women of the town, the annual race to the church with their cooking pancakes. Rules and regulations were laid out, and included a 415 yard course over a brick road, with each participant being over 18 years of age.

* * *

Buckwheat Griddle Cakes

3 cup stlrred buckwheat flour
2 tablespoons brown sugar
1 cup sifted all-purpose flour
3/4 teaspoon soda
1 teaspoon granulated sugar
1 teaspoon salt
2 tablespoons salad oil
1 package active dry yeast

Combine the flours and salt; soften yeast in 1/4 cup warm water (110 degrees). Dissolve the granulated sugar in 3 3/4 cups lukewarm water; add yeast and stir in dry ingredients, mixing well. Cover and let stand overnight at room temperature, (bowl must not be over 1/2 full). The next morning, stir the batter, adding the brown sugar, soda and oil. Refrigerate 1 cup batter for the starter (this keeps several weeks). Bake remaining batter on a hot, lightly greased griddle. Makes 20 griddle cakes.

To use the starter, add 1 cup lukewarm water, 1/2 cup stirred buckwheat flour and 1/2 cup sifted all-purpose flour. Stir batter until smooth and let it stand overnight as before. When ready to bake, add 1/2 teaspoon of salt, 1/2 teaspoon of soda, 2 tablespoons of brown sugar and 1 teaspoon of salad oil. Again reserve 1 cup of batter for starter.

* * *

New England Griddle Cakes

2 cups all-purpose flour
4 teaspoons baking powder
2 tablespoons sugar

1 teaspoon salt
1 cup milk
1/4 cup melted butter or margarine
2 well beaten eggs

Combine the ingredients and make large cakes, and spread while hot with soft butter and grated maple sugar; stack 6 high and cut like a pie.

* * *

Another trick the New Englanders use is to add some maple syrup to the batter, replacing the sugar and part of the milk. This makes four servings.

All in a Woman's Day--February 26, 1986

Pancakes have nourished nations

It would seem, that because of popularity, people have been consuming "hot cakes" almost since the discovery of fire. According to historians, flat, thin cakes of meal and water were the first foods created by human hands. So, down through the ages, pancakes, in one form or another, have been nourishment for almost every nation.

The first pancake was invented when a harried cook spilled a splat of batter on a hot stove. Whatever the origin, pancakes, griddle cakes, hot cakes, or whatever you call them, have made interesting and nourishing meals.

Pancakes, or griddle cakes, are the oldest form of bread. The first ones were made of pounded grain that were mixed with water and spread upon a hot rock to dry. Unleavened bread of the Hebrews was cooked on a griddle; in China, the egg roll, really a pancake, has been made for untold oriental ages.

Griddle cooking is an old form that developed in many countries, where cooking was simple and fuel scarce.

Here, in America, we associate such cooking with pioneer life. It was the griddle cakes that provided hot bread when circumstances did not prevail setting up a bake oven or taking time to use it.

The griddle should be heated slowly so that the heat is evenly distributed. If an ungreased griddle is used, it should be rubbed with a cloth bag filled with salt, after each batch of cakes is made. It is ready for use, when a drop or two of water is placed on it and the water begins to dance and sizzle swiftly about.

Today, most modern griddles do not need greasing; however, if found necessary just grease lightly. (I use a spray vegetable shortening).

If you want pancakes the same size, use a 1/4 cup measure to dip the batter to the griddle. If dollar-size cakes are wanted, use a tablespoon for dipping.

The cakes should be cooked until they are full of bubbles and the underneath sides are nicely brown. Turn them with a pancake turner or spatula, and then brown the other side. This takes only half the time to cook as the first half.

Batters for pancakes and waffles should be stirred quickly, and only until the dry ingredients are moistened. The batter should be a bit lumpy. An electric skillet, waffle iron or griddle make for perfect heat control when cooking the cakes. Some cooks would rather use a frying pan, however.

Whether you are making pancakes from a mix or an old family recipe, the trick to browning the cakes is in the making. Like all good golden pancakes, there must be shortening in the batter. But did you know that a little bit of light corn syrup added to the batter does even more for browning? If it is a mix or your own recipe, add about a tablespoon of light corn syrup for each cup of mix or flour. The heat should be moderately hot so that the cakes brown quickly, but not so quickly as to leave them raw inside.

Overbeating the batter makes the pancakes tough. The batter should not stand too long before using.

When making waffles, close the lid quickly and wait for the signal light or until the steam stops, before opening it.

If you desire a crisp waffle, allow it to remain on the grid for a few seconds after opening the lid, or let it bake a little longer.

To keep pancakes and waffles warm for a brief time, place them in a 250 degree oven after baking.

When milk is used in the batter, it should be room temperature.

* * *

Griddle Cakes

1/2 cup milk
2 tablespoons melted butter
1 egg
1 cup all-purpose flour
2 teaspoons baking powder
2 tablespoons sugar
1/2 teaspoon salt

Place in a mixing bowl the milk, butter and egg, and beat lightly. Sift together the dry ingredients and add to the milk mixture all at once. Stir just enough to dampen the flour. Add more milk if necessary to make the batter as thick as heavy cream. (Makes 6 to 8 cakes.) To vary, use buttermilk, sour milk or yogurt in place of milk. Use 1/2 teaspoon baking soda, instead of baking powder. Also, you can sift 1 tablespoon of corn meal in with the flour.

Cedar chests prove handy; all time 'Top Ten' sayings

Did you know that one piece of furniture that has been around more than 500 years is still popular? Do you know what it is? It's the cedar chest, also called a "hope chest" by generations of brides.

The versatility of the cedar chest has been rediscovered in recent years, probably because it is a great storage area for apartments and houses.

Traditionally, cedar chests were used to store linens, blankets and out-of-season clothing, especially woolens.

It seems that cedar chests fit into the same category as multifunction furniture and in addition to providing much needed storage area, they also perform other tasks. They are really appropriate for almost any room in the house.

There are a number of ways that cedar chests can be used in the decorating of the home or apartment. First of all, the cedar chest must complement the general look you have planned for the home. Contemporary European styled rooms will be highlighted by unadorned black lacquer or low-gloss teak chests. The soft tones of scrubbed pine or walnut chests are in tune with the country look. There are more than 100 different styles from which selections can be made; in fact, there is a cedar chest to fit any style of interior decor.

Some chests have upholstered seats on top; some have drawers on the bottom; there are extra wide chests for blankets and pillows; and believe it or not, there is even a chest with a shelf for the telephone.

The chest can be used as an end table between the sofa and a chair, with a slender lamp on top, for reading. Off-season clothes may be stored there, too.

In a small apartment, it can be used as a coffee table in front of a sofa bed. Pillows, blankets and sheets can be stored there as well as anything you might want to keep out of sight.

So, why not get in the mood and think cedar chests … they would be a great buy if you don't have one.

* * *

I have clipped the "Top Ten" sayings of all time and thought this might be of interest.

1. "Do unto others as you would that they should do unto you." (The Bible, paraphrasing Matthew and Luke)

2. "Know thyself." (Attributed originally to Socrates by Plato).

3. "Anything that is worth doing at all is worth doing well." (Earl of Chesterfield)

4. "If at first you don't succeed, try, try again." (William E. Hickson)

5. "The great essentials of happiness are something to do, something to love and something to hope for." (Unknown)

6. "The only way to have a friend to to be one." (Ralph Waldo Emerson)

7. "As a man thinketh in his heart, so is he." (The Bible, Proverbs)

8. "Knowledge is power." (Thomas Hobbes)

9. "Actions speak louder than words." (An ancient proverb, source unknown)

10. "An ounce of prevention is worth a pound of cure." (Old English proverb)

* * *

Beulah's Baked Chicken Breasts

Chicken breasts
1 1/2 cup raw rice
1/2 cup butter, melted
1 can chicken broth
1 can cream of onion soup
1 can cream of mushroom soup

Place chicken breasts on top of the raw rice, broth and onion soup mixture. Spread cream of mushroom soup over the top. Bake in a 350 degree oven 1 1/2 hours.

All in a Woman's Day--March 11, 1986

Eggs add sunshine to spring celebration

'Tis the season for thinking about and using eggs. They are a food that rates high on the list during the Lenten season.

Let eggs add sunshine to your spring celebration! After the decorated eggs lead the Easter parade, it's even more fun to enjoy them again in delicious, nutritious dishes. Eggs have been involved for hundreds of years in many of the traditional ways of celebrating this special season.

Most ancient people considered the egg to be sacred. It symbolizes the world and its elements. The earth is represented by the shell; water, the white; fire, the yolk; and the air itself, captured under the shell.

Easter, which occurs this year March 30, is such a joyous time and even for those who do not believe in the religious significance, it means—spring. For people around the world, Easter (or spring) is the time for celebrating.

There are unlimited tasty ways eggs can be used. Chowders and cream soups are pretty and also more nutritious with a slice or two of a hard cooked egg placed on top. Vegetables also can be dressed up with sieved hard cooked eggs added to the cream or cheese sauce.

Almost any kind of salad ... potato, tossed, molded or macaroni ... is prettier and tastier when hard cooked eggs are used in the salad or as a garnish.

After coloring Easter eggs, and the dye has dried, try rubbing the egg in a little shortening placed on a paper towel or in napkin or a dish. Then notice the results. The eggs will shine, and also it helps to take care of any uneven spots that possibly occurred in the dying.

When poaching an egg, add a little lemon juice to keep the egg white compact and prevent spreading.

Never wash eggs before storing. Egg shells are porous, and washing them permits germs to penetrate the shell more easily. If stored with the large end up, they will stay fresh longer. Also, they will stay fresh longer if stored in their own carton instead of in the refrigerator egg space.

Did you know that adding water, instead of milk, when scrambling eggs makes much lighter eggs?

In the event you are short of eggs, use one heaping tablespoon of coffee creamer for each egg needed.

When making an omelet, add a pinch of corn starch and a pinch of powdered sugar to the yolk before beating. This will keep it from collapsing and improves the staying power.

Omelets are generally of two different kinds: The puffy, in which the whites and the yolks are beaten separately resulting in a more fluffy omelet; and the French, when the yolks and whites are beaten together, thus resulting in a firmer, less fluffy omelet. Other omelets are variations of these basic kinds.

* * *

Puffy Omelet

6 eggs, separated
1/2 teaspoon salt
1/8 teaspoon pepper
11/2 tablespoons all-purpose flour
1 tablespoon water
2 tablespoons butter or margarine

Beat the egg whites and salt until stiff; however, not dry. Beat egg yolks with pepper, flour and water until fluffy. Then fold yolk mixture into the white thoroughly, but gently. Melt butter in a 10-inch skillet, tipping so the butter spreads over the bottom. Pour the mixture into the skillet, gently leveling the surface, and cover. Cook over very low heat until the omelet surface is dry and when a knife is inserted it comes out clean. Fold and serve immediately. Makes 4 servings. If cooking in an electric skillet, heat butter to 320 degrees and pour in omelet mixture, reducing the heat to 240 degrees for cooking.

All in a Woman's Day--March 18, 1986

Spring has arrived; how it is celebrated

It is getting that time of year when nature is edging towards a change, and human beings develop a behavioral pattern called "spring fever."

Spring, which arrives this week, through the centuries has been described by poets and philosophers as a curious mixture of cheer and woe. We have a few bright, warm days, followed by some more cold weather this time of year that seem to trigger "spring fever." This has been widely associated with mind wandering or day dreaming or restlessness. One poet put it this way: "March beckons spring that unlocks the flowers that paint the laughing sail."

Spring is the fading twilight of winter, and those animals that hibernate begin to thrill to the flute songs of their fine feathered friends returning from the southland.

This season is a rebirth ... flowers begin to peek through the ground, grass starts to take on a green tinge, and the buds on the early blooming shrubs begin to swell. Snowdrops and crocus also are making their debut.

Spring just seems to happen overnight. A writer for Encyclopedia Britannica has tried to say that there are really only two seasons ... winter and summer. Spring, he contends, as well as autumn, are merely transitional periods we unduly dignify with the season titles. The precious few weeks of spring seem to give new life to everything and spirits rise, and we are reminded that hope does "spring eternal."

Many years ago it was decided that spring was a good excuse for a celebration. These spring events have been with us long before Stravinsky immortalized "The Sacred Rites of Spring" in music. In ancient Roman times, a young man impersonated the god of sowing and husbandry for 30 days; then was put to death to symbolize the end of the old god and birth of a new one.

Greek maidens would dance wildly on Mount Parnassus to honor the great god Dionysus.

The Natchez Indians marked the season by putting out campfires, then solemnly relighting them as a symbol of rebirth.

In Japan it is the Cherry Blossom Festival that opens the spring season.

Morris dances have been big in England and Northern France, and the Chinese seem to have perhaps the best of all, the "Festival of Excited Insects."

In America, the spring dance must surely be performed on the baseball diamond.

Spring also means cleaning time, getting rid of the dirt and cobwebs, and making a fresh start, possibly turning over a new leaf.

Numerous midwesterners, who left the area, have found themselves coming back because the change of the seasons were missed so much.

It would seem that our great-great-grandpa had the right idea ... "Spring is a season worth noticing."

* * *

Pastel Spring Salad

2 (16-ounce) cans fruit cocktail
2 (11-ounce) cans mandarin oranges
2 (16-ounce) cans pineapple tidbits
1 large carton whipped topping
1 (22-ounce) can lemon pie filling
1 (10 1/2-ounce) package colored miniature marshmallows

Drain the fruits thoroughly, 1 to 2 hours. Mix whipped topping and pie filling, folding in fruit and marshmallows. Pour mixture into serving dish and refrigerate. Serves at least 10 to 12.

All in a Woman's Day--March 25, 1986
Easter is sunshine

To the Christian, Easter is the sunshine after the stormy weather; it is the freshness of spring after the long winter season.

Easter is a challenge to our faith; it is a challenge to renew our faith. Everywhere as we glance through the eyes of faith, we see the springtime evidence of renewal, rebirth, hope and expectancy.

The voice of Easter is but the echo of the words of hope that have been repeated over and over, "I am the Resurrection and the life ... " Those who hear and believe these words, will always find Easter to be the dawn of a new beginning, a putting away of things that trouble the mind, replacing them with a new hope of better things to come.

As we go forward to meet the spring, we can see the stone of winter being rolled from the door of the sepulcher to let life, warmth and beauty take over the land. From Easter we can gather strength to face the inevitable, to be able to salvage something good out of the winter just past, and to face the sunshine of a new beginning, letting shadows fall behind us.

A good exercise for Holy Week is to go through your Bible with a concordance and jot down pertinent scripture about the word "expectancy" or its derivatives. You will find advice there for almost any problem of today's confused period in history.

On Sunday, as another Easter comes, we will be reminded that Christ is still drawing men to Him. At each Easter season, many who rarely participate in life of the Christian Church will be in the sanctuaries to hear again the central fact of Christianity ... He arose!

And because He arose, because He lives, we shall live also!

* * *

May you have a blessed Easter!

It is always time for good 'hot cakes'

Spring, summer, fall or winter it makes no difference what season hot cakes, griddle cakes, Johnny cakes, pancakes or whatever your favorite name is for this special food, it is always good.

When you serve this food, something a bit sweet seems appropriate for the topping. Of course, plenty of butter must be included, and when the "cakes" are stacked with butter oozing out between them and drenched in molasses, honey, maple syrup or any other sweetening desired, this is a food that sets the taste buds working overtime.

Perhaps you have your own favorite topping to help make the "cakes" still a bit more luscious. Following are a few toppings you might enjoy trying:

Mock Maple Syrup: Boil until sugar dissolves (about 1 minute), 1 cup of light brown sugar and 1/3 cup of water. Then add a few grains of salt and a teaspoon vanilla. Serve hot or cold.

Honey Sauce: This is also good on cakes. It is made by mixing in a saucepan 2 tablespoons of melted butter and 2 teaspoons of corn starch. Stir until smooth and add 1/4 cup of honey. Cook 5 minutes.

Strawberry Butter: Combine 2 sticks or 1 cup butter or margarine with 1/2 cup of chopped fresh strawberries and 3 tablespoons of confectioners' sugar in a blender or food processor with a steel blade. (Frozen strawberries also can be used.) Whip until light and fluffy. This yields 1/2 cups of strawberry butter. It keeps well refrigerated. This also is good on biscuits.

Maple Syrup: Cook and stir until dissolved 1 cup of light corn syrup, 1/2 cup of light brown sugar and 1/2 cup of water. Then add 1 tablespoon of butter and a dash of maple flavoring.

Whipped Butter: Take 1/2 cup of butter and whip in an electric mixer until fluffy.

Honey Butter: Gradually add 1/4 cup of honey to whipped butter and beat until smooth; 2 tablespoons of grated orange peel also can be added.

Honey Peanut Butter Sauce: Combine and mix until smooth and of pouring consistency honey and peanut butter.

Orange Sauce: Combine 1/2 cup of butter, 1 cup of sugar and 1/2 cup of frozen orange juice concentrate. Bring to a boil, stirring occasionally.

All in a Woman's Day--April 8, 1986

Various weeds make edible food

The delight of children and the scourge of gardeners ... it is the dandelion, and here it is back again in all of its glory for another round of applause.

If dandelions were confined to a flower bed, we would undoubtedly say, "They are beautiful." However, since they are among the earliest so called "weeds" to sprout up, we just naturally think of them as such ... a weed! But that is not exactly right, as edible food comes from the plant, the root and the flower.

A familiar hardy plant of the chicory family, that has adapted itself to many climates, dandelions can be found growing throughout Asia, Europe, North America and the Arctic. The name dandelion comes from the French "dent le lion" or "lion's tooth," because of the sharply indented leaves of the plant.

No doubt the plant immigrated to America from Europe soon after the first colonists landed, arriving, perhaps in the earthen ballast then carried by many ships.

The plant is known by several other names ranging from the terse epithets of gardeners to blow ball, cankerwort, doon-headed-clock, fortune teller, horse gowan and Irish daisy.

Since it often reproduces by parthenogenesis (virgin birth), the dandelion needs not rely on the vagaries of wind or bees for pollination. Anyone, who has even attempted to grow a lawn, knows the tenacity of the dandelion.

In Europe, dandelion greens have long been accepted as a spring vegetable; to our colonial forefathers, a mess of dandelion greens was a spring tonic, a blood purifier and good for rheumatism. Dandelions also are used as an ingredient in laxatives.

No doubt many of you will recall how your grandmother, mother or perhaps even you yourself would go "greens" hunting in the early spring for the first signs of dandelions and other wild growing "weeds."

If you want to go "greens" hunting, be sure and look for the very young, fresh, green plants, with tender leaves.

Cultivated dandelion greens are more blanched and tender and not as bitter as wild varieties. Always avoid plants with wilted, tough or yellow leaves.

In the early spring, cultivated and wild dandelion greens can be found in the markets, and also during some of the winter months in southern areas. It is not easy to find dandelions growing in the wild, as many of them get sprayed with weed killer, making their use as a food nil.

Dandelion greens can be used just as greens from the garden. To cook, boil about a half-inch of water in a saucepan; add the thoroughly washed greens and salt; covering, and cooking 10 to 20 minutes or until tender. Drain and season to taste. A touch of vinegar is enjoyed by some partakers. For the very young and tender leaves use no water, just place washed greens in a covered saucepan. They will cook in the water that clings to the leaves after washing.

It has been said that dandelion greens make a tasty and delicious salad; however, again the leaves must be picked when very tender as they grow bitter with age. Blanched, chilled and served with a dressing, this makes what might be termed in some peoples' language a gourmet's delight. When using dandelions for salads, tear leaves into bite-size pieces; for cooking cut into 2-inch pieces.

The flowers often have been used for making dandelion wine. There is food value in the yellow blossoms as well as beauty. Some people prefer to eat the blossoms instead of the greens. Gather the blossoms early in the morning and rinse well in cold water, letting them soak in salt water about two hours. Roll in egg batter, flour and fry until golden brown. Supposedly they taste like fried mushrooms.

The roots are eaten as a vegetable or roasted and ground and made into coffee. To prepare as a vegetable, dig up the entire plant, root and all, then peel the roots with a potato peeler or a sharp knife; slice thinly crosswise. Cover with water and bring this to a boil and drain. Repeat the process and serve, seasoned with salt, pepper and butter.

To make coffee, roast the roots in a slow oven for about four hours. They should snap easily and show a dark brown interior when done. Grind and use as you would coffee. (This can be a bit bitter!)

How many people have heard of using the leaves of "dent de lion" to make tea? The tender leaves may be collected to be used fresh or dried and stored for winter use. In either case, the resultant drink is a pale green color with a delicate flavor that is a reminder of Oriental green teas. Never boil the mixture or the brew will be bitter. Place just enough dandelion leaves in a cup or nonmetallic pot and add hot water. Steep them three to five minutes, and enjoy them either plain or sweetened with honey.

Since it contains no caffeine, this tea is supposed to be good for indigestion and soothing to ruffled nerves.

Did you ever make dandelion jelly? Its taste resembles honey. In the early morning pick one quart of dandelion blooms without any stems. Wash and boil them with one quart of water three minutes. Drain off three cups liquid, add one package of pectin and one teaspoon lemon or orange extract and four and a half cups of sugar. Boil about three minutes and place in containers.

The dandelion is very high in vitamin

431

A and is a good source of calcium and potassium.

The silkworm even knows the value of the dandelion, using it for food in the absence of mulberry leaves.

Bees, no doubt, have a sense of epicureans, for they delight in gathering dandelion sweets for their "honey pots." According to some beekeepers, dandelions make about the best tasting honey of all varieties, even better than clover.

As sure as spring arrives, children all over our country can be found arriving home from school with sticky, green-stained hands, clutching a drooping bouquet of dandelions that they had picked just for "mother."

For generations, children and lovers have blown the fuzzy winged seeds from the hoary seed balls to know when they would get married, how many children they would have and whether or not their love was requited. Children often try holding a fresh dandelion blossom under the chin of a friend and announce that the yellow reflection means he likes butter. Because of this, they are sometimes called butter balls. Youngsters also tell time by the number of puffs required to blow away the down of the mature seeds, and they enjoy making bracelets and necklaces from the dandelion stalks with the flowers attached.

* * *

A few strange beliefs have emanted from the dandelion.

It will rain when dandelions don't open on mornings in Maryland, or when the down flies off the stalk on windless days.

Gathered on St. John's (Mid-summer) Eve in Silsesia, the dandelion wards off witches.

* * *

Knowing all the good things that come from the dandelion might make this lowly versatile "little feller" more acceptable to society.

In commenting on the life of the dandelion, one botanist ominously concludes that the "terrifying efficient" herb stands a good chance of inheriting the earth; to this grass growers will agree.

All in a Woman's Day--April 15, 1986

All about lettuce; ways to keep it longer

Some of you early gardeners are no doubt having fresh lettuce from your gardens by now; however, the cold blast of weather that blew in here last week stopped the growing process for the time being.

Lettuce lovers, and there are many, think there is nothing like fresh lettuce and radishes from the garden. Wilting the lettuce by using some bacon drippings, vinegar, sugar, salt and pepper, and a bit of onion, is a dish that is relished in the spring.

One of the oldest of vegetable crops, lettuce was introduced into America from Europe soon after the first colonies were established.

Lettuce, the common name of members of the herbaceous genus Lactuca, belongs to the chicory family, particularly the garden lettuce. The genus is a native to temperate regions of Eurasia and North America.

European wild lettuce, or prickly lettuce, is widely distributed throughout Europe and naturalized in the northeast United States. It has a slightly prickly stem, and its leaves have soft prickle margins. European wild lettuce is thought by most botanists to be the

432

parent species of garden lettuce. American wild lettuce or horseweed, a smoother, leafier plant, native to temperate North America, grows profusely in thickets and damp borders of fields.

Garden lettuce has been cultivated since the time of the ancient Greeks, and is a hardy annual herb. The four common horticultural varieties are head, leaf, Romaine and asparagus lettuce. Head lettuce forms cabbage like heads; leaf lettuce has free growing leaves that do not form a head; Romaine, or Cos lettuce, produces long, erect heads; and the asparagus lettuce has thick, edible stems and unpalatable leaves.

Most of the commercial lettuce produced in the United States is head lettuce.

The name lettuce has been commonly extended to include leafy vegetables, such as endive, and those that can be eaten raw in salads.

In the event you need some help in buying and storing lettuce, here are a few hints. In purchasing, always avoid heads of Iceberg lettuce that are very hard and that lack green color—these are signs of over maturity.

It is well to soak leafy greens from the garden in a solution of water and vinegar, using one tablespoon of vinegar to one quart of water. This kills any tiny bugs or worms that may still be clinging to the leaves. Also, it helps to crisp the greens. Rinse in cold water before using.

Most of us have a problem of keeping lettuce fresh and crisp. There are several different methods that you might like to try and then use the one that works best for you.

Always rewrap lettuce as soon as it is brought from the store. Throw away the adhesive wrapping and refrigerate in plastic bread bags. The lettuce is supposed to last twice as long with no wilting or darkening.

For crisping lettuce, and also celery, quickly place it in a pan of cold water with a few slices of raw potato.

Absorbent cotton terry cloth towels can be used to wrap lettuce, celery and other greens before storing in the refrigerator. The absorbent cotton fabric will keep the greens fresh and crisp for days.

It is possible to keep lettuce almost a month by storing it carefully. Break off any discolored leaves and make sure the head is completely dry. Wrap it loosely in plastic wrap or put it in a plastic bag and leave the top open. Place the head in a brown paper bag, folding it tightly around the lettuce and place it on the bottom shelf of the refrigerator, not in the crisper as it will draw moisture.

After bringing a head of lettuce from the store, wash and cover it with ice water for 30 minutes; drain about 15 minutes, then wrap it in several paper towels and place it in a plastic bag and refrigerate. After each use, rewrap in the same towels that are still damp. Lettuce should be crisp, and will keep longer than you may think it would.

Another hint is to leave the lettuce in the original plastic wrap and then wrap it in aluminum foil. Do not wash lettuce until ready to use.

Still another way: Core the lettuce and wash as usual making sure, however, that some water runs all the way down through the core. Then turn upside down, and drain. Place the lettuce head, with the core side up, in a plastic bag and leave the bag slightly open.

An average head of lettuce serves

four, and each serving has about 25 calories. It also adds calcium, vitamin A and iron to the diet.

Always tear off the amount you want to use and wash it thoroughly. Never cut lettuce with a knife as it bruises the leaves and speeds deterioration.

Too, torn lettuce is said to be better tasting than that which is cut.

A leaf of lettuce dropped into a pot absorbs the grease from the top of soup. Remove the lettuce as soon as it has served its purpose.

All in a Woman's Day--April 22, 1986

Mushroom season is about to arrive

Mother Nature seems to be on the early side this year, and while it is not quite time for the mushroom season, should the weather stay warm, and there is a humid rain, mushrooms will surely begin popping up.

Usually, when the first fingerlets of asparagus appear; the earth is moist, apple trees are taking on a blush of pink, and lilacs are about to bloom; it is the time to seek the morels, or sponges as they also are called.

Mushrooming comes only a few weeks in the spring and hits many folks like a fever. They take to the countryside in search of this gourmet eating. Hunters slip away quietly and silently to a destination that they never reveal, to seek and hopefully find that choice bit of eating that just can't be excelled, that is, if you are a mushroom eater.

Where do you find them? Well, that is a matter of opinion. Some say anywhere; however, if you know of an area that has really produced well in past years, it is most likely it will continue to be a productive spot that will bring forth fruit again and again. But don't be disappointed if you don't find them at this spot, for sometimes the beds have been known to quit overnight, and then again, some places that have been barren seem to come to life each year with the spore-bearing fruit.

Some authoritives seem to think that the most productive beds can be found in areas along creeks and rivers and on bottom land; however, many have been found on hills, knolls and even on bluffs. In areas where there are May apples growing, morels often appear. Too, they are sometimes found in old sawdust piles, and they seem to have an affinity for elm trees, particularly dead elm stumps. According to a veteran hunter, sunlight is a necessity, for when trees begin to leaf out fully, the season stops.

Squirrels enjoy taking them away to their nests to eat leisurely during the winter. Cows, too, like to eat the succulent varieties.

The morel is only a flower or bloom of a large multibranched underground fungus that has, no doubt, been growing years before it thrusts forward its first flower, according to experts. To reproduce, the fungus must send forth spores, and this is where the mushroom comes in; for it is the spore-bearing body that can appear above ground in a matter of seconds when conditions are just right. It seems that the microscopic spores the mushroom sends forth can be carried by animals, wind, and often by the mushroom hunters themselves. It has been found that only in rare cases does a spore take root and start a new fungus. Even after one is started, it is even more rare for it to flower or reproduce, so the supply is limited. This seems to be another case when Mother Nature is wiser than science.

The season is short for morels; here in Missouri it lasts sometimes only about four weeks. The first morels to appear are small, grayish to almost black. Then comes the large, more cream colored variety that can be found for a week or two. The edible morels can be readily identified by the spongelike characteristics. If you are lucky enough to find some, and you are a novice hunter, it might be wise to check your find with an experienced hunter, just to be on the safe side.

To the neophyte mushroom hunter; you will have to look carefully, for you can walk right over them as they blend into the leaves and the surrounding ground covering.

When you are a mushroom hunter, you have to move fast, for when they pop up, they only last several days, and if not picked will dehydrate and simply wither away. If you are among some of the lucky hunters to find this choice bit of eating, do you know how to store or prepare them?

One way is to hang them up to dry using a darning needle to go through the heaviest parts of the stem. Do not wash them before hanging them in a warm, dry place, where they should be left several weeks. They will shrivel as they dry. When completely dry, store them in coffee cans or similar containers and cover with a plastic lid.

To use, soak in hot water, drain gently and rinse until water is clear. Use hot water, not cold water. Drain on paper towels, cook as desired.

Mushrooms can be rolled in cracker crumbs, or coated with flour and then fried in a small amount of shortening (butter is best), or they can be deep fried. They also can be steamed in just a little beef broth. When sauteed in butter, they can be used to make about the best gravy ever tasted.

Mushrooms also can be frozen satisfactorily; so, if you get an extra supply, you might want to take care of them this way.

Morels are a delight to weight watchers, for they contain almost no calories, only minerals, protein and a flavor that makes everything else second best, that is, if you are a mushroom lover. The taste has a slight resemblance to domestic mushrooms; however, there is really no comparison.

Mushrooms bruise easily, but don't worry about brown spots as the flavor is not affected. Do not sautee them longer than three minutes.

This is a delicious, expensive and mysterious vegetable, and is closer to resembling meat than any other vegetable.

Now, if you think fishermen can spin some tall tales, just listen to morel hunters as they compare their mushroom finds.

All in a Woman's Day--April 29, 1986

Cabbage, called man's best friend, is ancient

It will still be a while before garden cabbage is on our tables in some form of tasty eating; however, most homemakers do use cabbage in some way several times a week. Raw cabbage is a good source of vitamin C and some vitamin A.

Cabbage, which has a Latin name of brassoca, is called man's best friend in the vegetable world. Learned scholars have argued about the origin of this great vegetable; however, the facts are both obscure and ancient.

Researchers have found that at least 4,000 years ago men were eating the leafy wild cabbage that was found on the coasts of Europe and northern Africa. In addition, cabbage also was eaten in China several thousand years ago. And, too, the Egyptians, Greeks and Romans all seemed to "adore" cabbage. Five pages were written by Marcus Porcius Cato, who was a great Roman statesman, seemingly a forerunner of the Americans' taste for coleslaw: "It surpasses all other vegetables. It may be eaten either cooked or raw. If you eat it raw, dip it into vinegar . . . It promotes digestion marvelously."

The Celts also thought highly of this vegetable, and took it into northern Europe. During the centuries it grew in Great Britain it became known as the national flower of England.

Cabbage arrived on the North American continent by way of Jacques Cartier, who planted it in Canada on his third voyage in 1541-42.

Early American colonists surely must have planted cabbage; if for nothing else than to feed their stock; however, there is no written record of it until 1669.

Cabbage comes in many varieties. Some have firm heads, some are loose, some are flat, egg-shaped or conical. Too, some have curly leaves and some are plain. In one form or another, cabbage is eaten in most countries, and it is the favorite food of the Slavic and the Germanic people as an important part of their daily diet.

Along with the versality of this vegetable, a number of myths or legends have been passed down. For instance, if you dream of cabbage, it meant sickness to loved ones and loss of money. It was told that babies were found in cabbage patches and young Scottish women guessed at the size and figure of their future husbands by drawing cabbages blindfolded on Halloween. Perhaps many of you know the story about the man on the moon. He was sent there because he stole a cabbage from his neighbor on December 24. It seems that a child in white surprised him doing this evil deed and said, "Since you will steal on this Holy night, let you and your cabbage go to the moon."

Sauerkraut that comes from cabbage, is said to have originated in Asia. Making kraut was a convenient way of preserving this essential food when no other method was available.

For many folks there is nothing that tastes better on a cold winter night than a big helping of tart and tangy sauerkraut. Served with a cracklin' crisp pork roast, frankfurters or sliced baked ham, it adds a delightful change of pace to a fall or winter menu.

To some people it tastes even better when it is homemade. The process isn't too hard. Just combine shredded cabbage with the right amount of pickling salt in a large stone crock and then let it cure in its own juice.

If you would like to make some quart jars of it just chop the cabbage until it is very fine; pack it in the jars and allow two teaspoons of salt for each quart. Pour hot water over cabbage, filling jars to shoulders. Seal. Sauerkraut will be ready for use after two weeks. This can be processed, in a hot water bath or pressure cooker.

* * *

Baked Kraut
No. 2 1/2 size can sauerkraut
1 cup sugar
Bacon

Place kraut in a greased casserole; place bacon and sugar on top of that. Bake 2 1/2 hours at 250 degrees. This is especially good with a turkey dinner.

All in a Woman's Day--May 6, 1986

Variety in cabbage; various ways of eating

Today there is more information available concerning cabbage.

Several kinds of cabbage are now found on the market. The Danish variety is a compact, solid head of late maturing cabbage, with leaves tight and smooth around the top, and with heads that are round and somewhat flattened or oval.

The heads of the domestic cabbage are somewhat angular and are usually not as compact as the Danish. The leaf tissues are more tender and brittle, and the leaves are somewhat curled or crumpled, and do not overlap as far at the crown as the Danish. This variety is largely an early or midseason crop.

The pointed cabbage is one that is called green or new cabbage and has a smaller head than Danish and the domestic; it is greener in color.

Red cabbage has leaves that are somewhat loose. There are several varieties of this reddish purple cabbage.

Savory cabbage is identified by crinkled leaves that shade from dark to pale, and the heads are loosely formed. People of Latin descent had this as a favorite, and it is becoming more and more popular in this country. This cabbage has a more mellow flavor than other green cabbage.

The celery or Chinese cabbage, as it is called, is a rather distant member of the cabbage family. The stalks are long and firm, tapering (about four-inches thick to about 12-inches long). It is a cross between oversized Romaine lettuce and celery. The leaves are tightly closed and are broad and crisp, ranging in color from pale green to white. It is used mainly in salads; however, many interesting and inviting dishes can be made from this vegetable.

When selecting cabbage, note that it should be solid and heavy for its size. Avoid heads that show yellow leaves, decay or injury. Should the base of some of the outer leaves be separated from the stem, the cabbage will no doubt be strong in flavor and coarse in texture when it is cooked.

Celery cabbage should be oval-shaped, firm and well balanced.

One pound of cabbage equals 3 1/2 cups raw or 2 1/2 cups when cooked.

In preparing cabbage, cut it according to the way it is to be used. Should it be old, cut round heads into wedges and remove the core in the center or shred it.

Never overcook cabbage.

It can be boiled in wedges, shredded or braised. Red Cabbage can be cooked any of these ways; however, a little vinegar or lemon juice added or a few apple slices will help hold the color.

To make ordinary fresh cabbage slaw fancier and different, add some cut up marshmallows or little pieces of pineapple.

For a different taste, try adding a little dill to each quart of kraut before sealing. Another variation is a small pod of red pepper.

To prevent a cabbage smell, put some walnuts, with the shells still on, into the pot along with the cabbage.

Also, a slice of bread on top of cooking cabbage will prevent odor from escaping.

A small bowl of vinegar placed near the cooking cabbage also helps to absorb odors.

A stalk of celery included in the pan when cooking cabbage, broccoli and other members of the cabbage family, will help lessen the odor.

To make cabbage easier to digest, cook it with the cover off about 7 to 10 minutes, which is enough to make it tender and still save vitamins.

Some homemakers freeze cabbage by cleaning it and then chopping it rather coarsely with a knife, not as fine, however, as for coleslaw. Steam it in boiling water three minutes, drain and chill it in ice water until cool. Drain in colander. Place it in plastic bags. This is good in stews or creamed.

If you are raising cabbage and have trouble with worms, you might try some of these methods: Pour cold wash water over them; it must be the soap that turns them off.

Try putting powdered sugar generously on the heads.

Another old-time method is to sift flour over the head every time it rains, from the time the cabbage first starts until it heads.

Nylon net held up by stakes with cans upside down over the top stalks will help protect from the white butterflies that lay eggs that later become cabbage worms.

* * *

Simple Baked Cabbage

1 pound cabbage, shredded
1 teaspoon salt
2 tablespoons butter
2 tablespoons flour
Dash of pepper
11/4 cups milk
1 teaspoon prepared mustard
1/2 cup cheese, shredded or grated
2 tablespoons crushed corn flakes

Cook cabbage covered in a small amount of boiling water until just barely tender, about 8 minutes. Drain and sprinkle it with 1/2 teaspoon salt. Melt butter and stir in flour, and remaining 1/2 teaspoon salt, and pepper. Stir in milk and prepared mustard and cook, stirring constantly, until mixture thickens. Combine cabbage, sauce and half of the cheese and spoon into a buttered 1-quart casserole. Sprinkle with remaining cheese that has been mixed with crumbs. Bake at 350 degrees 20 to 25 minutes or until hot and bubbly.

All in a Woman's Day--May 13, 1986
Barbecues could lead to more healthy eating

Have a barbecue if you have need for rekindling your family's interest in healthy eating.

Backyard barbecues always popular, provide a base for friendly, relaxed gatherings. Cooking and eating outdoors seems to offer an informal atmosphere that lends itself to congeniality.

In planning a menu, be sure to consider fresh, wholesome foods. Cooking outdoors also provides exciting opportunities for menu variations, as well as grilled creations.

Most folks, who do much barbecuing, are aware of the "regulars" for this type of cooking; however, it is the many fresh fruits and vegetables that can be grilled that make luscious additions to a barbecue. Corn on the cob and baked potatoes, the old favorites, are always good, but there are other possibilities, too.

Some vegetables have their own wrappings and can be cooked directly on the charcoal. These include baking

All in a Woman's Day--May 20, 1986

potatoes, sweet potatoes, hardshell squash, such as Acorn and Butternut, and sweet corn. Except for the corn, the only preparation necessary is washing. The corn, of course, requires pulling the husk back about halfway on the ear and removing the silk.

When the coals are ready, which takes about 20 to 40 minutes, spread them out in a single layer and lay the vegetables on top of them. Use tongs for frequent turning. About an hour and 15 minutes is the average cooking time for potatoes and squash. Sprinkle the roasting corn with unsalted water (salted water tends to toughen the corn) and it will be ready for eating in about 20 minutes.

This way of charcoal cooking of fresh produce is called ember-cooking.

Heavy duty foil can be used to cook other fresh produce, such as apples, peaches, plums, pears, bunches of cherries and grapes, as well as eggplant cubes, cauliflowerettes, broccoli, snap beans, peppers, mushrooms and zucchini slices.

A delicious combination of taste and texture can be found in grilled tomatoes. Use only those that are not over-ripe or too juicy. Should the tomatoes be large, cut in half and broil, open end up, over low fire, approximately 10 minutes. To keep the skins from breaking, place a sheet of aluminum foil under the tomatoes. Skewered cherry tomatoes need to be cooked only about 5 minutes.

For great main courses, side dishes or desserts, fix grilled fresh fruits and vegetables kabobs. Almost any combination of fresh produce can be skewered and grilled over a charcoal fire.

You might try beef or lamb chunks along with cherry tomatoes, small white onions, mushrooms and green pepper chunks to make traditional kabobs.

Another taste sensation is cubes of ham and fresh chunks of pineapple and grapes skewered and grilled over low heat.

When you are planning your menu for your backyard barbecue, make sure that it includes fresh fruits and vegetables that are nutritious, and colorful. They add texture and taste that will spark appetites.

Helpful hints to control pests

It is that time of year again when bugs and creatures make their appearance and take over. Here are a few helpful hints that might take care of some of the problems.

Wasps are flying around just looking for someone to sting. In the event you happen to be the chosen target, mix together equal parts of baking soda and table salt, moistened with water to make a paste. Apply it to the sting and place a small piece of cloth over it, using adhesive tape to hold it in place. If you don't happen to be where you can get this mixture, just moisten with any kind of tobacco (cigarette, plug or twist) and apply to the sting. This is to stop the pain and swelling. These suggestions also work with stings from other insects.

Another suggestion for relieving the sting of an insect is to make a paste of water and unseasoned meat tenderizer and apply to the bite.

If slugs are invading your garden, here is a suggestion to attract them so you can dispose of them. Save the rind of a cantaloupe and place halves upside down where you think you have slugs. The next morning remove the slugs from the rind, and continue to use until the rind dries up.

To get rid of slugs that crawl on the porch, sprinkle table salt around the edges. To get rid of them in flower beds, put shallow pans filled with beer among the plants.

For moles that keep popping up, take a stick of Juicy Fruit gum and roll it from end to end and place in the tunnels used most often by the animals. If the mole eats the gum it will "gum" up its digestive system and it will die.

To help get rid of those pesky little gnats that always keep bothering outdoors when you are fishing or hunting, take some imitation vanilla flavoring and just rub a little on yourself as a repellent. The little fellers don't like vanilla.

Since ants can cause so much trouble, so here are some helps. If you have been plagued with the little sugar ants in your cupboards and cabinets and on the floors, wipe the surfaces with white vinegar. Boric acid dusted in the cracks and crevices of the cabinets also helps; however, it must be kept away from food stuffs, as it is toxic.

Another suggestion for getting rid of ants is to put sage where they gather, and they will run like crazy.

Still another hint for them is to sprinkle garlic powder where the ants congregate; This will make them take off fast.

Too, sprinkling black pepper around the baseboards, under the sink and wherever ants invade, helps get rid of them.

Bay leaves placed in the area where ants frequent is another repellent.

Black pepper and baking soda mixed and spread around where the ants gather also will break up the reunion.

Powdered cloves have been suggested for getting rid of ants, as well as a good length of cigarette ash that is said to deter them. If a pail of ashes is left in the places where ants are likely to enter the house, the ashes will help stop them.

Boiling water poured in an ant hill also will help control the ant problem.

A favorite remedy with some people, is the use of cucumber skins. Too, some folks say ants will never cross a chalk line.

Ground cinnamon also is said to help chase them away.

To make a spray for bean beetles, mix two tablespoons of epsom salts and one tablespoon of soda to a gallon of water.

To make a spray to get rid of pests, put a garlic head in the blender with one cup of water. After this has been blended, add it to a gallon of water and spray plants once a week. This will help repel bugs and rabbits.

If house and garden haven't already been invaded, be prepared with some of the remedies suggested.

All in a Woman's Day--May 27, 1986

Preserve vitamins in all your veggies

Right now we are thinking fresh garden vegetables; however, if those are not yet available, the markets have all kinds of eye appealing vegetables to help spark those appetites that may be lagging. It behooves homemakers to be aware of how to take care of different kinds of vegetables so as to preserve the valuable vitamins.

When preparing vegetables for freezing, a French fryer is excellent to use for the hot water bath. The basket allows the vegetables to be quickly placed in and out of the hot water with no loose strays floating around, and no burned fingers.

When cooking two packages of frozen vegetables at a time in the same saucepan, do not double the quantity of water called for on the package. Use the same amount for the two packages as for one. Never try to cook more than two packages of frozen vegetables in one pot.

Don't wash vegetables or fruit that have just been purchased, when preparing to store them in the refrigerator, as the dampness or moisture is harmful and encourages spoilage.

When purchasing economy-sized packages of frozen vegetables, it might be wise to place them in smaller containers (possibly one-cup size or a yogurt carton). This is sufficient for one serving, and it is just about right for those who are alone.

After cooking vegetables, if there is any water left, save it for sauces, gravies or soups as it is full of nutrients. Too, this can be frozen and used at a later time.

If you have trouble removing corn silks from an ear of corn, just run a damp paper towel over the shucked ear.

When reheating vegetables, they should first be brought to room temperature. Perhaps the fastest way of reheating them is to stir-fry in a wok using a tablespoon or two of peanut oil.

You will find that the fewer seeds in eggplant the less bitter it tastes. In the event you don't know, there is a way to tell before cutting into it and this depends on the eggplant's sex! Check the bottom, that is, of course, the end opposite the stem, where there will be a grayish "scar" or indentation about the size of a dime. If the "scar" is oval or oblong, the eggplant is female and will be full of seeds; however, a round "scar" is a male, and it will have fewer seeds.

Sprinkle a little salt into the water in which you rinse vegetables from the garden. This is a good way to bring those little insects and worms to the surface.

To help keep vegetables crisper, line the vegetable crisper in the refrigerator with paper.

Cooked vegetables lose about one-fourth of their vitamin C after a day in the refrigerator.

If you want mashed potatoes in a hurry and do not want to use the ready-prepared kind, cut the raw potatoes with a French fryer cutter into small, even sized pieces and they will cook in a hurry.

When freezing corn, beans, or other vegetables or fruits that can be spread out separately on a cookie sheet to freeze, be sure to do so. Freeze about four hours and place in bags. By doing this, they do not freeze in chunks and it enables the "cook" to take as much out as needed. They also cook faster when separated, and some folks say corn tastes just as fresh as when it comes from the cob.

Green leafy vegetables such as collard, kale and broccoli, have a good calcium content.

If you are still crying when peeling onions, try this method. Peel the onion under running water and then freeze it about 20 minutes before chopping. If you do this, you should have no more tears.

To have less odor from onions, place them in a plastic bag in the refrigerator and leave for about 24 hours. They then should be less potent.

If you like to serve creamed vegetables in little cups, put slices of bread into muffin cups and brush them with butter and toast in the oven.

A tip for handling fresh vegetables . . . keep them refrigerated in darkness until used. If they are left in the daylight at room temperature for only a few hours, they lose much of the folic acid and vitamins B 2 and C.

Cook vegetables only in as little water as possible so that when they are tender they will have absorbed all the moisture in the pan.

Since some people cannot digest pepper skins, it is best to peel them before cooking. Place the pepper under a preheated broiler for just a few minutes; then drop immediately into a paper bag, closing tightly. You will find that the steam from the hot peppers will loosen the skins so that they just slip off.

Some "cooks" watch the season carefully to be sure to make the most of the fresh vegetables as they come into production. This lends the spice of variety to menus and the sparkle of well-loved flavors caught at the harvest of a new crop. Served by themselves, each vegetable is a jewel in itself. Eat and enjoy!

All in a Woman's Day--June 3, 1986

Discards add bits of flavor, nutrition

Since fresh vegetables and fruits are of much importance in a good diet, it is well to make the most of them each day.

Oftentimes homemakers discard parts of vegetables and fruits—leaves, peeling and stems—that can furnish fine food value and extra flavor if fully utilized.

As you purchase fresh vegetables and fruits, always do so with a discerning eye, and no doubt you will discover ways of your own to make the most of each one. Never throw away any part without first asking "Is there a way I can use this in my cooking?"

The outer leaves of a head of lettuce are often discarded when preparing it for storage in the refrigerator; however, the leaves do have important food value and often are richer in vitamin A than the paler, inner leaves. So, when you wash your lettuce, be sure to reserve the outer leaves to shred as a base for salads or to include in sandwiches.

The French take a whole lettuce leaf and lay it on top of green beans, peas and other vegetables when they are cooking as they feel it lends a fresh, subtle and sweet flavor.

The tougher outer leaves of a head of cabbage, too, have excellent flavor and food value. Just steam them until tender and use for stuffed cabbage with a favorite meat filling.

Parts of celery are many times discarded, but really should never be, for the greener, more fibrous outer part of the stalk has a delicious flavor for seasoning in cooking. The leaves serve as a fresh herb when chopped fine and added to soups and stews. The strings from the outer celery ribs are easy to remove with a potato peeler as they can be zipped off in a jiffy.

Many cooks use the woodier parts of asparagus and broccoli stems to make tasty soups, especially the creamy kind made with milk. After cooking the broccoli stems, they can be pureed in the blender and put into the soup. The stems must be peeled first, however, to remove the fibrous part.

Broccoli is often prepared in a wasteful way. Peel only the tiniest layer of the skin off the stems toward the flowerets; the rest is flavorful and tender. If there is any leftover broccoli, cut it up and place in an oil and vinegar dressing to marinate overnight. Next day you will have a delicious salad to please your family. This trick goes for many cooked leftover vegetables. They can be combined to make a delicious mixed vinaigrette salad, as you no doubt know it is called. Too, beets, carrots, green beans, as well as other vegetables, can all be prepared this way.

Whenever possible, always bake vegetables, such as squash right in the peeling; then you won't be discarding any edible parts. Acorn squash can be scooped out to the peel itself; and the crookneck, yellow squashes and zucchini should never be peeled. You will find that as soon as they are baked, boiled or steamed the peeling is flavorful and tender.

Whenever you find fresh beets in the market with tops, be sure to purchase them as the tops make delicius greens to eat as you would Swiss chard or spinach; in fact, sometimes they are even more tasteful than the others. They are cooked like spinach in a minimum amount of water.

Do you generally peel potatoes? Sometime try just scrubbing them and cooking whole, serving with the peeling on for the extra nutrition and good earthy flavor. Even when making mashed potatoes you will find that they can be peeled and mashed in the usual way as the skins will slip off easily if they are cooked tender. Even if you do peel potatoes, be sure they are well scrubbed. The peeling can be cooked and used to make soup or stock, adding nourishment.

From the tomato you can give a little touch of glamour by utilizing the peeling. Select a nice, red ripe tomato, and with a potato peeler take off the peeling in a continuous strip so that you end up with a spiral. These are delightful for making into a tomato rose. They also add a special touch as a garnish to cold cut plates, salads or hors d'oeuvre platters.

By now you have found out how important the peeling is in cooking. When using apples in salads and fruit cups never discard the peeling. Leave it on for a bright touch and for the extra bit of nutrition.

Oftentimes, after buying fresh fruit and it gets down to one apple, peach, pear or other fruit, they are sometimes discarded. Combine the different kinds to make a fruit cup, a salad or a cooked compote. See how easy it is to get an extra dish for your money, as well as a variety for mealtime!

It is always nice to have orange rind on hand for a delightful flavor. Use it in desserts, to flavor rice, pie fillings and also in other ways. When squeezing oranges for juice, first grate the peeling before cutting. This grated peel is easy to freeze for a nice orange flavor whenever needed. Orange and grapefruit peel are good in candy for a delicious confection. Too, try cutting citrus fruit in half, scoop out the fruit and use the shells as containers for salads or desserts.

Discards can add elegance and give a flair to your menus in real gourmet style. Don't be foolish and throw them away!

All in a Woman's Day--June 10, 1986

Serve vegetables to perk up meals

Fresh vegetables taste so good, they titillate the taste buds and also give important vitamins and minerals to the diet. Do you serve them often enough? When fresh vegetables are on the menu, meals perk up because of the flavor, texture, color and nutrition they add in various ways.

Vegetables are not difficult to prepare, though there are some unfounded and unfortunate ideas floating around that they are a lot of trouble. Some homemakers say they would serve fresh vegetables more often if they only knew more about cooking them.

There are several basic ways to consider when preparing fresh vegetables. If you want to cook them in water, there are rules to be followed. Use as little water as possible, add the vegetables and bring them to a rapid boil. Cover the pot and lower the heat to keep the vegetables only simmering. Proceed to cook until tender, never mushy. Among the vegetables to be cooked by this method are asparagas, peas, carrots, green beans, Swiss chard, cabbage, broccoli, brussel sprouts, kale, mustard greens, cauliflower, spinach, parsnips, collards, potatoes and squash—yellow crookneck, white button, butternut, and zucchini.

Another method is to stir-fry by using a heavy skillet, heating about two tablespoons of oil or butter, and adding about a pound of cut up vegetables. Stir over high heat for 3 to 5 minutes until crisp-tender. Vegetables especially good cooked by this method are celery, broccoli, cabbage, carrots, mushrooms, onions, zucchini and eggplant. A number of homemakers also use a wok to stir-fry. When vegetables are cooked this way, they take on a different taste and texture; so, it would be a new treat to try this method if you have never done so before.

Then there is cooking by baking. This generally includes potatoes and squash. Scrub the potatoes of baking size, and prick them in a few places with a fork, or you can wait and prick them when they are about halfway baked so they will be mealy. Do not wrap them in aluminum foil unless you want them steamed. Bake them at 425 degrees about 45 minutes to an hour.

For squash, including Butternut and Acorn, cut in half, discard the seeds, then place squash in a baking dish. Add water to about half-inch and bake about 45 minutes at 375 degrees. For the Hubbard squash, cut it in pieces and place in a pan as above and cook accordingly.

Fried vegetables are sliced or cut in suitable forms for serving. They can be sauteed in a small amount of fat or cooked in deep fat.

Also, vegetables can be cooked in a waterless cooker or steam pressure cooker, especially broccoli, cauliflower and green beans.

Roasting vegetables around meat also is a delightful way in cooking them as they take on the delicate flavor of the meat juices and turn a nice rich brown in the process. Potatoes, turnips, carrots and onions just seem to blossom when cooked this way.

Many homemakers like to cook vegetables crispy so they are batter-coated and deep fried. This makes a crunchy, light accompaniment for roasts and broiled meats. Zucchini, eggplant, cauliflower, broccoli flowerettes, mushrooms and green beans can all be cooked this way.

Vegetable custards make another tasty way in cooking, and these dishes make a meal in themselves. Broccoli in a cheese sauce is good and makes a light supper dish. Other vegetables also can be cooked this way.

Cooking vegetables in a pressure cooker is a time-saving way with some vegetables, and does help preserve the nutrients, but there are disadvantages, especially since you can't raise the lid to check and see or sample for doneness.

Don't forget the food processor. With a flick of the switch it will puree cooked vegetables in seconds. A blender also can be used to puree. Season it by adding butter, seasonings and perhaps some cream. This method also is good for combining some foods such as pumpkin and yams and turnips and potatoes.

It is sometimes rather mystifying to prepare fresh vegetables for cooking the first time. Most vegetables need a little mild barbering before being cooked, but try to make it only a light trim. Broccoli calls for trimming off rough, dry parts of the base, then slitting the stem upwards so that the stem will cook in about the same time as the flowery head. Cauliflower, too, calls for slicing off the coarse underpart and cutting off the stalks that cup the head. It can be cooked whole, or in pieces in water.

Most vegetables do not require peeling; however, carrots are an exception to the rule. The peel on the eggplant, zucchini and yellow crookneck squash have both flavor and good nutrition, so don't discard it.

While most vegetables are cooked best by the basic methods, fresh corn on the cob is a law unto itself. It is practically a religion with discriminating eaters that it be cooked to perfection. Fresh corn requires very little cooking, and it is important to cook it ONLY until the milk in the kernels is set. Most vegetables will become softer with longer cooking; however, corn does not; it just becomes firmer and tough when overcooked. The best way is to cook only one ear per person at a time. Half fill a large kettle with water, add one teaspoon salt per quart of water and bring to a boil; add corn and boil, covered, just until the milk in the kernels is set, from 3 to 6 minutes. Remove ears with tongs and serve immediately with butter or a favorite sauce. (I often add a little sugar to the water as this tends to improve the flavor, as well as it does with other vegetables). Then cook a second batch. Since the cooking time varies with the size and sometimes, with the variety of corn, it can be helpful to cook a "test ear" to determine the exact cooking time. If it is necessary, sometimes to cook the corn ahead of serving time, turn off the heat when the corn is added to the boiling water, then cover and let stand until ready to serve.

Another vegetable that is an exception to the rule is the artichoke, that fascinating object that looks like an ornamental top to a bedpost more than it looks like something to eat. It is, however, edible and is a delicious vegetable. It is cooked this way: Allow one artichoke per serving. Wash and cut half-inch off top of each, also cutting off stems. Using scissors, cut off sharp tips on the leaves and then add it to the boiling salted water, to cover, in a deep saucepan. Add a thick lemon slice for each artichoke. Cover and cook 30 to 40 minutes or until the outside leaf pulls off easily. Using two large spoons, remove from the water, drain and serve with lemon butter or Hollandaise sauce.

As Americans, we are fortunate to have fresh vegetables in season at our markets the year round. Just select your cooking methods and enjoy the wonderful bounty, good flavor, texture and the important nutrition added to the diet. Try to enjoy a fresh vegetable each day.

All in a Woman's Day--June 17, 1986

Raspberry, blackberry season is almost here

The "season of the seasons" of the year is fast approaching when raspberries and blackberries will be ripening, and on the market. And what could be more scrumptious than a dish of the berries with cream, ice cream or made into delectable pies or desserts?

Raspberries are the fruit of a bush of the Rubus genus that is a member of the rose family. Native of the North Temperate Zone, the European red raspberry was one of the first European plants to be introduced into America. The American red raspberry, native of eastern United States, is slightly inferior to the European species in the quality of fruit; however, it is better suited to the climate of the United States.

The b!ack raspberry of northern United States, also is hardy and productive. When ripe the cap-shaped fruit separates from the floral stalk or receptacle when picked.

Raspberries grow wild in many areas, including Missouri, where black raspberries are often found along country roads, in wooded areas, fence rows and ditch banks; and also in Europe, where there are many varieties; Asia; Australia; and in New Zealand, where they are considered pests.

The berry, made up of many small drupelets, is now found in several colors, including amber, red, black and purple. Raspberries are a delicately flavored fruit and are good raw, either plain or with cream. They can be used in making jellies, jams, puddings, pies and desserts.

Berries of any kind can be interchangeably used in recipes and also can be substituted in most recipes containing strawberries.

The height of the season is June and July, although they are available from June through November in some areas. When selecting, look for fresh, clean, plump berries that have a good color, with no mold, no wetness and no green spots. When a container shows stain, there is apparent spoilage of some of the berries. A pint of berries will serve three persons.

This should be a good year for raspberries, so you might want to use them in several ways. They are good with cream, sugar, in fresh fruit salads, compotes, with ice cream, mousses and sherberts; in all of the ways mentioned, use them raw. Cooked they are delightful in pies, tarts, cakes, puddings, souffles, pancakes, pureed, syrups and sauces, preserved in jams and jellies, and as juice.

The berries can be canned or frozen in syrup or with sugar, using three-fourths cup of sugar to four cups berries. Stir them until the sugar covers most of the berries; let them stand until the sugar is about dissolved, before spooning them into containers for the freezer. When freezing in syrup, place berries in containers and cover with a syrup made by cooking four cups water and six cups sugar. This is poured over the berries when cooled, and they are then frozen. You also can freeze the freshly washed berries, that are without any blemishes, by spreading in a single layer on a cookie sheet and freezing them until firm; then placing them in a container and continuing with the freezing.

Remember not to wash berries until ready to be used and then use cold water; never allow them to soak.

Blackberries, also from the rose family, can be used in anyway that raspberries are used. The height of the season for them is midsummer. When selecting, always look for juicy, plump dark berries. When using them raw, allow a half cup per person and when cooked three-fourths cup per person.

Blackberries, the last of the summer berries, is one of the oldest fruits known; well, that is not counting the apple that Eve gave to Adam. This succulent fruit is sought by many people in places such as you would find the wild raspberry; however, many plants have been killed when farmers do spraying to get rid of weeds.

The blackberry, not only is the oldest, but perhaps the most widespread, and traditionally in many parts of the country July 4 is the day to begin picking this succulent fruit, of course, providing the weather has been moderate. Should a late summer prevail, it often delays the ripening of the berries.

Blackberry patches are often called "bramble patches," and the plant, the bramble bush. The fruit is black or reddish purple. When picked it retains its stem or receptacle; that is a contrast to the raspberry.

If you plan to pick blackberries, you will need to be well protected with perhaps kerosene-soaked strips of cloth around the ankles and wrists to ward off "chiggers"; however, you will find that most berry patches are subject to those little "critters."

Although the blackberry is highly developed in the wild state, it was rarely grown as a garden fruit until about 1850. Since then it has been widely cultivated and has become an important commercial crop.

* * *

Raspberry Pie

4 cups raspberries
3/4 cup sugar
1/2 cup water
1 1/2 tablespoons minute tapioca
10 dabs butter or margarine
Unbaked pie crust
1 egg
1 tablespoon milk

Combine the washed raspberries, sugar, water and tapioca, and let stand several hours, overnight or even 2 to 3 days. This creates a nice syrup, dissolves the tapioca and the sweetness permeates the fruit. Roll out bottom crust for pie and place in pie tin; sprinkling with a little flour over crust in pan. Spoon the fruit mixture into crust and top with 5 dabs of butter or margarine. Place top crust. Combine egg and milk and brush mixture over top of pie crust; sprinkle it with a little sugar if desired. Bake at 350 degrees until nicely browned, about 40 minutes. This mixture is enough for two pies.

* * *

Raspberry Cake

1 package white cake mix
4 eggs

2/3 cup salad oil
1 package red raspberry gelatin, undissolved
1 (10-ounce) package red raspberries, thawed
2 teaspoons raspberry flavoring

Combine all ingredients in a large mixing bowl, using all the contents of the thawed red raspberries. Spread mixture in a well-greased 9x13-inch pan and bake it about 50 minutes in a 325 degree oven. Serve cake with whipped cream.

All in a Woman's Day--June 24, 1986

Blueberry crop is here; also other berries ready

This week's column concerns more about berries that make choice eating, especially blueberries, huckleberries and dewberries.

While we do not grow blueberries in this area, in the southern part of our state huckleberries and dewberries are harvested, and as people from that locality would say, "You haven't tasted nothin' if you haven't had a piece of huckleberry or dewberry pie."

Blueberries are an edible berry of a plant of the same name, and there are many varieties. They are bright blue in color, with a slightly frosted look, and they grow singly or in clusters on bushes ranging from one to 20 feet tall, in swamps and on mountains, needing acid soil to do their best. In their wild state, they are found from Alaska to Florida, and grow profusely on other continents, including the Arctic Circle. Blueberries are much prized where they grow. If you have heard of bilberries and whortleberries, they are merely blueberry varieties.

There is much confusion over the difference between blueberries and huckleberries as the words are sometimes used interchangeably. The huckleberry, generally speaking, is darker and blacker than blueberries. Outside of New England, both berries are sometimes lumped as huckleberries. You will find, however, that blueberries have real small unnoticeable seeds, while the huckleberries have 10 hard, seedlike nutlets. Huckleberries are always found wild; however, blueberries are cultivated as a commercial crop. The cultivated berries are larger than the wild; but the wild has the better flavor.

Blueberries, a food of the Indians, served as a major food supply for many tribes, who ate them fresh, cooked with meat or dried in large amounts for winter use.

It seems that blueberries are the only pleasant aftermath of forest fires, as they seem to grow in abundance on burnt over ground. The peak of the crop is June, July and August, with the major supply coming from New Jersey, Massachusetts, Washington and Michigan.

When selecting blueberries at the market, always look for berries that are firm, well-rounded and dry. Cultivated berries, are fatter and fleshier. Remember, when using raw berries, allow half cup per person; cooked, three-fourths cup per person.

Blueberries are especially good, combined with melon balls and/or strawberries. Blueberries and huckleberries are good served with sugar and cream or milk and are delicious with sour cream and powdered sugar mixed with a little ginger.

Huckleberry is the common name applied to shrubs belonging to the Heath family, named after the French chem-

448

ist, Joseph Louis Gay-Lussac. They are native to temperate North America. The fruit is dark blue to almost black and the lower surfaces of the leaves are sprinkled with resinous dots. Black huckleberry, native to woodlands and swamps of northeast United States and Eastern Canada, produces black edible fruit on shrubs growing one- to three-feet in height. Bear huckleberry, native to woodlands of southeast United States, is a slender shrub, less than a foot high that produces unpalatable reddish-black fruit.

Dangleberry, native to eastern United States, is a low shrub producing dark blue, sweet fruit.

Huckleberries are often cultivated in the United States for their foliage and also fruit. The he-huckleberry native to eastern United States, is another related species.

If you have never had the opportunity to go to the country "berrying," be sure to do so. And, if you are in a country where blueberries, huckleberries and dewberries grow wild, be sure to get a bucket and "go picking." No doubt the wild blueberries will spoil the taste for the cultivated variety, but the treat will be well worth the effort.

Dewberries also are grown in Missouri, and they differ from other types of blackberries, to which their fruits are similar, chiefly in having long, slender stems that trail along the ground. Often grown in gardens, where they ripen as much as two weeks earlier than those of other blackberry species, dewberry is a popular name for any of several trailing varieties and species of blackberries. The western dewberries also are trailing and by hybridization the Logan, Young and Boysen varieties have been derived from

them.

* * *

Canadian Blueberry Pie

4 cups fresh blueberries
1 cup sugar
3 tablespoons corn starch
1/8 teaspoon salt
1 tablespoon lemon juice
1 cup water
1 tablespoon butter
1 (9-inch) baked pie shell
1 cup whipping cream or whipped topping
3 tablespoons powdered sugar
1/2 teaspoon vanilla

Wash and drain berries; pat dry. Place 1 full cup of berries in a saucepan. Chill remaining berries. To the 1 cup of berries add sugar, corn starch, salt, lemon juice and water, cooking over medium heat until thickened and smooth; stirring constantly. Remove from heat, add butter and remaining ingredients. Cool 1/2 hour, then spoon into baked pie shell and chill. Before serving, top with the whipped cream sweetened with powdered sugar with the vanilla flavoring added, or use whipped topping.

If you are able to get huckleberries or dewberries, you can make them into the pie the same as with blueberries. (Check these berries for sweetness as you might need to add a little more sugar.)

When using cultivated blueberries, always use some lemon juice with them.

Fourth of July is barbecue time

That good old patriotic holiday, Fourth of July, is just the time for picnics and barbecuing. Everyone likes the casual, informal way of dining, and whether kids are cooking hot dogs on sticks or broiling steaks, family and friends will enjoy the festivities and fellowship that barbecuing brings.

Your own backyard is just the place to have a barbecue where you can have freedom of the wonderful outdoors atmosphere and still have all the conveniences of home.

To begin planning for the barbecue, think first of meat and, of course, there is a wide variety available of fresh and cured cuts. As roasting and broiling are usually the basic methods used in cooking outdoors, you will find that any cut that is usually cooked by dry heat method may be selected.

And while planning, always remember that the way a cut of meat is prepared influences the amount to purchase. For cuts with bone in allow three-fourths to a pound per serving; for boneless cuts you can allow one-third to one-half pound. You may need a few extra servings as the fresh air and the delighful aroma of outdoor cooking seems to sharpen appetites.

When preparing to start the fire, begin by lining the bottom of the fire bowl with heavy aluminum foil for easier cleaning. Place gravel or special insulation pellets on top of the foil. Since the foil reflects the heat, the gravel or pellets permit the charcoal to sort of "breathe," and also absorb the food drippings.

If your fire bowl is rounded on the bottom, use enough fire base to make a level bed out to the edge of the bowl. After four to six barbecues, always wash the fire base to remove drippings and ashes. Too, be sure the bowl is thoroughly dry before using, as gravel can "explode" if heated when wet.

Be sure and start the fire in advance, so you will have a good bed of coals at the time to start barbecuing.

The usual method takes about 45 minutes and that is to stack briquets in a pyramid shape, soak lightly with charcoal lighting fluid; let stand about a minute and light. Never place too many briquets in the firebox. This is a common fault of many outdoor cooks. For a roast it takes no more than 35 briquets to start; however, later you may wish to add five to 10 more at 30-minute intervals to keep the fire temperature the same throughout the cooking. For steaks and kabobs, only 25 briquets will be needed. As the surface of the briquets is covered with gray ash, spread the coals evenly and the fire will be ready for cooking. Mount the briquets at the back of the firebox for rotisserie cooking, and space them one to two inches apart for grill cooking. Allowing space between briquets for grill cooking helps to avoid flare ups. Should you want to catch the fats and juices for making a tasty gravy or sauce, use a drip pan.

If you would like extra smoke flavor when cooking meat, use wood chips or flakes—apple, cherry, hickory or oak—that have been soaked in water at least an hour before using in order to give the amount of smoke needed without burning. Just add it to some of the charcoal while cooking. Should the chips flare up, just replace them with wet ones.

Perhaps you would like to test the intensity of the fire. If so, you can use the old "Mississippi" method that is placing the palm of the hand over the coals at the height the food will be cooked. The fire will be ready for steaks, burgers and kabobs if you can count Mississippi one, Mississippi two, Mississippi three before having to pull your hand away. For spareribs and pork chops, a Mississippi seven is needed, while for roasts only a Mississippi five.

Don't forget, too, that the fire may cool off if the gray ash is left on the coals. Be sure to watch this and tap the briquets every now and then so the ash will drop off.

It might be handy to have a thoroughly washed spray bottle, that is filled with fresh water, in the event flames might get dangerously high so you can give them a good squirt.

Too, when barbecuing, always cook meats and poultry thoroughly, but slowly. Longer cooking over a low fire does mean less shrinkage and more thorough cooking. Don't forget that you are the chef, remembering always to follow safety rules for barbecuing and that way which is easiest and gives food the taste that to you is right.

* * *

Barbecue Sauce

2 tablespoons butter
4 tablespoons brown sugar
1 onion, grated
4 tablespoons vinegar
2 cloves garlic, minced
4 tablespoons Worcestershire sauce
1/4 teaspoon salt
1 cup catsup
1 tablespoon chili powder
1 teaspoon tabasco

Melt butter in a saucepan; add and cook the garlic and onion until soft. Add 2 cups water and the remaining ingredients; stirring until well mixed. Put on medium low heat and simmer 30 minutes. Makes about 2 cups. (This basic barbecue sauce is good on spareribs, hamburgers and pork chops.)

* * *

Chicken Barbecue Sauce

1 egg, well beaten
1/2 cup cooking oil
1 cup cider vinegar
1 tablespoon salt
1 teaspoon sage, crumbled
1/4 teaspoon pepper

Combine all ingredients in a jar and shake well. Let mixture stand several days before using it. Brush on chicken parts as they cook over the coals. This also is good with pork.

All in a Woman's Day--July 8, 1986

July weather gives call for ice cream

When Fourth of July weather arrives; it is time to make ice cream. Most of us do love that homemade product that tickles the palate and makes us "oh" and "ah" over the results.

Nature rewards those who turn the hand ice cream freezer crank (or the electric freezer) with a flavor delight that will melt into tasty memories of good old-fashioned fun.

No matter how ice cream is frozen, it is a great way to use milk products that have a wealth of nutrients. Included in this tasty food are vitamin A, calcium, riboflavin and protein.

Beginning homemade ice cream makers should plan to start with a basic vanilla. That is the easiest and always the most popular. Then later you can let your imagination take over. You can eat ice cream plain or topped with a favorite sauce or fruit.

451

To make good ice cream, always follow the instructions that come with the freezer as the design and type of material from which a freezer is made can make a difference in the salt and ice ratio to be used.

In addition to the freezer instructions, here are a few pointers in making you a "pro" at ice cream making.

So, that the ice cream product will not be grainy, icy or mushy, be sure to chop the ice very fine as it will melt more evenly and provide uniform coolness.

Use a glass measuring cup to measure the salt, as salt has a tendency to pit metal cups.

Use a wooden spoon for stirring and repacking ice cream to help retard melting.

Always protect the working surfaces with newspaper as salt is corrosive and also will destroy grass. As it also is harmful to your hands; it is well to wear rubber gloves as a protection.

A quart pan is helpful in measuring ice. Layer your ice and salt with about two quarts of ice to one cup of rock salt. Continue to add ice and salt as needed.

Always be sure the hole in the freezer bucket is open so that the brine will drain.

When freezing, turn until handcranking becomes difficult or until the electric motor labors.

Always remove the dasher, scraping the ice cream back into the container. Place wax paper across the top of the frozen ice cream and replace the cover. Drain off excess brine and pack with crushed ice and salt. Cover the freezer with a towel, rug or newspapers that will serve as insulation. Let it stand until hardened.

To prevent quick melting, add a tablespoon of unflavored gelatin. Soak the gelatin in one-fourth cup water, then melt over hot water and add to the milk used in making the ice cream.

To avoid overflow of contents, due to freezing expansion, never fill the freezer more than 1 1/2 inches below the top of the container.

After the mixture to be frozen has been made, be sure to let it chill before placing it in the freezer.

Store purchased ice cream today comes in more than 400 flavors and still more are being added; however, vanilla appears to be the favorite, with chocolate second.

Serve ice cream in a dish, a cone, topped with sauces or fresh fruit, in a soda, a banana split, frozen in a pie shell or just most anyway you would like it served.

Whether you make your ice cream, or prefer to purchase it at the market, just enjoy the goodness of each flavor and beat the heat with this tempting cool goodness called "ice cream." Even though the weather is cold in the wintertime, ice cream is still one of the favorite desserts here in America, for just anytime.

* * *

Vanilla Supreme Ice Cream
2 quarts milk (warm)
2 cups sugar (add to milk while it is warming)
4 eggs, beaten
1/2 teaspoon salt
1 teaspoon vanilla
4 rennet tablets (dissolved in 1/2 cup cold water
1(13-ounce) can Milnot
Cook the first five ingredients together over low heat until lukewarm. Pour mixture into freezer can; add rennet

and let it set about one hour until custard-like. Add the Milnot and freeze according to manufacturer's instructions. For fresh, fruit-flavored ice cream, add diced bananas, strawberries, peaches and other fruit before freezing.

* * *

Chocolate Ice Cream

1 quart milk
1 cup cocoa
1 cup light corn syrup
5 eggs
2 cups sugar
1 quart whipping cream
1 tablespoon vanilla

In a 2-quart saucepan combine 2 cups milk, cocoa and corn syrup; bringing to a boil over medium heat; stirring constantly. Cool. In a large mixing bowl. Beat eggs until foamy; gradually beat in sugar. Add cocoa mixture. Stir in 2 cups milk, cream and vanilla. Churn freeze. Makes about 1 gallon.

All in a Woman's Day--July 15, 1986

Tomato history is most interesting

Tomatoes, the beautiful, flavorful fruit from the garden, are now ripening plentifully, locally, and are they tasty and good!

Tomatoes are so much a part of our American cooking style that it is rather difficult to believe that people were once afraid to eat them. Their history is rather interesting.

They were probably first grown by the Incas in the lower Andes of Peru, with traders and explorers taking them from there to Mexico; the Aztecs and Mayans then adopted them. Pictures were carved in stone by the Mayans of this highly-prized "tomatl." The Spaniards, who gave it the present day spelling, were so intrigued by this bright South American fruit, they sent seed back to Europe, where they were grown as a curosity. Cortez was the individual who introduced the tomato to Europe in the 16th century.

It wasn't long until the Europeans soon developed superstitions about this relative of the deadly nightshade family. Some believed them poisonous or a powerful drug. Too, it was rumored that the tomato stimulated love, thus earning for it the name "love apple." Because the first tomatoes were yellow, they were called by the Italians "pomo d'oro" or golden apples.

Also the tomato was considered an aphrodisiac and the French called it "pommes d'amour" or apples of love.

The superstitions traveled to the colonies, and the early Americans grew love apples as ornamental plants. Later the Europeans eventually accepted the tomatoes. Recipes began to sail hither and yon, and North Americans began to nibble on them. As early as 1781, Thomas Jefferson was growing and eating tomatoes at Monticello.

Tomato cultivation became widespread by the 1830s, and by the mid 1880s they were being served regularly on dinner tables, after folks finally realized that they were good to eat and good for them. Even though they were raised in the gardens, it was the botanists, seed companies and experimental farmers that fully developed the tomato.

When purchasing tomatoes it should be done at least four days before using. Then they can be kept in a paper bag atop the refrigerator from three to seven days until they achieve the desired degree of ripeness. Once the tomato has ripened, it should be placed in the

453

refrigerator where it can be held for as long as two weeks. Tomatoes should be removed from the refrigerator at least an hour before serving, to return to room temperature, another flavor enhancing trick. (Some folks think they should never be refrigerated.)

Tomatoes are high on the list of best liked foods. Most popular is the red tomato, but even it comes in all shapes, sizes and shades. The yellow and the white tomatoes have a lower acid content than the red tomatoes. The small yellow pear-shaped tomatoes are good for making preserves. The cherry tomatoes are rather interesting, and they also bear from 150 to 300 of the small tomatoes. If you want to make an impression, just scoop out the centers of these small tomatoes and fill them with cream cheese dip and serve them as hors d'oeuvres.

One tomato plant is said to produce up to 20 pounds of fruit. So, if you have plenty and have shared with your friends and neighbors, who maybe do not have a garden, you might want to try some new recipes featuring tomatoes. They add a stimulus to main dishes and, yes, they can be made into a dessert from the unripened fruit. Also, they can be made into pickles, soup, stewed, breaded, fried, cocktail juice, and in countless other ways. They add distinctive flavor to various foods.

Perhaps one of the foods that we all know so well, and there are more varieties than spellings, is ketchup, kachup, catchup or catsup. Some homemakers use cider or white vinegar in making the condiment in which most teenagers bury everything on their plates. The cider vinegar gives it a little more zip; so, if you like a more mellow catsup, white vinegar would be the better to use in this great American cover-up.

Most of us think of catsup as being a strictly tomato product; however, that is not the case. Our grandmothers made catsup from a variety of ingredients, including apples, grapes, mushrooms, cranberries, gooseberries and walnuts.

If you want to make tomato paste, cook fresh tomatoes and then put them through a strainer. Then cook for at least two more hours until a paste develops.

A ventilated or paper bag is a good thing in which to place tomatoes to ripen. They also can be placed on a cabinet shelf. It isn't the light that is needed to ripen them, it is the warmth.

For a slice of tomato, without many seeds, slice vertically instead of horizontally.

If you have green tomatoes left in the fall, wrap them in newspapers. Place them in a cardboard box or bushel basket and store them in the coolest place in the basement or wherever it is coolest, in your home. By throwing a rug or old blanket over the box, you can keep the temperature more constant. Check them at two or three-week intervals and use as they ripen. You might even have them up until March.

* * *

Tomato Fritters

1 cup sifted flour
2 teaspoons baking powder
1/4 teaspoon salt
1 egg, beaten
1/2 cup milk
1 tablespoon melted butter

Sift the dry ingredients and add egg; stir in the milk gradually. Add melted butter and mix it well. Cut tomatoes in

454

thick slices and dip them in the batter. Fry them in deep fat (380 degrees) until brown on both sides. Turn heat low and cook a few minutes.

All in a Woman's Day--July 22, 1986

Sweet, juicy apricots can be a season delight

The juicy sweetness of apricots, especially those from California, as well as Washington and Utah, is one of the seasonal pleasures. They do grow in our area; however, more often than not, the freeze catches them as they are early bloomers. It happened again this year.

Drupes ordinarily make good desserts and this is especially true if the drupe is an apricot or any fruit with a hard woody pit.

A native of Asia, the apricot tree still grows wild on the mountains there. Some 4,000 years ago the Chinese cultivated apricots. From the native area, it came West to India, Persia, Armenia and Egypt. Alexander the Great took the tree from Persia to Greece, and from there it reached Italy. As far back as 100 B.C., Italy began growing apricots; however, they did not reach England until the latter part of the 16th century. They are grown extensively in the Middle East and all the Mediterranean countries, from Turkey to Spain to France.

Apricots were brought to the New World by the Spaniards, who planted seedlings at the Spanish missions in California about the 18th century.

Apricots have been a staple food in many countries. The remote little kingdom of Hunza in the high Himalayas, has drawn scientific attention because the people have superb health and have longevity. The chief food is apricots.

Another country where apricots are widely eaten is Persia, and there the poets have sung of the fruit called "the seed of the sun."

The Chinese feel that the apricot tree is endowed with prophetic powers. The famous Chinese philosopher, Lae Tse, was born under an apricot tree, and he attributed his gifts to it. Too, Conficius worked out his philosophy under an apricot tree, it has been said.

Among those people doting on apricots, and still do, are the Syrians, Lebanese, Turks, Greeks, Romans and Spaniards, who enjoy them raw, cooked, fresh, dried or made into ices. Most of us will agree that few fruits are more delicious or more beautiful to the eye. In Greek mythology the famous "golden apples" are thought to have been apricots.

Apricots that rank above other deciduous fruits in basic nutrition, can be purchased fresh, dried, canned, in juice (commonly called nectar), in dietary packs, baby food and preserves.

Almost 100 percent of the apricots in the United States are grown in California, with more than 25 percent of the crop dried. The season for the apricots is late May into August, with peak months being June and July.

* * *

Here is a recipe that you might like to try.

Mile High Apricot Pie
1 2/3 cups graham cracker crumbs
1/4 cup sugar
1/4 cup margarine, softened
1/4 cup chopped almonds
1 (1 pound, 1 ounce) can apricot halves
2 tablespoons lemon juice
1 envelope unflavored gelatin
Apricot preserves
2/3 cup sugar

1/4 teaspoon salt
4 eggs, separated

Blend together cracker crumbs, 1/4 cup of sugar, margarine and almonds. Press firmly against bottom and sides of a 9-inch pie plate. Bake in a preheated 375 degree oven 8 minutes. Cool. Spread apricot preserves over bottom of pie shell. Drain apricot halves, reserve the syrup, and finely chop the apricots. In the top of a double boiler combine 1/2 cup apricot juice and the lemon juice. Sprinkle gelatin over liquids and let stand 5 minutes. Add 1/3 cup sugar, salt and egg yolks. Beat slightly to blend. Cook over hot water, stirring constantly until mixture is thickened and coats a metal spoon. Remove from heat and add chopped apricots. Chill until thickened. Beat egg whites until foamy, and gradually add remaining 1/3 cup sugar, beating until the egg whites are stiff, but not dry. Fold into gelatin-apricot mixture and pour into pie shell. Chill 3 to 4 hours until firm. Makes 6 to 8 servings.

All in a Woman's Day--July 29, 1986

Use of apricots appears unending

Apricots are such a wonderful, delicate fruit that we need to find out a little more about them.

The fully, well matured apricot, has a true flavor, is plump and round, fairly firm and ranges from golden to a yellow orange color. They are a highly perishable fruit and are not always available in the market. Eight or 12 apricots make a pound.

They should be stored in a covered container in the refrigerator or in a perforated plastic bag. If apricots are green, let them ripen at room temperature and then store them in the refrigerator where they can be kept from three to five days.

Apricots are a highly nutritious fruit and are a good source of vitamin A, C as well as essential minerals, such as iron and calcium, and also high in natural sugars. You will find that three medium apricots have only 54 calories.

The fruit can be peeled by dipping into boiling water for 30 seconds, and then into cold water. A little lemon juice will accent its flavor.

For freezing, either peeled or unpeeled, cut into halves, removing the pits and pack in heavy syrup (five and a half cups sugar to five cups water). So that the fruit will not be discolored, add a half teaspoon of ascorbic acid to every five and a half cups of fruit. Fill container one-third full with syrup and then add fruit to within an inch of the top and finish filling with syrup. Top with crumpled wax paper to keep the fruit submerged.

Dried apricots have a large percentage of their moisture removed, and then they are treated with sulfur dioxide to retain the color. One pound of dried apricots equals six cups when cooked. In preparing them for eating, wash and cover with water; bring to boil and then lower heat and simmer 15 to 20 minutes or until apricots are tender. More water can be added to keep up the level of the liquid. Sweeten to taste.

A simple dessert is made by serving drained, canned apricots, with plenty of whipped topping that has been sweetened to taste. Flavor with vanilla.

To make a glaze for apricots, boil apricot preserves to between 225 and 228 degrees, stirring frequently, so they will not stick. This will cause them to stiffen slightly as it cools and will not be sticky. Use a pastry brush in applying. This simple glaze is used in France, both in home and professional cooking, as it gives a glitter and brilliance to any fruit tart, since the flavor of apricots blends well with other fruits. It also can be used as icing for cakes, cookies and pies or the inside of a pastry shell can be moistened with the glaze before placing the filling.

* * *

Glazed Apricot Cake

1 lemon flavored cake mix (2 layer size)
1/3 cup sugar
1 cup apricot nectar, heated
1/2 cup salad oil
1/2 teaspoon almond flavoring
4 eggs

Combine cake mix, sugar, nectar, salad oil and flavoring in a large bowl. Beat until creamy and smooth, about 2 minutes on medium speed. Add eggs, one at a time, beating well after each addition. Pour batter into a well greased bundt cake pan or a 10-inch tube pan. Bake at 325 degrees one hour until tested done. Cool cake in the pan 10 minutes; turn it out and glaze with the following while it is still warm:

Lemon Glaze

1 cup powdered sugar
3 tablepoons lemon juice
Few drops lemon flavoring

Combine ingredients. Thin with a teaspoon of water if needed. Pour over top and sides of warm cake.

* * *

Blue Ribbon Apricot Bars

3/4 cup butter or margarine
1 cup sugar
2 cups flour
1/2 teaspoon salt
1/2 teaspoon soda
2 cups dried apricots
Water to cover apricots
3/4 cup sugar
1 1/3 cups flaked coconut
1/2 cup English walnuts, chopped

Cream butter and sugar. Sift flour, salt and soda together and mix with creamed mixture. Spread 3 cups of this mixture into a greased jelly roll pan (15x10-inches) and pat down smoothly. Bake at 400 degrees, 10 minutes. Place apricots in saucepan and cover them with water, simmering until most of water is absorbed. Stir in 3/4 cup sugar and continue cooking until thick. Cool. Then stir in nuts and coconut and spread over baked layer. Sprinkle with remaining mixture over top. Bake in a 400 degree oven about 15 minutes or until light golden brown. Cut into squares or bars. Makes about 4 dozen.

* * *

Apricot Nuggets

1 pound box of powdered sugar
6 tablespoons melted butter or margarine
1 (8-ounce) package dried apricots, chopped
3 tablespoons orange juice
1/2 teaspoon vanilla

Mix sugar, butter, juice and vanilla in a bowl. Add apricots and knead; then mold the dough into 1-inch balls; roll them in chopped pecans and coconut. Place the balls in a covered container in the refrigerator. The longer they stand, the better they taste. They also can be frozen.

All in a Woman's Day--August 5, 1986

Melons wise fruit buy

Calorie watchers, gourmets and people who know what's good are, now enjoying the wide variety of fresh melons in season. Melons are, pound for pound, wise fruit buys. Nearly all of the flesh is edible and the size is usually sufficient enough for at least four servings.

The melons we are going to consider now are in the muskmelon-cantaloupe family. Selection for quality and flavor is difficult, challenging the skill of even the most experienced shopper. There is really no absolute formula; however, there are a few clues that will increase the possibility of selecting a "good" melon.

If it is picked when it is mature, it should have the following characteristics: Netting or veining should be thick, coarse and corky, and should stand out in bold relief over some parts of the surface; the stem should be gone, leaving a smooth shallow dip in the stem end; skin color between netting should have changed from green to yellowish buff, yellowish gray or pale yellow.

Too, be sure to look for signs of ripeness, for a cantaloupe might be mature and yet not ripe. A ripe cantaloupe will have a yellowish cast to the rind, have a pleasant odor and will yield slightly to a light thumb pressure on the blossom end of the melon.

For sometime now, cantaloupes and muskmelons, and other melons of this type, have been for sale at the markets. (It surely won't be long, if it hasn't already occurred, that some local early melon growers will have some fruits of their labor for sale.) Some of the melons on the market may be ripe; however, they may not have reached the best eating stage. Then be sure to keep them from two to four days at room temperature to allow the completion of ripening. Chill first prior to serving it. I guess the decision will be up to the individual!

When storing melons in the refrigerator, cover them so that the pungent odor will not penetrate other foods.

When you find the softening of the entire rind, large bruises and old growth, especially in the stem scar, you have clues to over ripeness and possible decay.

Remember, if you have leftover melons or extras from your garden, they can be saved at the peak of perfection by cutting them into chunks, packing in moisture vapor-proof containers or bags and storing in the freezer. Remember to serve before completely thawed.

The common American type of cantaloupe, has a thin, reticulated rind and yellowish-orange flesh, with the seeds attached to a netlike fiber in the center of the melon. When ripe, it has a sweet flavor and gives off a musklike odor. Muskmelon is the common name of several varieties of trailing, vine like annual herbs of the gourd family, native to Africa and Asia, and widely cultivated.

The most common variety of muskmelon in the United States, sometimes called nutmeg or netted muskmelon, has thin, reticulated rind and sweet flesh that is peach orange in color when ripe. It is often called "cantaloupe."

The Casabas melon has a yellow-ish ring covering that is webbed roughly; a little larger than cantaloupes, and are slightly pointed at one end. The flesh is a delicate cream color.

Then the Honeydews: When you think of them, something elegant seems to pop into your mind. Perhaps it is the pale, icy appearance, or maybe its subtle taste, or then it could just be the way it has of complementing other foods. Always select honeydews that are ivory or greenish white, and that turn to a cream color with pale streaks when ripe.

Honeyball melons are somewhat smaller than the honeydews. When ripe, they are slightly soft and fragrant and have finely netted rind covering their sweet, pink interior.

The Persian is larger than a cantaloupe, and you will find it has a finely netted and dark green rind that seems to become lighter in color when ripe. Its flesh is pink-orange and sweet; also, it is mildly aromatic.

Crenshaws or Cranshaws are a cross between Casabas and Persians. They boast bright salmon colored flesh when ripe.

The Santa Claus or Christmas melons have a light green interior and are very sweet and mild. They are football-shaped and appear to be somewhat like a watermelon.

There are many ways to serve this luscious fruit.

In the half of a cantaloupe, add chilled canned fruit cocktail (or fresh fruits). Squeeze lime or lemon juice over it.

Layers of cantaloupe and vanilla pudding served in stemmed glassware make a pretty dessert, with a sprinkle of coconut added just before serving.

Heap cottage cheese onto salad greens and surround it with wedges of cantaloupe.

For an appetizer, wrap bite size wedges of cantaloupe with thin slices of dried beef. Serve on a toothpick.

Half a cantaloupe filled with berries and topped with a scoop of lemon sherbert also makes good eating.

Add cantaloupe cubes to salads made with chicken, tuna or corned beef.

Make a tossed salad with salad greens, cantaloupe and cherry tomatoes.

Mix cubes of cantaloupe with other melons and plain yogurt, with walnuts added. Chill the mixture and serve it on lettuce leaf.

Cantaloupes also are great for breakfast served plain, with a little powdered sugar or with salt and pepper. The squirt of lemon or lime juice also brings out the natural flavor.

And last, but certainly not least, is the old tried and true delicacy—half a cantaloupe with the center filled with vanilla ice cream.

* * *

Melon Ball on 'Raft'

Slice a head of lettuce into 4 1-inch "rafts" crosswise. Beat 1 8-ounce package cream cheese with 2 tablespoons of sugar and 2 tablespoons of lime juice. Spread over each "raft." Top with watermelon balls, cantaloupe, crenshaw or honeydew, or use an assortment. Garnish with mint.

All in a Woman's Day--August 12, 1986

Ice cold watermelon is a nice hot day ending

Ice cold watermelon! What could be better on a hot summer day or evening than eating a luscious slice of chilled watermelon.

Melons are among the most refreshing fruits on earth. The juicy, red meat that is so sweet and speckled with seeds is a part of the summer season. And what could be more fun to serve on a picnic than watermelon, and then have the traditional seed spitting contest that is always popular.

The watermelon is the most highly appreciated fruit for sheer enjoyment, but also it has good nutrition. A 4x8-

inch wedge, a rather small piece for a real watermelon eater, provides half of the recommended dietary allowance of vitamins C and A, as well as a good contribution of other vitamins and minerals. The flesh of the watermelon is 93 percent water.

Even experts have trouble picking ripe watermelons; their recommendation is that you buy watermelon in a store where they provide cut melons so you can look for the good, red color inside and the dark brown and black seeds that show the melon has reached maturity. In selecting from a cut section, always avoid melons with pale colored flesh and white streaks or pale seeds that indicate immaturity. Dry, mealy, watery and stringy flesh are signs of over maturity or aging after harvesting.

If you are selecting a watermelon that is uncut, the surface should be fairly smooth. The end should be well filled out and rounded and the underside of the melon should have a creamy or yellowish color. If it is ripe, it also should give to a little pressure around the stem end.

A farmer, with his trick of plugging a melon, can judge accurately the ripeness of a watermelon before it is opened.

Thumping watermelons is a time honored tradition, but it is not the best way to check for ripeness. In the field, pickers can tell by the melon's tendrils turning brown, for that means it is about to get ripe. Another way for the untrained melon picker is to roll the watermelon over and without separating it from the vine, peel back a thin slice of the outer tissue. If it has turned yellow, that is a good indication the melon is ripe; if white, you better leave it alone.

To some, who are true connoisseurs, the secret lies in the brilliance of the stripes, whether dark green or light and netlike. They seem to think there is a fullness in color that comes with ripeness. With the dark green stripes there is a trace of yellow that begins to show. The same occurs in green netting.

You know, too, if all these methods fail, try scratching the melon with your fingernail, and if the rind come off under your nail, it is said that the watermelon is ripe.

Watermelon is the common name applied to the annual trailing vine citrullus vulgaris of the family of Cucubitaceae, and its large edible fruit. This vine, a native of tropical Africa, was cultivated for its refreshing sweet fruit.

There are many varieties; however, some are oblong, some round, some have thick green or striped rinds. There also are yellow meated fruit, as well as the small ice box variety with red and yellow meat. Too, there is a variety that bears white flesh fruit that is known as the citrus melon, and it is used like citron in preparing preserves.

Always keep cut melon wrapped to prevent it from absorbing refrigerator odors.

Some folks like to eat watermelon with salt or a little powdered sugar. They say it improves the flavor.

All in a Woman's Day--August 19, 1986
Homemade substitutes prove to be money savers

If you are in need of a substitute, or would like to have a homemade product instead of purchasing at the market, then these few hints may be of value.

In a previous column was a recipe for sweetened condensed milk. Here is another recipe for it, but just a bit different. It makes the same amount as the commercial kind (14 ounces) and will keep for several weeks under refrigeration. Use one cup of instant nonfat milk, one-third cup of boiling water, three tablespoons of melted butter or margarine, two-thirds cup of sugar and a pinch of salt. Put all ingredients in blender and process until smooth.

This might be a good time to make some homemade mustard. Take two heaping teaspoons of dry mustard, one heaping teaspoon of sugar and a half teaspoon of salt. Thoroughly mix all the ingredients and pour enough boiling water over them to make a thick paste. Cover and cool to room temperature. Dilute with apple cider vinegar to the consistency desired.

If you want to make your own cherry coke, just add grenadine syrup to the regular coke to suit the taste. The syrup can be found in the flavoring section of your supermarket.

Perhaps you ran out of an egg for thickening. If so, use one tablespoon flour.

To make cake flour use four tablespoons of corn starch in a measuring cup, then fill it with all-purpose flour. Sift together three times. This is equal to one cup sifted cake flour.

If you, have no corn syrup on hand, use one cup of sugar plus a half cup of water or liquid called for in the recipe.

In the event you have run short, and want to omit an egg in a recipe, increase the liquid by three tablespoons for each egg omitted. This is a bit risky; however, in delicately balanced cake or cookie recipes, or in recipes using lots of eggs, it can work.

If you have only cake flour and need all-purpose flour, use one cup plus two tablespoons of cake flour for each cup of all-purpose flour.

If you are out of vanilla, a batter or dessert can be flavored with grated lemon or orange rind and a little lemon juice. Or you can use one-fourth teaspoon of nutmeg for each teaspoon of vanilla extract or use just a dusting of cinnamon.

Should you have no catsup and need one cup, just combine one cup of tomato sauce or mashed canned tomatoes, one-fourth cup of packed brown sugar, one tablespoon of vinegar, one-fourth teaspoon of cinnamon and a dash each of ground cloves and allspice.

If in need of a tablespoon or two of Hollandaise for a sauce or glaze, just use a good quality mayonnaise (not creamy dressing).

No need to buy a bag of self-rising flour for one recipe, just make your own. To one cup regular flour, add half teaspoon of salt and one and a half teaspoons of baking powder. This equals one cup of self-raising flour.

You can make your own instant oatmeal and save money at the same time. Put old-fashioned or three-minute oatmeal into the blender and turn it to grind for a second or two; then use as you would instant oatmeal. For flavor variations add brown sugar, cinnamon, raisins or dried fruit or any combination; perhaps dried apples and cinnamon. Ounce for ounce, you will no doubt find that it costs less than the prepared packaged kind.

You also can make your own candied fruit. Use one lemon peel, two orange peels, one small can of sliced pineapple, one jar of maraschino cherries, two cups of golden raisins and one and a half cups of sugar. Drain cherries. Simmer citrus peels in water to cover for 15 minutes; drain and cut up fine. Combine ingredients and put mixture into a large, heavy skillet, cooking and stirring over low heat until fruit is glazed and liquid gone. Spread the mixture out on a large platter for two days and then keep in a glass jar in refrigerator until needed.

If you don't have any meat tenderizer, just sear the meat until it is well browned and pour in two cups strong tea. Put the lid on the Dutch oven and bring to a boil, then turn heat to simmer for several hours. When it is tender, sprinkle with salt and pepper, and cook for 20 minutes more. Cheaper cuts of meats, such as brisket, boiling beef and others, can be made tender and tasty. Delicious gravy also will result.

* * *

Apple Pie Filling

10 cups water
1 teaspoon salt
4 1/2 cups sugar
2 or 3 drops yellow food coloring
1 cup corn starch
5 1/2 pounds (approximately) apples, peeled, cored and sliced
2 teaspoons cinnamon
1/4 teaspoon nutmeg
3 tablespoons lemon juice

In a large saucepan, blend sugar, corn starch, cinnamon, nutmeg and salt. Stir in all the water; cook and stir until it comes to a boil and thickens. Add lemon juice and food coloring. Remove mixture from heat, and fill hot jars with apples, and then add hot thickened syrup up to the neck. Place lids and process in hot water bath for 20 minutes. Makes 7 quarts.

Get into the 'muffin act'

Are you a maker and a muffin eater? If not, this might be just the time to get into the "muffin act."

With the fall season fast approaching, perhaps it would be just right to make some of those "little gems," which by the way, a muffin is called, and then, of course, by the same token a muffin is a "little gem." The use of the words, gem and muffin, for this choice food really makes good sense, for according to Webster's dictionary, "gem is a perfect specimen of its kind." The definition of a muffin is "a little muff," used to keep the hands warm and that is what this quick bread does—keeps the hands warm as you hurry with it from the oven to the table so it can be served piping hot.

I never really thought much about muffins until a trip to Canada made me aware of their goodness. Muffins are featured at delicatessens, bakeries and various eating places, where the price ranges from 25 to 65 cents each, depending on the size and kind. In one large mall there was a shop of just muffins and it was called "Mmmarvelous Mmmuffins." I had no idea there were so many kinds. I have since found that there is a large range of assortments from the filled, that are typically Yankee in character, to tiny, crisp muffins.

In some places they were served warm; however, in others they were not, but that didn't seem to make any difference. People just munched away on a muffin of their choice. I had always thought of them being served "hot," with butter and perhaps jelly, jam or preserves. But I guess if they are good enough, it doesn't make any

462

difference—hot or cold.

Laying all jokes aside, they really are good to munch on, and with school-time here, they would make a nice addition to a lunchbox, as well as a tasty surprise for the "someone" in your family, who works and carries a lunch (brown-bagger).

When we think of muffins, the lore of the "muffin man" comes to mind. This was such a common sight on the streets of England, as well as in this country during the last century. Perhaps, too, you have heard or read of the traditional "ploughman's lunch" in England that consists of cheese and rolls and sometimes fruit. This combination of cheese, apples and nuts as a quick bread resulted in a delicious and filling muffin.

There are several different kinds of packaged muffin mixes to be found at the supermarket if you don't want to whip up a batch from scratch; however, you will find that they are not difficult to make.

Although these delicious goodies have been around for a long time, they are becoming more and more popular. And why shouldn't they? What other food can fill the bill for a hot and fragrant accompaniment for meals, easy and quick desserts, brown-bag goodies, and a perfect solution for either a leisurely breakfast or one on the go. They also fit in well for lunch or dinner (supper if you like). That is the magic of muffins. They are super!

* * *

If you want a tender muffin, use pastry flour and avoid overbeating.

The batter should always be stirred by hand until the dry ingredients are just moistened.

The perfect muffin will have rough, shiny brown crust, with the inside light and tender. Break open a perfect muffin and you will not see long holes, called tunnels, and the crumbs will be moist. If your muffins are tough, no doubt the batter was overbeaten, and there will be peaks on top with a tunneled texture and dull crusts.

If muffins cannot be served immediately from the oven, just tip the pan to one side so there will be no soggy crusts, and do keep them warm.

Should you want to reheat leftover muffins, just wrap them in aluminum foil and place in a 400 degree oven for 15 to 20 minutes. They also can be reheated in a microwave oven; or placed for 20 minutes or so in the top of a double boiler over boiling water; or they can be split and toasted and served buttered with jam, jelly or marmalade.

Too, if you do not have batter enough to fill all the tins, be sure and place water in the empty ones to prevent the heat from warping the pan.

Often tiny cakes, cream puffs and sandwiches are served at teas, but why not serve tiny fruit or spice muffins? Bake them in your smallest cupcake pans and serve them piping hot, they will be devoured.

Now you know it wouldn't be dificult to become "mad" about muffins if you just wanted to let yourself go and really get enthusiastic about this drop batter baked in individual pans and served as a quick bread.

* * *

Hawaiian Muffins

1 (14-ounce) package orange muffin mix
1/4 cup flaked coconut
1 (8 3/4-ounce) can crushed pineapple, drained
1 egg, beaten

2/3 cup milk

NOTE: If Orange Muffin mix is not available; use 3/4 cup candied orange peel, plus a little orange flavoring in a basic muffin batter.

Combine the muffin mix and coconut. Reserve 1 tablespoon of the pineapple syrup. Add pineapple, beaten egg and milk to dry ingredients and blend only until the dry ingredients are moistened. Fill greased muffin tins or paper baking cups 2/3 full, and bake them in a hot oven (400 degrees) for 15 to 20 minutes. Makes 12 to 16 muffins. Beat 1 3-ounce package cream cheese until light and fluffy; add the tablespoon reserved pineapple juice and beat well. Serve with the hot muffins.

All in a Woman's Day--September 2, 1986
How to mix muffins; variations are unending

What could be better than warm muffins tucked in a napkin on the breakfast table? After you get in the mood and swing of eating muffins, you will find that they grow on you and they are delightful eating, just anytime.

There are two ways to mix muffins. The first bears the muffin name and the other is the biscuit technique.

The muffin method is simpler and gives a good typically coarse and open texture. It is used for muffins containing large amounts of sugar and shortening.

The biscuit method, sometimes called the "cake method," gives a finer more cake like texture to the batter. This method is used for plainer type muffins.

For the muffin method, sift the dry ingredients into a bowl and make a hollow in the center. Combine the milk or other liquid, egg and melted shortening, and put all at once into the hollow, stirring just enough to moisten. The batter will not be smooth.

The biscuit method uses a pastry blender to mix the dry ingredients with the shortening, until it looks like coarse meal or crumbs that are about the size of a pea. Make a hollow in the center. Beat the egg until foamy and combine with the milk or liquid and pour all at once into the hollow. Stir the dry ingredients by pushing them with a spoon to the center of the bowl (to the hollow where the liquid is), slowly turning the bowl. After going around the bowl once, chop straight through the center with a spoon and mix ingredients. Stir, using as few strokes as possible and only enough to moisten.

There are a number of variations that can be used with a basic muffin recipe.

Orange Muffins: Cut in small pieces three-fourths cup candied orange peel and add to the batter.

Bacon Muffins: Add three strips of cooked and crumbled bacon to the batter. Too, bacon fat can be used as the shortening for a more distinctive flavor.

Date Muffins: Add to the batter half cup pitted dates cut up in small pieces or one-fourth cup raisins.

Peach Muffins: Add three-fourths cup peaches that have been peeled and cut into small pieces. Canned peaches also can be used. (You might try pineapple.)

Berry Muffins: Save one-fourth cup of flour and sprinkle over one cup berries—blueberries, huckleberries, and if you like, you might try using black raspberries or blackberries: fresh or frozen can be used. The berries are stirred into the batter last. Be sure to use a half cup sugar. If frozen berries are used, be sure they are thawed.

Pecan Muffins: Add half a cup chopped pecans and use only one-fourth cup sugar. After the tins have been filled, sprinkle sugar, cinnamon and more chopped nuts over the top before popping muffin tins into the oven.

Whole Wheat Muffins: Sub-stitute three-fourths cup whole wheat flour for the one cup of flour and do not sift. Add the whole wheat flour after sifting the other dry ingredients.

Jelly Muffins: After placing the batter in the muffin tins, top each muffin with a teaspoon of tart jelly.

Cheese-Caraway Muffins: Add one cup shredded sharp processed American cheese and a half to one teaspoon of caraway seed to the flour mixture.

Milk Muffins: Add a half teaspoon soda with three-fourths cup sour milk or buttermilk substituted for the sweet milk. Reduce baking powder to one teaspoon.

Cranberry Muffins: Fill muffin tins one-third full. Cut one cup of canned jellied cranberry sauce into half-inch cubes and sprinkle over the batter. Top with remaining batter.

* * *

Basic Muffins

2 cups flour
3 teaspoons baking powder
1/2 teaspoon salt
2 tablespoons sugar (or up to 1/2 cup)
1 egg, slightly beaten
1 cup milk
1/4 cup melted butter

Mix flour, baking powder, salt and sugar in a large bowl; add the egg, milk and melted butter, stirring only enough to dampen the flour. The batter should not be smooth. Place in greased muffin tins or use baking cups, filling each about 2/3 full. Bake 20 to 25 minutes in a 375 degree oven.

All in a Woman's Day--September 9, 1986

'Thoughtful' ideas are given about food

Some helpful hints concerning preparation, and caring for food should give some "food for thought."

Do you have leftover egg yolks and are you at a loss as to what to do with them? Just drop them in boiling water and let them cook until firm; cool and refrigerate. They will be ready to use in salads or for whatever needed.

Use a slotted spoon when making gelatin. This helps to make better gelatin as the slots pick up any undissolved granules.

When baking, sift dry ingredients onto a paper plate as this can be easily bent for pouring into a bowl.

Try adding a teaspoon of vinegar to the fat when deep frying. It helps to eliminate the greasy taste.

Ice coating on the outside of a package of frozen food may be an indication of some previous thawing, so the food inside may no longer be of top quality. Be sure to select another package.

Toast bread before grinding into crumbs and it will have a better flavor. Toasted sesame seeds also add to the taste. Keep some in a salt shaker and add to a piece of toast.

If gravy is too thin, just stir in a few instant potato flakes instead of flour.

Cereal and crackers sometimes become soggy. If so, just place them on a cookie sheet and heat them in the oven for a few minutes.

To prevent boil-overs, try adding a lump of butter or a few teaspoons of cooking oil to the water to prevent noodles, spaghetti or rice from boiling over and sticking together.

When making puddings or other sauces or jelly, spread a thin layer of melted butter or cream over the top after cooking. Then stir, and the scum and foam will disappear.

Try adding a pinch of baking powder to pie dough and it will make the crust lighter and fluffier.

A rib of celery placed in the bag with bread will help keep it fresh.

Having trouble peeling a plum? Try sticking a fork into it then lowering the fruit into boiling water until the skin cracks. Be sure the entire plum is submerged, so the skin will loosen.

When boiling pasta, try laying a wooden spoon over the top of the pan to prevent boiling over. Too, if you place a colander in the boiling water and then add the pasta, it won't stick to the pan and will be much easier to drain when the cooking is finished.

Frankfurters will frequently split when boiled. To prevent this, fill the pan with just enough water to cover. Bring to a boil and then add the frankfurters. Take the pan from the burner, cover, and let stand from 8 to 10 minutes.

A chocolate candy bar makes a good icing. Place the bar on a cake that is hot from the oven and it will melt. Spread while still warm.

A sprinkle of mace on the filling adds extra flavor to pumpkin pie.

An excellent fruit salad dressing can be made with just a couple of ingredients. Beat until stiff the white of an egg and add one teaspoon of plum jelly; mix well and serve.

If you are planning on cooking a turkey, after stuffing, insert a bread heel in the pocket. This will close the bird and eliminates trussing.

* * *

Cherry Salad Supreme

1 (3-ounce) package raspberry gelatin
1 (3-ounce) package lemon gelatin
1 (3-ounce) package cream cheese
1 (21-ounce) can cherry pie filling
1/3 cup mayonnaise or salad dressing
1 (8 3/4-ounce) can (1 cup) crushed pineapple
1/2 cup whipping cream or whipped topping
1 cup miniature marshmallows
2 tablespoons chopped nuts

Dissolve raspberry gelatin in 1 cup of boiling water; stir in pie filling; turn into a 9x9x2-inch dish. Chill until partially set. Dissolve lemon gelatin in 1 cup boiling water. Beat together cream cheese and mayonnaise. Gradually add lemon gelatin. Stir in undrained pineapple. Whip cream, or use whipped topping, and fold into lemon mixture with marsh-mallows. Spread on top of cherry layer; top with nuts. Chill until set. Makes 12 servings.

All in a Woman's Day--September 16, 1986

Fall season myths revealed

It has been said and written that soon after Labor Day, any warm day in the northern part of the United States is referred to by many people as "Indian Summer."

This, of course, although not really earth shaking, is not exactly a correct statement. There does happen to be certain criteria involved, as well as specific dates.

Of course, Indian Summer is a time when it is warm, the atmosphere is hazy or smoky, the barometer remains high, there is no wind, and the nights you will find are clear, as well as chilly.

Time seems to be one of the controversial aspects of this time of year. The warm days of fall do not, just by themselves, make Indian Summer as has often been the belief. The catch, however, might be unless the warm days follow the cold weather or a hard frost.

For the past 194 years, the Old Farmer's Almanac has adhered to the saying "All Saints bring out winter; St. Martin's brings out Indian Summer." And, so accordingly, Indian Summer can occur between St. Martin's Day, Nov. 11, and Nov. 20. Now, if the conditions that go to makeup Indian Summer, as described, do not occur between the mentioned dates, then there is no Indian Summer that year.

Too, if there should be a period of warm fall weather at a time other than between the dates mentioned, then you might described it as "being" like Indian Summer.

In American literature it seems to mean a time in late fall or after late October. This, of course, would seem to be in contrast with the time Indian Summer is in Old England. That can come in September, when it is known then as St. Augustine's summer; if in October, St. Luke's Summer; or if in November, St. Martin's Summer. These Saint days fall on Aug. 28, Oct. 18 and Nov. 11, respectively.

Has it ever occurred to you why a special time of year is called Indian Summer? There are various thoughts along that line. Some people think that it is from the early Indians, who fully believed that this condition was caused by a certain wind that seemed to come from the court of their god, Cautantowwit or the Southwestern god; however, some feel that it comes from the fact that this time of year, or possibly a little before, that the deciduous trees were all attired as colorful as Indians.

The most probable thought, in the way of origin, goes back to the early settlers in New England. It seems that each year they would welcome the arrival of cold wintry days in late October, when they would leave their stockades without worrying about Indian attacks and begin the preparation of their fields for the following spring plantings. It appeared that the Indians just didn't like attacking when the weather was cold. But, then, each year about St. Martin's Day, when it would unexpectedly turn warm again, the Indians would have just one more go around with the settlers, even if this was not the regular raiding season. The settlers called it, "Indian Summer."

You may have your own thoughts or folklore about this season of the year.

And while on the topic of weather, let's give a little thought to some weather lore that could possibly occur before the end of the year.

When sheep turn their backs on the wind, look for a cold spell.

You can predict a mild winter if the autumn onions have thin skins.

A white frost indicates rain.

If the breastbone of a goose is dark, the winter will be cold.

Frost clinging to trees late in the morning indicates snow.

If the sun appears during a snowfall, you can look for snow the next day.

Snow melting as it reaches the ground, indicates that the snowfall is only a flurry.

A green Christmas indicates a white Easter.

If worms tend to remain deep in the ground during the autumn or early winter, it will be a cold winter.

Walnut hulls that are loose and easily removed indicate a mild winter.

A severe winter is indicated by a large number of tumblebugs.

Fruit trees blossoming twice in a season indicates a hard winter.

Thunder in December means that cold weather is approaching.

* * *

Orange-Apple Cookies

2 3/4 cup flour
1 teaspoon salt
2 teaspoons baking powder
1 cup shortening
2 cups brown sugar
1 1/2 teaspoons vanilla
1 teaspoon orange flavoring
1/4 cup orange juice
1 egg
1/2 cup milk
2 large apples, peeled and cored
1 cup raisins

Sift together flour, salt and baking powder; cream sugar and shortening, adding the vanilla and orange flavorings. Add egg and beat well. Add the dry ingredients alternately with milk and orange juice. Mix well. Put apples and raisins through food grinder and fold them into the mixture. Drop from tablespoon on greased cookie sheet and bake 12 to 15 minutes in a 375-degree oven.

All in a Woman's Day--September 23, 1986

Appetite appeaser is now 'gingerbread'

As the days of fall begin to close in around us, we think of warm or hot foods to appease our appetites. What could be more inviting than a warm, delicious serving of gingerbread—plain, with butter, with ice cream, or whipped topping?

Whether you can say that a food is invented, I am not quite sure; however, that is the terminology that is given to a Greek from Rhodes, who, it is said that somewhere about 2000 B.C., "invented" gingerbread.

The fame of this delightful "bread cake" soon spread throughout the Mediterranean area and finally to England, where it became the custom to make gingerbread into shapes, representing people, animals or letters of the alphabet.

So, from this background, it is no wonder that gingerbread found its way to the American colonies and proved to be a favorite dessert. Of course, two of the necessary ingredients are ginger and molasses, both of which were linked with early American cooking.

In colonial America, the colonists displayed much pride in their wood gingerbread molds and their gingerbread, which was a favorite cake of colonial and postcolonial times. The mother of George Washington made gingerbread at home, and often served it to famous guests.

During colonial times, when sugar was scarce, or probably not available at all, molasses was used as the sweetener. Molasses often was called "long sweetening," while sugar was referred to as "short sweetening."

Makers of this spicy bread cake often used brown sugar or honey as the sweetening. Most generally it was cut into squares and served plain. Today we find it good served with hot applesauce, whipped cream or ice cream. A lemon sauce also is good as a topping.

This food is one of the oldest of cakes; however, the original gingerbread was not a cake, but a solid bread made with honey, spices and flour.

During the days when knighthood was in flower, the knights would fight tournaments to please their ladies, and gingerbread was one of the gifts that the fair maidens would bestow as a favor. The gift was rather elaborate and often looked like a tooled or gilt-piece of leather, with cloves and goldleaf often arranged in the shape of a fleur-de-lis.

In Europe, the great fairs were social events of the Middle Ages, and in the later centuries it was at these affairs that people in all walks of life—the rich, the poor, the young and the old—gathered for enjoyment. These events, however, would never have been complete without the gingerbread stalls. The holidays also featured gingerbread baked in special molds. These molds are now prize museum pieces.

As we think about the gingerbread, we remember the stories of the six-foot men and women gingerbreads of Begium and Holland that were baked for St. Nicholas Day; the panforte of Italy; the pain d'epices, the spice or gingerbreads of the French; the lebkuchen of the Germans, Swiss and Australians. Many of them were very elaborate and fanciful in shape and the decorations an inspiration as they were painted with colored sugar, often gilded.

From this comes the expression "the gilt on the gingerbread."

This 20th century recipe for gingerbread uses soft shortening or margarine rather than lard or butter.

It contains only one egg and therefore is an excellent dessert for those who want to lower their cholesterol intake.

* * *

Gingerbread

1/2 cup sugar
1 egg
1/2 cup shortening
1/2 cup light molasses
1 1/2 cups sifted all-purpose flour
3/4 teaspoon salt
3/4 teaspoon soda
1/2 teaspoon cinnamon
1/2 teaspoon ginger
1/2 cup boiling water

Cream sugar and shortening until light, and add the molasses and eggs; beat thoroughly. Sift dry ingredients together and add them to the creamed mixture, alternately with the water, beating after each addition. Bake in a lightly greased and floured 8x8x2-inch pan at 350 degrees for 35 to 40 minutes or until it tests done. Serve warm.

* * *

Lemon Creme Sauce

1/2 cup sugar
3 tablespoons corn starch
1/4 teaspoon salt
2 cups water
1/4 cup soft margarine
1 tablespoon grated lemon rind
3 tablespoons lemon juice
Few drops yellow food coloring

Mix sugar, corn starch and salt in saucepan; stir in water and cook; stir over medium heat until thick and clear. Blend in margarine, lemon rind, juice and food coloring. Serve over gingerbread. Makes 2 1/4 cups.

All in a Woman's Day--September 30, 1986

Enjoy apples in season

Just mention Pyrus Malus and you could sail into a discussion about the Garden of Eden, William Tell, American symbol or one of the best buys on the market this time of year.

Pyrus Malus, or apples, as they are

called, come into season in September and continue to be harvested in Missouri through November.

Apples are perhaps one of the most nutritious and delicious after school snacks you can serve hungry youngsters (oldsters like them, too).

Since peanut butter is one of the kids' favorite foods, as well as being packed with protein, just combine the two by preparing "Apple Goobers" that come from the National Apple Institute's Apple Kitchen. Just before serving, cut apples in wedges and cut out the core. Spread each wedge thickly with peanut butter. Serve them with mugs of chocolate milk or frosted milk shakes. (Apple Goobers, by the way, aren't just for kids; they make good garnishes for salads and cold cut platters!)

Johnny Chapman, or Johnny Appleseed as he was more familiarly known, may never have gotten as far West as Missouri; however, one of our first settlers and captain of one of the large wagon trains, a Captain Kuhn, planted several apple trees in his stockade. Little did he know he would be the first of many apple producers in his family here in Missouri.

Hints oftentimes help in the preparation of foods, so here are a few concerning this delicious fruit:

Two slices of fresh apple put together with a layer of cream cheese or slices of cheddar cheese makes a hearty and substantial snack.

Red apple cups make salads festive when you are having guests, and they are even nice to dress up the table for your family. Scoop out a Delicious, Rome or Winesap apple and fill it with a tasty fruit salad of chopped apple, white grapes, marshmallows and chopped nuts topped with mayonnaise and a sprig of mint.

Too, an apple cut in half and placed inside an airtight container with bread or cake will keep the bakery goods moist and flavorful for days.

When peeling apples, be sure to use a sharp knife, cutting out the bloom end first before starting to peel it. This way you won't have black pieces of bloom on the fruit that is peeled.

After cutting an apple, rub the exposed surface with a little bottled lemon juice and the fruit will stay fresh looking.

Another way to keep apples from turning dark is to peel, core and slice into a solution of two tablespoons of salt per gallon of water, and then drain. You can then pack the unsweetened fruit in containers and freeze. They will keep frozen for at least six months and when thawed tastes as if they were fresh. The salt seems to do the trick to give the fresh taste.

Here is something else you might like to try. Peel and slice apples one-fourth to a half-inch thick. Cook them in a can of imitation strawberry pop. Simmer until apples are tender. You can taste them to see if sugar is needed.

For a dessert you might try serving the apples in or with cheese or as a sauce or baked. Ounce for ounce, you can't top it for elegant taste and economy.

Apples can be served at any temperature you like; however, your reserve supply keeps best in the refrigerator, and not too close to the freezer, in plastic bags or the hydrator drawer. Apples keep well with reasonable care, and this helps make them one of the most economical fruits.

Have you ever really wondered just

how the Waldorf Salad originated? It was created by the Maitre d' at the opening of the Waldorf Hotel on Fifth Avenue in March, 1933, for the first public charity ball in history. The ball was given as a benefit for one of Mrs. William K. Vanderbilt's pet charities, St. Mary's Free Hospital for Children. According to the story, the Maitre d' was the congenial Oscar, who later became known as Oscar of the Waldorf. Back in those days; the salad was a revolutionary combination of foods, because most people did not eat fruit salads such as we do today. The Waldorf gave a light, different touch to a heavy meal. This is thought perhaps to be the start of the vogue of fruit salads.

* * *

The original recipe does not exist in writing; however, the official recipe from the Waldorf-Astoria, now located on Park Avenue in midtown Manhattan, follows:

* * *

Authentic Apple Salad

1 1/2 cups diced tart, red apples, unpeeled
1 tablespoon lemon juice
1 cup diced celery
1/2 cup mayonnaise
1 cup walnuts, chopped
Lettuce, chilled

Sprinkle apples with lemon juice to keep them from discoloring. Combine apples with celery; add mayonnaise, mixing well. Arrange leaves of crisp, cold lettuce on six salad plates and spoon on salad mixture. Just before serving, sprinkle with walnuts.

Apples seem to be tops

I am again going to delve into the subject of "apples." What could be nicer, this time of year, or any other time . . . they just seem to be a favorite fruit.

As you know, harvesting apples at just the right stage of maturity, and then cooling them immediately are the keys to successful long-term storage. The temperature and oxygen content of the storage rooms are controlled to slow down the breathing rate of apples.

Many people consider the flavor of apples from storage to be better than those of apples right off the tree.

If apples are stored too long and improperly, the result is mealy apples with brown cores. Apples in storage should be sorted occasionally so that those showing any signs of spoilage can be discarded.

Consumers can benefit from the spring and summer supply by using the fruit in a variety of ways.

For instance, keep apples handy for munching and include them in a school or worker's lunch box. Green salads can include apple chunks or wedges, and they can be added in chunks to chicken or seafood salads, potato salad and cole slaw. Too, apples can be used in bread pudding or rice pudding. A thinly sliced apple also is good on meat sandwiches. Take apples along on picnics with other summer fruits.

Delicious apples seem to keep their color longer than others after cutting; however, if necessary, a squeeze of fresh lemon juice will retard discoloration of any apple.

Too, any apple can be used for any purpose; but results will vary. Some apple varieties are better suited to different uses. Of the many varieties that are grown in the Unites States; however, only about a dozen provide almost 90 percent of the total production

* * *

Most folks have their favorite recipe for applesauce; however, you might like to try to unscramble this sauce or perhaps it might be a game for your club members to solve. There are 15 kinds of apples that went into this sauce. They are scrambled as follows: nantohaj, scnthoim, orme, hernnotr pys, lortndac, aid edr, dwil verri, nippip, loyewl soidilceu, sitanac, ginnegre, esnimad shubl, der licedisuo, wabdinl, aspinew and neb sidva. The answers (try to work the puzzle first) are: Jonathon, McIntosh, Rome, Northern Spy, Cortland, Ida Red, Wild River, Pippin, Yellow Delicious, Astican, Greening, Maiden's Blush, Red Delicious, Baldwin, Winesap and Ben Davis.

* * *

Apple Salad Deluxe

4 large, crisp red-skinned apples
2 teaspoons granulated sugar
1 teaspoon lemon juice
3 large stalks celery
1/2 cup coarsely broken walnuts or pecans
1/2 cup pitted, snipped dates
1/3 cup mayonyaise
1/2 cup heavy cream, whipped or whipped topping
Crisp lettuce leaves

Wash apples, cut out stem, then cut, core and dice unpeeled. Place in a bowl and sprinkle with sugar and lemon juice. Wash and cut celery stalks into small cubes; add nuts and dates to the apples. Mix well. Blend together mayonnaise and whipped cream or whipped topping. Fold it gently, but thoroughly into apple mixture. Spoon onto lettuce leaves on salad plates or into a lettuce lined salad bowl. Makes 6 servings.

All in a Woman's Day--October 14, 1986
Fall is sorghum time

It is the season for making and eating sorghum, that is made from a tropical Old World grass that has been used for fodder or syrup for centuries. But what could be better than sorghum mixed with butter and spread on hot biscuits? Mmmm! Good eating!

Perhaps you thought there was no difference between sorghum and molasses. But there is a difference; however, they can be interchanged in recipes. Although molasses is a by-product of sugar cane and sugar beets, sorghum can be used for making molasses; however, sorghum is made strictly from the sorghum plant.

The tall earless cornlike grass, with a terminal head of small seeds, supposed to be native of Africa and Asia, long has been cultivated in southern Europe and China as a forage plant, and for the syrup made from its sweet juice which does not yield a profitable quantity of sugar.

Sorghums were among the first wild plants that man domesticated, with the Egyptian cultivation going back before 220 B.C. The plants also were in India and China at an early date.

Sorghums are a genus of grasses that have a large number of species cultivated throughout the world for forage, food and syrup. This annual plant resembles maise and grows from three to 15 feet in height. The grains of sorghums are rounder and smaller than those of true cereals, with wheat as an example. Sorghums, found to be less nutritious than maize, can be grown in regions where maize will not flourish. It also requires very little water.

There are four types of sorghums, including grass, grain, broomcorn and sugar.

The grass sorghums are used only for pasture and hay, while the grain sorghums, grown in the United States since 1874, include milo, kafir, maize, durra, Egyptian rice corn, Jerusalem corn, broomcorn, shallu, kaoliang (Chinese sorghums), feterita and hegari. The seed, or the grain is used as feed for livestock, and the plants for forage. Commercially it is used in alcohol, oil, beer and starch. Grain sorghums in India, Asia and Africa are a staple food for human beings.

The broomcorns have a panicle with long branches known as the "brush." These branches are used for carpet and whisk brooms. They have been grown in the United States since 1797.

It wasn't until after 1853 that the sugar sorghum flourished in the United States. The sugar sorghum plants are tall and leafy, and the cane like stalk holds a sweet juice that can be boiled down into a syrup. It is this sorghum that is used as a substitute for molasses, and also it is often called molasses.

The syrup in sorghum is not crystalized into sugar, but is used in its pure concentrate form.

With the scarcity of sugar in the North during the Civil War, the sorghum syrup was used instead of molasses.

Have you ever visited a sorghum mill? If not, you should make an effort to do so. Not many remain in this area, and you might have to do a little searching to find a mill. In our area sorghum making time is generally late September or early October, so, it may well be over with for this season. However, it is possible the rainy weather might have delayed the process.

In preparation for making sorghum, the plant must first be stripped while it is still standing in the field. Then it is harvested, with the heads or flowers cut off and used for fodder. The fibrous stalks are run through a mill that crushes the reeds and forces the green sorghum liquid into large barrels.

Sorghum can be frozen; however, it also keeps well without freezing.

If it should go to sugar, place the container in a pan of boiling water and it will go back to the syrup form.

* * *

A recipe for "the best baked beans" has been shared by a family who operated a sorghum mill. You might like to try it as it is easy to make.

Best Baked Beans

2 cans pork and beans
1 teaspoon dried onion flakes
3 tablespoons sorghum
2 tablespoons catsup

Combine all ingredients and bake the mixture for 30 minutes at 350 degrees.

All in a Woman's Day--October 21, 1986

Time to think molasses

Last week sorghum was the topic; today, I am going to delve into that thick brown syrup known as "molasses."

This syrup is the result of being separated from raw sugar during the various stages of refinement. As it was noted last week, there is a difference between molasses and sorghum. Molasses is a by-product of sugar cane and sugar beet, with sorghum strictly from the sorghum plant. Sorghum also can be used for making molasses.

The sugar cane is cut close to the

ground as the lowest ends are the part of the plant that are richest in sugar. The stalks are cut or torn into small pieces and then put through rollers to extract the dark-grayish, sweet juice. This is boiled down until there is a thick syrupy mass that includes the crystals of sugar. This heavy syrup is then put into containers with holes through which the liquid can drip, leaving the raw crystalized sugar. This liquid is called molasses.

Molasses to Americans, means both the syrup that is separated from the raw sugar in the first stages of the production and the syrup that is taken from the raw sugar as it is refined. The second product is called "treacle" by the English. The word molasses is from the Portuguese "melaco" that is derived from the Latin root "mel" that means "honey," and "aceus," that means "resembling."

Sorghum molasses is the syrup that comes from the stalk of a group of grains that look very much like corn. It has been learned that this syrup is a pure product with no sugar extracted. It tastes, has the color and the consistency of molasses.

There are three major types molasses on the market. The unsulphured molasses is made from the juice of sun-ripened cane, cultivated in rich soil mostly in the West Indies, where it is grown under the hot tropical sun from 12 to 15 months. The juice is clarified and concentrated. The unsulphured molasses is then transferred to warehouses in this country, where it is skillfully blended to produce the finest quality, all sweet molasses. It is a carefully and deliberately manufactured product with no sugar removed and no preservatives or chemicals added.

Sulphured molasses is a by-product of sugar making. The very efficiency in modern sugar plants has lowered the quality of molasses by extracting most of the sugar from the original cane juice. Most of the sulphured molasses comes from areas other than the West Indies, and since the ripening season in these areas is not long enough to mature the cane, the sugar cane is treated with sulphur fumes during the sugar-extracting process. Strictly speaking, sulphur fumes are not necessary for the manufacture of molasses, but they are used in the making of sugar and, as a result, sulphur is present in the molasses.

There are two types of edible sulphured molasses—the first centrifugal and second centrifugal. The former is made by boiling sugar cane juice to the proper density in vacuum pans then passing it on to the centrifuge, which extracts a crop of sugar crystals and leaves an amber-colored molasses. This is the first molasses of the sulphured type; however, if this molasses is subjected to still another boiling and whirling, it is again robbed of more sugar crystal. The result is a darker molasses containing large percentages of natural gum and ash and less desirable flavor. This grade is the second molasses.

The third and last type is blackstrap molasses. This is what remains after all of the commercially available sugar has been removed from the cane juice. It is sold primarily to producers of animal feeds and industrial alcohol. This product has a black color and a harsh and bitter taste.

It seems that the quality of molasses depends on the soil in which the sugar cane is grown, the maturity of the cane and the amount of sugar extracted as well as the method of extraction. To a great extent, too, the quality depends on whether the manufacturer starts out to make, molasses or whether he makes sugar and ends up with molasses as a secondary product, or as in the case of blackstrap an end-product.

It is believed that molasses syrup was first eaten by the Chinese and the Indians. Its history in America began when Columbus introduced it to the West Indies and it turned out to be the prime sweetener of the whole Atlantic Seaboard, and continued to be such until after the Civil War. Often called the "life blood" of colonial trading, it proved to be an important crop. In addition to the molasses, also used regionally for sweetening, were local products—maple sugar, syrup, honey and sorghum.

Because of the importance of molasses to life in the colonial days it has been noted that the founders of the colony of Georgia "promised persons sent upon the charity for his maintenance in the Colony for one year 44 gallons of strong beer; 64 quarts of molasses for brewing beer." The mothers, wives, sisters and children of such men got no beer; however, they did receive the molasses.

One of the early day merchants, who got into the molasses business, was William Taussig, who was a baker. It was during the closing days of James Buchanan's turbulent presidency that Taussig established two bakeries in the Capitol. One of his most enthusiastic customers was President Abraham Lincoln, who frequently ordered the bakery's specialty, Molasses Pie. He also had a sweet tooth for gingerbread and other desserts made with molasses. In this respect, Lincoln was only following the footsteps of Washington and Jefferson, who were both very fond of molasses. A great deal of the cookery at Mount Vernon and Monticello was effected with the aid of that most delightful of naturally sweet substances, so the story goes. After the close of the Civil War, the two Taussig bakeries branched into the molasses business. The Taussig molasses enterprises officially became known as the American Molasses Company in 1905.

* * *

Dress Up Glaze For Ham

This instant dress-up glaze is for a whole ham and includes 1/3 cup molasses and prepared mustard. Forty-five minutes before end of cooking time for ham, score fat surface, stud wlth cloves and brush part of the molasses mixture over ham. Continue baking, brushing occasionally with the remaining glaze. This is for a whole ham.

All in a Woman's Day--October 28, 1986

Make unique treats; leaf, pumpkin cookies

Here it is almost Halloween time again and the goblins will soon be stalking the streets and making calls in their home areas; however, that is not always the case, some of those goblins must ride a broomstick to get as far away from home as they do.

Well, regardless, it is a time of fun for youngsters and oldsters alike. And if you are an oldster, make yourself have fun and be jolly when you greet those mysterious characters that ring your doorbell Oct. 31. You might be surprised how they will make your day!

Do you have in mind what you are

going to be giving as treats this year? Maybe you should think of something different.

Since autumn is such a festive season, you might try your creative urge by making some colorful leaf cookies. Shop for some leaf cookie cutters; however, if they are not available get some different leaves from the trees and make a pattern of cardboard or some other durable material, and you will be in business.

If you are giving them for Halloween treats, wrap them in plastic. And if they are placed in a basket, along with some pumpkin cookies, it will be colorful and attractive to the eye (also to tummy!).

If you don't want to make them for Halloween, the colorful leaf cookies are great to serve for luncheons, teas, bake sales, in your glass cookie jar and, well, for just plain eating.

When ready to roll out the dough, sprinkle flour on the dough board and roll lightly until 1/2-inch thick. It is best to not roll all the dough at once. Dip the cutter into flour each time; or if you are using a cardboard pattern, cut around it with a sharp knife. Place on a greased cookie sheet.

To get your colors for the leaves, mix food coloring—red, green, yellow and orange (orange is made by mixing red and yellow to the desired shade) in a muffin pan. Paint colors on cookies with a clean watercolor brush, using a flowing watercolor technique. Always wash the brushes after each color.

The following colors are to be used; however, they may not be quite true:

Elm: Brush the wider side with green, the narrow and shorter side with yellow;

Maple: Brush red into the veins then brush and blend yellow or orange over the leaf;

Oak: Begin at the tip with a flash of red blending into orange and finishing with yellow at the stem end.

Fill a salt shaker with granulated sugar and sprinkle over the moist leaf cookies. This will give them a glaze. Bake at 375 degrees for 10 to 12 minutes or until done. Be sure to check them carefully so they don't get too brown.

* * *

This same dough may be used for pumpkin cookies; however, a sugar cookie recipe can be used. Just be sure the dough is chilled thoroughly before rolling to 1/4-inch thick. If you do not have a pumpkin cookie cutter, use a glass or sauce dish or whatever to make the size desired. Place a stem on the pumpkin, frost it green. Bake the length of time designated in the recipe. Cool, then frost with orange frosting with coconut flavoring.

Pumpkin cookies would be interesting with the leaf cookies.

You may, through experiment-ing, work out more lovely color combinations. Have fun in your venture.

Happy Halloween!

* * *

Leaf Cookies

(A lady who has made the leaf cookies many times provided this recipe.)

1/2 cup shortening
1 cup sugar
2 well beaten eggs
2 1/2 cups flour
1 tablespoon milk
1/2 teaspoon baking powder
1/4 teaspoon salt
3/4 teaspoon nutmeg

Cream together shortening and sugar until fluffy; add beaten eggs and milk;

sift together the dry ingredients and add to creamed mixture. Shape into a mound and wrap in waxed paper and chill thoroughly.

All in a Woman's Day--November 4, 1986
Sweeten old-time way; use sorghum, molasses

Sorghum or molasses seem to enhance most everything in which they are used. (As I noted previously they can be interchanged in recipes, and still get that distinctive flavor.)

This type of sweetening gives. many foods that old-fashioned flavor as well as the rich, homey fragrance that envelopes the kitchen as foods are cooking.

With a jar of molasses or sorghum as a cupboard staple, you can make "Taffy Cow" that takes a big glass milk and one or two tablespoons of the sweetening goodness. This works equally well with whole or nonfat milk. Or you can make a "Taffy Molasses Cow" that teenagers enjoy. Combine in an electric blender one ripe banana cut in pieces, one tablespoon sorghum or molasses and three-fourths cup milk, blending until smooth.

If you are hungry for "Dame Nature's" touch with foods, go straight back to American pioneer days when sorghum or molasses was the prime sweetener. It was used to spread on bread, toast, muffins or crackers. And then try one or the other on waffles, pancakes or French toast to get an instant old-fashioned flavor.

Would you believe there is a barbecue sauce for outdoors and indoors that requires no cooking or refrigeration. Just blend one cup sorghum or molasses with one cup prepared mustard and stir in one cup vinegar. Keep in a covered jar, and when needed brush the sauce on hamburgers, franks, chicken, spareribs and chops when you grill or broil either indoors or outdoors. This yields about three cups of sauce. Or for variation you can add one cup catsup or a tablespoon of soy sauce or two tablespoons Worcestershire sauce and half a teaspoon tabasco pepper sauce.

Use sorghum or molasses poured over vanilla ice cream just as it comes from the jar. Nuts and marshmallow topping can be added. If you prefer something a little fancier combine pineapple tidbits and syrup (from a 9-ounce can) with a fourth cup molasses or sorghum and one tablespoon butter in a saucepan. Bring to a boil and simmer 5 minutes. Add half teaspoon rum flavoring. Serve hot or cold over ice cream. Yield about 1 y1/2 cups.

Molasses or sorghum is an energy food, plus it has available iron, calcium, thiamine and riboflavin. Children love sweets, and this craving can be transformed into a nutritional asset when molasses or sorghum are offered to assuage the childish appetite for something sweet. Here is a nutritious food fashion that can be started in your neighborhood. Mix one cup peanut butter with a third cup molasses or sorghum until blended and serve on bread. This makes about 1 1/3 cups of spread.

When you are baking or cooking and you would like to use some molasses or sorghum instead of sugar or other sweeteners in a recipe, here is a conversion story, and it couldn't be simpler. One cup molasses or sorghum equals one cup sugar or one cup corn syrup or one cup brown sugar. When using molasses instead of sugar in baking, add half teaspoon baking soda for each cup of molasses or sorghum, and reduce the other liquid in the recipe by a fourth cup for each cup of molasses or sorghum. Baking soda is used to neutralize the acid in the molasses or sorghum, and when more than half teaspoon is used per cup, it is added in most cases only to produce a darker color.

To replace brown sugar in a recipe, use one part molasses or sorghum and four parts granulated sugar. Just mix as needed and use as you would brown sugar. Mixture is always smooth, never lumpy and recipes are most generally improved. Molasses or sorghum also helps the good things you make stay moist and fresh longer.

There also is available bottled, light and dark molasses or sorghum. The light has a more delicate flavor and often is used as table syrup. The dark variety is tangy in flavor and is especially good for making foods that have many spices.

In the olden days after the making of molasses or sorghum was over, a batch of cookies was made. One family they obtained a recipe that became a tradition. The original recipe made a bushel basket of cookies. The basket was lined with oilcloth, with a clean feed sack put inside the lining and another white cloth over the top of the cookies that were stored in an above ground cellar at the end of the porch. A crumbled newspaper was the lid.

If you would like to make molasses or sorghum cookies, here is a recipe:

* * *

Blue Ribbon Molasses Cookies
3/4 cup butter or margarine
1 cup brown sugar
1 egg
1/4 cup mild molasses or sorghum
2 1/4 cups flour
1 teaspoon cinnamon
2 teaspoons soda
2 tablespoons sugar
2 teaspoons cinnamon

Place the first 4 ingredients into a bowl and mix and beat well. Add other ingredients, except 2 tablespoons sugar and 2 teaspoons cinnamon, and mix well. Clean hands can get into this dough and do the mixing, if desired. Chill at least 1 hour. Roll into balls about the size of a walnut. Dip into mixture of cinnamon and sugar and put on a greased cookie sheet. Bake at 350 degees for 8 minutes. Do not overbake. Remove just before you think they are done and slip off cookie sheet onto a clean tea towel or paper towel to cool. This under baking gives a chewy cookie.

All in a Woman's Day--November 11, 1986
Cider turns chills into good cheer
With the chill of fall in the air, a good warm beverage might be just the right thing to turn the cold chills into cheer.

What could be nicer than apple cider—cold, hot, mulled, hot spiced or, however you might prefer.

Back in the early days it was quite an event to make cider, and, too, it was a time for socializing.

Most families had apple trees, however, not all had a cider press. So, the apples were gathered into gunny sacks or baskets and taken to the press, and there it was that the good, golden liquid from the apples flowed into containers. In the earlier years, large amounts of cider were stored in barrels in the cellar.

Most often, however, cider was served fresh. When some was allowed to ferment, it formed what is called "hard cider," and was a popular alcoholic drink during the colonial era.

In the event you did not know, there are four main types of apple juice or cider that today are available at the market. They include fresh and unpasteurized; fresh and treated so as to retard fermentation (both of these types have to be refrigerated); the pasteurized, which is shelf stable; and the concentrated that is shelf stable or frozen.

Mulled cider is one of the ways it was prepared in earlier days. It is made by bringing to a boiling point, along with six whole cloves and a stick of cinnamon. This is for four cups of juice. After removing the spices, serve hot. Sugar may be added, if desired.

Hot buttered cider also is tempting. Make it by combining one quart of cider, one four-inch stick cinnamon, eight whole cloves, eight allspice berries (optional) and one quarter to one-third cup brown sugar, depending on taste. Bring to a boil and simmer 10 to 15 minutes. Strain into mugs and top each with about a teaspoon of butter.

Time is going by so fast that the Christmas entertaining will soon be upon us. Since cider or apple juice is the basic for making "Wassail," this might be the opportune time to include this beverage.

Christmastime in Merry Olde England found the wealthy Elizabethians toasting one another with mugs of hot, spiced wine from the traditional Wassail Bowl. This was a custom borrowed from the Saxons, who drank the same potion with shouts of "Waes Hael," good health.

So, it has been that down through the ages, the Wassail Bowl and Wassailing, or merrymaking, became an important English Christmas custom.

Groups of carolers would go awassailing from house to house, singing for their hosts in return for a cup of Wassail. The early day version of Wassail had baked apples floating in it and also included wine.

Today, it is found that an up-to-date Wassail Bowl is a distinctive way to provide steaming cups of cheer for holiday entertaining.

I am including two recipes for the making of Wassail. The first was discovered in an old diary and dates back to 1750.

* * *

Wassail I

2 gallons apple cider
3 cups dark brown sugar
8 sticks cinnamon
16 whole cloves
16 whole allspice

Put spices in a bag and place in the cider and boil 5 minutes. remove the bag; add sugar and boil 5 minutes more. Stud oranges with cloves, heat in the oven and put in the cider and boil. (Canned spiced crabapples can be put in each cup for serving.) This serves 30 to 40 people.

Wassail II

1 gallon apple clder
6 sticks clnnamon
2 tablespoons whole allsplce
1   tablespoon whole cloves
2 (lO-ounce) bottles lemon-lime
Soda or gingerale

Simmer flrst four ingredients at least 2 hours. Add soda or gingerale and serve warm.

479

'Kitchen helps' saves time, money

Kitchen helps that will possibly save the time spent there or to make food preparation a bit easier, as well as save money, are offered.

Hamburger will brown better if a teaspoon of corn starch is mixed into each pound of the ground meat. This also tends to keep hamburgers from tasting quite so greasy.

A pinch of baking soda keeps cream from curdling when poured over acid fruit or berries.

Bread chicken an hour before frying and refrigerate it; the coating will stay on better.

For a good bite, roll stuffed dates in fruit-flavored gelatin just as it comes from the package.

Toast oatmeal in the oven before using it to make cookies. It makes a great difference in flavor and you are sure to enjoy.

Add a pinch of sugar and some nutmeg to creamed spinach.

When making a custard sauce in a double boiler, don't let the water in the bottom of the boiler touch the pan over it; and use simmering, not boiling water.

The flavor of mayonnaise can be varied with chili sauce, catsup and prepared mustard to give new taste to sandwich fillings. Honey, jam or mayonnaise whipped into cream cheese is another fine treat.

For a nice, light brown pie crust, add one tablespoon sugar and a half teaspoon baking powder when mixing the crust.

Use one teaspoon vinegar in gelatin when using molds. This tends to make the gelatin firmer.

When making a cake, always add one tablespoon boiling water to the butter and sugar nikture. This makes a finer textured cake.

For a good flavor, add finely grated Swiss cheese to mashed potatoes.

This makes company chicken special: Fry one chicken until brown, then mix together one cup brown sugar and one cup orange juice (frozen). Pour over chicken and simmer 45 minutes.

A heated knife will cut through fresh bread more easily than one that has not been heated.

Sliced cooked carrots and cooked green lima beans makes an excellent vegetable combination.

Potatoes are baked faster if you soak them in hot water for 10 to 15 minutes before putting them in the oven. Slice the ends off before cooking and you will get extra mealy "taters."

If you have trouble with candy turning grainy, try adding a little vinegar to the ingredients and you will find it will become much more creamy.

If you are watching calories, but still like the taste of butter-seasoned vegetables, try adding a small amount of butter flavoring.

When making drop cookies or other dough mixtures, if you will dip your spoon in cold water each time before dipping in the dough, the dough will not adhere to the spoon.

To give color to cake frosting, add half teaspoon gelatin powder in any color. By adding more or less of the same color, you can obtain different shades of the same color.

Salads won't get soggy if you put a saucer upside-down in the bottom of the salad bowl first; then put the salad on top.

When making fudge, pour it into

small muffin pans that have been lined with paper muffin liners. This will make nice size fudge pieces without having to cut them. Peel off paper when fudge has set long enough to eat.

If cookies stick to the cookie sheet and are difficult to remove, quickly run the sheet over a top burner on the stove or return them to the oven for just a moment.

When candied fruit—dates, dried fruit or raisins—are called for in a recipe, it is easier to cut them with kitchen shears instead of a knife. Dip the shears in water between cuttings to prevent stickiness.

Milk stays fresh longer if a pinch of salt is added to a quart of fresh milk.

Eggs separate more easily when cold.

When making banana bread or cake, substitute banana baby food for mashed bananas. Two small jars of baby food equal one cup mashed bananas. Baby food is easily stored and always handy if you bake on short notice.

To keep boiled syrup from crystallizing, add a pinch of baking soda.

When a recipe calls for sharp Cheddar cheese and you have only mild, add a bit of pepper, dry mustard and Worcestershire sauce. You will then have a sharp cheese flavor.

When using commercial sour cream in a sauce or gravy, stir gently and as little as possible. Over stirring sometimes thins sour cream.

Add a cup of finely diced apples to a favorite muffin recipe, then top muffins with a sprinkle of sugar, cinnamon and nutmeg.

* * *

Caramel Corn

6 quarts popped corn
1/2 cup granulated sugar
1/2 cup firmly packed light brown sugar
1/4 cup butter or margarine
1 (14-ounce) can sweetened condensed milk
1/8 teaspoon salt
3/4 cup white corn syrup
1 teaspoon vanilla

In a heavy saucepan combine sugars, syrup, milk and salt; mix well and cook over medium heat, stirring constantly to 230 degrees on candy thermometer or until small amount dropped in cold water forms a soft ball. Remove from heat and cool slightly; then stir in butter and vanilla. Pour over popped corn and stir wlih a buttered spoon until it is evenly covered. Spread out on waxed paper to harden.

All in a Woman's Day--November 26, 1986
Say a holiday prayer

This is the time of Thanksgiving. The time to offer our praise and thankfulness for all the blessings bestowed upon us by our Lord and Saviour. Yes, it is time for us to bow our heads in prayer.

The true Thanksgiving is threefold— the home, the family and the bread that we speak of so often. For all the "little" blessings that we fail to recognize, let us express our deep appreciation. This Thanksgiving let us refocus our values and pause for Grace before our meals thanking the Lord for food, the life He has given us and every good blessing that has come our way. We often find that many of our blessings have been disguised in reverses that turn out to be better than anticipated.

* * *

A Currier and Ives print for "Thanksgiving" shows a farmhouse, the barn, a shed, the roofs covered with snow, a yoke of oxen and guests that had arrived in a horse drawn sleigh being welcomed by grandfather and grandmother. This was commemorated by a song familiar to chidren of the 19th century. Lydia M. Child wrote the verses and it was entitled—

"Thanksgiving Day"
Over the river and through the wood,
To grandfather's house we'll go;
The horse knows the way
To carry the sleigh,
Through the white and drifted snow.
Over the river and through the wood
Now grandmother's cap I spy;
Hurrah for the fun!
Is the pudding done?
Hurray for the pumpkin pie.

* * *

And speaking of food, it has been written that the custom of prayer before eating is as old as eating itself. The act of expressing thanks for the food we eat goes back for centuries with the practice of Grace handed down by oral tradition through the generations. However, later it was recorded, and in Deuteronomy 8:7-10 we find that Moses reminds his people to bless (thank) the Lord for their food and for all that He has given them.

It seems that the early day Hebrews had a special prayer that was said over each basic food, that, by the way, was in addition to the Grace said before the eating of each meal. To them this special blessing asked upon the bread was most important. For was not it the staff of life? In addition, the Hebrew meal also was finished with a prayer of length expressing gratitude. Therefore, it was natural that the early Christians continue the Hebrews' custom of prayer preceding a meal.

The old Hebrew ritual became a part of Communion services when Jesus took the bread and blessed it at the Last Supper. Christians repeatedly were asked by Paul, the apostle, to thank God for food and all the blessings. He said, "Whether you eat or drink or whatsoever you do, do all to the glory of God." "In everything give thanks," he wrote to the Ephesians and the Thessalonians.

Grace before meals has long been neglected here in America. In this land of abundance we've somehow become negligent in expressing our thankfulness and just take things for granted. We somehow forget as we often waste food, what it is like in many countries where famine reigns and where the food (the bread) for many has become a precious gift.

Walter Raunsfhenbursh has written a prayer of Thanksgiving that I would like to share. It reads: "O God, we thank Thee for the universe, our great home; for its vastness and its riches. We praise Thee for the arching sky and the blessed winds, for the driving clouds and the constellations on high. We praise Thee for the salty sea and the running water, for the everlasting hills, for the trees and for the grass under our feet. We thank Thee for our senses by which we can see the splendor of the morning and hear the jubilant songs of love and smell the breath of spring and winter as it comes to us. Grant, we pray Thee, a heart wide open to all this joy and beauty, and save our souls from being so steeped in care or so darkened by passion that we pass unseeing when even the thorn bush by the wayside is aflame with the glory of God."

* * *

Happy Thanksgiving Day!

Candles associated with Christmas holiday

Whatever we do this time of year, candles always add that special festive touch. The soft glow of candlelight just seems to impart a warmth and intimacy to almost any setting.

Candles always have been associated with Christmas, and many legends give them a place in the observance of the holiday.

For instance, in Ireland, on Christmas Eve a large candle was burned which could be snuffed out only by one named—"Mary."

An old verse repeats the tradition, that burning a bayberry candle on Christmas Eve would insure one of a long and happy life.

To learn your luck for a year, they say,

Burn a bayberry on Christmas Day.

If the flame burns bright and the light shines clear,

Good Luck will be yours throughout the year.

* * *

Some of you have been saving the remains of scented candles and melting them in a saucepan in order to give your kitchen a lovely fragrance. There are some warning rules about this procedure, however. For instance, use a deep receptacle that is not used for cooking food. Warm over a low burner. Do not melt too many candle stubs at once, and if the wax should catch fire, keep a cover handy to extinguish it.

Some helpful hints concerning candles might give some assistance.

Burning candles helps prevent a room from becoming smoke-filled.

Cut the fingertip from an old rubber glove and slip it on the bottom of a candle to keep it firm and steady in the holder.

Candle wax on metal candleholders is a real problem. If the candleholders are small, place them into a freezer. When the wax is frozen, it usually peels right off. Or, place under hot running water. This method melts off the wax.

One way of removing candle drippings from a table top is with a wooden paddle. Then remove excess was with a cloth that has been dampened with cleaning fluid. Wipe quickly with a dry cloth.

Small birthday candles will fit well into the little holes in the tops of some liquid detergent bottles. They make good candleholders for a birthday cake by catching the dripping wax and also holding them steady.

Use the same method of getting the wax film off of crystal candlesticks as you do other things . . . freeze. After getting the wax off, one of the best ways to clean crystal is to immerse it in a solution of one part alcohol an three parts water.

For a candlelight buffet, place aluminum foil under a lace tablecloth. Foil catches the candlelight and creates a soft, shimmery effect. The foil also protects the table from spills.

For a dining table or buffet, a candle can be placed in a bed of curly endive and accented with small cherry tomatoes or radishes for a touch of color—Christmas red.

Fresh fruits also go well with candles. Four forest green candles with pine fragrance can be placed in an arrangement of real or artificial greenery on which are placed polished apples, oranges and grapes.

* * *

Candles

Candles are such charming things,
They seem to shed their rays,
Upon the celebration
Of so many special days.
I love the tall green tapers
That with holly twine;
Or tiny birthday candles
In sugar-rose design.
Candles on a lighted tree,
Silver and blue and red,
Or the orange one that
blinks at me,
Through the pumpkin's
knifesplit head.
But slender Christmas candles
On altars, white and still,
Radiate Christ's spirit
And peace and an goodwill.
Lois Peck Eck'sten

All in a Woman's Day--December 9, 1986

Unique decorations create remembrances

Let's do something interesting this year in the way of decorations ... make something different ... unique ... something that will help create a memorable Christmas for your family.

It is well to try and keep things simple even though we are caught up in a society that would rather it not be, still that is the way it should be. The whole motivation of the season is that it must be realized it is not the material things in life that we are celebrating—it is the birth of Christ.

Try fixing some walnut decorations. They are unique. Walnuts that are gilded are a centuries-old tradition that can really give an antique look to your Christmas tree. In the early days, the original gilded walnuts were done by craftsmen with special ability and real gold was used; however, the effect can be duplicated by making them simple and inexpensive by using the techniques of the 20th century.

Perhaps the quickest, most inexpensive and practical way to gild walnuts (in the shell) is to spray them with a metallic spray. A hanger will be needed for each walnut, and that can be done by hammering a small brad into the top of the nut, placing the brad in the seam of the walnut for easier insertion. Only the head of the brad shows. Tie a string or a fine gold cord around the neck of the brad so it can be hung. After each nut is sprayed all over and allowed to dry, it will then be ready for your tree. They also can be used in table arrangements, wreaths or in swags of greenery along the rails on staircases and mantels. Too, they can add a bit of elegance for gift packages when used as ornaments.

Animal decorations for Christmas trees also are interesting and different. Trace animals such as elephants, horses, rabbits and the like from coloring books. Cut the pattern from felt using two pieces for the general shape. Glue pieces of felt for eyes, markings and spots along with sequins for detail. Then sew the two decorated sides together with an overcast stitch and stuff just enough to give dimension to the figures. These figures can be hung on the tree, placed on the mantel, table or windowsill. Next year, perhaps more animals can be added.

Tree ornaments—bells, stars, Wise Men and doves—can be made from styrofoam meat trays. Cut shapes with a utility knife. Cover the bells with bright felt, using spray adhesive and trim with fringe, rickrack and braid. Trim stars with stick-to-it metallic trim. The Wise Men can be made of felt, using black rickrack and metallic trim. Eyes can be small pieces of rickrack. The dove should be trimmed with silver sticky trim and, the olive branch is a spray of shirred green rickrack.

Perhaps you might like a pom pon tree. All white makes a beautiful delightful tree. The pom pons can be attractively arranged on the branches to fill empty places when used with other decorations. Where they add a pretty touch. Needed to make the balls are two 18-inch strips of nylon net for each ball. They also can be made of Christmas colors, red and green. A little glitter added to the edge gives a charming sparkle to any tree.

Another idea is to use burned out electric light bulbs. Paint with glue and roll in glitter of different colors. Let dry and then fasten a piece of colored ribbon to each one. These make attractive and different tree decorations.

Another idea to make different tree decorations is to take Christmas balls and space about six inches apart on a pretty ribbon—red, green, white or the color of your choosing. Thread each ball on the ribbon and secure with a knot. Then continue until enough balls are on the ribbon to trim the tree properly. Place the ribbon of balls on the tree as you would a string of lights. They can be quickly put into place as well as removed.

* * *

Butterhorn Cookies

4 cups flour
1 package dry yeast
1 1/4 cups butter or margarine
3 egg yolks
1/2 cup sour cream
1 teaspoon vanilla

Filling:
3 egg whites
1 cup sugar
2 1/2 ounces dates, chopped
1 cup chopped nuts
1 teaspoon vanilla

Dough: Combine flour and yeast. Cut in butter or margarine as for pie crust. Add egg yolks, sour cream and vanilla. Stir until dough forms. Divide dough into 6 or 8 equal parts. Chill at least 1 hour (or overnight) for easier handling.

Filling: Beat egg whites stiff. Add sugar, gradually beating until stiff and glossy. Fold in dates, nuts and vanilla. Roll portion of dough into a circle as for pie crust on pastry cloth or foil dusted with confectioners' sugar. Cut into 12 wedges. Place rounded teaspoon of filling at wide end of wedge. Roll into horn. Place on ungreased cookie sheet and bake at 350 degrees 15 or 20 minutes (depending on the size of the butterhorns) until lightly browned. Sprinkle with confectioners' sugar while horns are hot or frost with confectioners' butter icing. Store in tightly covered container.

All in a Woman's Day--December 16, 1986
Recreate ingenuity of colonists' yuletide

This Christmas try something different—try duplicating the colonists' yuletide ingenuity. The space-age shopper is accustomed to dashing to the store for just the right touch to complete holiday decorating; however, the colonial woman relied upon her own ingenuity to create the right holiday mood.

In the colonial days extensive and varied use was made of fresh fruits available at that time. Usually the table centerpieces and decorations for the yule tree were made of fruit.

Too, since the Christmas tree was a German custom and not introduced into this country until the 19th century, Christmas trees were fashioned by the colonists from fruit they had in plentiful supply during the winter months. The "apple tree," therefore, was often devised for the holiday season.

No doubt the whole family will enjoy making one of these trees, and it is a good way to increase family ties. Visitors will exclaim with delight at the delicious aroma that greets them.

To make a tree you will need a block of oasis, a green spongelike substance used in floral arrangements, about six inches high; pachysandra or boxwood; cinnamon picks or floral sticks; apples, approximately 24 two-inches in diameter; a cake stand; and one fresh pineapple. The cake stand is the base of the tree. Family members can help by washing the apples and shining them to a high gloss, then removing the stems. The oasis should be soaked in water so the arrangement will stay fresh for two weeks. Cut the edges of the top of the oasis to slant outward before placing on the cake stand. Then insert a cinnamon or floral pick in each apple, arranging them around the base of the oasis in a single row, sticking the picks in the oasis to firmly hold the fruit. Repeat for rows two and three. Be sure and make cetrain that all apples are turned basically the same direction. Insert pachysandra leaves or boxwood for trim in between each of the apples, then securely stick picks into the base of the pine-apple, affixing it to the top of the oasis.

So that the arrangement will stay fresh throughout the holiday season, it would be well to place it in the refrigerator when not in use. You will find that the combination of cinnamon picks; apples and fresh pineapple will scent the house with a delightful aroma.

Too, households in Colonial America often used colorful fruit boards on their doors during the Christmas season. One of the easiest and perhaps the most colorful was a lemon board.

To make this you will need a wicker or rattan flat Christmas tree, magnolia leaves, fine wire, a block of plastic foam about six or seven inches square, seven lemons and cinnamon or floral picks. Wire the square of foam to the middle of the back of the tree form, then wire and weave the leaves into the crisscrossed wicker of the tree form. Insert lemons onto the board, using the cinnamon or floral picks to hold in place. Be sure to place them so that they pierce the foam. Hang the tree on the door with the tip of the triangle pointing downward. Two would make a stunning display if you have double doors.

Since candles were the only way of lighting colonial households, lamp chimneys and hurricane lamps were plentiful. To make an attractive mantel or table centerpiece, gather fresh greens such as pine, hemlock, juniper, cedar or spruce. Also needed will be fresh fruit, a hurricane globe cradle. If you do not have a hurricane globe cradle and cannot find one, make a substitute by cutting green plastic foam (one-inch thickness) to conform to the shape of the globe. Place the hurricane globe lengthwise in its cradlle and lay a large bough of pine through it. Then carefully fill the inside of the globe with pears or apples or both, placing them at different angles for special eye interest. Place in the center of the table or mantelpiece. Arrange more pine or greenery around the base and use green grapes and leftover fruit for accent. Color can be added by using holly sprigs or nandina berries.

All in a Woman's Day--December 23, 1986

Gift of Christmas is a cherished time

The month of December brings thoughts of tinsel, colored lights and beautifully decorated Christmas trees. We find mistletoe, holly, bells, poinsettias, gaily wrapped packages and happy voices. But Christmas is much more!

Gaity, laughter and music seem to fill the air that has taken on an intangible magic. We find children scurrying and almost overwhelmed by everything and excitement reigns everywhere. There is bubbling childish laughter and adults smiling because they can still recall with just a "touch of nostalgia" the joyous Christmases of their youth. But Christmas is much more!

Some giving at Christmas is unselfish; however, some is done with the thought that something will be given in return. There are those whom we feel are twice blessed because they delight in bringing joy to others, for as the poet sang long ago, "the gift without the giver is bare" or "it is more blessed to give than to receive." While all this is significant, Christmas is much more! The giving of gifts at Christmastime has become so important in many lives that it has taken over the most beautiful, wonderful thing about the season ... the celebration of the birth of Christ ... that is Christmas!

Many years ago God gave us all a gift, the priceless, perfect gift of His son, Jesus. May we always cherish and hold dear this precious gift and never let it take second best in our thoughts and doings. Our giving should be because we remember that God gave us His Son ... gave Him to the world, and also because we know the story of the gifts that were brought to this newborn babe. It is not how expensive the gift is, but the love that goes with it. Let us reflect upon this thought "the smallest gift may yet be the most important gift of all." And that is what Christmas is all about!

And while we are giving our gifts of

love, let us not forget that the best things in life are free. The gift of the creation that has been bestowed upon us; yes, it is a gift, a gift that is always here—a gift we should always cherish. And it is free!

If you are searching for that perfect gift for a loved one, remember the words from the pen of Ralph Waldo Emerson: "The only gift is a portion of thyself."

* * *

May your Christmas be most blessed!

All in a Woman's Day--December 30, 1986
Ring in the New Year

It is that time again when we prepare to ring out the old year and ring in the new.

Some folks look forward to celebrating by drifting from party to party and some want to hold on to those last moments of the old year with folks to whom they are near and dear; however, if they are not available, then they would rather be alone with their thoughts and memories of the year that is leaving.

There are always so many memories to hold on to—some, so dear and intimate, some challenging, some full of sparkle and some that are filled with sadness that brings a tear to the eye.

The old is almost gone—finished. The new is yet to come, but it definitely will soon be here. A strange excitement and elation seems to surge through our being ... anticipation perhaps of what is in store for us.

This New Year will be no different than the others for it will give us a challenge to meet new goals and the opportunity to start fresh. So, it is up to each of us to take advantage and learn from the past and build for the future.

However, changing standards and values make us somewhat apprehensive concerning the future.

Many centuries ago, a man and his family faced the unknown. In response to a strange inward prompting they turned their backs on the rich and enlightened civilization of their great city; they abandoned their religion and security and, although not knowing whither they went, set out for a dream world—the land of Canaan.

We do not know about the road ahead of us as we move ever forward, but we have faith to believe that He has built our way with our strength and limitations in mind. So, let us all strive to do our best and make an effort to improve ourselves during 1987.

In the event you have not made any New Year's resolutions here are some written by Morgan Kizer that you might try.

Each day I will seek:
To be the love of God to some person.
To understand more than to be understood.
To be ears to someone who has a burdened heart.
To do some things I do not like.
To accept people with whom I disagree as persons.
To love more than I am loved.
To listen and look for good in each person.
To seek the friendship of some lonely individual.
To walk with someone along the road of sorrow.
To seek the grace of God to help me fullfill these intentions.

* * *

Happy New Year!

Goose significant
to holiday season

Did you get a goose for Christmas? If you didn't, you should have, for they are the "in" thing now. Geese are used in decorations on dishes, glasses, towels, knickknack items, napkins—well, you name it and there is a goose involved. Too, this popular fowl comes in various sizes. Some folks who are real handy, have been making geese in various styles for their home decor.

I have had inquiry concerning the relation of the goose to Christmas, and believe it or not, there is a legend about the role of a goose in this very special holiday just passed.

Accordingly, the goose was one of the animals present in the stable when the Magi arrived. All the animals fell silent and drew back shyly, as if sensing that these were not simple folks like Mary and Joseph. They were dressed in silken robes and brought expensive gifts for the infant. The goose was embarrassed because not one of the bigger animals stepped forward to welcome the distinguished company. So, the goose, it is said, swallowed its shyness and waddled out in front of the Magi. But, it was so nervous its voice came out squeaky and harsh as it uttered greetings. To this day its voice has remained the same.

So, in memory of this legend, roast goose has become part of the Christmas feast in many countries—a strange way it would seem to repay it for its gallantry!

* * *

Now, with the goose taken care of, let us think a little about Epiphany, which, by the way, occurs today, Jan. 6.

Epiphany, that comes from a Greek word meaning "appearance," usually is used in reference to the appearance of a deity in visible form. Twelfth Night is the popular English name for the Feast of Epiphany that falls 12 days after Christmas.

The earliest reference, according to research, was in the later years of the second century, when Clement of Alexandria in Egypt spoke of certain Christians observing the sixth of January in memory of the baptism of Jesus. The actual date seems to have been chosen in order to rival some of the popular pagan festivals of that day.

Also by the beginning of the fourth century, orthodox Christians in the East were observing the festival as a triple celebration. It became an all-inclusive feast, honoring the birth and baptism of Christ and His first miracle of Cana of Galilee.

In the West, however, the particular commemoration assigned to Epiphany was the visit of the Magi. During the Middle Ages, the Epiphany Festival was widely served by the performance of miracle plays in churches about the Three Kings. Especially in England, the day was marked by dramatic productions, though not necessarily religious ones, and this custom survived into the Elizabethan period. Shakespeare took the popular name of "Twelfth Night" for his play of that title that was written to be performed on that date.

Therefore, since Epiphany concludes the yuletide festivities, and its date coincides with many ancient pagan customs, it was often celebrated with strange ceremonies in which those customs mingled with Christian rites. Some of those old ceremonies are said to still exist in parts of Europe, where fixed rituals may have origins, often with an overlay of magic, that are lost in the past.

Haxey is a place in Lincolnshire, England, where it is said they still play on Jan. 6 the famous old hood game. Its origin harks back to pagan times, and the hood itself is thought to represent the head of a bull. In the game, 13 men take part, and one is called the "fool"; another the "lord"; and the 11 others, "Boggins." A two team scrimmage takes place, the object of which is for each man to succeed in placing a folded canvas hood into a particular goal, one after the other. The very last hood, the 13th, called "The Haxey," must be brought towards the final goal - an inn where there are drinks for all.

And speaking of drinks, there is another custom connected with Epiphany that is dated. It is wassailing the trees that is an unusual torchlight ceremony still observed, in certain parts of England on Jan. 17, which is the date of the "old Twelfth Night." This is another survival from very ancient times when prayers were made to the god of trees and fruit.

According to the legend, a glass of cider is thrown on the trunk of an old apple tree, while toast soaked in cider is fastened to the tree branches. Then guns are fired through the branches, while the old invocation of prayer to the tree is sung. Once the evil spirits have been frightened away by guns, according to the old tradition, one can settle down to the business of drinking cider—a real "wassail."

Acclaim prunes more than breakfast food

Among the special things to be observed in January is Prune Breakfast Month; however, prunes are not really just for breakfast ... they are good anytime, even for snacking.

The prune is a form of plum that is especially adaptable for drying; however, not all plums have the special quality for becoming good prunes, as some dry better than others.

The dried plum or prune, had its beginning in Asia, then migrated to Europe, where it quickly became a snack and also was used as a dessert, and for stuffing meats and poultry.

At one time when harvesting came, the prune plums were allowed to fall to the ground after which they were gathered by hand. Today, however, mechanical shakers are used, and in a short time the crop is shaken from the trees onto a large canvas, then placed on conveyors to go into bins.

After harvesting, the fruit is washed, placed on large wooden trays and put into dehydrator tunnels under controlled temperature, where they are allowed to dry 15 to 24 hours. To make one pound of dried prunes, it takes about three pounds of fresh fruit.

Prune plums are grown mainly today in California, where some 70,000 acres are under cultivation.

The California prunes provide approximately 75 to 80 percent of the world's supply of prunes.

This fruit has a lot going for it. Prunes contribute vitamin A, riboflavin and niacin, they are excellent sources of iron, and also provide copper, calcium and phosphorus.

Youngsters enjoy prunes "as is" to

eat out of hand, but oldsters like them cooked briefly with slices of orange or lemon. Most everyone enjoys prunes in a salad, especially, when they are stuffed with cream cheese and served with crisp greens, a slice of orange and rings of sweet onions.

Some folks have been found who did not like to eat prunes because of the seeds; however, now with the development of a special machine to pit the fruit, it has become a favorite with many people. Raw prunes are good for hand eating, in salads, compotes, stewed and as juice. They are especially good when dried and cooked to be used in cakes, muffins, cookies, pies and whips.

It is easy to cook prunes. Just place the washed fruit in a pan with just enough water to cover, and simmer gently until plump and tender and serve in its own juice, with heavy cream, if desired. Sugar can be added if you like the fruit a bit sweeter.

Too, prunes do not have to be cooked to be good. Just place the washed fruit in a dish in the refrigerator, adding as much water as the dish will hold and cover. They will eventually absorb the water, then add more. The water absorbs the natural sugar of the prunes and will become sweet and syrupy, even thick after a while.

To make pureed prunes, stem them, removing the pits and put through a food mill or in a food processor or grinder.

Prunes and figs may be stuffed for holiday feasting, for that matter, anytime, as well as dates. Prepare the prunes, dates and figs by steaming, covered, over boiling water for 5 to 10 minutes or until plump, but not soft. Make lengthwise slits; remove pits from the prunes and dates. All three of the fruits are good stuffed with peanut butter, candied orange rind combined with chopped nuts, mixed ground nuts and raisins, ground coconut and nuts or fondant. Pitted dates are good stuffed with a combination of a half cup of chopped maraschino cherries mixed with an 8-ounce package of cream cheese, then rolled in granulated sugar.

* * *

Perfect Prune Pie

2 cups uncooked prunes
Water to cover

Bring dried prunes to boiling point, cover and let simmer gently for 20 minutes or until fruit is tender. Remove from heat and cool.

9-inch unbaked pie shell
2/3 cup sugar
1/4 cup flour
1/2 teaspoon salt
1/2 teaspoon each maple and vanilla flavorings
1 cup light cream
1/4 teaspoon cinnamon

Line bottom and sides of pie shell with cooked prunes that have been thoroughly drained and pitted. Combine sugar and flour; then add to the remaining ingredients. Pour over prunes, and bake in a 400 degree oven until filling is set in the center. This is a delicious and unusual pie.

* * *

Prune Spice Cake
With Caramel Glaze

1 cup vegetable oil
1 1/2 cups sugar
3 eggs
1 teaspoon vanilla flavoring
1/2 teaspoon each of butter and black walnut flavorings
2 cups sifted flour
1/2 teaspoon salt
1 teaspoon each of baking powder,

soda, cinnamon, nutmeg and allspice
1 cup buttermilk
1 cup cooked, chopped, pitted prunes
1/2 cup chopped nuts

Cream together vegetable oil and sugar, adding the eggs, one at a time, beating well after each addition. Stir in flavorings; stir dry ingredients together and add to the creamed mixture, alternately with the buttermilk. Stir in prunes and nuts. Pour into a greased and floured 9x13-inch pan and bake 45 minutes in a 350 degree oven. Place on rack to cool and pour hot Caramel Glaze over the cake immediately.

Glaze

1 cup sugar
1/2 cup buttermilk
1/2 teaspoon soda
1 tablespoon white corn syrup
1/2 cup butter or margarine
1/2 teaspoon burnt sugar flavoring

Combine all ingredients in a saucepan and bring mixture to a rolling boil over low heat. Boil 10 minutes, stirring constantly. Remove from heat and pour over hot cake.

All in a Woman's Day--January 20, 1987
Month to 'think soup'

January is National Soup Month, so, let us think "soup." It is really refreshing after all the rich, sweet food that has been consumed during the holidays.

Some of us can remember when a formal dinner was served, there always was a "soup course," and most always it was a clear, delicately flavored soup; however, today with our informal living, we serve soup often with just a sandwich for lunch or perhaps a hearty soup can be the entire meal, most often in the evening.

If you are serving soup as a main course, count two cups; or as a first course, one cup would be suitable.

When you are preparing soup, just remember that you can use a little more of this or a little less of that or perhaps add something new. This versatility allows for the use of leftovers; however, keep in mind that food in the refrigerator ready to be disposed of will not improve your soup.

It is well not to salt or season until the soup is almost done. As the soup simmers down, the seasoning then becomes more prominent and concentrated; therefore, it is well to keep the salting and seasoning until it is almost finished.

Oftentimes, a thickening, or what is called a binder, is needed to give body to a soup. Flour is used for this, and for every two cups of soup use one tablespoon of flour. Melt the butter and stir in the flour, letting it cook approximately three minutes over low heat. Then add a little of the hot soup to the thickening, whisking well so it will not be lumpy; cook it until thick, then it can be added to the remaining soup, which should be heated and stirred until it is smooth.

Too, egg yolks can be used as thickening for some soups. This is done by beating one egg yolk with one teaspoon of milk or cream for each cup of soup. This should be added just before serving. So, it will not curdle, slowly add a little of the hot soup to the egg mixture, then whisk and pour into the pot. Be sure and reheat soup slowly, and stir it as it thickens. Do not boil.

For those of you who use canned soups, have you ever thought of adding fresh ingredients? Oftentimes, too, several compatible canned soups can be mixed together to make a delightful taste treat. Here you should follow your instinct and do some experimenting.

Most soups should be cooked in a covered pot so that the flavor and nutrients will be retained. You might only want to cover the pot part way so it will help reduce the soup to some extent. This also will intensify the taste of the soup.

There are all kinds of soups, hot or cold, lightly flavored or spicy, creamed, pureed, jellied, baked, thick or thin. Some soups receive their flavor from rich meat stock, some from water or milk, all that oftentimes brings out the real flavors. Some soups require a long, slow cooking process; others only a short time. Some need to mellow in the refrigerator.

When you make your next pot of potato soup, try adding a slice or two of American cheese just before serving. Stir soup until the cheese has melted. This adds a delicious flavor.

To remove fat from the top of soups and stews, wrap an ice cube in a piece of paper toweling and swish across the top of the mixture. The fat clings to the cold towel.

To help bouillon cubes dissolve faster, gently "crack" them with a nut cracker while it is still in the wrapper. It will be almost a powder when the foil is removed.

To get lumps out of canned cream soup, shake the can well before it is opened.

Some folks think oatmeal is not only a good thickener, but also it adds a nice flavor. Two or three tablespoons adds richness. Barley or rice make good nourishing thickeners, too.

What you serve with soups can add a lot of taste and texture. Perfect to serve with most soups are traditional steamed dumplings, a crusty loaf of dark bread or hot rolls. Some unusual tasty toppers to try instead are hot popcorn served plain, with butter or sprinkled with grated cheese. Kids like this very much; salty pretzels or pretzel sticks or garlic croutons, packaged or homemade. Bacon, onion or sesame flavored crackers are good; however, just plain old saltines spread with butter, and heated quickly, are tasty, too. Also, you might like to try crunchy corn chips, taco or tortilla chips.

For a modern soup made out of "nothing," keep a large saucepan full of water simmering on one of the back burners each evening while preparing the evening meal. Put leftover vegetables (except those of the cabbage family), or meat scraps into the pot as you cook. At the end of the meal, refrigerate the pot until the next day. After a few days you will have a savory broth to use as a base for other soups or to serve as is. The simmering sterilizes the soup, but, according to the recipe, start with a clean pot at least once every two weeks.

All in a Woman's Day--January 27, 1987

Fight off 'winter blahs'

Do you feel as if you might have or already are headed for the "winter blahs?"

If you can't get out of the house, you need to take some positive steps to fight off depression and keep your thoughts on the bright side; however, the weather so far has been more than could be hoped for, especially this time of year. If a snow should blow in, just chalk it up to the normal weather for our area.

If the weather is snowy, icy or cold,

many of us tend to stay inside; we do isolate ourselves from society, and it is then that depression can set in.

When the weather is not the best, and when activities have tapered off to some extent, it is nice to sit inside where it is warm and sip coffee. That is fine to a certain degree; however, sometimes more coffee is consumed than expected, and we become irritable, nervous and can't sleep. So, watch it!

If you live in a cold climate, learn to live with wintertime. And as the saying goes, "if you can't beat it—join it." So, what if it is cold outside, maybe a sleigh ride could be arranged, and age-wise, whatever it is, maybe ice skating could be in the plan.

There are ways to beat all of this if you put your mind to it.

Some of these hints could possibly be for those who "don't just grow old, just get better" and for whom "graying is all right."

Remember always to eat nutritionally, for as persons grow older their appetites tend to dull. If necessary, supplement your diet with minerals and vitamins, especially calcium and iron.

Try to keep physically active by exercising regularly, according to your individual abilities. Maybe you would want to take up swimming at an indoor pool, especially if you have arthritic bones, (and who of us hasn't?).

Visit with people on the telephone, and help brighten their day, as well as yours. Don't lose contact with others.

Try to rekindle old or former interests and possibly develop some new ones.

This might be a good time to start a hobby or a collection and lay the basic steps needed to becoming involved.

Listen to records or good stereo music.

Does your closet need cleaning? How about dresser drawers?

If you like to garden, you might do some arm chair planting. Even if you don't, the seed catalogs are arriving, and they are so intriguing and colorful—you can almost see the real flowers blooming. Some folks I know start spring house cleaning right after the first of January, and when the nice spring days arrive, they are ready to enjoy them.

If you are not of retirement age, take some time off so that you can be alone and not have to work with the children. Possibly you and your neighbor can take turns babysitting.

If you have a family, try to plan activities for them so they will be less likely to be romping or punching each other simply because "there is nothing to do."

Too, maybe you could help someone less fortunate than yourself, who can't be outside. Offer to do errands. If you are useful, you just seem to feel much better.

Do something special for yourself ... take a long, restful bath; plan a future activity.

Try to stay socially and mentally alert through contacts with family, by reading or joining groups.

How about trying some new recipes that you have wanted to do for so long, and just never got around to do?

If you live alone, when you cook, share with your neighbors, whether living in an apartment or a house. Invite them in for a snack and do some chatting.

Maybe some of these hints will help

you get started on a program that will take the blahs out of wintertime!

Christina G. Rossetti has written a poem about the months, and as we are headed into the new year, let us think about the words:

Months of the Year

January cold desolate;
February all dripping wet;
March wind rages;
April changes.
Birds sing in tune
To flowers of May.
And sunny June
Brings longest day;
In scorched July
The storm-clouds fly
Lightning torn;
August bears corn.
September fruit
In long October
Earth must disrobe her.
Stars fall and shoot
In keen November.
And night is long
and cold is strong
In bleak December.

* * *

Berneice's Green Bean Casserole

3 cans green beans
1 can mushroom soup
1 can mushrooms
1/2 stick butter
1/2 pound Velveeta cheese
1 teaspoon Worcestershire sauce
Salt and pepper to taste
Water chestnuts (optional)
Pimentos (optional)
1 can French fried onions
Bacon
3 tablespoons flour
Onions (optional)

Mix all together except the fried onions and they are sprinkled on top when ready to bake. Mix the other ingredients and bake 20 to 30 minutes in a 350 degree oven.

All in a Woman's Day--February 3, 1987
First valentine written in France

Dora T. Riddick has written a poem entitled "February" that seems to sum up the activities for this month.
Sugar and spice and everything nice,
That's what February is made of;
The shortest month of all the year
Snow-happy days that bring us cheer.
Here's what February is made of:
Beginning the second—Groundhog Day
Will clouds or sun hold full sway?
Abe Lincoln's birthday of record great,
From log-cabin fame to highest of State;
Valentine's Day—little hearts beaming;
Postmen laden—packages gleaming.
Then get your flags with hearts a thrill—
Parade for Washington, our leader still.
Last but not least, every fourth year,
Bashful bachelors hold this month dear.
(Leap Year when maidens do their parts,
By happily offering hands and hearts.)
Sugar and spice and everything nice,
That's what February is made of!

* * *

And since this is Cupid's month, Valentine's Day is the chosen topic. No doubt, Cupid as usual, is working overtime. Well over 500 million valentines will be exchanged on this special day, Feb. 14, according to Rust Craft Institute. One hundred years ago, 3 million were mailed in the United States.

While this has become a pleasant occasion for cards, candy and flowers, in earlier days for the maidens it was a time for serious husband hunting, and the maid would go to all ends to have her desires fulfilled.

Asking whether marriage was possible this year, the maid would peek through the keyhole to find out what she would like to know. She would arise early on Feb. 14, and set her eye to her keyhole. If she saw two objects, well and good; however, if only one; well, better luck next year.

Young men literally "wore their hearts on their sleeves" during early day celebrations of this special day. Men chose their valentines by drawing slips of paper with names from a vase. Each young man then wore the paper with his lady's name on his sleeve for several days.

You ask in what country Valentine's Day began? Some say it was like this: Young people in ancient Rome seeking the answer to the eternal query, "Who shall my beloved be?" held an annual lottery to honor their god Pan and goddess Juno. From this lottery, they hoped to discover their true love. Always held in February, the lottery survived through the centuries to become St. Valentine's Day.

With the coming of Christianity, the 14th of February was named in honor of several saints named Valentine; somehow the lottery came to be held on that day, but historians still scratch their heads about why any of the saints should be associated with it.

But like a kiss, St. Valentine's Day wasn't analyzed by our amorous ancestors. They just enjoyed it, and little did the young lovers realize that their "sweetheart sweepstakes" had taken the first step toward the establishment of the thriving present day greeting card industry.

In 1797, a book appeared in England called "The Young Man's Valentine Writer." This book was crammed with sentiments of all kinds in verse, arranged according to the sender's trade. For instance the village bricklayer might use the following:

> With mortar and trowel
> You know I do no ill,
> But a mansion can rise very high.
> Then, sweet Valentine,
> If you be mine

You shall have a fine house by and by.

In the mid-17th century, Velasques painted a picture of Cupid holding a mirror up to Venus. From that time on Cupid started to appear regularly on valentines. Down through the ages, the valentine styling has changed; however, Cupid is still pictured with his deadly arrow.

Shakespeare mentioned St. Valentine's Day in "Hamlet." Pepys alluded to the lotteries on St. Valentine's Day in his diary. The custom of sending anonymous love tokens was well established by the 16th century, when Edmund Spenser gave us the immortal line "Roses are red, violets are blue."

The first known English valentine was dated 1684, and carried this brief message:

> Good morrow, Valentine,
> God send you ever
> To keep your promise
> And be constant ever.

Valentines as we know them today, first appeared in the 18th century. They were made entirely by hand—from the message to the design, which usually consisted of cut-out pictures of flowers, doves, cupids and hearts.

The French are credited with creating the first written valentine, about 1400, and the earliest known "illustrated" valentine was published in 1500 in Milan. It appeared in a novel written by Pope Pius II. The illustration shows cupid getting in some of his traditional archery practice.

The first valentine was sent in the third century A.D. by a young Roman. His name was Valentius. For giving aid to Christian martyrs, he was imprisoned by Emperor Claudius II, and sentenced to death.

According to legend, while he was awaiting his execution he befriended the blind daughter of the jailer and restored her sight. On the night before he died, Valentius penned a farewell message to the girl, who had meant so much to him, and signed it "From your Valentine."

Valentinus was put to death on the 14th of February and was buried in what today is the Church of Praxedes in Rome. Near his grave, a pink almond tree, a symbol of abiding love, is said to have bloomed.

Thus the name of Valentinus has come down through the centuries as the word which stands for affection among friends and love between sweethearts.

Happy Valentine's Day!

* * *

Chocolate Puff Cookies

3 egg whites
1 cup confectioners' sugar
1/2 cup graham cracker crumbs
1/2 cup chopped walnuts
6-ounce package semi-sweet chocolate bits

Beat the egg whites until they hold straight peaks; sift and fold in the confectioners' sugar (sifted after measuring), a little at a time. Fold in the finely crushed graham cracker crumbs, the chopped nuts and the chocolate bits, that have been melted and slightly cooled. Drop the mixture by heaping teaspoons in tiny mounds about an inch apart on a buttered baking sheet. Bake them in a slow oven, 325 degrees, until they are firm, about 12 minutes. This makes 32 puffs.

All in a Woman's Day--February 10, 1987

Friday the 13th is feared

Another year and another Friday the 13th! In fact, this year has two other Friday the 13th's . . . in March and November.

The number 13 strikes fear in many people, and the word for this fear of this number is triskaidekaphobia, from the Greek, of course.

For many folks Friday, not just the 13th, seems to be unlucky, too.

Ancient manuscripts imply that Eve gave Adam the apple on Friday the 13th; it was on Friday the 13th that Cain slew Abel; and Christ was crucified on Friday the 13th. Some people who have triskaidekaphobia suffer actual physical reaction when Friday the 13th rolls around. They often suffer dizziness, rapid heart beat and light headedness.

Here are some legends, or lores that may assist you through that dreadful Friday the 13th.

Some people say that carrying an onion in the pocket wards off disease.

A rhubarb root worn on a string around the neck is said to ward off a "bellyache."

In the old country, it is said that they believe an empty egg shell, stuffed with hen's feathers, when worn around the waist, cures a stomachache.

Barley is thought by some people to cure a fever.

If you should sneeze before breakfast, it is believed that company's coming.

It is claimed by some folks that vegetables that grow underground must be picked on moonless nights or they will become sunburned.

Two ways folk wisdom suggests for getting rid of unwanted guests: a pinch of pepper under their chair or a broom stood behind the door.

In Newfoundland a sliced baked potato is placed in a stocking that is tied around the neck to cure a sore throat.

In Scotland it was once believed that throwing salt into brewing liquor would keep witches from it.

Some say it is good luck to burn onion skins in the fire.

Fruits and vegetables gathered in the dark of the moon will not spoil is another bit of lore.

Spilling salt is considered bad luck unless the spell is broken by throwing a pinch of it over the left shoulder.

Knock over the pepper box and superstition has it that company is coming. The direction in which the box falls indicates the direction the company will come from.

Dropping a dishcloth also has a superstitious meaning. It signifies something special is going to happen.

In Alabama, some folks believe that a dropped dishcloth indicates the approach of a sweetheart; while in some other locales, it is taken as an omen of an impending quarrel or a dinner guest.

The Chinese so highly regard rice that it is mentioned as part of the daily greeting. "How do you do?" they say. "Have you eaten your rice?"

Some people believe beech tree leaf tea will cure rheumatism.

Also, some folks declare it bad luck to burn sassafras wood.

People once thought the herb rosemary would help strengthen their memories.

In ancient Greece, students wore rosemary twined in their hair while studying for examinations because rosemary is symbolic of remembrance.

Indians used wild ginger to prevent ptomaine poisoning and to cure a toothache.

The English would mash the roots of hyacinths in white wine to hinder the growth of hair.

The daisy is an emblem of deceit in England.

The Welsh say that if the marigold does not open its petals before seven, it will rain or thunder that day.

It is believed by some people that eating daisies will cure the toothache.

All in a Woman's Day--February 17, 1987
Kitchen helps: odds, ends

How about some odds and ends for a little help in the kitchen?

One egg can do for a two-egg cake mix by adding two tablespoons of mayonnaise; and you will never know the difference.

Conserve liquid seasonings by putting them in a plastic squeeze bottle or a container with a spray pump.

To keep potatoes from sprouting and spoiling, store them in a brown paper bag in a cool, dark place.

When you are cooking any of the cabbage family (cauliflower, broccoli, kohlrabi, etc.) put a few celery leaves in the pan to keep the odor from permeating the air in the house.

Try adding three-fourths cup flour to generic cake mixes; and they will taste as good as the more expensive kind.

To prevent curdling in making scalloped potatoes, use a flour thickened white sauce instead of sprinkling the potatoes with flour, dotting with butter and adding milk.

Cabbage does not develop a strong flavor if it is not overcooked. It's mild and sweet flavored when shredded and cooked quickly and briefly with a little butter and a few tablespoons of water in a covered skillet. Watch the heat, and cook only until the vegetable is tender crisp.

If you are heating milk and don't want it to form a film over the top, cover the saucepan while the milk heats or stir it during the time it is being heated.

Yeast breads made with milk do not usually get stale as quickly as those made with water.

Lard is not a good shortening for cakes because air cannot be beaten into it easily.

Brown the butter, and weight watchers will be satisfied with half as much on their vegetables. Browning butter tends to heighten the flavor.

Make your own bread crumbs. Just save the stale bread (including the ends) and place them in the blender. Store the crumbs in a plastic bag in the freezer. The crumbs don't freeze together, so they can be used whenever needed.

A half teaspoon of coconut flavoring added to an envelope of whipped topping mix in place of vanilla takes away the artificial taste that some mixes have. Make this a few hours in advance; chill well, and the flavor will be especially good.

When making a cooked pudding from a mix (not the instant kind) and to make it go further, add one cup of milk and one beaten egg before cooking.

When baking purchased refrigerator biscuits that are found in the dairy case at the grocer's, place one on top of another. Bake a little longer and the biscuits will be nice and soft and more moist.

Save fruit juices and syrups from canned fruits and add to orange and grapefruit breakfast beverages. The juices also can be added to the batter for pancakes and muffins.

Keep citrus fruits fresh by wiping them lightly with cooking oil.

Marshmallows stored in tightly sealed glass jars will stay fresh for several months.

To make fresh berry pies so they will be less runny, try bringing the pie mixture to a boil and then simmer it for a few minutes before placing it in the shell.

To keep bread fresh, put a stalk of celery in the bread bag.

To prepare odorless fish, cover it with milk, add three tablespoons of lemon juice, and let it soak overnight in the refrigerator.

When cutting hard boiled eggs, the yolks won't crumble if the knife blade is dipped in cold water before cutting.

Rich, dark gravy can be made by adding a teaspoon of instant coffee to it while it is cooking.

Stretch peanut butter by adding margarine. It goes further and doesn't stick to the roof of your mouth.

Dip sausages lightly in flour, and they will have less shrinkage during cooking.

Flour keeps longer if stored in the freezer. This way it stays free of bugs and is always ready as it does not freeze.

To keep bacon from molding and to improve its flavor, rub it with a cloth soaked in vinegar.

When a recipe calls for dry oatmeal, toast it in the oven before adding it to the ingredients in a recipe. The oatmeal flavor is nutlike and the texture is crunchier.

Gently simmer a half cup of freshly squeezed orange juice, two tablespoons of butter and a half cup of marmalade until the marmalade is melted. Use this mixture to baste chicken, turkey or ham.

All in a Woman's Day--February 24, 1987

Household hints come in handy

Possibly you can use some more helps that would be handy around the kitchen.

A long handled, two-pronged fork becomes a handy kitchen tool with one simple alteration. Simply bend both prongs down at a 90-degree angle, about one-inch from the points. Use it to pull hot pans of food, cakes or baked potatoes from the oven, or to take down hard-to-reach items from high cupboard shelves.

After emptying contents of an opened can, rinse and cut out the bottom and then flatten. This takes much less space in the garbage and also cuts down on household pests and kitchen odors.

When cooking on top of the range, always turn the pan handles toward the center or the back of the stove so that they can't accidentally be bumped and spilled.

An egg beater will clean easily if soaked in cold water and then washed in warm, soapy water.

When cooking, to avoid warping your aluminum pans, don't run cold water into a hot pan. Don't let a gas flame get too high and don't keep a pan on high electric heat too long as that also will warp it.

If your refrigerator has a strong odor, put some fresh coffee grounds in a saucer or jar lid and place on each shelf. In a day or so the odor should be gone.

Scouring pads should not rust if they are dropped in a small container of baking soda.

Soak a stained enamel pan in strong vinegar water and it will come; clean and look like new.

For an inexpensive and effective household cleaner, mix one-fourth cup of sudsy ammonia with four cups of warm water in a plastic spray container.

To make liquid soap, combine leftover soap chips in water in a blender and pour mixture into plastic squeeze bottles.

Use a rubber band to secure a plastic bag to the ring collar on the meat grinder. The ground food will fall neatly into the bag.

To gather shreds of glass, go over the area with a piece of soft bread. Be sure and wrap the bread tightly before discarding so that no animals will eat it.

Dusting the light bulbs can increase your light by 50 percent.

To remove strong food odors from plastics, and other materials, place a crumpled sheet of newspaper inside and seal the lid tight, letting them remain overnight.

Never use an abrasive cleaner or steel wool to get stains off laminated plastic countertops since they could mar the finish. Try applying a solution of water, bleach and milk. Let it stand 60 seconds, then rinse with water immediately.

Silver polish will remove crayon

marks from vinyl floors.

Vinegar will help remove water spots from glasses. Just rub full strength vinegar on glasses until the spots are removed. Then wash glasses in suds and rinse.

Do you have a tabletop made of plastic? If so, just rub in some toothpaste and it should shine like new.

A toothbrush is just the thing to clean a food grinder.

To remove black marks from thermos bottles and lunch pails, put some margarine or other oily material on a paper towel, and wipe over the dirty areas. Wipe them clean and then wash them.

Peanut butter seems to be an inexpensive but powerful household cleaner. Should a bread wrapper or any other plastic touch a hot toaster or pan, it will leave a residue. Peanut butter is the answer. It will remove this as well as the residue left from tape, labels and stickers. Be sure to use smooth peanut butter.

All in a Woman's Day--March 3, 1987

The doughnut hole ... where did it come from?

Have you ever thought about the hole in the doughnut and who put it there?

There are several versions as to how it all came about, so, perhaps you can make your own selection of what sounds right to you.

It was centuries ago that doughnuts had no holes, and they were called fried cakes. They were round or square without a hole.

Crullers and fried cakes are closely related as both are made from the same dough and deep fried. Crullers, however, are shaped in a twist. In some parts of the country, fried cakes also are used for doughnuts, crullers and solid cakes. The filled fried cakes, oftentimes are referred to as doughnuts, for example, a jelly doughnut.

Doughnuts, as you may know, are just more than a good food. They have become a national institution and a state of mind. Because of their popularity, several nationwide doughnut shops have been opened, and they offer many different flavored delectables, including frosted and filled doughnuts. There are more kinds than you really can imagine.

There is no doubt that doughnuts are a genuine product of pioneer cooking. In fact, they were really bread cooked in a kettle or skillet on the top of the stove. In the early days, this was an important consideration, for oven cooking was never an easy task; and required long hours of firing.

The doughnut, seemingly the common fare of the working class, has had considerable speculation on its origin, or maybe it would be more correct to say on the doughnut hole.

When first prepared, the square or round pieces of dough came from the frying kettle soggy, heavy lumps that were just half done in the center. It is doubtful, that without the hole, the fried cakes would have become so popular as they are today. So, what about the hole in the doughnut?

In my research, it was found that there are several stories abounding about the hole in the doughnut. One story concerns Capt. Hanson Gregory of Rockport, Me., who lost men overboard from his ship after they had eaten some heavy fried cakes. They sank into the sea and were drowned. It seems that the disaster inspired the young captain to punch holes in the remaining cakes, making them resemble life preservers.

Another version is that the captain tried eating a fried cake while at the ship's wheel when a storm came up. Needing both of his hands on the wheel, he stuck the cake on a spoke of the wheel. Thus, the doughnut hole was born.

And still another version relates that Captain Gregory's mother was a famous cook whose culinary talents were well-known to sailors along the East Coast. She often prepared large quantities of fried cakes for her son to feed the crewmen while on long voyages. Concerned about the keeping quality of the soggy cakes, she pushed a hazelnut or a walnut into the center of each piece of dough before frying it and called it "dough nuts."

Doughnuts found popularity with the sailors, who dipped them in hot coffee or tea. Nuts, however, were expensive, so when the wily young captain made port again, he went to a tinsmith who fashioned a cutter that removed the center of the dough.

In 1847, a bronze plaque was placed on the old Gregory home in Rockport and it read thus: "This is the birthplace of Captain Hanson Gregory, who first invented the hole in the doughnuts in 1847." Americans hold Captain Gregory's invention in high esteem as millions of doughnuts are consumed each year.

Still there is another speculation. Historians have traced the doughnut ancestry back to a tribe of prehistoric Indians in the Southwest, where petrified fried cakes, complete with holes, have been unearthed.

It also has been thought that possibly the secret of doughnut making came to the United States with the colonists. Dutch settlers fashioned a cake, with a nut or raisin in the center, instead of a hole. Too, it has been said that the first true doughuts were made in New England. Raised with yeast, they were a little larger than walnuts and were spherical in shape.

Thus goes the story of the doughnut hole.

* * *

Here are a few hints concerning doughnuts.

Hang a glazed doughnut on a wooden dowl over a clean dishpan and allow it to drip dry.

For greaseless doughnuts, add one tablespoon of vinegar or one teaspoon of ginger to the oil before heating. This will prevent the dough from absorbing too much grease while frying.

For cake doughnuts, place liquid in bowl, then add dry ingredients. Do not mix too long or at high speed, as this causes doughnuts to be tough.

When frying doughnuts, turn them only once. Cool slightly before sugaring. If too hot, the sugar becomes sticky.

* * *

Doughnut Hole Muffins

Grease 12 muffin pan cups. In the bottom of each cup place:
1 tablespoon brown sugar
1 teaspoon light corn syrup
1/2 teaspoon water
1 teaspoon chopped nuts or
Pecan halves

Arrange 4 spudnut holes in each cup. Cover them with a cloth and let them rise until double. Bake at 350 degrees for about 25 minutes.

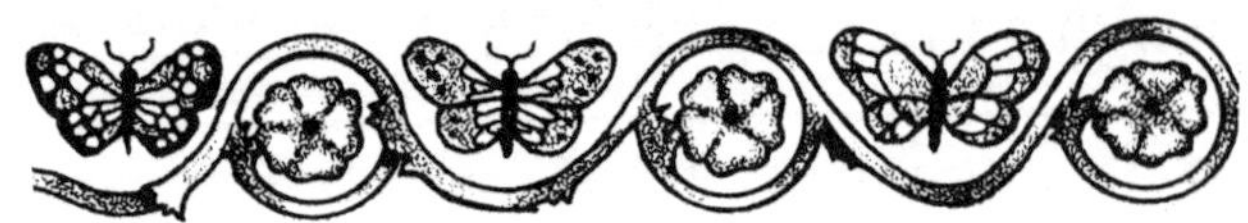

Tea leaves attempt
to foretell mysteries

This is the second Friday the 13th we've had so far this year, and we still have another to go—in November.

Have you ever studied the tea leaves and found from them in a rather mysterious way what they mean? The reading of tea leaves is just another form of foretelling, or maybe I should say, attempting to tell what is going to happen.

So, just for the fun of it, try reading your own tea cups this Friday the 13th. When the cup is empty, turn it upside down on the saucer, turn it around three times, and then place right side up on the saucer. These are the instructions for reading tea leaves. The tea leaves will form interesting designs, and most of the interpretations could easily appear in the leaves in your tea cup. If the tea leaves indicate a square, triangle, oblong or circle your "wish" will come true. Now, how about that?

I have come up with some interpretations about tea leaves that are rather interesting. If a star should appear, it denotes success in business and financial matters; an arrow, disconcerting news, maybe in the form of a letter; an airplane, beware of dangerous speculations in money matters; a key, an expansion in business; a ball, a warning not to change jobs too frequently; a pear, a marriage with riches; a chair, a visit from a friend; an arch, a long trip, probably by steamship;

A teakettle, a social gathering in your home; a castle, a surprise gift of money; a bridge, a pleasant trip; a windmill, be careful of hazardous undertakings; a heart, you have happiness due to a gift of money or love; a bottle, celebration; an apple, your recent business speculations should be a success; a triangle, a lucky omen, unexpected happiness; an anchor, a lasting happiness in marriage, a good sign in business affairs; a clover leaf, a symbol of good luck; a tree, look forward to an easy and sheltered life in old age;

Church, a good omen; a square, letters or parcels on the way; a bell, foretells a wedding; a ship, expect a visit from a friend; a dog, you have many good friends; a pitcher, you will continue in good health and happiness; a horseshoe, happiness or good fortune coming your way; a bird, indicates a departure for foreign lands very soon; and bubbles in a tea cup, foretell visitors.

Thus goes the reading of the tea leaves!

* * *

I also have found a few more omens that are rather interesting. Some people put stale bread in a baby's cradle in the hope of warding off disease.

It was thought lucky by some people for a butterfly to fly through their coat sleeve. It is supposedly good luck to throw a shoe over your left shoulder, but don't look!

It has been believed by some folks that they can ensure good weather on a particular day by eating everything on the table the evening before.

Another belief, is that when a knife falls to the ground, it brings bad luck to the person who dropped it; however, it brings good luck to the one who picks it up.

When the bottom of your feet itch, some people believe you are going to take a trip.

Folk wisdom says that if you sprinkle salt on a bird's tail, you will have good luck.

Then another about the birds; It is believed that if the first robin you see in the spring flies up, you will have good luck for the rest of the year. However, if it flies down, you won't!

If you sleep with your closet door open, some folks believe it's bad luck.

It is thought by some that dropping a knife will bring a gentleman caller.

Keeping fingers crossed ensures against disaster comes from the superstition that making the sign of the cross will avert bad luck.

An interesting superstition concerns the early Puritans, who believed that buttons were the invention of the devil and condemned them as vanities. Even today some Amish people use hooks and eyes as closures instead of buttons.

Some people believe that if you find your intitials in a spider's web, you will be lucky forever.

If you break a mirror and fear seven year of bad luck, here are three things that superstition holds will keep you immune. Wait seven hours before picking up the pieces. Throw the pieces into a deep, swiftly moving river where people do not swim, or bury them in a graveyard at midnight when there is no moon and no stars. That should save the situation.

* * *

Witches' Brew

Cherries
Lemon slices
1 quart cold tea
1 quart orange juice
1 (46-ounce) can Hawaiian punch

Place cherries and lemon slices in ring mold and fill mold with water. Freeze 24 hours. Mix remaining ingredients and pour into punch bowl over ice ring. Yields 25 punch cups.

St. Patty's Day has much tradition

Happy St. Patty's Day!

Faith and begorra it is that time again when the leprechauns are on the prowl and green shamrocks of all sizes can be seen. It is the time we proudly let our Irish heritage show (at least just a trifle, anyway).

Somehow we seem to be under the impression that the shamrock had its beginning in Ireland; however, that is not really correct. Historians have traced this symbolic three-leaf plant, that has a resemblance to the shamrock, to the ancient Egyptians.

Pictures of plants, that represent the shamrock, also have been found in the ruins of temples and pyramids. Too, found on early Roman coins and ancient Assyrian tablets, have been decorative motifs of a three-leaf plant.

When the shamrock was found in Ireland it was not the clover-type that we know today. It was a rather sharp tasting sorrel that grew in abundance in the woods that covered Ireland in those earlier days. This wood sorrel was used by the Irish folk for a food. They would grind it into a paste, mixing it with a butter-like ingredient and using the mixture to spread on bread and cakes.

When the wooded areas in Ireland began to become pastureland, the wood sorrel was replaced by a white clover that also was given the name of shamrock.

Through the years, the shamrock has had many names. It was called by the ancient Gaelics, seamrog, three-seamsrog, seamroge, shamrote, shamrocke, shamrug, semaroge and chambrock. Also wood sorrel, trefoil, white

504

clover and hop clover all have been classified as shamrocks.

It appears that the wood sorrel was the first shamrock, with the white clover second. Chances are today that if you wanted to purchase a shamrock for this special St. Patrick's Day, it will not be an imported shamrock plant. The white clover in the seedling stage often serves as our shamrock of today.

We know there are a lot of three-leaf shamrocks, but it is the four-leaf variety that is of special interest to everyone. When a patch of clover is found immediately begins the search for one with four-leaves, that is the kind that brings us our "luck," good luck!

* * *

A little poem by Josephine McEleer seems to set the stage for today.

Wearin' Of The Green

This mornin' I'll be wearin'
A little shamrock green,
That I might be a sharin'
With laddie and colleen.
This treasured Irish emblem
Significant and grand,
Because my folks ... God bless them
Once came from Ireland.
The green that I'm displayin'
Will stand out in the crowd,
And goes without the sayin'
Of heritage, I'm proud.
"Top of the mornin' to ye,"
Let me be first to say
E'en if no praise is due ye
On this St. Patrick's Day.

* * *

St. Patty's Salad

1 pound can crushed pineapple, drained and juice reserved
1 (3-ounce) package lime gelatin
1 banana, sliced
1 small bunch of green grapes, sliced
Add enough water to the reserved juice to make 2 cups. Dissolve gelatin in 1 cup of this hot liquid and then add the remaining liquid and chill until of the consistency of egg white. Fold in remaining ingredients and pour into a shamrock mold if you have one. Chill mixture until firm. Top with whipped topping if desired, maybe tinted green. Yields 4 to 6 servings.

All in a Woman's Day--March 24, 1987

Spirits lifted higher with arrival of spring

The year's at the spring
And days' at the morn;
Morning's at seven;
The hillside dew-pearled;
The lark's on the wing;
The snail's on the thorn;
God's in His heaven —
All's right with the world.
Robert Browning

Spring — it's the annual awakening; when spring has sprung. It reminds us that the "Fountain of Youth" is not lost. Our hopes and joys are renewed by the rebirth of the season.

The long awaited day of spring finally arrived on March 20; however, we have been enjoying springlike weather most of the winter, with the exception of a couple of flare-ups of cold weather. And as old-timers would say, we will probably have some more with Easter arriving as late as it will this year.

Just think how quickly spring does arrive; however, it takes only a second, or perhaps just a fraction of a second, and winter is gone and in its stead is that wonderful season of spring.

Mark Twain said: "(Weather) gets through more business in spring than in any other season. In the spring I have counted one hundred and thirty-six different kinds of weather inside of twenty-four hours." And that pretty much tells the story "of spring."

The early spring-like weather caused the budding of trees (and let's hope they were not killed in that earlier cold spell this month). Some flowers are showing more than their heads—violets and crocus are among the early bloomers, and forsythia is getting close to bursting into bloom.

Farmers have been busy in the fields in preparation for planting, the sunshine is beginning to warm the good earth, and some early gardens have been planted. Kite flying is always a part of spring; however, that already has been underway. Everything just seems to be rushing the season … it's all happening so early!

Most of us have been enjoying "spring fever" since the beginning of January. Of course, spring fever is just an attitude anyway; not a rite.

The weather has been so great we can't believe it is real. It must be a myth. Whatever it has been all these weeks is "just great."

Fresh, sweet smelling spring! These precious weeks of spring before the arrival of summer seem to lift our spirits higher and higher. Poets and philosophers have for centuries described spring in prose and poetry. In the book, "Twelve Moons of the Year," by Hal Boland, nature writer, it reflects on the seasonal change; "There is something in a mild March day that can touch a man to the very quick of his being. Just what it is cannot readily be stated, but it must be compounded by sunlight and air and warmth and immeasurable mystery that is partly summed by the word 'Promise'."

Spring housecleaning, if not already underway, will be soon. We don't have to hang the carpet over the clothesline anymore for a beating, but if you think spring housecleaning really doesn't exist, then you are wrong. Dead wrong! The garage and yard sales bear out that fact.

Just remember, spring is a season that is worthy of paying attention to!

* * *

Spring Salad

1 cup miniature marshmallows
1/4 cup pineapple (cut into 1/2-inch pieces)
3 1/2 cups shredded carrots
1/2 cup shredded coconut
1 cup seedless raisins
1 cup whipped cream or whipped topping
1 cup mayonnaise

Lightly toss together carrots, marshmallows, pineapple, coconut and raisins. Combine mayonnaise with carrot mixture and carefully fold in whipped cream or whipped topping. Serve in lettuce cups and garnish with coconut. Makes 6 to 8 servings.

Note: One pound of carrots should make the desired amount for the salad. If carrots are very moist, the amount of mayonnaise may be reduced. This salad also freezes well and may be served frozen or thawed.

All in a Woman's Day--March 31, 1987

Cake Month is cause for special celebration

Did you know that this is Cake Month? I didn't either until someone pointed out the fact.

Now, what do we do with it? Make cakes, of course, and give them away; this is what one lady has done to celebrate this special month. It is a little late this month this year to be making cakes to give away, but perhaps you can plan ahead and do it next year. That would surely gladden someone's heart to be thought of in such a special way.

Do you happen to have any problems with your cake making? Perhaps some pointers I am going to offer will be of help.

Do you have trouble with cakes made from a mix crumbling when you start to cut them? It might be caused by beating the batter too much, as this kind of abuse puts air in the batter and could possibly cause the crumbling.

If you have a cake come out of the oven with a sort of pyramid on the top, take a piece of thread by each end and run it through the cake to remove the hump.

Too, this can possibly be avoided if you will tape several thicknesses of wet folded paper towels around the outside of the cake pan. Bake as usual; the cake should come out even across the top, and the towels will not burn.

Cakes will be more flavorful if you always cream the flavoring, spice or grated fruit peel with the shortening three times.

If you are out of cake coloring, and really want to color a cake or frosting, try a little flavored gelatin or powdered drink. Start with about one-fourth teaspoon as more can be added to obtain the desired color. They are both good coloring agents. Taste is not adversely affected in the cake or the frosting. The flavor will be mixed into the batter more thoroughly.

To be sure your cake will stay fresh longer after it is cut, moisten a paper towel and wad it up a bit, then place it on the empty part of the cake plate, putting the cover over it. You might possibly have to redampen the towel as deemed necessary.

To make easy cake roses, shave colored gumdrops very thin and place them on a white frosted cake. They will curl like little roses.

To make soft, velvety textured cakes, proper creaming is a must. Make sure the shortening is at room temperature. With an electric mixer, cream the shortening on low speed; then add the sugar. Beat on medium speed until the sugar is dissolved and the creamed mixture is light and fluffy.

Dusting corn starch lightly on a cake before icing gives the cake a smooth, professional appearance, and also keeps the icing from running.

Here is an easy way to grease and flour cake pans: Thoroughly mix together a half cup homogenized shortening and one-fourth cup all-purpose flour. With this mixture you can grease and flour pans without a mess. Also, this gives a nice even brown crust. The mixture can be stored in a covered container on the cupboard shelf as it does not need refrigeration.

And still another coating for cake pans: Mix together a half cup of salad oil, a half cup of flour and one and three-fourths cups of shortening. Store in an airtight container in the refrigerator. A pastry brush will help in thoroughly coating the pan, or you can use paper toweling or even your fingers.

Still another mixture for greasing cake pans: Take one-fourth cup of salad oil, one-fourth cup of flour and one and one-fourth cups of shortening. Mix together and store it in the refrigerator.

For extra light cakes, try beating the cake batter with a wire whip. The results will be even better than obtained with a mixer.

If you have a tall, beautifully frosted cake that won't fit into the usual cake saver, cover it with an overturned canning kettle or spaghetti cooker.

No doubt you have heard about putting a glass of water on your cake plate to keep the cake fresh. Well, for your information, it is not water, but club soda or seltzer water. These bubbles keep the cake moist and fresh when stored.

To keep icings moist and prevent cracking, add a pinch of baking soda to the icing before spreading on the cake.

If you want to slice a cake for extra layers, use dental floss, holding it tight and drawing through with a sawing motion.

A steel knitting needle is a handy tool to loosen a cake from the tube of an angel food cake pan or from any other center tube pan. The needle slips easily; just slide it around the tube. It will not crack or break the cake, as a knife is likely to do.

* * *

Orange Slice Cake

1 cup butter or margarine
2 cups sugar
4 eggs
3 1/2 cups flour
1 teaspoon soda
1/2 cup buttermilk
1 pound orange slice candy, diced
1/2 pound dates, chopped
2 cups coconut
1/2 teaspoon butter flavoring
3/4 teaspoon almond flavoring

Cream butter or margarine and sugar together. Beat in eggs; add flour and soda. Then stir in buttermilk and add remaining ingredients, mixing well. Spoon batter into a greased and floured tube cake pan or loaf pans. (This amount is enough for one tube pan plus one bread pan, or three bread pans.) Bake at 300 degrees 45 minutes for loaves and 1 1/2 hours for the tube pan. Cool cake about 45 minutes in pans before turning out on cooling rack. This cake freezes well.

This is a moist and delicious fruit-type cake. It is delicious for a tea table or morning coffee.

All in a Woman's Day--April 7, 1987
Pretzel history reveals holiday ties

During the 12th century, no other food was so closely connected to a holiday as were pretzels to Lent and Easter.

In Chronicles at Tyrol, Switzerland, a reference is made to the practice in effect in 1132; everyone taking communion was to receive pretzels—eight for each male communicant and five for each woman.

In Bohemia, the day before the first Lenten Sunday, strings of pretzels were fastened to the fruit trees to make them bear heavily. There were even palm pretzels for Palm Sunday.

In Austria, children suspended them from palm bushes on Palm Sunday.

The lowly pretzel does have a special place in this celebration. They have a long Christian history; however, most of their Lenten significance has been forgotten during the last century.

The queer shape of the pretzel is due to a religious custom. In the early centuries, the old monks made and distributed pretzels to the children and the very poor on fete days; however, pretzels are no longer handed out on those special days. The pretzel shape is supposed to represent the arms crossed in supplication, a religious symbol. It was a reminder that Lent was a season of

508

penance and devotion.

The word pretzel has its roots in the Latin word for "little arms," bracellae. The German usage became "brezel" or "prezel," from which came the word pretzel.

Pretzels are made in bakeries today almost exactly as they were in the heyday of the Roman Empire. They are first boiled in a potash solution prior to baking, although, of course, the modern baker obtains his potash by a much simpler method than pouring water through hard wood ashes and then waiting for it to leach through as the monks did.

This interesting pretzel history might always have remained a hidden secret in dusty archives, were it not for the fact that during the first World War the sale of pretzels nearly ceased. That very important figure, "public opinion," almost gave the pretzel industry its death blow. Many people thought that pretzels were served only in German beer gardens, and almost overnight they imagined they could plainly see on each pretzel that forbidden trademark, "Made in Germany." You could not be 100 percent American, and munch a pretzel.

The blow fell hardest on the state of Pennsylvania because nearly every single pretzel served in this country came from the pretzel state, Pennsylvania. Nearly every town in that state supported a pretzel bakery and the pretzel bakery supported nearly everyone in each town. There, pretzel making and baking was considered an art. There was followed the Old World custom of a trade being handed down from father to son. All members of large families, from one generation to the next, were engaged in some step of the pretzel industry.

Historical records proved that the pretzel was not an invention of German brewers. An educational advertising campaign was waged so successfully that a national appetite was changed.

Today, pretzels have become so popular that they are made commercially in the form of sticks, Slim Jims, fish, animals, and alphabet letters. But the real article, the pretzel with the double twist, is still pretty largely made and bent by hand; a good pretzel bender is able to do 30 per minute.

Salt was originally added to the pretzels to banish demons, evil spirits, plagues and witches.

From the earliest times, the pretzel was made of a special dough consisting only of flour, salt and water, since fat, eggs and milk were forbidden during the Lenten period. Later it made its annual appearance on Ash Wednesday, sold by special vendors on the streets. In some cities they were distributed to the poor during the several days of Lent.

Today, some families and church groups reclaim the pretzel, and use it as a prayer reminder. There are some church groups that hold pretzel making parties on Ash Wednesday.

Today, we munch those salty bits of food, use them in niblet mixes, a crust for a dessert or salad and dipped in almond bark to be served as a cookie or candy.

* * *

Pretzel Salad

1 3/4 cups crushed pretzels
1/2 cup melted butter
3 tablespoons powdered sugar
1 (8-ounce) package cream cheese
1 cup sugar

1 regular-size carton whipped topping
2 (3-ounce) packages strawberry gelatin
2 cups boiling water
2 packages frozen strawberries

Mix together well, the pretzel crumbs, melted butter and powdered sugar, and press into a 9x13-inch pan. Bake 10 minutes in a 375-degree oven. Cool thoroughly. Soften cream cheese and mix in 1 cup sugar. Fold whipped topping into cream cheese mixture, and pour over cooled crust. Dissolve gelatin in boiling water and add frozen strawberries; stir until melted and spoon over the cooled mixture. Chill until set.

All in a Woman's Day--April 14, 1987
Let the bells ring out!

This Eastertime, let the bells ring out the glorious story of the Resurrection. Many church bells do not ring nowadays, for one reason or another, but this year let them tell the glad tidings.

Bells

Bells! Bells! Bells!
Listen to the bells:
the sunny peace
of a cowbell in
a summer meadow,
the deeptoned sorrows
of a bell that mourns
a great man, gone.
Listen to the bells:
the warning to birds
of a bell on the cat,
the changing of shifts
at the ship's bells,
and the old-fashioned
call to school bell.
But, oh, it is the ringing
of the Easter bells
that is the sound of joy!
They peal out a burst
of Hosanna—praise.
Listen! Christ is risen!
Resurrection Day is here!
The Easter bells are ringing.
—by Elizabeth Searle Lamb
* * *

Throughout the ages, bells have been the voices of history. They have pealed in victory or tolled to signal the beginning of battles. They have pealed at weddings, as the bride and groom left the church; at funerals to toll the age of the deceased as the procession left the church; on New Year's Eve, at midnight; or sunrise on Easter morning. They have announced curfews, celebrated births, summoned laborers to their work, given notice when the lord of the manor's oven was ready to bake bread, warned of fires, called attention to town criers, called soldiers together, signaled shop owners to open the market place and announced dinner.

Then, there is the delicious tinkle of the bell on the ice cream cart on a hot afternoon, the mellow tone of the cowbell at milking time, the sleigh bells on the bobsled or cutter that added joy to the Christmas season, the street car bell, the clanging bell of the locomotive, sounding the city that was perhaps two hours away, the ship's bells.

Also, there is the music of the telephone bell that young people especially enjoy, and the doorbell; however, it is not used as often anymore as people are too busy watching their favorite TV programs. Perhaps, we need a little more encouragement to press the doorbell of a neighbor, who might be lonely and offer that most precious gift that a friend can bestow, the gift of our time.

In addition, bells also are rung on other occasions when it is deemed appropriate and wise.

During the Middle Ages, bells were considered spiritual things. They received the blessing of the bishop and were washed with Holy water — a custom popularly known as the "baptism of the bells." The bishop prayed that the bell would summon the faithful to worship, drive away storms and frighten evil spirits.

Also during this era, church bells were rung to get attention and to announce fires, floods, and deaths.

Generally the largest bell in town belonged to the town, and not the church. A conqueror usually acknowledged the political importance of the bells by melting them down and casting his own.

Bells always have been closely associated with religious observances. Long before the birth of Christ, high priests of the Israelites, wore bells as a protection against evil spirits. Since the sixth century, Christians have used bells to summon worshippers.

In ancient China, batteries of small bells, kept in a temple or palace, served as standard pitches for tuning musical instruments. Some doubled as standard weights and measures of volume.

After 324 A.D., when Christianity was established as the state religion of the Roman Empire, the Christians began to use bells in their churches. At first the bells were small; however, they gradually became larger, and later one was hung atop a Christian church in the Italian Campania. The practice was approved in 605 by Pope Sabianus.

Some of the bells that rang out in England when World War II ended had previously sounded to celebrate the signing of the Magna Carta in 1215. Some English bells have tolled the death of every English ruler since King John died in 1216.

England's monotonous method of simply ringing, by repeating their order, finally gave way to "change ringing," with more elaborate variations played on five to 12 bells.

In the low countries, the chime grew into the carillon. The invention in the 15th century of the carillon machine or "chime barrell," turned the carillon into an oversized automatic music box, played by pegs that studded a rotating drum.

Then by 1600, wheels were used to distribute the weight of the large bells, and bell ringing in England became a game. English gentlemen even formed clubs to promote this hobby. London ringers in 1637 formed the Society of College Youths, later called the Ancient Society of College Youths, perhaps more because of the age of the members than the age of the club itself.

Prior to that, bell ringers, however, were in the lowest order of feudal priory, along with doorkeepers and floor scrubbers.

As trade grew in the 18th century, ringing spread to the colonies, although not as widely as in England. Old North Church in Boston imported eight bells in 1744, and Christ Church in Philadelphia imported a set 10 years later.

Paul Revere joined the first American "change ringing" group in 1750. "Change ringing" in Boston, however, didn't survive.

Since then, bell ringing has suffered its ups and downs in both England and the United States.

Perhaps the most famous American

bell is the Liberty bell cast in 1751 in London and arriving in Philadelphia in August, 1752. Even before it had proclaimed the Declaration of Independence in July, 1776, it had clanged defiance of British tax and trade restrictions and announced the Boston Tea Party. It also tolled the deaths of Washington, Jefferson, Adams and the other Founding Fathers.

A number of English or European folk tales tell of bells buried in the earth that can still be heard ringing if an ear is put to the ground on Christmas morning.

Too, there is the Easter legend concerning bells. According to European folklore, church bells that do not ring from Good Friday to Easter fly to Rome. On the way back they drop eggs for children to find.

And, so it is with the bells. But let them ring this Easter and tell the Good News to everyone.

* * *

May you have a blessed Easter!

All in a Woman's Day--April 21, 1987
Canned biscuits results amazing

It is amazing what a can of 10 biscuits, buttermilk, regular or country style, can do for you. Somehow, I seem to like the buttermilk style best.

You might like to experiment with a can of biscuits, and see what you can come up with that is new.

With some of the things that you can make, this exclamation might be heard, "Oh, you shouldn't have gone to so much trouble." That is what they might say when you serve something as delicious from the oven as Apple Coffee Cake.

The Czechs have been enjoying kolachy for years. It is often served at weddings and family gatherings in Czech and Bohemian areas; however, there is a knack to making the authentic kolachy. But now there is a simplified version, made from a can of biscuits, that you truly can enjoy.

And what could be better for a quick dessert than Quick Caramel Dumplings, also from a can of biscuits.

At a fair there was a division showing ways to use canned biscuits in a variety of quick hot breads. One that was especially liked was eclairs.

* * *

Apple Coffee Cake
2 cans refrigerated buttermilk or country style biscuits (10 to a can)
1/4 cup butter
3/4 cup sugar
1/3 cup finely chopped pecans
1 teaspoon cinnamon
2 tart (small or medium) apples, pared and cut into 20 slices

Butter the bottom and sides of a 9-inch round cake pan. Separate each can of biscuit dough into 10 biscuits. In a small skillet, melt the butter; remove from heat and cool. In a small bowl mix sugar, nuts and cinnamon. Dip biscuits, one at a time, in butter, then in the sugar mixture, and as you do so, overlap 15 of them around the outer edge of the prepared pan. Overlap remaining five biscuits in center. Tuck two apple slices between each biscuit so they do not extend over the dough. Bake in a preheated 400 degree oven until golden brown, 25 to 30 minutes. Invert on a round serving plate and remove pan. Serve warm with sweet butter.

* * *
Bohemian Raisin and
Biscuit Kolachy
1 cup raisins or currants
1/4 cup firmly packed brown sugar
1 to 2 teaspoons lemon juice
1/4 cup water
1 can (10 count) refrigerated flaky biscuits
1/2 cup sugar
1/2 teaspoon cinnamon
1/4 cup margarine or butter, melted
Glaze:
1/2 cup powdered sugar
2 to 4 teaspoons milk
1/2 teaspoon vanilla

In a small saucepan, combine raisins, brown sugar, water and lemon juice. Cook over medium heat 7 minutes or until mixture thickens, stirring occasionally. Cool. Separate dough into 10 biscuits. Combine sugar and cinnamon. Dip both sides of each biscuit in melted margarine, then in sugar mixture. Place rolls, sides touching, in an ungreased 15x10-inch jelly roll pan or a 13x9-inch pan. With thumb, make a wide imprint in center of each roll; fill with 1 rounded teaspoon raisin mixture. Bake in preheated 375-degree oven 15 to 20 minutes or until golden brown. In a small bowl, combine all glaze ingredients and beat until smooth; drizzle over warm rolls.

* * *
Quick Caramel Dumplings
4 tablespoons butter or margarine
3 cups brown sugar
3 cups hot water
1 teaspoon vanilla
1 can (10 count) biscuits

Combine butter, sugar and water in saucepan and boil 3 minutes. Add vanilla. Open biscuits and cut each one into fourths. Drop into boiling sugar.

Cover tightly, turn heat down low and cook 15 minutes. Serve warm with whipped cream. Makes 6 servings.

* * *
Lynda's Eclairs
1 can (10 count) biscuits
Shortening for deep fat frying

Separate the biscuits and roll each by hand into an elongated shape. Cover them with a towel or piece of waxed paper and let them rise 10 minutes; then deep fat fry until brown on both sides. Drain on paper towel.
Filling:
1/2 cup sugar
1/3 cup milk
2/3 cup homogenized shortening
1/4 teaspoon salt
1 teaspoon vanilla
1/2 cup powdered sugar

Place first 5 ingredients into bowl and beat 5 minutes. Add powdered sugar. Carefully insert knife into side of each cooked biscuit and gently slit lengthwise to create a cavity. With a cake decorator, insert some of the filling into each cavity. Chill.
Frosting:
1/2 ounce unsweetened chocolate, melted
2 tablespoons butter
1/2 cup powdered sugar
1 tablespoon hot water

Combine ingredients; beat well; frost chilled eclairs.

All in a Woman's Day--April 28, 1987
Old expressions contain meanings

You may not believe this to be true; however, many old-time expressions got their meaning across for many circumstances. I'm sure you will agree that the old-timers were the greatest linguists ever.

Since there were no I.Q. tests in those early days, folks often spoke of someone's intellect as he's as bright as a silver dollar; she's as green as a gourd; he's off his rocker; she's sharp as a tack; or he's as ignorant as all git out.

Some expressions used that were not quite so complimentary included: He's crooked as a snake; she's as slow as the seven-year itch; he's sitting on the fence; she's as skinny as a rail; he's as ugly as a mud fence; he's sheepish looking; she's as stubborn as a mule; you'll be laughing on the other side of your face; you won't last until the water gets hot; she's as tight as Dick's hatband; he is as poor as Job's turkey; plague take you; and I didn't know him from Adam's off ox.

These bits of wisdom may go for someone who is ill: I'm under the weather; I'm up against it; or I'm out of snuff. For those who are in good shape: Fit as a fiddle; I'm feeling my oats; and I'm as pleased as punch.

Sometimes when committee meetings drag on and on this might fit the occasion: Land O'Goshen let's cut the butter on some of these issues or we won't finish until the cows come home.

Some proverbs for good relationship include: A good example is the best sermon; write injuries in the dust, benefits in marble; approve not of him who commends all you say; modesty is a virtue; bashfulness is a vice; a lie stands on one leg, truth on two; if you would reap praise, you must sow the seeds of gentle words and useful deeds; a slip of the foot you may soon recover, but the slip of the tongue you may never get over; clean your finger before you point it at my spots; a good pair of ears will wring dry a hundred tongues.

About visitors: Fish and visitors stink after three days; give to your friends and lend to your enemies; a word of praise is equal to ointment on a sore; a little nothing will get you nowhere.

You will find no fools as troublesome as those that have wit; adversity makes men, prosperity makes monsters; what the fool does in the end, the wise man does in the beginning; better lose a jest than a friend; when the fox preaches, beware of your geese; every shut eye ain't asleep; the devil can cite scripture to suit his purpose; fate leads the willing, but drives the stubborn; pride goeth before destruction and a haughty spirit before a fall; when we do ill the devil is tempting us, when we do things we are tempting him; words may show a man's wit, but actions show his meaning.

For gains and losses: Many a man thinks he is buying pleasure when he is really selling himself a slice of it; when prosperity was well mounted, she let go of the bridle and soon came tumbling out of the saddle; after crosses and losses men grow humbler and wiser; keep the shop and the shop will keep you; a true friend is the best profession; an empty bag cannot stand alone; he who rises late must trot all day and will scarcely overtake business at night; he who loses money loses much, he who loses a friend loses more, but he who loses courage, loses all.

Some other expressions that can be vividly imagined are: I don't chew my tobacco but once (no repeating); bet your bottom dollar (assurance); cool as a cucumber (poised); great day in the morning (surprise); scared the living daylights out of me (fear); I felt knee high to a grasshopper (humility).

These you might give careful examination: Misfortunes seldom come alone; money is the root of all evil; it is much easier to go down than up; idleness is the beginning of sin; he that begins many things, finishes few; patience, time and money overcome everything; prosperity gains friends, adversity tries them.

Many of the phrases or expressions that folks use in their everyday conversation come from the Bible. For instance: In the twinkling of an eye (Cor. 15:52); den of thieves (Matt. 21:13); drop in the bucket (Isa. 40:15); no rest for the wicked (Isa. 48:22); a stone's throw (Luke 22:41); apple of his eye (Deut. 32:10); keep the faith (2 Tim. 4:7); old wives tales (I Tim. 4: 7).

* * *

Scripture Cake

3/4 cup Genesis 18:8 (soft butter)
1 1/2 cups Jeremiah 6:20 (sugar)
5 Isaiah 10 :14 (eggs, separated)
3 cups Leviticus 2:2 (flour)
3 teaspoons I Corinthians 5:6 (baking powder)
1 teaspoon each II Corinthians
 9: 9 (cloves, nutmeg, allspice)
3/4 teaspoon II Kings 2:20 (salt)
1 teaspoon Exodus 30:23 (cinnamon)
1/2 cup Judges 4:19 (milk)
3/4 cup Genesis 43:11 (blanched almonds, chopped)
3/4 cup Nahum 3 :12 (dried figs, finely cut)
3/4 cup II Samuel 16:1 (raisins)

Cream butter with sugar and beat in egg yolks, one at a time. Sift flour, baking powder, salt and spices, and blend into creamed mixture alternately with milk. Beat egg whites until stiff and fold into batter. Fold in almonds, figs and raisins, and turn into a greased and floured tube cake pan. Bake in a 325 degree oven 70 minutes or until cake tests done. (This delightful cake could be a real conversation piece at the next church supper.)

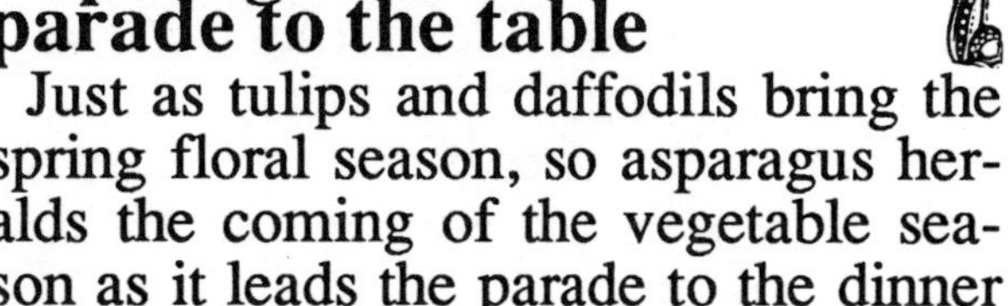

All in a Woman's Day--May 5, 1987

Asparagus leads parade to the table

Just as tulips and daffodils bring the spring floral season, so asparagus heralds the coming of the vegetable season as it leads the parade to the dinner table.

A number of years ago, when many plants were still wild and ground not cultivated so extensively, folks enjoying country living and could find asparagus growing wild. They learned that if the ground was warm enough for asparagus to grow, it was warm enough for garden making; and that is said to be the mental calendar that says, "It is spring."

Home grown asparagus is probably on the market by now, and will be the next couple of weeks. The cost of the fresh asparagus is high, but then, too, so is the frozen variety.

Early stalks of asparagus are most often willowy and thin; however, as the season progress stalks become meatier and fatter.

Which is better? No doubt it is matter of preference. Those preferring the stalks that are thin, enjoy the tenderness all the way from tip to stem. Those that like the thicker variety, declare that, while peeling an asparagus stalk is time consuming, it is well worth the effort as it is more flavorful and tender than the unpeeled. When a thick stalk is peeled, it generally is not necessary to break off much of the root thus having less waste.

Whichever way it is enjoyed, freshness is of the utmost importance; woody ends however, need to be cut away. With the thin variety, bend the spear until it breaks at a natural point, just where the tough root begins.

A brittle and easily punctured stalk of asparagus denotes tenderness. Always avoid stalks that have a large amount of white stem as they will no doubt be tough. Fresh asparagus also has a snap when broken.

If you need to peel asparagus stalks, lay them flat on a work surface. Scrap down the stalk, beginning just below the tip. A swivel bladed vegetable peeler is ideal for this sort of peeling. It is well to cut off an inch from the bottom after peeling.

If using canned asparagus, don't forget to open the can from the bottom. This let's the spears come out without breaking the tips.

Fresh asparagus and butter are compatible. If you desire to microwave, put a tiny bit of water in a loaf pan, place heads toward the center; microwave only five minutes and serve with butter.

Many recipes call for asparagus; and the rich, cutty flavor that it imparts to soups, salads, entrees in combination with eggs, pasta or meats. It does seem to be the best, however, when steamed or blanched and served hot with salt, pepper and butter it's still good. Capers, buttered bread crumbs, Hollandaise sauce or a bit of lemon never go a miss with this vegetable.

Another way of serving asparagus is to cover it with milk, swimming in melted butter (I would call it a white sauce) served hot over mashed potatoes, biscuits or toast. Chives added to the sauce gives emphasis to this delicacy.

A perennial plant, asparagus in many beds will last 20 years or more with minimum care.

A simple asparagus dish that also is elegant for company is an Asparagus Souffle. It is an interesting variation of the old creamed asparagus and spooned over-toast-dish. Line a baking pan or two-quart casserole with slices of the buttered bread. Place a layer of cooked asparagus over slices of buttered bread; add a layer of cheese slices along with another layer of asparagus and top with a layer of buttered bread slices. Beat two eggs with two cups of milk and salt and pepper to taste. Pour gently over asparagus and cheese layers. Bake in a slow oven (325 degrees) until firm.

* * *

Elegant Asparagus Casserole

3 cups asparagus, cut up
3 eggs, beaten
1/2 cup milk
1 cup bread crumbs
1/4 cup onions, diced
3 tablespoons grated cheese
Salt and pepper to taste
1/4 teaspoon oregano

Cook the asparagus in a little salted water until almost tender. Drain it and arrange it in a casserole. Combine eggs and milk and stir in remaining ingredients. Pour this over asparagus and bake it in a 350 degree oven about 20 minutes or until firm. More cheese may be added, if desired.

All in a Woman's Day--May 12, 1987

Sloppy Joes' beginning goes back to 16th century

Since this is Beef Month, let's think about a dish that has beef, ground beef that is, as its basis for that smoothin', sustainin', satisfyin' food … the Sloppy Joes.

In the early days of the American West, those words seemed to describe, and give the highest praise the cowboy had for the hearty meals that nourished him through the tedious tasks of ridin' and ropin' from sunup to sundown. The Sloppy Joe is a food that is truly American in origin.

During the long cattle drives of the 1870s, a lunch, that was "sustainin'" was made from leftover meat combined with beans and a spicy sauce that was served with the cooks' sourdough bread.

It is evident, and I'm sure you will agree, that the Sloppy Joe really was born on the range; however, the heritage of the Sloppy Joe goes back to the 16th century when Cortez came upon Indians cooking fish and fowl over an open fire—the origin or the beginning of the American barbecue.

The Spaniards then went a little further. After borrowing the technique, they dunked their meat in a thick tomato sauce made with spices that were described as exotic, along with accents of garlic and hot peppers.

Too, the Spanish settlers gave the refinement to the procedure and the "barbacoa" became that traditional fare served for festive events. Special cooking pits, with large rotisseries that could skewer a young steer or a pig, had been made by some of the ranchos and missions. Then when the meat was fully cooked, it was thinly sliced, topped with a spicy tomato sauce, and eaten with slabs of bread.

According to Western lore, however, the Sloppy Joe got its name the day a rancher had more neighbors to a barbecue than he could actually feed. It was then, in a moment of genius, that he ordered the cook to chop the meat, combine it with a spicy tomato sauce and serve between slices of bread. The outcome was such a successful venture that the rancher could no longer serve the traditional barbecued meat, and it was by popular request that "Sloppy Joes" were in demand.

It is understood that even today on some of the large cattle ranches, where the chuck wagon and roundup are still a part of the scene, the same as in earlier days, the Sloppy Joes are still a favorite lunchtime food.

But whether you are at home or on the range, Sloppy Joes make a convenient, tasty meal for lunch or supper. They can easily be prepared with a pound of ground beef (hamburger) and a can of that special sandwich sauce that is a combination of red, ripe concentrated tomatoes, bell peppers, onions and 14 different domestic and imported herbs and seasonings, with just a hint of garlic, blended into a thick, tangy sauce. Of course, if you are ambitious, it can be made from scratch.

Sloppy Joes are enjoyed by most families on hamburger buns or as an open-faced sandwich that can be eaten with a fork. It makes no difference how they are served or just what you choose to call them. Sloppy Joes are versatile, good, simple and inexpensive to serve when entertaining or to keep the family happy.

A survey reveals that other names for this glorious hot sandwich, include barbecues, chiliburgers, spoon, burgers, maid rites or tavern meat. Besides open-faced or as a sandwich, they can be served in Arabic or Pita bread "pockets," in tortillas or taco

517

shells, or on a French roll. Anyway, and by any name, they are Mmmmmmm, good!

The teenage set thinks they are great, and so do those folks at neighborhood get-togethers. Just add a vegetable salad, a beverage, that is a favorite, and your menu is complete.

Regardless of how you eat Sloppy Joes, just remember that the origin goes back to the early days in the American West.

All in a Woman's Day--May 19, 1987

Meat loaf has varieties

Still going along with May as Beef Month, the column this week concerns meat loaf; there are about as many recipes for it as Heinz has pickles.

Did it ever occur to you that whoever chopped that first piece of beef had the beginnings of "something wonderful?" Today, ground beef is probably the most popular, and possibly the most consumed form of meat used.

The idea of grinding beef originated in Northern Europe, in the areas that border the Baltic Sea. There the residents chopped their raw beef with dull knives and considered this beef a food of luxury.

As these people continued moving westward, they reached Hamburg, which at that time was one of Medieval Europe's busiest seaports. And it was there that the people adopted the custom of grinding meat, cooking it and serving it on bread. (Evidently this was the beginning of the hamburger.)

And from there the rest of the world took over, at least America did. This versatile kind of meat product had many roles. In addition to meat loaves and hamburgers, it also is used for meatballs, in all kinds of casseroles and skillet dishes, tacos and tamale fillings, chili, stuffing for green peppers, cabbage, pasta, hash, spaghetti sauce, pizza, Sloppy Joes, stews, soups, meat pies and even salads.

Whether it is hot or cold, this special kind of meat, dressed up in a loaf, with sauce or plain, fills the hunger void as few other foods can. Most folks like a king-size sandwich made from yesterday's meat loaf. I think you'll agree it is pretty good eating!

Beef is the main meat in a meat loaf; however, it can also be made from veal, ham, pork, sausage, turkey, chicken or a combination of meats. Oftentimes a recipe will call for a portion of sausage to be added along with the beef, which no doubt adds to the flavor.

For most cooks, onions are a must, of course, how much or how little is determined by the cook, who knows how the family likes this seasoning.

Meat loaves need a filler, which this can be several different kinds. Some fillers are cracker crumbs, cooked rice, raw oatmeal, soft bread crumbs, dry bread crumbs, ready-to-serve cereal, stuffing mixes or corn meal.

The liquid includes, milk—regular, two-percent or evaporated—tomato juice or sauce, canned soups, cream, wine, bouillon, apple or cranberry sauce, bananas, water, jelly, jams or marmalades.

Eggs most often are used as a binder; however, that is optional.

The meat loaf mixture should be moist; however, not "loose," but just moist enough to hold together. If the mixture should seem a bit too dry, just add a little more liquid, and if it should be too soft, add a bit more filler.

The loaves of seasoned meat can be

wrapped in cabbage leaves, topped with bacon strips or frosted with mashed potatoes. They can be stuffed with hard-boiled eggs, ravioli, rice mixtures, mashed potatoes, French fries, mushrooms or stuffing mixes. The loaves also can be basted and served with an assortment of sauces, including barbecue, mushroom, cheese, tomato, fruit (especially pineapple or cranberry). Seasonings generally include salt, pepper, catsup, parsley, mustard, garlic, chili, curry, horseradish, sage, or any herb that is especially liked.

* * *

Following is a heritage meat loaf recipe that from its meatball past has evolved as a favorite:

Heritage Meat Loaf

2 pounds ground beef
2 eggs
1 cup corn flakes
2 tablespoons salt
1/2 teaspoon pepper
2 tablespoon minced parsley
1 onion or 1 tablespoon dried onion
Sauce:
1/2 cup catsup
1/2 cup brown sugar
1 1/2 teaspoons prepared mustard
2 tablespoons cider vinegar
1/2 teaspoon ground nutmeg

Prepare the two mixtures separately and then add half of the sauce to the meat loaf and mix thoroughly. Place in a greased loaf pan (this could possibly be made into two loaves depending on the size of the pan). The remainder of the sauce tops the loaf. Bake in a 350-degree oven until it tests done. This may be sliced for sandwiches.

Pinch here and there for meat loaf recipes

Many homemakers will remember how their great-grandmothers, grandmothers and mothers did their cooking the way that follows:

I would like to share a bit more concerning the meat loaf. This item was written by Mary McDermott Shideler, who has authored many books and magazine articles. Enjoy the way she tells about her meat loaf: how to make a meat loaf for two persons. You can't; so start over. How to make a meat loaf for four to six persons or for two persons for two to three meals.

And this is the way she continued with her meat loaf recipe: "Buy 2 or 3 pounds of ground meat. If you like sausage, make half to a third of this quantity of meat to sausage. If possible, get ground chuck or ground round and not hamburger as it has too much fat in it.

"Dump meat in a bowl. Add to it 1/2 to 1 cup of somethings which (1) makes the loaf of a better texture-a bit lighter than if it's all meat and (2) soaks up the meat juices. Use anything that is convenient; bread crumbs, corn meal, oatmeal, corn flakes, grape nuts, cracker crumbs, rice might work, but I've never tried it (rice needs a good deal of liquid to cook properly.)

"Add liquid of some sort, enough that the meat and crumbs (or whatever) can be mixed easily but that the resulting mass will hold its shape. This will probably take a half or a quarter cup of something; an egg or two, or milk, or wine, or catsup, or any of these combinations. Or tomato juice.

"Add seasonings, (if you've used catsup for all your liquid, you may not

519

need any more-except salt); salt, pepper, Worcestershire, soy or tabasco sauce, Sauce Diable, a pinch of basil (if you have used catsup, especially), or sage or marjoram. By all means include a quarter of a teaspoonful-or more or less-of cinnamon. A dab of cloves and or nutmeg might be good. Cumin in highly desirable.

"Mix with your hands (sorry, but that's the only way that works) and smell it. If mixture smells sort of flat, add a bit more catsup, one of the sauces or herbs. If it smells sharp, add a bit more cinnamon or other spices (they are good blenders) or cover with a sauce as in next paragraph.

"Shape the loaf—round or square or rectangular—and place in a cake pan or something of that. I prefer to put it on a trivet, but if your trivets are all of the wire type, cover the trivet with aluminum foil and poke a few holes in it. The purpose of the trivet is to keep the loaf out of the fat as it melts out. Or plunk the meat into a bread pan or casserole and ignore the trivet. If you feel like it, dump over the meat (once it's in the baking pan) a can of undiluted cream of mushroom soup. Place loaf (in its pan) in the oven that you should have started heating before mixing the loaf.

"Baking directions: 1 hour at 350-375 degrees; 2 hours at 300-325 degrees; 3 hours at 250-275 degrees; 4 hours bake at 225 degrees.

"Serve hot the first night; cold the second night; heat in a can of gravy the third night. It may be desirable at some state of reheating to add a dab of cumin or curry. Or something.

"If desired, the first night instead of baking the loaf, take out enough to make "hamburgers" and broil them.

The next night, bake the rest of the loaf (which has been mellowing in the refrigerator in the meantime). Any meat loaf also can be baked in muffin tins; in that case bake at 400 degrees for half an hour or thereabouts.

"And there you have complete instructions for making a meat loaf.

* * *

I am going to include two recipes for meat loaves. These make good picnic fare.

Cranberry Glazed Meat Loaf

1 pound ground beef
1/4 pound bulk sausage
1/2 cup quick-cooking oats
1/2 teaspoon salt
1/4 teaspoon pepper
1 tablespoon Worcestershire sauce
1/4 cup evaporated milk
1 egg
2 tablespoons chopped onion
1 teaspoon paprika
1 can whole cranberry sauce
1/2 cup brown sugar
1 teaspoon lemon juice

Combine ingredients. Shape into a loaf. Spread with a topping made of one can of whole cranberry sauce, 1/3 cup of brown sugar and 1 tablespoon of lemon juice. Bake at 350 degrees for one hour. Serves 6.

* * *

Meat Loaf with Sauce

2/3 cup dry bread crumbs
1 cup milk
1 1/2 pounds ground beef
2 eggs, beaten
1/4 cup grated onion
1 teaspoon salt
1/8 teaspoon pepper
1/2 teaspoon sage

Put the bread crumbs and milk to soak. If it seems too dry, add more milk. Mix the ground beef, eggs, onion, salt, pepper and sage. Add the bread crumbs and milk mixture and mix well. Place in a 9 x 9-inch loaf pan.

Sauce:

3 tablespoons brown sugar

1/4 cup catsup

1 tablespoon prepared mustard

1/4 teaspoon nutmeg

Spread sauce on meat loaf. Bake it in 350 degree oven for one hour.

All in a Woman's Day--June 2, 1987

Wedding traditions have come a long way

While many traditions have fallen by the wayside, we still think of June as the favorite month for weddings.

* * *

"The time has come," the jeweler said,
to talk of many things;
Of shoes and rice and wedding bells
And diamond engagement rings ...

* * *

And that time does come, inevitably, to all young couples who are in love and think of purchasing that very important diamond ring as a symbol of love, according to the Jewelry Industry Council.

There was a time when a marriage was a business deal between parents of the bride and groom. The important thing was how much the groom's family paid for the bride and the size of the bride's dowry. Love wasn't given consideration.

Many wedding traditions date back to faraway lands and ancient rites.

For instance, the wedding ring dates all the way back to early Egypt, where the circular shape was a symbol of unending love. Even the finger on which the ring was placed goes back to an ancient belief that a vein in the third finger of the left hand ran directly to the heart. Too, back in those ancient times, men often kidnapped women from their tribes and forced them to be wives, placing metal bands around their ankles or wrists to impress upon the women that they were now the property of their captors. However, during the decline of the Roman Empire, this practice was replaced by the less barbaric one of simply placing a metal ring on a woman's finger to symbolize her submissive relationship to her husband. And, by the time the Roman Empire fell in the fifth century, the ring had completely replaced bands that had been placed on the wrists and ankles. The church, however, at first rejected this tradition; but in the ninth century, Pope Nicholas declared the wedding ring a symbol of the eternal bond between marriage partners and that is how it has stood since that time.

Still another tradition is the bridal veil, which was a symbol of virginity in ancient Greece. In America, however, it gained popularity after Nellie Curtis, George Washington's granddaughter, wore a veil because her fiance was enchanted by the sight of her through a lace window curtain.

It wasn't until the beginning of the 20th century that the white gown became a symbol of purity. In Victorian times, white was a sign of affluence, and it symbolized celebration in early Roman days.

The original bridal bouquet was made of a combination of garlic, chives and other strong herbs and was designed to drive away evil demons. The bride of today carries various flowers in her bouquet, many of which have had special meaning down through the ages. In centuries past, it was believed that myrtle was a favorite flower of the gods and it was used to symbolize constancy in duty and affection, with the apple blossoms symbolizing better things to come. Ivy symbolized good luck and eternal fidelity, and lilies stood for purity. The orange blossom, often used in bridal bouquets, symbolized fertility and happiness since the orange tree blooms and bears fruit at the same time. The ancient Greeks regarded a rose as the emblem of beauty and happiness.

Proper protocol, according to ancient Anglo-Saxon custom, had the maid of honor fashioning the bride's wedding wreath, as well as remaining with her for a number of days prior to the nuptials, tending to her needs, and making her beautiful for that special day. It was the bridesmaids' duty to stand guard over the bride the night before her being given to the groom to protect her from those who might think of capturing the maid for ransom. Today, of course, these attendants are on hand to give moral support and to help her look her best.

You'll agree that we have come a long way from those earlier days of courting and marriage.

* * *

Lavender Punch

1 package grape powdered drink mix
1 package lemon powdered drink mix
2 cups sugar
1 quart water
1(6-ounce) can frozen lemonade
1(6-ounce) can frozen orange juice
 16 ice cubes

Mix all, and at serving time add 1 quart gingerale. Serves 30.

* * *

Pink Punch

2 packages tropical punch powdered drink mix
2 quarts water
2 cups sugar
1 (46-ounce) can pineapple juice
1/4 teaspoon pineapple flavoring
1 quart 7-UP®

Mix all together, except the 7-UP® and chill. Add the 7-UP® or another carbonated drink, if desired, at serving time. This makes a delicate shade of pink punch; however, to give it a brighter tone a small amount of red food coloring can be used. This makes 25 half-cup servings.

All in a Woman's Day--June 9, 1987

Strawberry season is now underway

The season is well underway for those who have home grown strawberries, that are so sweet, juicy and tasteful. The recent rains; however, may have caused a bit of a problem.

These luscious red morsels that fill the air with their irresistible perfume (we might say), have been around for a long time, having originated in Europe in the 18th century, and grown in England, France and Italy before brought across the Atlantic. Strawberries seem to span the globe. Also long before the coming of the Europeans to the Americas, Indians in Chile were cultivating strawberries said to have been as large as walnuts; however, they were a pale red with firm flesh that was almost white.

Some of the early day colonists in this new country found big, bright, luscious red strawberries growing wild, and it was the Indians, who taught them the trick of sweetening the berries with the dew of the milkweed. Long before the arrival of the settlers, the American Indians were making

522

strawberry wine.

Strawberries make a colorful addition for every occasion, from breakfast through dessert. Whirred in a blender, they make a terrific, very berry puree to pour over vanilla ice cream. They also make late morning snacks and are elegant served whole and dunked into powdered sugar or dipped into plain yogurt, and then into brown sugar for a zippy, flavorful treat. Also they do something special for cereal.

No one seems to know who served the first shortcake (It is thought to have been originated by the colonists). Whoever it was had to be a good cook in some country kitchen. And, no doubt, it just had to be "divine providence" that led to combining garden fresh berries with warm baking powder biscuits and lathered with thick whipped cream. Or is it a dessert? Country cooks have been known to fill soup bowls with strawberry shortcake and serve it for an entire meal. And no one can question that it certainly is a man pleasing meal. Isn't that what cooking is all about? No doubt there are as many recipes for strawberry shortcake as there are cooks.

Experts agree that freezing is the simplest way to preserve the bright colored and delightfully flavored strawberries. Slicing the berries and covering them with syrup is the best way to retain the fruit quality as the syrup fills the spaces between berries, letting no air reach the fruit. A good syrup is to combine four cups of sugar and four cups of water or com-bining two cups of sugar with each four cups of fruit. Freeze immediately. It is recommended that ascorbic acid or an ascorbic acid mixture be added to the sugar or syrup before freezing. The acid is insurance against loss of flavor and vitamins. Most strawberries, if firm and bright colored, will retain their texture and flavor from eight to 12 months whether frozen packed, sliced, crushed or whole.

Some homemakers like to quick freeze them whole with the bright green leaves and stems intact. This way makes beautiful garnishes or appetizers throughout the entire year. Berries frozen this way, and served just before completely thawed are the next best thing to fresh berries from the market.

* * *

The shortcake recipe that follows is not quite biscuit or not quite cake; however, it has a nice, firm texture and a crusty sugary top. Best of all it is a cinch to stir up, when one is in a hurry.

Berry Patch Shortcake

1/2 cup butter or margarine
2 cups flour
1/4 cup sugar
4 teaspoons baking powder
1/4 teaspoon salt
Dash nutmeg
1/2 cup milk
2 eggs, separated
Additional sugar
2 pints fresh strawberries
1 cup whipping cream, whipped and sweetened, or whipped topping.

Rub a 9-inch fluted tart pan or cake pan with 1 teaspoon of butter. Sift dry ingredients into a mixing bowl and cut in remaining butter to resemble coarse meal. In a measuring cup, blend milk and egg yolks with fork. Stir into flour mixture to make a soft dough. Pat out in prepared pan, moistening fingers with left over egg white to prevent sticking. Brush surface with egg white. Sprinkle generously with sugar. Bake in a preheated 450 degree oven 12 minutes or until golden. Cool on rack. Top with sliced berries, sweetened to taste. Serve wedges of shortcake, topped with berries and cream. Serves 6 to 8.

All in a Woman's Day--June 16, 1987

Whipped topping tips

June is Dairy Month, so, think about products from milk, especially whipping cream-this is our point of interest.

Whipped cream appeared in Rome around the ninth century A.D. It was extremely expensive because the few chefs, who knew the secret, capitalized on their knowledge. In Vienna, some 300 years ago, an anonymous cook skimmed cream off milk and carefully whipped it into "schlagobers" or whipped cream. Today, Vienna is known for its lavish use of whipped cream, not only in countless pastries, but also as a sugared dessert served as a dish by itself or used in coffee.

Here are a few whipping tips:

A half pint carton of whipping cream contains one cup cream. It doubles in volume and becomes two cups of whipped cream, if whipped properly. And there is a "right" way to whip cream.

It whips best at cold refrigerator temperatures, 35 to 40 degrees; so, store it in the coldest part of the refrigerator. The cream, bowl and beaters should all be refrigerated for at least two hours before whipping.

You can use a rotary beater, wire whisk or an electric beater. If an electric beater is used, turn to medium speed, until the chilled cream begins to thicken, then lower the speed and watch it carefully, beating only until the cream forms soft mounds and is still glossy. Do not overbeat or the cream will turn to butter. Fold sugar and flavorings into cream after it is whipped. Adding sugar before whipping decreases stiffness and increases the whipping time.

Did you know that dairy sour cream will whip? It takes about five minutes to whip and will be thin before becoming fluffy. A little powdered sugar can be added to taste. This makes a light and healthy topping for gelatin or aspic.

To whip nonfat dry milk, beat equal amounts of powder and ice water into stiff peaks.

Instant nonfat dry milk can be sprinkled over partially set gelatin and the mixture whipped into stiff peaks.

Instant cocoa mix (about one teaspoon) added to a half cup of whipping cream will make chocolate whipped cream.

To make whipping cream beat up firm, and in about half the time, add seven drops of lemon juice to a pint of whipping cream.

For weepless whipped cream, add confectioners' sugar to whipping cream before beating. Cream stands up firm, even if it's not used immediately.

Another nonweeping whipped cream is obtained by whipping one pint of whipping cream until stiff. Combine one tablespoon of instant vanilla pudding and the amount of confectioners' sugar normally used, and beat into whipped cream. The whipped cream will stand up well.

Whipped cream can be frozen. Just drop spoonsful of whipped cream onto aluminum foil or waxed paper, cover with another sheet of foil or paper, and freeze. Next time when needing whipped cream the individual servings can be quickly defrosted for use.

To keep whipped cream stablized and prevent separating, soften package of unflavored gelatin in fourth of a cup cold water. Heat to dissolve the gelatin and add two tablespoons of sugar. Cool, then gently fold into whipped cream.

Flavor whipped cream with a little freshly grated nutmeg. It is delightful served as a topping for baked custard, bread pudding and apple or pumpkin pie.

If you are getting splattered when whipping cream, place a piece of waxed paper over the bowl and cut a slit in the paper to fit the beater or a hand mixer. A plastic bag over the entire bowl, with a hole cut in the top for the beaters, is another way of stopping the splattering.

* * *

If you use a lot of whipped topping you might like to make your own. Here is a recipe.

Whipped Topping

1 small can (2/3 cup) evaporated milk
2 teaspoons lemon juice
3 tablespoons sugar
1 teaspoon vanilla

Pour evaporated milk in a small mixing bowl. Chill in freezer until ice crystals form along the edge (about 20 to 30 minutes). Chill beaters. Beat icy evaporated milk with chilled beaters until soft mounds form, about 2 minutes on high speed of the electric mixer. Add lemon juice and beat until stiff peaks form, 2 minutes at high speed. Blend in sugar and vanilla. Serve immediately. Whipped topping is best if served within 1 hour after preparation. (Makes about 3 1/2 cups.)

Milk and butter history explained

The idea of having an annual celebration for milk began in the summer of 1937, when National Milk Week was proclaimed; however, by 1939, it had grown into a month long event, which it is today.

The observance was led by the National Dairy Council, with the American Dairy Association joining the ranks in 1940.

Cows arrived in the New World with the Jamestown colony, thereby setting up the beginning of the dairy production in this country. It was in 1851 that the first cheese factory in the United States was opened at Rome, N. Y. Then in 1856, Louis Pasteur began his experiments of killing microbes with controlled heat, thus resulting in a safer product, for the consuming public.

Condensed milk was patented in 1856, and in 1884, the first glass milk bottle was developed, representing a big step forward in making milk's quality readily available to the consumer. It was developed by Dr. Harvey Thatcher, Pottsdam, N.Y. Until that time milk was poured from open cans into the customer's open containers.

The ice cream cone was introduced in 1904 at the St. Louis World's Fair. In 1919, homogenized milk first appeared on the market.

Butter, a by-product of milk, is one of the oldest known dairy products having been discovered about 4,000 years ago by accident. To make butter, the nomads would take the milk from animals, such as the ewes or goats, placing it in animal skins as a sack for shaking the milk as it was hung over the back of a horse or camel. This pouch bounced around and as the animal moved the milk or cream, was churned into butter. Also, Bedouins' mirjahah and other similar skins are still used by Nomadic tribes in some areas of North Africa and the Middle East.

In its antiquity, butter was used as a salve for burns and various other skin injuries, an oil, a wrinkle eraser, a poultice, as money and, of course, as a foodstuff.

During Greek and Roman times, butter was a scarce commodity. Most often milk collected from the sheep or goats was drunk immediately or made into cheese.

Butter was not used extensively throughout Europe until the Middle Ages. It was the Scandinavians that first used this product, no doubt because of the cold climate it kept better. When it was first introduced into Europe, it was not widely used until the 18th century, as this dairy product would quickly turn rancid.

Butter was often associated with disease because of the lack of refrigeration. Parisians in the mid 17th century were warned by physicians that butter caused leprosy, a disease mistakenly linked with eating spoiled meat or seafood.

Butter, however, eventually became valuable. When the Pilgrims came to America, they had stored several tubs of butter on the Mayflower.

For many years butter making was strictly done as a home activity. The cream was sloshed in a wooden, crockery or glass churn until the cream or milk particles separated from the liquid, and butter was made. The fluid left was called buttermilk. An earthen pot, with a whirling wooden paddle, is still used today in some Indian villages as a process of making butter.

Salt was often added to the finished product as a preservative and the butter was stored in a container in the family well to keep it cool.

The first creamery in the United States that manufactured butter was built in the state of Iowa in 1871. Farmers would take their surplus milk to stations and sell it for conversion into butter and other dairy products.

The United States and the Soviet Union are world leaders in butter production.

There are several different types of butter packaged and available, including lightly salted, sweet cream, with no salt added and whipped butter that is sweet cream butter incorporating air or inert gas, thereby making it easier to spread.

Some, not all butter, is USDA graded and labeled accordingly to the quality. USDA AA, which is the very best, is made from fresh cream. It has a delicate, sweet flavor with smooth, creamy texture and spreads readily. It is either salted or unsalted; however, when salted the salt completely dissolves, and is distributed and blended in just the right amount to give an enhanced flavor. The USDA A is very good and made from cream that is only slightly less fresh. Although, rating second to the top grade, it will suit even the most discriminating consumers' taste. Too, it may be salted or unsalted. The USDA B is standard and made from sweet or sour cream; however, it does lack the flavor of the other two grades. It is either salted or unsalted.

Good butter should be a pale yellow, and should not show signs of "sweating" water.

All in a Woman's Day--June 30, 1987
Tips for milk and its by-products

As a conclusion to June as Dairy Month, in preparing foods a few tips might help in the use of milk and its by-products.

Buttermilk will freeze. If you purchase a quart or more of buttermilk and use only a portion of it, freeze the remainder. It would be well to use one cup containers as that is generally what is called for in a recipe.

If you want to save calories, use real sour cream to enhance taste and texture of a variety of foods. Try it as a replacement for higher calorie oils and mayonnaise in your favorite salad dressing recipe. There are 26 calories in a tablespoon of sour cream and 99 calories in a tablespoon of mayonnaise. A tablespoon of average French dressing has 65 calories.

If your commercial sour cream becomes outdated and tastes too sour for salads or dips, don't throw it away. Use it in place of sour milk in baking. Just add an extra half teaspoon of soda and a fourth cup of extra flour to the recipe.   Should you spill some milk, wipe it up immediately from enamel and porcelain. The lactic acid in the milk can stain these finishes.

Evaporated milk can be used in place of milk or cream in puddings and in cooking. It can really become a money-saving habit.

To make an inexpensive substitute for sour cream, use a cup of cottage cheese with two teaspoons of lemon juice and mix well in a blender until creamy.

Another way of making sour cream instantly is by stirring one tablespoon of vinegar, lemon juice or yogurt into an 8-ounce carton of real dairy cream.

A good way to melt butter is to turn an automatic coffeemaker on the warm switch and place a small pie tin or dish with the butter on the warming plate. The butter will slowly melt, and there is no risk of scorching or burning.

Since many people are interested in do-it-yourself projects, maybe you would like to make cottage cheese. Sour three quarts of milk until thick and put into a three and a half quart electric slow cooking pot. Set on low temperature and cover. Cook 2 1/2 hours, then drain in colander until curd is dry. Add cream, salt and pepper to taste. This is easy to do, and the cheese seems to turn out just right.

To keep cottage cheese or sour cream fresh after opening the carton, turn it upside down with the cover on tight. This keeps the air out of the container and the contents will stay fresh longer.

Weight is the most accurate way to determine the amount of cheese to use in a recipe. Four ounces of any cheese equals one cup firmly packed shredded cheese. The formula lets the cook know how much to buy for use in a recipe.

Thaw frozen fish in skim milk. The milk draws out the freezer-burn taste. The fish will have that fresh-caught flavor again.

No doubt we all have had trouble scorching milk. Try rinsing the pan with cold water before putting the milk in it and it won't come so near scorching.

What is ice milk? It is a frozen dessert made from milk, stabilizers and sweeteners. It contains between two and seven percent milk fat, and at least

11 percent total milk solids.

When milk has spoiled (and this holds true for any other odor in a room or car) just place a bar of soap so that it can absorb the odors. It has been suggested that Ivory® and Lux® work best.

Instead of putting cream or milk into mashed potatoes, try adding low calorie plain yogurt. It gives a sour cream taste without all the calories. Use a half cup for potatoes prepared for four servings.

When cooking with cheese, remember to keep it at a low temperature. Overcooked cheese becomes stringy and gluey.

When mixing dry powdered milk for drinking purposes, put in about eight ice cubes in place of one cup of water. It seems to dissolve better, and is good and cold for immediate drinking. Always be sure to shake the container good to help melt the ice.

Cheese wrapped in a paper towel dampened with vinegar keeps moist and fresh for a longer period of time.

As you know, real whipped cream has 10 times more calories than whipped nonfat dried milk, which is really easy to make. Mix a half cup dried milk and a half cup ice water for three to four minutes; add two tablespoons of lemon juice and beat three to four minutes. Then fold in a fourth cup of sugar and serve immediately. Always be sure the bowl and beaters are thoroughly chilled, and the water is ice cold.

Perhaps you already are aware that a new product is in the offing, although it may be several more years before it lands on the shelves in the supermarkets. It is sparkling milk, which may be the solution to the lagging dairy sales, and increased interest in nutrition. The dairy industry is developing a sparkling milk in cola, root beer, banana, coconut, peach, chocolate and pina colada flavors. The product is said to be more refreshing and thirst-quenching than regular milk. Too, it is supposed not to leave a film on the tongue.

People in the dairy industry are hoping that the bubbly milk will have an appeal to everyone, from the young to the elder.

* * *

This recipe for milk toast might be a bit different than you generally make, so you may want to try it for a change.

Milk Toast

Prepare a thin cream sauce that is made by melting in a double boiler top or small heavy saucepan, 2 tablespoons of butter or margarine with 1 tablespoon of flour stirred in, and blended over low heat. Then stir in 1 cup of cold milk or milk and cream, blending all together to keep smooth. Bring this slowly to a boil and cook 2 minutes, stirring constantly. Season to taste with salt and pepper. Into this white sauce dip 4 to 6 slices of toast. Place them on a plate or in a serving dish and pour remainder of the sauce over the toast. This can be sprinkled with parsley, chopped ham or diced hard cooked eggs.

All in a Woman's Day--July 7, 1987

Tasty beverages good all year-round

With summertime we think of cool refreshing beverages, that appease our taste buds. Perhaps the all around basic drink is iced tea, or it could be hot tea as many tea lovers enjoy that tasty beverage regardless of weather. No doubt, tea is the oldest surviving natural, prepared drink and is used by more people than any other drink throughout the world, with, of course, the exception of water.

Professionals may refer to tea as brisk, stylish, leafy; however, the average individual would call it relaxing, refreshing, soothing. The Chinese call it Ch'a, and the Japanese serve it in red lacquered cups at weddings.

The common tea plant is no doubt native to China, where it is said to have a magical cure for everything, and to drink it is, the "to taste sunlight, wind and clouds."

Most of our knowledge, however, about tea has come to us from England, or the English, where it is a time-honored beverage. The English tradition of teatime can be traced to the 17th century when Queen Catherine, wife of Charles II of England, was among the first to use tea and serve it to the English court.

Historical sources claim that this social custom should be credited to Ana, wife of the seventh duke of Bedford. In the mid-1840s, it was rather common to indulge in a large breakfast, then wait until late in the evening for the next formal meal. However, with the arrival of late afternoon, the duchess would often complain of suffering a "sinking" feeling, and to remedy this, she ordered tea, miniature sweets and sandwiches for the lords and ladies of her court. This ritual was greatly enjoyed over the daily gossip. And, so this most delightful afternoon break soon became an everyday ritual with English people of all classes.

Since then, several forms of teatime, both formal and informal, have evolved.

Following are a few ideas that perhaps you or friends might want to try as a part of this most cherished of customs:

There is Morning Tea: Perhaps you are waking up in England, if so, the sound of a whistling kettle is surely not far away. This early morning tea is a cup of hot tea with a cracker or a slice of bread and butter. Then, as morning nears an end, soon in sight is a break for tea. In England, this is known as "elevenses," and a cookie or two is served with the tea.

High Tea: This also is a favorite with the working class, even despite the fact that there is a formal sound to the name. This 6 p.m. event is actually a substantial evening meal that features meat pies and sandwiches, seafood (kippers and potted shrimp are favorites), hearty breads, savory sweets, assorted cheeses and cups of strong, hot tea. High tea does not require fancy bone china nor fine linens and lace.

Low or Afternoon Tea: Did you know that any tea other than a high or morning tea can be called a low or afternoon tea? It is served between 2 and 6 p.m. Many Americans are enjoying the resurgence of the popularity of this social custom, for they have the opportunity and pleasure of nibbling on treats and sipping a cup of soothing tea. Low tea can be formal or informal; however, it might be preferred. It is not determined by the manner of dress nor the presence of high society as one might be led to believe, but rather soley by the number of guests invited. When there are many guests, it generally is a stand-up affair; however, a small guest list permits them to be seated. Thus setting the tone for the high and low teas.

Nursery or Children's Tea: This simplest kind of fare, and the weakest of brewed tea, is the nursery or children's tea. In years gone by, often gingerbread, cinnamon toast or a modest slice of buttered bread with tea, softened the heightened appetites of children and their nannies.

Country Tea: Here we find homemade herbed and fruited breads dolloped with fresh whipped cream and jam or spread with seasoned butter, all of which tend to keep the teapot company when there is an afternoon country tea. A quilted cozy will keep the teapot warm. Always be sure the tea cannister (caddy) is filled, and the kettle ready, for there will most often be needed a second pot.

Cream Tea: We find the cream tea is simple, informal and delightfully pleasant. There is no better way to take a relaxing mid-afternoon break, than to sit down with a cup of tea and warm English scones topped with strawberry jam and Devonshire cream, which is a rich clotted cream made from nonhomogenized milk. Its flavor is slightly tart; however, yet similar to whipped, heavy cream. If you cannot find the true Devonshire cream in a gourmet or specialty shop, then just substitute unsweetened real whipped cream.

Russian scientists lay claim that tea helps the body rid itself of dangerous radioactive substances that are present in the system, and researchers at the University of California contend that drinking tea strengthens the blood vessels, thus preventing hardening of the arteries, as well as stopping deadly buildup of cholesterol levels in the blood, helping prevent many heart attacks and strokes.

Tea seems to be a beverage that grows more popular each year with all age groups. Hot, cold, spiced, plain or flavored, it is the drink that seems to suit almost everyone. It is considered a mild, but effective stimulant, as it contains 30 to 50 milligrams of caffeine as compared to 100 milligrams for coffee, depending, however, on the way it is brewed.

* * *

Cold Water Iced Tea

1 teaspoon of tea for each cup of water in a large pitcher. Add cold water, cover, and let it stand in the refrigerator 12 hours. Strain. This is an easy way to make very clear sparkling tea. This is an older version of making cold tea.

(Of course, we do not take this long most of the times, nowadays, as the instant teas seem to quench most thirsty appetites.)

* * *

Hot Tea

Rinse teapot with boiling water and measure tea into the pot or teaball, allowing 1/2 teaspoon of tea for each cup of freshly boiled water. Pour boiling water over tea; cover and allow it to steep 2 minutes. Strain and serve at once.

(Of course, again, this is the regular way for making tea, however, today's instant tea is used as well as tea bags, so it is less time consuming for most homemakers, who are so very busy.)

All in a Woman's Day--July 14, 1987

Easy tea recipes for all the seasons

Although this is the season for tea, especially iced tea; for some folks who enjoy tea, to its utmost, there is no special season for hot or cold tea.

Here are several hints that might be a

a:

ant cup of tea, ver the skin of es or lemons. n zest of the

d the sun just r tea bag in a vave on high ter to make

tea drinkers ," or "natu- But in case a bags in a set in the u will have

ea" in the ing direc- ot tap wa- with tags and set in s method the tea as fresh as that made in the sun, and you can continue to enjoy its freshness even in the wintertime.

Loose tea and tea bags should be stored in airtight containers and kept away from light. Tea that is fresh when purchased should keep about six months this way. Tea bags have a tendency to lose their flavor more quickly.

Iced tea is greatly improved if the cubes are made of tea instead of water.

Keep strong tea made from loose tea or tea bags in the refrigerator ready to make iced tea anytime. To make clear iced tea, run hot water until it clears and fill to desired strength with cold water. It's as clear as freshly made tea.

When making iced tea, add a tiny pinch (and I do mean tiny) of baking soda to the tea bags before pouring in boiling water. This will keep the tea from becoming cloudy in the refrigerator, and will not affect the taste.

To remove tea stains from china, dampen the spots with warm water, then rub briskly with table salt mixed with baking soda. Wash in warm soapy suds, rinse and dry in the usual way.

Remove the stains from china by soaking it overnight in a solution of denture cleaner.

When making iced tea, make it in the automatic coffeemaker for a change. Put the tea bag where you put the coffee and make as usual. You will get twice as much tea from one bag. You can use a quart size bag, and fill the coffeepot full. Unless you like strong tea, this will make two quarts.

And while this is not the kind of weather that most of us enjoy hot tea, the way the days, weeks and months slide by, it will soon be that time again. A cup of tea means different things to different people, and it is one thing that goes hand-in-glove with cold weather. To some it means a leisurely relaxing break in the day; a bracing warm-up drink, something special to linger over with friends; even a folk remedy for the sniffles.

For that time-honored tea, there have been some new twists added as some special blends have been put together to give teatime a new slant.

Never wash a tea strainer or a fine sieve in soapy water. Wash them in clear water to avoid an unpleasant flavor when the utensil is used again.

* * *

If you like Russian Tea or Friendship Tea, here is a recipe to be shared.

Russian or Friendship Tea
Mix 3/4 cup instant tea
2 cups dry orange breakfast drink

11/2 cups sugar
1 package (3-ounce) lemonade mix
11/2 teaspoons cinnamon
3/4 teaspoon cloves

Store in an airtight container. When ready to use it, take 3 teaspoons per cup of boiling water and add an additional teaspoon of sugar.

All in a Woman's Day--July 21, 1987

Vegetable ideas shared

Tiny vegetables have been dished up for some time in fashionable restaurants; however, some of them are just now becoming available in the supermarkets.

Among some of these miniature vegetables now offered to customers are baby golden beets, mini carrots, miniature turnips and baby kohlrabi. And, there is no doubt that shoppers can expect more varieties, and of course, even more competitive prices. Some of you gardeners perhaps have been harvesting some of these mini-veggies out of your gardens.

Fresh vegetables taste so good, they titillate the taste buds and bring important vitamins and minerals into the diet. They make meals perk up for flavor, texture, color and nutrition, when fresh on the menu. And, they really are easy to prepare, even though there are some unfortunate and unfounded ideas floating around that they are a lot of trouble.

Perhaps many homemakers would serve fresh vegetables more often if they knew more about cooking them.

Preparing and cooking fresh vegetables is really quite easy as there are several ways to consider.

The first method is cooking in water, which means using as little water as possible; adding the vegetables; bring-ing to a boil rapidly, covering the pot and lowering the heat to keep vegetables just simmering; cooking only until tender, never mushy.

Among the vegetables cooked by this method are asparagus, green beans, broccoli, brussels sprouts, cabbage, carrots, cauliflower, spinach, mustard greens, Swiss chard, kale, collards, parsnips, potatoes, yellow crookneck, white button, butternut and zucchini squashes.

The second method is stir-frying. This involves a heavy skillet (however, often used now is a wok). Heat about two tablespoons of oil or butter and add about one pound of cut up vegetables. Stir over high heat for 3 to 5 minutes until crisp-tender.

Vegetables especially suited to stir-frying include celery, green peppers, broccoli, cabbage, carrots mushrooms, onions, zucchini and eggplant. Vegetables cooked by this method have a different taste and texture, so this might be a new way to try.

Then there is the method of cooking vegetables by baking. Potatoes and squash are especially suited to this type of cooking. For potatoes, scrub the baking size, prick them in a few places with a fork and bake at 425 degrees for 45 minutes to one hour

For squash, butternut or acorn, cut in half, discard seeds and place it in baking pan. Add water to about half-inch and bake at 375 degrees for 45 minutes. For Hubbard squash, cut it into pieces, place in a pan as mentioned above and cook accordingly.

Another, up-to-date method, is the microwave. For instructions check your recipe booklet.

Preparing fresh vegetables for cooking are sometimes mystifying the first time around. Most vegetables need a little mild barbering before going into the cooking pot; however, try to confine the action to a light trim. Broccoli calls for trimming off the rough, dry part at the base; then slitting the stem upwards so that it will cook in about the same time as the flowery head. Cauliflower calls for slicing off the coarse underpart and cutting off the stalks that cup the head. It can then be cooked whole or in pieces in water.

Most vegetables do not require peeling, with the exception of carrots. The peel on such vegetables as eggplant, zucchini and yellow crookneck squash has both flavor and good nutrition, so don't discard the peeling.

While most vegetables are cooked best by basic methods; fresh corn on the cob is a law unto itself. It is practically a religion with discriminating eaters to cook fresh corn to perfection, and that requires the following procedure: Fresh corn requires very little cooking and it is very important to cook it ONLY until the milk in the kernels is set. While most vegetables become softer with longer cooking, not so with corn, it becomes firmer and tough when overcooked. It is suggested that only one ear of corn per person be cooked at one time. Half fill a large kettle with water, add one teaspoon salt per quart of water and bring it to a boil. Add corn and boil covered, just until milk in kernels is set, three to six minutes.

Remove ears with tongs and serve them immediately with butter or a favorite sauce. Then cook the second batch. The cooking will vary with the size of an ear of corn and oftentimes with the variety. It might be well to "test an ear" to determine the actual cooking time. If it is necessary to cook ahead of serving time, turn off the heat when the corn is added to the boiling water, then cover and let corn stand until you are ready to serve it.

Another vegetable, that is an exception to the rule is the artichoke, that fascinating object that looks like an ornamental top to a bedpost more than it looks like something to eat. However, it is edible and a very delicious vegetable, too. Here is the way to cook artichokes. Allow one artichoke per serving. Wash and cut half-inch off top of each artichoke. Cut off stems. Using scissors, cut off sharp tips on leaves. Add artichokes to boiling salted water, to cover, in a deep saucepan. Add one thick lemon slice for each artichoke. Cover and cook 30 to 40 minutes or until an outside leaf pulls off easily. Using two large spoons, remove from water and drain. Serve with lemon butter or Hollandaise sauce.

We, Americans are lucky to have fresh vegetables in season at our markets. Choose your cooking method and enjoy this wonderful bounty of good flavor, texture and important nutrition. Try to enjoy a different fresh vegetable each day!

All in a Woman's Day--July 28, 1987
Peaches are most plentiful this season

"How sweet it is," that of course, is speaking of Missouri peaches that are now in season.

Many of us presumed there would be few peaches this year after the freeze in the spring; however, Mother Nature seems to have a way of overcoming even the most difficult situations. So, regardless of the weather, there is a peach crop in Missouri, where some of the finest peaches are grown.

What could be more tempting than a peach highly colored with a red blush and delicious yellow fruit, or white meat, if it is preferred?

Peaches are nothing new as they have been around for a long time.

The peach tree is native of China, where it has been grown for thousands of years for its fruit and its beautiful decorative flowers.

It reportedly traveled along the caravan routes from China to Persia centuries ago, and thus its botanical name Prunus Persica. In the event you were not aware, peaches were once called Persian apples.

Too, the early Romans relished this fresh, delectable fruit and spread it throughout Europe, where it continued to increase in popularity. Peaches were brought to the New World by the Spaniards. The trees have been growing in Mexico since the late 1500s. Here the peach trees were carried inland by the Indians, with the French settlers in Louisiana and the colonists planting the trees in those areas. The plantings in the states were before 1629. Missouri settlers planted the trees in this state, where recipes using peaches have become a tradition.

Perhaps the best known variety is the Elberta, a freestone peach, that originated in 1870 in Marshallville, Ga.

Peach trees grow in most temperate regions, and are second only to apples in distribution throughout the world.

The peach, since time immemorial, has captured the imagination of the poets and artists. The peach in China was considered the symbol of a long life. Peach blossoms were painted on porcelain and given as birthday gifts to express the wish for many happy years. Chinese and Japanese poetry and art give lavish praise to the charming pink blossom and the fruit of the peach.

The peach is a rounded fruit, fuzzy, velvet skin that is creamy yellow when ripe, ordinarily. The nectarine, a variation of the peach, has a smooth skin.

There are hundreds of ways of serving peaches, canned, fresh, or dried—and all are delicious. Peaches also are distilled into a liqueur, as well as made into nectar.

* * *

Following is a recipe that is similar to a cobbler; however, it is called pudding. It is not rich like a pie, but has a good, delectable flavor. Too, any fruit can be used-fresh or canned.

Peach Pudding

1 cup flour
1 cup sugar
2 teaspoons baking powder
1/2 teaspoon salt
2/3 cup milk

Peel and slice as many fresh peaches as desired, and sugar to taste. Place them in a greased pan approximately 10 1/2x7. Mix ingredients and pour batter over the top of the fruit and bake it in a 350 degree oven 45 minutes. Serve with cream, ice cream, whipped cream or whipped topping.

All in a Woman's Day--August 4, 1987
Everything is peachy

Everything is coming up peachy! So, let us again think and eat peaches, for they are still on the market and will be for sometime yet. Some peaches ripen in early summer, some on into fall, and some as late as October; so, we should have peaches for several weeks.

The Chinese considered peaches a symbol of immortality and Alexander the Great dined on peaches while he was encamped in Russia. So, considering these facts, it is no wonder we enjoy this wonderful folkloric fruit. The lovely color of peaches and the fragrant aroma have led to many popular expressions such as "What a peach!" and "Everything's peachy!" Of course, all young girls want that "peaches and cream" complexion.

Fresh peaches have a lot to offer consumers, and although there are many varieties available, only an expert can distinguish one from another.

These varieties, however, fall into two general types: freestone (flesh readily separates from the pit) and clingstones (flesh clings tightly to the pit.) Most often the freestones are preferred for eating fresh or for cooking and freezing, while clingstones are used primarily for canning.

When selecting either type, always look for peaches that are firm or becoming slightly soft. The skin color between the red blush areas should have a yellow or creamy undercolor, with a well-designed crease. Always avoid very firm or hard peaches that have a green background color. They may be immature and won't ripen fully into the real peach flavor. Peaches really don't ripen much after being picked. They become softer and juicier, but still retain that unripe flavor, and often unripe peaches will shrivel with age. Also avoid very soft fruit as that indicates overripeness.

Many homemakers prefer to peel peaches; however, it is not necessary since superfluous fuzz is now removed before they reach the supermarket; however, some forms of preparation of the peach require peeling. To do so, just dip the peach in boiling water for 15 to 20 seconds, then plunge into a bowl of ice water. The skin should slide off easily.

Once the peach is skinned, it will darken in color, so to prevent this, dip peach slices into a citrus juice such as orange, pineapple or lemon. Some recipes call for ascorbic acid powder. This, too, is to keep the natural peach color bright and does not affect the flavor of the fruit.

Always handle the fruit gently as peaches bruise easily and decay soon develops. Don't choose a peach by its "blush," for many varieties do not turn red as they ripen.

Peaches should be stored in the refrigerator, where they will keep about a week. Soften peaches at room temperature and then move to the refrigerator.

When pureeing peaches, always add ascorbic acid before whirring them in the blender. Peach puree may be substituted for the liquid in cake or muffin mixes for a different and refreshing change. The puree used instead of water in both the cake and glaze for a bundt cake makes a pretty and exceptionally moist product.

Remember, when preparing recipes using peaches that about three or four medium-sized peaches will equal a pound. One pound will yield about two cups of sliced peaches or pulp. Approximately one to one and a half pounds of fresh peaches are needed for each pint of home canned or frozen peaches.

* * *

Here are two recipes you might enjoy trying:

Peach Punch

2 cups sugar
2 cups water

1 pint peach nectar (see note below)
1 (6-ounce) can frozen orange juice concentrate
1 (6-ounce) can frozen pineapple juice concentrate
3/4 cup lemon juice
2 large bottles of gingerale, chilled

Note: To make peach nectar, peel 1 pound ripe peaches, pit and cut into quarters, sprinkle them with 1/4 teaspoon ascorbic acid, or 1 teaspoon of commercial fruit fresh preparation. Place peaches in food blender, add 2 tablespoons of sugar, and blend on low speed 15 to 20 seconds. Freeze. To make punch, combine sugar and water, stirring to dissolve. Add nectar and juices, then, just before serving, add gingerale. Chill. Yields 20 to 25 servings

* * *

Simple Peach Swirls with Glaze
1 can refrigerated parker house rolls
1 to 2 fresh peaches (about 1 cup), chopped fine
1 teaspoon ascorbic acid powder or Fruit Fresh®
1/4 cup sugar
Dash of nutmeg, if desired

Remove all rolls from can to a floured board. Lightly work them together and roll into a rectangle about 1/4 inch thick. Sprinkle chopped peaches evenly on surface. Mix sugar, ascorbic acid powder and nutmeg. Sprinkle evenly over peaches. Roll up jelly roll fashion, beginning with long side of dough. Cut in slices and place in a well greased pan with sliced side up. Dot with butter if desired. Bake in 425 degree oven about 25 minutes. Ice with fresh glaze. Makes approximately 9 swirls.

Glaze:
1 cup sifted powdered sigar

1 1/2 tablespoons fresh peach puree
Mix until smooth and drizzle over baked swirls.

All in a Woman's Day--August 11, 1987
Sandwiches: the quick fix

This is Sandwich Month, and they are good whenever they are served; however, we make them work overtime during the summer months. They are the quick fix food for busy days.

Sandwiches have come a long way since John Montagu, the fourth Earl of Sandwich, refused to leave his gaming table for dinner, and bade his servants to bring him roast meat between two slices of bread. That was in the 18th century, and roast beef on rye is still a fine, hearty sandwich.

Today, however, we find that sandwich lovers everywhere use their imaginations to combine foods that are different in taste and texture. Many new breads are available, adding special accent to the choice of fillings.

Sandwiches are quick, easy to fix and please children, as well as adults, and they can be served hot or cold, just as the weather demands.

Most of them can be made ahead of time, making them perfect for picnics and busy days.

Too, most sandwich fillings and breads freeze satisfactorily; however, there are some foods that do not freeze, such as fresh lettuce, celery, tomatoes, carrots and other crisp vegetables that change in flavor and texture when frozen. These, of course, can be added after sandwiches are thawed.

Making a quantity of sandwiches at a time to freeze will save time, energy, making it is an easy way to have a variety of sandwiches on hand.

When freezing sandwiches be sure to

remember that jams and jellies soak into bread; mayonnaise and salad dressings tend to separate when frozen, although they can be used in small amounts as binders in frozen sandwiches. Hard cooked egg whites develop flavors and become rather rubbery when frozen. Cheese crumbles, so it should be grated, cubed or shredded.

If several sandwiches are to be made at once, lay out slices of bread in rows; spread them with softened butter or cream cheese. Then spread fillings on every other slice of bread. Close sandwiches with remaining bread.

Some fillings that might be of interest include peanut butter and crumbled bacon; peanut butter and applesauce; cottage cheese, raisins and chopped pecans; dried beef and chili sauce; diced beef, cream cheese and horseradish; tuna, salad dressing and orange sections; chicken, cream cheese and orange ring; and salami and cream cheese.

With back-to-school time almost here, for many youngsters it means brown bags and lunch boxes. This also goes for many adults, who tire of "eating out" and enjoy a lunch to suit their own taste buds.

Pita bread is the basis for a new adventure in sandwiches. The mainstay of many Middle Eastern cultures and a relative newcomer to our shores, it calls for unexpected combinations.

Pocket bread also is ideal for brown bag sandwiches. Prepare cooked, chopped chicken, diced scallions, mushrooms, greens and radishes, plus mayonnaise or salad dressing, and it is a meal-in-one.

For many hot sandwiches, a smooth and tasty white sauce is the foundation. The basic white sauce proportions are as follows:

Thin: One tablespoon of butter, one tablespoon of flour, a fourth teaspoon of salt and one cup of milk.

Medium: Two tablespoons of butter, two tablespoons of flour, a fourth teaspoon of salt, and one cup of milk.

Thick: Four tablespoons of butter, four tablespoons of flour, a fourth of teaspoon salt and one cup of milk.

In the top of a double boiler or in a heavy pan, melt the butter, add the flour and cook until bubbly. Then add milk slowly while stirring briskly. Cook and stir until the sauce has no starchy taste and is as thick or as thin as desired. If it becomes, too thick, add milk. If too thin, add flour. Then let your taste inspire the seasoning.

* * *

Baked Chicken Sandwiches

8 slices bread
Sliced, cooked chicken
4 slices American or cheddar cheese
4 eggs
2 cups milk
Salt to taste
Butter or margarine

Grease an 8x9-inch baking pan or dish. Trim crusts from bread, and butter. Place 4 slices of bread, buttered side down, in baking dish. Add layer of chicken and 4 slices of cheese. Top with remaining slices of bread with buttered side up. Whip eggs, milk and salt and pour over sandwiches. Cover with aluminum foil and store overnight in refrigerator. Bake at 350-degrees, uncovered for 55 to 60 minutes or until egg mixture is firm, and top is golden brown. Serve with a sauce made with 1 can of cream of mushroom soup mixed with 1/2 can of milk, heated. Makes four sandwiches. Tuna or ham cam be substituted for the chicken. This is good without a sauce; however, it could be used if desired.

* * *

Bun-Steads

These may be made ahead of time, refrigerated and baked when needed.

1/4 pound cubed American cheese
1 can (7-ounce) tuna
3 hard-boiled eggs, chopped
2 tablespoons chopped onion
2 tablespoons diced green peppers
2 tablespoons stuffed olives
2 tablespoons chopped sweet pickles
1/2 cup mayonnaise
10 to 12 hot dog buns

Combine ingredients, fill buns and wrap each in foil. Heat in a 250 degree oven for about half an hour.

All in a Woman's Day--August 18, 1987

Extraordinary ideas make impressions

We are still thinking sandwiches. There are so many good fillings that make them extraordinary.

For special tea sandwiches try various flavors, colors, textures and shapes, using nuts, parsley and sieved egg yolk for trim.

If you are making sandwiches for a cocktail party, make them as you do for a tea party; however, do not use sweet fillings.

It is always easier to cut bread into fancy shapes if it has been frozen ahead of time.

If the bread for sandwiches is not frozen, then chill it in refrigerator several hours so that it will be easier to handle.

When making peanut butter and jelly sandwiches, to prevent them from becoming soggy, always spread a thin coating of peanut butter on each slice of bread and then spread the jelly so it will be in-between.

You will find that ready-sliced bread most often is just too thick for any sandwich except lunchbox or picnic; however, a long sharp French knife cuts slices in half smoothly. A loaf of bread that weighs one and one-fourth pounds cut this way will make 16 to 24 slices, and a two pound loaf will cut into 45 or 48 slices.

As you know, butter for sandwiches should be softened at room temperature. Should you be making a large amount of sandwiches, beat the butter with an electric mixer or a spoon so that it is fluffy and soft.

Then beat into it a half cup of milk for each pound of butter. Allow approximately four tablespoons butter for 16 whole slices of bread.

To store sandwiches, place them in a tightly closed cellophane bag, aluminum foil or wax paper.

Party sandwiches prepared in advance can be arranged on plates, covered with wax paper and a cloth that has been slightly dampened. Store in the refrigerator or some other cool place. If they are to be frozen, wrap in freezer paper and they will keep at least three months. Thaw before serving.

Should the filling for sandwiches be very moist, make the sandwiches just before serving so that they will not become soaked.

Fillings that are good for toasted sandwiches are marmalade, chopped ham, peanut butter, sliced tomatoes, chopped meat, fish or chicken mixed with mayonnaise and seasoned.

French toast sandwiches also are good with any of these fillings.

For tea sandwiches always have the layer of filling thin so that it will not press out. Of course, for heartier sandwiches have the layer generous, cover and press slices firmly together.

Too, if you are making a smooth filling, such as cream cheese, butter only one slice of bread for each sandwich.

Some folks prefer to spread one slice of bread with butter and some with mayonnaise for certain sandwiches.

Baking powder biscuit sandwiches are a bit different. Make tiny biscuits using a packaged mix or your own recipe. Split, butter and put together with deviled ham spread, shaved maple sugar, thin slices of cheese or chopped chicken, which can be moistened with a hot gravy or cream sauce, (if desired), halved and sugared strawberries or jam.

Club sandwiches are definitely hearty and usually consist of two or three decks. They are generally made with buttered toast, plenty of sliced chicken or other meat, lettuce, sliced tomatoes and mayonnaise. They can be topped with a slice or two of crispy fried bacon. If you plan to serve a club sandwich with a fork, be sure and cut it diagonally in quarters, so that it can be easily handled.

If you would like to try making waffle sandwiches, just spread the outside of the bread lightly with butter. The filling, which generally is orange marmalade or a bit of cheese, perhaps dotted with a few drops of Worcestershire, is spread between the slices. Then toast in a waffle iron.

Banana, date and apricot breads are excellent for sandwiches.

* * *

Swiss and Ham Spread
1 cup coarsely ground cooked ham
1 cup shredded Swiss cheese
1/2 cup drained sweet pickle relish
1/4 teaspoon orange flavoring
3/4 cup mayonnaise or salad dressing
Dash of cinnamon

Combine all ingredients and spread mixture on bread, white, whole wheat or rye. This also is delicious with crackers.

All in a Woman's Day--August 25, 1987

Salt is important in the human diet

We have all heard the expression "He isn't worth his salt." Of course, the implication is that he isn't worth much, just as salt is inexpensive and a plentiful commodity. Then a quote from Matthew 5:13: "Ye are the salt of the earth," a statement made by Jesus, means in this instance, of course, "great worth."

Salt was very precious in Jesus' day, and for that matter, still is a necessity. At one time, salt was so highly prized that wars were fought for the possession of salt flats and springs. Often soldiers, back in the days of the Romans, were paid with salt as full or part payment for services rendered. As a result, the word salary is derived from the ancient word salarium, meaning salt money. In that era a bag of salt was considered as valuable as a man's life.

Salt has been most important as a seasoning and preserving agent since prehistoric times. It was commonly used in the altar offering of the ancient Greeks, Romans and Hebrews. It was an important medium of exchange in the commercial ventures across the Mediterranean, Aegean and Adriatic Seas, and it has been subject to severe taxation in Oriental countries from ancient to modern times.

Because of its usefulness in preserving foods, it was used by the ancients as a symbol of enduring faith. In the

539

form of salt cakes, it served as money in ancient Ethiopia and Tibet. Because of their need of salt, animals, wild or domesticated, often gathered at salt streams or surface incrustations of salt, called "salt licks," to lick the incrusted salt.

Because of the sacredness and dignity of salt, this mineral is like unto the four elements: earth, air, fire and water; so universal, so necessary to life, it has become known as the fifth element.

According to folklore, salt is supposed to ward off spirits, and throwing a pinch of salt over the left shoulder is a ceremony that in some countries means keeping the devil at a distance.

Too, the spilling of salt is a bad omen and is commonly interpreted as the sign of a quarrel, possibly because the acceptance of salt indicates friendly hospitality.

There seems little danger that we will run out of salt as all water contains a small amount of it, and beds of salt that were laid down in the past are to be found in many of our states, as well as numerous foreign countries. Such salt layers have been worked extensively in California, New York, Michigan, Kansas and Utah. Of course, if this source of salt should ever become depleted, there is a vast amount of ocean water from which it could be derived.

Salt, seems so important in our lives, but for health reasons we shy away from it all that we can. We use various spices, seasonings and herbs to cover up the lack of salt in our diet. However, if you go on a salt free diet for several days, you will know just how much salt does to bring out the fullness and flavor of foods.

Salt, widely used in the preservation of fish and meats, also is used in brine for making pickles and sauerkraut. Too, it is widely used in some refrigeration processes, in dyeing and in the manufacture of soaps and glass. In the chemical industry, salt is an important source of chlorine and is used in the manufacture of common sodium, common sodium compounds, such as soda cake or washing soda, sodium carbonate and sodium phosphate.

Today, we are lucky to have all kinds of toothpaste to suit our fancy; however, many will recall how salt was used for brushing teeth (it also was said to be good for the gums), and as a popular gargle.

Too, I am sure many of you will remember the old salt barrel for home and stock alike. The cost was about two dollars a barrel. That was a lot of money at that time; however, the livestock must have salt. Someone was always around to help load the barrel of salt on a wagon. The salt barrels were made of thin staves, with several wire bands around it to hold it together. One salt barrel would often last a year or two. The salt was carried to the barnyard in wooden boxes and the livestock always knew just where to find it.

Table salt, was available; however, it came in small sacks selling from five to eight cents a sack. A sack of salt could become hard because of the mositure, but if it did, a hammer would break it up. Salt in sacks was called "refined salt," and it was a little finer than salt in the barrel. Today, farmers mostly use blocks of salt for the livestock.

In previous columns the importance of salt has been told. There are some added things salt is known for, and that will help to make everyday living a bit easier.

Salt, or sodium chloride, perhaps has as its biggest use, deicing for highways and is among the cheapest and handiest of cleaning materials.

Foods will cook faster in salted water because it boils at a slightly higher than normal temperature.

A mixture of salt and cinnamon rubbed on oven burners helps keep them clean.

If you have bags under your eyes, so to speak, mix a teaspoon of salt in a pint of hot water and apply pads soaked in the solution.

If you want to prevent candles from dripping just soak them in a strong salt solution, letting them become well dried before using.

The sweaty odor in sneakers and other canvas shoes can be lessened by sprinkling salt inside of them.

Did you know that salt and olive oil mixed together in equal parts make a stimulating facial? Apply the mixture upward and inward.

Applied under medical supervision, salt is said to be able to remove tattos. The treatment is called "salabrasion." Several applications are needed.

Hot salt water will help relieve poison ivy irritation.

Mold can be kept from forming in cheese by wrapping the cheese in a cloth that has been soaked in salt water before the cheese is refrigerated.

Goldfish can be made happy and healthier if they are given a salt bath of a teaspoon of salt in a quart of fresh water. They should be left 15 minutes in the salt solution before they are returned to their own tank. (This you need to try at your own risk.)

Salt and lemon juice make a good cleaner for ivory piano keys and marble.

Good luck as you go about your "salty" way.

* * *

Chef's Salt

1 cup salt
1 tablespoon paprika, Hungarian or Spanish
1 teaspoon freshly ground black pepper
1/4 teaspoon white pepper
1/4 teaspoon garlic salt (not garlic powder)

Mix all ingredients well. Keep in a jar and use it instead of regular salt.

All in a Woman's Day--September 1, 1987

Fig history told; recipes are shared

Did you ever eat a succulent fresh fig? If not you have a treat in store for you. Fresh figs become available in midsummer, and of course, dried figs are available all year round.

When purchasing fresh figs you will find they can be purple or pale green. They should be a bit soft and look well filled out. When they are cut they should look pink and juicy inside. Fresh figs can be stored in the refrigerator, and the outer skin can be pared off with a sharp knife. Cut in slices and served with cream, is a favorite way of serving figs fresh. When figs are fully ripe, they need no sugar.

There are numerous varieties of dried figs. Especially good are the plump figs from the Mediterranean and Middle East. Sometimes they are sold packaged and sometimes in the bulk by stores that feature imported goods.

Another way to use them raw, and a tasty way, too, is to serve them sliced with thin pieces of country ham as an appetizer. Stewed dried figs are good eating as are figs in baked goods and puddings.

Canned figs also are available. Served chilled, they make a tasty change of pace.

The common commercial fig, a native of Southwest Asia, is widely cultivated in tropical and subtropical climates. Most of the figs grown in the Mediterranean region are dried before they are marketed. In the United States, California and Texas are the major centers of the fig produc-tion. The more popular California varieties are Calimyrna, Kadota and Mission. They are packed fresh or dried. Because of the humidity in the Texas fig-growing region, most of them are canned.

There is another species of figs, a taller tree, that also bears edible fruit. The figs are pear-shaped, sweet and slightly aromatic. This is the tree, sycamore, mentioned several times in the Old Testament. It is still a favorite shade tree in the Near East. The pipal, or sacred fig, is another member of the genus family growing in Southeast Asia. It is venerated by Buddhists and Brahmins. It is known as the Bo tree. The Banyan, or Indian fig tree, produces edible fruits that are occasionally eaten in India.

Several unrelated plants are sometimes called fig. For example, the plantain, a large edible tropical fruit resembling the banana, also is known as Adam's fig. A prickly pear is called the Indian fig because of its fig-shaped fruit.

California dried figs are a gift to the natural food lover. The wonderful vitamin and mineral rich figs are allowed to mature fully on the trees, and after partially drying, they are allowed to fall. Then they are spread on trays to dry naturally in the sun, concentrating the fruit sugar for energy and flavor.

There are simple or easy ways to enjoy figs.

A gray or Calimyrna and Mission dried figs served on a tray as a snack with dairy sour cream dip makes a delightful change. To make the dip add two teaspoons of finely grated orange peel, two tablespoons of orange juice, one tablespoon of honey and a fourth teaspoon of nutmeg. Blend thoroughly and serve.

To make a beautiful sandwich, without using bread, take layers of one and a half-inch squares of mild, natural cheese slices and thin sliced cooking ham. Top with dried Calimyrna or Mission figs split lengthwise.

Fig bars also offer unique snack ideas. For instance, toast and serve them warm for a taste change. Spread peanut butter on them to enrich them, or spread cream cheese on them for a new flavor. Also they can be crumbled in plain yogurt and eaten with a spoon.

* * *

Stewed Dried Figs

1 pound dried figs
1 tablespoon lemon juice
Cold water to cover
1/2 cup sugar
Sherry, vanilla or more lemon juice

Place the figs, water and lemon juice in a saucepan; cover it and simmer them until they are tender. Take out the figs and add to the juice the sugar and cook until thick. Flavor to taste with the sherry, vanilla or lemon juice. Pour this over the figs; cool and serve with cream. This will serve 6. Too, they can be served in a goblet with a bit of the juice and topped with sour cream or soft custard.

Stewed Figs

1 cup figs

1/2 cup sugar

Wash figs, remove stems, cover with water and simmer 20 to 30 minutes or until tender. Add sugar and simmer 10 minutes. Cool. Serves 4.

* * *

Fig Fritters

Prepare fritter batter and add 2 cups drained, preserved figs. Drop the mixture by spoonfuls into the deep fat at 365 degrees. Fry these until they are evenly browned. Drain them on crumpled absorbent paper, and sprinkle with powdered sugar. Serve with a lemon sauce. Makes 8 servings.

All in a Woman's Day--September 8, 1987

Cooking terms to clip

Some more cooking terms can be clipped to add to the list that was printed earlier.

A baking sheet is a thin oblong sheet of metal approximately 12x15 inches.

A pour batter contains one part flour and one part liquid.

A soft batter contains approximately one and one-third to two parts flour to one part liquid.

A medium batter contains three parts flour to one part liquid.

A stiff batter contains approximately four parts flour to one part liquid.

A soft or rolled dough is one that is just stiff enough to be rolled on a lightly floured board. Thoroughly chilled, a soft dough makes it possible to handle with a minimum use of flour on the board.

A stiff dough is one that is just stiff enough to be kneaded without sticking to a lightly floured board.

Cubing is cutting food by means of scissors or a sharp knife into small pieces of approximately the same width, length and thickness.

Lightly flouring is covering a bread board or other surface with a thin coating of flour.

Mashing is crushing food until its original form is entirely lost.

Slicing is cutting food into broad, thin pieces.

Lightly oiling is covering a baking sheet or other surface with a thin film of any melted cooking fat.

Well oiling is thoroughly covering a surface with any melted cooking fat.

Egging and crumbing is dipping molded food into beaten egg, then rolling in fine crumbs and again dipping in egg. This forms a coating that hardens immediately when food is immersed in deep hot fat, thus aiding in preventing absorption of the cooking fat.

Buttered bread or cracker crumbs are made by rolling dry bread or crackers into fine crumbs. Add melted butter or butter substitute and mix well, using the proportion of two tablespoons of butter to each cup of crumbs.

Caramelizing sugar is done by heating sugar in a heavy frying or saucepan, stirring constantly, until a golden brown syrup is formed. Remove it from the heat immediately.

A griddle or waffle iron is sufficiently hot for baking when it will snap with a drop of cold water on it. Drop the water on the utensil when it is smoking hot.

Scalding milk is done by placing milk over hot water until a film forms on the surface; when ready to use, stir film into the milk.

Scalloped foods are prepared by using finely shredded or chopped, cooked meat or fish and diced or sliced, cooked or uncooked vegetables. Fill a well-oiled baking dish with alternate layers of food and medium white sauce. Cover the top with buttered bread crumbs and bake it in a 375 degree oven until it is thoroughly cooked. Uncover and allow to brown.

Creamed foods are prepared by using freshly cooked or leftover meat, fish, poultry or vegetables. Leave whole or cubed as desired. Prepare a medium white sauce and add it to the food to be creamed. Mix lightly or add sauce to food after it has been placed in the serving dish. Allow from half to three-fourths cup sauce for each cup of food.

Souffles are prepared by using finely shredded or chopped meat, fish, vegetables or grated cheese. Prepare a thick, well-seasoned white sauce. Add the well-beaten yolks of three eggs and stir until blended. Fold in the stiffly beaten egg whites. Pour into a well-oiled baking dish and bake in a 375 degree oven until an inserted knife comes out clean.

Croquettes are made by grinding food material or separate it into fine shreds. Prepare a thick well-seasoned white sauce. Add one cup of sauce to each three cups of prepared food. Mix until well blended. The mixture should be as soft as can be handled. Cool. Allow from one to two tablespoons for each croquette. Form with two spatulas, on a lightly floured board, into cylinders, cones or balls. They should be uniform in size. Dip each into slightly beaten egg, diluted with one tablespoon of water, in crumbs and again in egg. Fry in deep fat 365 degrees, until brown. Drain on crumpled, absorbent paper.

* * *

Date Pie

2/3 cup sugar
1/2 cup butter or margarine
1 cup chopped dates
1/2 cup chopped nuts
1 teaspoon vanilla
2 egg whites

Soften the butter and then cream the sugar and butter. Add the dates, nuts and vanilla. Beat the egg whites until they are stiff, but not dry, and cut them into the other mixture. Spread in an unbaked pie shell and bake in a 350 degree oven one hour, or until the crust is brown. This is very rich and delicious. It can be topped with whipped cream or whipped topping.

All in a Woman's Day--September 15, 1987
More kitchen helps

It is again time have a few more helpful hints for the homemaker to use in the kitchen.

Kiwi fruit is great for tenderizing meat. Just slice it on top of the meat and allow it to stand 30 minutes for each half-inch of thickness.

When baking bread if you don't have enough loaf pans, try using a four-cup Pyrex measuring cup. Grease the cup, fill and bake as you would a loaf pan. You will have a nice round loaf of bread.

If whipped cream has to remain on the table for any length of time, mix in a small amount of gelatin. This will keep the cream from melting down too rapidly.

If in need of some marshmallow creme and you do not have any, take 16 large marshmallows (four cups) for one cup marshmallow creme and melt. (ten miniature marshmallows equal one large marshmallow.)

Muffins will be lighter if the muffin tins are placed in the oven and heated before pouring the batter into them.

To choose the sweet oranges, examine their navels. Choose the ones with the largest holes.

To keep meat loaf from cracking, dip your hand in cold water and rub the top of the meat loaf until smooth. Place loaf in oven and bake.

How do you select the best pears? With your nose. The fragrance tells you if they are ripe. This bouquet can vary in strength and character from variety to variety. Also, just press gently around the stem. If you find that it gives slightly, it is ready for eating. If pears are picked early, ripening can be hastened by placing them in a box or perforated bag with an already ripe apple.

Pot a few chives from your herb garden before winter comes. Place this on your window sill and you will have chives to snip all winter. By clipping them often and closely, they will be prettier and not become "leggy."

When making soup and broth, add a tablespoon of vinegar to the meat bones while cooking. Extra calcium will be drawn from the bones. The vinegar will not change the flavor.

A dampened tea bag has many uses. Hang it by a string from the lid of your brown sugar container, and it will soften the sugar. Also use a tea bag to soften molasses cookies or marshmallows that are hard. By the third day the marshmallows will be soft, except those on the bottom, so just stir them and let them stand a little while longer, and they will be softened.

Soak prunes in pineapple juice instead of water. Allow them to stand until quite plump and soft. You will like their unusual flavor.

Take advantage of sales of butter, margarine and peanut butter. All can be frozen. If you use peanut butter frequently, buy the large economy jar and freeze it in smaller containers.

Did you know you can make your own yellow rice? Just add half teaspoon of tumeric to one cup uncooked rice and cook normally.

Use a vegetable shortening to spray the top part of a double boiler when you prepare hot cereals, corn meal mush or steamed rice. Also spray the spoon for easy serving.

To test to see if your baking powder is old, put one teaspoon of it in a half cup hot tap water. Good powder will bubble with zip.

When canning or cooking pears for sauce, dissolve some red hots in the liquid. This adds a rosy hue.

When making custard, drop a regular size marshmallow into each custard cup before pouring in the custard mixture. During the baking, the marshmallow will rise to the top and melt, forming a crispy meringue.

Add a little sugar to tomato or vegetable soup to bring out the flavor and improve the taste.

If you will set pies and cobblers on racks to cool, the bottom crust will be less soggy.

Mushrooms will stay fresh longer if they are removed from the box and stored in a brown paper bag in the refrigerator.

* * *

Jewel Cranberry Salad

1 package cranberries
1 package raspberry gelatin
1 small can crushed pineapple
1 1/2 cups sugar
1/2 cup chopped nuts

Wash and drain the cranberries. Start to cook them with 1 cup of water. When nearly all have popped, add the sugar and let them cook a few minutes longer. Remove from the heat and stir in the gelatin, continue to stir until dissolved. Cool until syrupy, and add the pineapple with juice and the nuts. Chill. This is attractive served in a clear glass bowl.

All in a Woman's Day--September 22, 1987
Some more of those good kitchen hints

If you like making your own croutons from leftover or dried out bread, try this hint. The next time you fry bacon, drain the bacon on the bread. Put the bread into the freezer until you are ready to make the croutons. The bacon drippings add a zesty flavor. This is good when making salad dressings, too.

Don't you wish the yolks of an egg would stay centered when boiled? Simply stir them gently for a minute when they begin to simmer. This should do the trick.

Before you begin to measure a cup full of honey, wipe the cup with cooking oil and rinse with hot water. The honey won't stick.

Here's a simple, easy way to cook macaroni or spaghetti. Bring to a boil two quarts of water, then add seven ounces of macaroni or two cups broken spaghetti. Let water come to a boil again. Remove from heat and cover. In 20 minutes the pasta will be ready to drain and use anyway desired.

To take along a pie or any similarly shaped dish, slip it into your nine or 10-inch skillet. The skillet handle keeps you from having to grip the pie by its edge and risk damaging the crust. The skillet lid will keep it warm if necessary. This trick will let you take a fresh baked pie right from the oven straight to where it will be enjoyed, with no spilling in the car and harm to the pie.

Scissors come in handy here. After pizzas are cooked, take a large pair of scissors and simply cut the pizza into the desired sizes.

When catsup refuses to pour from the bottle, set it inside a fruit jar half-full of very hot water. This is good for using the last bit from the bottle, too.

If you don't have an easy way to cut up gumdrops, orange slices or dates, try putting about three tablespoons of flour into a small mixing bowl. Drop six to eight dates or candies into the flour. Use a spoon and roll them until they are thoroughly coated. Snip them into small pieces in the flour. Stir to coat. Place them in a strainer to separate the pieces from the excess flour. Store coated pieces in a covered jar in the refrigerator.

When you fail to soften butter or shortening for baking, just measure the amount of sugar the recipe calls for into a mixing bowl and place it in the oven or microwave, just until it is warm. Add the shortening to the sugar, and it will blend together in a hurry.

To help you make thinner pie pastry, lightly coat the board or waxed paper you will be using, with olive oil to make the dough stretch thinner without crumbling; then you are ready to roll the dough. The olive oil also makes the pastry easier to handle and gives it an attractive gleam when served.

For delicious marshmallow snowballs stick large marshmallows on a long kitchen fork. Hold in the steam of boiling water until sticky, then drop them onto flaked coconut, tinted pink, green, yellow or toasted, whatever suits your needs for a special occasion. Roll it over and over until it is coated on all sides. Place them on waxed paper until firm.

When a recipe says put spices and herbs in a "cheese cloth bag," use a tea ball strainer. It's more convenient and less time consuming.

Wide-mouthed peanut butter jars can be put to good use for leftovers. The see-through glass makes food easily identifiable and the screw lids keeps food fresh.

Try blending vanilla ice cream with a little peanut butter, spread between graham crackers, and freeze. Makes a good ice cream sandwich.

When you need to sprinkle fresh fruit that discolors easily with lemon juice try, using reconstituted lemon juice, in a small bottle equipped with a sprayer tip. Just shake it and start spraying and it covers more evenly and with not much mess.

* * *

Coconut Bars

1 cup nuts
2 cups graham cracker crumbs
1 cup coconut
1/2 cup butter or margarine
1/2 cup sugar
1 egg

Blend nuts, graham cracker crumbs and coconut. Place butter, sugar and egg in a double boiler and cook until the butter is all melted and the egg done. Mix the two mixtures and pat on a cookie sheet and chill. When it is chilled, frost with a powdered sugar chocolate frosting. Cut it in bars and serve. This is a rich cookie.

Fall harvest history told

American Indian Day was set aside for September as a way of honoring culture and heritage that precedes any other in this nation.

The American Indian played an important role in the first harsh New England winter the colonist encountered. The Indian crop was far from bountiful and many of their tribes lived very close to starvation; however, when the first wheat and pea crops of the colonists fared poorly in the new foreign soil, the Indians were there with their offerings of squash, corn and beans that helped to supplement the food supply.

The colonial women were anxious to learn the Indian ways in preparation of food using these vegetables. Many of the dishes are still popular today such as succotash, a mixture of lima beans and corn, and corn meal mush, as a basis for bread and cereals.

According to the United Fresh Fruit and Vegetable Association, squash was as important as corn to tribes, such as the Iroquois and other Indians of the East because of its nourishment and versatility.

Indians used boiling a great deal as a way of food preparation. Sweeteners, like the delicate milkweed blossoms or maple syrup tapped from the trunk of trees, were important flavors in the American Indian cooking. Honey also was another natural sweetener.

Squash is so versatile that from the pattypan to zucchini to the miraculous spaghetti that looks like a pasta-filled gourd, it serves as a basis for many dishes, appetizers, soups, entrees, side dishes and desserts. Few foods can claim this distinction.

Squash adds a splash of color to the season known for its hues. It endears itself to us when the season has ended. As we go into the cold monochrome (different tones of the same color) winter, we need a change, and the squash seems to fill the bill as well as providing color for the palate.

Squash, pumpkins and gourds are close relatives and members of the genus cucurbita, with cucumbers and watermelons also belonging. This 4,000-5,000 year old family, first was grown in the Mexican highlands. Squash seeds have been found by archeologists in the Mexican caves that date back to 9000 B.C. Squash was cultivated by the Pueblo Indians of the southwestern United States at least 2,000 or more years ago, it has been learned.

Long before white settlers arrived in North America, pumpkins lay in cornfields that were planted by Indians.

Columbus reported the first discovery of the squash vegetable; however, he did not know just what he had found. When he returned from a trip to America, he wrote about finding gourds and calebazzas in a village at the eastern edge of Cuba.

Since ancient times, gourds have been known throughout Europe (their historic roots go back to the hanging gardens of Babylon and in the domain of Charlemagne). Gourds also served as vessels for the ancient Egyptians when they were used as water flasks.

Amerigo Vespucci, an Italian navigator from whom the western continents received their name, in his writing describes small dried "gourds" seen hanging around the necks of Indians in the late 15th century in Trinidad. In Latin America, the hard rind squash still serves as cooking utensils.

The name squash comes from the Indian word askutasquash that means "eaten green." The acorn, a variety of winter squash, was eaten green by the American Indians, thereby giving it the name.

* * *

Indian Baked Acorn Squash

2 medium acorn squash (1 1/2 pounds each)
1/4 cup honey
1/4 cup soft butter or margarine
1/2 teaspoon salt
1/8 teaspoon pepper

Halve the squash lengthwise; scoop out the seeds and pulp. Trim the bottoms, if necessary, so the squash stands level. Blend together the honey, butter, salt and pepper, and divide among the halves. Place them in a greased baking dish and cover tighly with foil. Bake in a 375 degree oven 1 hour or until tender. Uncover and bake 15 to 25 minutes longer, or until slightly browned and soft, basting frequently with the butter mixture. Makes 4 servings.

* * *

Squash Bars

1 cup sugar
1/2 cup shortening
1 egg
1 teaspoon vanilla
1 cup cooked squash, mashed
2 teaspoons baking powder
2 cups flour
Powdered sugar
Orange juice

Cream together the sugar and shortening and add the other ingredients, except powdered sugar and orange juice, beating well after each addition. Spread this thinly on a large cookie sheet and bake at 350 degrees for 25 to 30 minutes. While the bars are still hot, spread them with a glaze of powdered sugar and orange juice, thin or thick as preferred.

All in a Woman's Day--October 6, 1987

More squash news given

Again, let us think about squashes. Oftentimes gardeners bypass squashes in favor of the more common vegetables; however, squashes are not only easy to grow, they also are good to eat. They are interesting to have in the garden because they come in many different shapes and sizes, long and narrow, rounded, flat and saucer-shaped. Children delight in the interesting forms.

Don't be fooled by the outer appearance of some squashes. Many are dark and rather an unappetizing green; however, the interiors are golden yellow and full of delicious flavor. Others like crooknecks, are mishaped and warty; however, the cream yellow interior provides a delicious dish when cooked and seasoned.

Squashes are categorized mainly by seasons, winter and summer.

Winter squashes are usually divested of their hard rinds, seeds and strings before cooking. They can be boiled 15 minutes until tender; however, the varieties are excellent baked, often with the rind intact. They can be filled with a meat stuffing for a main dish or with brown sugar or honey and butter for a side dish. Mashed squash can be flavored with marshmallows, raisins, pineapple, or nuts.

When baking squash, make certain to puncture the skin with a fork just the same as baking potatoes.

Squashes are not the best subjects for canning or freezing since they lose much of their flavor and texture; however, because of their maturity, when picked, winter squashes are suitable for storage for several months in a cool, dry place. They must be handled carefully, and those that become cut or bruised, or where bugs may have invaded the skin, should be removed, since rapid decay results.

Diverse in appearance and taste, the winter squash varieties are numerous. Among some of the best known are acorn, banana, butternut delicata (sweet potato), delicious Hubbard, winter crookneck and turban.

Summer squashes are thin-skinned when immature. They are best when used during the summer.

When you think of summer squashes there are zucchini and the yellow ones. Years ago, these were the main types of squash available during the warm months. Today, however, the array takes on a range of shapes and colors and subtly different tastes.

The traditional Italian green zucchini is one we are all familiar with; however, there are other varieties, the golden zucchini that has a distinctive color and a mild taste, and the green type, when shredded, gives soups, casseroles and even breads a special flavor and texture. Gourmet Globe is a spherical bright green-striped zucchini with a full sweet flavor. It is particularly tempting when filled with meat or fresh vegetable stuffing. Yellow squash, both crookneck and straightneck, are other well liked varieties.

Scallop or pattypan (or pattipan) has an appealing, plump bowl shape with scalloped edges. Within this group falls the white or button squash that is pale green when young, maturing a creamy white. Also there is the chayote.

Spaghetti squash is appearing more and more in the produce departments and is an intriguing novelty to shoppers. It gets its name from the spaghetti-like strands pulled from its flesh after cooking. It is being declared by many who have tried it as low calorie pasta substitute, since only 100 grams of boiled spaghetti squash has only 29 calories.

Summer or soft squashes, are available the year around; however, they are so plentiful through the warm months they have earned their seasonal name. They are low in calories, low in sodium, have a moderate amount of magnesium and vitamin C and are nutritious.

Summer squashes should be picked while young and tender. Always select those that are heavy, firm and glossy, using them as soon as possible after harvesting as they do not keep well.

Because of their tenderness, summer squashes should not be overcooked, for they loose their shape. To give the delicate summer squash its flavor, add one or two of the following: Parmesan cheese, basil, bay leaf, mace, marjoram, mustard, dill or rosemary.

* * *

Pumpkin or Squash Corn Bread

1/2 cup soft butter or margarine
3/4 cup honey
2 eggs, beaten
1 1/2 cups cooked mashed pumpkin or winter squash (canned works well)
1 cup milk
1 1/2 cups whole wheat pastry flour or whole wheat flour
1 cup corn meal
1 tablespoon plus 2 teaspoons baking powder
1 teaspoon cinnamon
1/4 teaspoon allspice
1/2 teaspoon salt
1/8 teaspoon powdered ginger

Preheat oven to 350 degrees. Cream butter and honey in medium bowl; add eggs, milk and cooked pumpkin or squash, and mix well. Add dry ingredients to the mixture and mix well. Spoon mixture into a large, buttered loaf pan, filling 3/4 full. Bake 1 1/2 hours. Check after 1 hour to see if it is done. If top browns too quickly, cover it with aluminum foil.

Note: Use leftover batter to make muffins. Bake them in greased and floured tins (or tins lined with paper cupcake liners) at 350 degrees for 15 to 20 minutes or until done. Serves 6 to 10.

All in a Woman's Day--October 13, 1987
Autumn and popcorn seem to be compatible

Popcorn and autumn go together; they are compatible. October was chosen as the month to call special attention to popcorn because traditionally harvest time has been the biggest popcorn eating season of the year; however, that really does not hold true anymore.

In earlier days, popcorn was a favorite Sunday night food when the family would gather together and enjoy this tasty morsel as a suppertime dish, along with crunchy apples. Oftentimes walnut or hickory nuts were cracked on Sunday afternoon in preparation for picking out that night, for choice eating. Games were played—dominoes, old maid, 42 and others—along with reading by the lamplight.

Families still enjoy popcorn as they watch television, read or listen to records, or the radio and enjoy the VCR's.

Plain popcorn is low in calories; however, some folks cannot even think of the word popcorn without drenching it with melted butter. I'll agree it does make it good, but sometimes the pounds are too difficult to shed. Of course, nothing smells quite so tempting as when corn is popping, and it really makes the taste buds work overtime. Since it is a natural nibbling food, it fits into most activities. Some folks almost have a "passion" or "devotion" for popcorn, eating it daily.

Remember when you went to the movies and paid five cents a sack for popcorn? Most of us still like popcorn when we go to the movies; however, the price now-a-days is somewhat higher.

Popcorn is a natural for it provides nutritional eating, has no sugar, no additivies, no preservatives, has high fiber and bulk and is an important carbohydrate, as well as having calcium, iron, minerals, vitamins and protein. And best of all, you might term it "in expensive."

In earlier days, the Indians used popcorn for food and decorations, besides eating it as we do. They also made popcorn soup and a fermented popcorn beverage. In addition, they wore popcorn necklaces and maidens adorned their hair with strands of popcorn.

Legend has it that the brother of Chief Massassoit took a deerskin bag of popcorn to the first Thanksgiving dinner, and thereafter the Indians continued to use popcorn as a "good will" gift when they would meet with the colonists.

Besides throwing kernels of corn into the fire and catching them as they popped out, some of the Indians would skewer an ear on a stick and hold it over the fire to pop. Too, some of the Indians used clay pots filled with hot sand as a popcorn popper.

Besides the traditional yellow and white popcorn, there also is a black popcorn called Black Jewel, and while it tastes the same as other popcorn, it does look a bit different before and after popping.

Some other kinds are rainbow, with red, white, blue and yellow kernels, and strawberry popcorn with red kernels on a strawberry shaped ear.

Yellow popcorn pops into two basic shapes, mushroom and butterfly or snowflake. The butterfly or snowflake is popular for home and theater use, while the candy corn manufacturers use the mushroom kernel.

* * *

Peanut Butter Popcorn Balls

1 cup corn syrup
1/2 cup sugar
1 teaspoon cream of tartar
1/2 cup peanut butter
1/4 teaspoon soda
3 quarts popped corn
1 cup small Spanish peanuts
1 cup coconut

Combine corn syrup, sugar and cream of tartar, and cook them until a spoonful dropped into cold water forms a hard ball. Stir in peanut butter and soda. Mix popcorn, peanuts and coconut. Pour syrup mixture over popcorn mixture; mix well and form into balls.

* * *

Presidential Popcorn

5 quarts popped corn
2 cups sugar
1 1/2 cups water
1/2 cup light corn syrup
1 teaspoon vinegar
1 teaspoon vanilla
1/2 teaspoon salt
1 1/2 cups jelly beans

Place popped corn in a large, slightly buttered bowl and keep it warm. Combine sugar, water, corn syrup, vinegar and salt in a saucepan and bring mixture to a boil, cooking it over medium high heat to a hard ball stage. Stir in vanilla; and then slowly pour syrup over popcorn, stirring well. Add the jelly beans and stir. Turn onto a lightly buttered large tray. Cool and break up to serve or form into balls if desired. (Makes 5 quarts.)

All in a Woman's Day--October 20, 1987

Ghostly Halloween tips

This might be a bit early to be writing about Halloween; however, it already seems to be in the air, so let's get with it and plan to enjoy this special holiday.

Halloween can be as much fun for grown-ups as it is for youngsters. Much enjoyment for adults comes when the "scary" little creatures come to the door for trick-or-treat. No child should be deprived of this special pleasure and the loot that goes with it. It is suggested, however, that the children stay in their own neighborhood or only go to those homes where they are known.

This custom of trick-or-treating by American children today, is nothing new, as this custom dates from the 17th century when Irish peasants asked for money to purchase luxuries for a feast to honor St. Columbia, who by the way, was a proselytizing priest during the sixth century setting up a monastery on Iona Island off the coast of Scotland.

And speaking of trick-or-treat, you might like to know what young Scots do to observe this ghostly celebration. They dress up as "guisers," that is in disguises, and go around to their friends' houses singing, dancing and collecting presents for their performances. In rural districts, they carry a lantern made from a hollowed-out turnip (no pumpkin) with a candle stuck inside.

A girl who wants to get married takes a lighted candle into a bedroom and places it in front of a mirror. Then she sits and looks into the mirror, and if she is lucky, she sees beside her own reflection the face of the man she is going to marry. If he turns out to be somebody she doesn't fancy, she may act like an ill-tempered fiend for a spell.

And about cats, they play an especially important role in this special holiday observance. Various superstitutions have developed through the years because of traditional association of the black cat as a companion of witches.

If you see a yawning cat, this indicates an opportunity that should not be neglected; however, if a cat rubs against an individual, that means good luck. If a cat is running away, this action signifies that a secret will be disclosed, possibly within a week. Now, if a cat sits beside an individual quietly, it indicates that peace and prosperity will be bestowed upon that person.

The C. J. Russells, Derry, N. H., have skeletons a plenty in their closets, and theirs is a "haunted" house for black cats, bats in the belfry, jack-o-lanterns, hobgoblins, witches and broomsticks that seem to thrive there. Some say they have a "ghost" of a chance.

These people are possibly the foremost collectors of Halloween memorabilia. Their collection includes some

10,000 items concerning Halloween, with possibly a third of them being postcards. The Russells say there are about 5,000 Halloween postcards in existence and they hope to get one of each, either by trick, treat, trade or commerical traffic.

Have fun on Halloween and welcome all the characters that come a-visiting. Don't forget to change the time on your clocks on the 25th, for on this special night goblins and ghosts will have an extra "witching hour".

* * *

Pumpkin Cookies

1 cup mashed pumpkin or sweet potatoes
1 cup sugar
1/2 cup oil
1 egg
2 cups flour
2 teaspoons baking powder
1 teaspoon cinnamon
1 teaspoon salt
1 teaspoon soda
1 teaspoon milk
1 cup semi-sweet chocolate chips
1 teaspoon vanilla

Combine the mashed pumpkin or sweet potatoes, sugar, oil and egg. Stir together flour, baking powder, cinnamon and salt. To the dry ingredients add the pumpkin or sweet potato mixture along with the soda that is dissolved in the teaspoon of milk. Mix well. Stir in chocolate chips and vanilla. Drop by teaspoonsful on lightly greased cookie sheet. Bake in a 375 degree oven 10 to 12 minutes. They can be frosted with an orange flavored frosting, if desired.

Fall is pear time

The ancient Greeks considered nectar the food of the gods; however, the poet Homer called the pear "A gift of the gods."

The pear is a member of the rose family, that also includes numerous favorite fruits, such as cherries, apricots, apples, raspberries, strawberries and plums.

The ancestral pear dates back centuries before Christ and by the time ancient Greek civilization reached its height, pears were actively cultivated. Later, however, victorious Roman legions carried pears back to their homeland and to conquered areas of the Old World.

Pears are native of the vast area stretching from central Europe to Asia, with most of the varieties grown in the United States developed from the European pear, Pyrus communis, that originated in the area of southeastern Europe and western Asia, or are hybrids of the European pears, and the sand or China pears. An example of the former are Bartlett and Anjou, with Keiffer, Le Conte and Seckel the latter.

The ancient Egyptians, Greeks and Romans were familiar with the pear. During the Middle Ages they were grown extensively in the orchards of monasteries and castles, the guardians of the civilization of their times.

Now, we find that pears are grown all over the world in temperate zones. There are more than 5,000 varieties grown in Europe. The leading pear country is France. It is a delightful sight, writers have written, to see a French pear orchard in bloom or trained pear trees that are pruned to grow on wires flat against a white-washed wall of a French farmhouse.

The Bartlett pear, a favorite, owes its origin to a very special delicate pear that was found growing wild by a schoolmaster at Berkshire, England, who sold it to a nurseryman. He propagated and distributed the fruit that was called Stair's pear after the founder. It was sometime in the late 1700s, that John Carter of Boston planted Stair's pears in the colonial territory of Massachusetts. Then in 1817, when the estate passed into the hands of Enoch Bartlett, he, not knowing its true name, gave it his own.

Pears were introduced to the West Coast by Spanish missionaries that moved North from Mexico, and later American migrants brought the pear West from the original 13 colonies.

More pears are grown today commercially in the United States than in any other place in the world, except Italy. More than two-thirds of all the pears harvested in the United States are Bartlett, which are grown in California, Oregon and Washington.

The sweet, juicy Bartlett pear is bell-shaped, with clear yellow skin that is sometimes blushed. The flesh is smooth and white. It is on the market from July through November. This pear is especially good for eating.

D'Anjou pears, available from October to May, have short necks that give them an oval appearance. Skin colors range from shades of yellow to green. The flesh is yellowish-white, with a sweet and spicy flavor. It is for eating, cooking and canning.

Bosie pears are yellow-skinned and heavily russeted with a cinnamon color. They have long tapering necks, are a melt-in-your-mouth buttery flesh that makes them a juicy choice. They are on the market from October to March and are especially good eating.

Some of the other more popular varieties are Comice, Seckel, Clapp Favorite and Winter Nelis.

The Comice pears, popular for holiday gifts, are sometimes quite large and almost round with thick greenish-yellow skins and very fine, juicy flesh. There season is from October to January. This pear is good for eating.

Seckel pears are in season from September to December and are delicious for eating, canning and pickling. They are small, quite sweet and highly russeted, almost reddish.

Clapp Favorite is in season from late August to September. It is a large symmetrical pear, yellow, with red blush, and is rather sweet. It is good for eating and canning.

Many homemakers have not mastered the art of ripening a green pear. The secret is rather simple. Just place green pears in a loosely closed paper sack or bag and leave them on the counter top for a few days and the green fruit will have turned yellow and be ready to eat. The sack or bag traps the ethylene gas that pears and other fruits give off in the ripening process. This natural hormone, ethylene, helps for fast and even ripening.

Scientists from the University of California, several years ago developed the California ripening bowl. The ventilated lid comes with the bowl and it traps the ethylene gas and also retains enough moisture to keep the pears from shriveling. It also is good for ripening other fruits, and will almost transform them right before your eyes.

* * *

The following recipe makes a delightful quick bread that is just right for an afternoon tea or a special home baked dessert:

Spicy Walnut Pear Bread

2 medium-sized pears, peeled and diced
1/4 cup apple juice or water
1 cup honey
1/2 cup vegetable oil
1 cup whole wheat flour
1 cup unbleached white flour
1 teaspoon baking soda
1/2 teaspoon salt
2 teaspoons cinnamon
1/2 teaspoon nutmeg
1/2 cup raisins
1/2 cup chopped walnuts

Preheat oven 350 degrees. Puree the pears and juice in a blender (only for a few seconds so the puree is not runny). Measure out 1 cup of puree. Combine the puree with the honey and oil and blend well. Combine the remainder of the ingredients together and add to liquid mixture. Blend thoroughly. Pour batter into a greased loaf pan and bake 50 minutes, or until inserted toothpick comes out dry.

All in a Woman's Day—November 3, 1987

Try pork today!

While many folks cannot eat pork, those of us who can, thoroughly enjoy its succulent goodness and the various ways it can be prepared. Try it today!

Some of the more popular cuts are loin roasts, pork chops, ham, ribs, liver, bacon, ground pork, sausage, pigs' feet, salt pork, as well as cold cuts that contain some pork.

When selecting pork, always look for light pink to white meat, white fat and pink bones. The graining in the pork is not fat but muscle. This, you will find, is the reason additional fat is needed when cooking such cuts of pork as tenderloin.

Fresh pork is high in protein and vitamin B and is flavorful. Pork should be cooked enough to destroy any trichinae; however, internal temperatures of 140 degree is considered safe. Overcooking makes the pork lose its succulence and is often tasteless and dry.

Almost every part of the "pig" is edible, and, I might add, delicious, from the lowly pig's feet to the most costly cut of tenderloin. A suggested serving should be one-third pound.

Salt pork—that is cured in salt or brine—is used to add flavor to several dishes, and it is especially good fried country style.

Leftover pork can be used in numerous dishes where other meat is suggested.

A picnic ham is a pork shoulder that has been cured and smoked. Since it has waste of bone and fat, about one pound per serving should be allowed.

Pickled pig's feet also have been a favorite dish of many people.

Today, many stores features cuts of meat in "family packs." The meat department will usually cut the loin into desired cuts, or at least make the saw cuts, so only simple knife work is required. Depending on the retailer, it may be displayed in individual cuts or left as whole "subprimal" (first original). Often cutting instructions are found on the package of subprimal.

The most popular way to divide a whole pork loin is into chops, country style ribs and a loin end roast. Any of the lean trimmings can be used for ground pork, cubes for kabobs or strips for stir-frying.

Pork chops are one of the most versatile pork cuts, and while they can be cut into various thicknesses, one to one and a half-inch chop is the best for dinner serving.

Country-style ribs yield more servings per pound than other ribs. They are equally good grilled or baked in the oven. Smoky country style ribs are basted with a tangy barbecue sauce while baking.

Fresh pork that won't be used within two days should be wrapped in moisture, vapor proof frozen wrap and sealed with freezer tape before being placed in the freezer. Always label the packages, noting the contents and date. Ground pork should be used within three months. Other fresh pork can be frozen up to six months.

You might try roasting pork and beef together. The gravy is good and the family has a choice of meats. Browned potatoes are good cooked with the meat.

Should the meat have an inspection stamp on it, you don't need to trim it off as the coloring is a harmless vegetable compound.

Always turn meat with tongs instead of a fork so that the juices will not escape.

Before cooking liver, marinate in milk several hours; then flour and fry. This takes away the strong liver taste.

Too, many cooks pour boiling water over the liver and let it set a few minutes, then wash it and dry before beating, flouring and frying.

Another tip about liver is to add one teaspoon sugar when it is seasoned and floured before frying it. Sugar also helps remove the strong flavor, and the liver will fry nice and brown.

Do not salt roasts until cooking is done. Not salting until it is done, helps keep the juices in the meat.

* * *

Ham Balls with Sauce

2 pounds ground ham
1 pound ground beef
2 eggs
1 cup milk
1 cup graham cracker crumbs
1 can tomato soup
1 cup brown sugar
1/4 cup vinegar
1/4 teaspoon dry mustard

Mix the ham, beef, eggs, milk and cracker crumbs together and then form balls from the mixture. Combine the other ingredients and pour over the balls. Bake in a 375 degree oven 1 hour.

All in a Woman's Day--November 10, 1987

Friday 13th: are you ready?

Have you looked closely at your calendar lately? If you have, you know that this is the week of Friday the 13th. It happens to be the third one we have had this year, the others occurring in February and March, which is really not too many times for "worriers" to get upset about.

This special day is often paralyzing for those folks who have a phobia for Friday the 13th. Did you know there are between 10,000 and 20,000 Americans that are superstitious and fear this day?

Let us think of some of the beliefs, omens or superstitions that cause a dilemma, good or bad.

There is one that says if you bite your tongue, you will tell a lie.

The herb doctors used parsley to give renewed health and strength to warriors wounded in battle.

For good luck when taking a written test, some say to use a new pen or pencil because it has never made a mistake.

Some people believe that a rooster crowing during the day means a friend will visit.

Folks often believe that cowslip roots will cure headaches.

Wearing coats inside out will ward off evil.

It has been thought by some people that if a honey bee zips around your head, you will soon be rich.

Some say that sneezing before a journey is a bad sign.

If you want good luck some people believe that you will get it by turning your hat around and then pulling out your pockets.

If you peel an apple and toss the peel over your shoulder, it will hit the ground and form the shape of the first letter of your future spouse's name.

Drop a piece of molten lead in cold water and it will take the shape of something in your future.

If you eat a piece of candy or cake just before bedtime you will have nightmares about snakes.

An itching skin is supposed to foretell visitors.

The gift of a knife cuts friendship.

It is unlucky to turn back from a journey, stub your toe, to wear peacock feathers, to leave a house through a window or to sit on a table.

It is supposed to be good luck if you find a horseshoe, pick up a pin or return money in payment of a debt.

Cold shivers indicate that someone is walking over the spot that will be your grave.

If you step on a crack, you will fail in your lessons.

A blister on the tongue means that one has told a lie.

The Germans, Hungarians, Jews and English are the most traditionally superstitious people in the world, with the sainted Irish running close behind, according to an expert in the field of superstition. However, the people of Thailand also are extremely superstitious. Some of their beliefs are baffling. For instance, a twitch of the left eye is good luck; however, not in the right eye.

Never, no, never get a hair cut on Wednesday.

To sign your name in red ink is bad luck.

To protect newborns from spirits that might be jealous of a beautiful child, they are often called unattractive nicknames. However, you feel about this special day, Friday the 13th, just be careful not to walk under a ladder or let a black cat run in front of you!

* * *

Cracker Salad

60 Ritz or Hi Ho crackers, crushed
1 stick margarine or butter, melted
1/2 cup sugar
1 (8-ounce) carton whipped topping
1 (8-ounce) can of frozen orange juice concentrate
1 can mandarin oranges, drained
1 small can crushed pineapple, drained
1 can sweetened condensed milk

In a 9x13-inch pan place half of the crushed cracker crumbs that have been mixed with the melted margarine, leaving the other half for the top. Mix the remainder of the ingredients together and place over the layer of crackers, sprinkling the remainder of the crumbs on top. This is a delightful salad, and also refreshing.

Walnuts: a fall treat

With the holiday cooking and baking soon to begin, this is a good time to learn about nuts, especially black walnuts, as they are most appropriate in this area for the season.

The harvest of black walnuts and hickory nuts in Missouri this year has been prolific. This means, of course, that folks, as well as the squirrels, are going to fare well this wintertime, regardless of the weather.

For many consumers, using nuts is one of the expenses and pleasures reserved for holiday times and used sparingly at other times.

Walnuts this year were a marketable item, and many pounds have been gathered and sold.

This nut, the black walnut, was cultivated for centuries in the Mediterranean area, and it was popular in Italy, as far back as the first century A.D.

The walnut was given much prestige by the ancient Persians, and proclaimed that it could be eaten only by royalty; however, with the fall of the Persian Empire, the walnut began to spread throughout the Old World and somehow it grew in stature.

It was consecrated to the god of Jupiter by the kings of Olympus; in Rome it was regarded as a symbol of fertility; and it was hailed in the scrolls of Solomon.

During the Middle Ages, walnuts became associated with alchemy and outright witchcraft were thought to possess great healing powers.

It was somewhere along the line that the walnut made its way to North America, and it has been found that the Indians made it a basic feature of their diet. Then when the Portuguese and Spaniards came to California in the late 1700s, they introduced other varieties; however, the Indian black walnut finally predominated.

Even though it was exploited commercially in the 1860s in California, the black walnut seemed to lag behind its European cousins for seven decades.

Consumers across the United States began to show a preference in the 1940s for using walnuts as an ingredient in confections and baking. From then on the production soared, especially during the World War II era when the growing areas of Europe had to curtail the output.

The black walnut has become known as the workhorse of the nut family and seems to be among the most popular in the supermarkets.

Probably the most important species is the Persian or English walnut, originally of southwestern Europe and China and widely cultivated for its superior thin-shell.

Here in the United States it is grown chiefly in California, where English walnuts also are an important crop.

Another American species is the white walnut, also known as the butternut.

Both English or black walnuts have many uses and are for the most part interchangeable; however, mostly in confections, which includes a wide variety of cakes, candy, ice cream and pie fillings.

The most unusual use for them is as a pickle, with their use in England for this purpose a common practice. This kind of pickle is most commonly served with cheese and cold meats. Walnuts also are used in catsup, and they are the base of one of the finest oils, walnut oil, known in France as hile de niox.

Enjoy your walnuts this year, for there is no flavor that is comparable to the flavor of a walnut.

* * *

Black Walnut Cookies

2 cups sugar
1 cup vegetable shortening
2 eggs
1 teaspoon butter flavoring
1 teaspoon vanilla flavoring
1/2 teaspoon black walnut flavoring
1 cup sour cream
1/2 teaspoon soda
4 teaspoons baking powder
4 1/2 cups flour
1/4 teaspoon salt
1/2 cup black walnuts, chopped

Cream together the sugar and shortening. Beat in the eggs until well blended. Add the flavorings and the sour cream alternately with the sifted dry ingredients. Stir in the nuts. Drop batter by teaspoons onto a greased cookie sheet and bake them approximately 15-20 minutes in a 350 degree oven. This makes a large batch of delicious cookies.

* * *

Black Walnut Dream Bars

First Layer:
1/2 cup butter
1/2 cup brown sugar
1 cup flour
Second Layer:
1 cup brown sugar
2 beaten eggs
1/4 teaspoon salt
1 teaspoon vanilla
2 teaspoons flour
1/2 teaspoon baking powder
1 1/2 cups coconut
1 cup broken black walnuts

Cream butter and 1/2 cup of brown sugar and work in 1 cup of flour until mixture is fairly crumbly. Pat smoothly into a shallow greased pan and bake 10 minutes in a moderate oven. Meanwhile, mix together 1 cup of brown sugar, beaten eggs, salt and vanilla. Sift together 2 teaspoons of flour with baking powder and mix it with coconut. Add black walnuts, blend them into the sugar and egg mixture. Pour this over previously baked mixture. Return pan to oven and bake 20 minutes longer. Cool and cut into bars.

All in a Woman's Day--November 24, 1987
Bless Thanksgiving

This is the season of Thanksgiving that is a recognition of God's love.

The words from Psalms 103rd chapter, verses 2-5 reads:

"Bless the Lord, O my soul; and forget not all His benefits;

Who forgiveth all thine iniquities; who healeth all thy disease;

Who redeemth thy life from destruction; who crowneth thee with loving kindness and tender mercies;

Who satisfieth thy mouth with good things."

* * *

The words are a wonderful comfort and assurance to repeat to yourself when the lamp of faith burns dim and your heart trembles at the threat of personal or national dangers.

These words have held true through the ages, and have never failed. And God shall not fail us today if we turn to Him as a people and as a nation and ask for guidance in problems and trials—great or small. "Blessed is the nation whose God is Lord."

* * *

Before the Pilgrims sat down to their feast, they observed the true meaning of Thanksgiving. They all gathered in their meeting house to give thanks for the good they had received, for survival through a long year of hardships, to pray for strength and courage to keep their faith in this strange new land.

May we be thankful people; may we as individuals, and as a nation, recognize our dependence upon God's bounty. May we at our daily bread give our Thanksgiving and bless the Lord for His loving kindness.

Thanksgiving is the festival of the garden, where God placed man to till it and dress it. It is the festival of the home, where peace and love and beauty of God are found. It is the festival of toil at rest, content with its reward— barns filled with the golden spoil of the fields; of families gathered in the old homestead; of reverent joy in the goodness and grace of our Heavenly Father.

This is a national day, not belonging to any party, sect or denomination; but a day when all differences are forgotten in the song of praise that we raise to our Father.

* * *

Sometime ago an old-timer on the 102 River bottom commented on the upcoming Thanksgiving holiday, and said his crops were the best they had been in years and that he was really thankful. He also philosophized, giving this formula for a happy life:

"Health enought to make work a pleasure;

Wealth enought to pay all the bills;

Strength enough to face difficulties;

Grace enough to observe and forsake wrongdoings;

Patience enough to see a job through to completion;

Charity enough to see good in others; and

Faith enough to plan for the future."

All in a Woman's Day--December 1, 1987
Brownies hold magic

There are brownies and then there are brownies. They are such good eating and are enjoyed by almost everyone at anytime. To me, however, brownies are just a little more special at holiday time.

Have you thought of brownies as a comforting food? They seem to give a soothing feeling for almost anytime. Whether for something very special or making peace with someone; Brownie and Cub Scouts love 'em. They are good munching after arriving home from school. "Kids" of all ages like brownies.

The thing that is especially nice about brownies is that anyone, whether you are a cook or not, can whip up a batch. You really don't need to be concerned about the sifting or when to add ingredients or how much to mix. Ordinarily you just put a few ingredients together, give a little stir and bake. There just seems to be no way you can do anything wrong in making brownies.

There are numerous taste and flavor changes that can be added to brownies that may make them seem a bit more special.

* * *

I am going to share several recipes that might be just a bit different from some you may have. Of course, there are recipes and more recipes for brownies.

* * *

Blond Peanut Butter Chip Brownies
1 cup butter or margarine, softened
3/4 cup white sugar
1/4 cup light brown sugar, packed
2 eggs
1/2 teaspoon vanilla
2 1/4 cups flour

1 teaspoon baking soda
1/4 teaspoon salt
2 cups (12-ounces) peanut butter chips
Cream together in a large bowl, the white and brown sugars, eggs and vanilla until light and fluffy. Combine flour, baking soda and salt and add them to the creamed mixture. Stir in chips. Spread batter in a 13x9-inch greased baking pan. Bake 35 minutes or until golden brown in a 350 degree oven until firm to the touch. Cool and cut in 32 squares. These can be frosted if desired.

* * *

Milk Chocolate Almond Bars

1 cup shortening
1/2 cup white sugar
1/2 cups brown sugar
2 eggs, separated
1 tablespoon water
1 teaspoon vanilla
2 cups flour
1 teaspoon soda
1/4 teaspoon salt
1 cup milk chocolate chips
1 cup sliced almonds
Cream shortening, gradually adding white sugar and 1/2 cup brown sugar; continue to cream until light and fluffy. Add egg yolks, water and vanilla and beat thoroughly. Sift flour with soda and salt, and add them to the creamed mixture; mix until blended. Spread evenly in a greased 15 1/2x10-1/2x1-inch jelly roll pan. Sprinkle chocolate chips over the batter and press into the dough. Beat the egg whites until soft peaks form and gradually add remaining 1 cup of brown sugar. Continue beating until stiff, but not dry. Spread meringue over the batter in pan and sprinkle with almond slices. Bake in a 375 degree oven 20 minutes. Cool on rack and cut into 40 2-inch squares. Remove from pan and let stand three hours or more before serving.

* * *

Deep South Brownies

1/2 cup butter or margarine
2 squares (1-ounce each) unsweetened chocolate
1 cup dark brown sugar, firmly packed
2 eggs
1/2 teaspoon salt
1/2 cup flour
1/2 cup chopped pecans
1 teaspoon vanilla
Melt butter and chocolate in a heavy saucepan over low heat. Remove from heat and add remaining ingredients, mixing well. Pour mixture into a well-buttered 9-inch square pan and bake in a 325 degree oven, 20 minutes or until firm to touch. Cool completely and frost with a mocha frosting. Makes 16 squares.

Mocha Frosting:

4 tablespoons margarine
2 cups powdered sugar
2/3 teaspoon vanilla
4 teaspoons hot, strong coffee
Cream margarine, add sugar and vanilla alternately with hot coffee. Control spreading consistency by adding more powdered sugar or more coffee.

All in a Woman's Day--December 8, 1987

Nut cluster treats

Peanut clusters, UMMMM! How good they are! They really are a holiday candy. In former years, the grocery or general mercantile stores did not carry them until along about Christmastime. Remember, too, most of them had fondant centers. You can easily make your homemade clusters with fondant, if you want to spend a little more time. Now, we can buy peanut

clusters the year around (not with fondant centers, however.)
* * *

In the event you like to make your own peanut clusters, I am going to share with you several recipes, all just a wee bit different. You might like to give some of them a try and then select the one you like best.

Take 1-pound white almond bark and a 12-ounce package of semi-sweet chocolate chips and melt together. Then add 1-pound peanuts, stir and drop by spoonful on waxed paper.
* * *

Another way is to take two 6-ounce packages butterscotch chips; one 6-ounce package chocolate chips, 2 or 3 tablespoons grated household paraffin. Mix and melt. Then add 10 to 12 ounces of Spanish peanuts. Stir and drop by spoonful on waxed paper.
* * *

Take 1 package almond bark, chocolate or white, 1 can sweetened condensed milk. Melt together and add salted peanuts, pecans, or almonds (as much as desired) and mix. Drop by spoonful on waxed paper. These also freeze well. The recipe makes a large batch.
* * *

Cook together to a softball stage, 1 large can evaporated milk, 1 stick margarine and 5 1/2 cups sugar. Remove from heat and stir in a 12-ounce package of chocolate chips, 1 pint of marshmallow creme and 1 teaspoon of vanilla and let melt. Then add a can of mixed nuts or 1 pound salted peanuts, and stir together. Drop by spoonful on a greased cookie sheet.
* * *

To make these peanut or almond clusters, use 1 pound almond bark, 1/2 cup of extra crunchy peanut butter, a few drops of butter flavoring and a few drops of almond flavoring. Melt all together and add 2 cups of rice cereal, 8-ounces of dry roasted peanuts or almonds and 1 cup of miniature marshmallows. Mix and drop by teaspoonful on two large greased cookie sheets.
* * *

Melt together two 6-ounce packages chocolate chips, one 6-ounce package peanut butter chips and add salted peanuts, as much as desired. Mix and drop by spoonful on waxed paper.
* * *

Melt together one 12-ounce package milk chocolate chips, 1 package almond bark and then add 1 pound of salted peanuts. Stir to coat. Drop on waxed paper by spoonful.
* * *

Take 2 pounds almond bark, chopped, one 12-ounce package semi-sweet chocolate chips, one 12-ounce package milk chocolate chips. Melt together in a heavy saucepan and stir in 2 cups Spanish peanuts. Drop by spoonful on waxed paper. Leave several hours or overnight to harden. Store in airtight containers.
* * *

Use one 6-ounce package chocolate chips, one 6-ounce package butterscotch chips, 1/2 cup peanut butter. Melt together in a double boiler. In the meantime, mix in a bowl 4 cups of miniature marshmallows, 2 cups of salted peanuts. Pour the hot mixture over this and stir. Drop by teaspoonful on waxed paper. Refrigerate until set.
* * *

Melt together one 12-ounce package semi-sweet chocolate chips, one 6-ounce package butterscotch chips, 1/2 teaspoon burnt sugar flavoring, 1/4 teaspoon butter flavoring. Combine the chips and flavorings in the top of a double boiler over hot water (not boiling). Keep water level below top pan of double boiler. Stir chips and flavorings gently until melted. Add peanuts and stir until coated. Drop by spoonful on a greased cookie sheet or waxed paper. Cool. Makes about 3 dozen clusters. Other nuts, raisins, dry cereal, peppermint chips, broken pretzels and chunks of almond bark can be substituted for the peanuts.

* * *

Use 1 cup brown sugar, a pinch of salt, 1 cup granulated sugar, 1/2 cup light cream, 1 teaspoon of vanilla and 1 1/2 cups of peanuts or pecans. Cook to a soft ball stage the sugars, salt and cream. Remove from heat and add the vanilla and peanuts or pecans. Stir until mixture thickens. Drop by spoonful on foil and let cool.

* * *

Take one 12-ounce package chocolate chips and one 6-ounce package of butterscotch chips and melt together. Then add salted peanuts as desired. Stir and drop by spoonful on waxed paper.

* * *

Use 1 can sweetened condensed milk, 6-ounce package of semi-sweet chocolate chips, 1 cup of roasted peanuts and 1 cup seedless raisins. Melt chocolate in double boiler, then add condensed milk. Cook until thickened, about 10 minutes, stirring constantly. Add nuts and raisins, stirring until coated. Drop by spoonful on waxed paper and refrigerate until firm. This makes about 20 clusters.

* * *

Use 2 tablespoons of margarine, one 7-ounce jar of marshmallow creme, 1/2 cup of butterscotch pieces, 4 cups of chow mein noodles and 1/2 cup of raisins. Melt margarine in 3-quart saucepan over low heat. Add marshmallow creme and stir until smooth. Continue cooking 5 minutes, stirring frequently. Add butterscotch chips and stir until melted. Remove from heat and add noodles and peanuts. Toss until well coated. Drop by rounded measuring tablespoonful onto waxed paper. Let these stand until firm. Store in airtight container. (Makes 2 1/2 dozen.)

* * *

This recipe calls for 1/3 cup soft butter, 1/3 cup light or dark syrup, 1 cup cocoa, 1 teaspoon vanilla, 3 tablespoons water, 1 cup nonfat dry milk, 2 cups sifted confectioners' sugar and 1 cup salted peanuts. Blend butter and syrup in a large mixing bowl and stir in the cocoa, then vanilla and water. Blend in the dry milk and add the confectioners' sugar. Mix well and add the peanuts, stirring until coated. If unsalted peanuts are used, add 1/2 teaspoon salt. Drop off tip of spoon onto waxed paper. Allow clusters to remain uncovered for 2 to 3 hours to dry. Store between layers of waxed paper in a covered container. Makes about 1 1/2 pounds or 2 dozen clusters.

All in a Woman's Day--December 15, 1987

Christmas facts told!

I have found some "Fascinating Facts About Christmas" that have been compiled by the editors of Funk and Wagnall's Dictionary. I want to share these interesting facts with you.

* * *

'Tis said Christmas cookies are a survival of the giving to the Roman senators during the Christmastime festivities in the early ages.

* * *

There is an old saying that if you quarrel on Christmas Day, things will go bad for you the rest of the year.

* * *

You want to know the names of the three men? They were Melchior, Balthasar and Caspar.

* * *

December 25 was originally a Mithraic feast date. The birthday of the unconscious Sun of Philocalus.

* * *

In Finland, Father Christmas is dressed as a Yule goat.

* * *

Christmas Island in the Pacific got its name because Captain Cook landed there on Christmas Day in 1777.

* * *

History records some great events happening on Christmas Day. Among others: The crowning of Henry II of England (1154); the time the barons forced King John to sign the Magna Charta (1214); the establishment of the Order of the Garter (1346); and the victory of General George Washington over the Hessians when he crossed the Delaware (1776).

* * *

There are only four hours of daylight in Iceland on Christmas Day, which means that Icelanders spend their entire holiday attending church services.

* * *

December 25 was a holiday in Britain long before the days of Christianity. It was known as Neodranecht or mother's night.

* * *

In Italy, the giving of Christmas gifts is advanced to Epiphany (the 12th night after Christmas).

* * *

There is a passage in the Bible that says Jesus was born on Wednesday, December 25 (in the 42nd year of Augustus). "'Tis in Hippolytus" commentary in Daniel.

* * *

The French call Christmas Noel; the Scotch, Yule; the Scandinavians, Juletide; the Dutch, Kerstmisse; the Welsh, Nadoliq; the Italians, II Natale; the Germans, Weihnachten; the Polish, Boze Navodzenie; the Bohemians, Bozic; the Slovaks, Vianoce; the Spanish, Navidad.

* * *

Legend has it that when the Virgin Mary bound her Infant Son with swaddling clothes and laid Him in the manager, the dry straw and hay with which it was filled were restored to freshness and life.

* * *

The first official mention of December 25 as Christmas is in the calendar of Philocalus (354 A.D.).

* * *

In the Balkans, the Croats and Serbs on Christmas Day go into the forest before sunrise and fell a tree. If it burns brightly in the home fireplace, prosperity (they believe) is in store for them in the year to come.

* * *

Danish children have no Santa Claus. Instead, a Christmas brownie called "Nisson."

* * *

The first Christmas pies were baked in the form of a cradle, with strips of pastry laid over the pie representing the manger.

* * *

Epiphany is often called "Little Christmas." It is the day the Magi arrived, they were not kings, but astrologers.

* * *

American Indians had a superstition that deer kneel and look up to the Great Spirit on Christmas Eve.

* * *

Santa Claus became a toymaker because poor children could not afford to buy toys, and he vowed he would make toys for them.

* * *

You may have some other interesting facts concerning Christmas; however, these should start you thinking.

All in a Woman's Day--December 23, 1987
Christmas message is hope

I would like to share with you some thoughts taken from a Christmas greeting; from a letter written by an Italian friar and painter, Giovanni da Fiesole (Fra Angelica, 1387-1455).

"Earth but cloaks your heaven.

"I salute you. I am your friend, and my love for you goes deep. There is nothing I can give you which you have not already, but there is much, very much, which though I cannnot give it, you can take.

"No heaven can come to us unless our heart finds, rest in today. Take heaven. No peace lies in the future which is not hidden in this precious little instant. Take peace.

"The gloom of the world is but a shadow. Behind it, yet within our reach, is joy. There is radiance and courage in the darkness could we but see; and to see, we have only to look.

"Life is so generous a giver, but we, judging its gifts by their covering, cast them away as ugly or heavy or hard. Remove the covering, and you will find beneath it a living splendor, woven of love, and wisdom, and power.

Welcome it, greet it, and you touch the angel's hand that brings it.

"Everything we call a trial, a sorrow, a duty, believe me, that angel's hand is there, the gift is there, and the wonder of an overshadowing Presence. Our joys, too, be not content with them as joys. They, too, conceal diviner gifts. Life is so full of meaning and purpose, so full of beauty beneath its covering, that you will find earth but cloaks your heaven.

"Courage, then, to claim it, that is all! But courage you have, and the knowledge that we are pilgrims wending through unknown country to our way home.

"And so, at this Christmastime, I greet you, not quite as the world sends greetings, but with profound esteem now and forever.

"The day breaks and the shadows flee away."

* * *

May your Christmas be most blessed!

All in a Woman's Day--December 29, 1987
New Year's nibbles

New Year's Day is the most important January holiday, and the only one the entire world observes, regardless of race or religious belief.

No doubt the greeting "Happy New Year" in various languages, has been heard around the globe.

New Year's Day is a legal holiday in all our states, as well as in the District of Columbia, Canal Zone, Guam, Puerto Rico and the Virgin Islands. In early times in such places as Cambodia, Babylon, New Guinea, Peru, Burma and Greece, there was a "period of suspended animation," observed with "fasting and austerity," before the dawn of a New Year. The Hebrews and the Natchez Indians in America also noted such a time.

Since the Advent of a New Year is symbolic of the fact that "life is in the end victorious and that death is swallowed up forever" (Theodore Gaster), the day has long been looked forward to, and greeted with joy.

Early men rejoiced because nature was taking on new life; they stopped work, and joined with families and friends in a season of good fellowship. Quarrels were settled; friendships renewed; rich and poor greeted each other; and many persons observed religious rites on New Year's Day.

This holiday is the oldest, and both primitive and civilized peoples have noted its arrival with some kind of festivity. Through the centuries, numerous traditions and customs have become associated with New Year's Day; therefore, when we moderns celebrate the day, we engage in some practices that are reminiscent of antiquity.

There is an old superstitition that some folks still follow, not only just at New Year's, it is the attempt to prophesy the future by "dipping" into the Bible at random. A person places his finger on a certain spot, reads the passage, and then tries to make it foretell his future.

The Romans sent friends good luck tokens, sometimes exchanging small copper coins with the head of Janus on one side, and a boat on the other; for he was the protector of ships and trade. Little Roman presents, such as gilded nuts were known as "strenaet." Gradually presents became more costly, and the Roman rulers were exorbitant in their demands for expensive gifts.

Making New Year's resolutions has long been an American custom. Even though some scoff at this idea and few succeed in keeping all of their resolutions, we are encouraged in the attempt by the poet, Alfred Tennyson, who wrote:

> I hold it truth with him who sings
> To one clear harp on divers tone
> That men may rise on stepping stones
> Of their dead selves to higher things.

* * *

It is always nice to have some nibbles for New Year's guests while watching ballgames and parades.

Nibbles

1 (6-ounce) package semi-sweet chocolate morsels
1 cup broken pecan brittle
1 cup raisins

* * *

1 cup milk chocolate chips
1 cup raisins
1 cup cashews

* * *

1 cup butterscotch chips
1 cup potato sticks
1 cup coarsely broken pretzel sticks

* * *

1 cup butterscotch chips
1 cup chocolate chips
1 cup broken corn chips

* * *

1 cup mint chocolate chips
1 1/2 cups sugar coated chopped dates
1 cup cashews

* * *

1 cup pretzel sticks
1 cup spiced miniature gumdrops
1 or 2 cups nuts, dry roasted peanuts, English walnuts, almonds, cashews, macadamian or mixed nuts or some of each
1 cup each M&M's chocolate and peanut covered candies
1 cup dried banana slices
1/2 cup dark raisins

1/2 cup white raisins
1/2 cup sugar coated date cubes
1/2 cup sugar coated pineapple cubes
1/2 cup coconut chips

This mixture gives a little bit of something for everyone to enjoy.

* * *

May the New Year bring the best of everything to each of you.

All in a Woman's Day--January 5, 1988

Homemade soups excel!

Most of us have eaten enough goodies to last for awhile, so it is time to count calories by eating smaller servings, pushing back from the table and exercising to get rid of some of those bulges that have shown up here and there. The eating bit, however, was fun while it lasted, and everything was so good we just had to indulge!

This is a good time to have soups or stews, whichever your family likes best, along with a sandwich. It is interesting to note that in a recent survey it was brought to light by a well-known soup company that a bowl of chicken noodle soup is as popular with kids as a peanut butter and jelly sandwich, and that could be mighty popular.

Generally we think of a lighter soup and sandwich for lunch, with a more hearty soup (the stick-to-the-ribs-kind) for an evening meal. The soup and sandwich meals needn't become monotonous; however, as there are a wide variety of nutritious, economical and dependable canned soups (what about your own?) available at the market. If you combine them in a number of unusual ways, they will provide youngsters and adults with an incentive to try some of the old favorites in various ways without even knowing that the palate is being treated and tempted with something new.

You might want to get adventuresome and try an old favorite transformed into something new, such as chicken noodle, cream of chicken or homestyle noodle soup into a hearty noodle muffin soup that is baked and is said to be a delectable combination. This particular soup is a sandwich and soup all in one. (Recipe is given.)

Most soups can be made in advance, in fact, oftentimes they are better the second or third day as they are reheated. Soups that have been refrigerated for a while or frozen may need diluting and also may need to be reseasoned before serving.

As soups cool they have a tendency to thicken, so a chilled soup may need to be thinned by using extra broth, cream or milk. Should the stock base be rich and meaty, it may jell when refrigerated; however, in that case it should be beaten with a wire whisk. Cold soups, like all cold foods, most often require additional seasoning, much more so than when soups are served hot.

Some soups need a binder, and in that case flour is good for that. The correct proportion is one teaspoon flour and one tablespoon butter for every two cups of soup. Always stir the flour into the melted butter and cook for approximately three minutes over low heat before stirring in a small portion of the hot soup. Whisk this well and cook it until thick, then add it to the remaining soup. Continue to heat and stir mixture with whisk until smooth.

Egg yolks also can be used as thickeners or binders. The proportion for this is one egg yolk to one teaspoon milk or cream for one cup of soup.

This is stirred into the soup shortly before it is served. So that curdling will be prevented, slowly drop or drizzle a little of the hot soup into the egg yolk mixture, whisking well before putting it into the pot of soup. Reheat soup slowly and stir until it thickens. Never boil it as the eggs will curdle.

Probably one of the most favorite soups is ham and bean. This method of cooking will help in degassing the beans. Soak the dried beans for at least three hours. Discard the soaking water and cook the beans in fresh water at least 30 minutes. Discard this water, add fresh water and continue cooking until the beans are done. The ham should be put in with the beans now. This method is supposed to destroy some of the gas causing chemicals with only a minor loss of nutrients.

* * *

Hearty Noodle Muffin Soup

1 can (10 1/4-ounces) condensed chicken noodle soup
1 soup can of water
1/2 teaspoon prepared mustard
3 English muffin halves, toasted
3 slices (about 1-ounce each)
 Provolone cheese
1 frankfurter cut into 18 thin slices

In a 1 1/2-quart saucepan set over medium heat, combine soup, water and mustard. Heat to boiling, stirring occasionally. Ladle soup into 3 oven-proof 8-ounce bowls. Top with muffin half, cheese slice and 6 frankfurter slices. Broil 3 minutes or until cheese begins to melt. Makes 3 servings.

* * *

New Englanders are proud of their clam chowder. Here is a recipe to try:

New England Clam Chowder

1/4 pound salt pork, diced
2 medium sized onions, diced
3 cups potatoes, diced
1/2 teaspoon salt
1/4 teaspoon pepper
2 cups boiling water
1 quart clams, chopped with their liquor
1 quart milk
2 tablespoons butter
1 pint light cream

Cook salt pork in pan until crisp; remove and add onions, potatoes, salt and pepper. Saute for 10 minutes. Cover with water and simmer 15 minutes. Add clams and their liquor and cook 20 minutes. Then add milk, butter and cream. Heat and serve.

* * *

Corn Chowder

4 slices bacon or salt pork
3 onions, sliced
4 medium sized potatoes, sliced
1 cup water
1 (No. 2 can) cream style corn
3 cups milk

Fry bacon or salt pork slowly and remove when crisp. Pour off all but 4 tablespoons fat and add sliced onions, sliced potatoes and cup of water. Cook 10 minutes. Add corn and milk. Garnish with bits of bacon. Diced and sauteed green pepper also may be added if desired.

All in a Woman's Day--January 12, 1988

Curing the Cold

The rubbing and the dripping, and the sneezing and the wiping, as depicted in TV commercials, seems to describe the season for flu, colds and all the other related respiratory diseases and illnesses.

It has been said that proper eating, getting plenty of rest, exercising and drinking lots of water will help fight off colds and the related illnesses that invade our systems along about this time of year.

Have you had your flu shot? It is recommended for older citizens and those folks having chronic diseases, such as diabetes, lung, heart and kidney ailments, to have flu shots as well as those taking cortisone or undergoing chemotherapy, who will have resistance reduced.

Too, you might need extra vitamins as well as mineral supplements to boost the resistance that does get a bit low about now.

Since away back, the cold has been bedeviled, and it has been found that the effects of the illnesses have been recorded in ancient literature. A 15th century writer described the plague of one Swanus, a pilgrim, who on the road to Jerusalem "dyed by the waye of colde that he had taken of goynge barefote."

According to records, most colds come about between September and May, with an abrupt increase found to be during September and mid-October. Some researchers believe that when people are indoors a lot as during the winter months, they are more likely to be exposed to people with colds as the warmer and drier air tends to dry out the protective mucous that lines the nasal passages, thus allowing the viruses that actually cause a cold to take hold.

It seems there are more than 100 different viruses that can cause a cold. The economic costs of colds, speaking in terms of work time lost, have been estimated in the millions of dollars.

There are lots of cures for colds along with many different kinds of remedies found on store shelves; however, none seem to be the ultimate answer to a real cure. Good old chicken soup seems to be the best thing to eat when you are "under the weather" with a cold or flu.

I am going to mention a few of the treatments that go back in time; however, in some areas some of them may still be practiced today.

One of the remedies is to go to bed. Melt a small amount of lard on the stove and add some turpentine. Then give the chest a good lubricating with this warm penetrating mixture, topping the chest with a flannel cloth that has been warmed to keep the grease from soiling the bed linens and sleeping garments.

Horehound candy was another favorite cure-all for colds. Although this wasn't kept in the medicine cabinet, it seemed to disappear fast!

Aspirin and Vick's Vaporub were old standby remedies. Patients would take an aspirin several times a day, as well as crushing some of the tablets in hot water and using as a gargle. The blue jar of Vick's was always kept close at hand. Again, the hot woolen or flannel "rag" was placed on the greased chest and fastened to the sleeping attire with safety pins. The rising vapor from the Vick's always brought tears to the eyes and it sure did help to unclog a stuffy nose. No bathing or shampooing would take place during the seige; however, when the hair became so stringy and greasy that it was unbearable; then corn meal was worked into the hair followed by a brisk brushing to help remove the dirt and oil.

Perhaps the only really pleasant part of having a cold was the freshly squeezed hot lemonade, laced with honey, and bowls of potato soup seasoned, with butter and celery, and served with crunchy oven toast.

Another remedy back in grandma's day was a mustard plaster used when you had a deep cold. Dried mustard or ground mustard seed was the base of the plaster, with a little suet added to make it stick. Oftentimes mustard and the white of an egg were mixed and rubbed on the chest to help get rid of a cold. This process really burned, so it has been said, but it seemed to do the job.

Honey was another item used to cure sore throats, and chewing honeycomb was prescribed to clear sinus passages.

When a cold got really serious, coal oil came to the rescue. Mixed with milk, it was drunk. This, of course, caused vomiting and was claimed to clear the throat.

Polecat or skunk oil mixed with suet was another combination used and those doctored with this remedy were sure that they did not smell like a bed of roses. A half cup of skunk oil also was used for a serious form of croup-membraneous croup.

In looking back through history, many folk remedies were used. I am going to share with you some found in the book, "Grannie's Remedies."

In some country districts, (England), there are still people who believe that swallowing a spider will cure a cold.

Several authorities on colds recommended that in order to reduce the length of illness and to avoid more serious ear and sinus infections, they should refrain from blowing their nose. Some colonial Americans would pare oranges and roll them inside out and stuff them up their nose.

Norman Lake, Lancaster, Pa., an inventor, in 1953 found that he could make a cold go away by wearing a clothespin on his nose. In 1977, he pat-ented a device he called the "cold clip." The Federal Food and Drug Administration, however, told Lake that he could not advertise his device as a cold cure but only as a way of keeping foreign particles out of the nose.

Another prevention for colds was to walk with the toes turned outward, walking with the chin slightly above the horizontal line as if looking at the top of a man's hat in front of you or at the eaves of a roof on a house. Walk a good deal with hands behind you and sit with the lower part of your spine against the chair back … this should help.

Onions seemed to play and important role in treating colds. A mixture of onion and butter was put on the chest and throat. Cooked onions also were placed in a muslin bag and worn around the neck, and to give protection to children, a large red onion was tied around the bedpost.

Some other old remedies included smoking, inducing shivers daily, rubbing "methylated" spirits into a bald head, rubbing the body with vaseline, wearing a gas mask for an hour a day, inhaling powdery dry licorice leaves, working with lime, avoiding people with poisonous auras, mental concentration (especially on mathematics), growing a mustache right up to the nostrils, sweeping chimneys, standing on the head under water and wearing as a pack between the kidneys a bag containing onions.

One of the traditional cures was known to some as the Hungarian Hat Trick. It was performed by placing a hat on the bedpost, getting into bed and to start drinking until you could see two hats. Then stop and hope for the best.

Still today, the search goes on and on for a desirable and seemingly unattainable cure for the common cold.

All in a Woman's Day--January 19, 1988
It's for the birds!

Have you remembered your fine feathered friends this winter? Don't forget they have to eat, too. The feeder may not help them survive, but it is nice to know that something is provided for them to eat. So far, however, we haven't had much snow to make their search for food difficult.

The thing about bird feeding, however, is if you do not want to keep up the feeding you should never start, for the feathered friends soon learn to depend upon you to provide food. Should you fail to keep this up during the winter, after starting feeding, some of the birds may perhaps die as they have learned to depend upon that source of food, especially so if their access of food is scarce, depending upon the weather, or if it is gone entirely.

If you are not already a bird watcher and would like to become one, just pull up a comfortable easy chair by the window in the direction you have placed a bird feeder or feeders, in a sunny spot, protected from the wind, and start watching.

But first, however, be sure the feeder or feeders are well stocked with a variety of seeds so that different species will be attracted. You will find that if you feed them you will have birds with you until springtime.

Don't forget that the birds need water, too. Some moisture may be obtained from dripping icicles, however, in real cold weather the bird bath should be filled several times a day with warm water. Of course, if you are lucky and have an electrically heated bird bath, the birds will think they are really in "bird heaven."

Folks having finch feeders are seeing a lot of those little fellows nowadays, and the other feeders are no doubt attracting chickadees, bluejays, woodpeckers, titmice, cardinals and nuthatches, and of course, those friendly little birds, the sparrows. They are all God's creatures, so they need to be taken care of if possible.

Should a new bird show up on the scene, it would be well to have a bird book close at hand to identify the newest member of the family.

Bird watching has become a national pastime. People can sit by the hour and watch the many capers the birds go through in their feeding.

You might like to do what many people do that like to bird watch. So they will have birds around to help control the insects when it is gardening time, they plant shrubs that bear winter fruit (berries that is) that attract birds.

Too, since the birds like sunflower seeds you might grow a sunflower or two this summer; however, if you don't, you can purchase the seed at the nursery or the markets.

If you grow sunflowers you can have some fun by cutting off the heads and hanging them upside down somewhere so that you can observe the antics of the birds. Those birds that can cling to the head or those not adverse to feeding upside down, such at nuthatches, will come to the sunflower head, and "put on a good show" for the viewers.

Many people have good luck putting out sunflower seeds, millet and cracked corn in attracting birds to their area. Hanging net bags of suet and other concoctions also will provide the birds with plenty of choice morsels.

* * *

Now, if you really want to make a good impression on your fine feathered friends, here are some recipes that you might whip up to their delight and that you might say are "strictly for the birds!"

(The following recipes are from the "Old Farmer's 1984 Almanac.")

Junco Corn Meal
(For the Birds)

3 cups corn meal
2 teaspoons baking powder
1/2 cup fat (lard or meat drippings)
3 cups water

Mix all together and bake them about 35 minutes in a deep pan at 375 degrees. Reduce the heat if the bread appears to be forming a hard crust. This recipe may be doubled or halved. Place it in mesh bags and hang it outdoors near the feeders.

* * *

Fine Feathered Entree
(For the Birds)

3 parts melted fat (suet preferred)
1 part corn meal or finely cracked corn
1 part peanut butter or other nut butter
1 part sunflower kernels or chopped nuts
1 part brown sugar
1 part chopped dried fruit (currants, raisins, prunes etc.)

Combine all the ingredients with enough water to obtain the consistency of cooked oatmeal. Cook mixture in a double boiler until well blended. Put it into small containers, such as tuna fish cans that can be securely fastened to feeders or trees.

'Rules of Thumb' help!

Perhaps you know some "rules of thumb," or at least have heard about them. If you do not know what it means, the "rules of thumb" are little bits of homemade knowledge that will help take the guesswork out of your life. Tom Parker has collected a number of these fascinating little gems in his book, "Rules of Thumb."

I am going to share some of the more interesting ones with you.

If you haven't worn a garment in a year, throw it out—you won't miss it.

Ten people will raise the temperature of a medium-sized room one degree per hour.

One inch of rain equals 10 inches of snow or vice versa.

The distance between your elbow to your wrist equals the length of your foot.

Your wedding ring size is the same as your hat size.

The heaviest rainfall usually comes three to five days after the new and full moon.

The thinner cheese is sliced, the better it is going to taste.

Plan to sit around for at least half an hour on any visit to a doctor.

You can check the fit of new pants without trying them on. With the top of the pants fastened, the closed waistband should just wrap around your neck.

People will eat one and a half to two times more mashed potatoes than baked.

You can mail five sheets of paper with a 22-cent stamp. (Times have now changed.)

To determine how many lights your Christmas tree needs, multiply the tree

To determine how many lights your Christmas tree needs, multiply the tree height by the tree width and multiply the resulting total by three.

To buy the right size socks, wrap the bottom part of the sock around your fist. If it is the right size, the heel will just meet the toe.

If you are not quite sure how deep to plant a flower bulb, try three times its length.

If you find your face dry and puffy when you awaken, put off shaving two minutes for each hour you slept.

Your body is eight times the height of your head.

On a new job, beware of those who might seem too friendly too soon.

When on a job interview, be sure you never spend more than 60 seconds answering a question.

The number of guests at a child's birthday party should be limited to the child's age-three for a three-year-old and five for a five-year-old.

Spring moves north at about 13 miles a day.

The number of stars visible inside the ring around the moon is the number of days before rain comes.

You will find that the deductible amount on auto collision insurance should equal one week's take home pay.

When first grade children get disruptive as a class, a major change in weather is near.

The height of a boy on his second birthday will be about half his adult height. Girls will be slightly shorter than that when grown.

When traveling, take twice the money and half the clothes you think you will need.

If a telephone rings more than six times, it probably won't be answered.

These little examples of "rules of thumb" are rather fascinating and the strange part is that these "homemade recipes" for making a guess seem to come out just about right. Some are handy and some you might say, are hilarious!

* * *

Mock Twinkies
1/4 pound butter or margarine
1/2 cup vegetable shortening
1 cup sugar
3/4 cup canned milk
1 tablespoon vanilla

Beat ingredients for 8-10 minutes. Bake a yellow cake mix according to package directions. Split and fill with the above filling. Cut into bars.

All in a Woman's Day--February 2, 1988
Cherries hit the spot!
Just as cranberries represent Christmas; pumpkins, Thanksgiving; strawberries, summer; the cherry seems to be the fruit for February.

With the birthdays of two Presidents, George Washington and Abraham Lincoln, occurring this month, (the birthdays are now observed as President's Day—this year on February 15), plus Valentine's Day, cherries have the opportunity to be the stars in a variety of foods prepared to celebrate these special holidays.

Since fresh cherries are available only for a brief time during the summer, at this time of year we have to use frozen or canned cherries. The cherry pie filling that you can purchase, or, if you prefer to make your own, has been brought into use in a number of food preparations.

So, whether you use frozen, canned or fresh cherries you will find different kinds—sour, sweet, white, red (and also deep red Bing cherries). The red cherries are the most used for preparing cherry desserts that are so popular during this month.

If you like cherry cokes at home you can make a good cherry coke syrup using a package of regular cherry flavored powdered beverage mix, adding only one and a half cups water and one cup sugar. Stir until the sugar is dissolved. Keep refrigerated. To make a glass of good cherry coke add two or three teaspoons of syrup to a glass of coke.

For an easy dessert, stir drained canned dark, red, sweet cherries and roasted diced almonds into whipped topping and garnish with chocolate curls.

A good cherry glaze for ham is made by using one package cherry gelatin, one cup boiling water and two cups brown sugar. Dissolve all together and baste over whole ham or pour over slices and bake one hour at 350 degrees.

* * *

Heavenly Cherry Pie

1 envelope unflavored gelatin
1/4 cup cold water
1 (20-ounce) can sweetened frozen cherries, defrosted
1 teaspoon lemon juice
1/2 cup flaked coconut
1/2 teaspoon almond extract
1/2 cup chopped nuts
1/4 cup sifted powdered sugar
1 cup whipped cream, whipped or whipped topping
1 baked pie shell, 9-inches

Soften gelatin in cold water. Drain cherries and add enough water to cherry juice to make 1 cup liquid. In a saucepan, combine lemon juice and cherry liquid and bring to a boil. Remove from heat and add softened gelatin, stirring until dissolved. Chill. When slightly congealed, whip until fluffy. Add cherries, coconut, nuts and extract. Beat powdered sugar into whipped cream or whipped topping and fold half of this mixture into the gelatin fruit mixture and spoon into pie shell. Marble the top with remaining whipped cream or whipped topping. Chill thoroughly.

* * *

Cherry Coffee Cake

2 cups sifted flour
2 teaspoons baking powder
1 egg
Milk
1 cup sugar
1/2 cup butter
1 can cherry pie filling

Sift together flour, sugar and baking powder. Cut in butter as for pie crust. Break egg into cup and add sufficient milk to make 1 cup of liquid. Beat egg into milk and add to the flour mixture, and mix well. Pour into a jelly roll pan (15x10-inches) that has been greased and floured. Cover with pie filling.

Topping:

1 cup flour
1/2 cup butter
1 cup sugar

Sift together the flour and sugar and cut in the butter. Sprinkle the mixture over the pie filling and bake in a 400 degree oven for 30-35 minutes. Serves 16-20.

All in a Woman's Day--February 9, 1988

Valentine's Day is special!

Valentine's Day stirs up thoughts of red roses, candy, chubby cupids and fancy red hearts. It is the special day of the year when lovers, as well as friends and relatives, express fellings of love.

It always has been a time for gift giving. Some of the gifts have remained the same through the years; however, there have been some changes. The earliest gifts given and received were most appropriately flowers and hearts. Sometimes a special valentine might bear a lock of the loved one's hair. Flowers given came from the giver's garden and this was made possible because on the ancient calendar, Valentine's Day occurred in the spring and flowers were blooming at that time.

Another version says the association grew out of the similarity between the word "galantin," meaning a lover of women, and the name of the saint.

In early Rome as the bird's mating began, a festival was dedicated to Lupercus, the wolf god or the god of shepherds and lovers. As a part of the celebration, the maidens deposited their names in a giant urn on the public square. Each young man drew a "card." Some maidens tried to attract attention to their cards by lavishly decorating them, thereby creating a lot of "ohs and ahs." This has been said to be a forerunner of our valentines of today. This observance was on February 15; however, gradually this Christian holiday became a time for exchanging love messages and St. Valentine emerged as a patron saint of lovers. Also there was a European belief that on February 14 each year the birds began to find their mates. In the "Parliament of Foules," Chaucer wrote, "For this was Seynt Valwntynes Day when every foul comes to chose a mate."

Another assumed theory that is most widely believed is that the first valentine ever written was composed as a farewell note on February 14 in the year 270 by a young Roman named Valentine, on the day of his execution, to the jailers' blind daughter and was signed "from your Valentine." Some say that Valentine wore an amethyst ring on which was engraved cupid, the Greek god of love, and that in this way cupid became associated with St. Valentine's.

Except for the jailer's daughter, almost everyone forgot the brave young Roman until Christianity had a firm hold upon the world. Then he was cannonized, and because he had been martyred on February 14, in his honor, that day was called St. Valentine's Day.

There was a period in England when much time and care were spent in the writing of valentines. Sometimes famous writers "ghosted" love messages for royal lovers to send to their ladies. It is said that King Henry V wooed Catherine of Valois with valentine greetings secretly composed by John Lindgate. For the unimaginative, a book, "The Complete Valentine Writer," published in London around 200 years ago, included a wide variety of love verses which were hand copied onto valentines.

Cromwell, the Puritan dictator of England at one time, practically stopped the sending of valentines during his rule because he thought they were "immoral." The custom, however, was reestablished during the reign of merry King Charles II, and gifts of scented gloves and jeweled garters as messages of love became popu!ar.

One English writer, some years after the telephone was invented, deplored the fact that the custom of sending valentines was slackening. He made this curious observation: "What really is killing valentines is the telephone.

When the telephone came into the house a valentine could not live in the same atmosphere."

Shoe laces, believe it or not, were one of the important gifts given on Valentine's Day. To us, shoe laces do not sound very much like a valentine gift; however, they may have been hard to come by in those days.

Gifts also were received by little children; however, they had to earn them. They, the boys and girls, would go around singing about St. Valentine's Day and collecting presents from those who invited them inside. It was very similar to the modern day trick-or-treat at Halloween.

If a suitor was really serious, small paper gloves or real leather gloves were given. The gloves, it has been learned, symbolized the asking for a lady's hand in marriage. If the lady in asking wore real gloves or carried the paper gloves when she went to church on Easter it indicated that her answer was "yes."

Ladies oftentimes gave their husbands or sweethearts a small circle of silk cloth that was embroidered with a heart and a floral design. This was used to keep the dust out of a man's pocket watch. The dust catcher gifts were highly valued by the men, who otherwise would have to use an ordinary piece of brown paper.

Among some of the superstitions about lovers that have persisted are these: If a long apple peel is flung over the left shoulder by a hopeful young lady, it could fall into the initial of her future husband; if a match burns from end to end without breaking or going out, the person who lights the match will have a happy marriage; if the last serving is taken from a plate of food, the one who takes it will never marry.

Some girls slept with mirrors under their pillows for three nights so that they would dream of their future husbands. Some went blindfolded into their vegetable gardens and pulled up cabbages by the roots. If the roots were straight they believed their husbands would be handsome; if crooked, ugly. Others, before going to bed, placed their shoes in the form of the letter T, the point of one touching the middle of the other. Then they would softly recite, "When I my true love want to see, I put my shoes in the shape of a T."

What Valentine's Day may evolve in years to come no one knows, but one thing for sure it will always remain a day for lovers, and love will be the theme. No doubt this year will be no different than others and postmen will be overloaded with thousands and thousands of valentines that will be delivered all over the country on this special day.

On Valentine's Day say, "I love you," in whatever way is special to you, but don't forget! One of the nicest valentine verses and also one of the oldest is simply, "Roses are red, Violets are blue, Sugar is sweet and so are You!"

* * *

Marshmallow Creme Divinity
1 1/2 cups sugar
1/3 cup water
Pinch of salt
1 pint marshmallow creme
1 teaspoon vanilla
1/2 cup chopped nuts
Food coloring optional

Cook sugar, water and salt to hardball stage; do not overcook. Pour it into the marshmallow creme that has been placed in a bowl, beating constantly. Add vanilla, nuts and desired amount of food coloring. Beat until thick. Drop by teaspoons onto waxed paper. Cool until set.

All in a Woman's Day--February 16, 1988

Cookbook news told!

Cookbooks, cookbooks and more cookbooks! Many homemakers have lots of cookbooks around, but they still continue to purchase them when a new one makes an appearance. Whether there is hopes of finding "that something special" in a recipe, or whether they just make good reading, may be a question as to why so many can be found around the home.

Some of the cookbooks purchased make homemakers feel real confident for the recipes in them have been tried and proven "good."

The first cookbook published in the United States was the "Complete Housewife" or "Gentlewoman's Companion," printed in 1742 in Williamsburg, Va.

A bibliography of American Cookery books list 490 books published from that time up to 1860. These were all written for the housewife, and not for a chef.

A cookbook published 100 years ago reports: "The average life in America would be about 80 years if proper care was taken of mind and body; at present it is only 34 years."

Along with the recipes, these old cookbooks always offered suggestions for a happier and longer life, and also remedies to cure anything that could go wrong with a man, his family or even his horse!

For example, If you want a girl baby put sugar on your bedroom window sill; if you want a boy baby put salt on your bedroom sill; for wind colds or night sweats, make sage into a strong tea and drink a cupful as emergency may demand.

For asthma sufferers: Sufferers of asthma should get a muskrat skin and wear it over their lungs, with the fur side next to the body. It will bring certain relief!

For red hands: Keep your feet warm by soaking them in hot water, and keep your hands out of the water as much as possible.

For hoarseness, palsy, dropsy and rheumatism: Make a syrup by boiling a horseradish root and add suffi-cient sugar to make it palatable. Take two teaspoonsful two or three times daily.

For sleeplessness: Lie with the head to the north, for there is no doubt something in the electrical effects of the earth that work upon the body in that position.

Well, so be it, for all those good remedies.

Cookbooks have continued to come from the press until it is said that books on foods and beverages rank second only to the Bible in number printed.

There has been a constant evolution in cookery, food preservation and cooking equipment. In the United States there is found in many of the cities, foods of every description from all over the world, and in book stores, books of recipes for dishes that are common in every civilized country. In the United States, with its population made up of people from many different countries, housewives may retain their own recipes, but so far as funds allow, everybody uses the most modern equipment for cooking.

No doubt the book that has had the greatest influence in raising the standard of American cookery is the "Boston Cooking School Cookbook," written by Fannie Merritt Farmer in 1896. This book featured for the first time level measurements in cups and spoons, and stressed the use of standard half-pint cups, divided into quarters and thirds, tablespoons holding one-sixteenth of a cup and a teaspoon holding one-third of a tablespoon.

The really early day cookbooks featured recipes measured by handfuls of ingredients, fat the slice of a walnut, a pinch or a smidgen of seasoning, and perhaps enough liquid to make a dough. Sometimes the recipe said to use your own judgement; naturally, an inexperienced person had some difficulty learning to cook.

With tested recipes and equipment of standard size, there can be little doubt in the cook's mind about the amount of ingredients to use or the method of preparation. The texture and flavor of foods are controlled to a large degree by the skill and cleverness with which ingredients are combined. Recipes of the great chefs can now be duplicated in the kitchen.

When applied to cooking, a recipe is a formula for preparing a dish. In old-fashioned usage the words "receipt" or "rule" were often used to mean the same thing.

And so, just as clothing and decorating styles change believe it or not, so do cooking styles. Grandmother's cookbook is fascinating to read; however, you perhaps won't use it. That is because grandma probably wasn't in as big a hurry in the kitchen as homemakers are today. To accommodate today's fast-paced lifestyles, preparation time for many recipes have been shortened and have become more streamlined.

If you happen to come across some old cookbooks or you have some in your possession, take care of them for no doubt they are priceless, and collectors would like to lay their hands on them. And if you want some pleasant reading, grab a good cookbook and the first thing you know you will want to whip up something as a surprise for your family. Just keep right on collecting cookbooks. It is a good hobby!

We all know that you can't judge a book by its cover, and that the proof of the pudding is in the eating, and that you had better look before you leap out of the frying pan into the fire!

All in a Woman's Day--February 23, 1988

It's February ... enjoy!

The month of February is almost gone, and if that is so, spring can't be too far away. Isn't that a good feeling?

Lots of things have been on the calendar this month. In fact you might say it is a potpourri month. First came Ground Hog Day, Lincoln's and Washington's birthdays, now both celebrated on President's Day, Valentine's Day and Ash Wednesday, the beginning of Lent. This month also is being observed as Potato Month, Canned Food Month, Oatmeal Month, Kraut and Frank Month and many others that perhaps I don't know about. And last, but not least, Leap Year Month, which, of course, is observed every four years.

How many folks are celebrating a birthday Feb. 29th? There should be some throughout the county that are observing this special day. To you we say "Happy Birthday," and may you have another in four years.

According to legend, this special Leap Year Day is a time when maidens happily offer their hands and hearts to bashful bachelors. Take care and beware fellows!

Like most everything a lot of lore goes along with this observance. It seems that St. Bridget was the first to propose to St. Patrick, and because of his personal vow of celibacy, of course, led him to decline her proposal. By the Middle Ages, the custom had spread throughout Europe. During this special month, and most especially on Feb. 29th, women not only talk about doing the proposing, oftentimes they do pop the question. This special time gave women the right to obtain their heart's desire instead of waiting for him to do the honors.

Today, however, about all that remains are the dances that celebrate Leap Year and Leap Year Day on Feb. 29th.

* * *

Since this has been a bit of a cold month, Oatmeal Month is rather appropos to think about. We all know that a hot dish of oatmeal is a good food to start a family off to work or study. Of course, the purpose of this special month is to celebrate nature's most perfect food, as well as encourage Americans to start each day with this nutritious, versatile and scrumptious cereal. And if you don't mind, it also is a good lunchtime dish as well as a light evening meal. Raisins or cut-up dates added to the cereal, does enhance its taste.

* * *

"Please pass the potatoes!" is a request or phrase that is heard almost as frequently as a request for the bread to be passed. The potato runs bread a close race in being the No. 1 food, called the staff of life. Potatoes are versatile as they can be used in so many different ways. Potatoes also have all the nutrients needed so they are healthful and good for you. It is what you put on them that adds calories to your diet.

Here are two ways to freeze potatoes. Cook potatoes just as you would when serving them baked; then allow them to cool thoroughly. Wrap each in foil and freeze. When needed, simply defrost and heat through. They taste fresh baked! They also can be peeled and fried, or however you want to use them.

Take small like potatoes and scrub thoroughly and cook with jackets on. Larger potatoes can be scraped or peeled. Boil quickly, and as soon as they are done, drain, cool and place them in plastic bags in the freezer. They can be frozen either with or without the skins. They may be used anyway fresh potatoes are used, from soup to salad. Try frying them in butter, too!

* * *

Cheese Potato Balls

2 cups cooked potatoes, grated
1 egg
1/2 cup grated American cheese (or any hard cheese)
2 tablespoons onion, grated
Salt and pepper to taste
Corn flake crumbs

Combine first five ingredients and form into small balls. Roll in corn flake crumbs. Bake them on a cookie sheet 20 minutes in a preheated 400 degree oven. This is a delightfully different way to serve potatoes.

All in a Woman's Day--March 1, 1988
Help for the kitchen!

This seems to be a good time to have some hodge-podge hints for the kitchen.

When a recipe calls for self-rising flour and you don't have any on hand, use this substitute: Three and a half cups all-purpose flour, plus one and three-fourths teaspoons baking powder, one and three-fourths teaspoons baking soda and one and three-fourths teaspoons salt.

To help cut down on the price of eggs, use only two egg whites for a meringue pie topping. Add about half teaspoon baking powder to the whites before beating them. This will swell the meringue, making it higher.

Remove potatoes from the plastic bags they come in at the store and put them in a paper bag to keep them from spoiling.

Are you tired of having lumpy soups and gravies? Tired of straining out those unwanted lumps? Well, you can make them lump free by using dried instant potatoes instead of flour. The gravies and soups will be smooth and lump free and be more flavorful, too.

When giving cookie platters for gifts, be sure to wrap each different kind of cookie separately in plastic wrap. This way, each cookie retains its special flavor.

Still hungry? After a big evening meal, you may still feel sudden hunger pangs while watching TV. Slowly eat a plain piece of bread, without anything on it. Then wash it down with a glass of water. For some strange reason this tends to satisfy your hunger and also relaxes you, too.

Hunting for a great vegetable dip? Try this. Combine one package (2.5 ounce) dried beef, chopped; one package (8 ounce) cream cheese, softened; a fourth cup of milk; one teaspoon dill weed or fresh dill; and a half teaspoon of horseradish. This makes one and a half cups of creamy dip.

Milk will stay fresh longer by putting it in the microwave and bringing it to 160 degrees. A cup of milk takes about 2 minutes. This seems to kill the micro-organisms that causes milk to have an off taste.

When preparing food, such as meat loaf or stuffing, use a heavy plastic bag instead of a bowl for mixing. Put all ingredients in a bag and hold the top closed with one hand while squeezing the outside of the bag with the other. No bowls or spoons to wash.

Ground pork may have 10 percent less fat than bulk pork sausage. So, if you like sausage, but hate the fat, to one pound of lean ground pork add three-fourths teaspoon of ground sage, a fourth teaspoon of pepper and a half teaspoon of salt (optional). For a country style sausage flavor add one teaspoon of ground sage, a half teaspoon of dried savory, crushed; a fourth teaspoon of pepper, a fourth teaspoon of cayenne and a fourth teaspoon of nutmeg. Just mix, make into patties and fry.

To freeze mashed ripe bananas add lemon juice or ascorbic acid or possibly a citric acid preparation to prevent them from turning dark. When ready to use, defrost and use in cooking where mashed bananas are needed as an ingredient.

Here's another way of making sweetened condensed milk. Use half cup of cold water, one and a half cups of nonfat dry milk solids and three-fourths cup of sugar. Gradually stir powdered milk into water, stirring until smooth. Microwave on high for 45 seconds to one minute. (Should be steaming.) Add sugar and stir until dissolved. This equals 1 can.

Use low to medium temperature when cooking with cheese, especially in the microwave. Do not overcook. If cooked too long or at too high a temperature, it will turn tough and rubbery.

Should you want a homemade taste from store purchased chili, brown half pound of ground beef and a small onion. Add one cup tomato juice and a family size can of chili concarne with beans. Heat thoroughly.

Red cabbage is a beautiful vegetable to add a little color and excitement to salads, as well as other dishes. However, when you boil it, some color is lost. Add a little vinegar or lemon juice and keep the color from bleeding.

Cutting a long sheet cake into squares is often messy and it is sometimes difficult to keep lines straight. The cut can be made simply by using dental floss. Wrap the floss around the index fingers, leaving a length slightly longer than the cake. Holding the line taut, draw it downward through the cake, until cut. This makes a clean straight cut. Change floss often to get clean cuts.

On the spur of the moment you decided to bake, but the butter or margarine is too hard to be creamed. Use the potato peeler or grater. By the time you have all the other ingredients measured, the butter or margarine will be warmed to room temperature and ready to be creamed.

All in a Woman's Day--March 8, 1988
Yogurt is surprising!

Yogurt has really caught on. Today it is the fastest growing dairy product in our country, and Americans have become one of the world's foremost yogurt consumers.

The history of yogurt is colorful. It dates back some 4,000 years. For many centuries it has been a dietary staple in India, and ruddy faced Europeans have bragged that it contributed to their virility and longevity.

The Phoencians spooned up yogurt for bemused foreigners traveling there 4,000 years ago; so, you can see it has been around a long time.

It is rather interesting and also surprising, however, that in viewing its long history that we find it was only in the late 1950s that it was more or less a novelty in this country, especially when it is contrasted with today's situation.

It has reached proportions of approximately five cups consumed by every man, woman and child in this country; however, it still lags behind the really avid yogurt eating countries. The Swiss really go for it by consuming about 200 cups on a yearly average; with the Dutch using 60, and the French 40 cups per capita. President Dwight Eisenhower was an occasional yogurt eater along with weight watcher movie stars.

Yogurt was once known as "sour milk with a college education" because it was a sophisticated by-product of the unseen workings of desirable bacteria. In fact, if you are not aware of it, yogurt is curdled milk that results from the acid formed in the conversion of milk sugar into lactic acid. It is the acid that thickens the milk and creates the tangy aroma and flavor that we know so characteristically to be yogurt.

The yogurt we have today is much different from the old world product of fermented milk from yak, goats, water buffalo, horses and sheep. Cow's milk is now used exclusively in this modern product that comes in various forms. Today, it is made from milk partly evaporated and fermented. Since it is thick, it is an excellent lower calorie substitute for sour cream.

An eight ounce serving of plain low fat yogurt has about 145 calories, with the flavored low fat yogurt having about 195 calories. Yogurt is an excellent source of calcium, riboflavin and protein.

One cup of milk equals one cup yogurt.

Yogurt, seasoned with lemon juice, salt and pepper to taste, makes a good dressing for vegetable or fruit salads.

To make a fruit cup, use fresh fruit cut in pieces, canned fruit or berries in old-fashioned glasses or small deep bowls. Cover with yogurt. If you like, this can be sprinkled with light brown sugar.

Perhaps you might like to try your hand at making your own yogurt. To do so, take one quart of milk and bring it to the boiling point for just one minute. Then cool to 115 degrees, and very carefully mix in two tablespoons of fresh, plain yogurt (this is a starter). Pour it into bowls. You can use a large crockery bowl, several small bowls or perhaps custard cups. Cover tightly and put them in a warm place where there are no drafts. The best temperature, 110 degrees, should hasten the incubation. It takes five to eight hours to be ready. To be sure the product is finished, just tilt the bowl and see if it holds together. It should be chilled for three hours, which also will make it more firm before using.

Yogurt must be handled carefully, for if it sets too long or too much starter is used, it will become watery and, too, the longer it is incubated the more sour it will become.

Yogurt also can be used in making soup, which is much lighter than the normal cold soup with a cream base.
* * *
You might like to try this dip:
Yogurt Dip
2 cups plain yogurt
1/2 cucumber seeded and chopped fine
1/2 teaspoon mint, dried and crumbled
or 1 teaspoon fresh mint, chopped
1 clove garlic, minced

Mix all ingredients and chill thoroughly, thus enabling the flavors to develop.

All in a Woman's Day--March 15, 1988
Irish pride shows
St. Patrick's Day
'Tis the birthday of St. Patrick
And as we commemorate,
A little bit of blarney
Is most appropriate.

Of the patron saint of Ireland
A good word we must say,
For love of Christianity
He spread along his way.

We'll be hearing of the shamrocks
And wearing something green,
And today above all others
Things of Ireland can be seen.

If for sure on this St. Patrick's,
Seems like Erin's everywhere,
On the tide of Irish laughter
You have been transported there
Virginia D. McCulloh
* * *
A long time ago a poet wrote: "A plenteous place is Ireland of hospitable cheer."

"Faith and begorrah" he was right, and it is that time when many of us let our Irish show just a wee bit (with pride) when we put on a little something green to wear on this very special day—St. Patrick's Day.

You don't have to be Irish, however, to join in the frivolity of the day. The most common tribute to the memory of St. Patrick is the wearin' of the green. Celebrants don green clothing or something green that is representative of the "Emerald Isle."

Much of our flamboyancy, associated with St. Patrick's Day in the United States, is not native at all to Ireland.

Originally, it was a Holy day and Irishmen celebrated it by attending mass and spending the day with their families. They usually wore something green and ate corned beef and cabbage. This was not a traditional St. Patrick's Day dish; however, both are standard Irish fare.

The Irish cuisine is varied and fine tasting, although folks often poke fun about the Irish cooking that consists of boiled potatoes. They have a wholesome and simple cuisine that reflects the country, its people and their way of life. Here we would call it "down home country cooking," and that is just what it is. Stews and delicious breads warm the body as well as the soul.

Emerald Isle food is meant for welcoming, for the kitchen is always the center of the Irish home. A softly spoken "Cead Miller Failte" (A hundred thousand welcomes) rests as easily on a Gaelic tongue as a pot of strong tea on the stove. Hospitality in the home is very much a part of Irish life, as much today as yesteryear.

Much has been said and told about St. Patrick, who himself is almost a legend. He is credited with the founding of 300 churches, including one at Dublin, where the famed St. Patrick's Cathedral now stands, and for the baptizing of more than a 120,000 persons.

So successful were St. Patrick's labors, that he came to be known as the one who "found Ireland all heathen and left it all Christian."

Many terms and phrases come from Irish folklore and culture, and they have been taken into use in the English language. For instance, a legend tells of the blarney stone, a stone in Blarney Castle, near Cork, Ireland, where it is said to make those who kiss it skilled in flattery. And then, of course, there is the gift of blarney that we know as a glib tongue. To be full of blarney, is comparable to the American slang phrase, "full of baloney."

Then, there are the leprechauns, known as "The Little People." They have charmed their way from Irish folklore to adorn greeting cards, posters, paper tableware, party hats and many other items for the celebration of this special day. According to legend, the leprechauns are mischievous elves that are believed able to reveal the whereabouts of hidden treasure, if caught.

Among some of the other phrases that originated in the Irish culture are "saints preserve us" and "faith and begorrah," a mild oath. Another is "getting your Irish up," which is a stereotype of a quick Irish temper. The Irish are often described as being hot tempered; however, they also bear the reputation of being lucky, hence the phrase "luck of the Irish."

There also are such words as shillelagh, a walking stick; a jig, a lively, springy dance in triple rhythm; hooligan, a ruffian (inspired by Patrick Hooligan, an Irish hoodlum of Southwark, London); lads and lassies, boys and girls.

Maybe you would like to surprise

your family on this special day and decorate your dinner table with things that "speak," of the Irish—shamrocks, pipes, a bowler (hat), maybe a little sprinkling of green confetti, and last, but not least, some pixies.

We know that Irish people are jolly folks and there is a saying that each March 17th, everyone who is not Irish, wishes he was! Happy St. Patrick's Day!

* * *

Blarney Stones

4 eggs
2 cups sugar
1/2 teaspoon salt
2 teaspoons vanilla
2 tablespoons butter or margarine, melted in 1 cup hot milk
1 teaspoon baking powder
2 cups sifted cake flour
Powdered sugar
Milk
Ground roasted peanuts or pecans

Beat eggs until light; beat in sugar, salt, vanilla and butter mixture. Sift flour and baking powder together and beat in quickly. Pour into greased 13x9-inch pan. Pound pan several times to remove air bubbles. Bake 25-35 minutes at 350 degrees. Cook and cut into 4x4-inch pieces. Cover all sides with icing made of powdered sugar and milk. Roll in ground peanuts.

This is an Irish recipe from settlers of Ireland at Old San Patricio, Texas.

All in a Woman's Day--March 22, 1988
Celebrate Easter!

This is the time of year that we are caught up in the deep religious significance of the season of Easter.

This very special event celebrates the Resurrection of Christ and it is at this time that we find Mother Nature beginning to awaken from a winter's sleep to rejoice with us.

Legends and stories abound pertaining to Easter, until it would seem that they would be exhausted. In my search for something new I did come across several thoughts pertaining to Easter, and they add to the wonderful story of the season.

It seems that "Near the Cross of Calvary," in a sheltered place, sat a mother bird brooding on her nest. The scene of the sorrow and cruelty so wounded her tender heart that she grieved and mourned. After a while she left her nest and flew from the scene of wickedness and pain. Those who looked into the nest found that the eggs were colored with drops of blood as if from the mother's heart.

* * *

Hot Cross Buns have become a tradition in some families, where the custom began as a daily "prayer." The father of the family would take a knife to cut a fresh loaf of bread; however, he first marked the top of the loaf with a cross. This was a sign of thankfulness to God for the bread. Later, however, on special occasions the cross was imprinted on the dough before baking. In England in the 14th century, rolls were baked on Good Friday and given to the poor. Later the custom spread to Ireland and then to other countries.

In Austria, people have a rather unusual observance. It is said that they gather on the mountainside for an Easter sunrise service, singing hymns as the sun rises, and then they shoot off cannons. (Why cannons? We'll probably never know!)

Also in that country eggs were used as rewards. King Edward I once had

450 eggs boiled and covered with gold leaf. These he gave as gifts to servants in the royal palace.

Red eggs in Persia were exchanged in observance of the spring equinox, a welcome to a new growing season. In early times, tender blades of wheat, that at this season were just beginning to show, were used for coloring eggs a lovely dark green. Then, along came the idea that other colors could be obtained by steeping leaves from the mulberry tree.

Chinese, Egyptians, Greeks and Romans all used colored eggs; however, in China red eggs were given out to announce a birth in the family. They would put an egg in the baby's first bath—one white for a boy and two red for a girl. This was done to insure good health, a long life and good fortune to the child.

The early Christians gave a religious symbolism to the red egg. The shell of the egg represented Christ's tomb; the red, His blood; and the hatching of the egg denoted the Resurrection.

Customs began to spread to use many colors of eggs to represent the aurora borealis and the colors of the rainbow.

In Italy eggs were carried to the church to be blessed, and then taken and set out with the flowers on the table. It seems that every visitor during the week of Easter was invited to eat an egg.

The coloring of Easter eggs in central Europe has become an important community event. The preparations, most often, begins many weeks ahead of time, when much visiting was done with friends and family in their homes. In some instances, the technique used by a family in coloring eggs was kept a closely guarded secret, and often passed on from one generation to another.

Too, these eggs sometimes became treasured works of arts and family heirlooms.

Most of the designs in the European countries are not on the trivial side. The patterns include flowers, messages of love, religious motifs, stars, symbols of happiness or good health.

In Germany, popular paper-mache eggs are filled with various goodies.

* * *

Glorified Scrambled Eggs

8 eggs
1/2 teaspoon salt
Dash of pepper
4 strips of bacon, diced
1/2 cup milk
2 tablespoons margarine
1/4 teaspoon butter flavoring
1(10 1/2-ounce) can cream of mushroom soup

Break eggs into bowl. Scramble lightly with fork and add seasonings. Bacon may be added to eggs. If you prefer crispier bacon, precook until about half done and then add to the eggs. Stir in milk. Melt margarine with butter flavoring in skillet. Add egg mixture and stir gently until cooked. Remove skillet from heat and add soup. Then return skillet to the heat a few minutes, stirring gently, until mixture is hot through. This is good served over toast or served as a supper dish with bread and butter.

All in a Woman's Day--March 29, 1988

This is an Easter Prayer

"Now faith, hope, love abide, these three, but the greatest of these is love." (1 Corinthians 13:13)

Christians believe that the love of God was most fully revealed in Jesus

Christ, and most dramatically expressed in the Cross of Calvary. The many dimensions of love are found in the translations of one's own life.

In its highest and finest expression, love is the fulfillment of all the cardinal virtues. It is never without justice, fortitude and temperance. Easter is a validation of the Christian hope. It is the universal day of love, for God was fully revealed in His Son, His Cross and His Victory over the grave. Easter has been said to be a six-letter word spelling "love."

* * *

A classic love prayer was composed and offered by Robert Louis Stevenson in the final months of his life on an island in the South Seas. Afflicted with poor health, and surrounded by domestic and political strife, he still had the great heart to pray. This prayer incorporates the cardinal virtues, so love sustains and directs the lasting elements of life itself. For as St. Paul says, "Love never ends."

This prayer could be for any of us, especially at this season of the year.

"Lord, behold our family here assembled. We thank Thee for this place in which to dwell; for the love that unites us; for the peace accorded us this day; for the hope with which we expect the morrow; for the health, work, the food and the bright skies that make our lives delightful for our friends in all parts of the earth and our friendly helpers in their foreign isles. Let peace abound in our small company. Purge out of every heart lurking grudge. Give us grace and strength to forbear and to persevere. Give us courage and gaiety and the quiet mind. Bless us, if it may be in all our innocent endeavors. And if it may not, give us strength to encounter that which is to come, that we may be brave in peril, constant in tribulation, temperate in wrath, and in all the changes of fortune, down to the gates of death, loyal and loving to the last. As the clay to the potter, as the windmill to the wind, and the children to their sire, we beseech Thee of His help and mercy for Christ's sake. Amen."

—By Robert Louis Stevenson

* * *

May you have a blessed Easter!

All in a Woman's Day--April 5, 1988

Hard-boiled egg hints

Wondering just what to do with the eggs the Easter bunny left behind?

Whatever you do, it is hoped that you placed the hard-boiled eggs into the refrigerator as soon as possible from their nesting place in the centerpiece of your holiday table. Because so many of the Easter eggs looks so pretty, we are tempted to leave them unrefrigerated for hours, after a meal has been finished.

It is claimed that Easter eggs should not really be boiled. Instead, the eggs should be pierced on the ends, then simmered gently over low heat for about 20 minutes. High temperature and overcooking toughens eggs. After cooking, pour off the hot water and fill the pan with cold water so that the shells will peel off easily when the eggs are ready to be eaten.

It is not hard to detect a rotten egg as the odor it gives off soon reaches the nose. It might not even be wise to use eggs that don't smell, when they have been used as Easter eggs.

Take for instance an egg cracked in transit, from the store to the home, should be used immediately, as well as any that might happen to crack during the cooking process.

No eggs should be left unrefrigerated for very long. Anytime they are kept out of the cold, lessens the eggs' keeping qualities and invites spoilage. So, be careful, and use your Easter eggs wisely.

I have a few hints concerning eggs.

Eggs, in the shell, raw or cooked, should keep for five weeks refrigerated. It is most preferable that they are stored in the carton in which they were purchased; however, the closed container slows loss of moisture to help preserve freshness.

Always store uncooked eggs blunt end up to keep the yolk centered.

Hard cooked Easter eggs should keep for about a week if they haven't been used as centerpieces and for egg hunts.

An egg is fresh if it sinks to the bottom of a pan of cold water when submerged. If it bobs, it is getting old, and if it floats, well, it is old. Older eggs, however, can be used in foods such as cakes and muffins where freshness is not critical.

Leftover egg whites can be used in cakes, meringues and souffles.

If you are frying eggs in butter or margarine, place two or three drops of oil in the pan and this prevents the butter from burning and turning brown.

When mashing egg yolks for stuffed eggs and the like, cut the hard-boiled eggs in half and then place the yolks in a strainer. Using a large spoon, push them through the strainer. This is easier than mashing them with a fork and is faster.

Instead of boiling eggs for potato salad, macaroni salad or egg salad sandwiches, poach them hard in an egg poacher. These can be mashed with a fork, cut up with a paring knife or pressed through a strainer. This does away with the peeling problems.

If you have cakes that sometimes fall, perhaps the eggs used might be too large. Medium and large eggs are best for cakes. The extra large eggs could be too much egg for the baking in which they are used.

If you want eggs that peel easily, first use eggs that are about three days old, which is a good age for hard-boiled eggs, and the age of most store eggs. After boiling, place them in the freezer 15 to 30 seconds, no longer.

When slicing hard-boiled eggs, dip the knife in cold water and the eggs won't crumble.

If short on eggs, use a heaping tablespoon of coffee creamer for an egg.

If you are cutting down on cholesterol, prepare chicken by rolling it in egg whites, unbeaten, then roll it in crumbs or flour or whatever desired coating you want, and bake it one hour.

If you have no egg, use half a cup of mayonnaise in its place.

To prevent the egg whites that are being poached from spreading all over, add a little vinegar (about a teaspoon) to the water and the egg whites will set and keep their shape. Vinegar also helps to keep the egg whites, white in color.

When you add eggs to a homemade bread mixture or any recipe that calls for yeast, make sure the eggs are at room temperature. If they are cold they will slow down the action of the yeast.

If you like fried eggs, and have a difficult time getting them to the table looking nice, try this method. Place one tablespoon of grease in a large size frying pan, use less in a smaller pan. When the pan is medium hot, never use a hot pan, drop eggs in the pan, one at a time and salt and pepper. Then add an eighth cup of water and cover tightly. Cooking time varies with desired doneness of egg. About four minutes will bring the egg to a firm center; less for softer centers.

National Egg Salad Week, April 4-10 is dedicated to the many delicious uses for all the Easter eggs that are still around. There are many ways of making them into egg salad to use for sandwiches. Some call for creme cheese, pickle relish, olives, mustard, pickle juice and salad dressing. Different herbs also add flavor. No doubt you each have your own special way of preparation.

Quiches are easier to make than they are to pronounce. Just sprinkle some chopped ham; flaked, drained tuna; or browned and drained ground meat into a pie shell. Add shredded cheese. Pour on a beaten mixture of six eggs, one and one half cups of half and half or milk or a can of condensed cream soup, along with seasonings, and bake about 35 minutes at 375 degrees. This is quick and good.

All in a Woman's Day--April 12, 1988

Have a piece of cheese

Most of us relish a good piece of cheese. Legends say that cheese was discovered thousands of years ago by an Arab. He started off on a long journey carrying milk in a pouch made of sheep's stomach. The enzymes in the sheep's stomach, the heat of the sun and the joggling of the camel turned the milk into the snowy white curd cheese and the thin liquid we call whey.

Another version tells of the pouch left in a cave, where cheese formed, possibly with some curing.

According to history, cheese was featured on stone tablets as far back as 4000 B.C.

The art of making cheese has undergone many refinements since those early times, giving us an almost endless variety of cheeses that range in texture from soft to hard, and mild to sharp flavored.

Cheese manufacturing in the United States evolved from a farm activity to a business when the first cheese factory was started at Rome, N.Y., in 1851. There are now approximately 400 to 500 USDA approved cheese plants in this country.

The cheese manufacturers across the United States successfully manufacture almost every type of foreign cheese, including Swiss, Camenbert, Blue, Parmesan and Mozzarella. In addition they have created some original varieties of their own such as Brick, Colby and Monterey Jack.

As American consumers continue to eat more cheese, particularly specialty cheeses, a few new varieties are making their way to the long and interesting history of cheese.

Some hints that might make handling cheese a bit more interesting have been gathered for sharing:

If cheese is stored in a tightly covered container with a few sugar cubes, mold won't form.

When grating cheese, put the grater into a plastic bag and grate the cheese into it. There is no mess or no extra bowl to wash. The bag also is a convenient place to store the grated cheese. This works well for bread crumbs, too.

Leftover cheese that has dried too much for sandwiches may be grated and used as topping for casseroles, soups, macaroni dishes, zesty grilled cheese sandwiches, chopped meat dishes such as meatloaf, meatballs and creamed dishes.

Cooking cheese is not a difficult process; however, there are a few things each cook should keep in mind when using this versatile food product, such as using a low heat, avoiding long cooking periods. To avoid them, add the cheese as a last ingredient, remembering that it melts faster if shredded, cubed, diced or grated.

* * *

Cheese Dressing

1 cup cottage cheese
1/2 cup French dressing
1/2 teaspoon salt
2 drops tabasco sauce
1/2 teaspoon onion juice
1/4 teaspoon celery salt
Dash of garlic salt
2 tablespoons cream

Combine all ingredients and blend well in mixer. Dressing should be very creamy. Serve over lettuce wedges or vegetable salad. Makes 1 1/2 cups of dressing.

All in a Woman's Day--April 19, 1988

Rice is versatile

Rice is a versatile food to be enjoyed at any meal in any course, salad, main dish, dessert. A good source of carbohydrate, it also supplies protein, amino acids, iron and B vitamins. Easily digested, practically all of it can be completely assimilated.

This ancient grain, along with wheat, barley and millet, domesticated before its time, was first cultivated in Southeast Asia about 4,000 years ago and arrived in the West with the "Moors" arrival in Spain. Too, as long as 2800 B.C., rice was a staple for civilizations from China to ancient Greece, to Persia, to the Nile Delta.

It's wild ancestor has been identified as semiaquatic marsh grass that is native to India and southeastern Asia. Most of the cultivated rice is grown in marshy or flooded lands, especially the sort of terrain found throughout the southern Orient and the southeastern United States. Too, it also can be grown in areas with a long growing season and much steady rainfall; however, this kind of rice gives a lesser yield of lower quality and is called hill rice.

The American or Indian rice is not a member of the family but an aquatic perennial grass. Never has it been successfully domesticated for large scale cultivation; however, it does have a long history of use by the Indians and today is considered a culinary delicacy.

It was only by perchance that rice came to the New World. About 1695, a cargo ship carrying grain from Madagascar to England was blown off course and forced to dock in the colonies, landing in Charleston, S.C.

The ship's captain expressed gratitude before sailing by giving the governor a handful of rough rice grains. These were used by the colonists for seed, and from this small beginning, the people grew enough rice to supply South Carolina and other neighboring colonies. The quality of the Carolina rice was high, and a seaport trade with England soon developed.

Rice, termed as a "giving" food, yielding more per acre than corn or wheat, has been grown where wheat would hesitate. Barley or wheat must be ground before using; however, rice can be eaten as a grain, thus eliminating the processing items such as tools, mills, yeast and baking ovens.

This cereal grass is the chief source of food for half the world's population.

* * *

Peppy Franks with Rice

2 1/2 cups prepared barbecue sauce
2 pounds frankfurters, sliced diagonally in 1-inch pieces
4 cups hot cooked rice

Combine the barbecue sauce and franks. Cover and simmer 15 to 20 minutes. Serve over beds of fluffy rice. Makes 8 servings.

All in a Woman's Day--April 26, 1988

Springtime asparagus days have arrived!

"Spring has sprung,
the grass has riz;
I wonder where
the asparagus is?"

No need to wonder anymore where the asparagus is for it is beginning to pop through the ground, and some folks already have been gathering this delicious vegetable.

Of course, when you harvest your own asparagus, you pick what you have; however, when you go to the market to make your selection there are certain things to keep in mind.

Choose fresh asparagus by looking for firm, straight spears with closed, compact tips. Avoid wilted, limp, flat or angular stalks. Thicker or more slender spears are equally tender; however, be sure to purchase spears similar in size in order to make more even cooking. If you always thought asparagus best when slender, now there is another train of thought, with some folks thinking the thicker the stalks the better. Now, just who is right?

Authorities, who think that thicker is better, feel this way because of higher pulp to fiber ratio; others still contend that slender is better. However, if you purchase asparagus of medium thickness, you're bound to be satisfied.

To have success in preparing asparagus use stalks of the same thickness so will cook alike and evenly when using the proper cooking methods. Cooking should be brief in order to conserve the nutrients in this delightful spring vegetable and to obtain the crisp tender texture.

Perhaps the best way to store fresh asparagus, prior to preparation, is to snap off the thicker ends and stand the spears in a glass or jar that has about one inch of water in it. Then loosely cover the spears with plastic and refrigerate. Since asparagus is a member of the lily family, it does continue to grow after harvest, so, treating it as if it is a flower will keep the spears at their freshest.

The secret to retaining its fresh color is to avoid overcooking. According to a legend, whenever Emperor Augustus of Rome wished to terminate some unpleasant business, he would exclaim, "Let it be done quicker than you can cook asparagus!"

If you will only make this tasteful lean green vegetable a part of your early springtime fare, you will find that it will pay off where it really counts ... flavor, nutrition and calories. A cup of cooked asparagus has only 35 calories, and it does contain 85 percent of an adult's recommended daily allowance of vitamin C, with half the requirement of vitamin A and about one-tenth of iron. It has been found that the rutin contained in this vegetable helps to strengthen blood vessels and the natural fiber aids digestion.

Here is a tempting skillet dish that makes the most of fresh asparagus. Combine it with sliced mushrooms and a bit of onion. Sauce it with lively tasting canned beef gravy ... ready to use right from the can. Add crunchy water chestnuts, ginger and tangy soy sauce for a captivating oriental flavor and texture. This company dish will especially complement lamb or veal.

All in a Woman's Day--May 3, 1988

Give a 'tribute to Mom'
"Behold Thy Mother!"

No greater tribute to motherhood can be found than that of Jesus' words spoken in the dark hour of His suffering and grief. Hanging upon the accursed tree, deeply conscious of the dreadful consequences of His assumption of our guilt, He expressed in His own words: "My God, My God, why hast thou forsaken me?"

Yes, even while enduring the terrible torment of that dreadful hour, Jesus was concerned about His mother. John tells us that when Jesus saw her and the disciple, whom he loved, standing by, He cried out: "Behold thy Mother."

How do we really thank God today for our wonderful Christian mothers, who gave so unselfishly and for the blessing of their influence? If you are fortunate enough to have your mother still living, tell her how much you love and appreciate her and that you thank God for all she means to you. If you do not still have your mother, make some other mother happy this special day coming up.

Duane Valentry has put together a story about how famous people that have paid tribute to their mothers. Here are some excerpts:

Lawrence Welk played many polkas for his mother, who loved to dance to that special kind of music. He has always given credit to her for his career. And he has said, "My mother was a wonderful person. She was so good she never even scolded any of us. The way we found she was displeased with us was a tear in her eye. She always had a tremendous faith and love for us, and I'm sure that's one of the reasons I've made good in my lifetime."

Often words by Ernie Ford defined mothers: "Mothers are women ranging in age from 15 to 100, in assorted sizes, shapes, weights and colors. A mother is truth with a mop in her hand, wisdom with an overdrawn bank account and a miracle with a sick child in her arms."

On Mother's Day in 1977, George Foreman, a one time heavyweight champ, announced he was retiring from the ring "because of his love for his mother and his newly found religious beliefs." He has commented that "she always was afraid I'd get hurt," and then he added, "I wanted to make up to her for a lot of heartaches I caused her as a youth when often delinquent." In his effort to reform, he joined the Job Corps, and then his boxing career followed. After retiring from the ring, he has been active as a preacher and helping hand for many youngsters.

Too, the great singer, Enrico Caruso adored his mother, who often went barefoot to pay for his music lessons, and who died when he was only 15. Carrying her picture all of his life, Caruso sang for her and gave the world much pleasure.

Although Mark Twain gave his mother worries all during his boyhood days, he always acknowledged that his humorous streak came from her. He has said "she had a sort of an ability that is rare in men and almost never found in women—that is the ability to say a humorous thing with the perfect air of not knowing it to be humorous."

And, of course, no one could top Anna Jarvis of Philadelphia, for it was she, who in 1907 arranged a memorial in honor of her own and other mothers who worked for her church. This gesture of gratefulness caught on and in 1914, President Woodrow Wilson designated the second Sunday in May as "Mother's Day for all the public to express love and reverence for mothers of the country."

* * *

Happy Mother's Day!
* * *

Super Mom Recipe

4 cups love
2 cups of helpfulness
3 cups of forgiveness
1/2 cup cheerfulness
1/4 cup tenderness
1 tablespoon of sadness
5 tablespoons of hope

Mix all together. Bake with sunshine and sprinkle with love. Serve every day. That is a Super Mom! And most Mom's are Super.

All in a Woman's Day--May 10, 1988

Celebrate with desserts; cooking terms defined

"How sweet are thy words unto my taste! Yea, sweeter than honey to my mouth!" Psalms 119:103.

We wonder just what kind of a world it would be without desserts, those simple puddings, pies, custards, souffles, ice cream, icy sherberts, gelatin, fruit, meringues, cheesecakes, sweet breads, cookies, cakes and all the good things that give us so much pleasure.

Desserts are made to please the palate; therefore, it is not just by accident that some of those tasty concocted delights end a meal—it is a grand finale. And those tasty sweet bits give us such a good feeling as we are ready to leave the table.

I have heard that some folks eat their dessert first just so they will "have room and can really enjoy."

Finding recipes for simple desserts that many families have enjoyed in the last century seems almost like finding a collection of old treasures. Most of the old-time desserts were simple, easy to prepare, more economical and even more delicious, we might say, than commercially packaged desserts can be. The old-time cooks put together, eggs, bread, milk, rice, or something of that nature, a sprinkling of sugar and flavor, and they wound up with something really good.

* * *

Here are processes and definitions for terms used in making desserts. Some of them include the following:

Al a mode: A dessert served with or garnished with a topping of ice cream.

Bake: To cook by dry heat in an oven.

Bavarian: A dessert pudding made with a gelatin-cream base.

Beat: To whip with a spoon, hand beater or electric mixer in order to combine food or incorporate air as in beating egg whites and whipping cream.

Blend: To mix ingredients until thoroughly combined.

Boil: To cook at boiling temperature which is 212 degrees at sea level.

Bonbon: A sweet made of or dripped

into fondant.

Broil: To cook by broiler or over coals or any other method of direct heat.

Caramelize: To heat dry sugar or food containing sugar until it is light brown and caramel flavored.

Charlotte: A dessert made by lining a dish with strips of cake, lady fingers or bread and filling it with fruit, whipped cream, custard or other filling.

Cobbler: A deep dish fruit pie made with a rich pastry or biscuit dough top.

Cream: To work or beat shortening until light and fluffy. Sugar and or flour and eggs may be creamed into the shortening.

Dredge: To coat with flour or a finely ground ingredient.

Eclair: A small custard or whipped cream-filled, finger-shaped pastry.

Fold: To combine ingredients by blending with a spoon or wire whisk, using an up and over motion.

Fondant: A preparation made from sugar syrup and kneaded to creaminess.

Glaze: To coat with a thin sugar syrup that has been cooked to the crack stage, or to cover with a thin icing.

Knead: To manipulate with a pressing motion plus folding and stretching.

Parfait: Ice cream, fruit and whipped cream dessert; or a frozen mixture of egg whites or yolks, cooked with hot syrup and combined with whipped cream.

Scald: To heat liquid that is just below the boiling point.

Torte: A cake or pastry made of many eggs, sugar and often grated nuts or dry bread crumbs instead of flour, and baked in a large flat form pan. Sometimes it is filled with jam and usually covered with frosting.

There are some elegant sauces that can be made, too, to accent the flavor of many desserts.

* * *

The recipe I am including is an old-fashioned one, I hoped you will enjoy!

* * *

Chocolate Bread Pudding

2 ounces unsweetened chocolate
1 quart scalded milk
2 cups homemade or good textured white bread crumbs
1/3 cup sugar
1/4 cup butter, melted
2 eggs, slightly beaten
1 teaspoon vanilla
1 teaspoon salt

Preheat oven to 325 degrees. Butter a 1 1/2-2 quart baking dish. Break the chocolate into bits and melt it in the milk, stirring until smooth. Add the bread crumbs and set aside to cool. When likewarm, add remaining ingredients. Mix well, pour into the buttered dish and bake for about 50 minutes or until set. Serve with whipped cream.

All in a Woman's Day--May 17, 1988

Make your meat selection

It seems there is no doubt that beef is the favorite American meat, no matter how it is prepared. Most families will have it served for at least one meal a day, generally the main meal.

Meat, however, is more expensive than other protein food, therefore it is important that it be selected carefully and wisely, and that the cooking is at its best.

Since May is Beef Month, we think the cooking of a juicy piece of meat is the pride of all cooks; however, the success and enjoyment of the meal does depend mostly upon the meat dish.

Because of the new breeding and feeding, techniques, according to the Missouri Cow Belles Bulletin, the calories, the fat and the cholesterol have been lowered in beef.

Meat supplies iron and other minerals as well as the protein for keeping the muscles and tissues in condition. Inexpensive cuts of meat may be cooked delicious and tender by several methods. Searing cuts of meat well, seals in the juices, and then cooking slowly until it is tender, makes it more succulent. Slow cooking softens the tissues.

After purchasing meat, it should be removed from the wrapping paper as soon as it can be and placed on a clean plate covered with aluminum foil and put in a cool place. When ready to prepare, wipe it with a damp cloth and avoid piercing it with a fork as this causes the loss of juice and flavor.

Which is it—veal or beef? The correct term that consumers sometimes find confusing is based upon the age of the dairy or beef animal from which the meat comes. Age also has a distinct influence on the taste and tenderness characteristics of the meat, as well as its price.

Veal is meat from milk-fed animals less than three months old, while beef is from animals past the veal age, but younger, however, than beef. Beef, that accounts for the really big consumer volume, is the meat from animals usually marketed at one and a half to two years old.

Tenderness of meat can be helped by adding a couple of slices of tomato to the roast. The acid in the tomato acts as a tenderizer.

You also can tenderize meat by adding a small amount of vinegar to the water in which it is being cooked. You won't taste the vinegar flavor.

It is well for a roast to stand about 30 minutes before carving and then make sure the platter is not cluttered with potatoes and carrots, so you will have room to carve. To do this, you must have a sharp knife, and cut across the grain.

When shopping for beef that is top grade, remember it should be a dull red, fine grained and firm. It also should have a good coating of fat and be well marbled, which means that a threadlike line of fat should run throughout the lean. The fat should be white or creamy, never yellow as that indicates the animal has been range fed, and the flesh will not be so tender. The fat around the loin, which is known as suet, should be dry and crumbly.

* * *

Pigs in the Blanket

Pound flour, salt and pepper into thin slices of round steak. Cut into strips 2-1/2 inches wide. Place diced onions and bacon on the strips. Roll them up and secure with a toothpick. Brown on both sides. Add a little water, cover with a lid, and cook slowly about 1 hour. Serve with gravy and potato dumplings.

All in a Woman's day--May 24, 1988
It begins with the sauce

Barbecuing time is anytime nowadays; however, it really gets into full swing Memorial Weekend.

Whatever you barbecue—chicken, ribs, hamburgers, bologna, steaks, chops, wieners—be sure you use the kind of sauce you like most for that is what makes the barbecuing delicious … it begins with the sauce!

Perhaps the most commonly, grilled meat is hamburgers. For the fluffiest, juiciest barbecued burgers, handle the meat gently, and as little as possible. Don't pack it. Medium or coarsely ground beef makes the lightest hamburgers. Furthermore, one-half cup of an extender such as nonfat dry milk, bread crumbs or crushed cereal added to one pound of ground beef is not only economical but also helps to keep the burgers juicy.

To make uniformly shaped hamburgers, try using a burger press or roll, or pat the hamburger about one-half to three-fourths inch thick between two sheets of waxed paper, using a light touch. Remove the top and bottom of a four-inch diameter pan and cut out the patties.

Hamburgers will hold together and retain juices better if handled properly on the grill. Turn them only once, cooking them over hot coals, about six minutes on one side and four minutes on the other side, or until they are to your liking. Never press a hamburger as it cooks. It will cause it to be dry and crumbly.

To avoid excessive flame-ups, take precaution. Spread the coals, allowing about one-inch of space between them. Have some water handy to extinguish flames; using your child's water pistol is one way.

Finally, exercise your imagination when serving hamburgers. They don't have to be round. Try shaping burgers to fit various types of bread—oval for French bread or square for white or whole wheat bread. Also you may want to experiment with various toppings, especially fun for summer guests.

Use lean 80 to 85 percent fat free meat to the least lean 70 to 75 percent. Ground chuck is perhaps the best to use, for it makes juicy hamburgers and costs less than lean. One pound makes four hefty hamburgers.

To help make juicy hamburger, use half pound beef, seasoned to taste, and add one slice of bread soaked in half cup of milk. Mix thoroughly. The hamburgers should be tender and delicious.

Try a little allspice in meat balls or hamburgers. It adds zip to the flavor, making these old favorites more interesting.

If cooking meat in a skillet, start it in a cold skillet over medium heat. Be sure to drain your patties well. A little salt added to the bottom of the skillet before adding the meat, will help to keep it from sticking, and the meat will absorb the salt flavor.

Herbs also may be added for variety.

Try barbecuing in a skillet. This is especially good for chicken or steak. Take one cup of barbecue sauce and one cup 7-Up or Pepsi; mix well and cook the meat in the sauce until it is tender. Cook all the way from 275 to 350 degrees.

* * *

The recipe for today is taken from Cherie Blanton's Cookbook, "A Little Fur in the Meringue Never Really Hurts the Fillins," and it is called "Hamburger Diane." It offers a marvelous way to prepare ground beef, and doing it in such an uncommon way that it becomes a gourmet experience.

Hamburger Diane
2 pounds ground round
1/2 teaspoon seasoned salt
2 teaspoons seasoned pepper
4 tablespoons (1/2 stick) butter
2 tablespoons vegetable oil
1 tablespoon prepared mustard

1 tablespoon lemon juice
1/2 tablespoon Worcestershire sauce
1/4 cup chopped parsley

Lightly mix ground round, seasoned salt and pepper in a large bowl. Gently shape into 6 large patties, 1-inch thick. Melt 2 tablespoons butter or margarine in a large heavy skillet; remove it from heat; blend in oil and mustard; return it to heat. Saute ground meat over medium heat 4 minutes on each side (for rare); remove and keep warm.

Stir lemon juice, Worcestershire sauce and remaining 2 tablespoons butter into the skillet; stir over low heat until well-blended; spoon over hamburgers; garnish with pimento and parsley sprigs. Hamburgers may be served on toasted slices of French bread.

All in a Woman's Day--May 31, 1988
Offer a handful of hints!

How about a handful of hints on a number of things that you might be needing to know as you go about your daily household chores!

It is time to get out your patio furniture, and if it happens to be wicker, you can clean it by rubbing it with a stiff brush and warm salt water. The salt will keep wicker from turning yellow as well as keep it clean.

A few moth crystals scattered around outdoor bushes and plants will repel bugs.

Did you know that you can use clean, squeeze type catsup and mustard containers for decorating cakes? Their spouts are great for writing and drawing with icing.

One of the more efficient, but less traditional ways of cleaning pewter, is with a cabbage leaf.

If you have some club soda that has gone flat it is good for watering plants. The chemicals that remain add vigor and color to the greenery.

To relieve the pain and swelling from a bee sting, apply a slice of onion. Too, you can moisten the skin and sprinkle it with meat tenderizer.

Catsup can be used to the last drop. Add enough lemon juice to dilute, horseradish to taste, shake well and you have a tasty seafood sauce. Or, you can add a little vinegar, and come up with French dressing.

If you need to measure something and don't have a ruler, you can use a dollar bill as an instant measuring stick. It is six and a half-inches long.

To remove chocolate from clothing, soak it in carbonated water and wash it as usual.

Self-rising flour has leavening ingredients and salt added to it, therefore, never use it in making yeast breads.

Old-fashioned recipes often call for a No. 2 size can. This is a can that holds one pound and 12 or 13 ounces.

Do you have caraway seed on your shelf in the kitchen? Use it with buttered noodles, in rye, quick or yeast breads, and in sauerkraut dishes.

A good meat tenderizer can be made by combining half a cup of vinegar with one cup of beef broth.

When cooking apples to make sauce or fillings, use apple juice or cider instead of water to intensify the flavor.

Many cooks have trouble with pie crust failure. If you will allow the dough to rest on the bread board or pastry cloth for about 10 minutes, the results will be much better. This seems to work regardless of the recipe used.

* * *

Chocolate Pie

1 cup sugar
2 tablespoons flour
1/4 cup cocoa
1 tablespoon margarine, melted
2 eggs
1 cup milk
1 teaspoon vanilla

Mix dry ingredients. Add beaten eggs and melted margarine. Blend well; add milk and vanilla. Pour into a 9-inch pie pan lined with pastry. Bake at 350 degrees for 20-30 minutes. This is an old-time recipe.

All in a Woman's Day--June 7, 1988

The strawberry ... is All-American fruit

Would you believe it if I told you that this time of the year strawberry shortcake beats out apple pie as the All-American dish! Well, according to statistics that is correct.

Homegrown strawberries, even though the crop is short this year because of the lack of moisture, are on the market, as well as the luscious shipped in berries that have been here for several weeks and still are in the produce departments of the super markets. But, there is something about home grown strawberries that appeals to the taste buds, and the aroma.

So often we think that possibly the larger the berry the better the quality; however, it is not a true barometer. Oftentimes the largest berries are not necessarily the ones with the most tempting flavor.

It has been noted that consumers purchase more strawberries frozen or fresh during the month of June than during any other month of the year. Also according to statistics, 83 percent of all households use fresh strawberries and 70 percent use frozen berries.

Again, according to statistics, the top five uses of frozen strawberries are in shortcake, as an ice cream topping, in salad, strawberries served with cream and whole sliced and sweetened berries.

While old-fashioned strawberry shortcake, topped with whipped cream, is a national favorite, there also are other variations. Some recipes call for flaky biscuits, pound cake, sponge cake, cream puffs or crisp waffles as the base on which to serve this delightful fruit.

Strawberries are one of the dieter's best friends, as a cupful of these delectable sweet berries has only 60 calories. These are not empty calories, however, as they are a terrific source of vitamin C, also vitamin A, potassium, iron and ascorbic acid.

Strawberries are best served slightly chilled, either alone or in combination with other foods Because they are so fragile, strawberries should not be washed until ready for use, and then very carefully. Also, hold them carefully for hulling.

Eat and enjoy this beautiful fruit!

* * *

Strawberry Angel Cake

1 package strawberry gelatin
1 cup hot water
1 cup ice water
1 teaspoon strawberry flavoring
1 cup whipped cream or the equivalent in whipped topping
1 cup marshmallows, diced
1 box frozen strawberries
1 tablespoon lemon juice
1 (10-inch) angel food cake

Dissolve gelatin in hot water; add ice water and flavoring and chill until syrupy. Then whip until fluffy. Stir in marshmallows, partially thawed strawberries, and lemon juice. Fold in whipped cream. Let this set, then place between layers of angel food cake or scoop out the cake and fill the cavity. This may be served topped with additional whipped cream. Fresh strawberries also may be used in place of frozen berries.

This also is delicious with red raspberries and raspberry flavoring.

All in a Woman's Day--June 14, 1988

Fathers are special

Father's Day will be observed all over the nation this coming Sunday, when gifts or special cards that say just what is most appropriate for you to say will be given in his honor.

We think of the first unofficial observance in 1910 in Spokane, Wash., by Mrs. John B. Dodd in honor of her father, a widower, who single-handedly reared six children.

The earliest forerunner of Father's Day cards was a clay tablet written nearly 4,000 years ago in Babylonia. The greeting was from a young man called Elmesu, wishing his father "good health and a long life."

Patriarchs elsewhere are sometimes recognized in some unusual ways. For instance, a young African Dinka tribesman would present to his father the most perfect present he could give, the skin of his first lion kill.

In old China, sons once showed their respect for an elderly parent by sewing a silk robe for him. Embroidered with Chinese characters for "Long Life," this "longevity robe," was thought to improve a father's chances of living to a ripe old age when it was put together by a person who was young enough to live a long time.

In our country, the offspring of strict Puritan parents were told to address their sire as "honored sir," instead of just "father." Children on the Trobriand Islands called their dads "My mother's husband," in the belief that spirits are the true fathers.

There are some special father's that we might recall. For instance Gideon, the Biblical warrior that had 70 sons for he had many wives.

One of this country's most famous soldiers and "father figure"—George Washington, known as the "Father of his country," died childless.

Then there was Philip of Macedon, whose exploits in conquering Greece made his son fear that his father would leave him no glories to win. However, Philip's son managed to amount to something after all by seizing the Persian Empire and much of India before he was 30. He is known in history as Alexander the Great.

Another father deserving a special gift from his son: Beethoven Senior, who encouraged little Ludwig to practice the piano, until Beethoven Junior became perhaps the greatest composer of all times.

No matter where you and your Dad stand in the annals of fathers and children, the time has come to give him something that will really say he is "Special!"

* * *

Happy Father's Day!

All in a Woman's Day--June 21, 1988

Dairy Month think milk!

June is National Dairy Month and it might be well to think about milk, generally.

There are several different types available on the markets and sometimes this can be a bit confusing. In fact, there are really five basic types of fluid milk available, and they are listed as follows, with their fat content:

Whole milk - from 3.3 to 3.5 percent.

2 percent milk - 2 percent fat.

1 percent milk-1 percent fat.

Low fat milk - 0.5 +2 percent fat.

Skim milk - less than 0.5 percent fat.

The calorie content increases as the fat content increases; thus, skim milk has the least number of calories. So, if you have to watch your fat intake, decide from the above list which would be best for your use. Remember, one cup of whole milk has about 150 calories, while skim milk has about 85.

Milk should be refrigerated as soon as possible after purchase. Containers should be kept closed so the food odors cannot be absorbed. Milk should be stored in protective containers, so it is not exposed to light that reduces some of the nutrients and sometimes gives an off flavor. Milk should be served cold.

One cup of reconstituted nonfat dry milk costs about a third the price of whole fluid milk. If dry milk is fortified with vitamins A and D, the two products are comparable nutritionally. Dry milk has lower calories and fat content. Milk drinkers, however, find it hard to tell dry milk from fluid "skim milk" if the dry milk is refrigerated 24 hours after mixed with water. For extra flavor a small amount of vanilla extract may added to the reconstituted milk.

Following are some milk equals:

1 cup buttermilk equals 1 cup milk.

1 cup yogurt equals 1 cup milk.

1/2 cup ice cream equals 1/4 cup milk.

1/2 cup iced milk equals 1/3 cup milk.

1 cup baked custard equals 1 cup milk.

1 ounce sliced Swiss cheese equals 1 cup milk.

1 slice American processed cheese equals 1/2 cup milk.

2 tablespoons cream cheese equals 1 tablespoon milk.

1/2 cup evaporated milk plus 1/2 cup water equals 1 cup milk.

Should you have to substitute, remember:

1 cup coffee cream may be substituted by using 3 tablespoons butter and 7/8 cup milk.

1 cup heavy cream may be substituted by using 1/3 cup butter and 3/4 cup milk.

1 cup whole milk may be substituted by using 1 cup reconstituted nonfat dry milk plus 2 1/2 teaspoons butter or margarine.

1 cup buttermilk or sour milk may be substituted by using 1 tablespoon vinegar or lemon juice plus enough sweet milk to make 1 cup (this should stand several minutes before using).

If you have on hand some slightly soured milk and you want to save it, just add a pinch of baking powder.

Should milk get scorched, add a pinch of salt.

Whipped butter, a by-product of milk, can be used in place of regular butter in recipes by using 1/3 to 1/2 more than the recipe calls for using.

To whip margarine, soften 2 pounds then slowly beat into it a large can of condensed milk. This makes about 3 pounds. Store it covered in the refrigerator.

* * *

Lemon Dessert

1 stick margarine

1 cup flour

1/2 cup chopped pecans

Combine and pat into bottom of a 9x13-inch pan. Bake at 350 degrees, about 15 minutes, if using a metal pan; 325 degrees if using glass pan. Cool.

1 (8-ounce) package cream cheese, softened
3/4 cup powdered sugar
1 cup whipped topping
1/4 teaspoon lemon flavoring
2 regular size packages instant lemon pudding mix
2 3/4 cups milk

Beat cream cheese and sugar and fold in whipped topping. Let this set 15 minutes before spreading on the cooled first layer. Beat together the lemon flavoring, pudding mix and milk. Pour over cream cheese layer; top with additional whipped topping if desired. Chill.

All in a Woman's Day--June 28, 1988

Taste of the exotic in fruits, vegetables

It has been said that eating should always be an adventure; and salads certainly are no exception!

Salads have come a long way, after beginning as a simple preparation of grasses, herbs and other plants, dressed up with salt, which was a favorite combination with the greens. The Latin word for salt in those ancient days was (sal) the forerunner of the word "salad," and salads have made their debut in many ways.

Through the centuries, however, salads have been mostly cold mixtures of greens with a vinegar based dressing, giving the accent. Now, we find warm varieties that are substantial enough even to be entrees. Not only are they healthful, but popular, and a delightful smart way to give nourishment.

With the arrival of summer (with all our hot weather, so far, we feel like it has been here for sometime) it is especially appropriate that this season is termed "salad days."

It has been said that Americans have taken the simple side dish of salad, that is served in Europe at the close of a meal, and transformed it into a meal itself for either lunch or a light dinner.

In thinking about salads and something different you will find that some of the lesser known delicacies of the fruit and vegetable families can add a delightful gourmet change of texture, appearance and taste, we might say, to those everyday salads with which we are familiar. So, why not try something different ... have an adventure!

Some of those new items on the market, that can make salads interesting and different, are available at different times of the year, so you might like to do some experimenting.

The kiwi fruit is now being used more and more as the flavor is a bit unusual, since it is crossed between a strawberry, a watermelon and a banana. This oval-shaped fruit with a fuzzy brown skin is available from June through March. The meat is a lime green color with miniature black edible seeds.

Snow peas, or as they are sometimes called sugar peas, are available all year, either fresh or frozen. These flat, broad pea pods, with their delicate flavor and crisp texture, are delicious, especially when used in many Oriental dishes.

Papaya is a pear-shaped fruit that not too many use in cooking. The flavor is crossed between a cantaloupe and a peach and is available at the market from May through June and October through December. It has a smooth green to yellow skin and is golden meated, with shiny black seeds.

The Jucama, that has a brownish root, resembles turnips. It is available from November through June. You will find that when it is peeled it has a crisp texture and a mild flavor that is very similar to water chestnuts.

The Mango is a rather elongated fruit with a skin of green, yellow or red tinged, depending, of course, on the variety. To use in salads, the skin of the fruit is scored, peeled and sliced or made into chunks. They are available on the market from May through August.

Water chestnuts can be purchased fresh or canned. Mostly used raw, they do have, however, a rather unique ability to remain crunchy even after cooking. They have a creamy white, crisp flesh and a chestnut colored brown skin.

Why not try some of these dlfferent items now on the market and see just how they will enhance some of your foods you prepare? You will find, no doubt, that they will give you a taste of the exotic, So, why not dare to be different, and see what happens!

* * *

Chicken Salad and Puffs

2 cups cooked chicken
1 cup shredded American cheese
1/2 cup blanched slivered almonds
1/2 cup chopped celery
1 can (9-ounce) crushed pineapple, drained
1 teaspoon salt
1 teaspoon soy sauce
1/2 cup mayonnaise or salad dressing
Combine all ingredients and chill. Serve on Puffs (recipe follows). Makes 6 to 8 luncheon servings or 24 snack puffs.

Puffs

1 cup water
1/2 cup shortening
1 cup flour
1/4 teaspoon salt
3 eggs
Combine water and shortening in saucepan. Bring to boil; add flour and salt all at once. Cook and stir over medium heat until mixture leaves sides of pan. Remove from heat; add eggs, one at a time, beating vigorously after each addition. Drop by rounded tablespoonsful onto a greased cookie sheet. Bake at 400 degrees, 40 to 45 minutes, or until deep golden brown. Cool. Split and fill with the well chilled chicken salad just before serving.

All in a Woman's Day--July 5, 1988

Ice cream sundae is born

Perhaps you know the story of how the ice cream sundae was born. Of course, it is understood that it depends with whom you are talking, those from Evanston, Ill., or Two Rivers, Wis.

It seems that the dessert, ice cream with different toppers, was a Sunday subtitutes for the ever popular ice cream soda, which most everyone desired; however, it was forbidden as a in pleasure unappropriate on the Sabbath. From that time on that delicious "bit of goodness" has come right into the hearts of Americans.

Somehow, it seems that it is the toppings that make the ice cream. Of course, there are the traditional toppings—nuts, fruit, syrup and piles of whipped cream, that is higher than most any sundae is wide. Your sundae repertoire can be expanded and can include anything from kiwi fruit and cantaloupe to raspberries to peaches and honey, and rum sauce. In fact, there are enough variations that one could enjoy a different sundae for everyday of the week and more.

Those good old days of cranking an ice cream freezer, and using ice that was once cut in blocks from the frozen river or ponds and stored for summer use, are gone.

Today that has been replaced by ice cubes from the freezer or a frozen insert. And you will find that table salt or no salt has replaced the rock salt that was formerly needed to make the ice cream mixture to freeze faster.

* * *

The Fourth of July is over; however, July is considered a patriotic month, so, you might want to make this special sundae.

Red, White and Blueberry Sundae

1/3 cup sugar
1 tablespoon corn starch
1/2 teaspoon salt
1/2 cup water
1 pint blueberries
1 cup miniature marshmallows
1 tablespoon fresh lemon juice

In a 1 1/2-quart saucepan combine sugar, cornstarch and salt, gradually adding the water. Stir in blueberries. Cook over medium heat, stirring frequently, until thickened. Boil 2 additional minutes. Remove from heat; add marshmallows and stir until they are melted. Cool, and stir in lemon juice. Chill. Yields about 2 1/2 cups of sauce.

Place one scoop each of vanilla and strawberry ice cream in chilled sundae dishes. Then drizzle the ice cream with blueberry marshmallow sauce.

* * *

Orange Almond Sauce

1/4 cup sugar
2 teaspoons corn starch
1 cup orange juice
1/4 cup orange marmalade
2 tablespoons butter
1/4 cup roasted slivered almonds

Combine sugar and cornstarch in a 1-quart saucepan; gradually mix in orange juice, marmalade; then cook over medium heat, stirring con-stantly until thickened. Cook 2 additional minutes and remove from heat; adding butter and stirring until melted. Chill. Just before serving, add almonds; 1/4 cup is a serving. (You might like to try this sauce served over vanilla ice cream. Um! Good!)

All in a Woman's Day--July 12, 1988
The versatile peach is the gold fruit of summer

A fresh peach is the gold of summer. So sunny and bright with its creamy color and rosy blush, the sweet succulent and fragrant peach is versatile, too.

It seems to have a kind of country charm when eaten out of hand, or sliced into a bowl and drenched with rich cream. And it can be the city slicker, in a brandy sauce served over French vanilla ice cream.

The peach is said to be the third most important fruit crop in the United States, with the apple, first; and the orange, second. It is a cousin of the cherry, the apricot, the plum and the almond.

Peaches have been in the New World since early history after Columbus and the Spaniards first planted trees in St. Augustine, Fla. The French in Louisiana, the English in Jamestown and the Pilgrims in Massachusetts all planted peaches as soon as their settlements were established.

Not only do peaches taste good, they

also are good for you. They are a good source of vitamin A and C, a fair source of potassium, and also low in sodium, which makes them an excellent addition to special and convalescent diets. And, also a big plus for the figure conscious person as there are only 38 calories in one medium sized peach. Their sugary, natural taste can be satisfying for a craving for something sweet.

The red color is not a sign of ripeness, and the blush often depends upon the variety of peach. When mature, it has a white or creamy yellow undercolor. Do not select green colored fruit, for peaches, if picked when immature do not ripen well; in fact, peaches that are green or hard will not ripen to a good flavor.

When they complete their ripening cycle, at room temperature, keep them until soft enough to eat (a paper bag will speed the process), then refrigerate and use as soon as possible. You will find that most of the volume of peaches comes in July.

Peaches for pies can be slightly firmer than those eaten out of hand. Fresh peach pie with an appetizing lattice crust is a jewel among pies.

For many people, it is hard to imagine a summer season without it when it is served still warm from the oven.

Peach pies came into favor only in the 1850s after Freestone peaches became available, making it easy to slice them. It was about this time that corn starch was developed (1842) and began to be used as thickening for fruit pies.

The basic rule for thickening is to mix the corn starch with the sugar and then toss the fruit with the sugar mixture. This will disperse the corn starch granules so they can swell evenly. Corn starch has no taste or color of its own; it thickens without a masking flavor or changing the rich peach color.

* * *

If you are a real peach lover, as most of us are, try to imagine the tender juicy slices of orchard fresh peaches combined with the rich taste and texture of homemade cake. The very thought is irresistible.

Fresh Peach
Upside Down Cake

3/4 cup butter or margarine, divided
1/2 cup packed light brown sugar
1/4 teaspoon nutmeg
5 medium peaches, cut in half and peeled
1/2 cup granulated sugar
1 egg
1 1/2 cups sifted all-purpose flour
2 teaspoons baking powder
1/2 teaspoon salt
1/2 cup milk

Melt 1/4 cup butter in an 8x8x2-inch square pan and sprinkle it with brown sugar and nutmeg. Arrange peach halves, cut side down, in pan. Cream remaining 1/2 cup butter with granulated sugar. Beat in egg. Sift together flour, baking powder and salt. Add to creamed mixture, alternately with milk, beating until smooth. Spread batter over peaches. Bake in 375 degree oven for 30 minutes. Let it stand 5 minutes and turn it out onto platter. Serve with whipped cream.

* * *

Peach Bread

1 1/2 cups sugar
1/2 cup shortening
2 eggs
2 1/4 cups fresh peach puree (see next page)
2 cups flour

1 teaspoon cinnamon
1 teaspoon baking soda
1 teaspoon baking powder
1/4 teaspoon salt
1 teaspoon vanilla
1 cup finely chopped pecans

To make peach puree: Wash 6 to 8 medium sized peaches. Slice, leaving skins on. Puree in electric blender.

Cream sugar and shortening; add eggs and beat until fluffy. Add peach puree and combine with other ingredients; mix thoroughly. Stir in vanilla and nuts. Pour into 2 greased and floured 9x5x3-inch loaf pans. Bake at 325 degree for about 1 hour.

All in a Woman's Day--July 19, 1988

National Baked Bean Month; hot dogs also recognized

What would a picnic be without baked beans? There is a world of difference between the cook who heats up a can of beans and the one who adds a touch of excitement to the same can of beans. What is the difference? Flavor and appetite appeal—that is the difference.

It was way back in 1875 in Maine that the first canned baked beans came into being. It seems that this was for the benefit of the men at sea in fishing fleets so they could have the same delicious Saturday night fare that they had while they were ashore. In many New England areas the Saturday night baked beans was a looked forward to event.

The beginning of today's real pork and bean enjoyment was back in 1880, when Americans got their first taste of beans baked in tomato sauce. That was the ultimate, and the way they had been prepared in England. Then in 1891 the Van Camp Packing Co. began processing in that manner, and since then, baked beans have been the top of the line.

Since this is National Baked Bean Month; it is time to pay tribute to one of our country's most nutritious and healthful food, baked beans ... an excellent food choice that is full of protein.

Most all kinds of beans are nutritious, including bean soup, kidney beans, lima beans, pork and beans, green beans and baked beans ... you name it. It could be said we are a "bean eating" country.

Many of us knew the lowly bean in our growing-up days when they were often served out of sheer necessity. There was no better way to feed a hungry family than to cook a big kettle of white navy beans, with a bit of bacon, pork or ham, and serve it along with a pan of corn bread. Sometimes if there were any beans left, they were made into baked beans for another day's enjoyment, with brown sugar, molasses, catsup, and perhaps a bit of mustard, added.

I am going to share several recipes for baked beans that I thought you might want to try, even though, no doubt, you have your own special concoction.

* * *

This **Ginger Baked Beans** recipe comes with several variations that can be used to tempt the taste buds. Take two one-pound cans baked beans, half cup dark corn syrup, one tablespoon finely chopped onion, one teaspoon ginger. Combine corn syrup and ginger. Spoon baked beans into a two quart casserole, stir in syrup mixture. Bake in 400 degree oven for about one to one and a half hours. Makes six servings.

* * *

One variation is **Ginger Peachy Baked Beans**. Follow the recipe for Ginger Baked Beans, top with peach halves, drained, from a 20-ounce can. Pour a little dark corn syrup over the beans.

* * *

Another variation is **Cardamon Peachy Baked Beans**. Follow the Ginger Peach Baked Beans, substituting one teaspoon ground cardamon for ginger. Place one heaping teaspoon of orange marmalade in center of each peach half, if desired.

* * *

Still another version is the **Pineapple Baked Beans.** Follow the recipe for Ginger Peach Baked Beans, substituting a 20-ounce can of pineapple chunks or slices, (drained) for the peaches.

* * *

Then the final way to use this recipe is **Ginger Baked Beans with Canadian Bacon.** Follow the recipe for Ginger Peach Baked Beans, substituting a half-pound sliced Canadian Bacon for the peaches.

* * *

Then there is a recipe for **Party Baked Beans** that is made with one cup firmly packed brown sugar, a fourth cup flour, a fourth cup prepared mustard, 1 tall can (1 2/3 cups) evaporated milk, two cans (1 pound, 12 ounce) pork and beans in tomato sauce.

Mix sugar, flour and mustard in a 4-quart baking dish, and add milk to the dry ingredients, mixing well. Add pork and beans and mix thoroughly, but carefully, so as not to mash the beans. Bake in a preheated 350 degree oven for 35-40 minutes, stirring occasionally, until beans are bubbly and beginning to brown. **Note:** When using an aluminum baking pan, increase oven temperature to 375 degrees. Makes 10 servings.

* * *

Another different recipe is **Applesauce Baked Beans.** Take one large can of oven-baked Boston-Style Baked Beans, one can (1-pound) applesauce and a fourth pound of salt pork. Arrange layers of beans and applesauce in four to six individual bean pots, depending on size. Remove rind from salt pork, score surface, and cut into chunks. Bury one chunk in each casserole, leaving only the scored rind exposed. Bake the beans in a 350 degree oven about a fourth of an hour or until pork is golden brown and beans are bubbly hot. Makes 4 to 6 servings.

* * *

Since this also is Hot Dog Month you might want to make **Baked Beans with Wieners.** Take three (one-pound) cans baked beans (pork and beans), three-fourths cup catsup, a fourth cup prepared mustard, half teaspoon garlic (optional), dash of Worcestershire sauce, three tablespoons brown sugar, eight wieners, sliced. Drain liquid from two cans of beans and turn them into a pot. Stir in other can of beans with the liquid. Add rest of ingredients. Fold together until well mixed. Sprinkle a little more brown sugar on top and bake uncovered at 350 degree for 50 minutes.

* * *

The last recipe is said to be "elegant eating" and is what is termed a "man pleaser" dish. This is one of those eloquent foods and an ideal way of converting a can of pork and beans into real company fare.

Baked Beans with Dates

1 (1 pound, 5-ounce) can of pork and beans with tomato sauce
1 teaspoon brown sugar
1 teaspoon molasses
1 cup chopped dates
4 strips of bacon, sliced
1 small onion (if desired)

Combine all ingredients and place in a bean pot (Do Not chop onion, just peel and "bury" in the beans.) Bake, covered 30 minutes at 350 degrees. Remove cover and continue baking for 30 more minutes. Serves 4-6. NOTE: Ingredients can be combined several hours (or even the day) before baking and kept refrigerated until time to put in the oven. This is an excellent emergency dish.

All in a Woman's Day--July 26, 1988

Great salad recipes take us into summer

This is the time when salads are rated high on the list of good things to eat. Often we don't want much when the weather is so warm, however, a good salad, along with a roll, muffin or cracker, can take care of our hunger needs.

I have several recipes that I want to share.

* * *

The first is a **Peach Filling Salad** that is made with one (21-ounce) can peach pie filling; one (11-ounce) can mandarin oranges, drained; one and a half cups miniature marshmallows; two medium bananas, diced. Combine all ingredients except bananas; add them just before serving. Chill.

* * *

Another salad that is a bit different is **Georgia Nut Salad** that comes from a plantation in that state. It takes two eggs; half cup of sugar; a third cup of vinegar; two tablespoons of cream; six large apples, pared and diced; one cup of pecans, chopped. Beat eggs in heavy saucepan until foamy and add sugar and vinegar. Cook until thick, stirring it with a wooden spoon. Remove from heat and beat until smooth. Let cool. Add cream and beat again. Pour sauce over diced apples and fold in pecans. Serve at once.

* * *

A **Mystery Salad** is made with one (16-ounce) can pineapple chunks; one can mandarin oranges; one or two bananas sliced; one cup small marshmallows; one box instant lemon pudding mix. Drain fruits, reserving liquids. Mix with banana slices and marshmallows. Mix reserve liquid from fruits with instant pudding mix and pour over fruit. Chill and serve immediately.

* * *

A **Gone With the Wind Salad** is a bit different and takes a regular sized box of lemon or lime flavored gelatin; one and a half cups water; one cup crushed pineapple; half cup sugar; three eggs, separated; one cup whipping cream, whipped, or whipped topping. Cook egg yolks, pineapple and sugar until thick. Cool. Set gelatin in refrigerator and let it cool until syrupy, then whip. Whip egg whites until stiff peaks form. Add pineapple to gelatin. Fold in egg whites and whipped cream. Blend until smooth. Line a 7x10-inch baking dish with Graham cracker crust and pour the mixture into it. This can be topped with whipped cream.

* * *

This is another salad that is interesting. It is **Cherry Mincemeat Salad**. Ingredients include 1 (9-ounce) package mincemeat; 1 cup water; 2 packages cherry gelatin; 3 cups water; 1 cup English walnuts, broken up. Break mincemeat up into small pieces and cover with 1 cup water, cooking over medium heat, and boil 1 minute. Cool. Prepare gelatin, using 3 cups water. When it is slightly thickened, add mincemeat mixture and nuts. Return mixture to refrigerator until set.

* * *

Next is a **Strawberry Gelatin Salad** that is made with 1 large package strawberry gelatin; 1 small can crushed pineapple, drained; 2 packages frozen strawberries, thawed; 1 pint sour cream, some small marshmallows; 3 bananas, sliced. Dissolve gelatin with 2 cups hot water and add 1 3/4 cup cold water. Cool. Add pineapple and strawberries.

* * *

Now for a **Hot Chicken Salad** that is made with 2 cups stewed chicken, cut up; 3 hard cooked eggs, diced; 1 tablespoon lemon juice; 1/3 cup almonds, slivered; 1 cup celery, diced; 1/2 cup mayonnaise, 1 can cream of chicken soup; salt and pepper to taste. Mix all ingredients and cover with crushed potato chips. Bake at 400 degrees for 20 minutes.

* * *

Opal E.'s Chicken Salad

8 chicken breasts
1 cup finely chopped celery
1/2 cup toasted sliced almonds
1 cup mayonnaise
1 teaspoon curry powder
2-ounces salt
1/2 teaspoon white pepper
2 1/2 cups chunk or tidbit pineapple, well drained
1 cup white grapes or white cherries
  Bake chicken breasts; chill and chop or dice; add celery and toasted almonds. Toss all items together lightly with mayonnaise, curry powder, salt, white pepper and pineapple. Just before serving add white grapes or white cherries and more mayonnaise if needed. This serves 10 to 12.

* * *

Fluffy Mayonnaise

1 egg yolk, beaten
1/2 cup mayonnaise
1/4 teaspoon No-Calorie sweetener
1 egg white, beaten stiff
  Combine the beaten egg yolk, mayonnaise and sweetener. Beat the egg white until stiff peaks form. Gently fold into mayonnaise mixture. Delicious served on gelatin salads with fresh fruit.

* * *

This unusual treat can be used as a dip for fresh garden vegetables. It is quickly whipped up and makes one and a half cups.

* * *

Vegetable Dip

Mix together 1 cup mayonnaise or salad dressing, 1/4 cup chili sauce, 3 tablespoons vinegar, 2 tablespoons chopped onion and 2 teaspoons sugar. Cover and chill.

All in a Woman's Day--August 2, 1988

Summertime helps for fruits, vegetables

It is a pretty sight to walk into a market and see all of the colorful, delicious fruits and vegetables ... fresh; crisp and tasty ... to satisfy our needs. Now we just need some help for their use.

When it comes to tomato canning time and you are wondering just how many fresh tomatoes to purchase, just remember it takes three pounds of tomatoes to make one quart when

607

canned.

To make a quick fruit dessert, top canned pear halves with vanilla or coffee ice cream and serve with chocolate sauce for company dessert. It's easy to do and good.

Fold some grated or finely chopped apples into each bowl of hot cereal if you are starting the day off with this kind of a breakfast. Sprinkle the top with a sugar and cinnamon mixture or drizzle maple syrup over it.

When you can fruits and vegetables at home, be sure and wipe off the outside of the jars with white vinegar after they are sealed. This treatment keeps mold from appearing if you perchance have a damp storage area.

You can store most fresh produce in plastic bags in your refrigerator if you punch holes for ventilations (a certain amount of air is needed to prevent sogginess). However, the exception to the rule is ... cucumbers, eggplant and peppers ... they tend to go soft in plastic bags.

The odor of cooking cabbage or cauliflower bothers many people. To help eliminate this add a tablespoon of white vinegar to the cooking water. In addition to helping to take away the odor, it also will keep the cauliflower white. Too, you might want to place stocks of celery on top of the cooking vegetables or try simmering a teaspoon of cinnamon in a pan of water during the cooking to lessen the odor.

Two vitamin C tablets dissolved in a bowl of cool water in which fruit is to be placed will keep it from turning dark.

Bananas can be placed in the refrigerator if they are put in a white or dark plastic bag. Clear plastic will not work. They will not turn dark as soon as they normally would.

If you have some cranberries tucked away in the freezer and would like to indulge before Thanksgiving rolls around, you might want to try this way of preparing them. For a pound of cranberries, mix two cups water, two cups sugar and bring to a boil, continuing for 10 minutes. Add berries and simmer until all have popped. Then add one teaspoon vanilla flavoring, half teaspoon almond flavoring and a dash of salt. They will taste similar to cherries. They also are good over ice cream.

If you want a quick and easy salad, slice fresh strawberries and bananas and add some melon balls. Mix three tablespoons frozen orange juice concentrate with three tablespoons water and pour over the fruit or place the fruit into the dressing. Chill and serve. The orange juice gives a tart refreshing flavor and keeps the fruit from turning dark. Sugar may be added if a sweeter salad is preferred.

To store raisins, prunes or dates, use a plastic container and add a crumpled wet paper towel before sealing. Fruit should stay plump and fresh and not stick together.

All in a Woman's Day--August 9, 1988
More secret helps for use in the kitchen

It is sharing time again for some secret helps in the kitchen.

If you will always wash cooking pans while they are still warm, they will come cleaner much easier.

The best way to keep sieves fresh, clean and odorless is to wash them in soda water instead of soapy water.

Save washing an extra bowl; mix salad dressing right in the salad bowl and then add the ingredients and toss them thoroughly.

Did you ever hard boil eggs and then get them mixed up with fresh ones? To sort them, hold a flashlight behind them. The beam will penetrate only fresh eggs.

Save time and energy. The next time you stir up a batch of cookies, double or triple the recipe of your favorite drop variety. Chill and shape the extra dough into rolls similar to those high-priced commercial cookie rolls. Wrap and freeze. When you need cookies, just slice and bake.

Your scouring pads will not rust if you keep them in an old plastic margarine container. They stay rust free to the very end.

A few grains of sugar mixed with soap lather will do a good job of getting grease from your hands.

Rubbing alcohol will remove sticky labels from jars.

Wipe your grater with salad oil before grating cheese. It helps keep the cheese from sticking and makes the grater easier to clean.

When storing glasses and dishes that are seldom used, place them in clear plastic food storage bags. They are easy to locate when you need them and remain clean and dust free.

A dry oven heats much faster, so always leave the door open a few minutes when you heat the oven for baking. This prevents moisture from forming on the oven walls.

To see if boiled eggs are done, lift one out of the water with a spoon, if it dries immediately it is done.

If you want fresh parsley, try this method. Cut an ordinary sponge in half, moisten with water and scatter parsley seeds into the various holes, then hang in a light airy place. Be sure to keep the sponge well moistened.

Keep a 12-inch ruler in the kitchen drawer. It will be helpful when you want to double check the measurements of cake pans, pie plates, molds and bowls.

To keep brown sugar soft and moist, store it in an empty three-pound coffee can and tape a "hunk" of cotton to the bottom of the lid. It will not harden for months.

When stainless steel cookware gets blue stains from too much heat, just rub them off with a cloth that has been dampened with vinegar. Good old vinegar comes to lots of rescues.

To help paprika and tabasco keep their bright colors, store them in the refrigerator.

In hot weather, stone-ground whole wheat flour and water-ground corn meal should be kept in a very cold place.

When making pizza, sprinkle the pan lightly with corn meal for a crispy crust.

When making spaghetti sauce or chili, add half cup vinegar and three tablespoons sugar. Cover and simmer for an hour.

Square containers in the refrigerator save space; however, round containers permit better circulation of air.

If the numbers on your electric fry pan, percolator, deep fryer etc., are worn off, rub them with a white or yellow crayon, and they can be read easily again.

* * *

Special Hamburgers
1 pound ground beef
2 tablespoons finely chopped green pepper
1/4 cup chopped onion

1/4 cup catsup
1 tablespoon prepared horseradish
1/4 teaspoon dry mustard

Combine ingredients and 1/2 teaspoon salt; mix well. Form into 4 to 6 patties. They can be broiled or placed in a greased shallow baking dish and baked at 375 degrees for 30 minutes.

All in a Woman's Day--August 16, 1988

Sandwich Month is during August

August is Sandwich Month, and what better time to indulge in a tasty bit of food as the weather stays warm and appetites are lagging. Often it seems that something cool and refreshing is all that is needed. However, it is well to have something hot for a meal, and this is where America's favorite foods—the hamburger and hot dog—come into view.

These two sandwiches can be dressed up or down, just as you choose. They can be served with all the fixins'—catsup, mustard, relish, onion, cheese or served without. Either way they are good!

The hamburger got its name from the German city of Hamburg. Perhaps it was because the city once carried on a lively trade with Russia's Baltic provinces, where the people ate a great deal of shredded raw meat, the ancestor of our Steak Tartare.

However, today it is regarded as an American creation. It is not really known just who invented the hamburger. During the eighth century, physicians in the Italian city of Padua began prescribing hand-chopped beef, fried with onions, as a treatment for a cold. (That was certainly a good prescription!)

Then in the 13th century, France's King Louis IX chefs came up with the idea of a food grinder, and had the royal armorer put one together.

Now, if you do not eat the ground beef in a bun, you will find that it is often called Salisbury Steak. This is a bunless hamburger, and was named after Dr. J. H. Salisbury, who more than 75 years ago recommended that ground beef be served three times a day for a whole list of ailments.

Ground beef, or hamburger, was first known as hamburger steak and was not served with a bun. At the beginning of the current century, the name was changed to hamburger steak and finally just plain "hamburger."

This great American hamburger is made from almost any part of the steer. No doubt some of you will recall how your grandmothers, would buy a piece of steak and then watch, very carefully while the butcher would grind it as ordered.

It is good when you have a meat market you can trust or a butcher in the supermarket who cuts the meat as you want it.

If you have a food processor, you can grind your own beef, and then, of course, you will know exactly the kind of meat that goes into your "hamburger."

It is important that you purchase ground beef with a low amount of fat. Twenty percent of the ground beef should be fat, according to dietitians. This amount is said to hold the meat together and give a good flavor. Too much fat, however, is a waste of money, as it melts away in cooking and does not improve the flavor.

But maybe you don't want a hamburger or hot dog. There are all kinds of other sandwiches, some of long standing, while others we can concoct on the spur of the moment with what we have on hand, for an "everything and anything goes" sandwich.

If you want to break up hamburger meat, or any ground meat for that matter, use a hand potato masher. It works better than a fork. The metal ones are recommended instead of a wooden masher.

When frying hamburgers, put them on a paper plate or paper toweling, after cooking to soak up the excess grease before serving.

Punch a small hole in the center of the hamburger patty and this allows it to cook through quicker and saves a lot of time, especially when you have several hungry mouths to feed.

All in a Woman's Day--August 23, 1988

'Back - to - School'; parents' help needed

It is time to think "back to school."

Perhaps parents will think it is back to "work" for them; however, you might help your child do a bit better in school if you helped him or her a little less.

Education experts say parents should not do their heir's homework, or the individual will not learn the subject. The role of the parent is to provide the proper setting and material for doing the homework. This includes the right lighting, a quiet place, pens, pencils, paper and reference books.

Also parents should be sure that their children are in good health as learning demands the best from the child that can be given.

Too, parents should not manage their child's allowance. Taking care of that is a good way to help him or her understand finance and mathematics.

A child needs to learn from the world around him or her.

Children do best in subjects that interest them. Parents of young travelers may find that their children have picked up geography, history, foreign languages, art appreciation and a taste for different foods, all from visiting other states and countries. Too, a better understanding of science, no doubt, will develop from seeing the places where great scientists have worked.

Let the world be their classroom, and you will find that it may make a difference in how well they do in their classwork.

Every year, literally thousands of health problems that are prevalent in students of grade and high school levels are first recognized by their teachers. Likewise, coaches and physical education instructors watch for and often detect health irregularities that might interfere with a child's physical performance and learning ability.

You may ask if this is a part of the teacher's job. No, not really. It's that extra sense of dedication that makes teachers already overworked public servants; they give your child that special attention, all because they really care.

Many children have health problems that retard their ability to learn or engage in sports effectively. And, unfortunately, many of these problems go unnoticed until they become serious. It is estimated that three out of every 10 school children have health problems that could affect their futures, if not directly, certainly in terms of diminished abilities.

Concerned parents should consider this before they admonish their children for lack of performance in school, lack of coordination, and poor work and play habits.

Not every child can be expected to be an Einstein in the classroom, or a Joe Namath on the playing field; however, everyone should be able to make the most of his or her abilities with ease and comfort.

* * *

A cookie and a glass of milk are good to have for a snack when your youngster comes home from school. Here is a cookie recipe for you to try.

Grandma's Cookies

1 cup shortening
1 cup white sugar
1 cup brown sugar
1 teaspoon vanilla
2 eggs
2 cups flour
1 teaspoon soda
1 teaspoon baking powder
1/2 teaspoon salt
2 cups rolled oats

Mix together shortening and sugars, add eggs and vanilla. Mix and make a pond in the center of the dough and add the flour, soda, salt and baking powder that have been sifted together. Mix well. Add oats, or nuts, if desired; drop by teaspoon on a greased cookie sheet, and bake in a 350 degree oven 12 minutes. This recipe may be varied by adding 1/2 to 1 cup or more of the following: Coconut, gumdrops, black walnuts or other nuts or chocolate chips.

All in a Woman's Day--August 30, 1988

Suggestions given for barbecue 'bash'

he last big bash of the season for barbecuing comes up right away—in fact, this Labor Day weekend; so, plan to take advantage and do some outside grilling with family and friends.

There is nothing quite so intriguing as the smell of burning wood and the food being cooked. It just makes you hungry, whether you want to be or not.

A different twist to the usual outdoor cooking is the use of aromatic woods. It seems that each wood has a distinctive flavor all its own, and thus adds that special touch when used in barbecuing.

The four most popular woods are hickory, alder, mesquite and oak. Apple and cherry woods are milder; therefore, they are good for cooking poultry and fish.

The red hot long lasting embers of hickory makes it the choice spice for the famous Southern style barbecuing. Hickory lends a tangy, smoky bacon like taste. And speaking of red hot, hickory enthusiasts claim that a cord of shagbark hickory produces almost as much heat as a ton of coal.

Southern barbecuing leans toward various cuts of pork, with hickory wood being most ideal. This kind of wood also is best when used for steaks, chicken, wild game, and even fresh tuna and halibut steaks.

The alder wood is a fragrant wood, with a somewhat more delicate aroma than hickory, and it does enhance the natural flavors of juicy pork chops, succulent chicken and Cornish game hens. The aroma does not overpower the flavor of the food. This kind of wood also is excellent for smoking salmon, oysters and other fish. In fact, certain American Indian tribes originally used this kind of wood for cooking and smoking fish, a northwestern version of the Hawaiian luau. At celebrations or "pot-latches," as they were called, salmon was, and still is often roasted over deep pits filled with the burning alder logs. Today, too, in northwestern areas, deep red strips of alder smoked salmon called, "squaw candy," is a favorite local snack.

Perhaps of all woods, mesquite is the most steeped in what we call "Americana." In the days of the western cowboys, when mesquite was a curse to them with its thorns and impenetrable brush; the most avid fans were the chuckwagon cooks, who used this sweet, smoky wood to step up the flavor of almost everything they cooked.

It produces intense heat, and chips and chunks of mesquite are used to flavor foods from pork to chicken and vegetables.

Oak is a versatile mellow wood that makes outdoor aroma cooking a joy. It brings out the natural flavor of thick steaks, halibut and plump Long Island ducklings when they are grilled slowly over the hot coals. It just seems to have a way of drawing out the naturally delicious flavor of foods.

I have found a few twists to help produce a good barbecue flavor. Soak the oak chunks in cider vinegar or red wine in place of water. Mix oak and hickory, or mesquite, to produce a special blend of woodsy aroma, or you can toss a few fresh herbs, such as thyme or rosemary, directly on the hot coals along with the wood chunks.

You can let wood chips or chunks be the sole source of cooking fuel or use them in combination with charcoal. The amount of wood needed depends on the size of the grill, the amount of food and whether it is used separately or with charcoal. By adding four to six wet chunks to the hot ash covered charcoal, you get an extra strong smoky flavor to the barbecued food.

Too, you can soak four to six wet chunks or one cup of chips in water two hours before cooking, and then place them on the hot coals. When the chunks start to smoke, that is the time to begin cooking. The more chips or chunks used the more potent the flavor. Should you desire a lighter flavor use less wood. You might need to do some experimenting to find the desired smoke flavor that your family enjoys most. The wood flavorings used in barbecuing make exceptionally tasty food.

If you keep the grill covered while cooking, the aroma from the wood will have a chance to fully penetrate the food.

* * *

There are many different kinds of basting and barbecuing sauces; however, the sauce I am going to give to you is for cooking in a skillet. Of course, it could be used for basting or to put on your barbecued food.

Barbecue Sauce

1 can cola or 7-Up
1 bottle of barbecue sauce

Mix the two ingredients together and pour half of it into the electric skillet. Arrange cut up chicken or other meat in the skillet and pour the remaining sauce over the top of the chicken. Salt and pepper if desired. Place cover on skillet; however, leave the vent open. Cook for three hours at 200 degrees. Toward the end of the cooking time be sure to check for sticking.

All in a Woman's Day--September 6, 1988
Two eating right

Regardless of whether you are cooking for one, two or a dozen people there are certain basic rules to be followed so that you will eat the necessary foods each day to keep in good health.

Neither food nor exercise can make you healthy and fit—it has to be good eating and a variety, along with regular exercise.

Often when there are one or two people in the family to cook for, it is easy to slide by and not always eat the foods necessary for maintaining good health. To do this, it is well to establish a daily eating pattern that includes the variety of foods needed from each of the four basic groups.

The meat group includes foods that are rich in protein and that also are a source of iron. Meat, poultry, fish, eggs, legumes and nuts provide the variation in this group.

The best source of vitamin C is found in the fruit and vegetable group. Citrus fruits, especially provides this vitamin; with vitamin A in yellow and leafy green vegetables.

The cereal and bread group includes cereal, breads, corn meal and pasta. You will find they are a good source of carbohydrates, the B vitamins, protein and iron.

And the last group, milk, includes all dairy products. From these sources we obtain calcium, phosphorus, protein, vitamin A and D and riboflavin.

So, to keep in good condition, be sure to establish good daily eating habits that will help in keeping weight under control by providing adequate starch and fiber, avoiding too much fat, saturated fat and cholestrol foods, as well as sodium and sugar.

When planning a weekly menu, a good procedure to practice is to check and see what is on hand and what is needed before going to the market. Be sure to read the labels on the packages so you will have knowledge of what you are buying.

It is easier to shop nowadays as many foods are packaged in smaller quantities, thus making it so you won't have to eat "leftovers" for several meals.

After making your purchases, be sure to store the foods properly for the best use.

Normally folks eat three meals a day; however, there are many who eat four or more lighter meals with smaller servings.

Regardless of how many meals you eat a day, remember that flavor, color and texture are important and add special interest to meals that might otherwise be rather bland and uninteresting. You might include something crisp, a softer food, mild to strong flavored foods, along with hot and cold foods.

Don't sit down to a table that is not attractively set. A table centerpiece, nothing very elaborate, makes for a special interest. Be sure the food that you serve looks attractive and that the plate is placed on a cloth or place mat that draws attention.

You might want to eat at different spots sometimes—the porch or patio, by a window, possibly watching television or maybe just listening to mood music.

Wherever or however you eat, just one or two or more, be sure to plan your meals around the four basic food groups that can be obtained from various foods that are cooked and prepared in different ways.

* * *

Here is an easy meat loaf that makes two servings.

Top of the Stove Meat Loaf
1 cup lightly packed ground beef
1 tablespoon finely chopped onion (optional)

3 tablespoons milk
2 tablespoons uncooked oats
1/2 teaspoon salt
Pepper
1/4 cup water
1/2 cup tomato sauce

Mix together all ingredients, except water and tomato sauce, and shape into 2 loaves. Brown on all sides in a frying pan or skillet, over medium heat. After pouring the drained fat off, add the water and pour the tomato sauce over the loaves. Cook covered over low heat for 30 minutes. More water may be added during the cooking if desired.

All in a Woman's Day--September 13, 1988

Always find room for more desserts

Despite all the modern efforts to reduce the calorie intake, still most families continue to enjoy topping off their meal with "something sweet."

There is a wide choice of desserts. Something delicate and light can follow a hearty main course meal or a "rich" dessert can be served following a lighter meal.

Desserts, however, don't need to be all sweetness. They can provide added protein and vitamins, along with skim milk, brewer's yeast or toasted wheat germ, all of which can be added to basic recipes.

No doubt America's favorite dessert is the "pie perfect." Pies can be rich and creamy or light and luscious. They are always the right answer anytime people gather for coffee and dessert.

A pinch of spice, a cup of fruit, a few chopped nuts added to puddings "plus" that can be cooked, baked, molded, layered—well, there are countless ways to make dessert time different "every time." Although we eat desserts for the good taste and enjoyment, remember those made with milk, eggs or fruit supply valuable vitamins.

When company comes for coffee and dessert or for some special occasion, then it is time to serve a dessert that is really something spectacular. A souffle, a cheesecake, or a Bavarian; each is a masterpiece of culinary skill. These kinds of desserts take a little extra time in preparation, so be sure and plan ahead when that special day comes along.

Then from the freezer comes all the icy cold desserts that are always good after a hearty meal. They are easy to prepare and store, and more than one can be prepared at a time. You will find an "extra" dessert in the freezer will be handy when unexpected guests drop by your home.

The finishing touches are made up of the little "extras" that turn a simple dessert into something very special. Sauces made to pour over ice cream, puddings and cake squares, along with toppings that come in delectable flavors, add a bit of glamour to an ordinary dish of fruit. And, of course, creamy, rich frostings and fillings make the plainest of cakes an extravaganza.

Now the microwave comes to the rescue and makes cooking so simple and fast. When women became breadwinners along with their husbands, they thought some of those good recipes of grandmother's day and earlier, that had been handed down from generation to generation, could not be enjoyed. It took too long to prepare and time was not available.

Now, because of the microwave, some of those wonderful, traditional recipes can be enjoyed again by families.

Give your microwave a chance to do the work for you so that you can enjoy all of the special holidays and have some extra time with your families.

* * *

Pumpkin Delight Dessert

32 marshmallows
1 cup pumpkin
1 cup whipped cream or whipped topping
1/2 teaspoon cinnamon
1/2 teaspoon cloves
1/4 teaspoon ginger
1/4 teaspoon nutmeg
14 graham crackers
1/4 cup melted butter

Melt marshmallows in double boiler; then add pumpkin and spices. Let Cool. Add whipped cream or topping. Crush graham crackers and mix with melted butter. Line pan with the crumb mixture; then pour in the pumpkin mixture. Sprinkle a few graham cracker crumbs on top and chill. This is a delightful and spicy autumn dessert.

* * *

Heavenly Banana Pie

1 cup sugar
1/4 teaspoon salt
1/4 teaspoon lemon juice
2 egg whites
2 large ripe bananas

Prepare a graham cracker crust and put in pie tin. Mash the bananas and add the sugar, salt and lemon juice. Beat the egg whites very stiff and fold into the banana mixture and then beat all well. Pour into the crust and bake at 350 degrees until set, about 35 to 45 minutes. Chill and serve topped with whipped cream or topping.

'Story of Bread' is told

Bread is deeply rooted in the story of our civilization. So important was wheat and its products, that they called for a sense of awe and reverence.

Throughout history, the making of bread has inspired minds and hands; poets and writers, who have romanced about it, and artists who have sculptured it.

The making of bread is a serious rite for those who truly appreciate fine food. There's a communion between maker and dough that seldom happens in other areas of cooking. Making bread is both a science and an art, and it has come to be a satisfying hobby, for men as well as women.

Since Neolithic people learned to grind grain between two stones; mixing the crushed grains with water and spreading the mixture on stones to bake in the sun, and later in hot ashes, bread has been a life sustaining element.

Making the first leavened bread is credited to ancient Egyptians. It is said to have happened this way: A batch of dough was allowed to stand before it was baked. Wild yeast cells settled in and grew, thus producing bubbles of carbon dioxide causing the dough to rise. They found that the dough was softer and more palatable, so, it then became the custom to let the dough stand for sometime before baking. There is no doubt that this was a hit-or-miss technique for some days the air bore no suitable yeast.

Later, it was discovered that the dough raised in this manner could be used as a starter for the next batch of bread to be made. The portion kept to start the next batch was called leaven

616

and was the forerunner of today's sourdough bread.

Romans sometimes used a leaven made of grape juice and millet that would hasten the fermentation of the bread. The juice contained the yeast from the skins of the grapes. Barm that forms on beer during fermentation was used as a leavening by the Celts in Britain.

By the time the colonists made their way to the New World, the yeast organism had been identified and the brewing industry had begun a by product of beer, making a brewer's yeast that could be used as a starter for bread. The yeast that floated to the top of the beer was skimmed off and placed in stone bottles. Bakers would purchase the yeast from their local breweries or make a "brew" at home.

Brewer's yeast, however, had a drawback, it had a bitter taste that was carried through the flavor of the bread.

In addition to brewer's yeast, homemakers in the 19th century used specially brewed ferments to make their yeast. The basis for these fermentations was a mash of grain, flour or boiled potatoes. Hops were often included to prevent sourness.

Self-rising bread was made from a starter of corn meal, milk and oftentimes potatoes. The term self-rising referred to the practice used of nesting the bowl of starter in a bed of heated salt to keep it warm overnight. Also a little salt was added to the starter to delay the growth of bacteria that might sour the milk.

* * *

Easy Cake Mix Bread

3 cups flour
1 small box cake mix (such as Jiffy)
2 packages dry yeast
2 teaspoons salt
2 cups warm water
1/4 teaspoon butter flavoring
Additional flour as needed

Place dry ingredients into a large bowl, stirring in water and flavoring. Beat, then add enough additional flour to make a soft dough. Turn out on floured bread board, and knead well. Grease bowl and place dough in it, turning it to grease all sides. Cover it with a clean towel and let it rise in a warm place until almost double in size. Knead down on floured board. Make into two loaves, rolls or whatever shape desired. Place in greased pans. Let them rise until double. Bake in a 400 degree oven 20 minutes or until they are golden brown and sound hollow when thumped.

All in a Woman's Day--September 27, 1988
Sourdough bread is regarded the greatest

Many folks think that sourdough bread is the finest bread ever devised by mankind.

To the frontier families, after the Bible, sourdough was the most important possession. Sourdough starters have been known to continue through generations in families. It not only made bread, biscuits and flapjacks, but it could be used to fill cracks in log cabins, treat wounds, brew "hooch," and even to feed the dogs.

During the Yukon Gold strike in 1897-98, the word "sourdough" became an important part in the American language, even though it had been a staple in the California camps for 50 years previously. It seems that the word could mean either man or his dough. Most often prospectors carried their starter buried in the top of a bag of flour or in a pot, strapped to their backs. Sourdough was an important part of their life.

It has been said that sourdough purists don't use yeast in their products; they just let the natural yeast from the air create the leavening in the mixture that had been left out long enough to collect the yeast spores. Of course, this is a chancy situation varied with successes and failures.

The starter or sponge, as it is sometimes called, simply consisted of a thick flour and water batter; however, some recipes called for sugar, salt, milk, potato water or even yeast. The starter was allowed to stand uncovered for one, two or more days, depending upon the ingredients and temperature. Then it was used in place of yeast in a recipe. Each time after it was used, the starter pot was replenished with flour and water to restore the mixture to its original consistency and volume.

The frequent replenishing is necessary to keep it alive. Take the mixture out of the refrigerator the night before you plan to use it. Then add two cups warm water and two and a half cups all-purpose flour per cup of sourdough mixture. Cover this and let it stand at room temperature all night, and it will be ready to use the next morning. Perhaps you would prefer a tangier taste, if so, the mixture can stand even longer.

Austrian chemists developed during the 19th century a system for massproduction of yeast. It was sown in vats containing fermenting brew. As it rose to the top, the yeast was removed and washed, with some of the water removed by pressure. It was then formed into ready-to-use cakes.

Bakers, however, were a little shy of this new product that was called dried yeast or German yeast, because it didn't keep well, and it was often bulked out with starch, chalk and pipe clay. However, by 1900 journals carried advertisements for yeast in which they claimed it was of the purest quality.

It was in 1863 that an immigrant named Charles Fleischmann went back to Austria in search of a good quality baker's yeast, returning to America with yeast cells in a test tube in his vest pocket.

He then began selling compressed yeast that was wrapped in tinfoil. With the onset of World War II, the U.S. government sought a dehydrated yeast that could be used on the battlefield to make bread. The Fleischmann Company produced in 1943, the first active dry yeast. Then after the war, dry yeast was introduced to the retail market and is now the form of yeast most used for home baking. This now has been improved to a rapid rise yeast that claims to be 50 percent faster than the earlier product.

There was a time each autumn after the harvest was completed and granaries stocked people paused to pay homage to the divine forces that brought them the blessings of abundance. So, it was that the "Day of Bread," began as a feast and thanksgiving. The custom, started in Europe, was revived there more than two decades ago. The idea also spread to the United States, to South America, Asia and Indochina. This day was one that was used to help relieve hunger in many areas of the world.

Bread often would symbolize a country, and a people by its shape and texture. Long slender loaves came from France and Italy; Sally Lund from

England; decorated varieties from Germany; and round unleavened loaves from the Middle East.

Only in the last hundred years has the making of light airy bread been a certainty, according to experts. Before this time, bread making, to be efficient, required years of experience, along with a generous amount of luck.

* * *

Here is a bread recipe that is excellent for a beginning cook.

* * *

Sourdough Starter

1 package dry yeast
2 cups all-purpose flour
2 tablespoons sugar
2 1/2 cups lukewarm water

Beat well, using an electric mixer if possible. Cover the dough and let stand with a cloth covering for two days. The starter is then ready to use. Stir down occasionally, if necessary. Store in refrigerator in a covered glass jar (Do Not Use Metal). This will keep indefinitely; however, the starter should be used at least every two weeks and equal amounts of water and flour added to remaining starter to keep it going.

* * *

Sourdough Pancakes

1 cup sourdough starter
2 cups milk
2 eggs, lightly beaten
3 tablespoons salad oil
1 teaspoon butter flavoring
2 tablespoons sugar
1 teaspoon salt
2 teaspoons soda
2 cups all-purpose flour

Combine all ingredients in order given and beat with a light hand to keep the bubbles in the sourdough starter. Bake on a hot griddle, turning once to brown on both sides. Add more milk if a thinner batter is desired.

* * *

Sourdough Sugar Cookies

1/2 cup shortening
1 cup sugar
1 teaspoon vanilla flavoring
1/4 teaspoon butter flavoring
1 egg
1 cup sourdough starter
2 teaspoons baking powder
1/4 teaspoon soda
1/4 teaspoon salt
1 3/4 cups flour

Cream shortening and sugar together, beating in flavorings and egg. Then add sourdough starter. Sift dry ingredients together and stir in; when well blended, drop by teaspoonful onto greased cookie sheets. Sprinkle with the sugar and cinnamon (2 teaspoons sugar and 1/2 teaspoon cinnamon mixed together). Bake them at 350 degrees for 12 to 15 minutes, or until done. Baking time depends on the size of the cookie. These also can be frosted or glazed, and they freeze well.

All in a Woman's Day--October 4, 1988
'Back to Breakfast'; let's make it good

Back to Breakfast !

All nutritionists say that breakfast, however, you eat it—leisurely, on the run, in bed or at a restaurant——it is important to your health and perhaps the most important meal of the day.

It helps to start your day, and after having breakfast, no matter how big your problems may have been, they don't seem quite so troublesome. Something in the "tummy" helps the way of thinking. For school children, breakfast for them is a big plus.

Now they tell us it doesn't make any difference what we eat for breakfast just so we eat. Sandwiches are okay, that we know by the breakfast sandwiches put out by the fast food restaurants. Now television is advertising a taco breakfast. Well that might be a bit different. It doesn't sound quite as sensational as maybe it should; however, for young folks who like this kind of food, it would no doubt be great.

A cup of coffee may help to awaken you and your senses, but something more is needed to really put the zing into your being—fruit juices, milk or hot chocolate, a cup of hot tea—all add to your diet. Even a big glass of water is good to start the day.

Perhaps you are a cereal eater. There are all kinds on the market, hot and cold, to sharpen your taste buds, along with fresh fruits, bacon, sausage, ham, eggs, pancakes, waffles, biscuits and gravy, rolls, muffins, toast and French toast. Yes, there are many appetizing foods that can tempt you. There also is a combination of foods for a breakfast casserole that can be prepared the night before, and then placed in the oven, upon arising. It will be ready by the time everyone is dressed for school or work.

Choose what you like best and then have something different each morning so you can enjoy a variation and not get tired of the same old routine.

However and whatever you prepare for breakfast, remember it is important that you eat something in the morning to help take you through the day.

Let's get back to breakfast!

* * *

A Thought To Ponder: The best way to be somebody is just be yourself.

* * *

Apricot Biscuits

1 package canned biscuits
1/2 cup sugar
1/2 cup apricot nectar (or puree)
2 tablespoons butter, melted (optional)
1/2 teaspoon orange flavoring
1/4 teaspoon butter flavoring

Combine all ingredients, with exception of biscuits, in a round 9-inch pie pan. Take each biscuit, punch a hole in the center and place on them the apricot mixture. Bake at 425 degrees until golden brown. Remove from oven and let stand about 5 minutes; then invert the pan and the apricot mixture will become the topping. This is delightful for a morning coffee, for breakfast, or for a simple meal.

* * *

Ham and Egg Casserole

6 or 7 slices of dry bread cubed to 1/2-inch
1 pound precooked ham cut into 1/2-inch cubes
1 1/2 cups cheese cut in small pieces or use sliced cheese
5 eggs
2 cups whole milk
1/2 teaspoon dry mustard
1/2 teaspoon salt

Arrange bread in a 9x13-inch greased pan, and place ham on top and then the cheese. Beat eggs, add milk, salt and mustard, and mix. Pour over the items in the casserole. Melt 3/4 stick butter or margarine and drizzle it over the top. Cover and refrigerate this overnight and bake it one hour in a 325 degree oven.

Crisp snap of fall means apples are ready

A convincing way to herald and welcome the change of season is to hear the crisp snap of the fresh new crop of apples as you take a bite.

Delicious apples are a great out-of-hand snack that satisfies the sweet tooth, provides valuable vitamins and minerals and makes a delectable low calorie dessert. A medium apple (2 1/2 inches in diameter) has about 66 calories.

Apple growers have superstitions the same as other folks. For instance, if the sun shines through the branches of the apple tree Christmas Day, there is going to be a good apple crop the following year. So, if this fruity bit of folklore is true, then the sun must have shown its brightest many times over the nations' apple orchards on Christmas Day.

Apples have an adaptability, flavor and economy that are hard to match.

The apple is often dubbed "king of fruits," and is no doubt the oldest fruit known to civilization.

Thousands of years ago in central and southwest Asia, China and the near East, apple trees grew wild. From there the apple found its way into Turkey, Israel and Europe. Fossilized apples found in Stone Age lake dwellings in Central Europe indicated prehistoric people ate and dried the fruit.

Perhaps more than any other fruit, the apple, is surrounded by myth and tradition. Greek mythology tells of a golden apple inscribed "to the fairest." This is reputed to have caused the Trojan War. Aphrodite's connection with the apple appears to be numerous, and the fruit, of course, has long been associated with love and fertility.

Apple trees begin to bear fruit when they are about four to six years old and peak at about 35 to 40 years. However, occasionally apple trees nearly 200 years old are still bearing fruit.

There is no such thing as a typical apple flavor. Each variety has its own distinctive taste and characteristic. Some are better suited than others for certain uses. For instance, the large mild, sweet flavored Red Delicious variety is excellent for eating fresh and for salads. The spicy, juicy Golden Delicious is superb for pies and sauces, as well as eating raw. Jonathans on the other hand are often considered multipurpose with their crisp texture, juiciness and tart flavor.

* * *

A Thought To Ponder: You're the apple of my eye. —anonymous

* * *

Apple Dabble Cake

1 1/2 cups oil
3 eggs
2 cups sugar
2 teaspoons vanilla
1 teaspoon burnt sugar flavoring
3 cups flour
1 teaspoon salt
1 teaspoon soda
1 cup chopped nuts
3 cups chopped apples

Mix oil, eggs, sugar and flavorings together. Sift flour, soda and salt together and mix with the first mixture. Fold in the nuts and chopped apples. Spray a bundt pan with nonstick spray and pour the batter in it. Bake 1 hour at 350 degrees. As soon as the cake comes from the oven, pour the following glaze over it:

1 cup firmly packed brown sugar
1/2 cup margarine

1/4 cup milk

Combine glaze ingredients and heat 3 minutes or until hot and bubbly and then pour it over cake. Let cake set 3 hours, them remove it from pan.

All in a Woman's Day--October 18, 1988

Glean more of those helpful kitchen hints

Let's glean a few more kitchen helps that will ease the work load.

A cotton-tipped stick is great for cleaning between the buttons on the blender.

A plastic bag or wrapper that has melted on a cooling pan will come off when placed over low heat. Rub briskly with a firm fabric. Never place the pan over high heat. The melted plastic does not harm the pan, but it does make it unsightly.

If the nozzle on your spray cans stick, just wash them in hot water for a few seconds and wipe. Always wipe the nozzle after each use and nine times out of 10 spray will come out easily.

To prevent the white water ring around the pan when boiling eggs, add a little vinegar and salt to the water. This also helps make the eggs peel easier.

If you should scorch a pan, enamel or otherwise, just fill it with water to cover the scorched part, add a small amount of liquid bleach and let it soak overnight. This cleans the pan easily and the scorched food disappears.

Fold a paper towel or a cleansing tissue and wrap it around the neck of the salad oil bottle with a rubber band to catch all the drips.

When wrapping a cake with foil, spray the foil with nonstick cooking spray so that the icing will not stick to the foil.

You will find that plastic wrap will cling better if the rim of the bowl or pan you are covering is moistened.

When a kettle cover loses its knob, just use a cork to replace it. Place a screw through the cover with the head on the underside. Push the screw into the cork. This makes a handy heat-proof knob.

After opening a glass of cheese spread, turn it upside down in the refrigerator and it will keep fresh longer and will help prevent mold from forming.

If you cannot get the top off of a fruit jar, just run hot water over it for a minute and the lid generally comes off easily.

Your left hand will not know what your right hand does and your dusting will be finished in half the time if you carry dust cloths or mitts on both hands.

To keep scissors working sharply, apply a drop of oil to the joint occasionally.

When using soap pads, cut them in half. That way they will be used before they can rust and also the cutting sharpens the scissors.

If your washing machine is oversudsing, simply put a capful of liquid fabric softener in the washing machine. The extra suds will soon disappear.

* * *

A Thought To Ponder: Laughing is the cheapest luxury one can enjoy. It stirs up the blood, expands the chest, electrifies the nerves and clears the brain.

* * *

Date Pecan Rolls

1 cup soft butter or margarine
1/2 cup sugar

2 teaspoons vanilla
2 cups flour
1 1/3 cups chopped pecans
1 cup whole dates, cut up

Cream butter and sugar and add vanilla and mix. Add flour and mix, then blend in pecans and dates. Roll spoonful of dough into balls. Refrigerate balls for 1-2 hours. Bake in a 350 degree oven for 20 minutes on greased cookie sheet. Remove from oven and roll in powdered sugar. Sprinkle them again after they have cooled. Yield: 60 cookies. (**Note:** There is no leavening agent needed and the dough does not rise.)

All in a Woman's Day--October 25, 1988

It's Halloween — here they come!

Here they come ... those traditional ghosts and witches, wild animals and skeletons, with astronauts sort of updating the parade that has no bands, no banners; however, it does have lots of giggles and high spirits. It will make more stops than the average parade; one at each lighted door, and perhaps some doors that aren't lighted. Woe to anyone who would dare to open a door without a treat in hand. It is Halloween!

This is a strictly fun evening; and treats handed out at the door or at a party should be in the mood of the day, amusing and casual ... these are the keywords.

Merry jack-o-lanterns will be grinning from doorsteps and windows and many trick-or-treaters will be carrying one. It's Halloween!

As it often has been mentioned, everything has a legend. So, according to Irish folklore, a stingy man, named "Jack" was barred from Heaven for his selfishness and very inhospitable ways. Too, he was expelled from Hell because he simply delighted in playing practical jokes on who else. . .the devil.

So, as the legend continues Jack, because of his bad traits, was condemned to walk the Earth, until Judgement Day, carrying a lighted lantern, Then, on Halloween "Jack" is said to be most often seen.

So, because of the legend, the Irish children took it on as a custom to go out on that particular night, Halloween, carrying a hollowed-out turnip with a carved grinning face, and lighted with a candle ... thus imitating the "Jack" folklore.

This custom was brought to the United States in the 1840s by the Irish immigrants. According to history, the children found large, orange pumpkins and these they learned made better jack-o-lanterns than turnips. As the celebration of Halloween became more popular, the name jack-o-lantern was given to the pumpkins that they adopted.

* * *

A Thought To Ponder: It's good luck to see a white cat on the road.

* * *

Orange Popcorn Balls

2 cups sugar
1 can (6-ounce) frozen orange juice
3/4 cup water
1/2 cup light syrup
1 teaspoon vinegar
1/2 teaspoon salt
5 quarts unsalted popped corn

Combine all ingredients, except popped corn, in heavy saucepan, and bring to a boil. Lower heat and cook to 250 degrees on a candy thermometer. Mixture will bubble and must be watched to keep it from boiling over. Slowly pour mixture over corn and mix well. Wait 5 minutes or until mixture can be easily shaped into balls. With buttered hands, form 24 small 2-inch popcorn balls.

All in a Woman's Day--November 8, 1988
Holiday nut crackin' hints

As the holiday approaches, we are reminded that is it nut crackin' time. Time to enjoy the goodness of different kinds of nuts.

Fresh nuts of various kinds are arriving at the markets, even our own pecans, and Missouri, by the way, is growing in that status.

All of this is in anticipation of the season, especially the holidays—Thanksgiving and Christmas.

There are a few hints that might be a bit helpful, especially if you are a nutcracker. It is fun to crack the different kinds of nuts and snack on the "crumbs." Picking them out is something else, but if you can plan to have a little help it can be a fun session.

The microwave helps in cracking walnuts and pecans. Place two cups of nuts in a casserole with one cup water. Turn the microwave on HIGH for one and a half to two minutes. It is well to soak pecans six to eight hours in cold water and use two and a half tablespoons salt to a quart of water. Even though pecans are not difficult to crack, this will enable the "goodies" to come out a little more easily.

Black walnuts are rather difficult to crack; however, another method that might make it easier is to soak them about 15 minutes in water, then place them in a wet towel overnight. Too, it makes a difference when cracking black walnuts-crack endwise, and then crack each quarter.

Another method is to use a vise, a bench vise, and place the walnuts in the opening below the vise. Hold your fingers over the nut to prevent scattering of pieces.

To make the cracking of walnuts, butternuts and hickory nuts easier, place the unshelled nuts on the rack in the pressure cooker, add one-third cup of water and pressure cook six minutes. When the air has been exhausted, cool and crack nuts right away. The shells should split with one easy tap and usually the nut meats will come right out of the shell.

English walnuts are not very difficult to crack; however, it will be an easier task if the pointed end of the nut is held upright and then struck sharply with a hammer.

Most nuts will always crack easier if soaked in salt water overnight. The water will not affect the crispness or flavor of the nuts.

Too, placing brazil nuts in the freezer makes them easier to crack.

Another method for cracking Brazil nuts, pecans and English walnuts is to place the nuts in a pan and cover with water, bringing to a boil and continue boiling about 10 minutes.

Drain and crack them when cool. This method helps the nut meats to come out in larger pieces. Another way with Brazil nuts is to place them in a 250 degree oven for about 20 minutes. The whole nut meat should then be easily removed.

Just a few hints for use after cracking:

After black walnuts have been cracked, let them set overnight, and the nut meats will come out more easily.

Pour water over nuts before adding

them to cakes, cookies and candy. Pieces of shell will float to the top of the water and can be easily skimmed off.

Use a magnifying glass to find bits of hulls in nuts you have cracked. Little pieces of wood stand out like a sore thumb.

To blanche almonds, drop them into boiling water, turn off heat and let them stand 3 minutes before draining. The skins will slip right off. Dry the nuts on paper toweling.

If you have a recipe calling for nuts, and are out of them, you can use a substitute. Use oatmeal, browned, in a small amount of butter or margarine and use just as you would nuts. This adds a rather delightful, crunchy nut-like flavor.

Always store shelled nuts in the refrigerator or freezer as they have a fairly high fat content and soon become rancid if stored at room temperature. Uncracked nuts, too, are best stored in refrigerator or freezer.

* * *

A Thought To Ponder: Character is not made in a crisis—it is only exhibited.

* * *

Spiced Nuts

2 1/2 cups pecans, almond halves or English walnuts
2 cups sifted powdered sugar
1/2 cup corn starch
1 1/2 teaspoons salt
1/4 cup ground cinnamon
2 teaspoons ground ginger
1 tablespoon ground cloves
1 teaspoon ground nutmeg
1 egg white
1 tablespoon almond flavoring
1/4 teaspoon orange flavoring

Spread nuts on a cookie sheet (prefer-ably one with raised edges so they will not slide off easily), and place them in a 200 degree oven for 10 minutes.

Beat egg white until frothy with water and flavorings.

Dip nuts, not many at a time, into this mixture and let them drain a few minutes in a coarse strainer. Then place them into a sack into which a portion of the first ingredients, powdered sugar, corn starch, salt, cinnamon, ginger, cloves and nutmeg, have been sifted together. Shake briskly as if you were flouring chicken. Spread out on cookie sheet and repeat until all nuts have been covered.

Bake them in a 200 degree oven approximately 3 hours. (Place a layer of the spiced mixture on the bottom of the cookie sheet ... then the nuts on top of this.) Some of the ingredients and amounts may seem incorrect, but they make a delightful confection. Store in an airtight container, (pound coffee can with a tight lid is good), if you have any left to store. This makes a delightful holiday delicacy.

All in a Woman's Day--November 15, 1988
Turkey 'talk' stuffings

In gratitude for the "plenteous" harvest of 1621, Gov. William Bradford, the first governor of Massachusetts Colony, proclaimed a day of Thanksgiving. Then in practical furtherance of this proclamation, he sent out four men in search of game, so the records say. Thus, early in the history of this special holiday, the turkey made its appearance.

It has come a long way from the wild birds the early Americans bagged in 1621; however, it has remained the traditional feature of the Thanksgiving meal through these many years. No doubt it has held its place of prominence because it was superbly prepared by conscientious cooks.

* * *

So that the breast of the fowl will not dry out while the legs are cooking, cover the white meat, after the first hour, with a cloth dipped in unsalted fat or oil. Always completely cook poultry at one time. Never partially cook, then, store and finish cooking at a later date.

You can tenderize a chicken or turkey by rubbing it with lemon juice.

* * *

A Thought To Ponder: The turnpike road to people's hearts I find lies through their mouths, or I mistake mankind. —Dr. Wolcot.

* * *

Of course, the feast is not complete unless stuffing is served. This year you might like to try a different dressing, "Orange Stuffing," it is called.

Orange Stuffing

Take 1/2 cup or 1/4 pound butter or margarine, 1/4 cup minced onions, 1/2 cup diced celery, 1/2 cup orange juice, 1 (8-ounce) package seasoned bread stuffing mix, 1 tablespoon grated orange rind and 2 cups diced oranges. Melt butter in skillet, add onion and celery, and cook them until tender but not brown. Stir in orange juice, add stuffing mix, orange rind and diced oranges. Toss lightly with a fork until all the crumbs are moistened. This makes enough stuffing for a 10-12 pound turkey. To prepare the oranges cut off peel in a spiral fashion and then go over the fruit again, removing any remaining white membrane. Then dice for the stuffing. Use the juice from the sectioning, adding more, if needed to make the 1/2 cup.

* * *

Generally you will have leftover turkey, and no doubt wonder just how to serve it so it will not be tiresome eating for the family. Here is a recipe you might try in place of sandwiches or warmed over turkey with gravy.

* * *

Prize Winning Escalloped Turkey

4 cups diced cooked turkey
14 cups cubed bread
1/3 cup butter or margarine, melted
1/4 cup turkey broth
1 1/4 teaspoons sage
Salt and pepper to taste
2 tablespoons chopped onion (optional)
4 cups turkey gravy

Make a layer of turkey in bottom of a 9x13-inch baking dish. Combine bread cubes, butter, seasonings, hot turkey broth and onions. Make a layer of dressing over the turkey and pour gravy over the dressing. Bake about 35 minutes in a 350 degree oven or until lightly browned on top. Cut into squares and serve. For a company meal, bits of pimento and green pepper may be added for color. Drained peas combined with the turkey create another variation for this interesting casserole. This can be frozen and then brought out at a later date for baking.

All in a Woman's Day--November 22, 1988

Thanksgiving reflects the spirit of America

The Thanksgiving observance has survived wars, crisis and depression. Perhaps more than any other national holiday, it mirrors American spirit and spirituality.

Sarah Josepha Hale, a writer and editor, waged a forceful 25-year campaign that finally caused Thanksgiving to become a regularly recurring holiday. As editor of Godey's Lady's Book, a monthly magazine, she wrote in 1827: "We have too few holidays. Thanksgiving like the Fourth of July, should be a national festival observed by all our people ... as an exponent of our republican institutions."

It might seem surprising to tie in our national Thanksgiving holiday with the poem, "Mary Had a Little Lamb"; however, the same woman who wrote this familiar little poem, also is known as the Mother of Thanksgiving, as we know it today.

Mrs. Hale lived to celebrate 15 Thanksgiving days. Her persistence and devotion to her ideals are today a blessing to each one of us.

A thundering row in 1939, was sparked when the late President Franklin Roosevelt proclaimed Thanksgiving Day for the third Thursday in November. Irate traditionalists maintained that Thanksgiving always has been on the last Thursday in November.

Since the first Pilgrim feast in 1621, Thanksgiving has been skidding around like a ball of butter on a hot skillet—once it even disappeared entirely for 47 years. The Pilgrims themselves skipped their own day in 1622 because the harvest was very poor and they didn't feel they had much for which to be thankful. It was reinstated in 1623.

There are only three months that haven't had Thanksgiving days: March, June and October.

Through the years, the Thanksgiving proclamations have faithfully reflected the personalities of the presidents. Hayes' proclamations were scholarly and lengthy; Grant's, short and homey; McKinley's, dignified and heavily flavored with religion; Theodore Roosevelt's, literary masterpieces of form and style; Wilson's, academic and serious minded.

Three hundred sixty-seven years have passed since the first Thanksgiving Day observance as it is known to us, and we need only to look back to see how far our great nation has come.

* * *

A Thought To Ponder: Thanklessness is a mark of immaturity of the spirit.

* * *

May you have a Thankful Thanksgiving Day!

All in a Woman's Day--November 29, 1988

Christmas holiday hints are suggested

Advent season has come, and that means we are heading into Christmas. It is a jolly time of year! It is the warm, wonderful time when old and young alike enjoy being involved with holiday preparations. And besides being a Holy time, also it is a fun time.

I would like to share a few hints to help in your planning for this very special holiday.

If you don't have a traditional fireplace on which to hang the children's stockings, use a planter pole. It can be decorated like a candy cane with each arm holding a stocking in anticipation of Santa's visit.

Fireproof a Christmas tree by spraying it with a half gallon lukewarm water to which has been added one cup alum, four-ounces boric acid and two tablespoons borax. Mix thoroughly. If there is any solution left, pour it into the water in the tree stand.

Red quilted, patterned or plain wraparound skirts make charming Christmas tree stand coverings.

An inexpensive way to provide name tags for a Christmas social is to use gift tags—the kind with string ties. Write a name on each tag with a felt tipped pen. Knot string ends to form a loop so each tag may be hung over a shirt or dress button.

A cute stocking gift for children is made by filling two baby food jars with different brightly colored candies; then with the lids securely screwed on, turn one upside down on the other. Fasten by using a piece of colored masking tape around where the jars meet. Tie a bow and attach a little tie-on ornament. Pimento jars also work real well.

Recycle Christmas cards by cutting the pretty front from old cards. Draw a line on the backside, using half the space for the address, stamp and return address. The other half can be used for a message. With postage so high, these postcards will save a bit of money.

Before Christmas, or even a birthday, children are always anxious to know how many days until the special occasion arrives. In France, mother's put as many stones in a container as there are days left. Then the child takes out a stone every day. As they see the number decreasing, they have a better idea than just hearing a number. Marbles also may be used.

If you have potted plants set around the home in plain containers, you might dress them up a bit by using Christmas paper wrapped around the pots. It adds to the festive atmosphere.

Perhaps you are planning on making a pecan pie for the holiday. Try this: Substitute the same amount of coconut and you will have a delightful pie. Dark corn syrup is often called for in the recipes; however, light corn syrup can be used just the same.

* * *

A Thought To Ponder: Christmas is love that flows from one heart to another.

All in a Woman's Day--December 6, 1988

Santa is a child pleaser

Whatever name Santa Claus goes by, depending on where he is, he always pleases the children.

He is known as St. Nick, Pere Noel, Father Christmas, St. Nicholas and Kris Kringle. He has been called Father Knickerbocker by Washington Irving; and to the Russians, he's Grandfather Frost.

This magical man of many names, not only brings gifts, he also has a lot of special gifts and powers, according to Christmas lore. He is gifted in guarding the fortunes of children, merchants and sailors, and also he takes a special interest in helping single girls find husbands.

The earliest pawnbrokers called him their patron. Today that idea is symbolized by the sign of the pawnbroker—the three gold balls.

The tradition of Santa Claus as the giver of Christmas presents comes to us from the fourth century legend of St. Nicholas, who was a real person. Nicholas, a bishop of Myra in Asia Minor, now Turkey, heard of a poor man, who was about to sell his three daughters into slavery because he could not provide a dowry for them. In those days this was not only customary, but obligatory in order to avoid disgrace. He saved them by gifts of gold which he threw into the house at night so he would not be seen. Soon after, they were all happily married. Unexpected gifts thereafter were attributed to St. Nicholas. The name Santa Claus itself, is an American derivation of the name St. Nicholas.

Santa was first brought to this country by the early Dutch settlers, who called him Sinterklaas. These Dutch burghers portrayed him as a merry old man, sometimes even with a wife they called Molly Grietje. Santa also looked a little different then: He wore a wide brimmed black hat, short Dutch breeches and smoked a long clay pipe.

Later the British brought their own Father Christmas to America, a happy roly poly Falstaffian figure. Inevitably, Sinterklaas and Father Christmas became one.

It was finally the task of American artists and writers to create an image of Santa Claus as we know him today.

In 1822, Clement Moore took out a poet's license and in his "A Visit from St. Nicholas," ('Twas the Night Before Christmas'), added a number of characteristics to the elf. No one has ever complained about what he did. This poem has become the foundation of our rich American tradition about Santa Claus.

In 1863, the famous cartoonist Thomas Nast, helped fashion the picture of Santa Claus as we envision him today. Yes, that's Santa all right, with his fur-trimmed suit, shiny black boots and long white beard. Just the way we've always known him, or so it seems.

* * *

A Thought To Ponder: A heart full of love always has something to give.

* * *

Santa Claus Punch

1 (46-ounce or 64-ounce) bottle cranapple juice
1/2 teaspoon whole cloves
1/2 to 3/4 cup cinnamon red hots

In a large saucepan, heat the juice and whole cloves to boiling. Add and stir in candies until completely melted. Remove whole cloves. Serve hot.

* * *

Cracked Bars

1 cup margarine
1 cup brown sugar
1/3 cup milk
1 teaspoon vanilla
1 teaspoon burnt sugar flavoring
Club crackers
1 cup crushed graham crackers
1 cup coconut
Nuts (optional)
Chocolate chips
2 tablespoons cream

Line a 9x13-inch pan with club crackers. Cook the first five ingredients to a boil; stirring. Add 1 cup crushed graham crackers, 1 cup coconut, and nuts if desired. Spread over crackers in pan. Melt 3/4 to 1 cup chocolate chips with 2 tablespoons cream. Frost bars and chill before serving.

All in a Woman's Day--December 13, 1988

Christmas foods hold appeal internationally

Feasting is an integral part of the Christmas celebration, symbolizing not only rejoicing at the coming of Christ, but also, the spirit of sharing, and brotherly love that is characteristic of the season.

Like so many other aspects of Christmas, it is a blend of Christian and pre-Christian traditions, strongly influenced by local custom and is observed internationally.

As we think about the food involved, traditional foods include almost everything, ranging from baked carp in Austria to roast pig in Hawaii.

In France, it is traditional to serve a Christmas supper after midnight mass, but the main dish varies according to the section of the country—roast goose in Alsace; turkey in Burgundy; oysters and sausages in Paris.

The people of Germany bake long cakes for this special holiday. The cakes are meant to symbolize the Christ Child wrapped in swaddling clothes.

The Danish Christmas Eve dinner features rice porridges, containing a "magic," almond that brings good luck to the one who finds it.

England has a mouth watering array of traditional dishes for Christmas feasting. Among them is plum pudding. The very first plum pudding was an answer to adversity, so legend says. An English king and his hunting party were lost in the forest on Christmas Eve. Commanded by the king, the cook prepared dinner, using the foods he had on hand—some meat from a stag, some bits of wild game, flour, bird's eggs, sugar, dried plums, ale and brandy. The cook not only created a delicious emergency dish, he also invented plum pudding, which tradition says must contain these same ingredients if it is to be the "real thing."

Christmas puddings, as we know them, today, date from about 1670, and began as a stiffened form of plum porridge. This was made of meat broth, raisins, fruit juices, wine and spices, thickened by bread crumbs.

Often as the pudding was prepared, it was customary for each member of the family to stir it, making a wish for the new year.

Roasted peacock was a Yule delicacy of early England.

The popular holiday party drink known as eggnog, is a modern version of an old English drink called syllabub, that was a spiced mixture of wine and milk.

As with many English customs, mince pie was first part of the Yule celebration of a British sovereign. Henry VIII popularized the pie as a Christmas dish. The first recorded recipe appeared in 1596, and the first mince pies were patterned in oblong shape after the manager in which Christ was born. It had a small figure of Jesus placed on top. The crust represented the gold brought by the Three Wise Men; the many spices—the frankincense and myrrh.

Some of the recipes stretched the imagination. One from 1394 instructs as follows: "A pheasant, a capon, two partridges, two pigeons and two rabbits. Separate meat from the bones and chop into fine hash. Add the livers and hearts of these animals, plus two kidneys of sheep. Add meat balls of beef with eggs. Add pickled mushrooms, salt, pepper, vinegar and various spices and pour all of this into the broth in which the bones were cooked."

The mince pie did, however, survive, although the Puritans of the 17th century tried to halt its consumption by arguing vigorously that it wasn't "A fit dish for men. "

In fact, Oliver Cromwell's parliament banned Christmas observance entirely, including church services, in 1644, to end what it called "pagan and heathen observances." It wasn't until Charles II was restored to the throne, in 1660, that the Christmas feast was revived.

"For food and fellowship, thank,

God," says the simplest of all graces.

A vast dinner of roast turkey, with all the trimmings, plum pudding and mince pies appear every year on countless tables throughout the world.

Turkey, though now traditional, is a comparatively newcomer, unknown in Europe before about 1542, and appearing then only as one among a variety of festival dishes.

Goose or beef for Christmas pies were the early favorites in ordinary families, while in the "great house" there were swans, venison, peacocks and the boar's head. The boar's head was eaten during the Scandinavian Yule in honor of the Sun-Boar. At great Medieval Christmas banquets, the head was garlanded with rosemary and bay and an orange or an apple was thrust between the teeth. The feast began with the ceremonial entrance of the hunters, musicians and the master cook, with the latter carrying the head of a boar on a silver platter. Sometimes, a lemon, the Norse symbol of plenty, was wedged in the boar's mouth.

More than 300 years ago King James I always had a turkey for his Christmas dinner. Gradually it replaced the boar's head of Medieval times as the favorite holiday meat in England. In Medieval England, Christmas feasts have been known to last several days and were extremely jubilant affairs.

In America, bringing a boar's head did not catch on. Instead the turkey became a favorite and an almost symbolic Christmas dish.

* * *

A Thought To Ponder: May there be enduring peace on earth and goodwill and love toward all persons.

* * *

Here is a recipe taken from a 19th century memo that reveals the tender loving care our ancestors afforded turkeys being prepared for the holiday feasting: "Coop up the turkey sometime before Christmas and feed it well. Three days before slaughtering, force an English walnut down its throat three times a day, and a glass of sherry once a day. The meat will be deliciously tender and have a fine nutty flavor."

* * *

Glazed Almond Treat

1 cup almonds
1 cup water
1 cup sugar

Heat water and sugar together until sugar is dissolved completely. Place nuts in mixture, not more than 12 at a time. Boil gently until tender. Remove with a slotted spoon, one at a time. Drain them on absorbent paper. Sprinkle more sugar over nuts, coating all sides. Dry in cool oven. Keep in closely covered metal container. This recipe was an early American favorite.

All in a Woman's Day--December 20, 1988

Christmas message is joy, hope, faith

Christmas is the most beautiful and beloved Holy celebration held by Christians throughout the world. Customs and traditions that have been faithfully handed down through generations are still a very important part of honoring the birth of Christ.

Christmas is a Holy Day, a day of grace and gratitude; however, most of all it means joy and hope for the world. We find that beyond the fun and festivities, there is the spirit of faith in the goodness and goodwill of people everywhere.

It seems that the spirit of Christmas is

a universal spirit, that each nation has shaped into its own individual customs and traditions.

In some of the observances, we can sense the gratitude that men feel for the hope of Christmas. We can know the prayers that they offer for peace and fellowship; and we can hear the warm greetings that come from the very heart.

As we think back to our childhood Christmastimes, we can remember, the uncomplicated, innocent joy we felt and how we anticipated that great day in our lives.

Now, as adults we find that we still look forward to Christmas, however, with a deeper feeling—a promise of love and goodwill in a world that is now filled with violence and chaos. We think of it as a joyous day to be shared with family and friends.

However, as we think and ponder about this special day, perhaps the most memorable part we cannot touch or see, the spirit of love and perpetual hope we all have.

* * *

A Thought To Ponder: "Glory to God in the Highest and on earth Peace among men in whom He is well pleased."

* * *

May you have a blessed Christmas with family and friends!

All in a Woman's Day--December 27, 1988

New Year's celebration has special traditions

In a few days we will be celebrating the arrival of the New Year. There will be gay festivities ... formal balls, teenage dances, midnight feasts, wassail bowls and house parties. However, more solemnly, people will gather at churches for Night Watch services of prayers, hymns and candlelight.

With the arrival of the first day of the New Year, there are certain traditions that are followed throughout the universe.

According to custom, southern housewives will be wearing colorful aprons and will whip up pancakes to serve to the late lingering guests. Then come early afternoon, they will offer their families black-eyed peas and hog jowl, a very much southern practice. The peas stand for peace and plenty; the hog jowls, for joy and happiness.

Too, to have plenty to eat come New Year's Day, you must eat the peas and hog jowl, and every family member must stir the pot.

Should you happen to take a bath between Christmas and New Year's Day, folklore says your spirit is purged and you'll have good luck in the coming year.

If you happen to light a bayberry candle on Christmas Eve and it burns to the end without going out, your luck should be good for the coming year.

Don't leave the Christmas tree up until after New Year's; that is a sign of bad luck.

Don't be taking up ashes on New Year's, as that, too, is a sign of bad luck.

Your income will be greater than your expenses, according to old superstitions, if on New Year's morning you gather a green bough and bring it inside for the whole year.

The first person you kiss after the New Year begins will love you most during the year.

Now this is one for all of us. If you place a piece of silver outside your door on New Year's Eve and get up the next morning without speaking to anyone and bring it in, you will have plenty of money all year long. Everybody get your coins ready!

If you should happen to see a man and a woman in front of a fire when you arise on New Year's morning, you will be married by year's end.

If you have company on New Year's Day or visit someone on that day, you will have similar experiences every day of the year.

The last day of the year, December 31, is called "Grand Last Day," and is truly a happy time, and time for merry-making that culminates in the Joya-no-kane, the 108 peals of the temple bells at midnight. The ushering in of the New Year has an extra special meaning in Japan for at the stroke of midnight, it means it's everyone's birthday.

* * *

A Thought To Ponder: "This is the Day (Year) which the Lord has made; let us rejoice and be glad in it."

* * *

May all good things be in store for you during this coming year!

All in a Woman's Day--January 3, 1989

Soup is comfort food

The holidays have come and gone and it is now time to get back into shape and eat "slim." Since January is National Soup Month, it is a good time to get started on easing up on calories, after all the good eating which we have enjoyed. But it was fun, nevertheless.

It has been said that to many folks happiness is a pot of soup or stew on the stove and perhaps a freshly baked batch of cookies.

Be that as it may, it is soup and stew time again.

No one wants to eat the fat that collects on the top of soups or stews, so in order to get rid of it just lay some paper towels over the top. They will absorb the fat and then they can be thrown away.

Waste not, want not with hodge-podge soup. Keep a container in the freezer and fill it with leftovers from each meal, a spoonful of gravy, an ounce of chicken or beef, spaghetti or chili, vegetables, rice or mashed potatoes. Then when you have enough for a meal, and it needs extra liquid, add spaghetti sauce, minced with mushrooms or au jus gravy mix along with enough water to give it a soup-like consistency.

Too, leftovers can be put in a food processor, and pureed meats and vegetables used later in soup stock.

When opening a can of cream soup if too much soup is left in the can, just turn the can over after cutting off the top lid and use an opener with a pointed end and make a hole in the bottom of the can. The soup will slide right out.

Homemade soup gets compliments when coupled with garlic muffins. Split four bakery English muffins in half, using a fork. Toast until slightly brown. Blend three tablespoons garlic spread concentrate with three tablespoons butter and spread on each muffin. Sprinkle lightly with grated Parmesan cheese and broil until golden brown.

Possibly some of you know about "Baby Soup." It is especially good to serve if children are ill, and is a comfort food. It is made with two cups of milk, three tablespoons of butter, salt and pepper to taste, four tablespoons of flour and one egg. Heat milk, butter, salt and pepper. Break egg into the flour and mix. Spoon the mixture into milk. Break up the dough with a spoon, but not too finely. Cook slowly until the little lumps (babies) are done.

That soup is similar to the Rivel Soup that our grandmothers and great-grandmothers used to make. To make it, use one egg, one teaspoon of salt and one cup of flour. Beat egg and salt and add flour, quickly; mixing with a fork until batter forms pea size pieces. Have chicken stock or broth (canned may be used), boiling. Add the rivels slowly and stir. Simmer gently for 10 to 15 minutes.

* * *

Since this is the beginning of the New Year, here are some "Good Memory Rules" to keep in mind.

* * *

'Forget each kindness that you do as soon as you have done it;

Forget the praise that falls to you the moment you have won it;

Forget the slander that you hear before you can repeat it;

Forget each slight, each spite, each sneer, whenever you may meet it.

Remember every kindness done to you what'er it measures;

Remember praise by others won and pass it on with pleasure;

Remember every promise made and keep it to the letter;

Remember those who lend you aid and be a grateful debtor.

Remember all the happiness
that comes your way in living;

Forget each worry and distress,
be hopeful and forgiving;

Remember good; remember truth;
Remember heaven's above you.

And you will find, through age and youth that many hearts will love you.

* * *

A Thought To Ponder: Every morning is a fresh beginning.

* * *

Following is a hearty fall or winter soup:

Linda's French Market Soup

2 cups mixed beans
1 smoked ham hock (optional)
2 chicken breast halves
1 teaspoon salt
2 bay leaves
1/2 teaspoon thyme
1 tablespoon dried parsley flakes
1/4 teaspoon red pepper (cayenne)
1/2 teaspoon black pepper
3 quarts water
4 stalks celery, chopped
1 large can undrained tomatoes, chopped
2 medium onions, chopped
2 cloves garlic, minced
1/2 to 1 pound smoked sausage

Pick over and wash beans. Soak overnight; drain. Put in large pot with remaining ingredients except for desired amount of smoked sausage. Cook mixture over low heat until beans are done, 2 to 3 hours. Slice smoked sausage, parboil for 5 minutes in separate pan, drain and add to soup. Add more salt, if needed. (Note: In using ham hock, use only 1/2 pound of sausage; without ham hock use 1 pound.) Remove chicken breasts, and ham hock if using, from soup; remove the skin and bones, discard; cut meat into chunks and return them to the soup. This is a hearty fall and winter soup.

All in a Woman's Day--January 10, 1989

Recipe story related

Recipes are like often told stories. It seems that no two people make or tell them the same way. Perhaps a pinch of some new ingredient or a different turn or plot only adds to the overall charm of a special dish.

It has been disclosed that several cookbooks tucked away in the depths of a Yale University library contain what are perhaps the world's most time-tested recipes.

The collection, inscribed on three Mesopotamian clay slabs, date back to 1700 B.C. These are no doubt the oldest cookbooks in existence; at least that is the conclusion of William W. Hallo, curator of the Yale Babylonian Collection. Scratched into the tablets are cuneiform figures that provide instruction for the preparation of dozens of Mesopotamian stews, meat pies and vegetable dishes.

The recipes are said to reveal "a cuisine of striking richness, refinement, artistry and sophistication."

The tablets, dating back to the Old Babylonian period of Mesopotamia, that was located in the area that lies between the lower Tigris and the Euphrates Rivers, in what is now Iraq, is often referred to as the cradle of civilization. Written on the best preserved parts of the tablets are 21 recipes for meat and four for vegetables. Instructions for preparation indicate that most of the food is prepared with water and fats and cooked slow, simmering in covered pots.

The recipes for meats include stag, gazelle, lamb, kid, mutton, squab and a bird called tarru. Also frequently mentioned are seasonings that include garlic, leek and onions. The stews often were thickened with grains, milk, beer or animal blood. Salt is mentioned occasionally.

Scholars have been unable to identify all of the ingredients used, including two seasonings, samidu and suhutinnu.

Jean Bottero, a French Assyriologist, has written that the most striking thing about all of this is the multiplicity of condiments that they added to one and the same dish, and the care with which they were combined into a blend of often complimentary flavors. No doubt these combinations presumed a demanding and refined palate—even when far removed from ours —betraying an authentic preoccupation with the gastronomic arts.

All of the blends and the preparation of those earlier day foods may make us a bit skeptical and perhaps a little superstitious. That might be all right, too, for this week is the first of the two Fridays the 13th occurring during this year. So, I guess we are entitled to a little skepticism.

* * *

And speaking of food, it seems at one time showering newlyweds with rice was an ancient magical rite. It was thought that scattering plentiful products over the couple immediately after the wedding would assure a fertile and productive marriage.

Being a bit superstitious also holds true with some kitchen inspirations that are no doubt folklore, too. A couple of these include "A poor man's table is soon spread" and "It is what you do with what you've got that counts. "

Other housewifely wisdoms include "One today is worth two tomorrows"; "Patience is a flower that grows not in every garden"; "Don't buy a pig in a poke"; "The empty barrel rattles the loudest"; "Life is not a problem to be solved, but a gift to be enjoyed"; and "If you would have a thing well done, do it: yourself."

* * *

A Thought To Ponder: Keep your words sweet you may have to eat them.

* * *

Great-Grandma's Ginger Cake

2 1/2 cups sifted all-purpose flour
1 3/4 teaspoons baking soda
1 teaspoon ground ginger
1 teaspoon ground cinnamon
1/4 teaspoon ground cloves
1/4 teaspoon salt
1 cup sugar
1/2 cup vegetable shortening (lard was used)
1 cup molasses
1 cup boiling water
2 eggs, well beaten

Sift flour, soda, spices and salt together and set them aside. Cream sugar and shortening with molasses, blend well. Add sifted ingredients to creamed mixture, alternating with boiling water, beginning and ending with dry ingredients.

Stir in beaten eggs. Pour them into a well greased 9x13-inch baking dish and bake it in a moderate oven, 350 degrees, for 30 minutes, or until center springs back when lightly pressed with fingertip. Cool upright in pan to room temperature. Cut in large squares and serve. It can be topped with whipped cream.

This is an old English recipe. It was economical 100 years ago, and it still is today.

All in a Woman's Day--January 17, 1989

Improve kitchen life by using hints offered

Kitchen life may be improved if you try some of the hints offered:

Add a little cottage cheese to ground beef for moistness and flavor. This is a meat stretcher, too, when needed.

When baking a casserole, try placing a pan of water under the baking dish so there will be no danger of a too brown crust on the bottom.

Instead of cutting pieces of cake the usual way, triangular, cut the pieces straight across the middle. After removing a piece just push the two halves together. Continue this process as you enjoy your treat.

Worcestershire sauce makes a good substitute for polish to clean small brass fixtures. Saturate a cotton ball with the sauce and wipe the fixtures. Use a soft cloth to wipe them clean.

If a plastic bread wrapper gets stuck to the toaster, coffeepot or pan, pour some nail polish remover on a facial tissue, hold it on the spot for half a minute, then rub until the plastic dissolves and disappears.

For a quick dessert idea, add one cup cooked rice to vanilla or chocolate instant pudding. A few raisins or chopped nuts also may be added or it is good just as is. It is a good way to use leftover rice.

If you want to clean your blender in a jiffy, add about a pint of water and a dash of detergent and run it for a few minutes. Then rinse and dry.

Always put leftovers on the top shelf of the refrigerator and this way they will never be lost or forgotten.

When a recipe calls for spices to be tied in a cloth bag, put them into a stainless steel tea ball instead. It can be used over and over and is easily emptied and cleaned.

Spray kitchen shears with nonstick cooking oil before cutting fruit, dates, marshmallows etc.

Pouring liquid from one container to another can be a disaster. To make this easier, put some butter or margarine on the side of the container from which you pour. This will help eliminate a mess.

A large metal salt shaker with a handle, makes a handy flour shaker for meats. Sprinkling the flour on the meat saves time and a mess when directions call for dredging or rolling meat in flour before browning.

Save empty salad dressing bottles; as they make nice vases for small bouquets to take to a hospital. Add a bit of ribbon and a bow to "dress up" the bouquet. A patient doesn't have to worry about returning a vase in this instance.

Do you use your ice cream dipper only when you serve ice cream? If so, then move it to a reachable place and put it into service every day. Use it to dip batter for cupcakes and muffins, to measure perfect size pancakes every time; to dip rice, macaroni or mashed potato servings; to dip cottage cheese, potato salad and other kinds of salad. Neat and attractive servings are made this way that can tempt reluctant appetites. Yes, and it does work well on ice cream and sherberts.

* * *

A Thought To Ponder: After dinner sit awhile; after supper walk a mile.

—Thomas Fuller

* * *

Date Pecan Balls

1 cup soft butter or margarine
1/2 cup sugar
2 teaspoons vanilla
2 cups flour
1 1/3 cups chopped pecans
1 cup dates, cut up

Cream butter and sugar; add vanilla and mix. Then add flour and mix; blend in pecans and dates. Roll spoonsful of dough into balls. Refrigerate 1 to 2 hours. Bake them at 350 degrees on greased cookie sheet for 20 minutes. Remove them from oven and roll in powdered sugar. Sprinkle them again after they have cooled. Yield: Approximately 60 cookies. No leavening agent needed. Does not rise!

All in a Woman's Day--January 24, 1989
This is Oatmeal Month

This is Oatmeal Month; however, it is a good month for cereals of all kinds to get back to the basics.

Oats are a member of the cereal family. Cereals are edible seeds that also are called grains and belong to the grass family. The most common cereal grasses are barley, corn, oats, rice, rye and wheat (buckwheat). Millet and sorghum are not true cereals; that is, in the botanical sense; however, they are used as cereals.

The word cereal goes back to Ceres, the Roman goddess of grain. Spring festivals beseeching her for a fruitful harvest were called Cerealia. Too, as far back as 8000 B.C. the Lake Dwellers of Switzerland cleared land for grain fields and used primitive plows with which to cultivate them; thus, they were providing food for themselves and also for their animals.

Before man grew cereals he had to spend his time hunting food enough to keep himself and family alive. When he began to grow cereals, he had foods that he could store and transport easily. Too, this let him have time to develop any skills or arts that he could. These, of course, distinguished civilized man from the savage.

And regardless, even to this day, cereal grains provide more food for less effort than any other food plants. They also contain proteins, some fat and vi-

637

tamins.

Cereal grasses grow in almost any climate from the Arctic to the tropics, but under many different moisture and soil conditions.

Cereals can be divided into three types: Hot or cooked; quick cooking and ready-to-eat. Oatmeal and Fatrina are examples of quick cooking, and or hot cereals. Quick cooking means they are made in smaller, thinner particles to decrease the cooking time. The ready-to-eat cereals are of a vast variety coming in puffs, flakes, shredded, nuts, sweetened and unsweetened, with various flavorings added.

Cereals requiring long cooking are generally less expensive than the ready-to-eat or quick cooking varieties. Individual homemakers are the ones that must decide on the cereal that is most economical and convenient for use. Ready-to-eat cereals come in packages with inner linings that should be kept intact. The lining should be folded to preserve the freshness of the cereal.

Whole grain cereals, dry or uncooked, even though unopened should be refrigerated because of the fat content. These can be kept on the refrigerator shelf five or six months. Dry or uncooked cereals may be stored on the kitchen shelf two or three months, with cooked cereals stored in refrigerator two to four days.

For best results, follow the directions on the package when preparing.

Because everyone is so conscious of cholesterol in this day and age, the cereal, oat bran, which is to be cooked, and oat flakes, a ready-to-eat cereal, both noncholesterol, are proving popular.

If you need instant oatmeal in a recipe and have only regular, place it in the blender, and it will serve the purpose just right.

Some folks cook cereal and what is left they let it set and later fry it the same way that mush is cooked.

There is a rather interesting story that goes along with flaked cereal. If you have had your corn flakes today, then you can express your thanks to the Kellogg Brothers, John and W.K., who revolutionized the way grains were converted into flakes during a kitchen experiment somewhere around the turn of the century.

The story goes that they had set up a laboratory in the kitchen of the Battle Creek Sanitarium for the Adventist Church, where John, a physician and health food pioneer, was trying to devise a vegetarian diet that would be less boring for the patients.

By perchance, one day while working with boiled wheat they were called away and upon their return a day or so later, they decided that instead of throwing out the panful of wheat grains that they would just run the mixture through rollers to produce a thin sheet of wheat.

Much to their surprise, that isn't what happened. Instead, the rollers discharged large, thin flakes with each grain a flake. The brothers came to the conclusion that the longer wait had caused moisture to be distributed evenly through each grain, allowing individual flaking.

This is how it happened that they stumbled onto the principle of "tempering" grain, and with only a slight additional refinement, the cereal flake was born.

A Thought To Ponder: The full use of today is the best preparation for tomorrow.

* * *

Cranberry Crunch

1 cup quick cooking oats
1/2 cup flour
1 cup brown sugar
1/2 cup butter
1 (1-pound) can cranberry sauce

Mix together until crumbly the oats, flour, brown sugar and butter. Place half of mixture in an 8-inch square baking dish. Cover with the cranberry sauce. Crumble on the remainder of the first mixture. Bake it at 350 degrees for 45 minutes. Cut in squares and serve it warm with vanilla ice cream.

All in a Woman's Day--January 31, 1989

Milady of the kitchen is offered assistance

Milady of the kitchen often needs a little assistance, so here is offered a few helps to make her work more rewarding.

Oftentimes you can find a good buy on endive, it makes a terrific salad. If you want to keep it from turning brown, rinse it in cold water before storing.

For wives, who have been detained at meetings or by shopping, here is a little suggestion: Always have the table set when your husband comes home for dinner. It creates the illusion of being on schedule, and he will be happy with the paper or the TV while you pop something into the oven.

To keep grease from spattering while frying bacon, sprinkle salt in a cold frying pan before placing the bacon in it.

Plants like bananas. If you want your house plants to bloom like crazy, put pieces of banana peel, white side down on the soil where your plants are growing. Discard when peel gets hard and black. Of course, it is a well-known fact: Bananas and their peels are loaded with potassium.

To prevent ham from becoming too salty, pour one cup of gingerale over it halfway through the cooking time.

Flavor a custard sauce with instant coffee (regular or decaffeinated) and serve the sauce over meringues.

Even when canned fruits and vegetables are on sale, don't overstock your cupboard! Remember that shelf life is about a year; after that, they may deteriorate in flavor, texture and color.

Always wash off the top of a can, or, in fact the entire can before opening it. Sometimes the lid falls into the opened cans and any dirt or dust on them will go into the food.

Always wash or wipe meat with a damp cloth or towel before cooking it. It goes through lots of hands and there just could possibly be some germs lurking on it.

Silverware should not tarnish if it is wrapped in waxed paper.

Keep peanuts in tightly closed containers in the refrigerator. They will retain crispness and flavor.

When a recipe calls for greasing pans, try sprinkling a few drops of the squeeze type liquid margarine into the pans and spread it with a pastry brush.

Did you know that chunk-light tuna is cheaper than solid-pack tuna to use in casserole dishes?

When items are reduced in price, they are near the end of their usefulness. Buy them only for immediate use.

Use chopped prunes instead of raisins in pastries. They are cheaper and they will taste just as good.

Don't overstock vegetables. They will shrink and lose much of their vitamin content.

* * *

A Thought To Ponder: Any woman who wants a little time to herself has only to begin doing dishes.

* * *

Lemon-Orange Delight Dessert

1 package lemon pudding mix
1 cup whipped topping
4 oranges

Prepare pudding mix according to directions. (Canned pudding mix can be substituted if preferred.) Fold in the whipped topping. Spoon into dessert dishes and chill. Peel oranges and separate into sections. Place orange slices on top of pudding in pinwheel fashion. Center with a maraschino cherry if a fancy dessert is desired. Serve this with vanilla wafers or sugar cookies. (If you really are in a rush, use mandarin oranges, drained.)

All in a Woman's Day--February 7, 1989
Valentine wishes!

Here it is almost Valentine's Day again!

It is the time of reflection of youth in an old man's eyes;
The blush on a young boy's cheek;
It's the sincere touch of a woman's hand;
The giggle in a girl's laughter;
It's flowers and candy for someone special;
It's lingering moments in search of just the right card or gift;
It's love—It's Valentine's Day.

—Selected

Age is no factor on this special day—the old, the young and the in-between celebrate the warmth of love.

There are many ways of saying "I love you" that perhaps are as significant and meaningful as candy and flowers or other gifts. Not everyone can express love in words. For some people, the words "I love you," are the hardest words in the world to say. But there are so many ways of showing love; other than words. There is the mother, who sits for long hours mending her son's jacket so that it will look almost new, or alters a dress for her daughter so that it fits well; the young wife, who spends the entire afternoon trying to make a special kind of dessert her husband likes so much; the daughter, who collects her elderly mother's washing and returns it with a bright, sunny smile; the husband, with his eyes twinkling as he tenderly whispers to his wife, "I don't know what I ever saw in you"; and the father, who spends all evening mending his son's toy train. All these acts are sincere declarations of love.

This little selected poem might bring a smile. Now, if some "feller" wants to send flowers to his valentine, he could be in a bit of trouble if he tells the florist to pick out a bouquet. Here is the reason:

Choosing a bouquet of flowers
For that Valentine, so dear,
Could cause you many problems,
And change your life, I fear.
Bachelor Buttons would be nice,
This message you could convey:
"I like being a bachelor
And that's how I'm going to stay."
Bleeding Hearts, how dramatic!
They could turn a heart to stone
And, before you know it
You would no longer be alone.

Then again, you might consider
Lovely Violets of blue;
Of course, she'd expect a note
Saying, "I love you."
Red roses by the dozen
Certainly would be dandy;
But if you want my advice-
I'd suggest you send her candy.

* * *

A Thought To Ponder: This Valentine's Day have a heart and let the trademarks of love show.

* * *

Happy Valentine's Day and may you be loved!

* * *

If you want something very special this holiday try this Hot Fudge Chocolate Sauce which a family I know serves at many special events.

Joy's Hot Fudge Chocolate Sauce
1/2 cup butter or margarine
1/2 cup cocoa
1/2 teaspoon salt
1/4 cup white corn syrup
3 cups sugar
1 (14-ounce) can evaporated milk
1 teaspoon vanilla

Mix together butter, cocoa, salt and syrup. Bring to a boil in the microwave. Take mixture out and add the sugar, stirring constantly. The mixture will be thick and gritty. Add the evaporated milk and vanilla. Microwave until sugar is dissolved and mixture is smooth. (Take the mixture out and stir occasionally.) Store it in a jar in the refrigerator. It may be heated if desired. This is delicious on ice cream.

Petroleum jelly has different uses

Have you ever thought how important petroleum jelly can be? This jelly like substance is really amazing and has dozens of uses around the home, indoors, outdoors and even in the workshop.

Petroleum jelly was discovered by Robert Chesebrough, a chemist, in 1859, when he happened to notice a substance that had accumulated on the oil pump rods, and that helped to heal cuts and scratches. Since that time it has been given a workout.

The homemaker will find that a bad grease stain on clothes can disappear by just rubbing the substance on the spot, letting it set overnight and then washing in hot water.

If you have a window in your home that sticks, coat the metal tracks with some petroleum jelly. Too, a thin coat also will protect metal tools and cooking utensils being stored.

This special substance can be used to keep kitchen and bathroom fixtures free of stains; clean them, let them dry and then apply a thin film of jelly.

It is good for removing lipstick from a garment by rubbing the stain with the jelly and then washing it in hot suds.

Petroleum jelly, along with toothpaste, makes it two of the likely (or should I say unlikely) products that remove all kinds of spots and stains.

A mixture of petroleum jelly, castor oil, lanolin and cocoa butter melted and put into a container and cooled, will help remove wrinkles, and in addition also will save some pennies.

Petroleum jelly, along with toothpaste, makes a fabulous lip gloss by taking your dried-out lipstick and mixing with the substance.

If your hands get grimy, just rub a bit of the jelly into them, leave it on your hands about 15 minutes; then wash your hands.

Women, who have very short or straight eyelashes, can apply this jelly before curling them and it will prevent eyeshadow from caking. Also, it will keep nails from splitting and soften the cuticles, as well as expensive creams, and can be used in lieu of lipstick. So you see, it has been around as a cosmetic for a long time.

It also can soothe windburn and blisters.

Apply a thin coat on bicycle handlebars, and it will prevent rust and also can lubricate the chain and gears. Smeared on the battery terminals and chromium of your car, it will prevent corrosion.

Petroleum jelly also can be used to remove tree sap from your car by softening it. The same treatment works for removing road oil, grease stains and tar.

If you happen to be doing some painting, you can end some of your problems by lightly coating door knobs, fixtures and window panes with the jelly.

Keep your synthetic shoes and boots shiny with petroleum jelly. Rub with a soft cloth to make them look like new.

Before installing an electric light in a socket that is exposed to the weather, rub a little of the jelly on the threads of the bulb. When it burns out and has to be replaced the bulb will unscrew easily and not chew up the socket.

In addition to all the helps mentioned (and I am sure there are more), it also can help keep a hunting blade or axe rust-free, lubricate a rifle and tempo-rarily waterproof a tent that has sprung a leak.

Vaseline® petroleum jelly is made by Chesebrough-Pond's® and some of these hints came from Jane Clancy, home service consultant for the company.

* * *

A Thought To Ponder: Delicious food that melts in your mouth also sticks to your hips.

* * *

Deloris' Pecan Delight Pie

4 egg whites
3/4 cup sugar
1 teaspoon baking powder
1/4 teaspoon vanilla
2 cups coarsely broken unsalted crackers
3/4 cup chopped pecans
1 1/2 cups whipped cream
1/4 cup chopped pecans

Whip egg whites on medium speed until soft peaks form; continue beating on medium speed while gradually adding sugar and baking powder. Continue to beat until very stiff peaks form and all sugar is dissolved. Add vanilla and mix thoroughly. Add unsalted crackers and 3/4 cup pecans; gently folding in by hand. Pour into a greased 9-inch pie pan and bake at 300 degrees for 30 minutes until center is almost firm. Remove from oven and cool. When thoroughly cooled, top with whipped cream and sprinkle with 1/4 cup chopped pecans.

All in a Woman's Day--February 21, 1989
The lowly potato: a perfect vegetable

What's highly nutritious, flavorful and filling, yet low in calories? It's the potato!

This vegetable comes close to being the perfect food. In fact, the U. S. Department of Agriculture states: "A diet of whole milk and potatoes would supply almost all of the food elements necessary for maintenance of the human body."

Potatoes are an excellent source of vitamin C and also supplies vitamin B6, iron, fiber, phosphorus, potassium, carbohydrates and protein.

They're great for diets, too. Besides being low in calories, there are only 76 in a medium sized potato. Eating potatoes lessens the appetite, and they're practically salt and fat free.

There are five basic kinds of potatoes—round white, long white, round russet, long russet and round red. When harvested early, reds and whites come to market as the "small new potato." All can be used in a variety of ways, including boiled, baked, roasted, creamed, mashed, stuffed, salad and fried.

Potatoes are always in good supply. Always select those that are firm, clean, relatively smooth and reasonably well shaped. Reject any with cuts, bruises, green color or sprouts.

Keep potatoes dry, in a kitchen bin or in any dark, cool well ventilated spot. Avoid placing them near hot pipes, radiators, extreme cold or direct light, which makes them turn green. Rinse them only before using.

Potato peelings are a wonderful fertilizer. After peeling them, let the peelings dry thoroughly. You can even run them through the food grinder on coarse sieve or the food processor before mixing with soil for indoor or outdoor use. The drying may be done with "free" heat after you've turned off the oven. Sweet potato and carrot peelings also may be used.

Add one grated raw potato to one pound of ground beef for juicy hamburgers.

Did you know you can rebake baked potatoes? The second time around just dip them in hot water and bake them in a moderate oven until they are piping hot.

Wash and dry baking potatoes, slice in half-inch slices; dip in melted low-calorie margarine; sprinkle with salt and place on cookie sheet. Bake in a 400 degree oven about 20 minutes. This does save energy.

Potatoes soaked in salt water for 20 minutes before baking will bake faster.

To improve the taste and texture of mashed potatoes, try adding a well beaten egg white. The result is surprising.

If you are short on instant potatoes, break up a few soda crackers and add to the hot potato mixture. It gives a little different flavor.

Yes, you can "bake" potatoes in your pressure cooker. Just wrap them in aluminum foil and place on the rack in the cooker. It will take only about 15 minutes, depending on the size of the potatoes. The water level should be up to the rack. They are tasty and very much like baked potatoes.

Try buttermilk in mashed potatoes instead of whole or canned milk.

A piece of raw potato makes a fine eraser of fingerprints on a painted surface.

To make gourmet potatoes, shape leftover mashed potatoes into balls or croquettes. Press a small cube of cheese into the center of each ball. Brush the entire surface with melted butter and roll in corn flake crumbs. Place them on a cookie sheet and bake them until they are well browned at 350 degrees. If desired, these balls can be frozen before baking. In this case allow extra baking time.

* * *

A Thought To Ponder: When you point a finger at someone, you are pointing three at yourself.

* * *

Harvest Potatoes

1 package (32-ounce) frozen hash brown potatoes, partially thawed
1 can cream of chicken soup
1 cup sour cream
2 cups shredded Cheddar cheese
1 1/2 teaspoons salt
1 medium onion, finely cut and browned in butter (optional)

Topping:
2 cups crushed corn flakes
1/4 cup butter, melted

Grease a 13x9-inch baking dish. Mix first six ingredients and put in dish. Combine topping ingredients and put them on top. Bake in 350 degree oven for 45 minutes.

* * *

Or you might do as I do: Make a white sauce and add as many hash brown potatoes as needed, along with some salt and pepper and some Philadelphia cream cheese. Place in baking dish and bake at 350 degrees about 45 minutes. Cheddar cheese may be diced on top.

All in a Woman's Day--February 28, 1989

Run out ... substitute

Has it ever happened to you? Right in the middle of a recipe you discover you need an ingredient you don't have on hand!

Well, then it is time to substitute; however, remember that substitutions may change the texture or flavor, or both, of a finished product.

To be on the safe side, always try to use the ingredients called for in a recipe whenever possible.

Mock Cream Cheese: 1 cup of low calorie cottage cheese, 4 tablespoons of margarine and a tablespoon skim milk. Mix all ingredients in a blender or food processor until smooth. This will yield 1 1/4 cups of mock cream cheese.

One tablespoon of Mock Cream Cheese will equal 1 tablespoon of cream cheese.

When a recipe calls for 1 cup of sour milk and 1 teaspoon of soda in making a cake, you may substitute 1 cup sweet milk and use 2 1/2 teaspoons of baking powder with perfect success.

If you don't have 1/4 cup of dry bread crumbs use 1/4 cup of cracker crumbs or corn meal or 1 cup of soft bread crumbs.

If you don't have a tablespoon of corn starch use 2 tablespoons of flour.

Should you not have a cup of corn syrup, use 1 cup sugar plus 1/4 cup liquid.

If flour is needed for thickening gravy or sauce, for 2 tablespoons flour you may substitute 1 tablespoon of corn starch, rice starch or arrowroot, or 2 tablespoons instant mashed potatoes, corn meal or quick cooking tapioca.

If a recipe calls for cooked or canned green peas or green beans, use some other fibrous vegetable: Cooked carrots, lima beans, corn or green pepper strips. Don't use turnips or parsnips as they may be too strong in flavor, while soft squashes will be too watery.

You may substitute, with good results, quick or old-fashioned rolled oats, corn or wheat flakes or other unsweetened cereal for about 1/3 of the flour in recipes for plain muffins and other quick breads.

For 1 cup of melted shortening you may use 1 cup of cooking oil, however, this should not be substituted in a recipe unless it does call for melted shortening.

There is no reason to buy a whole bag of self-rising flour for one recipe, so just make your own. To 1 cup of regular flour add 1/2 teaspoon of salt and 1 1/2 teaspoons of baking powder. This equals one cup self-rising flour.

* * *

A Thought To Ponder: Contentment is a matter of hoping for the best and making the best of what you get.

* * *

Carolyn's Orange Glazed Pork Roast

4 to 5 pounds boneless pork loin roast
1 1/2 teaspoon ginger
1/4 cup frozen orange juice, thawed
1/4 cup honey

Rub the surface of the roast with 1 teaspoon of ginger and place it on a rack in a shallow roasting pan. Roast uncovered 2 1/2 hours in a 325 degree oven. Meanwhile combine the orange juice, honey and remaining ginger and bring it to a boil; boil one minute. Brush sauce over roast several times, during the last 30 minutes of cooking. Let meat stand 15 minutes before slicing. Serves 8 to 10.

All in a Woman's Day—March 7, 1989

Top o' the morning is the wish extended

Ahhh, just to be Irish on St. Pat's Day! Being Irish for 364 days of the year just isn't visibly different from being French, Italian, Scotch, Jewish, Dutch or English. But come St. Paddy Day things change and Irish folk really become "Irish Folk." They live a lifetime of being Irish in just that one precious day. It is on this day that Irishmen just seem to grow taller and mightier.

Hundreds of years ago before the beginning of the Christian era, ancient tribes of people called Celts settled in Ireland and other parts of Europe. They were people of quick and skillful speech who loved to entertain one another by storytelling. Many of their colorful stories were about "Little People," tiny fairy folk, whom the Celts believed inhabited ancient mounds found throughout the countryside.

Of course, we know that these mounds that so puzzled the Celts were actually burial mounds built earlier by inhabitants of the country; however, to the Celts the mounds were the dwelling places of "wee" beings that possessed magical powers that could benefit the Celts or could go the other way and work mischief for them. It was for this reason that the Celts made every effort to be kind and friendly to these invisible folk.

Celtic tradition reminds us of a mythical storyteller named Ogma, who was so gifted at storytelling that he held his listeners spellbound by golden cords that ran from his nimble tongue, straight to the hearts of his audience.

When the soldiers of the Roman Empire overpowered the countries of Europe, the Celtic people and their traditions declined. The lovely stories were gradually forgotten and finally lost forever.

However, that was not true in Ireland, for the Romans did not overrun that country. There the legends lived and were passed down through the years. The Celts passed their stories on by oral tradition, meaning of course, that they taught the stories to their children, who in turn grew up and taught the stories to their children. It was in this way that the early Celtic heritage was preserved.

Then, when the Christian missionaries arrived in Ireland, they saw the cultural value of the Celtic folklore and realized these traditions might be forgotten and lost as the people adopted the new ways of Christianity. So, the missionaries sought out the best storytellers among the people and asked them to repeat the tales, which they carefully wrote down.

So, it was in this way that hundreds of the ancient Celtic tales were preserved. In the stories can be found the beginning of some of our St. Patrick's Day traditions, such as the wee leprechauns, the Irish harp, and the magical knowledge of the "Little People." Of course, some of the St. Patrick's Day traditions are of much more recent origin, including the "Paddy Pig," "The wearin' of the green" and Irish clay pipes.

Leapin' Leprechauns! If you want to make your leprechaun leap with delight just toast him with a goblet of Irish coffee. Here is a traditional toast that has a nice ring to it.

"Health and long life to you,
Land without rent to you,
The woman of your choice,
A child every year to you,
A long life, and may your
bones rest in Ireland."

The following bit of folklore tells the story of St. Patrick and how he banished the reptiles as if by magic:

"There's not a mile in Ireland's Isle where the dirty vermin musters; Where'ere he put his dear forefoot he murdered them in clusters. The toads went hop, the frogs went flop, slap dash into the water, and the rest committed suicide to save themselves from slaughter."

* * *

A Thought To Ponder: You can take the day off but you can't put it back!

* * *

Since potatoes, or the lowly "spud," as they are oftentimes called, are an important part of the Irish culture, here is a recipe using potatoes.

* * *

Golden Brunch Potatoes

2 baking potatoes
1 teaspoon oil
2 tablespoons butter, softened
2 tablespoons milk
2 tablespoons chopped green onion (optional)
1/4 teaspoon salt
4 eggs
1/2 cup shredded Cheddar cheese

Scrub potatoes and rub lightly with oil. Pierce in several places with a fork and bake at 400 degrees 50-60 minutes or until tender. Halve potatoes lengthwise and scoop out pulp, leaving 1/4-inch shells. Mash pulp and stir in butter, milk, onion and salt; season with pepper. Fill potato skins with the mashed potato mixture, making a hollow in the center of each. Break 1 egg into each potato half. Sprinkle with cheese. Bake at 400 degrees about 15 minutes or until egg is cooked to desired degree of doneness. Makes 4 servings.

All in a Woman's Day--March 14, 1989
Choose good nutrition

March is National Nutrition Month, using the theme "A Lifetime Decision; Choose Good Nutrition."

Each day we are faced with making decisions of our choices of food; however, we should select those that will contribute to our good health.

We often hear the saying, "that if you eat right you will feel and look right." But sometimes we wonder and are a bit doubtful.

It is so tempting during busy days for persons of all ages to eat meals, and yes, snacks, too, on the run, and often we do not even consider the nutritious value of the foods that we choose.

There is no question that more and more Americans are eating out, however, even if you do eat out, you don't have to sacrifice your waistline or even your diet. If you eat more than you really want, you will be eating unnecessary calories. Just forget your instilled habit of "cleaning your plate." Your extra food can be taken home in a "doggie bag." Perhaps you need to cover it well to keep from nibbling. It is such an easy thing to do ... nibble.

How do you eat your salads? Do you fork, stab and dip? Just a suggestion ... always order your sauces or salad dressings on the side. Then take your food that has been "stabbed" with your fork and just dip it into the dip or dressing. This will allow you to get a good flavor in every bite; however, calories will be notably less.

In the event you would hesitate to make this special request in restaurants, do not be shy, for most restaurants will be cooperative. In the event you did not realize it, this is how lowfat milk and nonfat milk became standard in most eating establishments; customers asking for them.

Salad bars, even if a good source of nutrition, can be pitfalls, especially when a ladle of dressing is placed on your salad. It can really increase the calories. This also holds true with buffets. The tendency is to get "our money's worth"; however, in so doing, it is difficult to control calories. If you can leave about half of the food on your plate when eating out you will be able to cut your calories in half.

Most of us have a struggle with snacks. When that "snack attack" strikes, just remember to stay away from sweets and high calorie foods. If you like to snack, don't feel guilty, but make it on foods that will give you good nutrition and that will satisfy your hunger such as fresh fruits, unbuttered popcorn, unsalted pretzels, cereal and fruit and raw crunchy vegeables. If you snack between meals, try to eat less at mealtime.

Also, when you go grocery shopping, be sure to eat something before you go —plain crackers or a bit of fruit. This is important, for if you tend to be hungry, there is no doubt that you will purchase items not on your grocery list and are really not needed.

Yogurt is fast becoming one of America's favorite foods. However you eat it—as a drink, frozen, in lowfat or nonfat forms or combined with different kinds of fruits—it is good.

Even in the fruit category there are choices—Swiss style means that the fruit is blended throughout the yogurt and in the sundae style the fruit can be found at the bottom of the container. Just like milk, there are yogurts to meet all of the demands of nutritional needs and the variety of preference. You will find the rich, egg yolk added type of custard like yogurt, as well as the natural fruit kind. Too, now even the nonfat plain yogurt is available at the market.

There are limitless ways that yogurt can be used ... salads, desserts, soups, dressings and entrees. So, do a little experimenting and maybe you will come up with something really elegant.

Let's "Make It With Yogurt!" With all the talk about calcium, yogurt is an excellent source; so, instead of eating it plain make a dip by using the mashed pulp of two avocados and one cup plain lowfat yogurt. Add garlic to taste. This is a good vegetable dip and makes a delightful topping for a taco salad.

Another good dip is one cup chutney to two cups plain lowfat yogurt.

Maybe you have never tried a sundae for breakfast, but here is one that you might like. Use assorted sliced or cubed fresh fruit such as kiwis, bananas, strawberries, cantaloupe or other fruit. Place these in the bottom of a glass or bowl and top with plain or vanilla lowfat yogurt. Then sprinkle with your favorite breakfast cereal or granola.

A quick dessert is to use cubes of a pound cake in the bottom of a stemmed glass topping with a scoop of frozen raspberry yogurt and pureed fresh raspberries.

Those in the business, say you can spoon it, lick it, scoop it and cook with it! Just try it for versatility!

Keep in mind that today's nutrition is important for tomorrow's good health. If you haven't already started on a good nutritional program, start today!

* * *

A Thought To Ponder: Be friendly with folks you know. If it weren't for them, you'd be a total stranger.

Hello! spring is welcome

Hello, Spring! Welcome back! It has been many months since you were here, but now you have officially arrived in all your glory. There were several days that we were a bit fouled up, for we thought that summer had arrived in your stead, since we did experience summertime weather, at least for a while.

What is spring?

Spring is plowing the fields and preparing the garden. The feel of warm earth on hands is as soft and rich as velvet, cool as spring shade and has a perfume that tickles the nose as well as the heart of those who truly love the earth.

A little later we will anticipate the early spring blossoms and perhaps some of them might even be blooming now in protected places. (The pussy willows are looking beautiful!)

Spring is fresh tender green grass and pale green grain fields where delicate shoots push through the ground to create a misty aura of at least 40 shades of green over the slumbering brown fields.

In this rural area, spring moves in with the melodic hum of tractors, great and small, caressing the earth with harrows, plows, discs and planters.

Spring is sudden rains splattering newly washed windows, (if the rain would fall in our area we really wouldn't care how splattered the windows became ... it would be such a blessing). We begin to wonder if there is enough moisture to even bring into view all those lovely shades of green we anticipate.

Spring is the capricious winds tossing kites about in a bright blue sky and sashaying through the tops of budding trees.

Spring is birds flitting here and there, swirling low, and then gliding only to soar again in the wind.

Each morning the sun rises a bit earlier and lingers just a moment or two longer before setting.

Spring is young animals born into this world, and that must be given tender loving care.

Too, when we think of spring, Easter just naturally comes to mind. This year it is coming a bit earlier than usual, but that is to be expected every now and then.

This Easter is no different from those that have gone before ... it is the renewal of our faith and our belief in the beauties of the season and for the goodness that He has given to us in so many, many ways.

Let us think of the anchor. It is the symbol of both Christ's cross and the hope of eternal life. From death on the cross to glorious resurrection ... all these are the beautiful messages of victory at Easter. He is risen! And Jesus does live! And because He lives ... we also shall live!

May your Easter be blessed!

* * *

A Thought To Ponder: Life is a flower of which love is the honey.

All in a Woman's Day--March 28, 1989
Peanuts rank high; have nutritional value

Because this is National Peanut Month what better time to think of peanuts?

The common name of peanut is applied to this annual herb, that is a legume instead of a nut. It belongs to the pea family. According to its various localities, it also is called groundnut, earthnut, ground pea, goober (the name southerners use), and pindar.

The plant grows from one to two feet high with thick greenish, hairy stems and spreading branches. After it blooms and the petals have fallen, the withered stock bends to touch the earth, pushing into the ground where the fruit or pods develop and mature underground. This is thought to be an adaptation of life in Africa, where swarms of locusts periodically devastated the land. However, the peanut is not native to Africa, as we sometimes think, but to Brazil and Peru, where it was discovered some 2,000 years ago.

Although pre-Columbian, South American Indians undoubtedly beat peanuts into a buttery pulp, and George Washington Carver, the famed botanist, concocted some of his laboratory experiments, the invention of peanut butter is attributed to a now nameless physician in St. Louis. It is said that in 1890 he whipped up a few dollops in a meat grinder to help patients in need of a booster of protein.

Still gaining more prestige, this high energy food got a more official approval, for it was in 1897 that John H. Kellogg was issued a patent for a process he had come up with for making "nut butter" for patients at Battle Creek Sanitarium in Michigan. About this same time the "Age of Peanut Butter" was still boosted when Ambrose Straub of St. Louis came up with an invention of a machine that could churn out Dr. Kellogg's concoction in a steady stream of nutrition.

A 100,000-year-old fossilized peanut has been found in China. Too, some pottery 3,500 years old, decorated with peanuts, has been uncovered in diggings at Inca burial grounds, where peanuts were buried by ancient tribes with the dead to provide a "well-balanced" meal in the afterlife and to give them strength for their journey ahead.

Pizarro's Conquistadors took the Ynchic (peanuts) back to Spain, and then they were carried to Africa on slave ships and traded with natives for various items, including elephant tusks. They were transported to the United States the same way.

Just when the peanut arrived in Africa is a bit uncertain; however, it was here that it was the prime source of nourishment. The raising of peanuts seems to be a main crop for obtaining cash in many of the underdeveloped countries.

Somehow we think of peanuts as nibbling food; however, they are much more than that. In Nigeria, peanuts are used in lamb stew and several African countries feature soups in which they are simmered with diced pork, smoked fish, onions and a wide variety of spices.

The Malaysians coat pork bits with peanut butter and serve them on a skewer. Closer to home, cooks in Louisiana oftentimes make a creole puff featuring peanut butter and grated cheese.

But it took the Americans to give this lowly peanut a gourmet status. Peanut butter and peanut butter chips are used in many ways to make rather elegant dishes.

The chip is made from peanut meal mixed with vegetable fat, nonfat milk solids and other ingredients. Chips are easier to work with than peanut butter. Who can resist a peanut butter sandwich with jelly or sugar? Pretty good eatin' I'd say!

The first commercially salted peanuts made their appearance in 1887, the first peanut vending machine and the first commercial candy bar appeared just after the turn of the century.

While most countries raise peanuts for oil, here in the United States they are raised mainly for food. Peanuts contain no cholestrol; however, they do contain a roughage or fiber that is valuable in assisting, the digestive system in regulating itself.

You have heard it said that willpower is the ability to eat ONE salted peanut.

* * *

A Thought To Ponder: If you love somebody, tell him.

* * *

Southern Peanut Pie

3 eggs
1/2 cup sugar
1 1/2 cups dark corn syrup
1/4 cup butter, melted
1/4 teaspoon salt
1/2 teaspoon vanilla
1 1/2 cups chopped roasted peanuts
9-inch pie shell

Beat eggs until foamy, add sugar, syrup, butter, salt and vanilla, and continue beating until thoroughly blended. Then add peanuts. Pour this into an unbaked pie shell and bake it in a preheated 375 degree oven for 45 minutes. It is delicious served warm or cold and may be garnished with whipped cream, topping or ice cream.

* * *

Peanut Fingers

1/2 pound unsliced white bread
1 cup milk
1/2 cup peanut butter
2 cups finely chopped salted peanuts
1 cup flaked coconut

Trim crusts from bread; slice 1/2-inch thick. Cut each slice into fingers, 1/2-inch wide. Blend together the milk and peanut butter. Dip bread in peanut-milk mixture, then in peanuts combined with coconut. Place these on a baking sheet and bake in preheated oven at 400 degrees about 5 minutes or until lightly browned. Makes 3 1/2 dozen peanut fingers.

All in a Woman's Day--April 4, 1989

A fork ... to use or not

The fork, the lowly fork, is a most important part of our civilization today.

Sometimes referred to as the "funny fork," you may not see anything funny about it, but if perchance you did, you would be splitting your sides at least three times a day and maybe more. Finally folks settled down and admitted it had a place on the table. This common bit of cutlery truly created its share of merriment before people sobered down and admitted to its usefulness.

For example, if you should happen to be eating peas with a doll sized rake or hoe, you'd cause a few giggles, too, you must admit. That seemed to be the way it was with the first forks to be seen in England. To the English this foreign gadget looked for all the world like the pitchforks that the peasants used to toss hay and clean barnyards. They felt that anyone having the nerve to hoist a mouthful of food from such a vulgar instrument could be certain of only one thing—to be the life of the party.

Our table fork, in various forms, is an ancient utensil; however, it never became popular in the civilization of antiquity: Some forks have been discovered in tombs of Egyptians priests.

Millions of people for thousands of years, from kings to shepherds, had always managed to feed themselves nicely and very well in the same way—with their fingers.

Even though King Solomon may have drunk his wine from a gold cup, he still picked up his roasted venison with his fingers, as did other famous people, Richard the Lionhearted, Caesar and Alexander the Great. Of course, there were spoons for stews and drippy sauces. It is easy to see why it became good manners to wash the hands twice at each meal—before and after.

The fork, supposedly, was introduced into Venice in the 11th century by a Byzantine princess. This two-pronged utensil became popular throughout Italy, and then Europe; regardless of that fact, it did not become common among the aristocratic until about four centuries later. It was then nobles of France found them a delightful, amusing novelty.

The English did not have a chance to laugh at them until the 17th century, and by then the fork had gained for itself quite a reputation.

A little later in history, those who could afford to own knives, placed food to their mouths on the sharpened points. The sharp prongs of the forks made them "dangerous," both to put food into the mouth and to have around children.

The Medieval fork was an article of great luxury, generally used in eating fruits and sweet meats. Owners of forks carried them on their persons, together with knives used for cutting food. This custom persisted until the 18th century.

Eating with a fork also was regarded as somewhat effeminate. Too, in some French and Scottish convents, the use of forks was prohibited as sinful for no one had found anything in the Good Book mentioning a fork, except the three-pronged "fleshhook" used to lift and turn food while cooking.

Early forks were made with a straight, shankless shaft, with a knob at one end and two straight tines at the other. Beginning with the late 17th century, the implement became heavier, a shaft was added to support the wider, tined end, and the number of tines were increased.

Fortunately to Queen Elizabeth, the French import was neither dangerous nor sinful but a wonderful new convenience. Her enthusiasm caught on; that seemed to be the end of the fork's fight for acceptance.

Even though the fork was brought to America as early as 1630 by John Winthrop, who became the first governor of Massachusetts, it was another 170 years before there could be found a fork at each person's place at the table.

The colonists in the meantime were very much contented to eat as they always had, with knives, fingers and spoons of horn or wood. The handy Indian spoon, a clam shell fitted to the split end of a stick, was adopted by many of the colonists.

Through the years the fork has changed in design from two, to three and at last to four tines.

In modern usage, a service of table silver has several types of forks; namely, the large dinner fork with four tines; the entree fork, similar to the dinner fork, but smaller; the short broad salad fork with three or four tines, with the extreme left tine being wider than the other three tines and made with a cutting edge. Some elaborate sets of silver possibly would include a fish fork and pastry fork, similar to the salad fork, and an ice cream fork, resembling a flattened spoon of which the bowl is divided into two broad tines sometimes with one or more narrow tines between them.

Regardless of this modern age, it still would not be correct to say that the fork is in general use, for there are millions of people who have never seen or used it.

* * *

A Thought To Ponder: Happiness is anywhere people take time to care.

—Nan Roloff

* * *

Emerald Salad

2 tablespoons gelatin
1 cup cold water
1 cup sugar
1/2 cup water
1/2 cup vinegar (scant) use vinegar from sweet pickles
1 medium can crushed pineapple (also juice)
1 cup nuts
1 cup sweet pickles, sliced thin

Let the gelatin soak in 1 cup of cold water five minutes. Then cook to a thin syrup the sugar, 1/2 cup water and vinegar. While hot, add to the gelatin mixture and stir until dissolved. When it begins to set, add the pineapple, nuts and sweet pickles. This is a tasty salad and good with sandwiches.

Handful of helpful hints!

Today, I have a handful of helpful hints.

If you are cooking for singles, here is a little suggestion: Beat four or five eggs thoroughly in a blender or with an egg beater. Then pour them into a jar with a lid and refrigerate and use by tablespoons. Three tablespoons plus one tablespoon of water makes it just right for French toast; four tablespoons makes a nice serving of scrambled eggs just for one.

To cook fish quickly and easily, poach it.

If you want to reheat cooked rice and keep it fluffy, just sprinkle two tablespoons of water over each cup of rice. Cover and heat over low heat five to eight minutes, or until hot.

Spray vegetable oil used to prevent foods from sticking is just great sprayed on the food grinder. For foods that tend to stick, it helps and makes cleanup easy, as well as washing.

Lemons will keep in the refrigerator for a long time without spoiling if you wipe them first with vinegar.

Remove gum from clothing by rubbing it with a beaten egg white.

Unsweetened breakfast cereal crumbled makes quick bread crumbs for a recipe.

Intensify the flavor of cooking apples for sauce or fillings by using apple juice or cider instead of water.

Add a little bluing to the dishwasher to make cut glass sparkle.

You can make your own breakfast cereals by purchasing plain cereals and adding chopped dates, figs or raisins.

No use to have a soggy salad. Just turn a saucer upside down in the bottom of your salad bowl and the water will drain under the saucer, leaving the salad fresh and crisp.

If you want to recycle a baked potato just dip it in water and bake it in a 350 degree oven 20 minutes.

You don't always have to have professional equipment to decorate a cake. Fill empty plastic squeeze bottles that have had catsup or mustard in them and go right along with your decorating.

Did you know that you don't have to waste time shucking corn and boiling it in a big pot? Just lay the ears on a sheet of aluminum foil in a medium oven and cook according to taste. The cornhusks help preserve the natural juice.

You also can cook the corn in the husk; however, peel the husk back and remove the silk, then butter and salt the ears, pulling the husks back up over the ear. You can wrap each ear in aluminum foil and bake 30 minutes in a 350 degree oven. This prevents the waterlogged taste.

A few grains of salt added to cream that won't whip will do the trick. It should make nice stiff peaks and doesn't taste salty.

A half cup of gingerale will prolong the life of cut roses.

If you are going to put muffins in the freezer, be sure to slice them in half. This way you can pop them right into the oven or toaster.

If you run out of eggs while in the process of cooking, a quick substitute can be either one teaspoon of corn starch or one teaspoon vinegar and increase the other liquid in the recipe by three or four tablespoonful. This works for one missing egg.

A pinch of sugar will balance the taste of an oversalted recipe, providing you are making a dish that can use a touch of sweetness.

To make sure your homemade cake doesn't stick to the pan, try placing the pan on a cloth wrung out of cold water immediately after taking from the oven. Leave only for a few minutes.

Warming a pie pan and dampening the edges should prevent your crusts from shrinking from the pan.

Plastic wrap placed in the refrigerator for storage is easier to handle.

* * *

A Thought To Ponder: All great accomplishments have simple beginnings.

* * *

Raspberry Swirl Cookies

1/2 cup butter or margarine, room temperature
1 cup sugar
1 teaspoon vanilla extract
1 egg
2 cups flour
1 teaspoon baking powder
1/4 teaspoon salt
1/2 cup raspberry jam
1/2 cup flaked coconut
1/4 cup finely chopped walnuts

In a medium bowl, cream butter, sugar, vanilla and egg until light and fluffy. Combine flour with baking powder and salt, and add to creamed mixture. Beat until well blended. Chill until firm, several hours. To roll, let stand at room temperature until slightly soft, then roll on lightly floured surface into a 12x8-inch rectangle. In a small bowl combine jam, coconut and nuts. Spread mixture evenly over dough, leaving a 1/2-inch border around the edge. Roll up from long side. Cut log in half crosswise and refrigerate until firm. To bake, cut chilled dough into 1/4-inch slices. Place them 2 inches apart on greased baking sheet and bake at 375 degrees 10 to 15 minutes or until edges are golden. Cool on wire racks. (Makes about 4 dozen.)

All in a Woman's Day--April 18, 1989

Share kitchen wisdoms

Here are a few kitchen wisdoms to be shared:

Save those plastic milk jugs for storing dry staples such as popcorn, rice, macaroni etc. You won't have to worry with torn bags or having a mess to clean up.

If you are getting ready to bake, be sure and measure each ingredient separately, then if the telephone rings there is no guessing as to whether you have already measured this or that.

Have you ever thought of using an old phonograph record wrapped in aluminum foil as a base for carrying a cake? Too, a new album with a special occasion cake would be a novel gift idea.

When measuring corn syrup, if you will flour the measuring cup, the syrup will slip out easily.

When measuring peanut butter, grease the measuring cup and it will come out easily.

When placlng newly purchased meat in the refrigerator, turn the package upside down so that the juice tray is on the top. The juice will flow back into the meat and will not drip onto other items.

If you want to store ice cubes, place them in a brown bag in the freezer, and they will not stick together. Cake frosting really isn't very appetizing when it gets sugary. To prevent this just add about a teaspoon of vinegar. By adding such a small amount it will not affect the flavor.

If you would like for fish scales to come off in a snap, just rub the fish thoroughly with vinegar before scaling.

You can pull the strings of the celery off easily if you will run warm water over it.

An old-time way of keeping stewed tomatoes from getting too watery is to crumble shredded wheat into the tomatoes while heating, and stir until thick.

When frying eggs, turn each egg over on another egg instead of flopping it over in the grease. Then the yolk will not break and the grease will not splash.

When baking in aluminum foil, be sure to turn the dull side out. The shiny side will turn heat in toward the food.

When baking ham, try basting it with slightly brewed tea. This beats some of the usual methods, and it's so tender you can cut it with a fork.

When making deviled eggs, put the yolks through a potato ricer to prepare them quickly.

Should your cake mix look too dry and crumbly, add two tablespoons of cooking oil to make it moist and of better texture.

After cooking any food containing protein, such as meat, eggs and cheese, remove them from the container and immediately run cold water in it. Let this stand a few minutes and the food will come right off.

When you serve hot rolls for dinner—really hot, try keeping them that way by lining a bread basket with aluminum foil before putting the napkin in the basket.

Never let the juice of raw chicken touch anything that is to be eaten. Some raw foods, especially chicken, can cause food poisoning.

When preparing to peel onions, place them in the refrigerator for an hour before peeling, then keep your mouth shut while in the peeling process. This way you are less likely to cry.

When you drop batter onto a cookie sheet, so that the dough won't stick to the spoon, try first dipping the spoon into milk.

* * *

A Thought To Ponder: A word of advice—do not give it.

* * *

Creamy Asparagus Salad

2 envelopes unflavored gelatin
1 cup water
2 (10-ounce) cans of cream of asparagus soup
1 (8-ounce) package cream cheese, softened
1/4 cup lime juice
3 tablespoons sugar
1/4 teaspoon hot pepper sauce
Green food coloring
1/2 cup minced celery
3 tablespoons minced onion

Sprinkle gelatin over water in medium-sized saucepan. Place this over low heat until dissolved. Add soup, undiluted, and stir until smooth. Beat cream cheese in a medium-sized bowl until very fluffy; beat in lime juice, sugar and pepper sauce gradually. Stir in soup mixture gradually. Add enough green food coloring to make mixture a nice soft green color. Stir celery and onion into the salad and pour into an 8-inch square pan. Chill until firm. Cut in squares and serve this on lettuce.

A tisket, a tasket, get yourself a basket

A tisket, a tasket, get yourself a basket!

Baskets are the "in" thing; they have been forever. Now their purpose is a bit different from former years.

In earlier times they were used for holding and carrying many different commodities; today, however, one of their main purposes is decorative.

Baskets of all shapes and sizes can be found in stores, markets, craft and gift shops; in fact, just about anywhere you might choose to go.

Do you have a basket? What kind do you have and how are you using it?

Basketry is one of the oldest handicrafts since prehistoric times. Folks have made baskets from grasses, leaves, stalks and other flexible materials that could be woven into a receptacle to hold a variety of things, including a basket for baby Moses.

Basketry is a popular handicraft, and as a hobby, people who make baskets are often referred to as basket makers; well, that really does make sense!

Some of the early American Indians covered tightly woven baskets with pitch so they would hold water. Even today some basket makers use many of the same materials and techniques used by the early day folks.

Baskets are used the world over for storing dry foods, such as fruit and bread. They also are used as plates and bowls if made waterproof by a special coating. With particularly close plaiting they can be used as containers for liquids. Such containers are found in various parts of Europe, Africa and among several groups of North American Indians. By dropping hot stones into the liquid the Hupa Indians of northwest California have even boiled water or cooked food in their basket containers.

Some open work baskets are used as sieves, strainers and filters. These, too, have been used in most primitive cultures.

Baskets can be used as transportation receptacles. Burden baskets are large, deep baskets in which heavy loads can be carried on the back. Too, there was a special kind of basket that was used long ago for harvesting crops … somehow it was pulled through the crop of grain and the seeds fell into the basket. In many countries baskets filled with commodities are often carried on the head of the bearer.

Baskets offer many decorative possibilities. Some baskets can be upended to make an occasional table; baskets such as those from the Philippines can be made into beautiful tables by placing a round glass on top of the upturned basket. A heavy basket can be used for holding wood by the fireplace.

Some baskets are beautiful containers for house plants or to use as an umbrella holder, a magazine rack or a toy box. They even make good wastepaper baskets. According to the kind of baskets used, they make attractive groupings in the family room or kitchen, as well in other rooms of the home. A display of baskets also may be arranged in a curio cabinet. Baskets with handles can be hung for special effects.

Used in the bathroom as a part of a decorative scheme, the right size basket make holders for guest towels, soap, toothbrushes, cleansing tissues and the like. To give a homey touch to a guest room, a fat basket placed on the dresser can hold a water glass, small box of tissues and a new bar of soap. Just before guests arrive, a pretty basket filled with fresh fruit, for both color and as a welcoming snack, might be placed in the guest room.

Some large baskets also can be used as clothes hampers.

Then there is the Easter basket; colorful baskets that hold all of the Easter treats. Baskets can be used for sewing needs, crayons, candy and to hold Christmas cards. Baskets also are used to carry food to those with whom we want to share.

All sizes of baskets, nested or otherwise, can be used as handy holders for odds and ends. Some of the miniature baskets, with a container inside might possibly hold an arrangement of pansies, or you might lay a small stem of silk roses across the basket as if they just had been picked from the garden.

Then there is the egg basket. Remember when eggs were gathered in a basket if you didn't have on an apron to hold them? A conversation piece could be an egg basket holding china eggs arranged on the counter in the kitchen reminiscent of other days.

Then, there is the laundry basket, garden basket and flower basket. Too, some purses represent baskets.

China and glass baskets also are popular; however, many of these are collector's items.

If you haven't guessed, yes, there are baskets for almost every need.

* * *

A Thought To Ponder: The reward of a thing well done is to have done it.

* * *

Apple Salad

2 cups diced unpeeled Red Delicious apples
2 cups cubed oranges
1 cup mild Cheddar cheese, cut up
1 cup mild Brick cheese, cut up
1 cup chopped dates
1/2 cup chopped walnuts or pecans
1/2 orange rind, grated
1/2 cup salad dressing, seasoned as desired

Combine fruits, cheese, dates, nuts and orange rind; add a little sugar to the salad dressing, if desired. Add it to fruit, toss lightly. Chill 1 hour; makes 6-8 servings. Place the chilled bowl of salad in a basket, it makes an attractive, appetizing addition to the noon or evening meal.

All in a Woman's Day--May 2, 1989

Basketry making is fun

This is a continuation of the column last week concerning baskets, to give a little more insight about this craft or hobby.

Two kinds of materials are used in making baskets. The hard kind and the soft. Hard material includes grasses, leaves, plant roots, strips of wood, tree bark and twigs. These all can be gathered or purchased. The hard materials require special preparation to make soft and pliable enough, as well as strong, with which to work. First, it must be dried at which time it shrinks and becomes brittle. Then it must be soaked in water so it will be easy to handle. The material is then ready to be used; however, it must be kept moist during the process of basket making.

657

Soft material includes yarn, rope, made from natural fibers, such as cotton, wool or such fibers as acrylic and nylon. These, too, are available in shops, and they come in various colors and sizes.

There are four basic basket making methods. Weaving is the simplest and the most common, with the basic patterns including plain, twill or herringbone. Twilling resembles plain weaving, but the weavers are used in pairs. Twilling produces a twisted pattern. Plaiting is like braiding or interwoven. Most plaited baskets are made of flat materials such as strips of leaves, paper, wood or ribbon. They generally are not as sturdy as woven baskets and need to have a rigid rim added to the top so that they will keep their shape.

Coiling is a sewing technique. The baskets begin from a core and winds around in a circle to form a coil. These are held together by a binding thread. Flexible materials needed for the coils are grass, rope, straw, twine or yarn. Fine, thin materials such as raffia, strips of cornhusks, yarn, string or rope are commonly used for thread binding.

Even in the modern, industrial world there seems to be a future in baskets because they are flexible, light, open, have firmness and volume. No doubt the basket will continue to be unsurpassed for some utilitarian tasks; however, some handmade baskets can become luxury items.

Basketry is really a folk art. It needs no investment or money, with the only essential requirements being a simple awl, nimble fingers and patience ... lots of patience!

Maybe now you will look a little more kindly at some of the baskets you have tucked away, and bring them out to enjoy.

* * *

A Thought To Ponder: Keep your face to the sunshine and you cannot see the shadow.

* * *

Chocolate Rice Bars

1/4 cup butter or margarine
2 ounces unsweetened chocolate
40 large marshmallows
1/4 teaspoon burnt sugar flavoring
5 cups puffed rice

Melt butter or margarine, chocolate and marshmallows, and add flavoring. Stir until smooth. Remove this from heat and stir in the puffed rice. Spread this in a greased pan, 9x13-inch, and let stand until firm.

* * *

Rhubarb Pie

2 cups diced rhubarb
1 1/2 cups sugar
Pinch salt
2 teaspoons minute tapioca
3 chopped maraschino cherries
1 teaspoon maraschino juice
1/2 cup sour cream

Mix ingredients together; place in a pastry lined pie pan and bake in a 425 degree oven 30-40 minutes. Serve warm with vanilla ice cream. **Note:** The sour cream takes the gritty feeling out of the rhubarb. It is very good. It is rhubarb time!

Recall the hanky; barefoot days of May

There are always some special things that are recalled as Mother's Day approaches.

For instance, do you remember how mother always was eager to know if we had a hanky (that was before the day of cleansing tissues) before we left home?

In those bygone days a handkerchief was a necessity and "no lady" left home without one. Of course, even though it perhaps played an important role in our society and culture, it is fast becoming obsolete, and just as well, for it no doubt was most unhygienic.

When Mother's Day came around ... or her birthday ... or Christmas ... the gift for mother was a hanky. A linen hanky was then no doubt the cheapest gift to be found. (A far cry from nowadays.) Most often it had her initial in the corner. The "kids" stood around so proud and awaited her approval.

Many women made handkerchiefs with fancy corners and then finished by putting a tatted or crocheted edge around the hem to add to its prettiness. Back in those days many women believed that a pretty, fancy handkerchief was as important as pretty gloves. Their fancy hanky needed to be seen so it went into a pocket where at least part of it would show, or they would gather it up in the middle as a jabot, fastening it at the neckline with a decorative breast pin.

A beautiful hanky was a must for a wedding; it was treasured as either something old or something new.

Many brides today carry one of grandmother's or great-grandmother's lovely handkerchiefs.

Did you know that the handkerchief was once the patron saint of romance? A young girl would accidently (oh, yes!) drop her initialed handkerchief for some dashing young man to rescue. Then she would drop her eyelids in a very coy manner, that was indeed rather bewitching; and soon the romance would blossom.

Sometimes when a lady cried, a gentleman would offer his handkerchief, since it was made of a large square of material, to dry her tears. She would very graciously accept and then would return it all laundered.

Some of you may recall that in rural schools, it was compulsory to have a handkerchief and the pupils had to stand inspection so the teacher could make sure that each one had a kerchief.

Too, this little square of cloth has been a much used piece of property throughout history in literature and drama.

* * *

Another practice that always occurred along about this time of year was going barefoot. Remember, again, how mother would always say "you can take off your shoes and go barefoot come the first of May!"

That was a day looked forward to with much delight, even if the ground might be a bit cool. That didn't really matter! This was the long looked for time of year awaited with anticipation when youngsters jerked off their shoes and long stockings. Somehow they felt that summer was almost here; too, it wouldn't be long until school would be over for the season.

When shoes and stockings were first pulled off, how good it felt to wiggle the toes and step on the cool grass. No thought was given to skinned feet or stubbed toes. So, what did it matter? "It was the first day of May and they got to go barefoot!" Sometimes, however, they had to tiptoe around.

Maybe the first of May was not so lucky for some of the youngsters as some had to wait until the first white butterfly made its appearance before they could yank off their shoes and stockings. Never forget there was a lot of looking for that butterfly!

* * *

A Thought To Ponder: Who can estimate the far-reaching influence of a godly Mother upon her child?

* * *

To all mothers everywhere ... "Happy Mother's Day."

* * *

A Love Cake for Mother

1 can of Obedience
Several pounds of Affection
1 pint of Neatness
Some holiday, birthday and everyday Surprises
1 can of running errands (The Willing Brand)
1 box of powdered "Get Up When I Should"
1 bottle of "Keep Sunny All Day Long"
1 can of pure Thoughtfulness

Mix these well, bake them in a warm oven and serve to Mother every day, not just Mother's Day. She ought to have it in big slices.

Helpful hints given

It seems as if homemakers never ever have quite enough helpful hints. Here are a few to add to your collection:

Keep fudge frosting soft and workable while using by placing the pan in hot water.

Boiling cloves in a cup of vinegar will absorb most kitchen odors.

If you are using a hand beater, place a dampened cloth under the bowl to keep it from walking. If you place the bowl in the sink, you will cut down on the splatters as well and make cleanup time quicker.

If your cake should turn out to be a failure, don't ever throw it away. Cut it into squares as for serving and top with whipped cream and serve as a pudding. A little fruit added to the topping also would improve the flavor.

Place stale, hardened rolls or biscuits in a tightly closed brown paper bag, sprinkle the bag with water and place it in a moderate oven for 5 to 8 minutes. This gives them new life.

You can clean up the cheese grater without shredding your fingers if you brush a small amount of cooking oil on the grater with a pastry brush, blotting off the excess oil. The cheese bits will fall away easily with a little soap and water.

Discover the easy way to slice beef paper thin. Simply freeze the beef slightly, then cut against the grain.

Mix chocolate syrup and prepared whipped topping for an inexpensive, quick and tasty cake frosting.

To store a frosted cake in the freezer, leave the goody uncovered until it is frozen. Then it can be covered without ruining the icing.

Don't fight that sticky bun dough. Before shaping rolls, try dipping your hands in cold water. Repeat as often as necessary.

Brown ground beef in half or pound amounts and freeze it in aluminum pie pans, for use in casseroles, spaghetti sauce. This will thaw faster than raw ground beef.

Whenever making packaged frosting or using the canned type, try adding about half a container of whipped topping, beating it into the frosting. It makes the frosting less sugary, gives it a creamier, more spreadable consistency and gives more icing for the cake.

To make whipped honey butter, cream a half cup of butter until light and fluffy. Gradually add three-fourths cup of honey, beating until well blended.

Did you ever try to oven-fry pork steak in the same way you prepare chicken? Dip the steak in milk, then in crushed corn flakes or prepared crumbs. Roast uncovered and turn once to brown on both sides. Use a moderate oven. The steaks turns out tender and not too greasy.

Whole chickens are your best buy. Not only do they cost less per pound, but they retain more of their juiciness and flavor. When you've cut the bird for cooking, unused backs and giblets can be frozen and reserved for making chicken stock.

Never carve any sizable piece of meat or poultry right after it comes from the oven. Give a roast turkey at least 20 minutes, and it will be much easier to slice.

Vanilla sugar, wonderful for flavoring, can be made by putting a vanilla bean in a jar of sugar.

* * *

A Thought To Ponder: The years teach much which the days never know.

* * *

Thousand Dollar Orange Salad

1 box orange gelatin
1 cup boiling water
3 ounces 7-Up®
1/2 pint whipped cream or whipped topping
1 small can crushed pineapple, drained
1 small jar maraschino cherries, drained
2 bananas, sliced
1/2 cup nuts, chopped
1 cup coconut

Dissolve gelatin in boiling water; add 7-Up®. Refrigerate about 45 minutes or until slightly jelled. Fold in whipped cream or whipped topping and the remaining ingredients into the gelatin mixture. Refrigerate until firm.

All in a Woman's Day--May 23, 1989

Cutlery is most essential

Cutlery, generally speaking, is a term applied collectively to all types of cutting instruments, especially referring to utensils used in the preparation and consumption of food.

Before the dawn of history, cutting implements, fashioned from flint stone and shells were utilized as weapons. Following the discovery of methods using metal instruments, they were made of bronze. Later the tools and weapons made from this alloy were replaced with iron, still the basic material in the manufacture of most types of cutlery.

The ancient Romans were extremely proficient people in the art of making cutting instruments. There have been found in the ruins of Pompeii, knives, shears and lancets of both bronze and iron. With the growth of the Roman Empire, the Romans conquered many countries and acquired skill in the fabrication of cutlery. Then, during the Middle Ages, a number of cities, notably Toledo in Spain and Damascus, became world famous for their cutlery products, especially swords.

The traditional center of cutlery manufacturers in England was Sheffield, which was well-known for the excellence of its knives and related products as early as the reign of Richard I (1189-99).

It was at a later period in history that Geoffrey Chaucer referred to a "Sheffield' thwitel" in one of his poems. The (thwitel) also called (whittle) is a crude form of a knife. This was followed by a type of folding clasp knife, much like the modern pocket knife.

The first cutlery factory in the United States, for the manufacture of pocket knives, was established in 1829 at Worcester, Mass. The manufacture of table knives began three years later at Saccarappa, Me. The industry steadily developed, notably in New England, as American steel improved in quality and decreased in price.

Early cutlery was hand forged, a method still used in the manufacture of certain high-quality products. In our modern times, all types of cutlery, including forks, table knives, scissors, carving knives and razors, are fabricated by machines, first in the United States and now extensively used in England and other countries.

Most professional chefs and cooks would probably agree that a "good knife" is the most important piece of equipment in the kitchen for it can just about make any cooking chore easier.

To keep your knives and cutlery in good working order, you might want to follow some of these tips from experts:

Sharpen knives regularly as needed. Dull knives can be more hazardous than sharp ones even when they are used properly.

Store knives in a slotted or magnetic rack to protect their points and edges. Do not store cutlery in drawers where the blades can become nicked or scratched and where someone may accidently pick them up by a sharp edge.

Wash blades in a degreaser solution and soapy water as soon as possible after using to clean away grease and food particles. Rinse well and dry with a cloth. Do not wash knives in automatic dishwashers and do not soak them as this damages and loosens the handles.

Cut foods on a wooden board to protect the knife's edge.

Do not hold knives in a flame or dip them in a pot of hot food—this may damage the blades.

Do not use them to pry jar lids or as substitute screwdrivers.

There are a few knives that are basic to any kitchen. A utility knife with a medium width blade that can slice fruit, sandwiches and trim meat; a slicing knife that has a narrow flexible blade that has a pointed end and is suitable for slicing various kinds of meat. There also are several length slicing knives. The paring knife that has a short, narrow blade is used for peeling, slicing, trimming and dicing vegetables, cheese and fruit. The cook's or chef's knife has a blade that makes it versatile for heavy-duty chopping, cutting, shredding and dicing. The boning knife features a narrow, curved blade that is used for cutting close to the bone and for easy removal of meat. The carving knife has a narrow blade shaped for carving and slicing meats. The bread knife has serrated edges so that the bread is not torn to pieces when cut.

Whether you use stainless steel or carbon steel is a matter of individual choice. You will find, however, that the stainless steel knives will not get rusty and are easy to keep looking good and shiny. Too, many of the newer ones seem to hold an edge as fine as carbon steel knives. Nevertheless, many cooks still prefer the fine quality of carbon steel knives that can be sharpened easily after using.

There are many knife sharpeners available; however, just an ordinary sharpening or whetting stone does a real good job. All you need to do to sharpen your knife is simply to draw the blade across the stone with a long stroke at angles varing from 15 to 25 degrees. Keep repeating until you have the edge desired.

No doubt many of you enjoy your electrical sharpeners, and that is great.

Maybe it is time to check your knives and see what you have and whether they need sharpening.

* * *

A Thought To Ponder: Destiny is not a matter of chance, it is a matter of choice.

* * *

So Simple Chicken

1 (14-ounce) box minute rice
3 small cans boned chicken
3 cans cream of chicken soup
Salt and pepper to taste
Grated cheese, optional

Cook rice according to directions. Add remaining ingredients. Heat and serve. (Tuna and cream of mushroom soup may be used in the same proportions with rice for a nice variation.)

All in a Woman's Day--May 30, 1989

Little more help is needed in kitchen

Perhaps you need a little more help in the kitchen, so here are a few tricks.

In baking, do you really know the difference between doughs and batters? If the mixture is thick enough to be rolled, it a dough, and if it's thin enough to be poured, it's a batter.

To keep chocolate cake brown on the outside, grease pans and "flour" them with cocoa.

Did it ever occur to you to use a new powder puff in your shortening can and also to use it to grease pans. Too, a new puff may be used to dust the pastry board and rolling pin.

Kitchen scissors are handy when making sandwiches. They may be used to cut slices of meat to fit the shape of the bread.

To avoid having a meringue fall, add

663

a fourth of a teaspoon baking powder to the mixture while beating the egg whites.

Use a decorating tube to fill deviled eggs or celery. It gives them a decorative look.

A bit of salt sprinkled in the frying pan will prevent fish from sticking to the pan while it is frying.

To make carrot curls, slice very thin lengthwise. Drop in ice water. The curl is natural and permanent.

Scoop out ice cream balls with an ice cream dipper or serving spoon, then roll them in long shreds of moist coconut or chopped English walnuts. Keep frozen until ready to serve. Just before serving, drizzle chocolate sauce over the top.

Both sliced bananas and undrained mandarin oranges are good, but try combining the two and sprinkling coconut over the top for a special treat.

For an extra sweet sandwich, use honey, and the same amount of peanut butter mixed together.

When gingerbread or applesauce cake comes back for the second time, you might dress it up with an elegant soft custard sauce.

It is easy to cut cake layers if you place a length of sewing thread all the way around midway along the layer edge. Pull on the ends until the layer is cut in half, and there should be no crumbs.

To keep marshmallows soft after opening, place them in a can with a slice of bread. Close the lid tightly.

Use a wooden spoon when stirring a mixture that is cooking on top of the stove. The handle of such a spoon stays cool to the touch. Too, sometimes a metallic taste could be given to the food.

If you have an old-fashioned ice pick on hand, it can be used for many other things. Test baked potatoes and squash for doneness; even use it to pierce the center of pies to check doneness. It can be used the same way for checking vegetables cooking on top of the stove. It also is good to test the doneness of roast turkey by sliding the point into the bird at the thigh, against the body. This does not harm the. meat but releases just enough juice to tell whether there is any pink.

Maybe you would like to have a make ahead white sauce. Combine one cup flour, one cup margarine, two and a half cups powdered milk and three teaspoons of salt. Blend until mixture has a crumbly texture and store it in the refrigerator. When needed, add half cup mixture to one cup boiling water and you are ready to make white sauce.

Electricity may be saved by shutting off the burner early so that the food can continue to cook without actually using the current. Burners stay hot quite sometime after they are turned off.

* * *

A Thought To Ponder: Many receive advice, only the wise profit from it.

* * *

Peanut Butter Candy

1 package butterscotch bits
1 cup nutty peanut butter

Melt the two ingredients together in the top of a double boiler. Stir. Drop by spoonfuls on cookie sheet. Refrigerate. Happy eating!

All in a Woman's Day--June 6, 1989
Diverse uses of mustard

Mustard! Really that doesn't sound very exciting or appetizing; however, with summer weather now in the picture and picnics happening, it is an important part of the food story. For many folks, mustard has been a favorite seasoning or condiment for a long time.

The word "mustard" is derived from the old French mostarde or moustard that meant a condiment made from the mustard seed and must, which was the juice of grapes or other fruit before and during fermentation.

This herb has a long and colorful history, both culinary and medicinal. Pliny the elder, the first century A.D. Roman writer, reportedly noted it to be effective in curing hysterical females, those who swoon from epilepsy or lethargy and those from any deep seated pains in any part of the body. In the latter part of the Middle Ages, mustard was prized as a cold cure, a therapy, by the way, that is still popular in some rural areas. No doubt many of you can recall your mother or grandmother making a mustard plaster and putting it on your chest to cure a cold or a deep seated cough.

Too, one of the most enthusiastic supporters of the use of mustard was John Evelyn, a 17th century Englishman, who wrote a treatise on "Sallets" (salads), in which he claimed that mustard, both the seed and the leaf, is of "incomparable effect to quicken and revive the spirits, strengthen the mem-

ory, expelling heaviness and preventing the Vertiginous Palsie." In short, he was writing that it was a necessary ingredient to all cold and raw "sallets," noting that it is very seldom, if at all, to be left out.

The Chinese used mustard for thousands of years, and the volcanic mixture we gingerly dab on egg rolls today is actually brown Oriental mustard combined with cold water and stirred to make a paste.

Mustard is the common name applied to pungent herbs of the pepper order, especially to several members of genus brassica, cultivated for the seed. This large family includes many well-known vegetables such as Brussels sprouts, broccoli, Chinese cabbage, collards, kale, kohlrabi, red cabbage, turnips and rutabagas.

The common hedge mustard has pinnate leaves, small yellow flowers and firm, thick walled pods. It grows as a weed in coastal regions of the United States. The tumble mustard has pinnatifid leaves, pale yellow flowers and long, rigid pods and grows abundantly as a pernicious weed.

The mustard of commerce is prepared mostly from black mustard and white mustard. Black mustard is a hirsute plant two to three feet high and has dark green lyre and lance shaped leaves, small yellow flowers and short pods. The seeds are dark brown and have a pungent odor. It is commonly found along the roadsides and wastelands throughout our country. White mustard is a somewhat smaller plant and has large flowers, pinnately lobed leaves, bristly pods and pale seeds. Another important member of the genus family is curled mustard that has crisp, cleft leaves and is used as salad greens, pot herbs and as a cooked vegetable.

Rather unique among the spices, unlike other aromatics, powdered mustard is no more redolent than corn starch as long as it is dry; however, mix it with cold water and it makes your senses tingle. Therefore, a wise cook makes only as much as needed if using the powdered variety. In just about 25 minutes after mixing the mustard, flavor fades with exposure to the air and room temperature.

Powdered mustard is used in preparing meats, gravies, sauces, creamed fish and vegetables, also in egg and cheese dishes, potato salad and molasses cookies.

Mustard plant species most commonly used for greens are known as leaf, Indian or Chinese mustard. The leaves are of many sizes and shapes. Some of the best known varieties include Elephant Ear, with large plain leaves, and Fordhook Fancy and Southern curly leafed varieties. The leaves have a peppery flavor and are boiled as a pot herb or used raw, chopped and added to green salads. Whole mustard seeds of the black and white plants are used for pickling, in boiling fish and vegetables and as a garnish for salads.

Prepared or table mustard, made from the powdered black and white mustard seeds, is mixed with water, vinegar and sometimes other seasonings. It is widely used as a table condiment and in cooking. There also are yellow mustard seeds used for seasoning.

In checking on the kinds of prepared mustards available at our local markets, you will find sweet, hot, spicy brown, stone ground, natural stone ground, horseradish, Dijon, mild yellow, herb, pure, Jalapeno and salad, and, of course, there could be other varieties. Some of the more highly seasoned mustards are Dusselford, English, German and Bohemian, with Creole or Louisiana and most other standard American types of the more milder kinds.

* * *

A Thought To Ponder: Cheerfulness is the atmosphere in which all things thrive.

* * *

Mustard and Mayonnaise

1 cup mayonnaise
2 teaspoons prepared mustard

Stir together until mixed. This combination is good to use on sandwiches, salads, vegetables and seafood.

All in a Woman's Day--June 13, 1989

Father's Day memories become more precious

As the years pass, memories of fathers become more precious, especially as their special day approaches. Possibly, according to age, we find ourselves recalling and using many things he taught as we were growing up, things that have stayed with us through the years.

Whether you call this special guy, father, dad, pop, daddy or whatever name you lovingly use, you can no doubt remember some of the "words of wisdom" that he often quoted. For instance, if he wasn't feeling well, he would say, "I'm under the weather." or, if feeling good he would remark. "I'm fit as a fiddle." Often he would describe city relatives who came visiting on the farm as "green as gourds." Whenever an off color joke was told out of place, he would say, "laughing on the other side of your face." The village Beau Brummel was referred to as "feeling his oats." If something proved to be too much for handling he would say, "They can't cut the mustard," or, if handling a situation well, he would comment, "Cool as a cucumber."

He would describe some folks as "sheepish looking," "skinny as a rail," "crooked as a snake," "can't be trusted as far as you can throw an elephant by the tail," "when they passed out brains, he was out to lunch," or "ugly as a mud fence."

Should action be insisted, whether prepared or not, he would say, "You won't last until the water gets hot," or, if a problem arose and not knowing where to commence, he would say he was "caught in the middle of the fence."

Also some of the expressions included "slow as the seven-year itch," "stubborn as an old gray mule," "poor as Job's turkey," "fools step in where angels fear to tread," and "he who lives in a glass house should not throw stones."

And speaking of money he would say "a penny saved is a penny earned," "great spenders are bad lenders," "two can live as cheap as one," "pennywise and pound foolish," "God helps those that help themselves," "never spend your money before you have it," "you always get what you pay for," and "don't judge a man by his worth."

The lives of old-timers were built around the many quotes that come from yesteryear. In speaking of children, he might say, "bright as a dollar," "sharp as a tack," "a regular show stopper," "knee high to a grasshopper," "little pitchers have big ears."

He also would say that you "need to practice what you preach," "haste makes waste," "there are two things for sure—death and taxes," "jack of all trades and master of none." If someone sort of piddled, he would say, "let's get with it."

No doubt many of you will remember some of these wise sayings; remembering Dad sometimes looking stern, sometimes with a smile touching the corner of his mouth and sometimes with a twinkle in his eye.

Rick L. Falk, a former television actor, drew up six "Beautitudes for Father". They are as follows:

Blessed is he who is given the ability to discern between needs and wants and the wisdom to choose wisely, for he and his family will reap the reward of prudence.

Blessed is he whose feet leave the soiled problems of his work day at the doormat of our Lord, for he will discover room in his heart to listen to the needs of others.

Blessed is he who dries the dishes of despair with the towel of tenderness, for he will find no lack of comfort from him who loves us all.

Blessed is he who foregoes the round of golf to become companion to his children, for a legacy of memories is bequeathed in these happy hours.

Blessed is he who trims the hedge of misunderstanding between himself and his neighbor, for the blossom of friendship has a sweet and lasting fragrance.

Blessed is he whose home is built upon the word of God, for his roof will be shingled with happiness and all who pass will see the goodness of the Lord.

* * *

A Thought To Ponder: There's a blessing on the hearth, a special providence for fatherhood.

—Robert Browning

* * *

Happy Father's Day to all Father's everywhere!

All in a Woman's Day--June 20, 1989

Secret ingredient is good buttermilk

Great-grandma cooked with buttermilk because she knew it made baked goods great, light, even textured and delicious! Buttermilk is every good cook's secret ingredient!

Since this is Dairy Month, it might be well to learn a little bit more about buttermilk. I am sure many of you use buttermilk in cooking. Most homemakers enjoy using this product for the results are a general better texture, the leavening is improved, with baked goods seemingly lighter and it also is more flavorful.

According to a nutritionist, buttermilk is misnamed; it should be called unbuttermilk.

This special milk, that is tart, generally the thickened liquid with the rich sounding name, is the residue leftover from churning butter. It is really cream with most of the fat removed.

Buttermilk is nutritious and is low in saturated fat; however, it is high in protein. Too, it has only about half the calories of whole milk. It is a boon to bakers!

That is a pretty good resume, don't you think, for a food that was once used mostly for "feeding the pigs."

In the earlier days of our country, almost everyone churned butter, and those who didn't made arrangements to purchase it. Generally, once a week, a nice mound or rectangular pound of butter, with a fancy emblem, would be delivered to their homes.

The fresh buttermilk, with flecks of butter floating around, was saved from churning. It made a delightful beverage and was wonderful for cooking.

Later, after the dairy industry modernized in the early decade of this century, most of the making of butter was shifted to rural creameries; the buttermilk was discarded or used for "slopping" the hogs.

Back in the 1940s, creameries began to dry the buttermilk and sell it in powdered form to commercial bakeries.

The cultured buttermilk in the dairy cases today also became available. This product is made of skim milk, thickened and acidified by adding lactic acid bacteria and bits of butterfat.

In more recent times a firm developed a powdered buttermilk made with real churned buttermilk and cultured with lactic acid to give the acidity needed.

Modern dairy scientists know why

buttermilk enhances most baked goods. It works in two ways: First, the acid content that is created by natural clabbering or by the addition of the lactic acid, reacts with alkaline baking soda or yeast and provides the additional leavening needed, thus making lighter cakes and breads. Secondly, the natural emulsifiers known as phospholipids, created by the churning process, disperses shortening more uniformly throughout the batter, creating what bakers refer to as "fine crumb."

Real buttermilk, you will find, whether powdered or a by-product of churning, acts as a leavening agent and an emulsifier; however, cultured buttermilk made from skim milk, does not contain the free phospholipids, thus causing it to just mostly enhance the leavening.

To use buttermilk powder in quick breads and cakes that call for regular milk, be sure and use four tablespoons buttermilk powder and one cup water to replace each cup of milk called for in the recipe; however, remember, too, that for each cup of liquid, to decrease the baking powder called for in the recipe by two teaspoons and add a half teaspoon of baking soda. Thus you will have the correct proportions, allowing the buttermilk to react with the soda and in turn to create a leavening.

If you need to substitute for one cup buttermilk, you can use one cup yogurt, which is fermented milk.

Keep in mind that buttermilk is the product that remains after sweet or sour milk has been churned and the fat removed. The cultured buttermilk is the soured product after pasteurized skimmed milk is treated with a suitable lactic acid bacteria culture.

* * *

A Thought To Ponder: A cookbook is a volume that is brimful of stirring passages.

All in a Woman's Day--June 27, 1989
Luscious eating comes from nectarines

Fresh California nectarines have arrived on the market in plentiful supply and they would make a delightful breakfast treat.

Just dice some of those juicy, colorful nectarines the night before using them so they will be ready for breakfast time serving. You might want to add some sugar and something to keep them from turning brown.

The season for this luscious fruit begins in May and lasts through September; however, the most abundant supply is available from July through August. Nectarines are a cross between a peach and a plum; however, some plant breeders believe that nectarines predate peaches.

Before World War II, this fruit took a back seat to their genetic cousins, the peaches; however, with the introduction of a new nectarine variety, the LeGrand, nectarines took off.

After 30 years of struggling for a foothold on the market, the California nectarines have now come into their own and have been outranking the California peaches in volume. They are no longer a victim of the "second fruit" syndrome.

The LeGrand nectarine is the father of every single modern nectarine varie-

669

ty, and at this time there are about 150 varieties. Fred Anderson is the father of the nectarine. A disciple of Luther Burbank, he did his plant breeding work near Merced, in the Central Valley of California. In addition, he also contributed much to the development of dozens of other plants—peaches, plums and roses.

It is agreed that the first nectarines grew thousands of years ago on the continent of Asia as did peaches; however, it has been found that these two fruits are intertwined.

Darwin has written that nectarines may spring from peach stones and peaches from nectarine stones. But who knows which came first. Hedrick, a famous plant specialist, has been quoted as saying that the nectarine, rather than the peach, represents the true ancestral form.

Not only Americans are California nectarine lovers, but according to statics last year for the first time in history, nectarines were allowed to be exported to the Orient.

The fruit must be picked mature; however, they cannot be completely ripe in order to survive picking, packaging and shipping. To completely ripen them use a California ripening bowl or a loosely closed paper bag. Then wait a few days, might even check every day to be sure, then upon touching the fruit, if it yields to the gentle palm pressure ... it is ready to eat.

One advantage of a nectarine is that it has a thin, tender skin that can be eaten along with the fruit; however, it can be slipped off by submerging it under boiling water for about 30 seconds, removing with a slotted spoon and then plunging it into cold water.

Nectarines are harder to grow than peaches. The fine, glossy skin is susceptible to hail damage, insect marks and various blemishes.

The name nectarine comes from nektar, the Olympic god's drink of choice. It is often referred to as "sweet and delicious."

The varieties that existed 50 years ago are no longer in existence, including the Jon Rivers and Quetta. Current varieties are May Grand, Firebrite and Spring Red. Maybelle is the earliest variety, with P-R Red the latest.

They are high in vitamin A, have some fiber, only 65 calories, no fat, no cholesterol, only a trace of sodium, with 271 milligrams of potassium.

Nectarines can be used raw for hand eating; cut up in fresh fruit salads, used in compotes and in tarts. Cooked, they can be used in any of the desserts and preserves that call for peaches.

* * *

A Thought To Ponder: We are all faced with a series of great opportunities brilliantly disguised as impossible situation.

* * *

Country Nectarine Jam
6 medium fresh California nectarines, finely grated
1 1/2 cups carrots, finely grated
4 cups sugar
1/4 cup lemon juice
1/4 teaspoon cinnamon
Combine all ingredients in large pot. Bring them to a boil; cook 40 minutes, stirring occasionally or until thickened

and mixture registers 220 degrees on candy thermometer. Pour into hot jars. Adjust caps. Process 15 minutes in boiling water bath. Cool. Makes 4 1/2 to 5 cups of jam.

All in a Woman's Day--July 3, 1989
Angel food cake ... is a heavenly delight

With summer days here, as well as Fourth of July time, homemakers might want to think of something to prepare that is easy, low in calories and delightful to eat!

How about angel food cake? It just might be the answer to the dessert problem.

This is to be a two-part column on angel cakes.

First, be sure to make your angel food the day before you plan to serve it; this way it can "ripen" to a finer texture and flavor.

The air incorporated into angel food cake batter is the leavening agent. When the egg whites are beaten, the sugar-flour mixture gently folded into them and the accurate oven temperature used—all of this helps to incorporate and keep the air in the batter.

There are a few tips to remember when preparing the angel food cake batter:

Never grease the pan unless specified; all utensils must be free of any kind of grease.

When the cake springs back, it is done.

If a brown crust is desired, remove cake from pan when it is completely cooled, as the longer the cooled cake is kept in the pan, the more crust will adhere to the pan.

An angel food may be cooled by slipping the tube pan over a tall glass bottle (soda) filled with warm water.

Too, when beating egg whites, do not tap beater on the bowl in which they are being beaten. The jar of the beater will cause the whites to lose a great deal of fluffiness. The beater should be tapped on the hand to clear off the whites.

Possibly you might have some problems such as the ones following:

If your cake is tough, perhaps your oven was too hot or the cake was overmixed.

If a coarse texture occurs, the egg whites possibly have been underbeaten or not sufficiently mixed.

A sticky crust is the result of insufficient baking, and an undersized cake can be caused by removing cake from pan before cooling, oven too hot, overmixing, underbeaten or overbeaten egg whites or perhaps the pan was too large.

You might keep all of these things in mind when you bake your angel food cake from scratch. (I'll admit it is mighty easy to just open a cake mix! But no doubt the taste is well worth the extra work.)

If you want to make an angel food roll make half the recipe and pour into a shallow pan, 10x15-inches lined with wax paper. Bake 20 minutes at 325 degrees and fill as for jelly roll.

You can spread it with lemon or orange filling or a thick layer of vanilla ice cream soft enough to spread but not melted, or some filling of your own choosing. Roll it up, serve with or without a sauce. Or you might spread it with whipped cream or whipped topping flavored with vanilla, instant coffee, maple syrup or chocolate. Chopped nuts also may be used.

You can make coconut snowballs by cutting angel food cake in three-inch cubes or pulling into irregular pieces. Roll them in seven-minute frosting, then in coconut. Place on waxed paper to dry.

* * *

A Thought To Ponder: A day hemmed in prayer is less likely to unravel.

* * *

There are several versions of angel food cake, with some requiring six, eight or 12 eggs. This recipe calls for 12 egg whites.

Angel Food Cake

1 cup sifted cake flour
3/4 cup sugar
1 1/2 cups (12) egg whites
1 1/2 teaspoons cream of tartar
1/4 teaspoon salt
1 1/2 teaspoons vanilla
3/4 cup sugar

Sift flour and 3/4 cup of sugar together two times; set them aside. Beat egg whites with cream of tartar, salt and vanilla until stiff enough to form soft peak, but still glossy and moist. Add remaining 3/4 cup sugar, 2 tablespoons at a time, continuing to beat until egg whites hold stiff peaks. Sift about 1/4 of flour mixture over whites and fold in. Repeat, folding by fourths. Bake in an ungreased 10-inch tube pan at 375 degrees for 35 to 40 minutes, or until done when tested. Invert cake in pan to cool.

Variation:
Chocolate Angel Cake

Prepare angel food cake, substituting 3/4 cup of sifted cake flour and 1/4 cup cocoa (regular type) for 1 cup sifted cake flour. Sift cocoa with flour and sugar two times.

All in a Woman's day--July 11, 1989
Mock angel foods also good eating

This is the second part of information on angel food cakes. This part concerns Mock Angel Food Cakes and Hot Milk Cakes.

Perhaps you won't agree, but an angel food cake can be made from two egg whites. This is called a Mock or Hot Milk Angel Food. There are several versions that I will give:

Mock Angel Foods

First: Sift together 1 1/3 cups cake flour, 1 cup sugar, 1/4 teaspoon salt and 2 teaspoons baking powder in a mixing bowl. Beat 2 egg whites; stir 2/3 cups of scalded milk gradually into the dry ingredients; add 1 teaspoon vanilla. Fold in stiffly beaten egg whites and pour mixture into an ungreased tube cake pan. Bake in a moderate oven, 350 degrees, for 45 minutes. Cool as for a regular angel cake.

Second: 1 cup sugar, 1 1/3 cups flour, 1/2 teaspoon cream of tartar, 1/3 teaspoon salt, 3 teaspoons baking powder, 1 teaspoon vanilla, 2/3 cup scalded milk, 3 egg whites. Sift the dry ingredients four times; add hot milk very slowly, beating continually. Add vanilla and fold in egg whites beaten until light. Turn into an ungreased angel food cake pan and bake in a very slow oven, 300 to 325 degrees, 25 to 30 minutes, until tested done. (The supplier of this recipe said that she does not use an angel food cake pan and has good results.)

Third: Sift 7 times—2 cups sugar, 2 cups cake flour, 1/2 teaspoon salt. Add 1 cup boiling water and let it stand until cold. Beat 5 egg whites until frothy and add 1 teaspoon cream of tartar, 2 teaspoons baking powder and beat again, then fold into the first mixture 1 teaspoon vanilla. Pour into an angel food cake pan and bake it 1 hour in a 350 degree oven.

Fourth: Sift 5 times—2 cups sugar, 2 cups flour; add 1 cup hot water; mix thoroughly and add 1 teaspoon vanilla or other flavoring (some like almond or lemon). In another bowl, beat 5 egg whites until fluffy; add 1 teaspoon of cream of tartar and beat again, add 2 teaspoons of baking powder and beat this until stiff. Fold first mixture into last mixture lightly. Bake in three layers in a moderate oven about 375 degrees for 25 minutes or until slightly brown. Put together with a favorite frosting. Coconut filling is good with this cake.

* * *

A Thought To Ponder: I know well that happiness is in little things.
—John Ruskin

* * *

This is a bit different recipe for angel food cake that you might enjoy.

Brown Sugar Angel Food

1 1/2 cups egg whites
2 teaspoons vanilla
1 1/2 teaspoons cream of tartar
1 teaspoon salt
2 cups brown sugar
1 1/4 cups sifted cake flour

Beat egg whites and vanilla, cream of tartar and salt until peaks form. Gradually sift 1 cup of brown sugar over egg whites and beat until stiff peaks form. Sift remaining cup of sugar with cake flour. Fold into egg whites. Pour into ungreased 10-inch tube cake pan. Bake in 350 degree oven 45 to 50 minutes.

Frosting: Blend 1/2 cup butter, 2 1/2 tablespoons flour and 1/4 teaspoon salt in saucepan. Cook this 1 minute—do not let brown. Add 1/2 cup milk and cook it until thick, stirring continuously. Remove the mixture from the heat and add 1/2 cup brown sugar. Beat well. Add 2 cups powdered sugar, sifted. Beat until thick. Add 1 teaspoon vanilla and 1 cup chopped black walnuts. Mix well. This frosting freezes well.

All in a Woman's Day--July 18, 1989
The bags ... 'have it'!

It's in the bag! Yes, I think you could say that there are so many things that we use paper and plastic bags for nowadays that sometimes we wonder just how we ever managed without them.

One of the first things to do is to purchase some different sized brown paper bags at the supermarket to do some of the things for which you might need to use a clean, fresh bag. Then there are things that you can put into your plain brown bag in which your groceries were bagged.

A brown bag is nice for flouring chicken and meat. Just drop in a few pieces at a time in the seasoned flour and shake the bag. The pieces will come out evenly coated.

Place an onion in a plastic bag and put it into the freezer 15 minutes before using or into the fridge the day before. This way you will reduce the spray of oils when the onion is cut and your eyes won't shed tears.

When crushing crackers or wafers, place them in a plastic or brown bag, use the side of a meat tenderizer hammer or the rolling pin and pound or roll the crackers into crumbs. The mess stays inside the bag. You might even make some extra crumbs while at it and refrigerate them in a plastic bag until ready to use.

If you want to coat bacon, it too, can be dropped into a brown bag to which flour has been added. Bacon, flour coated, will not splatter and shrink as much when prepared this way; then just fry as usual.

Fresh parsley or sweet basil tastes elegant with Italian food. Wash and use a towel for drying; then chop into desired sizes, placing them into plastic bags and then pop them into the freezer. They can be used anytime of the year and you will find that they defrost easily.

To reheat rolls, just sprinkle, rather lightly, with warm water, and place them into a paper bag, closing tightly. Heat in a 350 degree oven 10 to 15 minutes.

For ripening fruit—bananas, nectarines, peaches, as well as tomatoes—place them in a paper bag and keep in a warm place.

Make sure mushrooms are dry, then store them in a brown paper bag where the moisture will be confined and they will be allowed to breathe. This keeps them fresh longer. Do not place them in a plastic bag as this will make them slimy.

Since asparagus is so expensive, make sure that it is taken care of properly. Place uncooked stalks in a deep pot along with some ice water and place it in a plastic bag. Keep this in the refrigerator until ready to cook it, and the stalks should stay firm.

To keep cheese, just grate it and then store it in plastic bags in the refrigerator. This saves time when you need some in a hurry.

Vegetables also may be stored in self-sealing plastic bags after they have been cleaned and prepared. Heavier plastic bags are great for freezing fruits and vegetables.

When grinding foods that might fly about, just tie a paper bag over the mouth of the grinder to catch the bits and pieces.

Sandwich bags, of course, are for taking a sandwich to work or to a picnic. The sandwiches can be prepared ahead of time and refrigerated in the bag.

Hamburger patties also can be made by using sandwich bags. Place the amount of meat needed for each pattie in a bag and then flatten.

Remove paper from a frozen steak by placing it in a plastic bag and pouring hot water over it. The paper should peel right off.

For maximum flavor, appearance and nutritive value, store raisins in an airtight plastic bag and refrigerate to prevent them from drying out. If stored properly raisins will last up to 15 months.

* * *

A Thought To Ponder: Those who bring sunshine to the lives of others cannot keep it from themselves.

* * *

Easy Baked Turkey
1 frozen turkey, thawed
Salt and pepper to taste
3 tablespoons paprika
1/8 cup hot water (2 tablespoons)
1 cup peanut oil

Wash turkey and prepare for cooking. Season inside and outside of the turkey with salt and pepper. Dissolve paprika in water; blend in peanut oil. Baste turkey generously with oil mixture; greasing well. Place turkey in bag, breast side up; tie the end of the bag and place it in a baking pan. Bake in a preheated 325 degree oven for 15 minutes per pound approximatley. Test for doneness.

All in a Woman's Day--July 25, 1989
Put bags to good use

"It's all in the Bag" is a continuation with more suggestions offered for using brown or plastic bags in your everyday housework.

When purchasing a large bag of charcoal briquettes, separate them into several small brown paper bags and fold over the tops. Then when you are ready to start the fire, just place the bag in the grill and light a match. The heat from the burning paper lights the charcoal quickly.

When going on a trip, water your plants well and then cover them with a large plastic bag, making it airtight. The plants will go several weeks without having to be watered. Too, when you travel you might put your cosmetics and small items in a see through zipper bag.

If going on a trip, try packaging your medication in a sandwich bag. Fix a bag for each day you plan to be away and you will be in good shape, without having to dig around for your medication.

If you like to do the "search and find" puzzles, cut them out and place them in a clear plastic bag to take with you the next time you have an appointment; should you have to wait you will find waiting much more enjoyable.

Who would have thought there would be so many uses for bags? I'm sure that there are many more.

We wonder how we ever existed in earlier years without bags, especially plastic ones.

A paper bag manufacturing machine was developed in 1859 by William Goodale of Clinton, Mass.; however, up until that time groceries were placed in a cornucopia twist of paper, carried in containers or baskets taken along to the store, or carried in their arms.

Then in 1883, Charles Stilwell of Philadelphia made additional paper bag history when he invented a bag with pleats on the sides and a flat bottom. This improved bag would stand up when opened.

Then came plastic bags of various kinds; however, the history of plastics began about 1860, and continued through the years with various phases from 1895, 1909, 1929, 1940 and the late 1950s, with many more changes in later years. Work still is being done to bring better products and more of them into focus.

And, "It's all in the bag," seems most appropriate to say.

* * *

A Thought To Ponder: The stillness of nature speaks louder than a choir of voices.

* * *

Paper Bag Apple Pie

1 unbaked 9-inch pie shell
3-4 medium apples
2 tablespoons flour
1/2 cup sugar
1/2 teaspoon nutmeg
2 tablespoons lemon juice

Peel, core and quarter apples. Then cut each quarter in half cross-wise— you should have about 7 cups apples. Place them in large bowl. Combine sugar, flour and nutmeg and sprinkle this over apples. Toss to coat. Spoon into pastry shell. Drizzle with lemon juice. Top with the following mixture.

Topping

1/2 cup sugar
1/2 cup flour
1/2 cup butter or margarine

Work ingredients together until crumbly. Sprinkle over apples to cover top. Slide pie into a heavy brown paper bag, large enough to cover it loosely. Fold open end twice and fasten with paper clips. Place on large cookie sheet for easy handling. Bake it in a 425 degree oven one hour. Apples will be tender and the top bubbly and golden. Split bag open, remove pie, cool on wire rack and serve plain or with cheese or ice cream.

Enjoy versatile plums

August seems to be the month when fragrant, delicious plums, especially the darker skinned varieties, are most abundant.

Plums are grown on every continent, except Antarctic, and they may be the world's most versatile fruit.

Victorian lore claims that plum trees represent both fidelity and genius.

In the event you haven't noticed, the Japanese calendar of flowers, gave an entire month, February, designated to plums.

Belonging to the rose family, this fruit is distinguished from the peach, its near relative, by its smooth skin and unwrinkled stone.

Somehow this humble fruit pops up heroically in nursery rhymes—the Lion and the Unicorn and Little Jack Horner. According to the rhyme, the lion and the unicorn were making general nuisances of themselves in a certain town, fighting for the crown, until someone gave them, among other things, a plum cake that sent them out-of-town.

This fruit also has worked its way into American vernacular, and you can get "plum tired" or "plum crazy."

Speaking of color, plums comes in an array of colors, shapes, and sizes and more than 200 varieties, making an attractive eye-catching display in the markets.

The smallest of California's favorite and famous summer fruits, they are loaded with nutrition. They provide vitamins A and C, potassium, fiber and lots of refreshing water. They are a good source of quick energy as their carbohydrate content and the fiber makes for a feeling of fullness. All this for only 33 calories in a plum!

Speaking generally, the elongated blue varieties are European, and the red, black, purple and green are Japanese. The eastern states are especially suited to the cultivation of European plums, including such varieties as Lombard, Greengage and Damsons. Remember the delicious tiny blue Damson? They made such elegant jam, as well as the sweet small yellow-red sugarplums and the Kelseys.

Japanese plums are widely grown in the southern states, North as far as Vermont and West to California.

The majority of the California plum crop is made up of the Japanese plums.

Before 1870, there were no large red or crimson plums in the United States. It was the wherewith and curiosity of a gardener in Santa Rosa, Calif., Luther Burbank, who began the Japanese plum industry. Plums seem to be the passion of this great horticulturist and fruit historian and was called "his most lasting success." Burbank named his plums like Santa Rosa and Burbank, which would seem logical. However, Willard Sharpe, Vacaville, Calif., another fruit developer, named his creation of plums after old girl friends, and when he ran out of girl friends, he named them after counties in California.

This stone fruit has been grown for fresh consumption longer than either peaches or nectarines. Today's top five plum varieties, coming from California, where between 90 and 95 percent of the plums are raised, with the exception of Burbank's Santa Rosa, were introduced in the last 30 years. The others are Friar, Red Beaut, Casselman and Simka, all Japanese varieties. Another popular variety, however, is the Laroda, and it is said to be an excellent plum for cooking.

The Myrobalan is a prune like fruit that includes the weeping plum or the cherry plum type.

* * *

A Thought To Ponder: In every problem are the seeds of its solution.

* * *

Plum Tapioca

2 3/4 tablespoons quick cooking tapioca
6 tablespoons sugar
1 tablespoon butter
1 egg, well beaten
2 cups water
1/4 teaspoon salt
1/2 teaspoon vanilla flavoring
1 cup drained, canned plums

Rub plums through sieve. Combine tapioca, water and salt and cook until transparent. Combine sugar and egg and add to tapioca. Cook 5 minutes. Add butter, plums and flavoring. Cook this mixture 5 minutes. Remove from heat. Chill. Makes 6 servings.

All in a Woman's Day--August 8, 1989
Plums make precious bits for summer goodness

Plums are those "precious bits of goodness" on the market from mid-May through September.

When you are shopping, beware of the very large fat plums for they are not necessarily the best.

All of the California varieties fall

into two categories, Japanese and European.

The skin color of the Japanese plums that mature early and into mid season, range from yellow to red. The flesh is juicy and tart.

The crimson skinned Santa Rosa, also a Japanese hybrid, has remained the most popular California plum since it was developed at the turn of the century.

European plums, most abundant at mid season, were brought to California missions by way of Spain and Mexico. They come in shades of blue to purple and tend to be sweeter and slightly smaller.

Washington, Oregon and Utah supply small purple prune plums that are most readily available from mid August through September. Also known as Italian prune plums, the oval shaped fruit is freestones, meaning that the stone separates freely from the fruit. This plum is excellent in desserts, sauces, sherberts and as an accompaniment to roast poultry and pork. Because they are firm fleshed and meaty, the Italian prune plums also make great jams and preserves, requiring a short cooking time.

Dried prunes are made from freestone plums, such as the Italian prune plum. When this variety is cooked for a long time, they tend to taste similar to a prune, however, they are less sweet.

When purchasing prune plums, always look for fruit that is almost ripe, with skin free of wrinkles and blemishes, that yields lightly to pressure to the palm and is slightly soft at the tip. It has been said that plums will not ripen if picked green. For prune plums it is recommended that if the plums are not quite as ripe as desired, place them in a loosely closed paper bag at room temperature. When the desired ripeness is reached, and be sure to keep check closely, store immediately in plastic bags in the refrigerator. You might try this with other plums and see if it will work.

The medium prune plums average only 20 calories each.

Plums do not have to be peeled, regardless of how they are used.

For starters you can use plums in popsicles, adding pureed fruit to lemonade and freezing; in plum punch by adding coarsely chopped plums to cranberry juice and whirling in the blender; for a fruit platter with other fresh fruits sliced to dip in fudge and marshmallow sauces; in shortcakes using plums with a small amount of sugar to form juice; serving on a split biscuit with cream; and for ice cream bars that are made by combining chopped plums with softened vanilla ice cream between oatmeal cookies and frozen. Then there are breads, cakes, pies, compotes, jams, jellies, preserves; salads and hand eating. So, you can see that plums are versatile.

Whatever variety of plums you choose, it will probably have a light dusting on its skin and this is called "bloom." This occurs naturally as nature's own protective coating and is perfectly safe to eat.

* * *

A Thought To Ponder: Like life, few gardens have only flowers.

***

Plum Conserve

2 pounds Italian plums
1 cup seedless raisins
1 medium orange
3 cups sugar
1/2 cup coarsely chopped walnuts

Pit plums; grind all fruits; add sugar and bring this to a boil. Cook it until thick, about 10 minutes. Stir in the nuts. Pour it into hot scalded jars. Seal; makes 6 half pints.

All in a Woman's Day--August 15, 1989

Try cutting it up!

Do you like to cut up? Do you have cutting ways? Are you on the cutting edge? Do you need some snip tips? Whatever it is in the way of cutting, you'll find help here.

If you want butter to be cut so it comes out in really nice, clean squares, just place waxed paper over the knife blade.

No special gadget is needed to cut pizza … just use your kitchen shears … they are a great substitute.

Pinking shears also can often be used for cutting out patches for kids' play clothes and work clothes; pinking the bottom edges of shirts and blouses that are worn inside skirts and pants. It makes the line smoother and less bulky.

Double the life of flowers by cutting their stems at a long slant … this way they absorb more water.

Scissors are just right for cutting a variety of sticky fruits, such as raisins, dates and figs. Just dip the scissors in water every now and then during the cutting process. Another sticky food that scissors are good for cutting is marshmallows. Dip the scissors in hot water.

A grapefruit knife is ideal for cutting and hollowing out vegetables or fruits for stuffing.

Cutting fresh bread is always difficult to manage; however, it is easier if you use a thin bladed knife that has been heated. Too, a heated knife or scissors should be used to cut warm coffee cake.

We always want our party variety of sandwiches to be especially dainty, with nice shapes and smooth edges. This can be accomplished by using scissors instead of a knife. You will find an electric knife also is very good for cutting tender, delicate sandwiches.

Kitchen shears are wonderful for snipping things: Fresh herbs for measuring; cutting up poultry; trimming excess pastry from around a pie plate and cutting off fat from meat and poultry.

Cheese can be cut easily with a heated knife. A piece of waxed paper placed over the knife blade helps in turning out even slices.

Meringue on a pie can be a rather difficult thing to handle sometimes and often sticks to a knife blade. To help avoid this problem you can either sprinkle sugar over the meringue, when baking, cut pie with a knife blade that has been dipped in cold water or butter the knife blade.

Never cut salad greens with a knife as it bruises them and makes them bitter. Just gently tear them by hand into bite size pieces.

Onions are really tear-jerkers. Try this method and see how well the tears are controlled: Cut an end slice from a peeled onion, then cut the exposed surface of the entire onion into tiny squares by slicing into the onion to any desired depth, then cutting crosswise into thin slices.

Cake sometimes can be rather trying to cut. To avoid crumbly cake slices, try heating the knife blade in very hot water. Then, without wiping it dry, slice the cake.

Often cutting a sky-high angel food cake can be a disaster. This delicate cake needs careful attention. Instead of a knife, try using a wire thread, a piece of silk thread held taut, or even try just plain everyday thread, again held tightly.

* * *

A Thought To Ponder: When you are through changing, you are through.

* * *

Lemon Dessert

1/2 cup nut meats, crushed
1 cup flour
1 stick margarine

Mix the margarine with the flour until crumbly. Add nut meats. Spread and pat into a 9x13-inch pan. Bake at 375 degrees about 20 to 25 minutes. Watch so it doesn't get too brown. Cool.

1 (8-ounce) carton whipped topping
1 cup powdered sugar
1 (8-ounce) package cream cheese, softened

Add creamed cheese and powdered sugar to the whipped topping and stir it until smooth. Spread on cooled crust.

2 packages instant lemon pudding
3 cups cold milk

Mix ingredients at low speed with electric mixer 2 minutes or beat by hand. Pour over the cream cheese mixture. Top with whipped topping, and if desired, nuts. This can be made the day before using.

All in a Woman's Day--August 22, 1989
Wild and luscious blueberries delight

Wild and luscious blueberries! So elegant! What good eating!

Blueberries have been on the scene as a part of American cooking since the days of the Indians. This, of course, was long before the Pilgrims landed when the Indians used the berries, the Maine wild blueberries, for eating fresh, cooked, the juice to treat venison before it was smoked, drying for winter use and ground into powder for medicinal purposes.

Of course, it was the Indians who introduced the early settlers to this important, and no doubt, a major part of their food supply. The colonists, too, used this delicious food in various ways.

Related to the huckleberry, they have some interesting and most unlikely relatives. For instance, the cranberry, the mountain laurel and the azalea are related.

There does seem to be a bit of confusion concerning the difference between blueberries and huckleberries since the words are used interchangeably. Generally speaking, the lighter colored berries are called blueberries and the darker, blackish berries, huckleberries. You will find that outside of New England, they are lumped together as huckleberries.

The wild low bush blueberry is harvested by hand with a rake about 18-inches wide, and it is a tedious, back breaking task. The pay is reportedly up to $10 an hour; however, even then growers find it difficult getting enough help to harvest the crop.

Unlike the cultivated blueberries that grow on bushes up to five feet and higher in the Midwestern states, the wild Maine blueberries are not more than a foot high. They grow in large open places called "barren," not in cultivated fields as would be assumed; growing haphazardly, not in rows as the cultivated blueberries grow.

Visitors to Maine this month will have the opportunity to drive by one of that state's most interesting sights, and perhaps will never realize, it is here that the nation's largest crop of blueberries is harvested. Approximately 98 percent of all the wild blueberries come from Maine.

More blueberries are produced throughout the United States in cultivated patches.

In Ellsworth, Me., the center for wild blueberries, some of the locals have been quoted as saying, "God meant blueberries to be."

The native Americans learned that the burning of the fields increased the productivity. No doubt this is one of the few pleasant things that come as the aftermath of a fire. This burned over ground produces the largest amount of berries.

They grow singly or in clusters on mountains or in swamps, with acid soil needed. In their wild state, blueberries are found from the northern tip of Alaska down to Florida. The blueberries grow profusely on other continents, even above the Arctic Circle. Wherever they grow they are highly prized. Bilberries and whortleberries are varieties of blueberries. Huckleberries always grow wild; however, as we know, there are many cultivated varieties of blueberries.

The cultivated blueberries have a rather bland taste in comparison to the delicious wild berries grown in Maine. It is thought that perhaps the exceptional taste of the wild blueberries might come from the mix of berries in each "barren." It seems that one farm might have as many as a thousand varieties and during the harvest they become mixed, thus accounting for the delightful flavor.

* * *

A Thought To Ponder: Love isn't love until you give it away.

* * *

Blueberry Grape Salad

2 packages grape gelatin
1 package pineapple gelatin
3 cups boiling water
1 small can crushed pineapple
1 can blueberry pie filling
1 cup pecans, chopped

Dissolve the gelatins in boiling water and cool. After it thickens, add the other ingredients and chill. Serve with whipped topping.

* * *

Year-Round Blueberry Pie

Pastry for 9-inch pie
3/4 cup sugar
1/3 cup flour
4 cups frozen unsweetened blueberries
2 tablespoons butter

Little lemon juice

Mix sugar and flour then mix with blueberries. Turn this into the bottom crust. Dot with butter, add the lemon juice and top crust, seal and flute. Bake in a preheated 450 degree oven 40 minutes. Serve slightly warm, with scoops of vanilla ice cream or whipped topping.

All in a Woman's Day--August 29, 1989
Blueberries are tops!

Today we are going to take a look at just how delightful blueberries can really be.

A blueberry should be plump and full with a light powdery grayish hue bloom; they should be free of any kind of mold. Good quality fresh blueberries have a shelf life of up to three weeks, that is, of course, if they are given proper care. They are the longest lasting of all berries. The secret is refrigeration.

They can be dry packed frozen at home with little or no loss of flavor, and be kept for as long as two years. To home freeze for a year long use, simply place the berries into your favorite size container and place in the freezer, or you can take the boxes just as they come from the market, tightly cover them with a clear plastic and freeze. Do not wash berries before freezing, otherwise, they will freeze into one solid lump and become mushy when thawed. Correctly, berries should be individually frozen so that they pour freely from the container. Wash them just before using.

Large cultivated blueberries are available fresh from the middle of May through September; however; in processed form they are available the year around. Canned blueberries are available with or without syrup, too.

This special delicacy is low in calories, and believe it or not they are packed with nutrition. There are many varieties and they range in color from blue-black to a purplish-blue.

While traditional blueberry recipes are still part of nearly every cook's repertoire, today consumers are looking for quick and easy blueberry recipes to fit their contemporary lifestyle.

Here are some quick, easy ways of preparing this fruit.

The frosty purple blue of the berries is perfect to use with contrasting colors and flavors of cantaloupe and seedless green grapes for a fruit cup.

For a special occasion you may want to serve the combination with lemon, lime or pineapple sherbert.

Angel food cake may be given similar treatment. Slice the cake into three layers, then put them together again with blueberry studded whipped cream or whipped topping. Frost the entire cake with whipped cream or topping and garnish with a generous amount of blueberries. You can have this ready well ahead of time as it is better if refrigerated several hours.

Perhaps you might like to make a creamy no cook sauce to go with the berries. Blend together three ounces of softened cream cheese, half cup firmly packed light brown sugar; one cup sour cream and a half teaspoon vanilla. This makes one and a fourth cups. Cover and chill. When ready to serve, fill sherbert or parfait glasses with blueberries and top with this tempting sauce.

When cooking blueberries, the larger berries often tend to sink to the bottom of the batter; however, if they are frozen individually and coated with flour before adding to the mixture, this can be prevented.

Ginger, nutmeg, cinnamon and lemon tend to bring out the natural goodness and flavor of the berries. They are available as a muffin mix with canned berries; then, too, there is the canned blueberry pie filling that is so good. Frozen berries are available with or without syrup. Allow six to eight hours to defrost them in refrigerator or three hours at room temperature.

Most cooks have more than one way of using blueberries beyond the beloved pancakes, muffins, coffee cakes and pies. Some blueberry lovers insist that the very best way is to eat the fresh berries by the handful right out of the bowl. Others say that you can't beat blueberries over cereal, ice cream or cottage cheese for getting full pleasure from this All-American fruit.

* * *

A Thought To Ponder: Learn from yesterday; live for today; hope for tomorrow.

* * *

Spectacular Blueberry Cream Pie
1 baked 9-inch pie shell
1 package vanilla pie filling
1 1/2 cups milk
1/2 teaspoon vanilla flavoring
1/2 cup cream whipped or whipped topping
2 cups blueberries
1 tablespoon corn starch

2 tablespoons sugar
1/2 teaspoon lemon flavoring
1/2 teaspoon blueberry flavoring

Prepare pudding mix according to directions on the box; however, use only 1 1/2 cups of milk. Cool. Fold in whipped cream or topping and vanilla flavoring. Spoon into baked pie shell. Refrigerate until firm. Combine 1 cup blueberries (frozen, canned or fresh) with corn starch, sugar and just enough juice to combine the dry ingredients, 1-2 tablespoons. Cook over low heat, stirring and mashing berries until mixture is thick and clear. Stir in the other cup of well-drained berries and the lemon and blueberry flavorings. Cool slightly; spoon over top of the vanilla layer in pie shell. Keep pie chilled until time to serve it.

This is really a spectacular pie and can be made with the prepared blueberry pie filling by simply adding the lemon and blueberry flavorings to the mix and spooning it over the vanilla layer as directed. A no calorie sweetener may be used in place of sugar in this recipe with excellent results.

* * *

**Margaret Chase Smith's
Blueberry Cake**
1/2 cup shortening
2 eggs
1 cup milk
2 cups sifted flour
2 cups blueberries, washed and drained
4 teaspoons baking powder
1/2 teaspoon salt
1 teaspoon nutmeg

Cream the shortening, add sugar; beating until creamy. Add eggs and beat until light and foamy. Sift together, baking powder, salt and nutmeg, and add alternately to the creamed mixture with the milk. Then fold in blueberries. (Remember to flour the blueberries so they will not sink to the bottom of the pan.) Pour the batter into two well greased, 9- or 10-inch layer pans and bake at 375 degrees for 25 to 30 minutes or until tested done. Allow cake to cool in pans for 10 minutes, then turn them out onto cake racks and continue cooling. Put together with a favorite frosting.

All in a Woman's Day--September 5, 1989

September ...
is Chicken Month

There are a lot of special days, as well as a number of special happenings, designated for the month of September. One of them is Chicken Month.

To me, however, it always seemed that it should be July, for that is the month for good old country fried chicken. It was in this month, on the Fourth, that homemakers in the earlier days always tried to have the first fried chicken of the year. After waiting so long it was "lickin' good." Too, it was a far cry from today when we can have fried chicken every day if we so desire.

However, contemporary lifestyles have changed the way Americans now cook and eat. If you are trying to keep pace with today's times, chicken, seems to be the smart meat choice for several reasons; namely nutritionally it is good, economical, tasty and convenient.

When you go to the market now to purchase chicken, you no longer choose between the whole bird or its cut-up parts. It might be fair to say that chicken now comes in literally dozens of different forms. You may select the parts you want ... breasts, thighs, drumsticks, drummettes quarters, halves, boneless breasts, thighs, nuggets, cutlets, patties, ground, diced. These are all ready for cooking and only takes a minimum of preparation time.

Today nearly four out of every five broilers leave federally inspected processing plants in forms other than whole ready-to-cook chicken. And that isn't all; new chicken products are continually being introduced to the public as the broiler industry responds to the demands of the time pressured, two income families for easy to fix, quick healthful and tasty meals.

Nutritionists continue to recommend low calorie chicken for all ages. Since we are more conscious of the health and fitness way of life, we tend to substitute chicken for red meat more often in our diets. So, because of its versatility, chicken can be used repeatedly in a seemingly endless variety of ways.

Today, perhaps, chicken is safer and more wholesome than ever. Like most meat products, it requires thoughtful care in handling and cooking.

The National Broiler Council offers some practical guidelines that might help "cooks" in taking care of chicken they are preparing. No doubt, many, or most of you, do the things they suggest; however, these are reminders:

First, always be certain that the chicken you are cooking is well done; never, never, let it be "medium" or "rare" cooked. The recommended internal temperature for a whole chicken or parts with bones is 180 degrees; boneless parts, 105 degrees.

Too, always wash your hands, countertops and utensils in hot, soapy water between each step taken in the preparation of the chicken. Never cut up raw chicken and then use the same knife and cutting board to prepare other foods without always washing thoroughly.

Do not place cooked chicken on the same plate or tray used for raw chicken without thoroughly washing.

Cooked chicken, that is not eaten immediately, must be kept either hot, 140-160 degrees or refrigerated at 40 degrees or less. Do not leave it at room temperature for more than two hours.

Chicken for picnics should be stored in insulated containers or ice chests and kept refrigerated until ready to eat.

After purchasing raw chicken, be sure to promptly refrigerate. Tray packed chicken can be refrigerated two days in its original wrapping. If you want longer storage, wrap chicken in freezer paper, securely sealing with air pressed out; use it within six months for the best quality. Frozen cooked chicken should be used within two months.

* * *

A Thought To Ponder: The only person who saves time is the one who spends it well.

* * *

Scalloped Chicken

2 tablespoons butter
2 tablespoons flour
1 1/2 cups chicken broth
3/4 teaspoon salt
2 cups cooked or canned chicken
1 cup bread crumbs, stirred in 1 tablespoon melted butter

Prepare sauce of butter, flour, broth and salt. In a greased shallow baking dish, place a layer of chicken, then add some sauce; continue these layers until all ingredients are used. Top with buttered crumbs; bake in moderate oven, 350 degrees, until sauce bubbles and crumbs are brown. Serves six.

All in a Woman's Day--September 12, 1989

Chicken is good eating anytime

Again, let us think about chicken. As noted previously, chicken is good eating anytime of the year. A poll showed that seasons are "all equal" as a favorite time to eat chicken.

Aldrovandi, a noted Italian scientist of the 16th century, has written "If there is need for an elegant and groaning board, you have in the chicken the most praiseworthy, meat." Chicken with almonds, by the way, was one of his favorite dishes.

Chicken long had been making an appearance on American dinner tables years before the 13 original colonies became a nation. According to history, records noted that there were chickens on the Mayflower with the Pilgrims; that Jamestowne (the way the Pilgrims spelled the town) settlers raised small home flocks of chickens; at that time they were raised mostly for the feathers that were used to stuff feather beds; and that chicken was served at a reception held at Mount Vernon for General Lafayette.

685

Regardless of the records, however, there is still no agreement on whether chickens preceded Columbus to the New World or whether they were brought by Spanish and Portugese explorers landing on the coast of Brazil in 1500. It has been theorized that they were indigenous to America, brought across the ocean by Polynesian sailors or even Egyptian adventurers whose voyages are not recorded in historical annals. It is known, however, that Captain Cook found chickens on Pacific Islands and that by the time the Spaniards had conquered Mexico, the Incas were familiar with chickens.

This wild fowl that crowed and strutted very similar to our Banty roosters, is said to have originated from the Red Jungle fowl as early as 3000 B.C. in the jungles of Southeast Asia amidst the dense bamboo forests and thickets. This bird, no doubt, provided a tasty morsel for hungry hunters, who later as they became explorers, carried birds with them eastward from island to island across the Pacific and westward as they followed the mountain valleys and rivers across Asia and Europe.

There is, however, evidence that domesticated chickens had a multiple origin with other wild birds involved in the development of various breeds. Some birds were domesticated very early in China and spread by military and commerical contacts.

This small jungle bird must have been somewhat of a rarity in Europe; in fact, it was looked upon as sacred, and had won its place there by the 16th century. Henry of Navarre, the French king, could envision as a goal, a chicken cooking in every Frenchman's pot. Then by the 18th century French farmers were force-feeding their birds with aniseed and other fragrant spices so as to provide more flavorful chicken.

Publius Claudius, commander of the Roman fleet during the first Tunic War in the third century, B.C., who desired to bring about good fortune, offered food to his sacred birds. According to the records, the birds would not eat so he hurled them into the sea. Then Claudius suffered a devasting defeat in the battle of Drepanum. It was later that the Romans found a more satisfactory use for the sacred birds ... they made an excellent addition to a banquet table.

And so, as the American cuisine developed, chicken became a preferred dinner dish; however, in various parts of the country it was prepared differently. Too, it is a Sunday favorite, whether roasted in cold weather or served chilled in sumnertime. Fried chicken has been a longtime American favorite. It can be deep-fried in fat, sauteed in butter, dipped in batter or even simmered in champagne.

Chicken is an economical dish to serve. Most fanciers regard the breast as the choicest part of the fowl; however, some believe that the meat from the wings are featured in many cuisines, including, Southern Creole, Spanish and Chinese.

Here are a few hints on preparing chicken:

When frying chicken, it will brown much better if the pieces are carefully dried. The pieces will not brown if damp.

For a crisp crust on chicken, rub it with mayonnaise before baking it.

When you find after purchasing a, chicken that it is real tough, just soak it in vinegar, and it will become tender.

For a lemony chicken, just puncture a fresh lemon several times and place it inside the poultry cavity. The lemon juices baste the chicken while it bakes.

A small amount of baking powder added to the flour when coating chicken for frying will help make a crispy crust.

When frying chicken ahead of time for a meal, place browned pieces on a broiler pan, with water in the bottom of the pan. Set the oven at 300 degrees; this will cook the chicken inside and will keep it hot indefinitely. The chicken will be well browned, yet moist inside.

To get a thin crust on chicken, coat pieces with seasoned flour before frying.

For a crisper, heavier crust, lightly dust chicken with flour and dip pieces in buttermilk or in a mixture of one egg beaten with a third cup of milk and two tablespoons lemon juice. Roll pieces in seasoned flour and place them on wire racks. Let chicken stand 30 minutes for coating to dry. Roll pieces in flour again if the chicken is still moist. Then proceed as usual for skillet fried or oven fried chicken.

Some homemakers render the chicken fat and use it as cooking oil. Always melt it before measuring. Some advise when making pie crust, use one-fourth as much chicken fat as flour for the "flakiest crust you have ever tasted." Render the fat and freeze it for later use.

Some good cooks like to soak the chicken pieces in cold water, rolling them in flour and then letting the coated pieces rest on wax paper for 30 minutes in the refrigerator before frying.

* * *

A Thought To Ponder: Reputation is precious, but character is priceless.

* * *

Chicken Salad

2 cups cooked chicken (or you can use tuna) diced
1 1/2 cups carrots, grated
2 cups celery, finely diced
1/4 cup green pepper, chopped (optional)
1 small onion diced (optional)
1 cup salad dressing (enough to moisten)
1 1/2 cups canned shoestring potatoes

Combine all ingredients with exception of the shoestring potatoes. Chill this well. When it is ready to serve, stir in potatoes. Crisp potato chips, corn chips or cheese crackers could be coarsely crumbled and substituted for the potatoes. Be certain they are crisp at the time the salad is served to add a special crunchy texture.

All in a Woman's Day--September 19, 1989

'Tricky ways' ...
for handling food

There are "tricks to all trades," and food is no different than anything else. There are tricky ways in which to handle various kinds of food.

Sift powdered sugar over meringue before putting it in the oven to brown and it will cut easier.

Icing will not run off a cake if a little flour is sifted over it before the frosting is added.

Instead of grating rind from a lemon when it is required in a lemon pie filling, wash and cut it in strips and drop them into the filling as it cooks. Then remove. This little procedure brings out the flavor.

Sprinkle unbaked cut out cookies with different flavors of gelatin, then bake them, for a tasty treat with a fruity flavor.

Try shaking together tag ends of several boxes of cereal to create a new mixed cereal. The kids will love it if you invent an imaginative name perhaps like "Monster Crunch." Stale cereal also will taste fresh if it is heated on a cookie sheet for 15 minutes in a 300-degree oven.

Try making your roast tender by adding two slices of tomato.

Should too much salt be spilled into something when cooking, drop in a few slices of raw apple to absorb the excess. Remove the apple slices before serving.

Place large marshmallows on top of a freshly frosted cake and the foil or plastic wrap that is placed on it will not stick.

To retard mold on cheese, try using vinegar in a plastic bag. Shake it well and then empty it before placing wrapped cheese inside the bag.

Too, a slice or two of bread in the bottom of the meat loaf pan will absorb some of the grease that cooks out of the meat.

For a cheesy taste, melt thin slices of cheese over hot vegetables instead of making a cheese sauce.

A pair of tweezers makes a handy kitchen gadget for removing bones from fish fillets before cooking.

Leftover egg yolks may be baked until they are hard and then chopped fine and used as a garnish for cooked spinach, broccoli or asparagus.

Wash fruit in one cup of vinegar diluted with a fourth cup of water to get rid of any bacteria or insecticide.

Broil fish fillets on lettuce leaves so that the fish will remain moist and doesn't stick to the pan. Cut the leaves the size of the fillets.

When rolling out cut out cookies, use confectioners' sugar instead of flour. It makes the cookies sweeter and helps keep them moist. Also the dough doesn't get tough.

To make soda or graham cracker crumbs, place crackers between foil or in a sandwich bag and press them with a rolling pin or other round objects.

* * *

A Thought To Ponder: The means some people use in getting ahead in this world probably means they are getting behind in the next.

* * *

Coconut Almond Carrot Ring
(a coffee cake)

1 1/2 cups flour
1 1/2 teaspoons baking powder
1/2 teaspoon salt
1 teaspoon cinnamon
1 cup sugar
1 cup oil
2 eggs
1 cup finely grated carrots
1/2 cup almonds, chopped
1/2 cup dates (cut up) or raisins
1 2/3 cups coconut
1 (16-ounce) can cream cheese frosting

Mix flour, baking powder, salt and cinnamon. Beat sugar and oil at medium speed until well mixed; stir in flour mixture; add eggs, one at a time, beating well after each addition. Stir in carrots, nuts, dates or raisins and 2/3 cup of coconut. Pour into a greased and floured 9-inch bundt pan or 6-cup ring mold. Bake it at 350 degrees for 35 minutes or until it tests done. Cool it in pan 15 minutes; remove and finish cooling on rack. Frost with cream cheese frosting and cover with remaining coconut plus more if needed.

All in a Woman's Day--September 26, 1989

This is Egg Month

Among other things, September is Egg Month. So, this must be the right time to write something about eggs.

It is a good idea to leave eggs out of the refrigerator so they will warm to room temperature before cooking. If you are boiling eggs, shake each egg vigorously before covering with cold water and a lid, and the yolks will remain centered.

Try egg whites to loosen sticky chewing gum that has stuck on clothing.

If you have difficulty in peeling hard-cooked eggs, it might help to pierce the eggs before cooking. Either use an egg piercer, a punch, a pin or a carpet or thumb tack. Piercing the large end of the egg before cooking will help prevent the eggs from cracking by providing an outlet for air pressure that builds up during cooking. Too, a small amount of water may seep into a "pierced" egg during the cooking and this tends to help separate the egg from the shell, making peeling easier.

Experts say the best way to store eggs is in the closed carton in which they are purchased. They should then be placed in an area of the refrigerator where the temperature is more constant. The special egg slots in the refrigerator door, unless they are covered, allows drafts each time the door is opened so that is not the ideal place for storage. Too, you might check the eggs to be sure they are stored correctly in the carton with the large ends up as this helps center the yolks. Also less movement and temperature change help eggs to stay fresh longer.

You will find that for hard-boiled eggs, the older the better as they peel more readily. Because the shell of the egg is porous, eggs do breathe and absorb odors that affect their taste.

Many homemakers cook hard-boiled eggs by starting them in cold water with some salt added. This keeps the shells from breaking and also keeps the whites from leaking out just in case an egg should crack.

If egg whites go limp while beating, try adding a teaspoon of cream of tartar for every cup of egg whites. This should keep them nice and foamy.

To make a meringue that is different, beat three egg whites until stiff; add three tablespoons brown sugar, gradually, then fold in an eighth of teaspoon salt and two tablespoons powdered sugar. Brown it in a 325 degree oven about 15 minutes. This meringue does not "weep" and is especially, good on butterscotch pie.

Another use for egg whites is to rub your shoes with them as it will keep them looking new.

To make quick scrambled eggs, rinse a clean jar with cold water then break eggs into it; add seasoning and a little water, and shake vigorously until thoroughly mixed. Just rinse the jar with cold water and no more having to wash an egg beater. Did you know that using water instead of milk makes light scrambled eggs?

If you are having trouble steaming open your envelopes, they most likely have been sealed with egg whites. This is one way of protecting your mail from would-be letter openers.

Tomato time is over with, almost, anyway; however, you can get some extra mileage out of your eggs if you will save the egg shells, crush them and put a handful under the tomato plants. This will help control blossom end rot.

When making deviled eggs, try using softened cream cheese. If you have six hard-boiled eggs use one-half of a large-size package or one small size. Blend it together with your eggs; then add the necessary salad dressing, along with pickle relish or pickles or whatever else you like to use.

Do you find it troublesome carrying deviled eggs to a picnic or a meeting? If so, just place each one in a colored paper cupcake holder. They make an attractive display on the table and they are easy to serve as each person can pick up a paper cup.

Here is a little bit of "eggs" for thought. Where do you belong in the following list?

Do you like your eggs sunnyside up? Then you are healthy, happy and wise.

Do you like your eggs hard cooked? Then you are a persistent, dynamic and sincere soul.

Do you like your eggs soft cooked? Then you are gentle, kind and patient.

Do you like your eggs medium cooked? Then you are calm and collected.

Do you like your eggs poached? Then you are speedy, peppy and intelligent.

Do you like your eggs scrambled? Then you are nervous, passionate and artistic.

Do you like your eggs over-easy? Then you are versatile, magnetic and like to dominate.

Do you like your eggs shirred? Then you are sensitive, romantic and fastidious.

Do you like your eggs in omelets? Then you are steady, reliable and conservative.

Where did you belong in this "egg cooking" deal?

* * *

A Thought To Ponder: You can do anything if you have enthusiasm. Enthusiasm is the yeast that makes your hopes rise to the star.

—Henry Ford

* * *

In the event you have lost or mislaid your egg substitute recipe, here is one you might like to use.

Egg Substitute

3 egg whites
2 tablespoons dry powdered milk
1 teaspoon water
Few drops yellow food coloring

Blend egg whites and add the dry powdered milk, water and coloring.

Mix well. You can either scramble this mixture or use it in place of eggs in recipes. This amount is equal to two eggs.

All in a Woman's Day--October 3, 1989

Don't forget ... this is apple time

Fall is here again. How time does fly! In the spirit of the seasons, the Monarch butterflies are enjoying the late flowers, as well as the humming birds; finches, too, some folks say are back. Birds that travel South for the winter have been gathering in preparation for the journey. There is a touch of chill in the air, and there have been some cool nights. Since our weather has been rather unreal this year, no season can really be predicted. This just has to be Indian Summertime, however.

This we know ... Fall has arrived ... and come this season we think of crunchy, cold apples (yes, and a bowl of popcorn, too).

In our immediate area, apples haven't been as good as in previous years; however, beautiful apples are available at the markets. And, for those who like to go to the orchard to pick, or just buy, there are apples not too far away. Don't forget this is Apple Month.

The flavor of apples is best when they are at their peak of maturity. Background color is the key to maturity. Those with green-yellow to yellow background color are mature. Ripe apples usually have a dull and extra yellowish appearance.

While apple size is not a maturity indicator, size is related to use. Small apples are good choices for snacks or for packing in a school lunch. Medium sized and large apples are desired for eating fresh, baking or using in desserts.

In Missouri, more Jonathans than any other kind of apples are grown, with Red Delicious, next. When those two varieties are mixed to make apple cider, the result is a great combination.

Golden Delicious apples are the most underestimated of all Missouri apple varieties. They are a spicy, sweet apple and are delicious eaten fresh or cooked. Like their cousin, the Red Delicious, they are typical, large apples; however, they have more flavor and a more crispy, juicy flesh than the red variety. Many Missouri cooks believe that the Golden Delicious makes the very best baked apples, salads and apple butter. Yet, despite these characteristics, the Golden Delicious is among the lowest in production in the state.

If you are having a group in for fellowship, why not do as one hostess did ... give an apple as they are ready to leave.

If you are doing a recipe that calls for rum but you do not want to use that flavoring just substitute with one can apple juice. It is much less expensive.

Apples make delightful decorations for fall. An attractive centerpiece can be made with Golden Delicious. In a pretty bowl, along with some fall colored leaves. Then, of course, at holiday times, use shiny red apples with sprigs of evergreen.

In the event you are wondering how many apples make a pound, it takes two or three medium sized apples to make the poundage.

When preparing apples for pie, be sure to add the amount of sugar needed immediately after peeling so the apples will not turn brown. Too, if you are working with a large amount of apples, just drop the peeled and sliced apples into water to which has been added one tablespoon of fresh lemon juice. This will do the same trick in preventing them from turning brown.

For a tasty treat try mini-carameled apples. Core and slice them, then cut each slice in a suitable size for eating. Place them in a dish and dribble over them hot caramel sauce made by melting a bag of caramels over hot water. This is easily eaten with a fork. Or you can put a toothpick in the apple pieces and dip them into the caramel sauce.

* * *

A Thought To Ponder: Anyone can, count the seeds in an apple, but only God can count the apples in a seed.

* * *

Golden Delicious Apple Pie
Crust:
2 tablespoons soft butter or margarine
1 1/2 cups flaked coconut

Spread 9-inch pie plate with soft butter or margarine. Press coconut firmly into butter. Bake at 325 degrees about 10 minutes or until golden brown. Cool.
Filling:
1 tablespoon unflavored gelatin
1/4 cup cold water
4 egg yolks
1/3 cup sugar
1/4 teaspoon salt
1/2 cup lemon juice

1 1/2 teaspoons grated lemon peel
4 egg whites
1/2 cup sugar
2 Golden Delicious apples, pared, cored and coarsely grated

Soften gelatin in cold water. Beat egg yolks slightly; add 1/3 cup sugar, salt and lemon juice. Cook in a saucepan over medium low heat, stirring constantly until thickened. Add lemon peel; then add gelatin, stirring until it is dissolved. Cool until it begins to jell; then stir in grated apple. Beat egg whites until frothy; add 1/2 cup sugar, gradually, beating to soft peak stage. Fold into lemon-apple mixture. Pile into baked coconut shell. Top with whipped topping if desired.

All in a Woman's Day--October 10, 1989
Sugar fills that 'sweet tooth' craving

This time of year we begin to think about having some extra sugar on hand for bazaar and holiday cooking. Any bargains in sugar we will be ready to "gobble up" immediately, so we will be prepared.

It is nothing new to think about sugar, for it seems that Americans have always had a "sweet tooth."

The history of sugar goes back to antiquity, when sugar cane was cultivated in India several centuries prior to the birth of Christ.

The derivitive of sugar is from the Sanskrit word Sarkara; and it was from India that sugar moved westward to Persia, where it was called shakar. And, yet it went further West to the Arab nations bordering the Mediterranean Sea, from whence the seafarers took their prized shakar across the water to Europe, with this no doubt happening at the beginning of the Middle Ages.

The Europeans, especially the Greeks and Romans, were aware of the sweet sticky syrup that could be taken from sugar cane many centuries before they actually had an opportunity to have a sample.

Too, the soldiers of the army of Alexander the Great observed it without identifying it during their foray into India. The Roman Pliny wrote this about sugar, "It is a kind of honey which collects in reeds, white like gum and brittle to the teeth; the largest pieces are the size of a filbert. It is used only as a medicine."

There is no doubt that the Moors were certainly cultivating sugar cane in Spain by the eighth century; however, because of the lack of communication with the Moslem and Christian territories in Medieval Europe, the remainder of Europe got its sugar from the East.

As would be expected, Venice, a center of importing activity, was close to having a monopoly on the transporting and the refining of this new rare "spice," as it was called and which they obtained in the process of transporting Crusaders to and from the Holy Land.

The creative cooks of Italy, needless to say, went for the sugar, using it without discretion in a wide variety of dishes; and in their capacities as chefs to the very rich, for whom the use of this precious substance, sugar, was a status symbol.

The young lords and ladies of Boccaccio's Decameron are therefore depicted as feasting upon sugar sweet-ened delicacies; a portrayal in fiction of an overwhelming fact that sugar was the most important factor; that it was the most important new taste sensation to hit the Italian banquet table, thereby making its influence felt even in macaroni. Because this preference reached such an extreme, one Cardinal Ascancio Sforra, feted his compatriots in a fashion which displayed both his wealth and his sense of macabre: He gave a dinner at which each diner drank out of a skull-shaped cup paired with bones made from sugar.

On another occasion a French king, Henri III, visited Venice, where he was treated to a dinner in which spun sugar had been used to create everything from napkins to utensils, of course, not forgetting the dinner plates.

The French also developed a sweet tooth once sugar came into their culinary scene, adding sugar to virtually everything from hors d'oeuvres to dessert.

King Charles V of France also enjoyed sugar. He liked toasted cheese enhanced by a combination of cinnamon and sugar, also the combination of sweet and salty or savory flavors which were commonplace in European cookery from about the Middle Ages until the end of the Renaissance.

One of the first cookbooks dealing with sugar was penned by Nostradamus. The first part was concerned with the use of sugar in cosmetics, fragrances and medicines. The second part dealt with recipes for among other things, fruit preserves, candies, Spanish nougats and marzipan tarts.

Columbus brought sugar to the New World in the form of sugar cane that he planted in the West Indies. This was an act that had far greater reverberations in the course of history than Columbus could ever possibly imagine.

The cultivation and refinement of sugar became one of the major industries of the West Indies, and was especially lucrative for the planters. It seems that Cortez, Spanish explorer, was the first European to present himself at the Zatec ruler Montezuma's court after first having scoffed at the idea of becoming a planter. He is quoted as saying, "I have come to gain gold, not cultiviate fields like a peasant." Still he settled down to the planting of sugar cane that eventually led to his prosperity.

It was some centuries later that King George III of England is said to have succumbed to a fit of jealousy on discovering that the owner of a carriage far more elegant than his was a man, who had made a fortune planting sugar cane.

Even with the nearness of the West Indies, the American colonists did not have the opportunity to enjoy sugar in their early years in the New World. Because of the shortness of money they had to find other ways to sweeten their food.

* * *

A Thought To Ponder: We cannot direct the wind, but we can adjust our sails.

* * *

Mincemeat Golden Cookies

1 cup mincemeat
1 1/2 cups sugar
3 1/4 cups flour
1 teaspoon soda
1 cup shortening
1 egg

1/2 teaspoon salt

Cream shortening and sugar; beat egg; blend with the shortening mixture, and mix. Sift flour, salt and soda and stir into egg mixture, blending thoroughly. Fold mincemeat into mixture. Add a little water if mixture is too stiff. Drop by teaspoons on a greased cookie sheet, a few inches apart, and bake in a 400 degree oven about 8 minutes. Makes 3 dozen cookies. (This is a rather old recipe.)

All in a Woman's Day--October 17, 1989

Halloween ... is 'meet and treat'

Each year as Halloween nears, thoughts turn to ghostly spirits and we somehow think of Salem, Mass., with it witch trials and executions. So, why don't we get on our broomsticks and fly there this Halloween?

It is here that its celebrated witches have made Halloween a year-round industry for this seaport town where Nathaniel Hawthorne retold his "Twice Told Tales" and first spooked out the House of Seven Gables as a tourist haunt.

Hawthorne may have been feeling a bit guilty about his great-great-grandfather, John Hathorne. He was the hanging judge, who presided over many of the infamous witchcraft trials in 1692, when 164 accused witches languished in local jails and 14 women, five men and two dogs were hanged on Gallows Hill as disciples of the devil. This novelist Inserted a "w" in his name while attending Bowdoin College to rid the family closet of this skeleton, who later provided so much inspiration for his writing and unwittingly did so much for the economy of Salem.

In Salem, witchcraft has been a growth industry ever since the pragmatic Puritan fathers forced the families of the condemned to pay the hangman's fee before retrieving the body of the late "witch" for burial.

When the month of October rolls around, it has been related that the red brick streets of restored Salem town echo with the sinister tread of such doings as "horrible parade," "a bewitching ball," a witches brew competition, a pumpkin carving contest, ducking for apples, midnight visits to the Old Burying Grounds and other haunted happenings. And, in addition the town has such permanent attractions as a Witch House, the Salem Witch Museum, the Witch Dungeon Museum, several certified historic haunted houses, the wharf and the Peabody Museum with its collections of witch doctor masks, voodoo dolls, Hindu puppets and funerary artifacts brought back by the old New England sea captains. Too, the Chamber of Commerce sets up a haunted house on Salem Common, complete with a vampire's coffin and humorous epitaphs on wooden tombstones.

You ask, where else but in Salem and its environs, where herb gardens are known to flourish and be popular, could one learn that plants such as parsnips, nightshade, monkshead, aconite and belladonna are said to give brooms their climbing power and enable witches to get up over the trees. And, to get a better liftoff, on Halloween spice up their broom handles with herbs and fireplace soot.

You probably already know that Halloween was derived from the early Christian "All Hallow's Eve," that is the day before the religious feast of All Saints, November 1; however the history of this special time goes back even further to the time of the Druids. Members of a priesthood of ancient Gaul, Britain and Ireland, the Druids were said to worship nature and to celebrate the new year on October 31.

According to legend, the Druids believed that on the last night of the old year, the "lord of death" gathered together all of the souls of the dead and freed them to roam.

Also, it was believed that witches soared through the skies on broomsticks or took the form of black cats.

In order to protect themselves from these evil spirits, superstitious peasants made offerings of food and sweets, and disguised themselves as goblins, ghosts and witches, so that the "real" spooks wouldn't be able to recognize them.

Thus arose the Halloween tradition of "treating" and masquerading in costumes.

Tradition has it that huge bonfires also were lit at this time to ward off demonic spirits and protect the crops, flocks and herds from evil influence. Because the spirits were thought to be loose on Halloween, this holiday was believed to be a favorable time for telling fortunes concerning marriage, luck, health and death. Even the name, occupation and hair color of one's future spouse were predicted.

Some of the present day games stem from those superstitions. For example, bobbing for apples originated with the practice of dropping apples and a sixpence into a bucket of water. Anyone who could retrieve them with the mouth, without using the teeth, was said to be in for good luck in the coming year.

In the early days of our nation, Halloween was celebrated with taffy pulls, corn popping, apple bobbing parties and hayrides. A few pranks were thrown in for good measure, such as changing house numbers or street signs and taking gates away to let cows and pigs wander into the streets.

In the 1930s, however, Halloween had come to be a time for young children in costumes, to call on neighbors with the greeting "trick or treat."

Several decades later, in the early 1970s, in order to preserve the most wholesome aspects of the ever evolveing Halloween, a nationwide "Meet 'n Treat" campaign was launched and designed to take any connotation of "tricks" out of treating by "meeting" the neighbors and "treating" the kids. This encouraged parents to accompany their children on the treating rounds, promoted the observance of Halloween safety rules as set forth by the National Safety group and called for family, neighborhood and community parties to climax the celebration of Halloween.

Have a safe and happy "Meeting" and "Treating" Halloween!

* * *

A Thought To Ponder: A Cornish Prayer—From ghoulies and ghosties and long-leggety beasties that go bump in the night; Good Lord, deliver us!

All in a Woman's Day--October 24, 1989

Everything you need to know about pies

Anytime is pie time; however, in the fall, as cooler weather approaches, we think more about having a piece of pie. Almost everyone dotes on a good pie, and someone must have been thinking along that line, too, for Saturday (October 28) is National Pie Day.

But don't wait until "Pie Day" or for a special occasion to come along, just put one of your lip-smacking pies together any day of the week and treat your family to a taste of the good life.

Some tips for making this dessert that is "tops" for most folks might be in order. So, here are a few:

When making cherry pie, make your favorite crust, then put cherry pie filling into a bowl and stir in one box of cherry gelatin and 3/4 cup hot water. Put mixture into a 9-inch crust, top and bake. This makes more filling for the larger pie pan.

When making pastry for apple pie, try adding some grated Cheddar cheese to the dough.

If you have trouble making the crust, then you perhaps should purchase a ready-made crust from your grocer or prepare one quickly from cake, cookie or graham cracker crumbs.

Creamy filling for pies makes good use of pudding mixes and whipped toppings. And remember, these don't need to be cooked. Just mix, fill and chill.

Try buttering your pie pan before putting in the bottom crust and it will make it brown nicely and will not be soggy.

Another trick with cream pies is to spread a thin layer of cream cheese over the baked crust before adding the filling. This too, prevents a soggy crust.

Also to avoid a soggy crust, sprinkle a little sugar on the lower crust before putting in the filling.

Too, you can brush the bottom crust with a little egg white before adding the filling. The crust won't become soggy and you will have a nice light crust.

Bake the bottom crust of your pie 10

minutes before adding the filling and then bake it as usual. This will help prevent a soggy crust.

Also for a crust that won't absorb the moisture of juicy pies, substitute one egg yolk for one tablespoon of water in the dough. Mix the yolk with the water and let it chill before using.

Vanilla pudding used as a pie filling is especially good when it has sliced bananas or coconut added.   In place of flour try using a teaspoon of tapioca for thickening fruit pies.

Sometimes homemakers roll out the crust and place it in a pie pan for freezing; then some roll out the pie crust and lay it singly on a flat surface like a cookie sheet. When frozen it is stored in a container and taken out as needed for making a pie. This saves space.

If you have a trouble with a creamy pie becoming a little runny, just dissolve a package of unflavored gelatin in a fourth cup of cold water. While this is dissolving, make the pie filling and when it is taken off the stove add the dissolved gelatin.

Pastry will roll more easily if the rolling pin is cold. Place it in the refrigerator for a short time before using it.

When preparing pie crust, roll the pastry from center to outer edge; however, don't roll back over it to the center. Lift the rolling pin and again roll from the center. This insures a pastry with an even thickness all over.

If you want your pie crust to be extremely flaky, measure the flour and shortening into a bowl and chill them at least an hour before mixing.

When rolling pastry between waxed paper, always sprinkle the work surface with a few drops of water. The waxed paper will adhere to the surface and will not slip when you are rolling the dough.

When making a graham cracker crust, instead of using granulated sugar, try using four tablespoons of powdered sugar.

If your diet restricts the use of spices, but you still want to eat pumpkin pie, try adding a teaspoon of vanilla. It gives a nice flavor.

To make a delicious pie crust, try substituting lemon-lime flavored carbonated soda pop for the water called for in the recipe. Be sure the pop is cold before using. The fizz in the drink makes the pastry light and fluffy.

One of the difficult things about baking a pie is getting the crust to stay even on the bottom of the pan while baking. Try rinsing your pan with cold water and see if that doesn't help.

To make a flakier pie crust add a tablespoon of cold orange or lemon juice as a part of the liquid.

Don't save your pumpkin pie spice for pies only. Use it instead for cinnamon in cakes, cookies, fruit pies and compotes; yes, even on cinnamon toast. If you do this, you might begin to use pumpkin pie spice more often than some of your other spices

Happy pie baking!

* * *

A Thought To Ponder: Memories are windows of the past.

* * *

Angel Food Pie

1 1/4 cups sugar
1/4 cup corn starch
2 cups boiling water
2 egg whites
1 cup crushed pineapple, drained
1/4 teaspoon salt
1 teaspoon vanilla

Sift sugar, corn starch and salt; add boiling water and cook until thick, about 5 minutes. Pour over the beaten egg whites and beat well. Add pineapple and vanilla. Pour into baked pie shells. Serve it with whipped cream or whipped topping. Maked 2 pies.

All in a Woman's Day--October 31, 1989
More tips on using sugar

More about sugar!

Whether you realize it or not, if you use much sugar, you can quickly use up your calorie allowance for the day. Few nutrients are received from sugar; however, it does supply calories.

It would be well to cut back on the use of sugar in your daily preparation of foods. At the table, too, learn to use less sugar and other sweetenings—honey and molasses. You will soon find that it tastes as good without so much sugar as what you were using.

When shopping, take notice, too, in the amount of sugar or sweetening that are in the various items purchased. It might take a little more time to shop, but it will be well worth the time spent.

Lots of experimenting has been going on with sugar to bear out the fact that it has been a folk remedy for wounds. Evidently it kills bacteria and simultaneously nourishes the tissues. You might try placing a bit of just ordinary sugar on a wound and see how it responds.

Now, for a few hints concerning sugar:

When sugar gets hard and lumpy, put it in the refrigerator for a day or two and it will come out soft.

If real hard, large lumps show up in your sugar do not waste this precious sweetener, just run the lumps over a slaw cutter and you will have measurable granules again.

If you are making cake icing and have used up all the powdered sugar, and the icing is still too thin to spread, quickly make more by putting granulated sugar in the blender. Blend on high speed until the sugar is a fine powder. For extra body add about a tablespoon of corn starch.

If you are trying to cut calories, add a little less sugar to a recipe and substitute a little extra vanilla. It will give the impression of sweetness. If you run out of brown sugar or want to make your own you can try this:

As you know, commercial brown sugar is commonly made by blending molasses with white sugar crystals. All you need to make your own is unsulphured molasses and white sugar. For the equivalent of one-half cup of brown sugar blend one-half cup of granulated sugar with two tablespoons of unsulphured molasses.

In recipes calling for brown sugar to be mixed with several other ingredients, just add the molasses and sugar separately. There is no need to pre-blend the sugar and molasses.

Although homemade brown sugar can be stored for a brief period in a plastic bag, it is best to make it as needed.

In some of the recipes you can substitute unsulphured molasses for white sugar; however, the amount of liquid should be reduced by one-fourth cup for each cup of sugar called for in the recipe.

That should take care of the making of your own brown sugar and how to use it.

If you have a microwave, soften brown sugar in 30 seconds by putting a cup of hardened sugar in a glass dish with a slice of white bread or a wedge of apple. Cover and microwave on

HIGH for 30 to 40 seconds. Then, of course, discard the bread or apple.

Too, brown sugar often is an ingredient found in chewy cookies. Here are two interesting ideas that make use of this moist sugar: First, brown sugar placed in a bread box will keep the bread fresh. Cookies and cakes that have become dry and stale may be made fresh again by putting them in the box with the bread and brown sugar or by dipping them into milk and lightly rebaking them.

Unless the recipe states otherwise, always firmly pack brown sugar into a measuring cup or spoon. The packing should be firm enough so that when the measuring tool is inverted, the brown sugar is released and holds its shape.

A good method of storing granulated sugar is simply to pour a five-pound bag through a funnel into a clean, dry empty plastic milk container. The sugar will stay dry and is easy to pour.

* * *

A Thought To Ponder: In the end, the things that count are the things that you can't count.

* * *

Date Cookies

1/4 cup margarine
3/4 cup brown sugar
1 egg
1/2 cup sour cream
1/2 teaspoon vanilla
11/2 cups sifted flour
1/4 teaspoon baking powder
1/2 teaspoon soda
1 pound dates
Pecans, halves (for 50 cookies)

Cream shortening and sugar; add egg, sour cream and vanilla. Blend in dry ingredients. Drop dates that have been stuffed with a pecan half into the dough and cover with batter. Place on a greased baking sheet and bake 10 minutes at 400 degrees.

There is enough dough to cover 50 dates. When cool, frost with vanilla or brown sugar frosting.

All in a Woman's Day--November 7, 1989
Bring back memories of the kitchen apron

Remember the old kitchen apron, the coverall apron or the one that tied at the waistline? We don't see many of them anymore as the average housewife doesn't take time to put on an apron as she goes about her housewifely duties.

There was a time, however, when this utility garment was a must. Every housewife wore an apron and she had them for different occasions.

The everyday apron was indeed a utility garment and was worn to the garden where the wearer would gather a mess of peas or green beans or even perhaps, mustard greens or spinach. In using it as a basket she would gather up the hem of the apron in her left hand while doing her picking with the right hand. Then she would head for the house, and there on the back step she would take off her bonnet and sit down to prepare the vegetables for dinner that day. If shelling peas, she would deftly slip them into one of the pockets, and by the way, all the aprons had pockets ... they were essential ... with the hulls left in the apron. When finished she would give a quick flip of the apron so that the hulls went over the fence, most often into the chicken yard.

Too, as she would pass the apple tree on her way back to the house, often she would again fill her apron ... this time with apples, if they were ready, for a luscious apple pie.

When it came time to feed the chickens, again her apron was used as a basket, and in it she placed ears of corn that she shelled for feeding. The grains were then thrown out to the chickens. As they were busy clucking and making sounds of contentment; she would then use the apron to gather eggs to be carried to the house.

This apron also made a great, as it was called, "flutter apron." It was used in shooing chickens back into a coop if they had escaped or if found foraging in the garden or flower beds.

The housewife always had a fresh, clean apron hanging behind the door in the event a caller came. She would quickly yank off the one she was wearing and slip on the fresh apron, making a good impression.

Do you remember how the lady of the household, when she wanted to call her husband from the field, she would take off her apron, climb up on the fence and wave it madly to catch his attention? You know the horses seemed to even know this sign, for when they reached the end of the row, they waited patiently to be unhitched before starting on a slow trot to the barn. Generally when a lady was seen waving an apron rather wildly, it was a distress signal ... a good Morse SOS sign.

The healing powers of an apron cannot be duplicated for holding a throbbing stubbed toe or for using a corner to dry tearful eyes and wipe a dripping nose. If an accident had been real serious there have been times when an apron was quickly whisked off and torn into bandages or made into a tourniquet. Aprons also were used to gather cobs or wood that were used to keep the stove going or to start a fire.

We've always heard of apron strings and how some sons were tied to their mother's apron strings. Remember?

Often babies were cuddled in the apron on their mother's lap as she sang a lullabye.

Aprons also often have been used for fanning and there have been times when they could create more breeze than a palm or mortuary fan.

Too, they could be pulled over the head and used as a sun shade or to keep off a sudden summer shower.

On Sundays the lady of the house often put on a stiffly starched white apron that sometimes was decorated, most often with crossstitch at the hem and pockets. Ties were wider on the Sunday apron so a prettier bow could be tied. The sash was a little longer, and how it did flutter and dance here and there as the mother of the domain hurried to prepare Sunday dinner on the old wood stove after coming home from church.

On wash day, there could be seen a line full of everyday kitchen aprons and the Sunday best, all starched and waiting for ironing day on Tuesday. There also were those fancy little aprons that were all frills and lace. . .those were for company best or teatime.

At bazaar time, aprons were a big item, and all the women who could sew tried to make theirs the prettiest or the most usable. However, as their usefulness became less needed, the aprons began to disappear from the scene.

Young girls wore aprons to school to keep their dresses clean—Remember?

Women wearing aprons tied at the waist put them to good use, too. At naptime. they would lie down on the bed and pull their apron up over their shoulders as a protection—like a blanket.

Regardless of what kind of apron it might have been, the old kitchen or coverall, or fancy, with all the memorable stories it will be treasured in many hearts for years to come.

* * *

A Thought To Ponder: Home is where the temperatures should be maintained by hearts instead of hot heads.

* * *

Family Pie

One handful of Forgiveness,
One heaping cupful of Love,
One pound of Unselfishness

Mix together smoothly with Faith in God. Add two teaspoons of Good Nature for flavor; then sprinkle generously with Thoughtfulness. One complete pie serves any size family.

All in a Woman's Day--November 14, 1989

Bittersweet ... is something special

Have you ever thought of bittersweet being a special Thanksgiving decoration?

Along with turkey, cranberries and corn, bittersweet is a native American that deserves and should have a prominent place at Thanksgiving. It is an outstanding ornamental vine that provides excellent decorations indoors and out.

There was a time when bittersweet could be found growing natively in almost every county in our state. Many folks still try to collect berries from the wild; however, that is rather difficult as farmers have cleaned out fence rows and sprayed here and there to get rid of unwanted plants. As a result, bittersweet took its toll and is becoming more difficult to find in most areas.

But there is an answer to that. There are some people that are growing it to be sold. This year some of the bittersweet offered for sale included cuttings of long strands of berries that made a picture of beauty. Since bittersweet is an excellent ornamental plant, it is a worthwhile addition to the home landscape. By growing your own, if you can find a place, you will help prevent depletion of this native plant. You will have enough berries for indoor decorations, and maybe some to share, as well as provide a bright spot of beauty. Too, they also provide food for the birds, our feathered friends.

Bittersweet is a vigorous vine that climbs by twining. It should have plenty of room. It can climb up to 20 or more feet. It tolerates sunny and shaded locations; however, it will not fruit well in heavy shade.

You may be asking, "Is it a hardy plant?" Yes, it is and can be planted spring or fall in many types of soil. In the fall the leaves are yellow. The berries you will find also are yellow until they split open to reveal the bright orange-red fruit. These bright fruits usually persist on the vine throughout the winter and, as already noted, provide food for the birds.

There are several types of bittersweet, with two of them most frequently found for sale. The most popular of the two is the American bittersweet—Calastrus scandens, which is the one found in the woods. The other is an introduced type called Oriental bittersweet —Calastrus orbiculatus.

You will find that the Oriental bittersweet has leaves that are more rounded than the American type. Also you will note that the fruit clusters of Oriental bittersweet are produced in small lateral clusters, while the American bittersweet produces, large terminal clusters. You will find, too, that the Oriental bittersweet is a more vigorous grower and often produces more color in the garden than the American type that is preferred for arrangements.

Bittersweet may be grown from seeds planted outdoors in the fall, from softwood cuttings taken in midsummer or from hardwood cuttings taken in the fall.

Do try to use some of this bit of native American heritage in your home this Thanksgiving time. It is nostalgic and a good conversation piece, as well as a home brightener.

Let's celebrate Thanksgiving with bittersweet!

* * *

A Thought To Ponder: Thanksgiving is an open gate into the love of God.   —Robert N. Rodenmayer

* * *

We Thank Thee

For the gifts of wood and field,
Autumn's ever bounteous yield;
For the friends who, through the year,
Have made glad our sojourn here;
For the joy and sweet content
With which grief and pain are blent,
We thank Thee.

For the visions of our sires,
And the dreams their faith inspires;
For the heroes who have wrought
Toward the kingdom Thou hast wrought;
For Thy patience as we grope
Toward Thy one world, our great hope,
We thank Thee.

—Thomas Curtis Clark

Breads ...
from start to finish

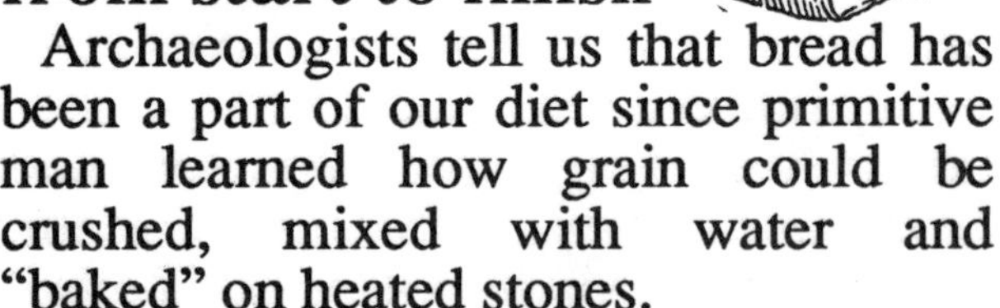

Archaeologists tell us that bread has been a part of our diet since primitive man learned how grain could be crushed, mixed with water and "baked" on heated stones.

Although the later discovery of leavenings transformed bread into the plump, airy loaves that we know, flat bread never has lost it's allure in many parts of the world.

With modern cooking methods, today's flat bread undoubtedly beats its counterpart in flavor and texture. However, even more interesting is the way it has taken on new characteristics from each culture that adopted it.

For instance, the Germans top flat bread with buttery cooked onions, cubed ham and a touch of caraway seeds. The end result is a German Onion Bread. A thick wedge served with spicy sausages and a crisp salad, makes a hearty meal. Or you might just cut the wedges thin for an "anytime" snack.

Then in the Scandinavian countries, flat bread was devised to be stored. These northern lands have such a short growing season that grain often was harvested unripened. Since grain spoils quickly at this stage, it had to be used to make a dry bread that would keep well. Flat bread proved to be the answer. Rolled paper thin and baked, a cracker crisp bread was produced that would last through the long winter.

As indicated by its name, unleavened bread contains no leavening. Made of a mixture consisting essentially of flour and liquid, it is best known at matzoh, originated by the Israelites and eaten at Passover. Among other types of unleavened bread are the dampers of Australia; Indian corn bread; and Swedish rye bread.

As we know, the preparation of baked grain products have been used as food since prehistoric times. The first "bread" foods were believed to be made from acorns or beechnuts, crushed and mixed with water and subjected to natural or artificial heat to consolidate the grain into a cake.

Fragmentary portions of unleavened bread have been unearthed in the ruins of the Swiss Lake dwellers, builders of the earliest known civilized communities of Europe. Too, among the ancient Egyptians the craft of baking was known before the 20th century B.C.

The bakers of ancient Greece were world famous. Also in Rome, public ovens were established in the time of the Republic. Bread was made chiefly in the home or in the small neighborhood bakeries until the end of the 19th century A.D., when the trend for "factory" bakeries began.

At that time manual labor was superseded in many of the operations by bread making machinery, including mixing machines, chain conveyors for carrying dough through temperature controlled areas during the rising periods, automatic baking ovens, and cooling, slicing and wrapping machines.

However; certain modern innovations cannot be regarded as improvements; for example, change in the process of flour milling, mainly to produce a white flour, eliminated many of the natural vitamins and minerals from the grains.

During World War II, the Federal government required as a public health measure, the enrichment with vitamins and minerals of all breads offered for sale to the public. However, after the war, it reverted to State control. Nowadays, there are newer machinery and ways in bread making, and now most of us are looking for "how many calories," and wanting to know if the bread is cholestrol free.

Just a few hints for bread making:

When bread comes from the oven lay the loaves on their sides on cake racks and cover them with a clean, dry cloth for about 20 minutes. The lines from the cake rack show where to slice the bread. It really is best not to cut the loaves until they are cool as the texture is not stable until then. Who in the world can resist sampling a slice of fresh, hot homemade bread? After it is cool, wrap and store it (for awhile).

If you like a soft, bright tender crust, brush the baked loaves with butter. For a crisp crust, let the bread cool naturally—do not butter it. Should you like a glazed crust, brush the dough before baking with a mixture of a slightly beaten egg yolk and four tablespoons of water.

Too, when using a recipe calling for bread, note whether soft or dry crumbs are specified. They should not be substituted for each another. Soft bread or chunks are preferred when the bread itself is a major ingredient, such as bread puddings, timbales, poultry stuffing or stewed vegetables. Dry bread crumbs are a fine grind that are used as an accent ingredient to enhance flavor and lend texture interest. Dry bread crumbs are used to bread meats, extend meat loaves and croquettes, or to add a crunchy topping to a hot vegetable dish.

* * *

A Thought To Ponder: Work is the yeast that raises the dough.

* * *

Rhubarb Bread

1 1/2 cups brown sugar, packed
2/3 cup cooking oil
1 egg
1 teaspoon salt
1 cup sour milk
1 teaspoon vanilla
1 1/2 cups diced rhubarb
2 1/2 cups unsifted flour
1 teaspoon soda
1/2 cup nuts, chopped

Mix ingredients in order given. Divide dough and put into greased and floured loaf pans. Bake in 350 degree oven for 40 minutes.

All in a Woman's Day--November 28, 1989

Christmas is season of giving and caring

There are so many beautiful things that relate to Christmas; however, we especially think of giving and caring.

With Thanksgiving over, and as you enter this holiday season, think about your gift giving.

* * *

What shall I give? You ask each year as Christmas days draw near. What can I do for those I love—what present can I buy? "What shall I give my feelings to express and to convey for the festival of love we keep on Christmas Day?"

"What shall I give," said God, "unto my children there below—struggling in the dark? What gift of joy can I bestow? ... " "I will go myself," He said, "as one of them to be. I will visit my creation. They, My face shall see."

"This will I do to prove my love and teach them how to live. More I cannot do for them and more I cannot give. I myself will be the gift within a human frame. I will give them Christmas to remind them that I came."

—Patience Strong

* * *

Have you every wondered why giving is so much a part of this wonderful holiday season? It is because, as the poem said, the coming of Christ represents the highest form of giving. God so loved the world that He gave His Only Son, that all men might be saved.

Christ gave Himself through a life of service, dedication, and a cruel death on the cross.

Mary gave her free consent to God to do His will, in love to bear the Child and to guide Him until He would be about His Father's work.

Joseph gave love, understanding and protection. No one could have done more that first night to find shelter and comfort, nor later expend more effort to protect mother and Child from those who sought so desperately to destroy them.

Therefore, the first Christmas was a day of giving in many ways, but most importantly it was the unselfish giving that it represented in dedication and service to the will of God.

If we but take a look at ourselves, we will find there are so many ways that we can share, that we can give. A bit of love is the most impressive present that we can give. A hug, too, wouldn't do any harm.

The best Christmas gifts are still those that come from the open heart, as well as the open hand, and the warmth of a friendly smile. The words of a cordial greeting add priceless meaning to whatever the gift may be.

It is so easy to get caught up in the materialism of Christmas that we forget to take time to enjoy important traditions of this most special time in our lives.

704

Sit down and think what you might be able to do, remembering that money, while important, is not everything.

Give a "certificate" redeemable for a service to some special someone. Maybe if it is someone with whom you live, promise to give up a habit the other person doesn't like or offer to stop nagging about something that upsets you.

Offer a night or a weekend of baby-sitting to good friends so that they can be alone or do something special they would enjoy that they seldom have the opportunity to do.

For family members, make up a photograph album with pictures of the past and the present with all individuals identified. This would be something they could treasure for a lifetime.

For faraway relatives, tape a message, and if you have a family, be sure to include the youngsters. Do not over-do the giving of gifts to children. Give only a few gifts so they will not be overwhelmed and end up not appreciating any of them.

Cook a favorite dish and share it with someone, possibly in your home or theirs.

Too, you might plan a special activity a day or two after Christmas to lessen the inevitable feeling of being let down when it's over. This, too could be shared as a giving experience.

And don't forget there are two sides to every coin. It may be "more blessed to give than to receive"; however, also it is true there is such a thing as being a "gracious receiver," and that in itself is an important attribute.

* * *

Somehow, not only
for Christmas,
But all the long year through,

The joy that you give to others
Is the joy that comes back to you;
And the more you spend
in blessing
The poor and lonely and sad,
The more of your
heart's possessing
Returns to make you glad.

—John Greenleaf Whittier

* * *

A Thought To Ponder: Joy is not in things. It is in us. —Wagner

* * *

Friendship Recipe

Take some morning sunshine,
Add a sprinkle,
some kind words, too ...
Then put in some happy hours,
It's not too hard to do ...
Add a little thoughtfulness,
Stir just enough to blend ...
Serve it warm with loving hands,
Giving it away
to family and friends.

All in a Woman's Day--December 5, 1989

It is time ...
for holiday baking

Christmas baking always has been a serious business. In earlier times one was not supposed to work on Christmas Day and as little as possible during the "Twelve Days of Christmas."

Consequently, great stores of baked foods, as well as roasted meats, were under preparation for weeks ahead. Today it is easier for the homemaker, not only because of labor saving equipment, but also, because of modern outlook.

Although the homemaker often follows traditions, she is no longer bound by inconvenient superstitutions, as for example, the Scandinavian women. Their baking had to be done in the

705

light of a new moon.

In Sweden, some families still follow the old observance of decorating the table with "Christmas pile," for each member of the household. This pile includes a great variety of cookies, candies and nuts.

Many of our British cousins eat turkey at Christmas; however, the roast goose of Dickens' "A Christmas Carol," long has been a favorite alternative.

The French have a big meal after church on Christmas Eve to usher in the holiday. Baked ham is a favorite; however, many people shun meat that night and serve eel, baked on a bed of leeks, moistened with white wine.

In Germany, where wild game abounds, hunters try to bag a deer or wild boar for Christmas.

We find that in Brazil, below the equator, Christmas comes during their summer and usually people serve a fish pie on Christmas Eve and celebrate the day with a picnic.

Too, there are many differences in Latin America. In Nicaragua for instance, the Yuletide feast is often built around a platter of tamales.

A Yule roast in Sweden may be ham, and a featured dish is highly flavored red cabbage. This meal begins with the traditional smorgasbord, including such delicacies as spareribs, sausage, pickled herring and liver paste.

Fancy Christmas cookies were introduced to America in the 18th century by the early German settlers, who counted their old cookie molds made of clay, tin or wood, among their most treasured heirlooms.

The industrious Pennsylvania Dutch housewives baked cookies by the wash basketful in such varying shapes as fish, rabbits, men smoking pipes, horseback riders, hatchet bearing Indians, stars, dolls and, of course, all the characters and animals associated with the nativity scene. They even made some reindeer that were more than a foot long. Outstanding cookie displays were proudly used to decorate windows. They were tucked into Christmas baskets for the poor, and it was customary to include several dozen cookies when returning molds that had been borrowed.

Many cookies were handed out to the Belsnickles, those costumed visitors like mummers, who went from house to house checking on the children's behavior during the year. Some of the Belsnickles were so terrifying that children were known to confess to hitherto unsuspected misdoings.

Candy canes have been one of the most popular symbols of the Christmas holidays. It began with an old superstition during the Middle Ages. Europeans of that period carried glass canes filled with colored candies to distract witches. They believed that the witches became so interested in sorting the candies that casting of evil spells was forgotten.

An orange in the Christmas stocking for many years in some families has been a tradition. A fresh orange was, indeed, a special treat for any child in the days when they were not quite so plentiful. Nobility oftentimes had potted citrus in glass houses to provide this midwinter treat.

The Swedish tradition of a "wishing cookie" is rather delightful. To make a wish, place a cookie in the palm of your hand and press in the center with one finger of the other hand. If the cookie breaks into three pieces and you eat all three without saying a word, you get to make a wish.

The recipe for the "Wishing Cookies" will follow, but first, however, I want to give you a "Christmas Scent" you might like to make. It is a holiday fragrance for your home. Take two cups water, one tablespoon whole cloves, three cinnamon sticks, one whole nutmeg or one teaspoon of ground nutmeg. Simmer all ingredients in a medium sized pan. Add additional water and spices when needed. It will make your home Christmasy fragrant.

* * *

A Thought To Ponder: Christmas began in lhe heart of God. It is complete only when it reachcs the hearts of people.

* * *

Wishing Cookies

3 1/4 cups flour
1 teaspoon baking soda
1 teaspoon ground cinnamon
3/4 teaspoon ground ginger
1/2 teaspoon ground nutmeg
1 cup butter or margarine
1 1/2 cups sugar
1 egg
2 tablespoons molasses
1 tablespoon water
1/2 teaspoon finely grated orange or lemon peel

Stir together flour, baking soda, cinnamon, ginger and nutmeg. In a large mixer bowl, beat butter or margarine until softened and add sugar, beating until it is fluffy. Add egg, molasses, water and peel; beat well; gradually add flour mixture, beating until well mixed. Cover and chill about 2 hours or until easy to handle. On lightly floured surface roll dough 1/8-inch thick. Cut it with cookie cutters. Place cookies on ungreased baking sheet and bake them in a 375 degree oven about 8 minutes or until done. Remove and cool. With a decorating bag and writing tip, pipe on a design with the icing that follows.

Lace Icing:

Stir together 2 cups sifted powdered sugar, 1/2 teaspoon vanilla and enough light cream or milk (about 2 tablespoons) to make icing of piping consistency. Makes about 100 cookies.

All in a Woman's Day--December 12, 1989
Beautiful legends give special meaning

During the Yuletide season, numerous legends come to light. Always there seems to be new ones, and this year is no different.

Each of the legends is beautiful and gives a special meaning to Christmas.

Those about animals are especially noteworthy and touching.

It has been told that the night of the birth of Jesus was the darkest ever known, but when the Child was born, a great light spread across the skies. Black branches put out green leaves; blossoms and berries appeared on withered vines; flowers never seen before sprang out of the dry earth. At that moment the cattle kneeling down in stalls of the little shed, spoke to each other. A cock crowed, "Christ is born!" and the animals whispered "Let us all worship together."

Another legend tells us that the barnyard animals show their adoration of the Child by falling on their knees just at midnight on Christmas Eve.

When the American Indians learned of the Baby Jesus, they naturally believed that the deer knelt at midnight on Christrnas Eve.

The folks in Norway honor all animals, even fish, at Yuletide. Cattle, birds and fish are assured of safety during the time that is known as the "Peace of Christmas." No snares are set during this period of time. The farmers feed their cattle salt from a cowbell in the belief that they would be able to find their way home at night.

In Old Italy on the Eve of Christmas, a curious ceremony takes place in the farmer's barn. The farmer and his shepherd would carry lighted candles, into every corner of the animal shelter, holding the tapers high so that the light was shed into every dark corner.

Too, in Scandinavian literature there is a story of Jesus as a boy helping his playmates to make clay birds. When he had finished modeling his bird, he would clap his hands and the bird would take wing and fly off into the skies.

Even the bee has its niche in the Christmas folklore. In England long ago it was believed that the bees sang to the Christ Child at midnight on Christmas Eve. Sprigs of holly were placed in beehives at Christmas. This comes from a legend that at the manger, bees gathered to hum a hymn of joy. Today holly growers still keep hives near their orchards.

One legend tells of a busy mother living in Germany, who cleaned her house until not a bit of dust remained and all the spiders fled to the attic. However, on Christmas Eve, when the tree was decorated, the poor spiders in the attic were heart broken because they could not see the tree or be there when the Christ Child made His visit. So, they finally crept through a crack in the door and sneaked into the room. But they had a problem ... they could only see one ornament at a time. Then they began to move up into the tree to see the beauty and, alas, everywhere they went, they left a trail of dusty, gray cobwebs.

When the Christ Child came to bless the tree, He was pleased to see that the spiders, whom he loved, for they were God's creatures, too, had found so much pleasure in the tree; however, he knew the mother would be heartbroken when she found the tree looking so dingy. So, he reached out His hand and touched the webs and they all turned to shimmering silver and gold. And that is how tinsel came into being. Since that time, however, many people have followed the custom of having a spider among the tree decorations. Some even use gold and silver spiders and webs as the only decorations. A group once made spiders that they packaged to sell and included the legend with this thought: "For you, this Christmas spider will turn all dusty gray thoughts into happy shimmering ones."

Then according to another legend, on December 26th it is the custom of "Feeding the Wren." Children place a wren in a cage in a bush and go collecting money in order to release the bird.

And, so the legends go on and on.

* * *

A Thought To Ponder: Christmas is the season when people take the milk of human kindness out of the deep freeze.

Warmest Wishes

Enjoy the special feelings of Christmas

Christmas gives the feeling of excitement that something glorious is about to happen. It is in the air, in the falling of the early dusk and the millions of twinkling lights everywhere.

Christmas is a house gaily disordered—paper, bits of ribbon, unmailed Christmas cards, berries that have dropped from holly boughs.

Christmas is the coming home of the family—the children, grandchildren, yes, even great-grandchildren that fill the old home with laughter and mirth, the glow of expectancy on faces and the love in the smile of a neighbor.

Christmas is the smell of food—pies, cookies, mincemeat and apple cider.

Christmas is the wrapping of packages, hanging of wreaths, the trimming of the Christmas tree, the lighting of thc candles and writing notes to old friends and loved ones.

Too, Christmas is the sound of carols, the chimes of "Jingle Bells" and "Silent Night" and the music so unique, that comes from the faraway stars.

Christmas is renewed concern for the welfare of our fellowmen, the desire that is burning within us for peace on earth and goodwill toward all men and nations.

* * *

A Thought To Ponder: Christmas is Christ living in the hearts of all persons.

* * *

The Work Of Christmas
When the song of the angels is stilled,
When the star in the sky is gone,
When the kings and princes are home,
When the shepherds are back with their flocks,
The work of Christmas begins:
To find the lost,
To heal the broken,
To rebuild nations,
To bring peace among brothers,
To make music in the heart,
—Dr. Howard Thurman
* * *

May each of you have a blessed Christmas!

Counting down the days!

Not many days until Old Father Time will be making his demise; and we will be looking for a Baby New Year that is full of promises for all good things.

As we think of Father Time, grave and determined with a scythe in his hand, he goes forward, with never a look back. On his forehead hangs a solitary lock of hair, and at the back of his head he is entirely bald—just a reminder to us that time is proverbially flying, that it never stands still. "Time and tide wait for no man."

Time seems to pass slowly and wearily for many. They do this or that, rushing here and there to "kill time." They follow certain pursuits that give them no real satisfaction and leave them disillusioned and disappointed.

People in this modern age seek reality in the present moment, here and now, believing in the old proverb, "A bird in the hand is worth two in the bush." But the present moment is the smallest individual moment or fraction of time.

Many devices have been invented to give folks the exact moment at a given time, that immediately dwindles into space. By the exact radio or television time, watches are set correct to the second. Time vanishes every second, and we strive to use profitably every passing moment in the time that may yet remain for us.

And so, as Father Time trudges ever onward and the old year steps aside, the new will move in. And to mark the transition, as always, there will be celebrations symbolizing our hopes for a clean slate that lies ahead.

There will still be 12 months in the year, seven days in the week, 24 hours in a day and 60 seconds in a minute. However, our conception of time is a bit different today from what it used to be. Through Einstein's theory of relativity and our discoveries in space, we have come to the conclusion that time—and space—are endless.

* * *

Let's think less this year about Number One,

Let's all help someone else have fun.

Let's never speak of the faults of a friend,

Until we are ready our own to amend.

Resolve to laugh with and not at other folk,

And never hurt anyone just for a joke.

Let's hide our troubles and show only cheer,

Then surely we'll have quite a Happy New Year.

* * *

From the Virginia Almanack (1773) comes this "Holiday Toast:"—"We wish you health and good Fires; Victuals; Drink and good Stomachs, innocent Diversion, and good Company; honest Trading, and good Success; loving Courtship, and good Wives, and lastly a happy New Year.

* * *

A Thought To Ponder: Each year is a new beginning ... a golden dawn on the horizon of life.

* * *

May each of you have a wonderful New Year!

* * *

Bubbly Cranberry Punch

2 cans jellied cranberry sauce (16-ounce size)
1/2 cup lemon juice
1 1/2 cups orange juice
2 large bottles chilled gingerale (28-ounce bottles)

Beat cranberry sauce until smooth and stir in lemon and orange juices. Empty several trays of ice cubes into a punch bowl and pour mixture over them. Carefully add gingerale and mix. Makes about 20-25 cups.

All in a Woman's Day--January 2, 1990

The olive ...
is the oldest fruit

Perhaps one of the richest heritages from ancient times is the olive that ranks among the world's oldest fruits.

This popular fruit has earned a place in history; however, the martini drinker probably has little realization of the years of history that bob about in his glass.

Olive trees were first cultivated 6,000 years ago in the Mediterranean basin.

Those first wild olive trees were low, thorny, gnarled shrubs, as well as being puny; their fruit was low in oil. The Syrians and Palestinians developed the compact oil rich and beautiful olive tree as we know it today about 4000 B.C., and it still grows in the Mediterranean countries and California.

The Mount of Olives takes its name from a grove of olive trees that stood on its western flank, but has now in most part disappeared. It was here that most sacred associations of Christian history converge.

The olive was cultivated in Crete from about 2500 B.C., where the island prospered from its exportations of olive oil and the timber felled to make room for the olive groves.

Reay Tannahill in her book "Food in History," has this interesting sidelight: "At the onset of the sixth century B.C., a statesman prohibited the exportation of any agricultural product other than olive oil. So the trees were quickly felled to make room for olive trees. The deep taproots of the olive tree couldn't preserve the precious topsoil as well as the roots of the trees they replaced, so by the fourth century B.C., Plato was gloomily contrasting the bare white limestone of the Attic countryside he knew with the green meadows, woods and springs of the past. The pure and brilliant light, which is so startling a characteristic of Greece, today has been bought at the expense of the trees that had once kept the land fertile."

The apple or plum shaped olive has been a basic food in all the Mediterranean countries, even in modern times. It was in the 1800s that olives became important to the agricultural economics of Mexico, Argentina, Chile and Australia.

The Spaniards brought the black or ripe olives into the New World through Mexico in the 18th century and into California in the year 1769. The Franciscan monks first planted them at the San Diego Mission. Then 100 years later the groves were large enough to be of commercial importance; and at the turn of the century a processing method was discovered.

In Syria, the olives' native habitat, the possession of a strain of cultural olive, yielding much more oil and commercial wealth than the wild variety, was regarded as a symbol of cultural and economic advancement; the offer of an olive branch, from which such trees were propagated, was regarded as a symbol of friendship and came to be accepted as a token of peace.

Among the ancient Greeks the olive was regarded as the gift of the goddess Pallas Athena, to whom it was sacred, and a crown of olive branches was a symbol of the highest honor bestowed by the state. The Roman writer Pliny reported that a long and pleasant life depended upon "wine within and oil without." Later the use of olive oil came to be regarded more as a necessary substitute for butter and other animal oils than as a luxury.

The wood of the olive is hard, often variegated, and is valued for cabinet work.

In those ancient times, from one large tree, a family could obtain a year-round supply of green olives, also the ripe black ones, as well as the oil. In fact, such a tree could produce as much as half a ton of oil and all the fruit a family could use.

In those lands, where dairy products were scarce, olives provided the fat vital to the human diet. The oil was a key part of the cuisine and still is in Spain, France and Italy.

Olive trees are late starters and don't

bear fruit until they are eight years old. Thus, an olive grove, that eventually becomes highly profitable, represents considerable outlay of money at the beginning.

* * *

A Thought To Ponder: You're never too old to learn—and what you learn is what makes you old.

* * *

Olive Surprises

1/4 cup soft butter or margarine
1 cup grated sharp Cheddar cheese
1/4 teaspoon each of salt and paprika
1/2 cup sifted all-purpose flour
3 dozen medium-size stuffed olives

Cream butter and cheese until blended. Add remaining ingredients except olives, and mix well. Chill for 15 to 20 minutes. Shape a small portion of dough around each olive. Bake in preheated hot oven 400 degrees about 15 minutes. Good hot or cold. Makes 36.

All in a Woman's Day--January 9, 1990
Learn more about olives

We are going to learn a little more about olives for which, it has been said, you have to acquire a taste. (This I believe.)

In the event you didn't know, olives all begin life green in color.

Right off the tree they are too bitter to eat and must be "cured" to take away the bitterness. Green olives are not soaked as long, and that is why they are more bitter than black, ripe olives.

In the process of curing and fermentation as they are oxidized (exposed to air), they turn black. They can be kept green by avoiding oxidation.

When olives are allowed to ripen on the tree, they go through color phases similar to those of the apple—from green, they turn a strawberry blond, then deep red, then red, purple-black, and finally black.

Hand picking the black ripe olives is necessary to avoid bruising, and processing them takes about three weeks. When the finishing process is varied to inhibit darkening, the resulting brown flecked light green olives are sold as "green ripe."

Black olives are packaged as whole unpitted, whole pitted, sliced and chopped. There are nine different sizes available.

In many of the olive growing areas, homemakers put the fruit to many uses besides canapes. For instance, there is olive stuffing, olive bread and olive soup.

Even though featured in cooking, the olive oil also was used for light in lamps and fuel for stoves. In the days of Caesar, Romans rubbed themselves with olive oil, which they believed contributed to longevity.

Egyptians made more extensive use of olive oil than we do today. Oil from the first pressing was used to baste meat roasts, dress vegetables and make sauces.

The second time around the fruit was pressed to produce an oil to moisten the skin and dress the hair. A third pressing yielded oil for lamps and fuel for stoves.

Americans generally think of olives as a condiment, appetizer and for seasoning. Europeans are more versatile and have long used the fruit in cooking meat dishes, especially stews and meat loaves.

Foreign suppliers long have cornered the market on olive oil. A staple in

Mediterranean diets, olive oil has become quite popular with connoisseurs in large cities who willingly pay up to $20 or more a liter for the finest extra-virgin oils.

Extra-virgin is expensive because it is made with the finest hand picked fruit and is pressed on stone hand presses. Olive oil is cold pressed, a low pressure technique that doesn't heat the oil and thus prevents loss of flavor, color and nutrients.

The cold pressing process is carried out in stages. Water is added in subsequent pressings of the olive pulp to help the flow of oil. The water is drawn off after the oil is collected.

Oil labeled "virgin" comes from the first pressing and is less expensive than the extra-virgin as it is not generally pressed by hand and the fruit is not hand picked with the same care. "Pure" oil may be made from second or third pressings, and in the United States it may contain chemically extracted oil. The final pressings produce oil useful only in the manufacture of soap, textiles and other nonfood applications.

That is the story of this strange fruit, the popular olive, that adds that extra touch to the relish tray. Few are the pantries that cannot boast at least one bottle or jar of olives on a shelf.

* * *

A Thought To Ponder: Coming together is a beginning; keeping together is progress; working together is success.

All in a Woman's Day--January 16, 1990
Teapots can be elegant

The hustle and bustle of the holidays is over, so why not settle down, and relax with a cup of your favorite tea?

There are so many different, delightful kinds and blends on the market nowadays that you should have no trouble finding the one that is special for you.

And the brewing? How do you do it? What kind of a teapot do you use? Oh, there are all kinds of teapots.

Since the Chinese created them some 4,000 years ago, this special container for brewing tea has been recreated endlessly in a variety of imaginative forms, especially during the 200 years or more they have been manufactured in the western world.

The one used today, however, is essentially the same shape as the first ones brought here from China in the 1600s. It is a pot or a vessel of some size, generally short and stout, that has a cover, a handle and a spout.

The favorite material for teapots here, as well as in China, is pottery or porcelain. In the West, silver became a second choice only for families who could afford a teapot made of such valuable material. To some extent, pewter also was used in America until about 1859, with copper and tin known to have been used in some parts of the world. There also have been some wooden teapots, however, these, no doubt, were oddities and displayed more than used.

The early teapots were small. Since the price of tea was high and it was very scarce, tea was made only in small amounts.

Along about the 1730s, silver teapots that were pear-shaped made their appearance. Later, however, about the 1750s they were made in an inverted pear-shape, usually footed. During the 18th century, about 1757, teapots were made of mottled shades of brown and buff into a glaze distinctive earthenware. A similar mottled glaze was used in 1849 in American pottery in Vermont, Maryland and along the Ohio River Valley. Perhaps the most coveted by collectors was a teapot made here and known as Rebecca at the Well.

The 18th century was a favorable time for the western potters; however, before the turn of the century many of the English potters had created a new attractive kind of earthen and stoneware. This stoneware originated in Germany and its distinctive glaze and color was due to the table salt that was thrown over it before the final firing. Earlier salt glaze of a rather gray-white tone was being molded into teapots in such odd shapes as a house, a camel and a ram. Some small teapots with floral decorations were made of the English Delft. Agate ware of the same period also was being made.

Following the end of the Revolutionary War, a straight sided cylindrical teapot, with the monogram of the purchaser in a shield surrounded by a ship flying the American Flag, made its appearance. It was after the war that the United States began to trade directly with China, and to our country was brought the typically Chinese canton, a porcelain teapot with blue decoration.

It was during the 1740s that porcelain teacups and saucers were first manufactured in England; however, prior to that tea had been served, for the most part, in drinking glasses set on glass plates. It was only the wealthier that could afford the Oriental and Continental porcelain. The English glassmakers were forced to compete with the making of more delicate and colorful wares. They replied with a skillfully ornamental glass porcelain; however, the cordial glass remained part of the tea table equipment for an additional quarter of a century.

In the late 1700s the straight-sided cylindrical teapots, not much larger than the pear-shaped teapots, appeared with the boat-shaped teapot following in the early 1800s. Along about 1830, even silver teapots were made larger in size with decorations of gadroomg and fluttering. These were very popular. As attractive as metal teapots may have been, the western potters began to turn out teapots in earthen and stoneware to find out if that material could be as popular as porcelain. (The porcelain won.)

Not all of the teapots were marked. Many of the luster and gold banded tea sets quite likely carried no markings of a potter or maker. Neither do a great many of the teapots that were used and loved during the 19th century. We do think, however, of the Meissen in Germany; Wedgewood in England; and Haviland in France, all of which had their marks as to shape, kind of pottery or type of porcelain glaze and the style of decoration applied.

I am sure you will agree that there is something about a teapot that seems to have charm, whether it is whimsical, quaint, graceful or elegant. Even those folks who are nontea drinkers oftentimes wind up by acquiring a collection of dozens of teapots.

There is a sort of curious body response to a teapot, don't you agree? Garth Clark, a New York City art ceramics historian and author, has said that a teapot's shape is so human that it lends itself to caricature and is often used as a form of satire or political protest, with part of the attraction being the warm fuzzy aura that surrounds the tea-drinking ritual.

He further commented that even those who do not drink tea have learned to think of tea as comforting or celebratory, and to associate the tea ceremony with mother, home and a sense of well-being.

The same elements that give a teapot its human form make it an attractive challenge to artists, with each part of the pot—body, handle, spout and lid—offering design opportunity to let the imagination roam fancy free. Perhaps you have never seen any teapots shaped like birds, buildings, fish, cabbages, kings, crowns and cars. But some like that do exist. This kind of distinctive styling seems almost beyond imagination.

* * *

A Thought To Ponder: Too many people don't care what happens, so long as it doesn't happen to them.

* * *

Friendship Tea

2 cups sugar
2 cups instant orange breakfast drink
3/4 cup instant tea
1 (3-ounce package) instant lemonade
1 teaspoon cinnamon
1/2 teaspoon ground cloves
1/4 teaspoon salt

Combine all ingredients and store them in a tightly closed jar. Use as you would instant tea. This is good either hot or iced.

All in a Woman's Day--January 23, 1990

Facts of interest related about tea

A little something about tea goes well with the teapot story.

There are several legends or stories concerning tea. It has been written that without a doubt the world's first cup of tea occurred when a wild tea bush fell into a pot of drinking water as it was being boiled. The flavor was enjoyed, and from then on it might be said that the beverage "took off."

Then there is another story that notes the use of tea was discovered by Emperor Shennog or (Shen Nung) of China about 2737 B.C. However, the earliest known mention of tea appeared in Chinese literature about 350 A.D.

A book mentioning tea was published in Venice in 1559. The first reference in writing to tea drinking in China dates from the eighth century A.D. So, there is some discrepancy.

Tea was known in Japan as early as the sixth century, but was not widely used as a beverage until the 11th century, when Buddhist priests began to encourage its use for medicinal reasons and because it was thought the ritual of tea drinking was morally uplifting. Another account notes that tea was grown in Japan in the ninth century from plants imported from China.

Tea drinking was introduced into Europe and America in the 17th century, and it became a great commercial item in England in the 17th century and in the United States in the 18th century.

The first shipment of tea was made to Europe in 1610 by Dutch traders, who imported it from China and Japan. By 1650 the Dutch were importing tea into the American colonies.

In 1657 tea was sold for the first time in a coffeehouse in England, and it went on to become the national beverage of Great Britain, with some people drinking tea at the rate of 11 pounds per person per year.

In 1767 Britain placed a tax on the tea being used by the American colonies and the resistance to this tax is what brought on the Boston Tea Party in 1773, and also contributed to the American independence movement.

In 1839 a tea bush was found growing wild in India by a British major named Robert Bruce. Within the next few years, many tea plantations were established in India. In that year, eight chests of tea, the first ever to come from India, were auctioned off in London.

Traders from Europe, sailing to and from the Far East in the 16th century, began to take back word of an unusual Oriental beverage called tea. The price was as high as $8.50 a pound; however, it wasn't until 1880 that tea became an important part of India's economy.

The first tea on the island of Indonesia was planted in 1684. But on the isle of Ceylon, now Sri Lanka, coffee was the chief crop until a few years following 1869.

It was in that year that a severe blight attacked the coffee trees and killed all of them. Since the farms had to be replanted, this time tea plants were used instead of coffee trees. Today tea is this island's principal crop.

Attempts to grow tea in North America failed because of high labor costs, however, it has been grown successfully in Brazil, where it is economically increasing in importance.

The people of the Far East have a legend about how man began to use tea. According to the story, there was a saint in India, who prayed without stopping for many years.

Then, one day he fell asleep. The saint was so upset that he had fallen asleep that he cut off his eyelids and threw them away. For five years more he continued his prayer without sleep; then he again felt sleep coming over him.

He chewed some leaves from a shrub nearby and began to feel bright and wide awake. When people found out about the shrub, many others began to chew its leaves.

The manner in which folks drink tea differs all over the world. The English speaking people usually drink their tea with sugar and sometimes with cream, milk or lemon juice added. The English commonly drink tea for breakfast, the midday meal, the four o'clock tea hour and supper.

The people of the Orient almost never use sugar in their tea. Dried, Jasmine blossoms are sometimes added to tea to give it a delightful fragrance.

Japanese tea drinking has become a social custom among the people, and there are strict rules or manners for tea drinking. The Scots often brewed tea so strong that it resembled black coffee.

A few people like to add liquor; such as rum, scotch or cognac. In Tibet a cup of tea is served with a lump of yak butter floating on its surface. The Tibetans are so fond of this that they drink a great many cups—at least 10 to 20 and sometimes more a day.

The French drop a small sweet cake, called a Madeleine, into the tea to sweeten it.

* * *

A Thought To Ponder: Praise, like sunlight, helps all things to grow.

* * *

Cherub Coin Cookie

3/4 cup butter or margarine
1 1/2 cups firmly packed light brown sugar
1 egg, beaten
2 cups sifted cake flour
1/8 teaspoon baking soda

1/2 teaspoon salt
1/4 cup finely chopped pecans

Cream butter or margarine and add sugar, add egg; mix well. Mix and sift flour, baking soda and salt; add gradually, mixing well after each addition. Stir in chopped pecans. Chill overnight. Shape into tiny balls, 1/2 inch in diameter. Place them on a greased cookie sheet; flatten them slightly with thumb. Bake at 375 degrees for 8 to 10 minutes. Let the cookies stand a few minutes before removing from cookie sheet. Makes about 10 dozen.

All in a Woman's Day--January 30, 1990

Tea appears in many varieties

The tea story, like Topsy, just grew and grew, but this is the end of that story, I promise. For your information, teas are divided into three kinds, brought about in the process of curing. They are green, brown and black.

The green tea leaves, after gathering, are quickly dried over a fire. They do remain green in color. The tea has a pale green tinge and is delicate in flavor. Most often green teas are served plain.

This variety includes hyson, young hyson, hyson skin, imperial caper, gunpowder and the teas known as Chinese green and Japanese green.

Brown tea leaves are dried for a time in the sun and air before drying a second time over a fire. The leaves are brown in color, and the tea is darker than the green tea. Its flavor is aromatic. Brown teas, including ooling and Ceylon, most generally are served plain or with lemon and no sugar.

Black tea leaves are dried in baskets in the sun and air until a fermentation occurs; then they are roasted over charcoal before a final drying over a fire. This blend is considered fruity and is served with milk, light cream, cloves, sugar and orange peel or lemon. The leaves are black.

Among the varieties of this tea are pekoe, congou, bohea, darjeeling, souchong, and the teas labeled as English or Irish breakfast, and Earl Grey (this tea is more aromatic and needs very little or no sugar).

The use of iced tea and tea bags began in the United States. Richard Blechynden, an Englishman trying to increase the use of tea in this country, first served iced tea at the St. Louis Exposition (also called the St. Louis World's Fair) in 1904.

That same year Thomas Sullivan, a New York City coffee and tea merchant, sent his customers samples of the tea leaves in small silk bags instead of the usual containers. The customers began to order tea leaves in bags after finding that tea could be brewed easily from them.

Instant tea developed in this country; first marketed in 1948. Now the tea bags are made of a special filter paper and come regular or decaffeinated.

Many people used tea balls or muslin strainers in earlier days when brewing tea.

About 150 to 200 cups of tea can be brewed from each pound of tea, according to statistics.

* * *

A Thought To Ponder: A lie can take care of the present but it has no future.

* * *

Angel Whisper Cookies
1 cup butter or margarine
1/2 cup sifted confectioners' sugar
1 teaspoon lemon extract

2 cups sifted all-purpose flour
1/4 teaspoon salt

Cream butter to consistency of mayonnaise; add sugar gradually while continuing to cream. Add remaining ingredients; blend well; chill. Measure a level teaspoon of dough; round into balls; flatten slightly and place them about 1 inch apart on ungreased baking sheet. Bake at 400 degrees for 8 to 10 minutes or until edges are lightly browned. Put together with the following Lemon Filling. Makes about 5 dozen double cookies. This is a delightful cookie to serve with tea.

Lemon Filling

1 egg, slightly beaten
Grated peel of 1 lemon
2/3 cup sugar
3 tablespoons lemon juice
1 1/2 teaspoons soft butter or margarine

Blend all ingredients in top of double boiler. Cook over hot water, stirring constantly until thick. Chill until firm. Spread on cookie, placing another on top of filling.

All in a Woman's Day--February 6, 1990

Enjoy Valentine's Day to your heart's delight

Amidst all the dark and dreary days that often make up the month of February, there is one day that seems to stand out, that shines through like a beacon of light: It is Feb. 14, Valentine's Day.

No one really seems to know just why this special day is associated with romance and love; however, it is and that makes a nice respite during the wintertime.

The name Valentine evolved from the Latin word for healthy, strong. It has been used occasionally ever since the days of ancient Rome; however, never frequently. Most Valentines in this country are called "Val" by friends and family.

Hearts are a symbol of love and so are birds. Folklore tells us that Feb. 14, the most romantic holiday of the year, is supposed to be the day when each little bird "chooses its love mate."

Still another story or theory concerning Valentine's Day is that it is celebrated in honor of the oldest and best loved of the Roman gods, Faunus, the god of nature.

Since hearts depict love, no doubt that is the reason for so many of them being everywhere at this special time of the year.

There are so many ways to say "Be My Valentine," You Are My Valentine," or "I Love You." Select the way that suits you best

Since amethyst is the birthstone for this month, you might like to consider giving jewelry, especially featuring this stone. That would light up the eyes of that someone special in your life. It seems that the tint of this stone varies in color from an almost colorless violet to a deep purple.

Colorful cards, with endearing sentiments, are available almost everywhere. Their popularity has increased since the widespread use of valentines began sometime during the 18th century. There are cards for husbands, wives and sweethearts. There are musical cards that play "Love Story," "You Light Up My Life," and the old, but familiar love song, "Let Me Call You Sweetheart."

Flowers are another way of showing love, with roses, the flower of romance, the most popular. Carnations provide a less expensive alternative that conforms to the lovely red valentine color.

It takes a little bit of doing to get roses ready for this special time of year. The supply of red flowers are most often depleted because of the Christmas holidays, so a new crop must then be started. It takes approximately 57 days of perfect sunlight to develop and mature a rose. This is rather difficult to achieve during the short and cloudy days of winter.

There are flowers in every price range, potted plants, mixed bouquets, and if you are planning on going dancing, a lovely corsage of silk flowers is a delightful gift.

Balloon-o-grams also are popular. And there are singing telegrams; however, those probably are not accessible here.

Then there is candy! Chocolates just seem to say that sugary sentiment you want to convey to your loved one. There are red heart shaped boxes of candy as well as conversation heart candy.

A dinner and a show is another way of expressing affection.

Sunday School or Church School teachers might make a valentine box with a slit in the top for the youngsters to drop in their offering to show God they love Him.

A valentine signature tree is an inexpensive project that could be done at school, Sunday school or at home to be sent to a classmate, who is ill, or to an elderly shut-in. Print your name; or little messages on hearts cut from red construction paper and on the other side paste a picture of a flower cut from a magazine. Use a gummed, sticker or perhaps just make your own.

Tie these on the limbs of a forked tree branch about a foot high, and anchor well in clay or plaster of paris.

The kitchen might be the place from whence comes a sweet gift ... heart shaped cookies or candies. Mother also might prepare a dinner of special foods.

Heart shaped valentines have long been a familiar way of expressing love. Red, the symbol of love, denotes the life blood, and thus the sincerity of the giver. Folklore reveals that in earlier years when you chose a valentine, it was the same as choosing a wife. So, you should be a bit careful!

Perhaps many of you will remember the "Vinegar" cards. Some of them were pretty cutting and cruel. For instance here are a couple that reveals the sting implanted in them:

> You clumsy, puffy porpoise
> So flabby, fat and lazy,
> It's too bad you're not a hog,
> For you'd then be quite a daisy.

* * *

> To an oleo-margarine factory
> I warn you don't go near
> You'd be such a prize,
> They'd seize you and melt you down,
> I fear.

* * *

There is really no way you can put a price on love, but some of the ways mentioned might help you to say "Be My Valentine."

* * *

A Thought To Ponder: Love will find a way ... indifference will find an excuse.

* * *

For that bit of sweetness for this special time of year, you might try this Date Roll, which is a candy.

DeLoris' Date Roll Candy

4 cups sugar
1 cup milk
1 cup chopped dates
1 cup nuts, chopped
1 tablespoon butter
1 teaspoon vanilla

Cook sugar, milk and dates over slow heat, stirring constantly until the mixture forms a hard ball in cold water. Then add butter, vanilla and chopped nuts, beating until creamy. Spread on a wet, cold towel and roll up. Wrap the roll in waxed paper and keep it in the refrigerator. After it cools, it is ready to be cut and eaten.

This recipe was given to her by her mother-in-law, Julia Teson Eickholt.

All in a Woman's Day--February 13, 1990

Kitchen tips help

It's always nice to have a few hints to help get the homemaker out of the kitchen a little quicker.

Here are a few that just might do the trick.

If you must peel potatoes ahead of time and have to leave them overnight, a slice of bread in the water will stop them from discoloring.

When making gelatin, always add the powder to the boiling water instead of pouring the water over the gelatin. The granules will dissolve quickly as they hit the water, so you don't have to stir and stir. Besides, there shouldn't be a rubbery layer at the bottom of the dish or bowl if done this way.

To make meat loaf fluffier, add a little baking powder to the recipe.

If you have a cake mix or any other ready mix that you feel might be getting a little too old for the best results, just try adding an extra teaspoon of baking powder to the mix. Too, a little flavoring also will help. Fix your mix as usual. It should turn out fluffy and fresh tasting, as well as flavorful.

Use a coffeemaker—one with a warming plate—to keep a dish of food warm. They also are ideal to make a hot pot of tea when you are not in a real hurry. Just fill a glass with water, drop in the bags, and set on the plate.

We all know the secret of apples keeping brown sugar fresh and bread to keep cookies fresh, but now it is said that celery will keep bread fresh. Put a piece in the bag and tie tightly.

A dab of peanut butter—smooth or crunch—added to your favorite chili recipe lends a nutty characteristic to the dish.

Use a vegetable peeler to slice cheese from a brick. The thin slices spread easily and melt quickly in recipes being prepared. For a quick cheese sauce, simply place some of these extra thin slices on top of a bowl of hot vegetables.

If perhaps you have to drink powdered nonfat dry milk, the taste can be improved. Add 1/2 teaspoon of coffee cream to your glass or milk or 1/2 teaspoon of vanilla extract.

Add a heaping tablespoon of wheat germ to each serving of cooked cereal. This adds nutrition.

A dab of anchovy paste, blended with mayonnaise, transforms a mild condiment into a snappy taste delight.

Never slice a tomato until just before eating. About three minutes after slicing, the pleasant aroma and flavor starts to fade. Also keep them at room temperature rather than in the refrigerator because cold also causes loss of aroma.

Combine a few drops of Worcestershire sauce, plus a pinch of flavor enhancer, in melted butter for boiled corn and seafood to provide an extra zippy taste.

Brush plain steak with a blend of flavor enhancer and prepared mustard for a spicy addition before broiling, which reduces the hotness of the mustard to a savory, tangy flavor.

Add flavorings to cooked cereals like oatmeal and wheat cereals. They might include black walnut, coconut, maple, vanilla or burnt sugar flavorings.

You might place the flavors on the table at breakfast time and whichever takes a person's fancy can be sprinkled into the bowl of hot cereal.

Don't try exotic new recipes for guests. Make a trial run for the family. This precaution will help you be a happy hostess.

Keep your sugar from getting lumpy by putting a soda cracker in with it.

Wire cheese cutters make slicing frozen dough much easier.

For an easier and speedier cleanup, try using a potato peeler instead of a grater when grating small amounts of hard cheese.

* * *

A Thought To Ponder: Opportunity knocks. Temptation kicks the door down.

* * *
No Knead Rolls
1 1/2 cups warm water
2 packages dry yeast
4 cups sifted flour
1/4 cup sugar
1/3 cup soft shortening
1 1/2 teaspoons salt
1 egg

Pour water in large mixing bowl; add yeast and let it stand a few minutes; stir to dissolve. Add half of flour, then the sugar, salt, shortening and egg. Beat until smooth, 1 1/2 to 2 minutes.

Add rest of flour. Scrape sides of bowl. Cover the dough and let rise in warm place until double in bulk, about 30 minutes. Grease muffin pans, spoon in batter, filling about half full. Let rise until they reach the top of the muffin cups. Bake in hot oven 10 to 15 minutes.

All in a Woman's Day--February 20, 1990
Macadamia nuts ... flavor delights
This is Macadamia Nut Month; however, it is a nut we don't hear too much about.

Native of Australia, it was named for John Macadam, a Scottish scientist and physician, who lived and worked in Australia.

This shiny seed, that has a creamy colored kernel, has a hard, smooth shell and grows on a tropical evergreen tree. The kernel is round and very rich in flavor.

Sometimes known as the Queensland nut, it has been cultivated in Hawaii as that state's commercial crop. Approximately 50 million pounds have been produced there each year in the past few years. There are some 660 macadamia nut farms now in Hawaii.

This nut is rich in oil and has a sweet flavor similar to that of the Brazil nut. The seeds can be eaten after roasting and salting; however, they also are good eaten raw. This nut is especially enjoyed as a cocktail snack.

Outside their place of origin, the macadamia nuts are almost always sold shelled and roasted.

They can be used in making pie, a Hawaiian spinoff of the traditional pecan pie, with a hint of orange; a macadamia nut cream turnover; a pastry shell of Bavarian creme laced with the tropical, soft white nut.

In addition they are used in cakes, candies, cookies, brownies, as a garnish for seafood and chicken, a crumb coating for fish and vegetables, and as a topping for dips and sauces.

They are available in supermarkets in vacuum packed tins and jars. Unopened they will keep indefinitely in these containers in a cool place; however, once opened the nuts should be used within one month or frozen for longer storage.

* * *

A Thought To Ponder: "'Tis an ill cook that cannot lick her own fingers."

* * *

Following is a recipe that sometime you might like to try.

United Airlines
Macadamia Nut Cake

1 1/2 cups corn oil
2 cups sugar
3 eggs
1 1/2 cups shredded carrots
2 teaspoons baking soda
2 teaspoons salt
1 teaspoon ground cinnamon
1 teaspoon ground allspice
1 teaspoon vanilla
1 tablespoon corn starch
3/4 cup chopped macadamia nuts

Combine all ingredients and mix until blended. Turn batter into a 9x13-inch baking dish and bake 45 minutes to an hour at 350 degrees. Let it cool and frost with the following cream cheese frosting.

Cream Cheese Frosting

1 (8-ounce) package cream cheese
3/4 cup butter or margarine
2 cups powdered sugar
1/2 teaspoon vanilla
1 teaspoon lemon juice

Cream the cheese and butter with the powdered sugar, vanilla and lemon juice until slightly fluffy. Spread on the cooled cake.

All in a Woman's Day--February 27, 1990

Ways to beat the egg, just try substituting

With so many people conscious about eating eggs, possibly because of an allergy or needing to watch their cholesterol, I have found several "how to beat the egg" suggestions that might replace this "hen fruit."

There are commercial egg substitutes on the market to replace eggs in your recipes; however, here are a few you can make at home.

If you have a recipe that calls for one egg you may substitute by using two tablespoons water along with a half teaspoon baking powder.

Or one egg white plus two tablespoons polyunsaturated oil equals a whole egg.

One egg white, two and one-fourth teaspoons nonfat dry milk powder and a teaspoon of vegetable oil mixed together will equal one egg.

Two egg whites may be substituted for a whole egg. One to three teaspoons vegetable oil may be added for every yolk that is omitted.

If the recipe includes two or three eggs, for each egg, the following substitution may be made: two tablespoons water, milk or other fluid, a half teaspoon baking powder, one and a half teaspoons vegetable oil and two tablespoons flour.

For two eggs you may substitute with the following: Three egg whites, two tablespoons powdered milk, one teaspoon water, few drops yellow food coloring if needed. Blend together the egg whites and powdered milk and then add the water and food coloring.

Another substitute for two whole eggs that makes a half cup of liquid substitute is four egg whites, one tablespoon oil, one tablespoon nonfat dry milk powder and three drops of yellow food coloring. Combine and mix together until well blended.

Since eggs are a binding for cookies and cakes, you might want to try using one-third cup of water and one tablespoon flaxseed. Bring this to a boil, reducing to low heat and cooking for 5 minutes or just until the mixture is of the consistency of a raw egg white.

Omelettes made with egg whites are practically cholesterol free. Whip the whites until stiff, but not dry. Heat your omelet pan and spray it with nonstick coating. Cook whites until set on top and nicely browned on the bottom. Top with a mixed vegetable or other filling, fold and serve immediately.

* * *

Here are some other substitutes that might be of interest:

As a substitute for dairy case cottage cheese, try clabbering the milk and then heat slowly until the whey rises to the top. Pour off and place curds in a bag and let them dry six hours. Do not squeeze. Pour into a bowl, season and store in the refrigerator.

Low fat yogurt is an excellent substitute for mayonnaise and cream in salad dressing recipes. You may also dollop it on a baked potato in place of sour cream.

Many good cooks prefer sour cream to sweet cream for certain recipes. Often sweet cream when left to sour by itself develops an undesirable flavor and odor. However, you can sour your own cream with consistently good results by shaking up five teaspoons of buttermilk in a fresh pint of the liquid cream. Let the mixture stand 24 hours at a temperature between 70 and 85 degrees before using.

* * *

A Thought To Ponder: The best way to grow old is not to be in a hurry about it.

* * *

Cherry Pie Substitute

3 cups apples, sliced
1 1/4 cups cranberries
1 1/2 tablespoons flour
1 cup sugar
1/2 teaspoon cinnamon
2 tablespoons margarine

Mix the ingredients and place the mixture in an unbaked crust, then place top crust. Bake for 10 minutes in a 400 degree oven and then at 350 degrees for 30 minutes.

All in a Woman's Day--March 6, 1990

Hiccup remedies given

It makes no difference how you spell it—hiccup, hiccough, hicke up, hiccop, hickok, hickup, hicket, hickhop, hikup, hecup or hickop—it's a situation that is most uncomfortable and annoying. Most of us spell this word hiccup.

Having hiccups is nothing new, for folks have been having attacks for, well we might say, from the dawn of time.

The different spellings are those in English, and date back possibly as far as 1544. At this time the accepted medical practice for this occurrence was to "cast colde water in the face of him that hath the hicket." The British persist in spelling the word as hiccough; however, it has nothing whatsoever to do with a cough, and is still pronounced hiccup.

Hiccups are caused by spasm of the

diaphragm, the muscle under the lungs that controls breathing. This condition appears to cause a sudden intake of air that ends with a "hic," as the glottis snaps to a close.

This can happen or be brought on by rapid eating, eating spicy foods, pneumonia, alcoholism, stomach and intestinal upsets, pregnancy, bladder infections, perhaps using tobacco or a hearty laugh after a large meal.

Prolonged hiccups can be stopped by surgery; however, it has been said it can inhibit breathing.

There are dozens of folk remedies that are supposed to help stop the hiccups. A lot of them might seem to work because the hiccups usually do go away by themselves, except in unusual cases.

Lots of the remedies can be found right in the kitchen. If you have a tendency to have hiccups, keep some of these home remedies in mind, just in case.

Eating a teaspoon of peanut butter, sugar, salt, vinegar, Worcestershire sauce, crushed ice, lemon juice or eating dry bread (not all at once).

Several of the remedies involve water. For instance, drinking water through a folded handkerchief, drinking water rapidly, drinking water out of the wrong side (this is the far side) of a glass, holding your ears and nostrils and drinking water, taking a mouthful of water and swallowing in three gulps, then repeating three times, and in the meantime stand perfectly still and breath through your nose.

Drink a glass of water while standing on your head, hold your ears and drink water using a drinking straw, lay a chair on your stomach and drink a glass of water, drink a glass of water with a pencil in your mouth; stick your head under water and count to 25, stick your hand in ice water, place an ice bag on the diaphragm below the rib cage or drink nine swallows of water from your grandfather's cup without taking a breath.

There are some other rather unusual remedies—pant like a dog; place a wastebasket over your head and have someone beat upon it; cover your head with a pillow; put the head of a burnt match in your ear; place a matchstick on top of your head and count to nine; turn your pockets inside out; spit on a rock, then turn it over.

Try holding your elbow seven minutes; try to induce fright, so the the victim will catch his breath; place a pinch of salt on the back of the tongue; cough; sneeze; bite your thumbs and blow hard against them for a minute; hold your breath and stick out your tongue.

Lay a broom on the floor and jump over it three times; walk around the broom once and then leave it where it is. Too, try laying a broom on the floor, the bristles to the right and jump over it seven times. Place a dime against the roof of the mouth and hold it for 30 minutes, or wet a piece of red thread with your tongue and stick it to the forehead and then, look at it.

You might try saying several little lines, that are said to help. For instance, say "Nine sups from a cup cures the hiccups." Do this three times without taking a breath.

Or stand in the middle of the road and say "Hiccup, stickup, not for me, hiccup, stickup."

Or say "Hiccups, hiccups, stand straight up, three sups in a cup are good for the hiccups." Also do this three times without breathing.

Then if everything fails you might resort to eating a lemon wedge that has been soaked in angostura bitters.

No doubt there are many more cures, but this is a start anyway.

Many years ago when someone had been helped with the hiccups it was told about. For instance, in 1584 it was noted: "The hickot is cured with sudden scare or strange newes." Then in 1626, "Sneezing doth cease the Hiccough." Or, "You must in the very instant that the hickup seizes the party pull his ring-finger and it will go off. (1727)

* * *

A Thought To Ponder: It isn't necessary to blow out the other person's light to let yours shine.

* * *

Peanut Butter Chews

16 large marshmallows
1 cup crunchy peanut butter
3 tablespoons butter or margarine
2 tablespoons milk
1 teaspoon vanilla
1 cup flaked coconut
1 cup quick rolled oats, uncooked
Whole peanuts

Melt marshmallows, peanut butter and butter over very low heat or over hot water. Add milk and vanilla; stir well. Remove mixture from the heat, stir in coconut and oats. (Mixture will be very stiff.) Drop from teaspoon on waxed paper. Decorate with whole peanuts. Makes 3 1/2 dozen

All in a Woman's Day--March 13, 1990
St. Patrick's Day is potato planting time

Potatoes somehow always seems to enter into the picture when St. Patrick's Day is mentioned. No doubt it is because it often is the time (the only time) to plant potatoes, according to many folks.

The Incas, Peru Indians, as we know them, first cultivated the potato, and it had many uses. Ranging in size from a small nut to an apple, the coloring varied from red and gold to blue and black.

They used raw slices of potatoes to place on broken bones, slices were carried to prevent rheumatism and eaten with other foods to help prevent indigestion. They also used potatoes to measure time (judging from the time it took to cook them.)

In 1537 when the Spanish Conquistadores discovered the potatoes in the Andean village of Sorocota, they took them along on their return trip to Europe. The folks there did not readily accept the new vegetable, thinking, since it was a member of the nightshade family, that it was evil or poisonous. Too, it was considered a dangerous aphrodisiac and was thought by many people to cause syphilis or leprosy.

It took the help of Germany's King Frederick William, France's Parmentier and England's Sir Walter Raleigh to promote this vegetable; however, it did eventually gain popularity throughout Europe.

Germany's king ordered peasants to plant and eat potatoes or else have their noses sliced off. In France the Parmentier worked with King Louis XIV to help popularize potatoes in that country. One of the things done was to prepare a feast using only potatoes, even potato liqueur. Among the guests were Benjamin Franklin and Marie Antionette, who wore potato blossoms in her hair, it has been told.

725

Sir Walter Raleigh introduced potatoes in Ireland. He was given 40,000 acres of land there by Queen Elizabeth, on which he was to grow potatoes and tobacco.

In 1621 the first potatoes were said to have arrived in North America. Captain Nathaniel Butler, who was governor of Bermuda, sent to Francis Wyatt, governor of Virginia at Jamestown, two large chests containing potatoes, along with other vegetables.

It was around 1719 that the first permanent North American potato patches were established in New England by Scotch-Irish immigrants. It has been thought it was possibly near Londonberry, New Derry, in New Hampshire.

Thomas Jefferson introduced French fries to the United States when he served them at the White House.

Potatoes, too, were once the unofficial currency on the South Atlantic Island of Tristau da Cunha.

And in the event you didn't know, potatoes were almost worth their weight in gold during the Alaskan Klondike gold rush. Miners traded their gold for potatoes.

The invention of potato chips came about by a mistake. Commodore Cornelius Vanderbilt, railroad magnet, was dining at a fashionable resort at Saratoga Springs, N. Y., when he complained that his fried potatoes were too thick. He sent them back to the kitchen. The chef, George Crum, in order to spite his haughty guest, sliced some potatoes paper thin and fried them in hot oil, salted and served them. Everyone was surprised by Vanderbilt being delighted with the Saratoga Crunch Chips. Potato chips have been popular ever since. They survived World War II despite the rationing conditions that were severe on practically every material necessary to produce chips. The industry had itself declared "essential" since chips were the only ready-to-eat dehydrated vegetable available at the time.

As far as a true Irishman is concerned, "A day without potatoes is a day without nourishment."

* * *

A Thought To Ponder: A new broom sweeps clean, but the old brush knows all the corners. An Irish Proverb.

* * *

Parmesan Potatoes

6 large potatoes (or equivalent)
1/4 cup flour
1/4 cup Parmesan cheese, grated
3/4 teaspoon salt
1/8 teaspoon pepper
1/3 cup margarine or butter
Chopped parsley

Quarter potatoes if you use large ones, or if quite small new ones, they can be used whole. Mix flour, cheese, salt and pepper in plastic bag. Moisten potatoes with water and shake in bag, coating well. Melt margarine or butter in a 9x13-inch pan. Place potatoes in pan and bake at 375 degrees for 1 hour, turning once. When golden brown, sprinkle them with parsley.

All in a Woman's Day--March 20, 1990

Kiwi fruit reaches new dimensions here

Today is the beginning of spring and time to think of something that is refreshing, and also attractive lo use in meal planning.

What other than the strikingly distinctive kiwi fruit, for both taste and appearance, that adds colorful and delicious new dimensions to many recipes.

The kiwi is a strange looking fruit

with its fuzzy brown coat, (looks as if you should either step on it or pet it), has a pleasantly sour taste with all of the fruit edible. For out-of-hand eating it is advisable to rub off the fuzz and, of course, for salads kiwi fruit should be peeled.

This fruit once a favorite in the court of China's great Khans, is now becoming popular in America and can add glamour to most any dish.

The season for this delicacy generally begins in October, when harvesting starts in California; however, even now the markets have a good supply of this tangy, sweet berry, studded with tiny black seeds encircled with brilliant green flesh, that makes a colorful addition to all kinds of food.

The kiwi fruit was discovered by an English botanist in China about 143 years ago. The fruit grows on trees, is about the size of a lime and has a thin brown skin covered with fuzz, as I have previously noted. It can be peeled and then sliced for a tasty snack.

Kiwi fruit, also called the Chinese gooseberry, became known in the Western world in the 19th century, and it was in New Zealand that it was discovered how tasty the fuzzy brown ball became when the outer skin was removed, revealing, of course, the brilliant green pulp.

In New Zealand, where the fruit is especially popular, a favorite way of serving it is to top with meringue, baked until crisp, with sweetened whipped cream (you can use topping) and peeled, thinly sliced kiwi fruit.

American agriculturists began testing kiwi fruit in 1935; however, it was not until the 1960s that the first commercial vineyards were planted in California. Today this western state has more than 6,000 acres under cultivation, and acreage is still increasing.

The berries, as the fruit is called, receive special treatment during harvesting. Handpicked, they are shipped to market when mature, but still firm, to prevent punctures and bruising. To ripen, leave at room temperature for several days until the fruit yields to the gentle pressure of the finger, or to hasten the procedure they can be placed in a bag or fruit ripening bowl. The full enjoyment of the kiwi fruit is best when it ripens at room temperature.

Kiwi fruit will keep for a week or more in the refrigerator. They also can be slowly ripened in the refrigerator, a process that takes several weeks.

The average size kiwi fruit contains 45 calories, is low in sodium and is a good source of vitamin C. It is especially popular with those persons watching their diet. It is high in potassium and a good source of dietary fiber, too.

Kiwi fruit is now generally available at all supermarkets as well as in gourmet fruit stores.

This fruit is delightful in fruit salads, but also is good in other salad combinations. You might experiment with kiwi fruit slices in your favorite recipes for chicken, waldorf, tossed green, cole slaw or molded salads. The bright green color provides an artistic accent. If you use kiwi in a molded gelatin salad, do remember to cook it a few minutes before adding to the gelatin mixture, just as you would fresh pineapple. These fruits contain an enzyme that prevents the gelatin from setting unless it has been cooked previously.

Kiwi slices add special culinary flair to many entrees, including fish, poultry, lamb, veal and pork. Slice it into Polynesian dishes, too, or glaze ham or spareribs with fresh kiwi jam.

This exotic fruit creates a dazzling dessert. Fresh kiwi pie, kiwi glazed cheesecake and a colorful parfait, using chopped kiwi fruit, are just a few of the ways to use this beautiful fruit in enchanting desserts.

Of course, the rich vitamin C content of kiwi fruit, which is about the same as a good-sized orange, is an excellent reason for serving it often. Try kiwi in combination with fresh orange, lemon, lime, coconut or pineapple juice. It makes a tangy addition to iced tea and cocktails, too.

Did you know that nurseries are now offering hardy kiwi plants for growing even in the far North? They are advertised as being sweeter than regular kiwi, but minus the brown, fuzzy skin, and they can even cope with 25 degree below temperatures. They are almost immune to disease and pests. They have glossy green foliage and fragrant white flowers. The flavor of the kiwi is much like a strawberry or melon, with edible skin. You might try your hand at growing your own kiwi fruit.

* * *

A Thought To Ponder: "Happy art thou, as if every day thou hadst picked up a horseshoe." —Longfellow

* * *

Kiwi Fruit Crush

1 kiwi fruit, peeled and sliced
1 banana, peeled and sliced
1 papaya
1/2 cup orange juice
Crushed ice
Kiwi fruit slices for garnish

Place all ingredients in a blender and beat until frothy. Serve in tall glasses over ice. Garnish with kiwi fruit and banana slices on long picks. Makes 2 8-ounce servings.

All in a Woman's Day--March 27, 1990

Try using today's many new fruits

As spring makes its debut, we think of something different in the way of food that might sharpen the taste buds just a wee bit.

More and more homemakers are using the new fruits that are appearing at the supermarkets. They are a bit different in various ways, and if you have a thought of buying, you no doubt would wonder just what to do with your purchase.

Have you tried the Angeleno Plum? It is a late maturing plum that was developed at Bakersfield, Calif. This plum has a luscious taste and is deep purple in color. It will be in the supermarkets long after summer plums have disappeared.

Cherimoya has a taste that is described as a cross between a pineapple and a banana. The outside will vary from smooth to knobby. This fruit is generally eaten raw.

The Atemova is a special hybrid of the Cherimoya and the Sugar Apple. It can be heart shaped, conical or irregular in form; however, the taste is pudding sweet and it has creamy white pulp centered with black seeds. The pulp of this special fruit, native to Asia and also grown in Florida, can be spooned out as you would a cantaloupe.

The exotic golden waxy Carambola or Star Fruit comes in sweet and sour varieties, that range from mild to tart. The sweet variety tastes much like a combination of apples, grapes and plums. Because of its shape when it is sliced, each piece is a star. The deeper the orange color, the sweeter the taste.

Sweet Star Fruit is delicious sliced, sprinkled lightly with sugar and served raw or in salads.

Asian Pears may be eaten out-of-hand or peeled and thinly sliced for salads and desserts. They are crisp like an apple. This fruit can be cooked and made into chutney or relish and used instead of the traditional cranberries.

Papayas are not really new, but they haven't been used as much as they could be. When selecting, choose those of moderate size; they should be larger than a good sized pear. Select fruit that is at least half yellow, with as little green as possible. Naturally, avoid any that might be bruised or showing signs of shriveling or decay.

If papayas are not yellow, they should be kept at room temperature for a few days until the skin color is fully yellow and yields to slight pressure. Placing them in a brown paper bag or ripening bowl hastens the ripening process. By giving the fruit ample ripening, papayas can be refrigerated and stored for a week or more.

Fresh figs are not really new either although they have been readily available in Europe for centuries. They are now becoming more popular in this country. There are two seasons for figs, early in June and late summer, that continues until frost. The Mission figs, both black and green, are named for the California mission where they were first cultivated by Spanish missionaries. The Calimyrna fig also known as Smyrna (an ancient city in Turkey, now called Ismir) is smaller than the Mission figs and is green-gold in color.

Kadota figs are excellent eaten raw and out-of-hand. They are low in calories and high in vitamin C. They also are delicious paired with sliced prosciutto or ham as a first course, poached in wine or sugar syrup or in dessert tarts.

You might like to experiment with some of these fruits and find out just how delightful they are for eating.

* * *

A Thought To Ponder: We will never find time for anything. If we want time, we must make it.

* * *

Fig Mousse

2 cups whipped cream or whipped topping
1/2 cup sugar
Lemon flavoring or juice
Few grains salt
1 cup chopped well-drained preserved figs

Whip cream until stiff or use topping; fold in sugar and salt and add lemon flavoring or juice to suit the taste. Mix thoroughly. Fill mold and pack in ice and salt. Partially freeze, then carefully fold in 1 cup chopped, well drained preserved figs. Repack and let it stand 4 hours. Makes 8 servings.

All in a Woman's Day--April 3, 1990
Partners in fun
Easter, decorated eggs

Eggs generally are associated with Easter; however, because of the cholesterol problem, perhaps folks will not be eating quite so many this year. But what can top a deliciously deviled egg, especially at Eastertime?

Well, there is one thing for sure, if we can't eat 'em, we can decorate them to suit our fancy.

Perhaps you are not aware of the fact that the easy to dye coloring that is used extensively today came about by accident more than 100 years ago; in fact, it occurred before Easter in 1879.

According to the records, William Townley, who was owner of a drugstore in Newark, N. J., was weighing egg dye for a customer when a powdery piece fell from the jar he was holding, splattering the white marble counter, with some bits also flying onto his suit. The counter was eventually cleaned with hard work; however, the spots could not be removed from his suit.

He was so disgusted that he thought he might even quit selling the "messy stuff"; however, losing other business caused him to reconsider and to think of some other procedure to measure the dye.

When the weather became warm enough for him to work outdoors, he set up a table in the backyard, and when business was dull in the store, he and his assistant weighed and wrapped small packets of various colored dyes. At Eastertime he sold these for five cents each, not only to his own customers, but also to friends who operated similar shops in the area.

His customers were so pleased with the handy packets that were just right for dyeing a few eggs, that they told their friends about their new Paas egg colors. (Paas being an old Pennsylvania Dutch word for Easter.)

Townley's Easter egg dye business increased to such an extent that he finally gave up his drugstore operation so he could spend all of his time working in the new found business.

Today many companies carry on his good work of making and packaging nonpoisonous beautiful colors for decorating Easter eggs. Some companies, too, now press the powdery dyes into pills that are easily dissolved in boiling water.

* * *

Now let's dye some eggs!

Here are some of the things needed … water, vinegar, piece of kitchen sponge, strip of cardboard, toothbrush, wooden skewer or popsicle stick, scissors and two large egg coloring kits with nine colors in each.

If you think you would like to preserve the eggs, be sure to blow them out; otherwise, use hard cooked eggs. If you are going to cook the eggs, be sure and use enamel, steel or glass pans; never use iron or aluminum because of the chemical reaction that keeps the color from adhering properly.

Prepare two batches of egg coloring, one to be used as a background or base color. This should be mixed according to the package directions using one tablespoon of vinegar with a half cup water for each color. The second batch is to be used to create the design and is prepared in a concentrated form using one tablespoon vinegar and one tablespoon of water for each color.

Immerse the egg in the background color until it has the desired tint; set aside and allow it to fully dry before decorating it.

Following are three different kinds of decorating:

Combed Eggs—Cut a piece of card board to resemble a comb and dip into the concentrated dye. Blot excess with paper towel or newspaper. Draw comb across the egg; then repeat. Should the lines be too pale, dip comb again into the concentrate and allow cardboard to absorb more color. Complete with one color, allowing egg to dry before adding a second color.

Sponged Eggs—Cut a piece of sponge into strips 1/2x1/2x2-inches long and cut off square edges of one end. Dip sponge into concentrated color, blotting out excess. Imprint pattern on the egg by gently pressing sponge against the egg. As you work hold the egg vertically between thumb and index finger and turn the egg gently when applying the imprint.

Spattered Eggs—Place the colored egg on top of a bottle and dip an old toothbrush into the concentrated shade. Run the stick over thc bristle to spatter the color on the egg. Again allow it to dry before repeating with a second shade. Be sure to rinse the brush in fresh water before using another color.

Have fun with your egg coloring!

* * *

A Thought To Ponder: Some folks are like Easter eggs ... ornamented on the outside and hard-boiled on the inside.

* * *

Opal's Noodles

2 eggs
2 tablespoons cream
1/2 teaspoon salt
1/8 teaspoon red cayenne pepper
1 1/2 cups flour

Beat together eggs, cream, salt and the red cayenne pepper; add flour and knead about 5 minutes. Form into a ball and place in a tightly covered container for 20 minutes. Divide the ball in half and roll each one separately on a lightly floured board until each is paper thin and can be picked up like a chamois skin. Let them dry for 5 minutes. Roll up like a jelly roll and cut into desired strips. Spread strips out to thoroughly dry, possibly 2 hours. Then drop in boiling broth and cook.

All in a Woman's Day--April 10, 1990

God's love ... is the promise of Easter

Easter is the Christian festival of joyous worship proclaiming the age-old affirmation: "Christ is Risen!"

Holy Week ... a significant season! What does it mean? It was during this time that the last fellowship meal was served, prayers prayed, the betrayal, the trial, the Crucifixion and the Resurrection when Jesus stood in their midst and spoke to them the comforting words, "Peace be with you," (John 20:19). This amazing news leaped swiftly from person to person. He is alive. Alleluia!

These events are more than a matter of the faraway and long ago. Human beings today experience broken fellowships, have urgent prayers for deliverance, betrayal by friends, damaging falsehoods, pain, sorrow and despair. They are written into the very fabric of human life.

But there is another side to consider ... the golden moments that came from all of the experiences that enhance lives.

Golden moments may include neighborly kindness, the flash of a redbird hidden in the evergreens, a rare friendship, a baby's smile, a beautiful sunset, a chance to lend a helping hand to someone in need, watching a rosebud unfold, giving deepest love to family and friends.

Golden moments come to us through God's great love, and they are tucked between our times of discouragement, strife, disappointments, tears, hard work, sorrows and adverse times.

Oftentimes, we perhaps feel things are better on the other side or that someone has less strife or discouragement than we have. That most often is not the case. Many people carry heavy burdens but continue to give golden moments to those who come into their lives.

I would like to relate a story that is so like most of us. It is entitled "The Golden Windows."

"Once a boy lived in a small house on a mountainside. Each morning he stood and looked across the valley where there appeared the most remarkable house. This house seemed to be crowned with glistening golden windows. How the boy yearned to get a closer view of this beautiful home, with those shining golden windows.

"One morning he left his home and started the long hard climb down the mountain and across the valley toward the house. It was evening by the time he arrived. To his dismay the house seemed smaller and less attractive than his own, and it had only ordinary window panes. Surely he had made a mistake, he thought. This was the wrong house.

"Can you tell me where I can find the house with the windows of gold?" he asked a child playing in the yard.

"The child nodded and pointed across the valley to the boy's own home. The light from the setting sun was reflected on the window panes of his house and they shone like shimmering gold. The boy had seen only the gold across the valley, failing to see that in his own house."

We, too, do not see the gold in our windows when we are looking beyond instead of within.

Are golden windows and golden moments making the journey through life revealing to us God's great love? ... that is the promise of Easter.

* * *

A Thought To Ponder: God has written the promise of the Resurrection not in books alone but in every leaf in springtime.   —Martin Luther

All in a Woman's Day--April 17, 1990

Put a little sizzle in your skillet today

If you would like to put a little sizzle in your skillet here are a few tips.

It makes no difference what kind of a skillet you use, the old-fashioned cast iron (and they are really great for some things), an electric skillet, a teflon coated skillet or wok, which some folks feel is almost like a skillet.

So if you haven't been using your skillet for a while, get it out and start cooking.

To saute vegetables until golden, heat oil over medium high heat and then stir in the vegetables and cook for five minutes in the skillet.

To saute vegetables until soft, cook at medium high heat and brown until top shines, then turn once.

To brown uncoated meat: Dry meat, place in skillet on medium high heat and brown until top shines, then turn once.

To brown ground beef, shape meat into a large patty, place in hot skillet over high heat for five minutes. Then cut patty into quarters, turn and brown it for five minutes; drain off fat and crumble.

To brown chicken, place it in oil over medium high heat until top of the food shines, then turn once.

If you line a skillet with foil to cook bacon or sausage, it will cook with less heat, and you can discard the whole mess without cleaning the pan. (Always remember to use paper toweling to absorb and press out the excess grease.)

Weave bacon strips together to squeeze them into a skillet. You can turn the whole skilletful with one flip of the spatula.

Invert a colander over a skillet when frying. It will catch spatter but will let the heat escape.

Grill a pound or two of bacon; divide into portions; wrap it in aluminum foil with a bit of grease added. This can be frozen and warmed as needed for bacon, lettuce and tomato, bacon cheeseburgers or grilled cheese and bacon sandwiches.

Add a little cooking oil to your skillet to keep food from absorbing so much of the shortening. Use about one teaspoon in a 10-inch skillet, when ready to fry potatoes, chicken or the like.

When frying fish, add one tablespoon vinegar to the cold shortening and more corn meal will stick to fish instead of ending up in the skillet when the fish is done.

Chill croquettes before frying them in the skillet, and they will hold their shape better.

Before frying potatoes, sprinkle them lightly with flour ... this makes them a delicious golden brown.

Before frying chicken in the skillet, to make it golden brown, roll it in powdered milk instead of flour.

Use the skillet for browning butter. Browning brings out the flavor of the butter, so use only half as much as needed for seasoning vegetables if it is browned before it is added.

And popcorn! Remember how a skillet was used for popping corn. Maybe some of you still do it this way.

In a previous column I gave a recipe for skillet cookies. In addition you can bake a cake in a skillet, make gravy, bake corn bread, cook a roast, make Spanish rice ... there are just so many ways you can use your skillet to prepare wonderful food for your family.

So, keep your skillet handy for you don't know when the occasion will occur you will need it. Oh, such good things can come out of a skillet!

* * *

A Thought To Ponder: You will always stay young if you live honestly, eat slowly, sleep sufficiently, work industriously, worship faithfully—and lie about your age. (from Life Today).

All in a Woman's Day--April 24, 1990

Needed odds and ends

Sometimes we need odds and ends of hints, so here you will find a few.

Add vinegar to a dish pan of water if you have exceptionally greasy dishes. Several tablespoons of the vinegar will cut the grease.

Rinse a cup with cold water before you measure a sticky ingredient such as shortening. This way it is not supposed to stick to the cup.

You can almost use your rhubarb now for this hint. A handful of rhubarb cooked in about a quart of water will help clean silver. Place the silver for five to eight minutes in the mixture after it is cooked.

When you open a new can of shortening or coffee, save the plastic lid from the old can and put it on the bottom of the new can. It will help save the shelf, where it is stored, from nicks and scratches.

For a delicious drink, slice and peel an apple and put it through the blender with one cup of milk, six small ice cubes and liquid sweetener to taste. You also can substitute one-half cup strawberries.

To prevent bacon from curling, dip the strips in cold water before frying.

Bacon will lie flat in a pan if you prick it thoroughly with a fork as it fries.

A quick way to separate bacon is to heat a spatula over the burner on the stove, then slide it under each slice to separate it from the others.

When cooking macaroni or spaghetti, add a tablespoon of cooking oil to the boiling point. This prevents it from sticking together when drained.

When making yeast dough for bread, rolls or doughnuts, add some instant potato flakes. This makes a good textured dough and adds delicious flavor.

Use buttermilk for the liquid called for in the directions for a chocolate cake mix. Add one teaspoon baking soda. You will have a wonderfully moist, tender cake.

Try adding one-half teaspoon cinnamon to your favorite graham cracker pie crust. It gives an added zip.

When peeling boiled potatoes, grease the knife and your hands with a little shortening before you start. The skins will not stick as readily to the hands and the knife.

Garlic has a tendency to dry out. Try freezing the buttons in a small glass jar. They will keep indefinitely.

If some of you homemakers are still using lard for a pie crust, use one-fourth cup butter or margarine with three-fourths cup lard and three cups flour. The crust will be flaky and have a nice color.

If you need to slice hot bread, heat the blade of your bread knife and slice it direct from the oven. You will have nice, thin slices.

When making a white sauce for creamed carrots, try adding about a teaspoon of peanut butter.

To remove visible fat from meat, cut it off when the meat is partially thawed. The task will be less messy. Scissors are a good thing to use for trimming the fat from meat.

Add one cup plain yogurt instead of a cup of cold water to a gelatin dessert for a creamier, tart flavor.

To get stains off your favorite china dishes, rub the spot with a cork or soft rag that has been dipped in baking soda.

To prevent lumps when cooking hot cereal, start with cold water instead of boiling water as directed. The texture of the cereal will be much smoother.

To soften butter, place it first in a bowl of warm water before removing the wrapper.

Rub the skin of a chicken with mayonnaise before baking to make it crisp and brown.

To improve an inexpensive cake mix, add one tablespoon of butter for a richer tasting cake.

* * *

A Thought To Ponder: Pray for a good harvest but keep on hoeing.

* * *

Sea Breeze Salad

3 packages lemon or lime gelatin (or combination)
2 cups boiling water
2 cups cold liquid
1 cup drained crushed pineapple
1 can lemon pie filling or a large package of lemon pudding mix
8-ounce carton whipped topping

Dissolve gelatin in boiling water; add cold liquid (water and juice from pineapple). Let set until gelatin begins to thicken; stir in lemon pie filling or pudding prepared as directed on package. Whip with electric mixer. Reserve one cup of the mixture. To the remainder, add crushed pineapple. Place in a 9x13-inch pan and refrigerate until set. Fold whipped topping into reserved cup of gelatin mixture and spread over first layer and refrigerate.

All in a Woman's Day--May 1, 1990
Grandma knew her 'receipts'

We can never give up the fact that Grandma knew what she was talking about. No, she really didn't believe in "receipts" as she called them. She said that if you want a "receipt," buy a cookbook.

Of course, we all know how Grandma cooked—a smidgen of this, a pinch of that and a handful of something else. She didn't believe in jotting down a "recipe" as we do today. And by the way, she wasn't referring to a slip of paper that was proof of purchase. No siree! She meant that "receipts" came from cookbooks, and to her, like perhaps so many of our older generation, regarded the words "recipe" and "receipt" as synonymous.

It really is quite understandable for there is a similarity between the two words as they both come from the Latin word "recipere," meaning "to take back or receive."

The Dictionary of Word and Phrase Origins explains it thus: "recipe" is the present tense of the verb, meaning literally "take." The word "receipt" comes from the past participle of "recipere," and originally meant "that which has been received."

Originally the word also was used as reference to a list of medical ingredients and it eventually came to mean the cooking formulas that have been handed down by experienced cooks to inexperienced cooks. "Receipts" therefore were "received" by culinary novices.

Too, the word also shows up in another common usage. Since the very earliest days of medicine, "recipe" has been used as the first word in prescriptions, as "Take Three Times Daily." In former years, the word was spelled out; however, today it is more often abbreviated by the familiar "Rx" that actually is the letter R with a slant mark across its base to represent the remainder of the word.

Today, we find the word "recipe" is increasingly used to mean any list of ingredients as in "recipe for success." However, the most common use still is culinary. For those who think the "receipt collectors" are just mispronouncing "recipe" you need to think again. The Oxford English Dictionary notes that "receipt" first made its appearance in print in 1582, while "recipe" did not appear until about 1652. So you've got to hand it to Grandma. She was right after all.

And speaking of "receipts" and "recipes," with family gatherings soon to get in full swing, wouldn't it be nice to put together some of the old family favorites from away back, yes, from Grandma and Great-grandma's times. They would be something to be cherished. Use recipes from the various categories if you should want to do it that way, or just hit and miss from each family, with a little comment about the recipe, anecdotes about childhood and also home life. If there is a story with a recipe that would be great to include, and it could become a treasured memory book as well as a treasured cookbook. It also would be nice to include some pictures.

If you have some heirlooms but you don't know for sure who should receive what, have a special time for heirlooms at the family gathering and let those who want this or that, have the items, and it will bring much happiness into their lives. (And no doubt yours, too.)

You could make this family reunion one of the most memorable occasions ever by collecting and keeping those "receipts" or "recipes" held dear by family members throughout the years.

* * *

Have a Happy Day.

* * *

Black Walnut Bars

1 egg, separated
2 cups flour
1 cup sugar
1 cup butter or margarine
1 teaspoon vanilla flavoring
1/8 teaspoon butter flavoring
1/4 teaspoon black walnut flavoring
1 cup chopped black walnuts

Place egg yolk in large mixer bowl with flour, sugar, margarine and flavorings. Blend well and then stir in 1/2 cup walnuts. Spread mixture in ungreased 10x15-inch shallow pan (jelly roll pan is ideal.) Beat the egg white until frothy and brush over dough. Sprinkle with remainder of the nuts. Bake at 350 degrees for about 25 to 30 minutes. Cuts into almost 40 bars.

All in a Woman's Day--May 8, 1990

Flowers, mothers complement each other

When we think of Mother's Day, so often comes to mind flowers. Somehow we just seem to associate mothers and flowers, and remembering that seems to be one of the tenderest times to recall.

On her special day, Sunday, May 13, some of us will be wearing a pure white flower in her memory. Others will be wearing a red flower to signify that she is still letting her light shine here upon her loved ones and friends.

Many mothers will perhaps recall their first bouquet from their youngsters, a bouquet of yellow dandelions, and at this time of year they are most prolific. This, no doubt, was the best bouquet ever to be received and one that will be held dearest.

Many of you are planning to give flowers again this year for her special day. So, if she receives a bouquet it is important that she be able to preserve it, for longer enjoyment.

Maybe some mothers are already bringing flowers into their home for enjoyment. To keep them pretty and fresh as long as possible, there are a few ways to preserve those lovely blossoms.

The suggestions were provided by a friend, also a mother, who was a flower lover, both inside and outside the home.

Maybe these hints she provided for cut flowers will help mothers enjoy nature's beauty a little longer.

Apple Blossoms - Use two tablespoons ammonia to two quarts of water (cut in bud: crush stems).

Amaryllis - Use two quarts kitchen ammonia to one quart water.

Begonias - Two tablespoons salt to two quarts water.

Carnations - Place them in cool water up to flower heads; do not immerse blooms.

Chrysanthemums - Place 10 drops of oil of cloves in two quarts water before placing the flowers.

Evergreens - (of all types) Use one tablespoon glycerine to one quart water.

Gladiolas - Place in a solution of five tablespoons vinegar to one quart of water.

Grape Hyacinths - Plunge them into hot, then cold water; add eight drops alcohol to one pint water.

Hyacinths - Squeeze substance from cut ends soon after gathering. Plunge into very cold water to which five drops of oil of peppermint is used to one pint water.

Iris - To one quart of water, add three drops of oil of peppermint.

Marigolds - Use two tablespoons sugar and one tablespoon salt to one quart water.

Narcissus - Arrange them in no more than one-inch of water. They like very little.

Peonies - Place three tablespoons of sugar into one quart of water.

Petunias - Place them in one teaspoon of sugar to a pint of water.

Bird of Paradise - To a quart of water add a half cup vinegar.

Roses - Use two tablespoons powdered alum or two tablespoons salt to one quart of water.

Snapdragons - Place two tablespoons of salt into two quarts water.

Sweet Peas - Plunge the flowers into hot then into cold water.

Dahlias - Use five tablespoons of alcohol to two quarts of iced water (burn ends of stems).

Daisies - Place eight drops of oil of peppermint to one quart water.

* * *

A Thought To Ponder: God could not be everywhere and therefore he made Mothers. (An Old Saying)

* * *

My Mother's Garden

My Mother has a garden fair;
So many flowers are blooming there.
She knows, from early morning sun,
How each has fared when day is done.
I used to pause and wonder why,
She loved it so, and I would try—
To see the beauty in each flower,
That she admires hour by hour.
Now, years have passed and I have learned,
That to her garden she has turned.
For courage in her hopes and fears,
In prayers for loved ones through the years;
Her garden's not just flowers and sod,
But a living altar to her God.

—Nellie Chapman

All in a Woman's Day--May 15, 1990

Life can be ...
a bowl of cherries

Life can be bowl of cherries if you just let yourself go and enjoy the fruits of the season ... the season of cherries, and it will soon be here.

By the way, cherries seem to rate high on most folks' list of favorite fruits.

There is nothing really new about cherries. This small, smooth, round fruit, with a stone in the center, comes from white or pink flowers. It originated in Asia Minor and was named for the Turkish town of Cerasus, now called Giresun located on the Black Sea.

The earliest known mention made of cherries was in 300 B.C., when Theophrastus, the Greek "father of botany," described both the tree and the fruit. Pliny credited Lucullus, Roman lover of food and luxury, with bringing the cherry to Rome following his victory over Mithridates, King of Pontus.

Birds also were a factor in spreading the fruit throughout Europe.

The cherry was brought to this country by early settlers, and goes as far back as 1629, when the Red Kentish cherry was cultivated in Massachusetts.

Back in those earlier days most of the colonial homes had one or two cherry trees growing in their backyards; George Washington's family home was no exception.

Of course, we all know the story of how a cherry tree there became immortalized by Parson Weems, who wrote the story of the "Life of George Washington: With Curious Anecodotes; Equally Honorable to Himself and Exemplary to His Young Countrymen."

Also, numerous painters and poets have been inspired by Europe's favorite fruit, the cherry. Robert Herrick, the 17th century English poet, picked up the words of the cherry vender as he wended his way through old London, and then turned them into a lyric of praise of the fruit and a certain lady. The words went thus:

> Cherry ripe, ripe, ripe, I cry
> Fall and fair ones; come and buy;
> If so be, you ask me where
> They do grow, I answer, there,
> Where my Julia's lips do smile;
> There's the land, of cherry-isle.

* * *

And continuing our thinking about cherries, we must never forget the loveliness of the flowering ornamental cherry trees, such as those grown by the Japanese. Each year many many people travel from near and far to Washington, D. C., for a glimpse of the blossoms of the 3,000 ornamental cherry trees planted along the Tidal Basin.

It was in 1912, as a token of goodwill, from one capital to another, Tukio Ozaki, governor of Tokyo, made the presentation. Since then they have been a springtime joy for many people.

It was in 1847 that the sweet cherry industry began on the West Coast. Henderson Luelling, a pioneer horticulturist, took cherries with him in a covered wagon load of fruit to be planted in Oregon.

From there came the rich, juicy Bing and Lambert cherries, that now have been crossed, and are grown in the volcanic soil of the Northwest states that also include Washington, Idaho and Utah. Cherries from these four states begin appearing on the market in mid June, and usually last through early August.

The more prolific Bing cherry is known for its large size, plump shape and mahogany hue. The Lambert has the same rich taste; however, it is usually elongated or sometimes heart shaped.

If these cherries are to maintain their flavor and firmness, they must be kept cool; they are chilled in ice water and placed in storage areas awaiting packaging.

Cherries are divided into two groups, the sour and the sweet. The sour cherries are rounder, softer textured and grow in this area. The sweet cherries are the larger of the two groups, heart shaped and firm, yet they retain their tenderness: Sweet cherries are red, white, golden or dark red, and, of course, they are used fresh or cooked.

Among some of the other varieties are Chapman, also called Early Chapman. This cherry is very large, sweet and flavorful and matures early. This variety is said to have been produced from a seedling of the Black Tartarian.

Then there is the Republican, also known as the Black Republican or Lewelling, with purplish or black fruit, mild, crisp and sweet.

Royal Ann, also known as Napoleon, has light golden colored flesh, with a pink or light red blush. They are meaty and flavorful. This is the only light flesh variety that has commercial importance. This variety is mainly for canning.

Also in the sweet cherry category is the Tartarian, also called Black Tartarian, with purplish to black flesh, excellent flavor, tender and sweet. This is the most popular of early mid-season varieties.

Among the sour or tart cherries is the Early Richmond, clear medium red, with tender flesh. It ordinarily is the first sour cherry on the market in late spring and is often confused with the Montmorency, which is a full clear medium red and very juicy. It is especially good for pies, tarts, jellies and all cooking, and perhaps the most popular sour cherry in the United States.

Then there is the English Morell that has a very deep red coloring, becoming almost black, with dark red flesh that is tender and melting. It also is good for all cooking purposes.

There are no doubt some later and newer varieties; however, these mentioned have been around for sometime and are proven fruits.

Be ready for the cherries and enjoy.

* * *

A Thought To Ponder: Happiness is not perfected until it is shared.

* * *

Cherry Dessert

20 coconut or vanilla wafer cookies, crushed

1/4 cup butter or margarine
1/4 cup sugar
1 (8-ounce) package cream cheese
1/2 cup powdered sugar
1/2 pint cream, whipped or whipped topping
2 cans cherry pie filling
1/2 teaspoon cherry flavoring

Crush cookies; melt butter and combine with sugar and crumbs. Press into a 9x13-inch baking dish and bake at 300 degrees, 15 minutes. Combine softened cheese and powdered sugar and beat them until fluffy. Whip cream or use whipped topping and fold into cream cheese mixture. When crumb crust has been cooled, spoon this mixture over the crust. Combine cherry pie filling with cherry flavoring. Add a little red food coloring if a brighter color is desired. Spoon over cream cheese layer in pan. Refrigerate until time to serve. This is a large recipe and will serve 12 to 15.

All in a Woman's Day--May 22, 1990
Little red poppy is memorial flower

Poppies are an important part of the Memorial Day observance. They are memorial flowers that are for remembrance; and that is what Memorial Day is all about ... remembering.

Veterans returning from World War I found that the contrast of the bright red poppies growing wild among the white wooden crosses in cemeteries in Europe was a scene that could not easily be forgotten.

Col. John McCrae wrote the poem "In Flanders Field," and it immortalized the poppy as the symbol for those who died so that we might have freedom.

R. W. Lillard wrote a response to the

poem and it was entitled "America's Answer," in which he dedicated the living in a continued struggle for freedom.

The American Legion and the Veterans of Foreign Wars and their Auxiliaries adopted the poppy as their official memorial flower. It was in May, 1922, that the Veterans of Foreign Wars conducted a nationwide dispersement of poppies made in France. The American Legion held its first distribution of poppies made in France in the spring of 1923.

The first poppies given for a contribution in the United States and Europe were for the benefit of children in war torn France and Belgium. The Franco-American Children's League had charge of the poppies, which were made of silk by widows and orphans of the French veterans.

The first wearing of the poppies for remembrance took place on Nov. 9,1918, in New York at the 25th conference of the Y.M.C.A.

At one time the daisy was the memorial flower of the American Legion and its Auxiliary; however, at the American Legion National Convention in 1922 the delegates also made the poppy their national memorial flower to replace the daisy. The American Legion poppy is made of red crepe paper petals that are formed around a green crepe paper center.

It was in February, 1924, that the name Buddy Poppy was registered with the United States patent office by the Veterans of Foreign Wars.

The organization still has trademark rights of the name Buddy under the classification of artificial flowers.

The Buddy Poppy was made of a circle of glossy red paper, stamped to show seven petals behind a green center. This past year, however, they changed to a silk poppy. Both veteran groups' poppies have paper ribbons attached stating that the flower was made by a disabled veteran and the name of the organization.

Some of the persons serving in the Armed Forces were not able to go home because of injuries, some physical, some mental, that made them incapacitated for the remainder of their lives. The government program assists with some of the problems; however, it was the American Legion and the Veterans of Foreign Wars and their Auxiliaries, who first began showing concern by providing care that changed many of the lives of the disabled veterans.

Poppies cannot be sold; however, volunteers from the two organizations receive a contribution for a poppy, with the contributor deciding the amount to give.

In many areas each group arranges the distribution of the poppies for a different time; however, in Maryville, the two organizations work together to make this a special time for remembering. Poppy Days are held just prior to Memorial Day and before Veteran's Day; however, here, poppies are dispersed at only one time, the Thursday prior to Memorial Day.

All money given for poppies goes into relief and rehabilitation funds of the local Auxiliaries, and it is then administrated as the need arises.

Material for making the poppies are provided by the organizations for the hospitalized veterans who assemble the poppies as a therapy in Veterans' Hospitals in almost every state. The veterans are paid nominal fees for their work, thereby letting them earn some money as well as keeping their minds and hands busy.

Perhaps this year as we contribute our money for such a worthy cause, we can accept this bright little flower with thanksgiving and compassion; thanksgiving for the life that we enjoy here in our United States and compassion for the sorrow and suffering of others because of wars.

So, poppies for remembering are a way we can help those individuals who have given us the peace we so desired, but who cannot now help themselves.

Following is an excerpt from a poem written by Doris Lowe:

Little Red Poppy

The Little Red Poppy is like a rose,
Though no aroma fills the air,
It has the sweet smell of America,
For it was made by hands that care.
Made by the boys who left their home
To protect this land for you and me,
Who returned with pride in their hearts,
For they kept our great land free.
They didn't say they had other plans,
Nor ask, "What is in it for me?"
They didn't say that the weather was bad,
Or "forget" where they had promised to be.
Remember these things each year
When poppies go on sale,
Put a smile on your face, give of your time,
And be there without fail.

* * *

A Thought To Ponder: The real meaning of the external remembrances can only be measured in the depth of personal feeling that comes within each American.

Enjoy the great taste of cherries

This is a continuation of cherries as there are more things I wanted to bring to you about them.

It has been said that cherries, any way at all, are very special. Of course, folks who are not cherry "lovers" perhaps don't think that way.

Cherries are a pretty fruit. When they come in cans or jars they are mostly light and dark sweet cherries with or without pits. The red sour or tart cherries always are pitted. Among the other canned or processed cherry products are pie fillings, sauce, some juice blended with other fruit juices, preserves, candied, glazed and maraschino cherries.

And speaking of maraschino cherries, these are made from sweet cherries, generally Royal Ann, that are bleached, pitted and steeped in a sugar syrup with a touch of oil of bitter almond, along with food coloring.

This delicacy has a history that dates back more than 300 years to Italy, where a white sweet cherry was soaked in a cordial called "maraschino," which was made from another cherry known as Marasca. It seems that the name was derived from the Latin word amarus, that means "bitter."

The French later created another version, using cherries that were soaked in a sugar syrup. And it was the French who named their version "maraschino cherries."

After being imported to our country, maraschino cherries were very popular. Later home grown cherries and syrup were developed into an all-American product.

These special cherries are used in

cookies, cakes, sauces, candies, along with salads, fruit cups and alcoholic beverages. A maraschino cherry makes an attractive addition to special desserts and salads as a garnish.

When selecting cherries, be sure to chose those that are fresh appearing and good color for the variety, as well as plump and ripe. Sour cherries should be medium firm and sweet cherries should be firm. Cherries with stems keep better: however, if used right away, stem-med cherries are a better buy. A quart of cherries with stems equal one and one-half pounds, or three cups stemmed and pitted, or two cups juice. One quart of stemmed cherries equals two pounds or four cups pitted or two cups juice.

Be sure to select top grades if the cherries are to be used in cocktails, compotes, salads, desserts and as garnishes. However, if they are to be used chopped or mixed with other foods, as in sherbets, cobblers and sauces, other grades are a thriftier buy.

* * *

Following is an old-time version of a **Mock Cherry Pie** recipe:
If you've ne're et mock cherry pie
Here's a receipt I wish you'd try.
Two cups of cranberries you will need.
One cup of raisins free from seed.
One cup of sugar more or less—
Now put in a tray and chop the mess.
Add two-thirds cups of water cold,
One tablespoon of flour to hold,
Vanilla, added to your taste,
And all enclosed in a nice rich paste.
Now open your mouth and close your eye—
You'll think you're eating Cherry Pie.

* * *

As I said previously, when thinking of cherries we just naturally associate them with George Washington from whom our special thought comes.

* * *

A Thought To Ponder: If you can't have people as you want them, you must take them as they are.

* * *

Out of this World Pie

1 can cherry pie filling
3/4 cup sugar
1 large can crushed pineapple and juice
1 tablespoon corn starch
1 teaspoon red food coloring
1 box (3-ounces) raspberry gelatin
6 bananas, sliced
1 cup chopped pecans
2 baked pie shells (10-inch)
Whipped topping

In a saucepan, combine cherry pie filling, sugar, pineapple and juice, corn starch and food coloring. Cook until thick. Remove from heat and add gelatin. Allow to cool. Add bananas and pecans. Pour this into two baked pie shells and top with whipped topping. Chill.

All in a Woman's Day--June 5, 1990
Wedding cakes reflect tradition

Traditionally June just seems to be the right month for weddings; however, there are other months when there are possibly just as many.

Have you ever wondered why June has been said to be the month of weddings? Could it be because the weather is warm and sunny, the flowers are blooming in splendor and vacation time is upon us? Maybe, it is just tradition that makes it so.

No matter what the reason, the wedding cake is an important part of the wedding. It should be the reflection of the wedding from the colors to the individual fancies of the bride and groom.

There are such a wide variety of cakes to select from ... the traditional, the multitiered, the domed Australian cake. The little fountains make the cakes especially interesting, and excitement comes when the cake is put together, with each layer placed just where it belongs, with extra frosting used to cover where the layers join together.

And, of course, cake is always fun to eat. Perhaps, maybe it is because of the happy occasion, but somehow wedding cake just seems to taste a little better than other cakes.

The wedding cake had its origin back in the Roman era. In those early days, a simple wheaten cake was broken during the ceremony. The first morsels were eaten by the bride and groom, with the rest of the cake crumbled over the bride's head in a fertility rite to guarantee many children and a life of plenty and happiness.

Cakes first appeared at weddings in the "higher society" in which it was known as confrarreatio, which translates as "an eating-together time."

It was an unleavened scone made of flour, salt and water, with no decorations. After the crumbling of the cake, the guests could scramble for the fragments that were scattered here and there. If they were lucky to get a piece, it was thought they would get a share of the blessings.

Not much was said about wedding cakes until the Anglo-Saxons began to supply a basket of small dry biscuits at weddings. Each guest could take one home, and what was left was given to the poor.

When Elizabethan times came in England, guests would bring their own cakes to weddings, and they were very similar to what our buns are today. These small sweet buns were the centerpiece of the table and the bride and groom were playfully challenged to kiss each other over the cakes that were arranged in a mountainous bundle. If the stack remained standing, the marriage would be a good one. Then as weddings grew larger, the stacks often fell over.

It was about 200 years ago that a chef from France created a multi-tiered cake that looked like a stack of buns; however, it didn't fall over. This is no doubt why we have multi-tiered cakes today in the United States.

Today in France, however, croquembouche, a cake composed of cream puffs is held together in a cylindrical form with melted caramelized sugar. This is still the wedding cake of choice there.

The top layer of the cake is known as the bride's and groom's cake, and most often it is saved for the couple's first anniversary. So, because it is special, some couples want the layer to be chocolate.

Too, there was a time that the groom's cake of chocolate had to be a separate cake; however, it now has become acceptable for the individual cakes of the wedding cake to be both of white and chocolate varieties.

The basic color of cakes often depends on whether the bride will be wearing a white or ivory dress. Flowers, ribbon, pearls and even glitter have been used to accent the wedding cake.

There is an old Scottish wedding superstition that the mother of the groom prepares a batch of small cakes to be consumed by the bride and her wedding party on the morning of the ceremony. These cakes, originated in the northeast county of Aberdeen, are called "bounty cakes." Made from butter, sugar, flour, Drambie (a Scottish liqueur) and, in the original recipe, crushed heather buds, the flower plentiful in Scotland. These cakes were said to bring good luck and fertility.

* * *

A Thought To Ponder: In all the wedding cakes, hope is the sweetest of plums. —Douglas Jerrold, 19th century English humorist and playwright.

All in a Woman's Day--June 12, 1990
Recall Dad's proverbs

Father's Day is fast approaching; a day when we think back over the years, with many things coming to mind. In earlier days, often he came up with sayings that have held true. Today, however, we do not hear much of this kind of talk.

Following are some proverbs or sayings that some of you might enjoy remembering and thinking about, and possibly some of which you no doubt heard your father or grandfather express.

* * *

Silence is the finest reply to folly.

A skilled cheat needs no assistance.

One eyewitness is better than 10 hearsays.

Sometimes the best answer is no answer.

A cheerful word does the good of medicine.

Three may keep a secret if two of them are dead.

A clean mouth and an honest hand will take a man through any land.

People who are wrapped up in themselves make small packages.

Great talkers are like leaky pitchers—all runs out of them.

* * *

Long ago some of these were said:

The Golden Age is never the Present Age.

A fog cannot be dispelled by a fan.

You can't catch the wind in a net.

He who never climbed, never fell.

We may delay, but time will not.

The rose is beautiful, but the thorn is sharp.

It is better to have been a has-been than a never-was.

* * *

You might examine some of these sayings:

Marry in haste, repent in leisure.

Beauty is only skin deep, but ugly goes clean to the bone.

Weather and women's thoughts change often.

Keep your eyes wide open before marriage, half shut after.

A fool and a dry stick can be broken, not bent.

A pebble and a diamond are alike to a blind man.

Speech is silver; silence golden.

From small beginnings, come great things.

In trying times, don't quit trying.

Lost time is never found.

One is never too old to learn.

* * *

Following are a few gentle hints and small talk.

Memories temper prosperity, console adversity, caution youth and delight old age.

Glass, china and reputation are easily cracked, never well mended.

He that won't be advised won't be helped.

To lengthen thy life, lessen the

meals.

Figures never lie, but liars can figure.

Laziness moves so slowly poverty soon overtakes it.

Money isn't everything.

Great spenders are bad lenders.

* * *

And, so the sayings or proverbs could go on and on. No doubt they recall memories of the wonderful things that your father or grandfather stood for in life.

* * *

HAPPY FATHER'S DAY!

* * *

A Thought To Ponder: You are rich who still have your father.

* * *

Recipe for a
Happy Father's Day

3 cups love
2 cups hugs
Kisses galore
5 spoons tenderness
1 cup kindness
4 spoons hope
2 spoons of loyalty
A barrel of laughter
A little sparkle

Take love and hugs and kisses; too, Mix them together for something new; Blend in tenderness, along with hope, Making it a day on which he dotes! Then add loyalty and laughter gay, that should help make his day! Sprinkle a little sparkle here and there, And there will be joy beyond compare. Let this mixture bask in the sunlight bright. And serve generously to his delight. Don't let this recipe be just for this day alone, But one that will last day after day and be his very own.

Summer fruits ...
offer flavor, variety

Have you ever given a thought to the fresh fruits that are now in season or will be? They are so tantalizing in color and flavor and are the gems of the season.

Let's think a bit about some of these summer fruits that make for such luscious eating.

A native American fruit, the blueberry is related to the cranberry. It was used by the Indians to make pemmican, a meat mixture that was carried on hunting trips.

And the watermelons! Of course, we relate them to the Fourth of July when they are considered a special treat, along with homemade ice cream and fried chicken. Now these foods can be enjoyed the year round. It seemed fitting for the watermelon to be a Fourth of July special because they were first grown in the 1600s by our country's Puritan forefathers. More varieties of watermelons are grown today in the United States than anywhere else.

And strawberries! Folks have been enjoying their goodness and delectable eating. It was Izaak Walton, who wrote of the strawberry, "Doubtless God could have made a better berry, but doubtless God never did." And that just seems to say it all. Cardinal Wolsey, a man who understood eating well, introduced strawberries and cream to the English table.

Henry VIII's gardener can be given the credit for popularizing cherry trees for English gardens. In London, "cherries, ripe," was the cry of young women selling this ruby fruit on the streets. Of course, the tart cherries like those early English fruits now are usually canned or frozen for pies and other baked desserts.

No doubt you have heard peaches called the "queen of fruits" by the Chinese, who were the first to cultivate them nearly 3,000 years ago. This blush-skinned fruit was taken along the old silk-trading road to Persia, then into Europe, where it was known as a "Persian apple." And for the westward settlers, the wild plums were a welcome fruit. This naturally sweet fruit was free, just for the picking. They were called Indian cherries or beach plums, and this native-American fruit made delicious preserves. Today, many of the varieties of plums grown in orchards have more distant roots. In fact, some have come from China.

Blackberries! You can almost taste the delicious flavor in pies and cobblers. They were at one time so common in England that Shakespeare made them a "symbol of abundance." However, in America, a similar profusion of wild blackberry bushes were such a nuisance to colonial day farmers that they were not thought worth cultivating until about the 1830s.

Apricots were Chinese, too. They claim a royal beginning in China in 2200 B.C., and even today they grow wild on the mountain slopes around Peking. From China the apricot traveled to the part of the Persian Empire now known as Armenia, and years later it won the title of the "Golden Apple" in Greek mythology. The apricot industry began in California more than 175 years ago. Apricots are nutritious, as well as a delicious food.

All these fruits are so attractive in appearance, as well as in flavor. We should utilize them as much as possible.

* * *

A Thought To Ponder: Without kindness there is no joy.
* * *

Here are two versions of the mystery salad. No doubt you would like to try them both as they are quick and easy to make as well as good summertime eating.

Mystery Salad I
1 can (16-ounce) pineapple chunks
1 can mandarin oranges
1 or 2 bananas, sliced
1 cup small marshmallows
1 box lemon instant pudding mix

Drain fruits, reserving liquids. Mix with banana slices and marshmallows. Take reserved liquid from fruits and mix with instant pudding. Pour over fruit and chill or serve immediately.

Mystery Salad II
1 can pineapple chunks
Seedless grapes
Bananas, sliced 
Marshmallows
Nuts
Coconut
1 box instant lemon pudding

Drain pineapple, save juice. Combine all the ingredients or any other fruits desired. Mix pineapple juice with instant pudding and toss with fruit.

All in a Woman's Day--June 26, 1990
This is salad time!
As the weather warms up, degree by degree, cool salads are enticing to serve as we tend to want to get away from foods that are "heavier" in texture.

When selecting foods for salads, remember that there should be a pleasing blend of flavors; there should be a contrast of textures (soft foods should be mixed with those having fibrous and

746

crisp texture). Too, there should be a contrast of color. This may be accomplished by combining foods of vivid colors such as carrots or beets, with those having little or no color. This may be accomplished by topping the salad with a colorful food, dressing or seasoning.

Too, special attention should be given in the arranging of the ingredients. Fresh fruits or vegetables are the foundation of the salad. If fresh, they should be washed and placed in a cool spot to become crisp. They may be sliced, diced, cubed or shredded in order to be easily eaten.

Canned or cooked fruits and vegetables should have crispness and be well drained. They are prepared the same as fresh produce.

Dried fruits can be used cooked or uncooked and they can be used whole, halved, diced or shredded.

In using cooked meat and chicken, when the meat is freed from the bone and gristle, it should be diced or shredded. Fish should be flaked or shredded.

Macaroni, rice and spaghetti offer bulk to many combinations of foods. Too, cheese, nuts, prepared cereals and candies lend flavor when many combinations of foods are bland. Hard-cooked eggs offer bulk, color and flavor.

Be sure and have prepared salad foods thoroughly chilled before they are combined. If a combination is to be marinated, the separate foods should be mixed with a well seasoned French dressing and should stand one hour before serving.

Ingredients are mixed by tossing lightly together with two forks. Be sure and pile loosely on crisp salad greens and top with salad dressing Oftentimes salads are mixed with a mayonnaise or boiled salad dressing before being placed on the salad greens. If using this method, then the salad should be served immediately.

Well blended combinations of food, such as fruits, vegetables, meats, chicken and fish, are added to a gelatin base that is a carrier of flavor. The gelatin gives solidity to the salad, thus giving it individual character.

Frozen salads are often served and they are made with a combination of foods that have been blended with a creamy salad dressing. The salad should be kept at freezing temperature only until the dressing has become solidified. Ordinarily this requires about four hours.

Commercially prepared dressings offer an excellent way of adding flavor and seasoning to any salad combination. They can be purchased in three types—French, boiled and mayonnaise. They lend themselves to the same variations as homemade products; or variations may be purchased.

There also are three general types of homemade salad dressings: French, boiled and mayonnaise. When these are combined with salad ingredients, the use is interchangeable. Their use is determined by individual likes and dislikes. The only requisite is a pleasing flavor.

When using French dressing you can get variety by the use of or addition of fruit juice, honey, grated cheese and various combinations of seasonings.

Boiled dressing often can be varied by the use of whipped cream, whipped topping or whipped evaporated milk, chopped hard-cooked eggs, relishes and chopped pickles.

Mayonnaise dressing can be varied in

the same way as boiled dressing. It forms the fundation for Thousand Island and Russian Dressing.

* * *

A Thought to Ponder: Very little is needed to make a happy life.

All in a Woman's Day--July 3, 1990

This is America's 'Happy Birthday'

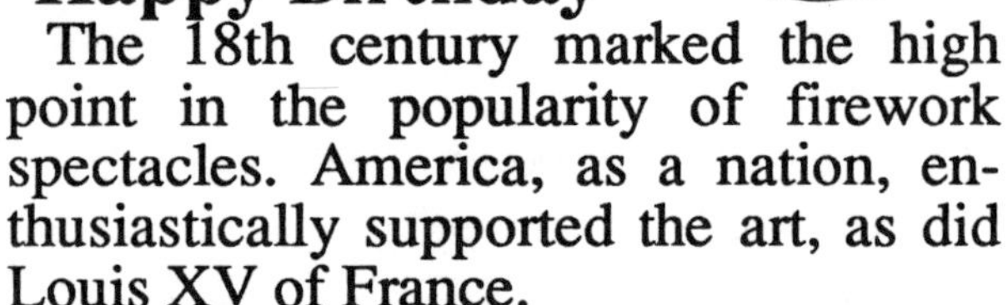

The 18th century marked the high point in the popularity of firework spectacles. America, as a nation, enthusiastically supported the art, as did Louis XV of France.

Beautiful firework displays throughout the country now help make the birthday of our independence the spectacular celebration that we have come to expect.

The date of July 4 is significant in American history for many reasons other than the signing of the Declaration of Independence.

It was on this date that John Adams, second president of the United States, and Thomas Jefferson, third president, signers of the Declaration of Independence, both died in 1826. James Monroe, fifth president, died in 1831.

United States and British troops went into action together in World War I in 1917. First American troops landed in Britain in the summer of 1917; then they went on to the shores of France in July, 1917, under the command of General Pershing.

The Statue of Liberty was presented by France to the United States in 1884 to commemorate the French and American Revolutions.

The Navy's first raising of the Stars and Stripes was in 1777, when John Paul Jones hoisted the banner on his ship, the Ranger.

Fourth of July is the traditional day when stars are added to the flag to denote a new state admitted to the Union.

In 1802 the United States Military Academy was opened at West Point, N.Y., with 10 cadets enrolled.

In 1817 Gov. Dewitt Clinton of New York state turned the first sod for digging the Erie Canal, which later spanned 352 miles from Buffalo to Albany, N.Y.

It was in 1828 that the first spadeful of earth was turned for the first railroad built in the United States for the general transportation of passengers.

The song "America" was sung publicly for the first time in 1832 in Boston.

The cornerstone for the Washington Monument was laid in 1850.

In 1854 the cornerstone was laid for the present House of Representatives of the nation's Capitol.

Then in 1865 the cornerstone of the Soldier's National Monument at Gettysburg, Pa., was placed, and this is where Abraham Lincoln made his famous Gettysburg Address.

In 1898 the United States flag was hoisted on Wake Island in the Spanish American War.

In 1942 the United States Air Force made its initial Second World War assault on Europe.

In 1946 the United States gave the Philippine Islands its independence.

The United States Bicentennial was observed July 4, 1976, marking the 200th anniversary of its independence with festivals, parades and New York City's Operation Sail.

There are no doubt other happenings that fall into this Fourth of July historical category; however, all of these events mentioned make the celebration monumental.

748

* * *

A Thought To Ponder: Observe good faith and justice toward all nations; cultivate peace and harmony with all. — (George Washington)

* * *

Ragged Old Flag

I walked through a country courthouse square; on a park bench an old man was sitting there. I said, "Your courthouse is kinda run down." He said, "Aw, it'll do for our little town." I said, "That flagpole has leaned a bit, and that's a RAGGED OLD FLAG you got hanging on it." He said, "Have a seat," and I sat down. "Is this the first time you've been to our little town?" I said, "I think it is." He said, "I don't like to brag, but we're kinda proud of the RAGGED OLD FLAG.

"You see, we got a little hole in that flag there when Washington took it across the Delaware …

"And it got powder burned the night Francis Scott Key sat watching it and writing "Say Can You See" …

"And it got a bad rip in New Orleans with Packingham and Jackson tuggin' at its seams …

"And it almost fell at the Alamo, beside the Texas flag, but she waved on through …

"She got cut with a sword at Chancellorsville, and she got cut again at Shiloh Hill …

"There was Robert E. Lee, Beauregard and Bragg, and the south wind blew hard on the RAGGED OLD FLAG …

"On Flanders Field in World War I, she got a big hole from a Bertha gun …

"She turned blood red in World War II, and she hung limp and low by the time it was through …

"She was in Korea and Vietnam. She went where she was sent by her Uncle Sam …

"She waved from our ships upon the briny foam, and now folks just don't seem to wave her anymore back here at home …

"It's in her own good land that she's been abused …

"She's been burned, dishonored, denied and refused …

"And that government for which she stands is scandalized throughout the land …

"And she's getting threadbare and wearing thin …

"But she's in good shape for the shape she's in. Cause she's been through the fire before, and I believe she can take a whole lot more …

"So we raise her up every morning, and take her down every night. We don't let her touch the ground, and we fold her up right …

"On second thought, I do like to brag …

"Cause I'm mighty proud of that RAGGED OLD FLAG."

All in a Woman's Day--July 10, 1990

Make everyday tasks lots easier

Sometimes tasks that are everyday can be made a bit easier with just a new twist that will turn around the everydayness.

When preparing baking powder biscuits from scratch, instead of cutting them into rounds, cut them into squares with a knife. It won't take so long, and you won't have scraps of dough left to knead together and roll out again.

Perhaps your microwave has just high and low settings. You can get the medium setting by placing 3/4 cup water in a custard cup in one corner of the

749

microwave. This will give a 70 percent or medium high when it is turned on.

Did you know that peppers are one of the easiest vegetables to freeze? They do not need to be scalded; just clean, break into pieces, tie into plastic bags and pop into the freezer until needed. If your family likes peppers, they can be purchased when they are low priced and kept for using during the astronomical cost season.

Do you really know how to brown meat? The trick to the whole thing is not to put too many pieces of meat in the skillet at once. If you don't give the pieces of meat "elbow" room the meat will boil instead of brown.

Perhaps you need to store ice cubes for later use. Place them in a brown paper bag, the kind in which you bring your groceries home from the market. If you find there is an excess of moisture, put the cubes on a paper towel before storing in the bag. They do not stick together when placed in the freezer. There is really no rhyme or reason why but they just don't stick together and are easy to take from the bag.

If you have some milk that is only slightly soured, it can be freshened with a pinch of baking powder; however, it must be used pronto.

Pieces of white bread placed in the refrigerator will absorb odors.

Dental floss is good for something else besides flossing our teeth. It is good for trussing a bird for grilling or roasting, since it is strong and doesn't burn easily.

Is your knife a little dull? Sharpen it on the rim, of a clay flower pot. Keep the blade almost flat on the rim and it will become razor sharp.

If you have a blender, use it wisely. Don't overprocess as you usually can blend in seconds only; cool hot vegetables or liquids before placing in the container; place cover firmly on before using; place your hand on the cover of the container when using; and lastly use a rubber spatula when blending heavy mixtures.

For a change of pace from a sweet cake icing, make a powdered sugar frosting and add unsweetened powdered drink mix to taste. This is good on a white cake.

Sometimes favorites, like chili con carne or a special curry sauce, seem to lose their zesty appeal. To give them a little zip, simply blend in a dash or two of liquid hot pepper sauce.

To make shopping easier, when making out the grocery list, use a red ink pen for the items that are on special or that you have coupons for; use black or blue for the other items.

When mashing fruits for jam, work with only a small amount at a time. Use a potato masher and place berries in a flat bottom cake pan; Freeze extra berries for use later.

Leftover poultry dressing can be used by pressing it into a pie pan and making a main dish pie shell. Fill with creamed vegetables; just heat and serve.

Substitute canned broth for water in recipes for a fuller flavor.

Old-timers had a trick for telling if melons were ripe. They placed a broom straw across the highest part of the melon. If the straw turned around, it was ripe. Try it and see if it works for you.

* * *

A Thought To Ponder: Freedom is important when you don't have it; it should be just as important when you do.

***
Date Torpedoes

2 tablespoons butter or margarine
7 1/2 ounce box dates, finely chopped
1 cup brown sugar
1 teaspoon vanilla
3 cups Rice Krispies
1 can flaked coconut

Melt butter in skillet over low heat; add dates and sugar. Cook over low heat until dates are lightly browned and mixture is thickened. Add vanilla and Krispies; mix well. Form into small balls and roll in coconut. Yields about 60 balls.

All in a Woman's Day--July 17, 1990

It is fair time ... from past to present

It is fair time in Nodaway County and a lot of other places. In some areas folks call them picnics; however, they are not as intricate or as involved as county or state fairs, and do not include as many things of interest for the participant or the viewers.

Back in those early days of the fair, (Maryville has had several different tries at promoting this venture) the entire family prepared for the fair and came by wagon, buggy or even horseback to attend this annual event. Most of the fairs lasted two or three days, and oftentimes families brought things along so they could stay over for all the activities.

The midway was always such an interesting place to visit. There could be found the shooting gallery, the skill game of throwing darts, where you could generally win a prize if you hit just right. Then there were the side shows, with the unusual characters and freaks and then, too, of course, were the forbidden shows where young people were cautioned "not to set foot inside that tent." (Bet most of them did!)

And the roller coaster and the ferris wheel that possibly made their debut in this area in the 1920s. The merry-go-round, with its tinkling music that went along with the up and down of the various animals which were being ridden. It was such fun!

Too, there were always special acts that generally included animals such as dogs, ponies, horses, bears and monkeys. This, too, was interesting and exciting. Lots of preparatory work was involved in getting these acts readied for the fair.

Exciting was the flying trapeze or the man on the highwire! Sometimes folks could scarcely look it was so frightening!

Some of the places that held fairs had special buildings for some of the exhibits. Maryville at one time had a Floral Hall, which was a two story building at the fairgrounds at the southeast edge of town. Besides flowers, also exhibited there were all kinds of intricate fancywork, displays of fruits, vegetables, jams and jellies, along with that special chocolate cake or the delicious cherry pie, all awaiting to be judged. It was great to receive a blue, red or white ribbon, along with a little monetary assist. How thrilled were the winners!

In those earlier days also sack races and pony races were a part of the activities. Men and their sons brought their most elite livestock for display and judging along with seeds and fowls.

Harness horse racing was one of the important events at the county fairs, and at one time Maryville was fortunate enough to have a fairgrounds with a grandstand. There was no starting gate for those early day—races_they just soared down in front of the grandstand until the starter thought they were even and then he shouted, "Go!" If they had to be brought back for another start, a bell was rung. That, of course, is a far cry from the sophisticated starting gates that are at the fairs and race tracks today.

Then there were the ice cream cones, pop and the cotton candy. Yum! Yum! Good! Oh, yes, and the lemonade! How it was enjoyed! Some folks felt a little uneasy about the water, so lemonade just seemed to take its place and really "hit the spot"!

Public weddings were often held at the earlier fairs, and the couple would receive almost enough merchandise to set up housekeeping. Too, there were the queen contests. At one Nodaway County Fair, Mrs. Harvey Dowden, the former Florence David, was the first Miss NOCOMO.

Machinery eventually entered the picture, with dealers arranging displays. And the fiddlers were busy.

Fairs today have a lot of the things going on that have been mentioned as well as tractor pulls, horse shows, car shows, and parades.

State fairs always have been more elegant than the county fairs, and to be a winner there sort of placed the individual in a class all by himself.

It was in October, 1855, a Missouri state fair was held at Boonville. The Missouri present day fair has been held in Sedalia since 1901.

Funds for this first fair came from the treasury of the Missouri State Agriculture Society, according to the State Historical Society of Missouri. Too, it relates how a legislative act of Feb. 24, 1853, provided $1,000 for the space of four years for the premiums at those fairs. The act was repealed in 1855, when rivalry between the counties caused the state to be divided into five districts for five state fairs. The five districts then received funds through the district treasuries.

The first legislature that provided for the establishment and maintenance of a Missouri State Fair was made in 1899, and the first fair thereafter was held in September, 1902, at Sedalia. Moberly, Sedalia, Chillicothe, Centralia, Boonville, Mexico and Marshall competed for the location for the annual celebration; however, on Oct. 10, 1889, Sedalia was finally decided upon, so writes the Society.

Fairs though are nothing new; however, they were held for a periodic or occasional meeting of buyers and sellers, with their merchandise for purposes of trade.

Originally they were held in conjunction with religious festivals. However, because of travel, it was impossible for would-be purchasers to acquire desired commodities at will, and for merchants to renew their stocks continually. Fairs, therefore, logically developed, taking place when quantities of goods had been accumulated and where great numbers of potential purchasers were present.

They were established as annual events throughout Europe and also became institutions in the East, notably in the religious center of Mecca. So important were they to commercial life that secular and religious authorities granted the merchants special privileges, including the fact that as a court of their own they could settle disputes that arose while fairs were in progress.

It was during the Middle Ages that

the European fairs were prominent, especially during the 13th and 14th centuries.

It has been found that the fairs of Champagne were the most famous during the latter period; however, later, the fair at Geneva became important, along with fairs held at Pavia and Milan in Italy; Frankfurt, Strasbourg and Leipzig in Germany; and Stourbridge and London in England.

Some fairs were established for the sale of a particular kind of merchandise, such as cattle, horses or cloth; while others emphasized general merchandise. Many fairs, in addition to their trading activities, maintained labor exchanges, and it was there that domestic or agricultural servants hired themselves out for a year.

Now and then a "pleasure fair" was held for amusement in connection with the trade or commercial fair. They later lost their commercial aspect and became almost entirely pleasure fairs.

By the 18th century, when the number of shops and markets had increased and transportation and communications were improved, commercial fairs had lost their importance; however, fairs were still maintained because trade could be concentrated in a single place, and market conditions could thus be gauged and fixed.

The trade fairs of the 20th century, especially in the United States, were more on the nature of exhibitions than true fairs; various industries, such as the automobile, radio or textile, held annual fairs to show their latest products and promote sales, with a greater part of the activity taken over by the regional, national and international exhibitions and expositions. Some European fairs became exhibitions for spe-

cialized merchandise and admitted only those connected with a particular industry.

In the United States the most common type of fair was the county or state agricultural fairs. The county event was originated by Elkanah Watson, a prosperous merchant of Albany, N. Y., who organized the first rural fair at Pittsfield, Mass., in 1811.

Today, too, we have the World Fairs or Expositions, and while there is much to see, they again are promoting the selling of merchandise.

* * *

A Thought To Ponder: Remember the fair in Nodaway County, July 19-22. Plan to attend and enjoy!

All in a Woman's Day--July 24, 1990
Wise snacking can be healthy

Snacking is one of the favorite pasttimes of Americans. Of course, that is not all bad, only according to the kind of food that is used for snacks. This subject of snacking is important, and it seems that parents are becoming increasingly more interested in the snack foods they are providing for their children.

This American way of life finds a vast array of foods available. Snacks can help contribute to a nutritionally balanced diet, and they are just as important as the choice of foods consumed at mealtime. It already has been established by the National Nutrition Survey that 12-to 16-year-old boys and girls derive at least as much of the recommended dietary allowance of protein, riboflavin and ascorbic acid from snacks as from traditional meals.

Young children, because the stomach capacity is limited, literally cannot eat enough food three times a day to supply the nourishment their bodies need. At home and at school, mid-morning and afternoon snacks, as well as another at bedtime, is not unusual.

There is yet another benefit from snacking. Research shows "that smaller, more frequent meals are utilized in such a way that depresses the formation of adipose tissue (fatty tissue) as desirable during the growth as a prevention of obesity." Too, failure to meet the traditional requirement for protein is believed to be an important cause of loss of resistance to infections.

Snacking also has a role as a social occasion, especially for teenagers. The choice of food for snacks can be those that supply essential nutrients and that will not spoil the appetite for meals. Snacks should be considered a part of the day's food, contributing to the total nutrient supply.

It should be emphasized that there is no one perfect food. The best diets draw nutrients from a great variety of foods, namely, meats and dairy products, grains, fruits and vegetables.

Here are a few suggestions that should help when the snacking urge strikes: Slice a cantaloupe or honeydew wedge; bite into a velvety peach, nectarine or apricot. Grasp a bunch of delectable grapes; peel a flavorful orange or enjoy the sweet taste of dates, prunes or raisins.

Fresh crispy celery sticks, apples and carrots are snack time favorites.

Slice a banana into bite size pieces and dip into either fresh lime, lemon or orange juice to which a little honey has been added, then coat them thoroughly with chopped walnuts or pecans.

Make fresh juice pops. Place freshly squeezed orange or grapefruit Juice into small paper cups and partially freeze it before inserting wooden popsicle sticks; return to the freezer until thoroughly frozen.

Spread peanut butter on bite size apple wedges or inside celery ribs.

String toothpicks with alternating cubes of cheese and fresh fruit such as apples, pears, pineapple, grapes and melon.

Add diced green pepper to a peanut butter sandwich.

Experiment with other fruits and try some other vegetables, including green beans, broccoli, turnip, cauliflower, zucchini or yellow squash rounds, sweet potatoes and others. These can be dunked into a vegetable dip. Many vegetables taste differently raw, so homemakers don't be surprised if your child likes them this way, but not cooked.

* * *

Add a fresh twist to snack-time with a fruit pizza. Press pie crust into a pizza pan or cookie sheet. Prick the crust with a fork and bake it 10-15 minutes until lightly browned. While crust is baking, soften cream cheese with fresh orange juice; beat to a creamy consistency. Coat the baked crust with the cream cheese mixture and top with any combinations of fruit ... peaches, plums, pears, berries or other fresh fruits.

* * *

The days when children were welcomed home from school or wherever with freshly baked bread or ice box cookies just out of the oven, are gone. No doubt, gone forever! However, in these days of microwave, children can return home to stocked cupboards with ingredients they can easily heat up for fast snacks that are healthful.

Parents often can even plan on having something leftover from meals that youngsters can have that will not spoil their dinner. For instance, spaghetti can be portioned out in advance and it is a good nourishment food. Also, there can be a bowl of soup, baked apples, plain or filled with a marshmallow, peanut butter or raisins, with a sprinkle of cinnamon on top, hot dogs, a small hamburger, as well as a pizza and cheese sandwich. The sandwich can be made by using a slice of whole wheat bread, spread with spaghetti sauce, sprinkled with Mozzarella or Monterey Jack cheese, Polish sausage or lunch meat. Then put a slice of toasted bread on top and pop it into the microwave about 35 seconds. Another snack is a slice of toast buttered and sprinkled with cinnamon and placed in the microwave 10 seconds. Store purchased cookies also can be popped into the microwave for 10 seconds, and they will be soft and warm.

Let us not forget that the snacks mentioned also are healthy for parents, as well as children. Try to stay away from foods that provide excess amounts of sugar and fat.

* * *

A Thought To Ponder: It isn't your position that makes you happy or unhappy. It's your disposition.

* * *

Noisy Nibble Mix

1/4 cup butter or margarine
1/4 cup chunky-style peanut butter
5 cups cereal (bite size shredded corn, wheat, rice or bran squares or round toasted cereal)
1 cup small twisted pretzels
1 cup peanuts
1 cup sunflowers nuts
Place butter and peanut butter into a large nonmetal mixing bowl and do not cover. Place in the microwave oven, set on full or high (100 percent) power. Set timer for 1 1/2 minutes. If the ingredients are not soft, microwave on high for 30 seconds more. Use rubber scraper to stir until mixed well. Add the other ingredients, toss gently with 2 rubber scrappers until coated with mixture. Microwave uncovered on high, stirring often, until hot and crisp, 4 to 6 minutes. Spread mixture in a large shallow pan to cool. Store it in tightly covered container. Makes 7 1/2 cups.

All in a Woman's Day--July 31, 1990
Kitchen ingredients accomplishes wonders

It is amazing what some of the things found in the kitchen can do to help homemakers.

Did you know that lemon extract will remove black scuff marks from luggage?

Heavy white syrup will remove grass stains from clothing. Just apply the syrup generously to the stain and allow to remain until the stain can easily be removed. Light scrubbing may be necessary.

Vinegar also will remove grass stains from washable clothing. Saturate the spot with vinegar, wash as usual.

Cooking grease can be absorbed by dry corn starch. Just apply to the spot; let it set a few minutes and then brush lightly to remove the corn starch.

Ginger ale will remove mustard stains from clothing. Soak the stain with ginger ale and allow to set until the stain is easily removed. Again, some scrubbing may be necessary.

Light scorch stains on linen can sometimes be removed by rubbing with the cut side of an onion. Then soak the material in cold water.

Stains from ballpoint pens may be removed by sponging the area with milk until it disappears.

Clean an electric coffeepot with Kool-Aid. Run it through the entire cycle, then rinse and dry thoroughly.

The inside of a dishwasher may be cleaned by filling the dishwasher cup with Tang (an orange drink) instead of detergent. Wash it without dirty dishes and run through a complete cycle.

Coffee grounds also come to the rescue. When chopped onion leaves an odor in thc freezer, just place 1/2 cup fresh ground coffee in a dish and set it inside the freezer. This method also freshens a china cabinet that might have a peculiar odor that you had not been unable to be removed previously.

As soon as a bruise occurs, apply a bit of butter. The bruise will heal and there will be no discoloration.

Chewing gum on clothing may be removed by rubbing peanut butter on the spot or by rubbing an egg into the spot. Ice cubes rubbed over gum will help loosen it.

Price tag glue can be removed from glassware with several different things. Apply bacon grease, lighter fluid, rubbing alcohol or mineral, salad or cooking oil to the gummed areas and then rub it to remove the glue.

Musty odors in plastic containers can be removed by bleaching. Then sprinkle the container with cinnamon, closing it for several hours. Then wash. The cinnamon takes the bleach odor out, and its scent disappears in a short time.

If you pat the skin around where a splinter entered the body with olive or baby oil, it will slide out more easily.

For greasy work clothes, pour a bottle of cola into the wash water to loosen the stains.

Suede shoes can be given a lift by rubbing them with a sponge slightly moistened with cold black coffee.

Remove burned-on foods from a pan by generously applying baking soda on the place that has been barely moistened with water. Let the paste stand overnight, then wash.

Rusted bolts can be worked loose by pouring a carbonated beverage on them.

When food in your frying pan sticks, loosen it right away by placing the pan on ice or something that is very cold.

After using the conventional polish on the furniture, sprinkle a little corn starch on the surface, then rub to a high gloss. Corn starch absorbs the oil and it leaves a glistening surface.

The lipstick smear on fabric can be helped by rubbing the spot with a slice of white bread or dab with petroleum jelly, and follow with a dry-cleaning solution. Putting salad oil on the spot, and laundering the fabric after 5 minutes also will work.

* * *

A Thought To Ponder: Keeping your chin up does more than boost your moral—it helps maintain the firm lines of the chin and neck.

All in a Woman's Day--August 7, 1990
Fresh, ripe peaches arrive in all their glory

They are here in all their glory—those luscious, fresh, ripe peaches that are so much a part of the summer scene.

If you want to thoroughly enjoy peaches, perhaps you might like a few helpful hints about how to select the

756

fruit and how to bring out the flavor if they have been picked slightly immature.

Since this fresh fruit bruises easily, it is up to the producer to know just when it should be picked so it will reach the customer in good condition and still give the most flavor possible under the circumstances.

You will find that a peach, with an undertone of green, has been picked too soon, and no matter how long it is left on the kitchen cabinet, it will not ripen. So, in purchasing peaches be sure to look for those with a smooth, velvety skin that has a creamy undertone. A good sense of smell doesn't hurt either. Do not squeeze peaches to determine the maturity. Even if you are going to buy the peach you squeezed, it will be bruised, and nobody else wants bruised fruit, so, it can't be sold; thereby, a squeeze makes the cost go up. A little squeeze can be costly!

When peaches are not quite ready to use, place them aside in a warm, but shaded spot and leave them to ripen. They will not ripen in the cool confines of the refrigerator.

There are many new varieties of peaches that have been and are being developed that have deeper red skin color that adds to the beauty; however, it also makes it more difficult to judge maturity.

Tree ripened peaches are most likely to become soft almost within minutes; and a basket or bag of such peaches will have some bruises by the time they are moved from the orchard to the kitchen.

So, the most flavorful fresh peaches may therefore sometimes show a minor bruise or two, but this will not take away from the overall quality. So, remember when you shop, always give the peach the tender loving care it so much deserves ... no squeezing, please. The red blush on peaches does not mean ripeness.

Avoid peaches with wrinkles, brownish spots or traces of green on the skin.

The peach is the third most important fruit crop in the United States (the first is apple, the second orange, according to statistics). And, if you are not aware of the fact, the peach is a cousin of the cherry, the apricot, the plum and the almond. So, it has lots of relatives.

There are hundreds of ways to serve peaches—fresh, canned or dried, all of which are delicious. Peaches also are distilled into a liqueur, as well as made into nectar.

Fresh peaches will not turn dark if you peel them into a syrup that includes a little powdered fruit drink mix. Use the orange flavored powder and put about one-fourth teaspoon for each pint of syrup. This also can be done when canning peaches.

Another way to prevent fresh sliced peaches from discoloring is to make a simple syrup of the desired sweetness.

A simple syrup is made by bringing to boil equal parts of sugar and water. Then dissolve two tablespoons of corn starch in a bit of water and add to the syrup, which has come to a good boil, and cook until the syrup is clear. Add one or two drops of yellow or pink food coloring. The syrup is ready to use hot, warm or cold. Simply slice the fruit into the syrup. It is the corn starch that does the trick. Store the syrup in the refrigerator until it is used up.

Also there is a fresh fruit pectin on the market that will prevent darkening when sprinkled on the fruit.

I have learned of another way to

freeze peaches. Take them right from the box or basket and put them on trays in the freezer. Then when frozen, put them in plastic bags. When you want to use them, take the peaches to the sink and let cold water run over them. The skin can be pushed off. Put them in a dish and let them thaw at least an hour. They will stay bright and taste like a fresh peach should. Don't let them thaw before you take the skins off because they will cling.

When canning peaches save the pits and make Peach Pit jelly. Fill a gallon container (not aluminum) with pits. Add five cups boiling water, cover and let stand overnight. The next day add seven cups sugar to the bright red juice and a package of pectin. Make jelly according to the directions on the box.

* * *

A Thought To Ponder: Marriage: An institution held togther by two books—cook and check!

* * *

Peaches and Cream Salad

1 (3-ounce package) orange gelatin
1 cup boiling water
1/4 teaspoon orange flavoring
1 (3-ounce package) cream cheese, softened
1 (8-ounce carton) whipped topping (use only 2/3 of container)
1/4 cup chopped pecans

Dissolve the gelatin in the boiling water; add the orange flavoring; cool and refrigerate until slightly thickened. Whip the softened cream cheese and fold into the two-thirds of the whipped topping. Add the pecans and fold all into the gelatin. Pour into 9-inch baking dish. Chill until almost firm.

Peach Layer

1 (3-ounce package) peach gelatin
1 cup boiling water
1/4 teaspoon peach flavoring
1 (21-ounce) can peach pie filling

Dissolve the gelatin in the boiling water; add the peach flavoring. Chill slightly and add the pie filling. Pour over the top of the cream layer. Chill until firm. Note: Red gelatin can be used with cherry pie filling.

All in a Woman's Day--August 14, 1990

A bouquet of useful ideas

How about a spicy bouquet fashioned of some useful ideas?

Many fruits and vegetables make good pickles. Take for instance pickled cherries; spiced grapes; dilled green beans; chutney; a mixture of fruits; chopped mixed garden vegetables; pickled okra, onions, cauliflower and carrots, all make delicious pickles, according to each individuals special tastebuds.

Carrots can be frozen by grinding and shredding. They must be fresh. For each cup of carrots add one teaspoon sugar. Place in plastic bags and freeze. When you are ready to make a salad or stew, add the carrots in the amount desired and allow to thaw. Stir to combine with other ingredients.

And when making pickles, be sure always to use the freshest picked cucumbers. It is best to make the pickles immediately after picking the cucumbers, for even if the cucumbers stand overnight they do deteriorate, and, of course, that makes less than a perfect pickle. When cucumbers get too old, they get seedy and have too much water content, especially so during a rainy season; however, on the other hand, if there is too little rainfall, that, too, makes a difference in the finished product.

Should freezing be your favorite way

of preserving, just try freezing cucumbers. Peel, slice and place a cup of cucumbers in a plastic bag, seal and freeze. When ready to use, cover while still frozen, with a solution of one teaspoon sugar, an eighth teaspoon salt, half cup mild vinegar and half teaspoon dill seed (optional). Place mixture in the refrigerator and use as needed.

You will find that peppers and onions can be frozen, too. Just grind or grate and freeze in ice cube trays with only enough water to moisten. After freezing, place the cubes into plastic bags and return to freezer. A cube or two at a time can be used in salads, soups and stews.

It is a simple task to make pimentos from homegrown sweet red peppers. Just wash and quarter the ripe sweet peppers, removing the seeds. Soak overnight in a strong solution, using five tablespoons salt to one quart water. In the morning, drain and rinse them. Make a solution of a half cup vinegar, a half cup sugar and a half cup water. Make amount needed to just cover peppers. Combine with the drained peppers and simmer 5 to 7 minutes. These can be placed in a jar, and they will keep well in the refrigerator.

Some of you will no doubt remember that Grandmother used grape leaves in making pickles, and they are still a useful product. There seems to be something in the grape leaves that helps keep the cucumbers firm. Add to cucumbers placed in brine, they are as helpful today as they were those many years ago. Discard the leaves when cucumbers are taken from the brine for the next step in the pickle making process.

A dash of powdered ginger can be added to most foods, and it accents the taste; however, it is not detectable, but just seems to work magic.

Marinating also helps to spice up meals. Here is one that is called **Southern-Style Vinegar Marinade**. It is made with 2 cups apple cider vinegar, 1 cup Kansas City-style spicy barbecue sauce, 2 tablespoons lemon juice, 1 tablespoon dry mustard. Combine ingredients in a saucepan and simmer the mixture on low heat until well blended. Cool. Pour over meat and marinate up to 24 hours in the refrigerator.

Believe it or not nasturtiums give a delicious flavor to salads. The young flowers and leaves add a special note; and the seeds, if pickled when young and green, can be used as a substitute for capers.

Basil, a peppery herb, goes great with tomatoes, eggplant, eggs, fish and cheese dishes. The flavor of this herb gets zestier when cooked.

Potato salad is generally made with each cook using a preferred special (doctored-up) dressing concocted to give it a one-of-a-kind flavor. Some cooks believe that the potatoes should get cold before the dressing is added as it does take less dressing this way; however, others feel that to get the best flavor the salad should be put together when the potatoes are still just warm enough to handle.

* * *

A Thought To Ponder: Variety is the spice of life.

* * *

**Elizabeth Ann's Cheese
Topped Molded Salad**
No. 2 1/2 can apricots
No. 2 1/2 can pineapple chunks
1 cup juice reserve

2 packages (3-ounce) orange gelatin
2 cups boiling water
1 1/2 cups miniature marshmallows
1 egg, beaten
1/2 cup sugar
4 tablespoons flour
2 tablespoons butter
2 cups whipped topping
Grated cheese

Drain juice from fruit; dissolve gelatin in 2 cups boiling water and add 1 cup juice combined from fruit. Let this chill until it begins to set; then add 1 1/4 cups chopped apricots, 1 1/4 cups diced pineapple and 1 1/2 cups marshmallows. Let set until firm. Cook 1/2 cup sugar and 4 tablespoons flour with 1 cup fruit juice; and beaten egg, cooking one minute until thick. Remove from heat and add 2 tablespoons butter; cool. When chilled, fold in whipped topping. Spread over top of gelatin mixture and top with grated cheese. Use 9x9-inch pan. Serves 12-25.

All in a Woman's Day--August 21, 1990

Bygone school days recalled in memory

Here it is school time again, however, it is a far cry from those years of long ago.

For a long time we have been aware of the decline of the rural school and knew it was becoming a "vanishing breed," and now it is practically extinct.

In the earlier days in the settlement of our country, rural schools were generally located two miles apart and youngsters walked or rode a pony or horse; however, the father of the household often would take them in the wagon or sled if weather was extremely inclement. When roads became better, traveling was easier by automobiles; consolidation took over in schools, and that was the beginning of the end of rural schools.

There are still a few of those old schools left, with some still used for community gatherings, some for storage and some for museums, with the remainder gone by the wayside.

In a few isolated areas there are still a few of the old rural schools left; however, they are now modernized.

Some folks have always felt there were advantages in having fewer pupils and smaller classes as the teacher could take more time with the pupils and there would develop a family-like atmosphere.

In those earlier days, teachers had only to pass an oral or written examination, and they were allowed to teach. Quite often the teacher was just out of school or perhaps not yet even graduated, and oftentimes only about 16 years of age. In later years teachers had to pass an examination before a teaching certificate was awarded. Then as time went by, the colleges offered 30-hour teaching certificates, as well as a 60-hour or a lifetime certificate. These are no longer a part of the educational scene. Today's teacher must have one of various degrees and as a part of becoming a teacher must do student teaching.

Teachers in those bygone days found that older pupils were a consolation for they helped to tutor the younger children; in fact, they helped do everything, thus showing tolerance and compassion.

The school year was divided into terms ... fall, winter and spring, and often the older boys got to attend only the winter term as they were needed to help with the farming.

As schooltime came around in those days, most families shopped from the Sears Roebuck catalog. Youngsters spent hours thumbing through the catalog and drooling over all the pictures of what they would like. Some things were ordered; however, it had to be early because it took quite a while for mail to come through. Girls' dresses and boys' shirts often were made out of feed sacks. Too, it was difficult to fit "summer barefoot feet" into new shoes. Long underwear and long cotton stockings were purchased early for sometimes winter didn't always wait.

Lunch boxes were regular school equipment and the highlight of getting ready for school was selecting one that was special. They came in various colors with different kinds of designs and pictures as decorations. If a lunch box was forgotten and left at school, the next day's lunch was sent in a half-gallon syrup or lard bucket. The first day of school lunch had to be something special. One treat was peanut butter and crackers; this was not a part of an ordinary meal, mostly just a special school treat. Sometimes, too, in cold weather, the teacher would heat food on the top of the stove so there would be a warm meal.

During school days, games were played out-of-doors; among them were drop the handkerchief, follow the leader, ante over, fox and geese, blackman, sheep in my pen and tug of war. When the weather was bad and pupils had to stay inside, they would often play hide the thimble and I spy.

Friday afternoons when lessons were over, that was the time for spelling bees and ciphering matches.

A portion of the social life in the community centered around the school, and when gatherings were held; the pupils would entertain with programs.

School rooms were equipped with homemade benches up in front where pupils would go to recite their lessons. Lamps were used in those earlier days until electricity came along. Bathroom facilities, were not very great. They had boys' and girls' outhouses that were two-holers with a moon and star cut into the buildings. At one time school lighting had to be approved, and instead of having windows on both sides it was thought better to have them just on one side. We'll probably never know just for sure how that project worked out.

I guess we can say that gone is the day of the one-room schoolhouse, the old water bucket, the dipper, the tin cups and the pot bellied stove. Many folks still have in their possession some of the old desks of yesteryear.

In today's modernized world, teachers, while they still have many extra duties to do and be responsible for, do not have to fire up the stove, carry water and do all the odd jobs and chores of a janitor. Because teachers in those days had this work to do, they generally roomed and boarded at a home near the school.

Some of you will remember the old slates and slate pencils of those olden days. Often the slate was bound in red felt and it was not always as clean as it could be; sometimes it was rather musty smelling. They were really not very sanitary articles.

There were three things that were very much a part of the scene ... the Big Chief pencil tablet, pens and pencils.

The tablet seems to have deep roots.

It was in 1906 that William Albrecht founded the Western Tablet Co., in St. Joseph. For many years it was known as Westab and later Mead, St. Joseph Division. Although many changes were made through the passing years in locations, names and products, Big Chief tablet continued to remain the same.

The array of tablet covers, varied through the years; they have been numerous; but Big Chief, one of the first, has remained unchanged. Patterned after no living person, it was purely original. Among some of the featured covers have been movie greats—Billie Dove, Rudolph Valentino, Shirley Temple and Our Gang kids. There have been political figures, presidents, patriotic designs with flags and doughboys in uniform during World War I, as well as Indian braves and maidens.

Each cover fad just seemed to fade away as the years went by; all except Big Chief, and it has remained unchanged through the span of time, and has continued to go to school.

It is a wonder that Big Chief was able to exist with all the competition in this space age and modern school items such as spiral notebooks, magical plastic that seals so easily and zippers that interlock all so sophisticated. The only competition that Big Chief really seemed to encounter was a gag at a sales conference, the Son of Big Chief was printed. So, it was that Big Chief and Son of Big Chief went to school together, and both can be found in Maryville stores.

Slates were replaced with pens and pencils. Long ago in Mesopotamia, there were cuneiforms (wedges) that were used to help communicate ideas that had a retainable form. The wedge-like marks were made on tablets of clay by using a sharp bone or piece of metal.

In the seventh century someone came up with the idea that a good writing pen could be made from the wing feather of a goose, and so for more than 1,000 years the quill pen was the popular instrument for writing.

School desks also were equipped for pen and ink writing as the desks had holes in them that was made especially to hold the ink well.

It wasn't until the 1800s that a steel pen appeared. They were first made by Samuel Harrison, a locksmith in England, who made them in the form of small steel barrels into which replaceable steel nips (something pointed) could be fitted. The first metal pens were manufactured in the United States in 1810, by Peregrine Williamson, with the production taking place at several plants along the East coast. Back in 1888, John Louis, Weymouth, Mass., received a patent on a ballpoint pen; however, it was not until after World War II that it received much promoting.

The lead pencil is really nothing new for it existed back in 23 A. D. and the Aztecs were using them when Cortez arrived in Mexico in 1520. The pencil; however, as we think of it today, dates back to 1812 when William Monroe, Concord, Mass., came up with the idea of enclosing graphite in a wood casing. This idea was not long in catching on. Some of you will remember the pencil of earlier years that was a small wooden deal with an eraser fitted down into the top and was called the "penny pencil."

The pencil became a favorite instrument for writing; the pen and ink took a back seat and was left to the use of penmanship classes.

All of these items were so important in an ordinary school day long ago; now, of course, it is calculators and computers that are used in this modern age. There is no doubt, however, that the tablet, pen and pencil have a continuing future.

All in a Woman's Day--August 28, 1990

Cooking with fish can be quick, easy

Whether the fish is catfish, pike, bullhead or whatever the variety, they must be handled in about the same manner.

It seems that cooking fish intimidates most cooks; however, it really is quick, easy and fun, so, if you can broil a steak or fry a chop you can cook fish. Don't be shy about this cookery as there is really just one secret to the success of this particular food. And that secret is "Don't Over Cook." It will ruin the flavor, texture and eye appeal. Just remember fish and seafood are juicy and tender before they are cooked.

Cooking seems to bring out the full flavor of fish. But remember, keep your kitchen fork handy so you can make the "fork test" for doneness. To test with a fork, gently probe the thickest portion of the fish and be sure that you make the test no later than halfway through the suggested cooking time. You will find that when the fish is done it will not only be fork tender but also flaky. When making the test there is a division of the flesh but this does not present a problem. Just gently push it together and serve at once.

Baking, broiling and frying are the basic forms of cooking, and no doubt the most popular is panfrying. Dip fish into a liquid "wash," coat it with breading and place it in a shallow pan in hot, but not smoking oil. Fry it until it is golden brown on both sides and crackling crisp on the outside, flaky and moist on the inside. Because time varies in the cooking with the thickness of the fish, be sure the fork is handy for testing the doneness for the perfect panfried fish.

Baking is another method of cooking. Place fish into a greased baking dish, brush with cooking oil or sauce and place it in a moderate oven. If the fish is not yet thawed, start it frozen and increase the baking time. Just remember the fork test.

Fish, too, can be broiled indoors or outdoors on a grill. Baste generously before and while broiling to keep it juicy and moist. For holding and handling during the charcoal broiling, use a well greased, long handled hinged wire grill. It is most useful.

Poaching and planking are less basic methods of cooking fish. Poaching requires less than 15 minutes for filets or steaks. Place the fish in a shallow pan and pour over it, a liquid such as lightly salted or spiced water, white wine or milk. Cover and simmer until the fish passes the fork test. Cooked this way, it can be served hot; with a sauce, or chilled and flaked for a salad.

To plank a fish simply means to bake it on a special hardwood "platter." If you are unable to find a plank at a department store, a bake-and-serve platter will serve the same purpose. A succulent dressed salmon or other fish steaks and filets are especially good planked.

So the fish will fry straight and not curl, place the skin side down in the pan first.

Several hints concern fish odor. To remove fish odor from hands and skillet by using a small amount of vinegar in the wash water. To eliminate odor in the kitchen, dice a stalk of celery with leaves, add water and cook it in a saucepan, uncovered on the top of the stove. Still another way is to add a cup of vinegar to a quart of water and let it simmer over a low flame. Also adding a teaspoon of peanut butter in the pan with the oil helps prevent odor in the house, and the fish will look and taste better, too.

When freezing fish, freeze them covered in water; they will keep their good flavor.

A tablespoon of vinegar added to cold shortening when frying fish will help more corn meal stick to the fish instead of ending up in the skillet.

When baking fish, brush it with a little mayonnaise, it adds moisture and has a pleasing flavor.

Watch for the color changing in the doneness of fish. Raw fish appears watery and translucent, while cooked fish looks opaque and white.

As with most everything, there are always bits of folklore, omens, beliefs, charms and superstitions or whatever term you might like to use, connected with fishing.

Commercial skippers, or fishermen have a qualm about Friday. Some won't begin a trip on this day because they believe it means bad luck.

Also dreaded is a crow that flies across the bow. There was one skipper who ran his vessel ashore so that occurrence would not take place.

Too, some think that if a ship is watched out of sight it will begin the very worst kind of luck and will never be seen again.

To go aboard a ship with a suitcase or wearing gray gloves meant all hands will be lost.

Then, if a hatch is turned upside down or dropped into a hold, it is felt that misfortune will be sure to follow on the trip.

If a cake of ice is dropped overboard by accident, while getting ready for a trip, good luck and a big catch will result.

If a girl or a widow catches an eel it is a sure sign that she will be married to a widower.

Many skippers believe that "whistling in the pilot house" will attract favorable winds; others think that tossing a penny overboard will bring the wind.

It seems that all fishermen know that stolen fishing tackle is really the only equipment that will always insure a good catch. A stolen hook will catch twice the number of fish that a hook bought in any sporting goods store will capture.

Should a fisherman wait to get his bait, after reaching the fishing area, it is predestined as miserable luck.

If fishworms appear in number atop the ground, some fishermen believe the finned hordes are ready to bite; however, in the New England area during the past century, one of the most popular baits was flakes taken from the scab that grows on the inside of a horse's leg.

Spitting on a fishhook is a very ancient superstitution and relates back to the most primitive times. There is a little couplet that originally must be said as a part of the spitting ritual. It goes thus:
Fish, fish, fish, come bite my hook!
You'll be a captain and I'll be a cook.

By many fishermen it is considered bad luck should someone spit into the water ahead of them as this is believed to drive the fish away. Then some believe that the catch will be greatly enhanced if they spit into the mouth of the first fish caught.

One of the most unusual beliefs: Eat the eyes of a fish and you'll never be afraid of the dark.

Many American fishermen have been known to name their ships after sons or daughters or other near relatives believing this signifies good luck. Some like to have the name of their boat begin with the letter "E" as an omen of good luck and some believe that a name containing two "R's" will bring home good fortune.

* * *

A Thought To Ponder: Things that are natural are never without a certain grace and excellence.

* * *

Fish Batter

1 cup ice water
1 egg
1/4 teaspoon soda
1/4 teaspoon salt
1 1/3 cups unsifted cake flour

Combine the ice water and egg; beat them well and then combine mixture with the soda, salt and 1 cup flour. Mix until just blended, leaving a few lumps. Sprinkle the remaining 1/3 cup of flour over the top of the batter and stir only lightly with a fork. Some flour should float on top. Place bowl of batter in a large bowl in which you have placed some ice. Keep batter cold while dipping the fish.

Fresh pears always give succulent taste

Fresh, juicy pears are real mouthwatering delights, and the taste may be sweet, buttery, acid or spicy. They are one of the few fruits that improve in flavor and texture when ripened off the tree.

For culinary purposes, the pear is very similar to and perhaps just as versatile as the apple. Both may be prepared the same—pear butter and pear sauce, the same as you would apple butter and applesauce.

Of the many popular varieties, Bartlett, D'Anjou (pronounced "an joo" or "an zhoo," French) and Bosc (pronounced Bosh) are the most frequently available, with the Anjou and Bosc most preferred for baking.

All alone, the Bartlett pear boasts an elegant image. It is often associated with those things continental and also it is classically pictured with a slice of Brie, a crust of bread and a glass of Chardonnay; however, for the more simple tastes, it also is delicious sliced over a bowl of cereal for breakfast or eaten from the hand.

It seems the only trick to success with fresh Bartletts is learning the technique of ripening. This fruit does not ripen properly on the tree; therefore, it must be picked mature, but firm. If kept at room temperature for several days it will ripen quite well; however, a ripening bowl or a loosely closed paper bag will help to accomplish the ripening process.

When pears are fully ripened on the tree, often the quality is poor and has a grittier texture.

Kieffer pears seem to be one of the most popular homegrown varieties;

however, for the best quality, they, too, must ripen two to three days after picking at temperatures ranging from 55 to 65 degrees.

A pear that is perfectly ripe should have a "springy" feeling. Be sure to select pears that are firm, well shaped, but beware of soft spots and blemishes. Pears bruise easily and must be handled with care!

You will find that pears are grouped in two classes. Those of the fall varieties that mature in August and September and the winter varieties that are picked in late September and October. Among some of the varieties found in the fall group are Tyson, Bartlett, Seckel, Moonglow, Stark-Crimson and Delicious. Winter varieties include Kieffer, Bosc, Comice and Duchess.

Canned pears are available whole, quartered or sliced and they come packed in water, juice and syrup. They also are available in diet packs and baby food, as well as nectar, spiced, pickled and in fruit cocktail. Dried pears are packaged in halves and also are mixed with other dried fruits.

Three or four pears equal one pound or two cups sliced. To easily remove the skins from the fruit, put them in a wire sieve or cheese cloth and dip into boiling water. Bartlett pears require about a minute, in the boiling water. Kieffer pears; however, require three to five minutes. Other varieties may require different timings, so it would be well to experiment with one or two pears.

Fresh Bartletts are a natural choice for roast meat or poultry, in fact, they complement all types of food.

You might note: Pears take on the flavor of other foods with which they are stored. For instance, if near potatoes, they easily acquire an earthy taste; and if stored near meat, this rather objectionable taste is taken on from the meat. So, beware where you store this fruit!

Juicy, delicate flavored pears go a long way towards making the brown bag lunch a more alluring prospect. Perhaps if you choose to be more daring, you could try coring a whole pear and stuffing it with cream or cheddar cheese, deviled ham or peanut butter. Add some grapes and prunes to a pear half, and you can do away with a sandwich. A handful of nuts or a slice of bologna will give the added benefit of protein. Chilled pears served with imported cheese make a simple, but delightful dessert.

It is not often that you come across a food like pears that will fit well into breakfast, lunch or dinner. Too, just imagine it being equally at home as an entree, salad or dessert, or all by itself.

It is the pear that moves gracefully, and we might say, tastefully through our meals.

* * *

A Thought To Ponder: A day of worry is more exhausting than a week of work. —The Pepper Box

* * *

Fresh Pear Cake

1 cup brown sugar
1 cup white sugar
3 cups flour
1 1/2 teaspoons soda
1/2 teaspoon nutmeg
1 teaspoon salt
1/2 teaspoon cloves
1/2 teaspoon cinnamon
3 eggs
1 1/4 cups vegetable oil
1 teaspoon vanilla
3 cups pears, chopped or grated

1 cup nuts, chopped

Mix the first eight ingredients. Add eggs, oil and vanilla. Mix well. Add pears and nuts. Bake in a well-greased bundt pan in a 350 degree oven one hour and 15 minutes or until done.

Glaze

1/2 stick margarine
1/2 cup sugar
1/2 cup evaporated milk

Combine the three ingredients in a saucepan and boil until of glaze consistency. Pour over cake. If you prefer, use your favorite frosting.

All in a Woman's Day--September 11, 1990

Kitchen 'siftings'

It is time to have some "siftings" from the kitchen.

When making sauces always add flour to melted butter off the heat so that you will have a smoother mixture. Too, when adding any liquid to a sauce base, stir it in, off the heat. Add hot sauce to cold sauce, two tablespoons at a time so the cold warms up gradually and doesn't curdle. The secret of a good sauce is to use low-to-medium heat, never use high.

If you need to correct a separated sauce, Hollandaise or chocolate, beat in a tablespoon or so of cold water; use hot water for mayonnaise. In correcting a too thick a sauce just heat until simmering, then beat in, using a spoonful at a time, a little cream or stock until the desired consistency is reached. Then, if you must correct a too-thin hot sauce blend a teaspoon of flour with a teaspoon of soft butter. Beat into the hot sauce off the heat until smooth. Then simmer.

Add a slice of lemon or lime to your favorite pot roast or beef stew recipe for a zippy, tangy gourmet flavor.

Meringues that have lost crispness may be dried in a preheated 225 degree oven 15 to 25 minutes.

If pasta you are cooking is ready before the sauce, just drain and place in a bowl and cover with hot water. It can be held this way up to 15 minutes.

If a molded gelatin salad does not set, pour it into a saucepan, heat gently, then add a fourth-ounce package of plain gelatin that has been softened in a fourth-cup water. Stir well, return to the clean mold and try it again.

Try combining salt and pepper in a large shaker to save time seasoning foods. Mix one teaspoon pepper to a four-ounce shaker, or to suit your taste.

Coat bacon by shaking it in a bag of flour; then fry it as usual. It will not spatter or shrink and also gives it a different good taste.

You might try this. Add one to three tablespoons corn meal to cream style corn. It not only thickens the corn, if it should be too thin, but adds a delicious flavor.

If food, has burned in the oven, sprinkle cinnamon in the oven while it is still warm, but not hot. Too, you can put a half cup of ammonia in a pot of boiling water on top of the stove. This will help eliminate the burned smell.

For a crispier bacon, try soaking it in milk or water half an hour before cooking and then dip it in flour to create a crisp, flavorful treat.

You will have super tender baked chicken if it is marinated in buttermilk, cream or milk for several hours before cooking.

Soak liver in tomato juice for about an hour before cooking if you want moist and tender liver.

Before baking potatoes, rub the skins with olive oil for moister and tastier skins.

Your green vegetables will be greener if you lift the lid on the pot a few times when they are cooking.

To keep bread fresh, place a rib of celery in the bag with it.

It is best to use glass pie pans for two crust fruit pies that require longer cooking; however, tins are best for one crust custard pies that should bake more quickly.

If you don't have enough filling to fill a pie shell, just add some apples as they can be combined with almost any fruit for a delicious filling.

To avoid damage when baking stuffed peppers, just coat them with salad oil before stuffing. This will keep them bright and green.

Always make it a policy to serve great tasting salad dressing; just mix a pinch of sugar to cut the vinegar's acid taste and to blend the seasonings.

For a better meringue stir two tablespoons boiling water into the beaten egg whites just before spreading over the pie and the meringue will not run.

* * *

A Thought To Ponder: We must learn to be still in the midst of activity and to be vibrantly alive in repose.

* * *

Chocolate Angel Food Cake

1 package white angel food cake mix
1 1/2 cups water
1/4 cup cocoa

Prepare cake mix using the 1 1/2 cups of water for the moisture and then mix as usual. Add the sifted dry cocoa to the first addition of dry ingredients. Bake in a 10-inch tube pan as directed. Cool and frost.

Honey has been tops throughout history

Throughout history the delicious sweet taste of honey has been enjoyed until sugar (known only since the 13th century A.D.) came into being.

That honey was gathered in prehistoric times has been evidenced by paintings in caves, that have been found near Valencia, Spain, that depict hives of wild bees being tapped by an intrepid climber.

In early civilizations, honey also was treasured for its natural sweetness.

Too, honey was reserved for only the rich, who could afford such a luxury. Taxes too, were often paid in honey because of its value.

The Bible discloses that honey was one of the things deemed necessary for the life of everyone. This was along with water, fire, iron, salt, milk, bread of flour, clusters of grapes, oil and clothing. We all know the reference made to the "land of milk and honey" as promised the Israelites and of King Solomon's advice to his son, "use thou honey for it is good. '

The Egyptians also appreciated honey, for dating from the third millennium B.C. there has been found on the walls of one temple sculptures showing methods of beekeeping, a science that was founded early in the history of civilization. Also noted has been the fact that the bee and its honey were so important to the Egyptians that one symbol of royalty was the honeybee (many centuries later this symbol was adopted by Napoleon for his insignia). Too, what seemed good for the Egyptians also was good for the Greeks for they were especially fond of honey, notably wild honey for Hymettus, for this is where the bees drank the nectar.

So, what was nectar for the Greeks, was ambrosia for the Romans for it was this group of people, who created the art of beekeeping, into a science.

Pliny, the Elder, a Roman naturalist, during his travels amassed such a large amount of material on the effects of honey that it encouraged him to draw the conclusion that honey was a food that increased longevity. He cited a group of devout beekeepers in northern Italy who lived extremely long lives, with more than 100 persons over 100 years of age, with the eldest 135.

The Medieval Emperor Charlmagne, keeping with the royalty preceding him, favored honey, and issued a royal edict that his estates should always have a supply of honey and beeswax available. Every Medieval manor house had its hives, and by the 1500s various European principalities required peasants to raise bees for honey.

In the monasteries that dotted the face of Medieval Europe, the taste of honey also was kept alive with the reason seemingly to be as a source of wax for candles that they used in their religious ceremonies. However, because of this, they produced prodigious amounts of honey, much of which was disseminated outside the monastery walls.

The European civilization did not maintain a monopoly on honey, for it was valued in both the Moslem and Hindu worlds. The high esteem of honey was revealed by the Islamic, prophet Mohammed when he taught that honey is a remedy for illness of body, and that Koran is a remedy for illness of mind, and recommended both remedies.

A ceremony involving honey is a part of the Hindu wedding ritual in India. A dish of honey is fed to the bridegroom when he arrives at the home of his betrothed. It is during the ceremony that he speaks these words "Honey, this is honey, the speech of thy tongue is honey; in my mouth is the honey of the bee, in my teeth lives peace. "

The early inhabitants of the Americas, when the Spanish conquistadors arrived in the New World, also enjoyed honey. When they arrived on the shores they found the Mayan and Aztec Indians feasting on honey they had taken from hives of domesticated bees.

Did you know that tiny honey bees have been used to carry messages in time of war? The Chinese, who have been the first to do numerous things, used them during World War II to carry news across the Japanese lines. The messages were printed in tiny letters on very thin paper that were enclosed in small capsules and fastened to their bodies. Bees have a homing instinct, as do carrier pigeons.

Cold sufferers drink honey as tea; the Chinese mix it with rice flour cakes; the Finns stew prunes in it; the Turks, who say, "Bal tutan parmagini yolar" ("who eats honey licks his fingers") put it in pancake batter; and the Jews all over the world enjoy it in celebration of Rosh Hashanah, the Jewish New Year. And so goes the story of honey.

* * *

A Thought To Ponder: A land flowing with milk and honey. Exodus 3:8.

* * *

Honey Glazed Lima Beans
2 cups dried lima beans
1 cup chopped onions
1/4 cup shortening
3/4 cup honey

1 1/2 teaspoons salt

Wash beans and soak them about two hours in water, drain. Cover beans with water and bring to a boil. Cover and simmer over medium heat two hours, drain. Melt shortening and saute onions until tender. Mix beans, onions, honey and salt together and pour into a casserole. Bake in a preheated 350 degree oven until beans are glazed and tender; about one hour.

All in a Woman's Day--September 25, 1990

Honey's history is interesting

This is a continuation of the bee and honey story that I hope will reflect some additional interesting facts and offer a few helps concerning this sweetener.

In the earlier days the honeybee brought something new and welcome to the scene. It was the bee tree, and it became a permanent fixture in the superbly wooded countryside; therefore, it was easy for settlers to keep a "sweet tooth" well supplied.

Bee trees, as well as the wild honey, were plentiful and not hard to locate. All folks needed to do was glance skyward toward the heavens and they could see the industrious little honeybees flying home to their storehouses … the bee trees.

Both honey and beeswax influenced the economy of the early 1800s. Beeswax sold for about 25 cents per pound, while honey was valued from 10 to 37 cents per pound.

Honey was generally stored and transported in barrels; however, as a substitute often used were cleaned skins of a dressed deer as containers. Too, honey sometimes was stored in large troughs hewn out of logs.

At that time bees were known as "English flies" and the "white man's fly." The Indians believed that the appearance of bees foretold further invasion by the white man.

The early settlers also used honey for money, barter, wagon grease lubricant, wine and as a substitute for soap. So, as noted, it was most versatile and important in the lives of the settlers.

The Bible proclaimed the Promise Land to be "flowing with milk and honey." Hippocrates prescribed wine and honey for pain; and athletes in ancient Greece proceeded to eat honey before entering the arena. Throughout the ages honey has been a prominent symbol of robust health.

Ancient Greeks called honey the nectar of the gods, and ordinary folks throughout the centuries have agreed to its goodness.

The nectar is the sweet substance that bees drink from flowers; pollen is the yellow dust that fertilizes the bloom that grows to be the fruits and vegetables we enjoy eating today. Bees also use pollen as food and they store it in combs along with the honey.

Honey is the condensed nectar. To evaporate the water, bees use their wings to fan the air inside the hive until the nectar is of a certain consistency. At that time they store the substance in cells of the comb, seal or cap them with wax; thus it will keep indefinitely in the capped combs.

A comb is not only used to store honey and pollen, but also it is where eggs are deposited. The combs used for raising the young or brood are located in the lowest portion, called the hive body, and that is where the bees live. The supers placed on top are shallow boxes for bees to work in and store honey.

Honey is sold in different forms. One is the liquid, or we know it better as strained honey. This is made by forcing the honey out of the combs and straining to remove crystals.

There is the creamed or solid honey. This honey has been strained and is partially or entirely solidified.

The comb honey you will find is sold as it is stored by the bees. Chunk honey is a combination of strained and comb honey.

Mildly flavored honey always has been most desirable with delicate flavors predominating; however, stronger flavored honeys are used in spreads and other recipes where a distinct flavor is desired.

The color and flavor of honey differs depending on the type of blossoms visited by the honeybee. As a general rule, light colored honey is milder in taste, while dark colored honey is stronger. Some of the most common honey floral sources are:

Clover, the most common that has a mild taste; alfalfa, mild flavored, aromic and light in color; orange blossom, mild and fine flavor and light colored; Acacia, pale yellow with a delicate flavor, produced in China and California; tupelo, a premium honey from the Southeast that is white and heavy bodied and high in fructose; and buckwheat, a dark full-bodied honey from the Midwest. Some of the other flavors are locust, maple, sage, blueberry, blackberry, and fireweed.

Refrigeration of honey will hasten granulation; however, it does not inhibit the taste or purity of the product. It should, however, be stored at room temperature and in a dry area. Should it crystalize, remove the lid and place the jar in warm water until the crystals dissolve. Too, you can microwave one cup honey in a microwave-safe container on high for two to three minutes or until the crystals dissolve. Stir every three seconds and do not boil or scorch.

A 12-ounce jar of honey equals one standard eight-ounce measuring cup. A pound of honey equals approximately 1 1/3 cups.

When measuring honey, be sure and use oil or moisten the cup for easy pouring.

The best results in cooking with honey is to use recipes that specify honey; however, if substituting for granulated sugar use honey up to 1/2 of the sugar. If you want to do a little experimenting, honey can be substituted for all the sugar in some recipes.

When using honey, instead of brown sugar, always use some molasses with the honey.

In making cakes you can replace half the sugar; however the liquid must be reduced to one-fourth cup for every cup of honey. When it comes to replacing sugar in cookies the amount varies with the kind of cookies. For a crisp cookie use no more than one-third cup of honey; however, in fruit cookies honey may replace up to two-thirds of the sugar; and in brownies half the sugar. It is important to mix the honey with the liquid and then add to the other ingredients, thus preventing sogginess forming on the top of the baked item.

Honey may be used in canning and it also can be used to replace one-half the sugar in the syrups for fruit and up to one-half the sugar in syrups when freezing.

Add one-half teaspoon baking soda

for every cup of honey; however, if the recipe calls for soda do not add more.

So that baked goods do not get too brown, reduce the oven temperature by 25 degrees. Honey does absorb and retain moisture easily, therefore items baked with honey stay fresh longer.

Honey also can be used as a substitute for sugar in many other things, pie fillings, candied sweet potatoes, salad dressings, glazes, sauces, vegetables, custards, puddings, in fact, in most of the recipes.

Some folks like to substitute two-thirds as much honey as sugar. This is a matter of individual taste.

Corn syrup may be substituted for honey in most recipes; however, the syrup is not as sweet as honey and the texture and flavor will be altered to a certain degree. You cannot substitute corn syrup for granulated sugar.

Try spreading honey on hot toast, or if you chop up sections of comb honey, mix with sunflower seeds, nuts, raisins, wheat germ or a crunchy cereal for a tasty snack.

Whipped cream will stay firm longer if honey is used as a sweetener instead of sugar.

Honey is an incredibly powerful healer that fights infections in deep cuts, wounds and burns.

After all that has been learned about honey, there is no doubt that it is made by the most efficient factories to be found anywhere.

* * *

A Thought To Ponder: Even bees, the little almsmen of spring flowers, know there is richest juice in poison-flowers. —Keats

* * *
Honey Fudge
2 cups sugar
4 ounces unsweetened chocolate
1/4 teaspoon salt
1 cup evaporated milk
1/4 cup honey
2 tablespoons butter

Combine sugar, chocolate, salt and milk. Boil five minutes; add honey and cook to a softball stage (240 degrees on candy thermometer). Add butter and let mixture cool to lukewarm. Then beat until creamy, pour into a buttered pan. If desired nut meats may be added after beating.

All in a Woman's Day--October 2, 1990
Helpful food tips
Helpful food facts and tips are always worth considering. Think about them!

To make soup go further, add some cooked macaroni or noodles. To one can of vegetable or chicken soup, add a can of milk and a cup of cooked macaroni or noodles.

If you have trouble with your mixer beaters holding the cake or cookie batter, just spray them with nonstick spray before starting and it won't gather on them.

Try adding a dollop (per bowl) of liquid smoke to potato or bean soup for a different flavor.

Corn flakes can be an inexpensive substitute for nuts in many cookie recipes.

Cut meringue on a pie with a knife that has been buttered on both sides and it won't tear.

If you don't want cookie dough sticking to your spoon to be used to drop the batter on the cookie sheet, just dip the spoon in milk before starting.

Instead of siphoning fat from meat drippings just pour it into a cup or bowl and place in the refrigerator. The next day the fat will be solidified and can be lifted off and discarded.

Try placing flour, corn meal, oat meal and other such foods in the deep freeze for about four days after bringing them from the store and you will have no bugs in them.

If you think your baking powder may be loosing its potency, test by dropping a teaspoonful in a cup of hot water. If it bubbles, it is still good.

Use a slightly warmed knife to cut cheese that is moderately hard, such as cheddar.

Add a tablespoon of salad dressing to your pie crust to make it flakier. A little less liquid will be required.

Pie will slide easily out of a pie plate that has been lightly dusted with flour before using.

If cake should be a bit stubborn in letting loose of the pan, just set it over a pan of boiling water for a few minutes.

For a lighter, fluffier cake try replacing a fourth of a cup of butter with three tablespoons of sour cream.

Cooked icings will not crystalize if you add a pinch of salt to the sugar.

A delicious flavor will result if you use equal amounts of lemon, vanilla and almond flavorings in your recipes.

Fudge can be made extra creamy if it is placed into a cold bowl before beating.

Try adding a sprinkle of finely chopped mint leaves to green beans or peas just before serving. It will be a delicious new flavor.

To unscrew a stubborn jar lid, hold it over a flame for a minute to soften the rubber seal, and it will come off easily.

Remove odor from hands after chopping onions or preparing garlic by quickly rinsing them under running water and then rubbing them along the chrome spout of the faucet.

If rust gets on cooking knives, just jab the blades into an onion and let it stay for about an hour, then work it back and forth to remove the rust.

A topping for waffles or pancakes can be made by placing equal parts of soft butter and honey into a blender. After they are combined, pour it over the waffles or pancakes for a delicious topping.

When making meringue, for every three egg whites add one teaspoon white vinegar for a fluffier finished product.

Tuck a piece of aluminum foil under the napkin in your bread basket to keep the bread warm. A preheated ceramic tile also can be used.

* * *

A Thought To Ponder: There is many a slip twixt the cup and the lip. —William Hazlitt

* * *

One More Chocolate Cake

2 cups sugar
5 tablespoons cocoa
1 cup butter or margarine
2 eggs well beaten
2 teaspoons vanilla flavoring
3 cups cake flour
1/2 teaspoon salt
2 teaspoons soda
1 cup commercial buttermilk
1 cup boiling water

Combine sugar, cocoa and the margarine until mixture is like whipped cream. (If using margarine, add a few drops of butter flavoring.) Then add the well-beaten eggs and vanilla. Sift together the cake flour, salt and soda and add alternately to creamed mixture with 1 cup of buttermilk. Add the boiling water. (This will be a thin batter but don't add anymore flour.)

Turn into a well-greased and floured 9x13-inch baking pan and bake at 325 degrees for 1 hour. Frost with your favorite chocolate icing.

All in a Woman's Day--October 9, 1990

Enjoy popcorn snacks

Beside apple pie, what is more American than popcorn? So, during this month of October you can "eat your heart out" on popcorn as this is National Popcorn Month. Of course, you just might do that the other 11 months of the year, too.

October was chosen for the observance of "Popcorn Month" because it is traditionally harvest time, as well as one of the largest popcorn eating seasons.

Popcorn poppin' an' munchin' has been ongoing in the United States for many many years. In fact, long before Columbus sailed into the New World, American Indians were popping corn in hot sand, on hot stones, in shallow clay pots or even right on the cob over the open fire. Popping urns, undoubtedly several thousands of years old, have been unearthed by archaeologists. Evidently those original Americans knew a good thing when they got a taste!

Did you know that a kernel of corn when popped takes 37 times as much room as it did before being popped? One report noted that if you have enough kernels to cover the state of Wyoming it would cover the entire United States when popped. Now, how is that for statistics?

Popcorn is the number one night study snack food for college students; creative cooks turn it into delicious desserts like popcorn cakes and pies; a great before dinner appetizer; a party nibble; a substitute for croutons or crackers in soup; and of course, moviegoers consider a bag of warm buttered popcorn an important part of the theater outing and in our homes watching TV, it is just about as important.

I am going to share several ways of fixing your favorite snack food the All-American favorite ... popcorn!

For those of you who might tend to serve something less fancy, hot buttered popcorn can be sprinkled, with various accenting flavors—garlic, celery salt, chili powder, grated Cheddar or Parmesan cheese, bacon bits, barbecue powder, or even dry soup mix. All of which gives an interesting change of pace.

* * *

Peanut-y Popcorn—Two quarts popped corn; one tablespoon creamy peanut butter; two tablespoons butter. Place popped corn in a large bowl; melt peanut butter and butter in a small saucepan and drizzle over the popcorn. Stir and mix well and serve at once.

* * *

Cajun Corn—Two and one-half quarts popped corn; one-fourth cup butter, melted; one-fourth teaspoon paprika; one-half teaspoon onion powder; one-half teaspoon garlic powder; one-fourth teaspoon cayenne pepper, and teaspoon lemon pepper. Pour butter over warm popcorn and combine the remaining ingredients and sprinkle over the corn tossing to mix. Bake in a 300 degree oven for crispy popcorn, if desired. Makes two and one-half quarts. (Note: Have plenty of beverages on hand as this snack makes you thirsty.)

* * *

Oven Caramel Corn—Ten cups popped corn; two cups brown sugar; two sticks margarine or butter; one-half cup white sugar; one teaspoon salt; one-half teaspoon soda; one teaspoon vanilla. Mix the margarine and sugars together and boil five minutes, then add the salt, soda, and vanilla, stirring into the sugar mixture. It will swell slightly; then pour at once over corn and stir until coated. Spread on cookie sheets and bake in a 250 degree oven for one and one-half hours, stirring every 15 minutes. Cool. Store tightly covered.

* * *

Poppycock Caramel Corn—Thirty cups popped corn; two cups brown sugar; two sticks margarine or butter; one-half cup white syrup; one teaspoon soda; one teaspoon salt. Mix ingredients; pour over popped corn that has been placed in a large pan. Mix and spread on two greased or teflon cookie sheets and bake one hour at 200 degrees. When cool, break it apart. If desired add walnuts, pecans or almonds.

* * *

Chocolate Popcorn—Five quarts popcorn; one and one-half cups sugar; one-third cup syrup; two and one-half tablespoons cocoa; two-thirds cup water; three tablespoons butter; one teaspoon vanilla. Place sugar and syrup over heat and stir until sugar is melted. Boil three to four minutes with the lid on; remove cover and cook until it forms a hard ball in cold water. Add cocoa that has been melted over hot water and the vanilla. Pour over corn. It can be left in "Cracker Jack" form or made into balls.

* * *

Chocolate Popcorn—Seventeen-ounce jar marshmallow creme; a 12-ounce package of milk chocolate or semi-sweet chocolate chips; two tablespoons water; one teaspoon vanilla. Melt marshmallow creme and chips in a double boiler; then stir in water and vanilla and pour over five quarts popped corn. Stir until coated.

* * *

Cinnamon Popcorn—Four quarts popped corn; one teaspoon cinnamon; one-fourth cup butter or margarine; one-fourth cup sugar; one-fourth teaspoon salt. Place popped corn in buttered or greased 9x13-inch pan. Then in a heavy saucepan melt margarine or butter over low heat; then stir in sugar, cinnamon and salt. Stir until sugar is dissolved. Pour over popcorn, tossing to coat. Bake in a 300 degree preheated oven 10 minutes. Cool.

Don't forget that however you eat popcorn it is poppin' good!

* * *

A Thought To Ponder: A warm smile is an invitation to draw up a chair before the log fire.

All in a Woman's Day--October 16, 1990
This is cobbler time!

This is cobbler time. Cooler weather brings on the desire for a cobbler made from a fruit that is especially liked and enjoyed.

Cobblers are a traditional American dessert similar to the deep-dish fruit pie; however, in place of a pastry crust, cobblers generally are topped with a rich biscuit dough.

They go back to the Pilgrim days and have remained a favorite through the years. The popularity of this easy dessert gives it a place in American history.

The origin of the word "cobbler" is unknown; however, it may have come from the expression to "cobble up," that is, to put together quickly, since these desserts are easy to make. Another version is that perhaps the clumps of dough on top of the fruit resemble a cobblestone street. Wherever the name came from it makes no difference; only that it is good eating!

Cobblers can be made with any number of fruits, including cherry, apple, peach, rhubarb. These fruits have always been favorites, along with blackberry.

This mixture of fruit and biscuit like dough, can be served either hot or cold.

There will be little resistance to this type of dessert that will please almost anyone that has a sweet tooth.

Here are a few cobbler recipes that are a bit different.

Apricot-Nut Cobbler

6 cups (2 pounds) apricot halves
3/4 cup sugar
2 tablespoons flour
1/2 teaspoon cinnamon
3/4 cup all-purpose flour
1 1/2 teaspoons baking powder
1/4 teaspoon salt
1/4 cup unsalted butter or margarine, softened
1/2 cup chopped walnuts
1/4 cup nonfat milk

In large bowl, combine apricots and next three ingredients; pour mixture evenly into ungreased 1x7x11/2-inch baking dish. In a medium bowl, combine the 3/4 cup flour and next three ingredients. With a pastry blender cut in the butter until the mixture resembles fine crumbs. Stir in milk; mixture will pull away from sides of bowl and be clumpy. Gently stir in walnuts; drop 8 spoonsful of dough on top of the apricot mixture. Bake in a preheated 425 degree oven for 30 minutes or until dough is golden brown and apricots are bubbly. Makes 8 servings.

* * *

Peach Cobbler

1 1/2 cups flour
1 teaspoon sugar
1/4 cup milk
1 cup sugar
2 tablespoons butter
1/2 teaspoon salt
1/2 cup oil
1 quart frozen peaches, thawed
1 tablespoon flour
1 cup water

For the crust: Combine the 1 1/2 cups flour, salt and teaspoon sugar. Add to this the milk and oil; combine well and press into the bottom and sides of a square pan or oblong baking dish. Place peaches in a saucepan over heat and add the water. Mix the 1 tablespoon flour with 1 cup sugar and add to the hot peaches. Pour the thickened peaches into the crust, dot with butter and bake at 425 degrees 15-20 minutes. About 5 minutes after removing from the oven, break the crust into the filling, if desired. Serve warm.

* * *

Strawberry Cobbler

1 1/2 cups sifted flour
2 teaspoons baking powder
1/2 teaspoon salt
1/2 cup sugar
1/4 cup shortening
1 egg, beaten
1 pint frozen or fresh strawberries
1 tablespoon lemon juice
2 tablespoons melted butter or margarine
1 tablespoon quick-cooking tapioca

1/3 cup milk

Sift and mix flour, baking powder, salt and sugar; cut in the shortening. Combine the milk and egg; then add to dry ingredients, stirring until all the flour is dampened. Spread the strawberries in a shallow baking dish. Sprinkle the strawberries with the tapioca, lemon juice and melted butter or margarine. Drop the batter in six or eight mounds on the fruit. Place in a preheated 400 degree oven and bake for 30 minutes. Serve with whipped topping or ice cream.

* * *

Apple Cobbler

6 cups apples, sliced
1 tablespoon flour
Pinch of salt
3/4 cup flour
1/4 teaspoon baking soda
1 cup white sugar
1/2 teaspoon cinnamon
3/4 cup oatmeal or any dry cereal
3/4 cup brown sugar
1/4 teaspoon baking powder
1/2 cup butter or shortening

Combine tablespoon flour, cinnamon, white sugar and apples in a deep baking dish. Mix the remaining ingredients until they are crumbly. Pour over apples and bake in a 350 degree oven until apples are cooked Serve with whipped cream.

* * *

A Thought To Ponder: He who forgives ends the quarrel.

All in a Woman's Day--October 23, 1990

Goblins, ghosts will be roamin'

We now begin to think of ghosts, goblins and superstitions. It just seems naturally.

But cats, too, have always been a part of is season, especially those that are black.

Black cats carry the burden of being bad luck because several hundred years ago people believed witches used these cats to carry out their evil spells. An old belief was that witches could change themselves into cats. In this altered state they could prowl unmolested and cast spells on unsuspecting victims.

Not all spells; however, were evil. Some witches used their powers for good and they were very popular. For instance, it has been told that one kept a kitchen garden especially to grow flowers and plants for the benefit of friends and neighbors. She would give a sprig of St. John's wort to maidens to put under their pillows to dream of their future husbands. She presented thyme to prevent nightmares; southernwood for good luck; and caraway branches to cure warts and skin blemishes.

If a black cat comes into your house and stays, it is said that you will have good luck; however, remember, it is bad luck if a cat dies in your house.

Cats seem to come in for more than their share of superstitions, the Egyptians even had a cat goddess, Bast, who protected men from contagious diseases.

Ancient Hebrews believed that the ashes of a black kitten would enable persons to see demons. The Azande tribe of Africa believed some women gave birth to cats. No one can deny it, for to see one of them is to die.

It has been written that on Halloween the dead walk that night; so, if you hear footsteps behind you, don't look around. If you meet the walking dead, you too, will die.

Also if you go to a crossroads and listen to the wind, you will learn all the things that will happen to you in the coming year; however, if you sit on a three-legged stool, you'll hear spoken aloud at midnight the names of those doomed.

Some Scots believe that people born on Halloween have the gift of second-sight.

Ghosts can be kept away, some say, by reading a verse of the Bible backwards, folding the page, putting a knife and fork on the place and putting the book under a pillow.

Halloween, however, has its good side, too. If a man crawls under a blackberry bush on that night, he will see the shadow of his future wife. A girl can see her future mate's image by standing in front of a mirror, combing her hair and eating an apple.

Witches were kept at bay by a cross of two twigs of the rowan tree fixed to the outside doors. And if the farmer's wife was churning butter and it wouldn't churn properly she would break the witches spells by stirring the cream with the twig of a mountain ash and then beating the poor cow with another twig from the same tree.

Even a little more than a hundred years ago many farmers and their wives, in fact the majority of country folk over in England, were a very superstitious lot. One of their daily prayers, well known at that time, were these words: "From witches and wizards and long tailed buzzards and creeping things, that run in hedge bottoms, Good Lord, deliver us." All kinds of protection was used to save the house and stables from the Evil Eye, the Powers of Darkness and Evil Spells. Necklaces of "holy stones,"

stones containing a natural hole, were hung behind the house door and in the stables to protect the animals from sickness and to keep the "Night Mare" from riding the horses. The horses also wore symbols on their harness as charms to protect them from evil. These charms can be seen today in British museums.

Whatever the sign may be ... walking under ladders, broken mirrors, spilled salt, and, yes, black cats, all of which seems to be bad luck superstitions; however, there is another side to it, you might say the good luck side. Salt is purposely spilled in Japan; broken mirrors are believed to be a protection from death by the Scandinavians; walking backwards under ladders is done by the Egyptians; and it seems that the British welcome a black cat to cross their path. So, whether it is good luck or bad, superstitions continue to be passed by word of mouth from one generation to another, and each region has its own particular belief.

Have a ghostly (Happy) Halloween.

* * *

A Thought To Ponder: The wisest man is generally he who thinks himself the least so.   — (Boileu)

* * *

Peanut Butter Cups

1 package graham crackers (10 graham crackers), finely crushed
1 pound powdered sugar
1 cup chunky peanut butter
1/2 pound margarine or butter
12-ounce package chocolate chips

Combine the finely crushed graham crackers with the sugar; melt margarine and butter and add peanut butter. Stir until melted. Pour over the cracker-sugar mixture and stir until moistened. Pour into an ungreased 9x13-

inch pan or muffin tins. In a double boiler melt a 12-ounce package of chocolate chips and 1/4 bar of paraffin (if needed). Pour over the first mixture and let harden.

All in a Woman's Day--October 30, 1990

Pumpkins have Halloween glow

Pumpkins now are taking on a Halloween glow. The harvest seems to have been plentiful as there are all shapes and sizes of them for sale.

The pumpkin, called a fruit, (I think most of us regard it as a vegetable), adds a delightful bit of color here and there when arranged in the yard or on the porch around a bale of hay or straw. The clown like characters sometimes added for atmosphere, gives a touch of nostalgia to the setting.

The cutting of eyes, nose and mouth in a pumpkin, with a light placed inside, no doubt was done by someone in a spirit of fun as a joke or a prank; however, the idea "caught on" and soon took hold. Today, however, there is not as much carving of the faces as there is of painting them on the pumpkin. They are cute and adorable and this, too, is "catching on."

It has been found that the word pumpkin comes from the French word "Pompion." or "Pompon" that is derived from the Greek word "Pawpon," meaning ripe and mellow.

The Chinese have a charming name for the pumpkin, calling it "Emperor of the Garden." To them this fruit symbolizes health and fruitfulness.

Slang terms have been created because of the pumpkin. We use the expression "pumpkin head" to denote a dull, stupid person; however, it originally meant a description of an early day haircut. Colonial New England has a Blue Law that decrees that every man must have his hair trimmed in a round version around a cap. Then, an ingenious Yankee hit upon the idea that the dried half of a pumpkin shell worked better than a cap for this purpose, and so, the resulting round haircut tagged New Englanders with the nickname "Pumpkin Heads."

The phrase, "some pumpkins," described persons or things of importance. Reportedly originating in 1853 in New York City, it happened when the public viewed a display of giant pumpkins at the Crystal Palace Exhibition and the phrase "some pumpkins" was used to express their wonder at the sight of such large fruit.

The famous Capt. John Smith, who thought the pumpkin was to be eaten raw, described it lukewarmly as "A fruit like unto a muskmelon but lesse and worse."

Folks use pumpkins in different ways. For instance, the Israelis stuff pumpkins with ground meat; in Sri Lanka it is curried; the Greeks fry it in oil; the French puree it; in the Caribbean they make it into bread; the Chinese turn it into delicate dumplings; the Russians boil it slowly with rice to form a thick breakfast porridge; and here in our country, it is dried, pickled, spiced, made into pudding, bread, cookies, cakes, ice cream, doughnuts, pies and other desserts.

It is a fruit of longevity for Spanish conquistadors took pumpkin seeds back to Europe in the 17th century; however, pumpkin fossils dating back thousands of years B.C. have been found in the Peruvian Andes.

* * *

If you have youngsters you might

like to try this song, "Down in the Cornfield," that is a parody to "Up on the Housetop."

Down in the Cornfield

Down in the cornfield, frosty white
Witches prowl on Halloween night.
If I should spot one, what a fright!
I'd run like a turkey, afraid to light.
Chorus:
Ho, Ho, Ho! Who Wouldn't go?
Ho, Ho, Ho! Betcha I know,
Down in the cornfield frosty white,
Where witches prowl on Halloween night.
Down in the cornfield, shiver and shake,
The rattle of bones doth a coward make.
If I decide a peek to take,
I'll be ready to take a fast break.
Chorus.

* * *

A Thought To Ponder: Many has been the poet that has sung the praises of the pumpkin, not just baked in a pie, but "smilin' on the vine."

* * *

Pumpkin Ice Cream Dessert

1 1/4 cups flour
1/4 cup sugar
1/2 teaspoon salt
2/3 cup butter
1/2 cup nuts, chopped
1 cup pumpkin
1/2 cup brown sugar
1/4 teaspoon EACH nutmeg and cloves
1 quart vanilla ice cream

Sift flour, sugar and 1/4 teaspoon salt; cut in butter; add nuts. Reserve 1/2 cup crumb mixture. Press remaining crumbs in a 10-inch pie plate. Bake at 350 degrees 10 to 12 minutes. Cool. Combine pumpkin, brown sugar, remaining salt, nutmeg and cloves in a saucepan and cook for 1 minute. Cool. Beat cooled pumpkin filling into the ice cream. Spread over cooled crust; top with reserve crumb mixture. Freeze until ready to serve. Yields 8 servings.

All in a Woman's Day--November 6, 1990

Baking is an ancient profession

Baking is a very ancient art, and bake ovens are about as old as baking. More than 2,000 years ago, the Egyptians, who were always proficient bakers, used simple ovens without flues, and in early Greece, baking was done in heated, large bowls, like clay ovens.

Throughout the history of Roman Medieval times, as well as into our own day, baking took place in a simple masonry chamber that was placed above a fire box, in other words an oven of some description.

In colonial America, baking was done in Dutch ovens, in front of the fireplace or connected with it or in alcoves with flues that were built into the backs of the wide masonry kitchen fireplaces. These ovens were heated by a wood fire that was built within them. When the bricks were thoroughly hot, the ashes were swept out into an ash pit that was below or into the kitchen, after which the flue of the oven was closed and the food to be baked pushed in by a long handled shovel. There is no doubt about it that the colonial housewife knew just the exact spot in her oven in which its heat would give her the best roasts, pies and bread.

It seems that metal ovens and kitchen ranges first appeared in England and the United States in the late part of the 18th century; however, they were first dimly viewed by housewives. In an early day cookbook a warning was written to the unfortunate owners of one of those new fangled contraptions not use it but to send the bread to the baker, instead, which seemed to be the custom in those days.

Always, baking has been a highly skilled occupation, with bakers seeming to be key figures in a community. It has been noted that such professions were highly regarded by the governments even to the extent of having constant rules and regulations of the trade, even from the days of ancient Egyptians, so as to insure honest bread, as well as to prevent bread riots.

Until the more recent years it seems there has been a close connection with baking and cleanliness. In those earlier days the women had definite days for doing chores, and it appears that Saturday was the day set aside for baking and baths. In those days when hot water did not come from a faucet, the kitchen range not only provided the heat for baking, but also the hot water needed for "pampering."

There were a lot of good things that came out of those early day ovens, besides meat and bread, namely flummery, grunt, slump, switchel and shurb, along with mock apple pie and vinegar pie to name a few. Our ancestors had to be inventive and imaginative not only in naming the item but in making good use of the harvest, or maybe just making do when the crops were scarce and possibly the pantry being on the bare side.

Those recipes are treasures and no doubt many of you have some traditional hand-me-down recipes that would seem to invoke a taste of history of our country as well as heritage from the colonial times.

When the harvest would come around, the homemaker would "put-up," store in the cellar or possibly the attic, all they could harvest from the garden, the orchard, the woods or the fields. The meals prepared reflected the seasons and the dearth or abundance of crops.

Along the coastal areas moss was gathered by the housewives and dried and then used for thickening puddings or blanc mange.

In the spring, everywhere the fresh and tasty wild greens, poke, dandelions, fiddlehead ferns and tender shoots of milkweed, that were much like delicate asparagus, were gathered.

This was followed by the season of berries, when flummeries, grunts and slumps were made. Flummeries were made from any berry that was boiled until tender, simmered a bit along with cornstarch for thickening, then sugared and eaten cold with cream or milk. Grunts and slumps were made with apples or berries, stewed with sugar and water and then dumplings or squares of biscuit dough dropped into the aromatic mixture and cooked until done.

Oftentimes the very richness of the harvest added to the problem of having variety. If there was too much buttermilk to drink the cook concocted buttermilk pie, or cake frosting, along with griddlecakes.

Piles of golden pumpkins brought rows of pumpkin pie and for a change of pace puddings and preserves. Or, if there was no pumpkin, an inventive cook tried squash and found it couldn't be told from the original. As for the improvident, who had neither pumpkin or squash, they used wild persimmons. After a frost it was found that they could be picked and were delightful in cakes, pies, puddings and marmalade. And, then there were the pawpaws. With some venturesome cooks trying them, and I might add, succeeding with custard, jam and the old favorite, pie.

When lean times came along with nothing to make pies from, again that our ancestor cooks improvised and came up with vinegar pie, mock apple pie, made with sugar, water, butter and crackers, along with chess pie made with sugar, butter, eggs, a touch of corn meal and lemon or the old stand-by, cider vinegar for flavoring.

In those early days of our country, corn meal was a common staple used the year round. It appeared in many disguises ... sweet Indian pudding, johnnycake or journey cake, eaten cold on a journey or at home hot for break-fast, dinner or supper, or as just plain mush carefully watched as the slow bubbles plopped to the surface during the long process of cooking, and then eaten hot with milk or sweetening. The leftover, if there was any, was sliced and fried the next day.

* * *

A Thought To Ponder: Better half a loaf than no bread. —John Heywood

* * *

I am going to give a recipe for Buttermilk Pie that is as we might say, "an oldie."

Buttermilk Pie

1 cup buttermilk
1 cup sugar
1 egg
1 tablespoon flour
1 tablespoon butter
1/2 teaspoon lemon flavoring

Mix sugar, butter, flour and beaten egg. Beat in the buttermilk and flavoring. Bake in one crust until firm; top with meringue and brown.

All in a Woman's Day--November 13, 1990
Turkey is ...
All-American bird

Believe it or not it is turkey time, however, nowadays that is about 12 months out of the year, so I guess that having turkey, is really nothing new.

We, here in America, have long associated the turkey with Thanksgiving for the simple reason that it seems to be an All-American bird.

This regal fowl has had a long and colorful history in North America, and though it, too, is colorful, it is not nearly as exotic as the Oscellated species found in the tropics of Central America. These turkeys have heads of bright blue with orange warts and wattles, and their beautifully colored plumage is iridescent and truly resemble a peacock.

It was after the Spaniards came, that turkeys were sent to the European market and it was there they received their name, or at least so goes the story. It seems that the Hebrew vendors of Spain took to selling the birds, not as food, but as a curiosity of nature...a kind of peacock. And, since they thought it resembled the peacock, they called it by the name they used for peacock, tukki.

The Spaniards found the turkey such an oddity many were taken back to Spain in the early 1500s, reaching England a few years later. Because of the turkey's colorful plumage, the Spaniards, too, called the bird after a peacock—"galloparo." Even today in Latin American countries, the big bird is known as "pavo."

It made its appearance in England

during the reign of Henry VIII, almost a century before the Pilgrims arrived in the New World. The English seem to have a tendency to believe that anything bizarre, exotic and succulent surely must have come from the East. The new bird fitted the description and was believed to have come from Turkey. Thence the name they gave to this new fowl.

This great bird made its debut on a royal menu in 1524, where it was served as a minor item for a banquet at which there were 16 different kinds of meat and some 30 kinds of fowl. From this elegant and extensive array, the turkey came out a favorite.

The Azetcs lay claim of discovering the turkey. In addition to hunting the bird for food, they also domesticated it. Cortez and other Spanish explorers arrived in what we now know as Mexico, Yucatan and Central America, where they found wild and tame turkeys among those people.

The Pueblo Indians of the Southwest valued the turkey for its unusual feathers and they were used in making blankets and decorating their ceremonial costumes. Other Indian tribes looked to this fowl primarily for food. None were hunted for the sport of hunting.

The Tewa tribe also held the turkey in high esteem as was made evident by an early legend that concerns an Indian Cinderella, who was befriended by turkeys. She was dressed in fine clothes and sent off to a dance where she met her Chief Charming.

There also is another turkey legend that was Indian related. Why is the turkey bald? The legend concerning this fable goes like this: It seems that long ago the Great Spirit for some unremembered reason extinguished all fire on earth, with one exception. He left a single spark in a hollow tree. A turkey belonging to a noble chief discovered this spark by accident. Knowing how badly man needed fire on earth, this intelligent bird gathered bits of dried grass and moss and piled them around the spark. Then it blew its breath upon the spark until it blazed up and ignited the grass and moss, thus saving fire for man. In the process, however, the blaze burned the feathers off of the turkey's head and left him with the "bald and blistered" look that we now see.

Today's version of the turkey is a plump and succulent bird, with the early day wild turkeys being wiry, tough and sinewy because of living in the dense forest and being forced to move around a great deal. Trees were cut down and the desire of many Americans for hunting wild game meant staying in one place almost impossible. For a number of years wild turkeys were almost extinct, however, now here in Missouri, as well as in other places there is a reason for hunting them.

There have been years of scientific breeding and poultrymen have been able to produce birds that are now pleasingly tender. Too, the color, has changed in the process, with many of today's birds almost all white.

Through the years, the turkey seems to have found a way of being a part of some of our expressions, even though a few may be passe.

Did you ever hear the "talk turkey" expression? It means down-to-brass-tacks business discussion. Too, anyone strutting about with an overly confident swagger, has been referred to as "walking turkey" or "turkey walk" simply because it resembled the manner of the bird. Also there was a dance called the "turkey trot." Remember? An old—time saying was "saying turkey," that meant a swain paying his lady love a flower compliment probably derived from the turkeys own courting method.

A bundle of personal belongings that lumbermen toted from camp to camp often was called a man's "turkey" and if a lumberjack "hoisted the turkey," that meant he had packed up his belongings and left camp. In more recent years when a Broadway production failed, it is said to have "bombed" or "laid an egg," but one may still hear of it as being a "turkey."

This expression began in the days when amateur acting groups produced special shows for Thanksgiving Day that generally left much to be desired in the way of production and acting talent. Actors involved in such ventures were called "turkey actors" because of their exaggerated histrionics and also the fact that they had their moment of glory on this special holiday. Later, however, the name was shortened to "turkey," designating any mediocre or failing thespian effort.

And, so, it would seem that this strutting, fantailed bird, apparently is the one that has made Thanksgiving famous.

* * *

A Thought To Ponder: To give thanks sincerely, one must give more than thanks.

All in a Woman's Day--November 20, 1990

We relate thankfully to the 5 grains of corn

Thanksgiving time has arrived. The time when families join together in fellowship and love to express thankfulness for all the blessings bestowed.

Harvesttime is almost over and it has been, in most instances, bountiful. Because we are grateful for all our blessings, this might be a good year to add a symbolic touch to our Thanksgiving table by placing five grains of dried corn at each place. No doubt most of you know the story about the five grains of corn and this just might be a good time to refresh our memories of what happened those many years ago.

Corn played an important role in the lives of the Pilgrims, as well as in our lives today, and it has been said, "without it they might have starved."

When the Mayflower landed on our shores, a scouting party of 16 men was sent out to explore the area. Led by Miles Standish, they did catch glimpses of a few Indians, but there were no encounters. Perchance they came upon what William Bradford described as certain heaps of sand. Digging soon uncovered a basket of corn. Additional digging brought forth still another large basket filled with what was termed as "fair corn, some yellow, some red, and other mixed with blue."

Even though the Pilgrims had included wheat and barley seeds in their supplies brought along to America, they also were aware that corn was a crop that grew best in America. So, because of this they were delighted with their findings. They felt that if they should have a failure with their wheat and barley, this newly found corn might just save them from starvation. However, being honest men, they did hesitate before gathering up the cache. Realizing they had chanced upon a hidden store

784

of Indian corn, they pondered the thought that if they took some of it this would mean they had stolen from the Indians. The temptation, however, proved too much, so they decided to carry away as much as possible. To ease their conscious they told each other that when they met the Indians they would explain why they had taken the corn, and offer so they said, something "to satisfy them" for their loss.

From all accounts, the winter of 1620-21 was a year of hardships and misfortune for the newcomers, with about half of the small band of Pilgrims stricken by disease, exposure, cold and privation. Food supplies got so low that rations of only five kernels of corn were distributed daily to each person.

Conditions, however, changed for the better with the arrival of the first touch of spring in 1621, and also with the arrival of Squanto, an English speaking Indian, who gave the settlers Indian corn seed and showed them how to plant, using fish as a soil fertilizer. He told the colonists that the corn was to be planted when "the leaves of the oak were the size of a squirrel's ear," and warned them that they must post a guard over the field for 14 nights, until the fish could rot, otherwise the wolves, who were ravenous, would dig them up. Because they followed his advice, their crops grew and flourished.

Governor Bradford, so the story goes, thought it would be most fitting to celebrate with a Thanksgiving Day because conditions were so much improved and there was need for rejoicing in a special manner after "we have gathered the fruits of labours."

Later in New England's earlier days, the five grains of corn they had given to the colonists became a symbol of a Thanksgiving custom. Five grains of corn were placed at each person's empty plate before dinner was served as a reminder of what the forefathers had survived. Each member of the family would pick up a grain of corn and tell what blessings had been received.

These five grains of corn, also had another symbolic meaning. The first grain picked up at the first Thanksgiving celebration was for thankfulness for posterity; the second reminded them to be grateful for peace; the third, to be grateful for Jesus Christ; the fourth grain reminded them to thank God for the power of his presence; and the fifth and last grain reminded them to be grateful for God's pardon.

Today in Plymouth, Mass., there is a site called "Corn Hill," which many of the readers have probably visited. It is marked with a bronze plaque that reads "Sixteen Pilgrims, led by Miles Standish, William Bradford, Stephen Hopkins and Edward Tilley, found the previous Indian corn on this spot, November 16, 1620."

We, too, have so many reasons to be thankful, both materially and spiritually, and as we place our five grains of corn let us be ever mindful of all those things that have gone before to make possible what we have today.

* * *

A Thought To Ponder: "O beautiful for spacious, skies, for amber waves of grain."

To each of you ... Happy Thanksgiving!

785

Time to make holiday fruit cake

For those homemakers who make their own fruit cakes it is time to think about getting that bit of cooking out the way for the holidays—Christmas and New Year's.

Some people don't seem to care about this bit of lusciousness; however, for those of us and friends who do, it is choice eating.

Fruit cakes date at least to the Romans, who blended raisins, pine nuts, pomegranate seeds and honey wine into a cake known as "satura." This word, satire, a literature form invented by the Romans, comes from a mixture of many ingredients both sweet and sour. It has been only in recent years; however, that fruit cakes have developed a more contemporary reputation of being a parody (an imitation). Some of the best imitations of fruit cakes are prepared in a variety of ways and are known by such disparate names as panforte, that is Italian; black cake, that is Caribbean; and plum pudding, that is British.

Fruit cakes have been prized over the centuries, probably because the dried fruits always have had, shall we say, "an edge of luxury to it."

In Britain fruit cake is still the traditional wedding cake and has been otherwise linked with romance.

Even as late as in the 19th century, young men and women have been known to put slices of fruit cake, known as the groom's cake, under their pillows in the belief that whomever they dreamed of that night they would marry.

Some homemakers have been making fruit cakes for many years as part of the holiday ritual. It has been said that fruit cakes keep so well some of them could be kept forever which could be a blessing or a curse.

Of course, we have all heard the expression "nutty as a fruit cake," where this came from I do not know, but more than likely it dates back many years.

Some fruit cakes have a high alcoholic and sugar content that makes them able to be preserved for a year or even longer, provided they are moistened from time to time with additional spirits and are stored in airtight containers. It has been recommended that a medium grade of brandy is good for the moisture in cakes. Many of the cakes do not require alcohol. Although many fruit cakes are better if prepared in advance, there are a number of recipes that can be prepared and eaten in the same day.

Should the candied fruit often used, be too sweet for some people to enjoy, then the fruit should first be soaked in boiling water to remove some of the sugar and preservatives before baking.

Too, it has been suggested that instead of candied cherries, citron and pineapple that sliced peaches, apricots, mangoes and pears could be used.

A piece of cheesecloth dipped in cider and placed in the container with the holiday fruit cake will keep it moist.

Should you have some fruit cake on hand, cut it in small squares and dip is melted white chocolate. The pieces are attractive and the taste is changed. Too, a dip can be made and poured over slices of the cake to make another change.

In preparing the fruit for the cake always leave the seedless raisins and the currants whole. Seeded raisins should be cut in half with wet scissors.

Cut dates and nuts in quarters; cherries in half, and slice candied pineapple, citron and fruit peels thin. Some markets sell fruit already prepared for the fruit cake, especially at holiday time.

If preparing the pans for baking, use a deep loaf pan, butter lightly and line with aluminum foil. If you want to use glass or ovenware casseroles, small or large, they are attractive to use, especially if you are planning on giving it as a gift. These should be buttered lightly but not lined with foil. After the cake is baked, cool completely and then put it in airtight containers to ripen. The cakes can be wrapped in a juice soaked cloth and then in foil. The cloth should be moistened once a week.

When serving thin perfect slices, chill fruit cake before cutting.

Fruit cakes are always tastier, or so it seems, if made and aged at least two weeks before using. They can be stored in the refrigerator, freezer or a cool area of the house.

When serving fruit cake, the same day that it is baked, be sure to cool the fruit cake before slicing to avoid crumbling. For easier slicing and improved flavor, wrap the cooled fruit cake and store in the refrigerator for at least one day.

Fruit cake keeps well, so you can prepare it ahead of the holiday rush. Refrigerate fruit cake up to two weeks or freeze it up to three months. Before serving, thaw fruit cake at room temperature.

Why not make several of these contemporary fruit cakes for the holiday season. They're great on the holiday buffet table, when guests drop by and for Christmas morning breakfast or brunch. Chances are your taste-tempting, new fruit cake won't even be recognized as fruit cake.

Remember, don't reserve fruit cake for special occasions. Fruit cake, a sort of pound cake with fruit can be served anytime of the year. If you have a good fruit cake recipe that you bake or if you have found one that is delightful and can be purchased, just remember, it is not just for Christmas anymore.

* * *

A Thought To Ponder: Would ye both eat your cake and have your cake? —John Heywood

* * *

Unbaked Fruit Cake

1 pound dates, cut fine
1 pound marshmallows, cut fine
1 pound orange slices or gum drops, not licorice, cut fine
1 pound graham crackers, crushed fine
1/2 cup sugar
1 cup whipped cream or topping.

Stir all and knead. Press into pan lined with waxed paper and let set for six days.

All in a Woman's Day--December 4, 1990

Romantic history belongs to candy making

You won't believe it but candy has a romantic history. In fact, it has one of the most exciting stories known to historians, for no other food can trace its beginnings to so many different countries.

Natural sweets, such as honey, have been known from the earliest times; however, it is thought that candy making started in Egypt for it was in 156 B.C. that confectioners in that country were selling sweetmeats from baskets in the market places.

Paintings in ancient Egyptian tombs depict candy makers using rough and rudely shaped molds to make the delicacies of honey mixed with nuts, chopped fruits, herbs and spices.

Romans often finished their very lavish feasts with candy. This was the origin of the saying "topping off," that is, finishing the meal with something sweet.

The Persians and the Arabians introduced sugar to candy. It seems that some of Alexander the Great's soldiers brought back a sweet reed from India and this combined with spices became a popular dessert.

One of the earliest functions of candy was to disguise unpleasant medicine with the doctors using it to make their potions sweeter. Medieval doctors also often used for this purpose a "sugar-plate." This was sweetmeat made of gum dragon, white sugar and rosewater, beaten to a paste.

In 1519 when Cortez conquered the Aztecs, he also discovered the cacao bean. His physician friend, Maradon, combined the beans with equal amounts of sugar, cinnamon and cloves. This, perhaps was the first chocolate confection. In the early 16th century, Emperor Montezuma proffered a golden goblet of "chocolatl" to Cortez, who took some of the cacao beans back to Spain. The pods of the cacao beans are the fruit from which is derived the world's chocolate and cocoa. They appear on the trunk of the trees and the main branches.

A display at an exhibition in 1851 of English boiled sweets, stimulated manufactures in France and other countries. At that time in the United States, 380 small factories were making lozenges, jujube paste and stick candy. By the way, the word candy is said to have derived from the Persian word for sugar kandisefid.

America's baseball fans in 19]1 were sold the first candy bars. They were made of almond, nougat and chocolate covered marshmallows with peanuts.

Today there are more than 2,000 varieties of candy made. So, we should have no trouble in making our selection of a favorite.

Many folks will go to great lengths to find their favorite flavor of candy. In a survey it was found that men seek out solid chocolates, while women lean toward fruit flavored cremes and jelly-filled candies. Too, adolescents like crunchy candies, such as toffees or chocolate and nut combinations; with the more elderly individuals preferring cordialtype cherries. Children go for sweet, simple confections like solid milk chocolate, caramels and marshmallows candies.

* * *

In Europe many of our Christmas traditions originated, and it was customary to decorate the tree with symbols of the newborn Christ. Candles represented the light of the world; the star recalled the first Christmas night. Those who came to visit the new King were portrayed in symbols—musical instruments represented the angels; crowns and golden caskets signified the Magi; the shepherd's hook or cane symbolized the shepherds of Bethlehem; and the three Wise men who came with gifts.

* * *

A Thought to Ponder: Talking about reducing won't work. You have to keep your mouth shut.

* * *

Coconut Bonbons

1 1/2 pounds confectioners'
1 cup butter
4 cups pecans, finely chopped
1 (7-ounce) package of coconut, chopped
1 (14-ounce) can Sweetened Condensed Milk
2 (12-ounce) packages chocolate chips
1/2 bar parrafin, shaved

Combine first five ingredients; mix well and refrigerate overnight. Next day, remove only a portion of the candy at a time. It softens quickly. Roll into small balls and dip into chocolate coating. To make coating, melt chocolate chips in saucepan over low heat, stirring until smooth; add paraffin, stirring until mixture is combined. Place candy on cookie sheet until chocolate coating sets up. Wrap and store in cool place. These ripen if allowed to age a few days.

All in a Woman's Day--December 11, 1990

'Visions of sugarplums danced in their heads'

And "visions of sugarplums danced in their heads!" Remember that line from Clement C. Moore's "T'was the Night Before Christmas?"

Well, maybe you have been wondering just what is a sugarplum? Do you really know? There are a number of versions, some claiming it is a candy and others saying it is a fruit.

Some folks have contended that "sugarplums are better than candy," which by the way was not so plentiful in those earlier days and in many homes was only served on Christmas. It is said, too, that sugarplums are very sweet and about the "closest thing to heaven that could be."

Too, some say sugarplums grow on a bush and the plum is smaller than a regular plum. Other folks declare that the flesh is golden in color and that it is a task to be able to pick any sugarplums as the birds, bless their hearts, know just the very second that the fruit is ripe. Many of us remember, too, that fruit in earlier days was not picked until it was ripe.

Then we find those that say the sugarplum is a pitted prune stuffed. Others say that the sugarplum is actually a fruit, and that it is a large yellow-green plum, very sweet, with the juice sticky and thick like syrup, and, oh, yes, they grow on trees.

Then there is a sugarplum candy that is like a small bonbon that no doubt is made from maple sugar or the juice of a sugarplum fruit.

In earlier days some homemakers felt they could make so many different things out of sugarplums, and with all the different recipes, no doubt that is just what they could do.

This 19th century treat still remains but a name not identifiable as glaced fruits (originally either plums or figs), often wrapped in glittering foil. Recipes today combine fruit and nuts.

So, again, the question is asked "Just what is a sugarplum?"

* * *

A Thought To Ponder: To eat, and drink and to be merry. Ecclesiastes 8:15

* * *

I am going to share several recipes for sugarplums. Read them, try them and then decided, if you can, "just what is a sugarplum.

* * *

Sugarplum Surprises - (makes 3 dozen) 1 cup butter; 2 cup sifted confectioners' sugar; 1 1/2 teaspoons vanilla; 2 cups sifted flour; 1/2 teaspoon salt; 1 cup quick cooking oats; 3 dozen candied cherries. Stir butter to soften; add sugar and vanilla beat until fluffy. Sift flour and salt together; add to butter mixture. Stir in oats (dough will be quite stiff). Shape 1 heaping teaspoon of dough into a ball around a candied cherry. Place on ungreased cookie sheet and bake in slow oven, 325 degrees, until brown, about 30 minutes. While still hot, roll in sifted confectioners' sugar,

* * *

Sugarplums - 1 cup chopped dried apricots; 1 cup dark raisins; 1 cup light chopped raisins; 1 cup chopped dates; 1 cup chopped pecans or walnuts; 1/4 to 1/2 cup honey and ginger sauce; 1 to 1 1/4 cups unsweetened coconut. Combine first four ingredients and mix well with hands. Add nuts, honey and ginger sauce. Shape into balls 1 teaspoon at a time. Roll in coconut. Keep in an airtight container in refrigerator. Serve in paper cups or wrap in cellophane wrappers and tie on Christmas tree. Makes about 2 dozen.

* * *

Sugarplums - 2 large boxes gelatin (any flavor, but preferably strawberry); no water; 1 cup sweetened condensed milk; 1 cup shredded coconut; 1 cup chopped pecans. Mix together; chill at least 2 hours. Make into balls and roll in sugar.

* * *

Christmas Sugarplums - 1/2 cup butter or margarine; 1/3 cup light molasses; 1 package (15-ounce) yellow raisins, ground twice; 2 cups graham cracker crumbs; 60 pecan halves; powdered sugar; flaked coconut. Mix butter, molasses, raisins and crumbs by hand until well blended. Pinch off pieces the size of a large olive and wrap each piece around a pecan half. Roll 30 in sugar, the rest in coconut. Makes about 60 sugarplums.

* * *

Sugarplums - 1/2 cup butter; 5 cups powdered sugar; 1/4 cup whipping cream; 1 teaspoon vanilla. Cream butter, add sugar slowly. Add cream and vanilla while adding sugar. Beat until completely blended. Make into 1-inch balls and roll in colored sugar, etc. They freeze well.

* * *

Sugarplums - 1 package (6-ounce) dried apricots; 1/2 package (4-ounce) dried apples; 1 cup walnuts or pecans; 2 tablespoons rum; 1 cup raisins; 1/4 cup sweetened shredded coconut. Use blender, food processor or knife to chop fruits and nuts until fine. Put all ingredients back into the blender and add the rum. Blend for a few seconds. Turn into a bowl and form into balls 1/4-inch in size, pressing firmly into shape. Roll balls in granulated sugar. Store in airtight container for up to 2 weeks or freeze.

* * *

Sugarplums - 2 eggs; 1 cup sugar; 1 tablespoon corn starch; 1 can (8-ounce) crushed pineapple, well drained; 1 cup dried apricots, cooked, drained and chopped; 1/2 teaspoon finely shredded orange peel; 1/2 cup coarsely chopped nuts; 1/2 teaspoon orange extract; 1/4 teaspoon salt; 4 cups Corn Chex cereal, crushed to 2 cups; 1 1/2 cups (3 1/2-ounce can) shredded coconut. In a saucepan beat eggs, slightly; add sugar, corn starch, pineapple, apricots and orange peel. Cook over medium heat, stirring constantly, until it comes to a boil. Boil 2 minutes. Remove from heat and stir in nuts, salt and extract. Add cereal, mixing well. Cool. Drop by teaspoons onto coconut and shape into balls. Makes 4-1/2 dozen.

All in a Woman's Day--December 18, 1990

Touching Christmas narrative is related

It was a long journey from Nazareth to Bethlehem, leading up to the Christmas event. There was heavenly music filling the air, the fluttering of angel wings, the star shining so brightly, the shepherds, the Wise Men, Mary and Joseph and the blessed newborn Child.

This special season took on a new awareness when a visit was made to a nursing home to provide entertainment for the residents.

It was Christmas Eve. Snowflakes were gently falling, descending ever so softly to the ground. It was a world of beauty outside with multicolored lights twinkling here and there among the flakes.

When the violinist began playing his instrument, his wife picked up the tune on the piano. And, so, as the songs and hymns of Christmas filled the air, residents of the home began quietly gathering in their wheel chairs to join in the festivities and the singing of songs so dear to them. No song books were needed by this group, as the words were indelible on their minds and hearts.

Finally the director led to the piano a frail, thin, blind woman. She was attired in a faded housecoat and house slippers. The director asked if she would sing "Silent Night" with the group. As she consented, softly the pianist touched the keys from which came music that filled every corner of the big room. This dear lady began singing this favorite Christmas hymn in the most beautiful soprano voice ever heard.

Her rendition held everyone speechless. They were stunned by the wonderfulness of the occasion. As she finished, tears were streaming down her face and she said, "Please, would you let me sing it again?"

Everyone applauded consent, and when the second rendition was concluded there were no dry eyes—she had brought such beauty into their hearts—hearts that had been scarred and hurt through the years. Nothing had to be said; however, everyone knew that she was filled with glorious memories of the past.

Later it was learned that this slightly stooped figure, who had been out of touch with the world for so many years, once had been a professional singer having done many operatic musical dramas during her younger years.

All those present that blessed night realized that Christmas for them had taken on a new awareness. (P.S. The basic facts of this story are true.)

And so, may this holiday bring to each of you, too, a new awareness.

* * *

A Thought to Ponder: Those true to God seldom appeaer false to others.

All in a Woman's Day--December 24, 1990

'It wonders me that . . . '

"It wonders me that ... " This is an apt Pennsylvania Dutch expression used to indicate surprise or difficulty understanding some act or situation.

As we stand at the threshold of a new year with its uncertainties and challenges it is only natural to reflect and project.

And would you believe that out of the reveries come some puzzling thoughts and some things at which we could do better. So, as we are ready to enter 1991 "It wonders me … "

—That in some instances the church speaks so softly about man's basic alienation from God—that is his sin.

—That some folks can be so much for National and International peace and yet can act so inhumane toward to office or business associates.

—That parents demand that their children not experiment with drugs when they themselves tip the glass or light up for a smoke.

—That there should be a lighter side to life and we should try to bring more joy and happiness to other people, which would in turn bring it into our lives.

—That God can be so patient with us, His bungling, arrogant children when all the time He continues showering us with so many many blessings.

—That there surely must be some way to have more patience in all that we do and say and that we will have the wisdom to know when it comes.

—That we will have the power to laugh; however, not at the expense of others.

—That we use the month of January to revitalize ourselves, resolving to achieve, to arise to new heights and to elevate our way of life.

—That there will be a few friends who understand us, and yet remain friends.

Yes, "it wonders me that … "

As we start another year, let us think, too, of what time means in our lives. Let us hope that it is no too late to …

—Take time to worship; It is the key to reverence.

—Take time to work; It is the price of success.

—Take time to think; It is the source of power.

—Take time to read; It is the fountain of knowledge.

—Take time to help; It is the key to happiness.

—Take time to play; It is the secret of youth.

—Take time to live; It holds life's secret.

—Take time to dream; It hitches the soul to the stars.

* * *

May the New Year bring to each of you the best of everything, even "it wonders me that … "

CANNING, FREEZING

CASSEROLES

COBBLERS

COOKIES